WILSON: CHILDREN AND THE LAW

WILSON: CHILDREN AND THE LAW

A completely revised and
re-written second edition

by

Jeffery Wilson and Mary Tomlinson

of the Ontario Bar

Butterworths

Toronto

Wilson: Children and the Law, Second Edition

Printed and bound in Canada.

The Butterworth Group of Companies

Canada
Butterworth & Co. (Canada) Ltd., Toronto and Vancouver

United Kingdom
Butterworth & Co. (Publishers) Ltd., London and Edinburgh

Australia
Butterworths Pty Ltd., Sydney, Melbourne, Brisbane, Adelaide and Perth

New Zealand
Butterworths (New Zealand) Ltd., Wellington and Auckland

Singapore
Butterworth & Co. (Asia) Pte. Ltd., Singapore

South Africa
Butterworth Publishers (SA) (Pty) Ltd., Durban and Pretoria

United States
Butterworth Legal Publishers, Boston, Seattle, Austin and St. Paul
D & S Publishers, Clearwater

Canadian Cataloguing in Publication Data

Wilson, Jeffery.
 Wilson: Children and the Law

Includes bibliographies and index.
ISBN 0-409-87762-X

1. Children — Legal status, laws, etc. — Canada.
I. Tomlinson, Mary. II. Title. III. Title: Wilson:
Children and the Law.

 KE512.W54 1986   346.7101'35   C85-099003-3

Sponsoring Editor — Ruth Epstein
Managing Editor — Linda Kee
Supervisory Editor — Marie Graham
Editor — Priscilla Darrell
Cover Design — Marguerite Posner
Production — Jim Shepherd

Foreword

In 1974 and 1975, I served as Chairman of the British Columbia Royal Commission on Family and Children's Law. We studied and made recommendations on virtually every aspect of family and children's law. At that time the idea of children's rights was in a sense in its infancy.

Although our work at the time was confined to our own province, we felt the need of a complete examination of children's rights throughout Canada. There has been a good deal of writing in journals and periodicals, but no attempt to analyse the law and the social policy underlying the law in the field.

Jeffery Wilson's book is one written for lawyers and other professionals who deal with children and the law. Their work is carried on within a framework of statute law. Within that framework, the most profound questions of human rights arise within the field of children's rights. It is only necessary to refer to the custody of children, the obligations of marriage partners to their children, the rights of adopted children to seek out their natural parents, artificial insemination, test tube babies, and so on, to realize that these are areas where intensely private matters are exposed to legal analysis; that analysis should provide not only dissection of the language used in the statutes but also consideration of the assumptions underpinning the statutes.

Examination of the condition of children under the law raises in its most graphic form the question of state intervention. When can the state take a child from its parents? When the law perceives people as dependent, it usually endows a guardian appointed by the state with substantial powers over their lives. Women used to be treated this way.

Such measures have historically been the product of liberal reform, and their purpose has been entirely benevolent. But children are the most helpless of such special interests. If the family cannot care for the child, or if the family unit itself breaks down, the law allows the state to intervene and assign the child to parental substitutes. These may include foster parents, adoptive parents, group homes or other institutions.

A number of questions arise: When ought the state to be allowed to intervene to remove a child from its parents? We would all no doubt agree there are cases where this should be done. But then there are cases where we might disagree. Take the case of alleged neglect of a child. Who is to say that a child's parents are not bringing the child up properly? By whose standards should the care that parents are providing to a child be measured? What evidence should be admissible: see *Hopkinson v. Superintendent of Family and Child Services*, B.C. Court of Appeal, Vancouver Registry, No. CA 001431, September 4, 1984, reported in *The Advocate*, Vol. 43, Part I, January, 1985, pages 131-132.

Then there is the question of custody. Certainly the best interests of the child are the test. But what really is in the best interests of the child? Who is to say? What are the criteria? And is the child to be heard?

In my view, what occurs in the early years of life will determine much that occurs afterward. These years are vital to their growth or their failure to grow in pre-adolescent and adolescent years. The providing of love and security and direction in the early years is essential to the child's own development of a sense of identity, to a child's own notion of self-worth. If a child's emotional development in those very early years is impaired or injured, the consequence may well be an attempt by the child in pre-adolescent or adolescent years to assert his identity in anti-social behaviour. The child may be a failure at school, he may be a failure among his peers, it may be that the only way in which he can attain a sense of identity, or achieve any kind of recognition, is by an overt violation of the norms that we have come to think should govern us all. These formative years are crucial; when the full story is told, the Child is father of the Man. When the law is brought to bear, it must be with sensitivity and insight, as well as firmness.

Any rational approach to the problem is one which seeks to deal not only with the effects, but with the causes as well. The causes often lie within the family, and the remedy often lies with the family. Thus we have seen throughout Canada the development of new perceptions in the field of children's rights and child welfare. Indeed, in the 1970's these perceptions brought in nearly every province recommendations for reform: unified family courts; family and children's advocates; modernized definitions of neglect; changes in the law relating to custody, guardianship and adoption; and a greater measure of community control over resources, especially for Native communities. Some of these proposals have been implemented, some not.

Legislation ought to set out the needs of children, and the rights of children. What are the needs of children? I do not think it is all that difficult to spell them out: the need for food, clothing and shelter, and for warmth and affection, for emotional security and mental health, for education.

Should these needs be spelled out as legal rights? Should children have a legal right to a permanent home, or to adequate services in their home, or to decent care and treatment if they are institutionalized? In B.C., we said they should be. Moreover, where a child is handicapped, we urged that his handicap should in no way diminish his rights as a child. Legislation dealing with children's rights should be sufficiently elaborated to indicate the application of such rights to handicapped children. Children's rights should apply equally to any children who may be institutionalized or who may be in care.

It is, of course, the primary responsibility of the family — of the parents — to provide for these needs. The function of governmental institutions and agencies is to supplement the family in meeting these needs whenever the family is either temporarily or permanently unable to meet them. Provision of resources by the state should not be regarded as a last resort. So where are we now? The era of reform has been overtaken by the era of diminished resources.

But the era of reform did affect the way people think about these questions. I know that in British Columbia, although our Commission's recommendations were not by any means all of them adopted, our hearings and our recommendations made an impact on the thinking of lawyers, social workers, health professionals — all those who are engaged in administering the law and in making it work. I think something very similar happened throughout the country.

The 1970's were productive of social experimentation and change. Some may be skeptical of what was achieved. Those of us urging reform found that both the law and social work professions were sometimes inclined to resist change. Some practitioners in both fields remain unreconstructed. But, on the whole, there was progress in acceptance of new ideas and in the establishment of innovations.

In this book, Jeffrey Wilson covers all of the ground that has been traversed in the last 15 years. He has done so in a scholarly, readable fashion, and in a way that will make the book useful not only to lawyers, but also to all professionals in the field.

Perhaps the most important new element in the field — one common to every province — is the Charter of Rights. This may turn out to be the leading edge in the field of children's rights. If the courts are to examine the implications of Charter provisions, in particular Section 15, in a way that goes beyond mere dissection of the language, they must comprehend the ideas that inform the law today. Jeffery Wilson's book offers an opportunity for them to do so.

Thomas R. Berger
1985

Preface

This book, an expanded and rewritten second edition of the 1978 volume, deals with most areas of the law which affect the child and his or her family in Canadian society.

We must offer the usual but nonetheless heartfelt apology of basing the discussion primarily on Ontario law. However, we hasten to add that every province is faced with the same issues discussed in the book and many have adopted or are considering legislative approaches similar to those in Ontario.

The book is a legal text intended for practical use by professionals although there were many instances when the temptation was great to digress. Does the impact of the law aggravate rather than ameliorate the hurtful situations which children find themselves in? Is the law really relevant when the obvious need is for dollars, not words? One hopes that this book can at least assist in formulating some baselines from which to proceed in tackling these more important questions.

We would like to thank Barbara Jackman, a Toronto lawyer specializing in immigration law, for her assistance in vetting Chapter 9, given our lack of experience in the area. In addition, our thanks to Michael Cadesky of the Toronto chartered accountancy firm of Mintz + Partners, who vetted the section on income tax implications connected with children. And finally, our inexpressable thanks to Betty Krieger who typed the manuscript and who somehow managed always to squeeze in one more draft in her spare time.

Finally, it should be noted that for the most part, the law as discussed in the book must be taken as of January, 1985, with the exception that the following Bills have been incorporated into the text in anticipation of their becoming law: Ontario's *Child and Family Services Act* (passed but not yet proclaimed); Ontario's proposed *Family Law Act, 1985* (received first reading on June 4, 1985); and the federal *Divorce and Corollary Relief Act* (received second reading on May 22, 1985).

JEFFERY WILSON
MARY TOMLINSON

October 1985

Table of Contents

Table of Cases

List of Statutes

Adoption Act, 1921, S.O. 1921, c. 55
Adoption Act, 1958, S.O. 1958, c. 11
Age of Majority and Accountability Act, R.S.O. 1980, c. 7
Apprenticeship and Tradesmen's Qualification Act, R.S.O. 1980, c. 24
Banks and Banking Law Revision Act, 1980, R.S.C. 1980-81-82-83, c. 40
British North America Act, 1867, 30 & 31 Vic. c. 3
Business Corporations Act, 1982, S.O. 1982, c. 4
Canada Elections Act, R.S.C. 1970, c. 14 (1st Supp.)
Canada Evidence Act, R.S.C. 1970, c. E-10
Canadian Bill of Rights, R.S.C. 1970, App. III
Canadian Human Rights Act, R.S.C. 1976-77, c. 33
Change of Name Act, R.S.O. 1980, c. 62
Charter of the French Language, R.S. Q. 1977, c. 11
Child and Family Services Act, 1984, S.O. 1984, c. 55
Child Welfare Act, R.S.O. 1980, c. 66
Child Welfare Act, S.M. 1974, c. 30
Children of Unmarried Parents Act, R.S.O. 1950, c. 51
Children's Law Reform Act, R.S.O. 1980, c. 68
Children's Law Reform Amendment Act, 1982, S.O. 1982, c. 20
Children's Maintenance Act, R.S.O. 1937, c. 213
Children's Mental Health Services Act, R.S.O. 1980, c. 69
Children's Residential Services Act, R.S.O. 1980, c. 71
Citizenship Act, S.C. 1974-75-76, c. 108
Constitution Act, 1982 (en. by the Canada Act, 1982 (U.K.) c. 11, Sched. B)
  (Charter of Rights and Freedoms, ss. 1-34)
Corporations Act, R.S.O. 1980, c. 95
Courts of Justice Act, 1984, S.O. 1984, c. 11
Criminal Code, R.S.C. 1970, c. C-34
Criminal Records Act, R.S.C. 1970, c. 12 (1st Supp.)
Day Nurseries Act, R.S.O. 1980, c. 11
Deserted Wives' and Children's Maintenance Act, R.S.O. 1970, c. 128
Developmental Services Act, R.S.O. 1980, c. 118
Divorce Act, R.S.C. 1970, c. D-8
Education Act, R.S.O. 1980, c. 129
Election Act, R.S.O. 1980, c. 133
Estates Administration Act, R.S.O. 1980, c. 143
Evidence Act, R.S.O. 1980, c. 145
Extra-provincial Custody Orders Enforcement Act, S.B.C. 1976, c. 17
Extra-provincial Custody Orders Enforcement Act, S.M. 1975, c. 4
Extra-provincial Custody Orders Enforcement Act, S.N.B. 1977, c. E-15
Extra-provincial Custody Orders Enforcement Act, S.P.E.I. 1975, c. 68
Extra-provincial Custody Orders Enforcement Act, S.S. 1978, c. E-18
Extra-provincial Enforcement of Custody Orders Act, R.S.A. 1980, c. E-17
Family and Child Service Act, S.B.C. 1980, c. 11
Family Benefits Act, R.S.O. 1980, c. 151

Chapter 1

Introduction: Children's Rights*

The chapters which follow discuss the laws that affect children in Canadian society with reference largely to Ontario and federal legislation. Laws that affect children, like other constituencies, often reflect a compromise of competing political or economic interests in the community at large. However, these laws, unlike those for other constituencies, find their political validity in the test of what is in the child's best interests as opposed to what the particular constituency itself is directly demanding. This difference is due to the dependent and immature state of childhood which compels adults in a democratic society to legislate for children those rights which children would pursue themselves if they were capable. However, by this very approach which theoretically is highly moral and admirable, the legislation and its method of implementation may more often reflect the interests of every other constituency but children. It is the rare elected body or bureaucracy that acts only in the interests of an economically powerless, non-voting, and essentially silent constituency.[1] Further, even if the motivation is pure, the assumptions underlying "best interests" may uncon-

---

*For a more detailed discussion of children's rights, particularly as they relate to s. 15 of the *Charter of Rights*, see J. Wilson, "Age Discrimination: Children", *Equality Rights in Canada*, eds. A. Bayefsky, M. Eberts (Toronto: Carswell Co., forthcoming).

[1]For literature on the fallibility of adult caretakers see J. Goldstein, A. Freud, A. J. Solnit, *Beyond the Best Interests of the Child* and *Before the Best Interests of the Child* (New York: Free Press, 1974 and 1979 respectively); R. H. Mnookin "Foster Care: In Whose Best Interests?", *The Rights of Children* (Cambridge: Harvard Educational Review, Reprint Series No. 9, 1974), at pp. 29–48; S. Katz, *When Parents Fail: The Law's Response to Family Breakdown* (Boston: Beacon Press, 1971); M. Garrison, "Why Terminate Parental Rights" (1983), 35 *Stanford Law Review* 423; R. H. deLone for Carnegie Council on Children, *Small Futures* (New York: Harcourt Brace Jovanovich, 1979); E. Schur, *Radical Non-Intervention: Rethinking the Delinquency Problem* (Englewood Cliffs, N.J.: Prentice Hall, 1973); J. Holt, *Escape from Childhood* (New York: Ballantine, 1974).

sciously have more to do with an adult's biases, prejudices and myths about childhood than with any objective, empirical evidence. Even with respect to the latter, there seldom exists a consensus among professionals who study children as to their nature, capacity and needs.[2]

History alone gives some indication of the invalidity of any one particular society's concept of childhood. For example, in the Middle Ages in Europe, childhood *per se* was an unknown concept. Once children reached six or seven years of age, they were dressed like adults, mixed with adults and possessed the rights and responsibilities of adults. Multi-aged communal and peer group living eased the child over the hurdle between infancy and adulthood. Schooling existed only in the form of apprenticeships. The seven-year old was expected to work. Subsequently, major economic and political upheavals such as the Industrial and French Revolutions produced an urban, nuclear family, as distinct from the rural, extended family, and a huge class of working and unemployed poor. Various philosophies emphasized the need to protect the innocence and vulnerability of the child from the evils of sloth and idleness. Children of the fourteenth and fifteenth centuries who regulated themselves (or at least worked side by side with their parents in order to avoid starvation), were replaced by the children of the sixteenth and seventeenth centuries whose perceived innocence required protection and guidance.[3] Modern day examples are the children of war-ridden societies. For example, over the decades of decimation, Vietnamese children have become their country's soldiers and breadwinners at eight and nine years of age.

The laws in North American society are unabashedly discriminatory in that they limit or withhold from persons under a particular age, usually 16, 18 or 19 years in Canada, those fundamental rights and freedoms which are integral to every person over that age living in a "free and democratic society." Due to the dictates of universality in our justice system as well as practicality and efficiency, the lawmakers choose watershed ages at which a "child" is deemed competent to handle the rights and accompanying responsibilities of being an "adult" in our society. Hence, a person under 16 years may not drive a car, purchase tobacco or marry without parental consent. A person under 18 cannot drink, vote or enter into binding contracts. (For a full discussion of this aspect of children and the law, see Chapter 5, "Property and Civil Participation".)

The laws are based essentially on the premise that, until the person reaches an age representative of competency, the parent, or whoever has legal custody of that person will stand in his stead with respect to determining his best interests subject to the type of state-imposed limitations noted above and subject to the courts acting as the final arbiter of "best interests" when the state suspects that a child is at risk. (See the chapters on custody, financial support and child

---

[2]See e.g. A. Skolnick, "The Limits of Childhood: Conceptions of Child Development and Social Context" (1975), 39 *Law and Contemporary Problems* 38, at p. 42.

[3]P. K. Naherny, J. Rosario, "Morality, Science and the Use of the Child in History", *Schooling and the Rights of Children*, eds. V. F. Haulrich, M. W. Apple (Berkley: McCutchan Publishing Corp., 1975), at pp. 5, 11, 13, 35n, 29. See generally Phillippe Aries, *Centuries of Childhood: A Social History of the Family* (New York: Random House, 1962); C. J. Ross, "Of Children and Liberty: An Historian's Views" (1982), 52 (No. 3) *American Journal of Orthopsychiatry* 470.

protection.) The criminal law alone singles out the child as an independent entity separate and apart from the family who, if between the ages of 12 and 18 years, is held responsible for his anti-social acts, albeit not to the same degree of severity as his adult counterpart. This may be due to the fact that the protection of society from criminal acts is an objective that must take precedence over the usually paramount "child protectionism" objective. (See Chapter 7, "Crime and the Child".)

In the past few decades a novel lobby has emerged with respect to the status of childhood which advocates children's rights rather than child protectionism due to the fact that the latter can often be ineffective and unjust. The United Nations' "Year of the Child" spawned many such calls to the barricades, and in Canada, even prior to the international promotion, a 1975 *British Columbia Royal Commission Report on Family and Child Law* included a part entitled "Children's Rights" which suggested radical changes to the legal status of children in society.[4] "Best interests" protections were transformed into entrenched rights and the child was to become a separate legal entity, who was given the status to pursue and enforce those rights in court. Due to the inevitable pendulum swing of political and societal mores, what remains today is something between "child protectionism" and "children's rights."

The wild card on the horizon is the *Canadian Charter of Rights and Freedoms* which not only entrenches the rights and freedoms of all "persons" which includes any age, but also prohibits discrimination under s. 15 before and under the law as well as equal protection and benefit of the law based on the specifically enumerated category of age. The question will be whether the "reasonable limitation" test of s. 1 or the "affirmative action" exemption of s. 15(2) will be used by state and court alike to entrench the "best interests" tautology as well. In other words, will the bench go behind the rubber stamp "best interests" label to determine in an objective, empirical and judicial fashion just what are the child's best interests as well as whose "best interests" the impugned legislation actually serves. Under the *Canadian Bill of Rights*, the courts were asked to strike down provisions of legislation discriminating against children in the criminal system which basically allowed for more severe punishment for minors than for their adult counterparts.[5] The courts declined to do so on the basis that the intent of Parliament was to act in the child's best interests which was a valid federal objective. The disposition which the appellants labelled punishment was labelled as beneficial treatment by Parliament, a label behind which the courts did not intend to go.

To date, cases concerning the rights of children brought under the *Charter of Rights* have, for the most part, dealt with the criminal law as determined by the now repealed *Juvenile Delinquents Act*. In the criminal sphere, the courts appear willing to pierce the "best interests veil" by way of the "reasonable limits" test, no longer endorsing parliamentary immunity based on legislative intent. Such decisions have essentially recognized no inherent distinction based on age in the

---

[4]*Fifth Report of the British Columbia Royal Commission on Family and Child Law: Part III*, Chairperson Mr. Justice Berger (as he then was), 1975.

[5]*R. v. Burneshine* (1974), 44 D.L.R. (3d) 584, 15 C.C.C. (2d) 505.

applicability of the *Charter's* provisions and, for the most part, they have specifically recognized proceedings under the *Juvenile Delinquents Act* as criminal, thereby deserving of all of the protections which the justice system extends to an accused person.[6]

There have been very few non-criminal Charter cases dealing with children's interests that have been reported. Of those few, most might be classified as reflecting parental interests (as well as or instead of children's interests) in controlling his or her child's upbringing in the face of state objections. Such cases consider the issues of consent to medical treatment[7] or education in a particular language,[8] religion,[9] or child welfare.[10] An issue clearly of interest to the child which may potentially be fought in a Charter context by parents on behalf of their children is the right to an education appropriate for a particular child's needs. (See Chapter 8, "Education".) Then there are those issues in which the child and the parent may find themselves in opposition to one another such as consent to mental health treatment or committal[11] (see Chapter 5, "Property and Civil Rights: Consent to Treatment") or the custody/access arena in a family breakdown situation[12] (see Chapter 2).

An essential thread runs through all of the issues. While the courts must recognize that children like some other constituencies must be treated differently under the law in recognition of their dependent status, the courts must also determine when and how the infringement of rights and liberties and unequal treatment is justified in the context of the language of the *Charter*. To do this the court must go behind the intent of the legislation to its impact on children, necessitating the introduction of socio-economic, psychological and/or empirical data and opinion[13] in order to challenge long-held assumptions about childhood and the infallibility of adult caretakers. To do otherwise is to revert to the *Canadian Bill of Rights* approach of "valid government objective" or the "rational relationship" test applied by U.S. courts when dealing with a constituency which attracts only "minimal scrutiny." Many Canadian courts have already established as a general proposition that legislative intent and valid

---

[6]*R. v. M.* (1982), 70 C.C.C. (2d) 123 (Ont. Prov. Ct.) (s. 9, *Charter*: protection against arbitrary detention); *R. v. KS* (1982), 8 W.C.B. 502 (Ont. Prov. Ct.) (s. 10(b), *Charter*: right to retain counsel); *R. v. D.G.* (1983), 11 W.C.B. 275 (Alta. Q.B.) (s. 11(h), *Charter*: "double jeopardy"); *Re Edmonton Journal and A.-G. for Alberta et al.* (1983), 42 A.R. 383, 4 C.C.C. (3d) 59 (Q.B.); *R. v. R.J.* (1982), 37 O.R. (2d) 173 (Prov. Ct.) (s. 11(d), *Charter*: privacy of proceedings).

[7]*Re D.* (1982), 30 R.F.L. (2d) 277 (Alta. Prov. Ct.).

[8]*Société des Acadiens du Nouveau-Brunswick Inc. et al. v. Minority Language School Bd. No. 50* (1983), 48 N.B.R. (2d) 361, 126 A.P.R. 361 (Q.B.); *Marchand v. Simcoe County Board of Education et al.*, summarized in (1984), 24 A.C.W.S. (2d) 196 (Ont. H.C.).

[9]*R. v. Jones* (1983), 43 A.R. 64 (Prov. Ct.) (On appeal).

[10]*Re T. and C.C.A.S. of Metro. Toronto*, summarized in (1984), 26 A.C.W.S. (2d) 86 (Ont. Prov. Ct.) (ss. 7, 20, 8, 9, *Charter*); *Re W and C.A.S. of Regional Municipality of York*, summarized in (1982), 17 A.C.W.S. (2d) 147 (Ont. Prov. Ct.) (ss. 1, 8, 24(2), *Charter*).

[11]For an American case see *Parham v. J.R.*, 99 S.C. 2493 (1979). For a Canadian case which held that s. 10(c) of the *Charter* ensures that *habeas corpus* applies to persons involuntarily detained under a *Mental Health Act* see *Reference Re Procedures and the Mental Health Act* (1984), 5 D.L.R. (4th) 577 (P.E.I.S.C.) (in banco).

[12]For an inter-parental Charter issue in the area of custody see *Brown v. Brown* (1983), 29 Sask. R. 265, 3 D.L.R. (4th) 283 (C.A.) (court found no contravention of s. 2(a) religious freedoms in limiting access by prohibiting the taking of children to religious services).

jurisdiction are not the determining factors and that the courts are now supreme in deciding whether the broad rights and freedoms of the *Charter* have been infringed beyond ''such reasonable limits prescribed by law as can be demonstrably justified in a free and democratic society.''[14] Further, due to the specific enumeration of ''age'' as a category under s. 15 of this Act, it seems doubtful that the courts would adopt a minimal scrutiny approach to this constituency especially if fundamental rights and freedoms are at stake, if indeed Canadian courts develop U.S.-like gradations of scrutiny at all.

One final note. An inchoate ''defence'' to which the state may eventually resort is the ''affirmative action'' exemption to equality rights, found under s. 15(2). The essential difference between this ''defence'' and the s. 1 ''reasonable limits'' test is that the ''affirmative action program'' need only ''have as its object the amelioration of conditions'' of the ''disadvantaged'' constituency which may bring one back full circle to ''legislative intent.''[15] Nevertheless, even this subsection must meet the s. 1 ''reasonable limits'' test although it is conceivable that by bringing the legislation within s. 15(2), the scrutiny under s. 1 may be less rigorous.

As a bottom-line position, and as a starting point, the effect of s. 15 and the advent of a concept of ''children's rights'' must be to test, if not neutralize, the long-held untested and blanket presumptions of incapacity for those constituents of society identified as children.

---

[13]*Reference Re Education Act and Minority Language Education Rights* (1984), 47 O.R. (2d) 1 (C.A.) (court can consider historical background of Charter provision including relevant political, economic, social and cultural developments as an aid to interpretation); *Public Service Alliance of Canada v. R. in Right of Canada* (1984), 11 D.L.R. (4th) 337 (Fed. Ct. T.D.); (must assess benefit resulting from restraint to society as a whole against the cost of infringement to individuals and economic evidence can assist in the balancing exercise; note that the Fed. C.A. in affirming the decision expressed doubt as to utility of using economic evidence to decide *Charter* issues: 11 D.L.R. (4th) 387 (Fed. C.A.); *Re Southam Inc. and The Queen (No. 1)* (1983), 41 O.R. (2d) 113, 3 C.C.C. (3d) 515 (C.A.) (in determining the reasonableness of the limitation, the court must be satisfied by the terms and purpose of the limiting law, its economic, social and political background and, if helpful, references to comparable legislation in other free and democratic societies). In the U.S. case of *Wisconsin v. Yoder*, 406 U.S. 205 (1972), Mr. Justice Douglas in a strong dissent relied on the psychological and sociological findings of Piaget, Kohlberg, Kay, Gessel and Ilg regarding the capacity of children to exercise moral and intellectual judgment in holding that the Amish children should be heard by the court in a decision affecting their education.

[14]*Re Southam Inc. and The Queen (No. 1)* (1983), *supra*, note 13 (''presumption of constitutionality'' has no application); *Re Jamieson and The Queen* (1982), 70 C.C.C. (2d) 430 (Que. S.C.) endorses *Quebec Association of Protestant School Bds. v. A.-G. of Quebec (No. 2)*, (1982), 140 D.L.R. (3d) 33 (Que. S.C.) (test that a limit is reasonable if it is proportionate to the objective to be attained by the law); *Re Reich and College of Physicians and Surgeons of Alberta*, unreported, April 6, 1984 (Alta. Q.B.), as cited in *Canadian Charter of Rights Annotated*) (''reasonable limits'' test does not turn on what is necessary or the only possible course of action to meet the social need but it is more than mere reasonability; the legislative objective must be important or ''compelling'' and the means chosen to achieve it are preferable to some other means of achieving it); *Public Service Alliance of Canada v. R. in Right of Canada, ibid.* (s. 1 test more than reasonable rationale and more than showing that in Legislature's judgment, the limitation was justified which only goes to showing ''prescribed by law'').

[15]See *Bill of Rights* cases *R. v. Mackay; R. v. Willington* (1977), 36 C.C.C. (2d) 349 (Alta. C.A.), in which a provision of the *Juvenile Delinquents Act* making it applicable to boys under 16 and girls under 18 was upheld on the basis that Parliament did not discriminate by distinguishing unfavourably but, in fact, singled out one group to confer a benefit on it.

Chapter 1: Readings

"A Basic Youth Law Library" (biblio) (Mar/80), 13 *Clearinghouse Rev* 866.

American Law Division, Cong. Res. Serv. of the Library of Congress, *Constitutional Rights of Children* (Prepared for Subcommittee on the Constitution of the Committee on the Judiciary, U.S. Senate, 1979).

Aries, Philippe, *Centuries of Childhood: A Social History of the Family* (N.Y.: Random House, 1962).

Bayefsky, A. and Eberts, M. (eds.), *Equality Rights in Canada* (Toronto: Carswell Co., to be published in April, 1985).

Berkeley, H. *et al.*, "Children's Rights in the Canadian Context" (1978), 8 *Interchange* 77.

Boli-Bennett, J. and Meyer, J.W., "The Ideology of Childhood and the State: Rules Distinguishing Children in National Constitutions, 1870–1970" (1978), 43 *American Sociological Review* (No. 6).

Bremner, R.H. (ed.), *The Legal Rights of Children: An Original Anthology* (N.Y.: Arno Press, 1974).

British Columbia Royal Commission on Family and Children's Law (Berger Commission), *Fifth Report* (Victoria: Queen's Printer, 1975).

Catton, Katherine, "Children and the Law: An Empirical Review", *The Child in the City: Changes & Challenges*, Michelson, W. *et al.* (eds.), (Toronto: University of Toronto, 1979), pp. 201–08.

Clive, E., "What Has Happened to the Age of Minority" (Scotland), (July, 82) 27 *Jur. Rev.* 51.

Cohen, Howard, *Equal Rights for Children* (Totowa, N.J.: Rowman and Littlefield, 1980).

Davidson, H. and Horowitz, R., *The Legal Rights of Children* (Shepard's/McGraw-Hill, 1984).

De Lone, Richard H., Carnegie Council on Children, *Small Futures: Children, Inequality, and the Limits of Liberal Reform* (New York and London: Harcourt Brace Jovanovitch, 1979).

Dickens, B., "Modern Function and Limits of Parental Rights" (July, 81), 97 *L.Q. Rev.* 462.

Erickson, Erik, *Childhood and Society*, 2nd ed. (N.Y.: Norton, 1964).

Foster, H.H., *A Bill of Rights for Children* (Springfield, Ill.: Chas. C. Thomas, 1974).

Freeman, M.D.A., "The Rights of Children in the International Year of the Child" (Great Britain) (address at University College London, Nov. 15, 1979).

Gaylin, W. "The 'Competence' of Children: No Longer All or None" (March, 1982), 21 *J. of Am. Ac. of Child Psychiatry* (No. 2) 153.

Henning, James S., (ed.) *The Rights of Children: Legal and Psychological Perspectives* (Springfield, Ill.: Chas. C. Thomas, 1982).

Institute of Judicial Administration, American Bar Association, *Standards Relating to the Rights of Minors* (Ballinger, 1981).

International Year of the Child — Child Advocacy, 1979: Proceedings (Yale Child Study Center, New Haven, 1980).

Kahn, A., Kamerman, S. and McGowan, B. *Child Advocacy* (Aronson, 1975).

Katz, S. (ed.) *The Youngest Minority: Parts I and II* (Lawyers in Defence of Children) (American Bar Association, Family Law Section, 1974).

Keiter, "Privacy, Children and Their Parents: Reflections On and Beyond the Supreme Court's Approach" (March, 82), 66 *Minn L. Rev.* 459.

Kenniston, Kenneth (Carnegie Council of Children) *All Our Children — The American Family under Pressure* (N.Y.: Harcourt Brace Jovanovich, 1977).

Leon, J., "Canadian Children — Prospects for Legal Rights and Representation" (1979), 2 *Fam. Law R.* 16.

Margolin, C.R. "Salvation vs. Liberation: The Movement for Children's Rights in an Historical Context" (1978), 25 *Social Problems* (No. 4) 441.

Marks, F.R. "Detours on the Road to Maturity: A View of the Legal Conception of Growing Up and Letting Go" (1975), 39 *Law and Contemporary Problems* 78.

Melton, G.B. "Toward 'Personhood' for Adolescents: Autonomy and Privacy as Values in Public Policy" (January, 83), 38 *American Psychologist* 99.

Mnookin, R., "Children's Rights: Beyond Kiddie Libbers and Child Savers" (Fall, 1978), *Journal of Clinical Child Psychology* 163.

——————, "Thinking About Children's Rights — Moving Beyond Kiddie Libbers and Child Savers" (Spring/Summer 1981), 16 *Stanford Lawyer* 24.

Mnookin, Robert H. and Coons, John E., "Toward a Theory of Children's Rights" (1977), 28 *Harvard Law School Bulletin* 18–21, Spring.

Rosario, J. "Morality, Science and the Use of the Child in History", *Schooling and the Rights of Children*, Haubrich, V.F. and Apple, M.W. (eds.) (Berkeley: McCutcheon Publishing Corp., 1975).

Ross, C.F., "Of Children and Liberty: An Historian's Views" (1982), 52 *American Journal of Orthopsychiatry* (No. 3).

Skolnick, A. "The Limits of Childhood: Conceptions of Child Development and Social Context" (1975), 38 *Law and Contemporary Problems* 38.

Stodolsky, S., "Age-related Changes in the Individual: Childhood and Adolescence" (Symposium on Age Discrimination) (1981), 57 *Chi-Kent L. Rev.* 851.

Stone, O.M., "Warsaw Conference on the Legal Protection of the Rights of the Child" (1979), 17 *Alta. L. Rev.* 555.

Sutton, J.R., "Social Structure, Institutions and the Legal Status of Children in the U.S." (March, 83), 88 *Am. J. of Soc.* (No. 5) 88.

Teitelbaum, L., "The *Age Discrimination Act* and Youth" (Symposium on Age Discrimination) (Fall, 81), 57 *Chi-Kent L. Rev.* 969.

Wald, M., "Children's Rights: A Framework for Analysis" (1979), 12 *U.C.D.L. Rev.* (No. 2) 255.

Westen, P. "The Empty Idea of Equality" (1982), 95 *Harvard L. Rev.* 537.

Wingo, H., Freytag, S.N. "Decisions Within the Family: A Clash of Constitutional Rights" (March, 82), 67 *Iowa L. Rev.* 401.

Worsfold, V.L., "A Philosophical Justification for Children's Rights" (1974), 44 *Harvard Educational Review* 142.

Wringe, C.A., *Children's Rights: A Philosophical Study*, (London, Boston: Routledge & Kegan Paul, 1981).

General: Special Issues of Periodicals on Children's Rights.

Law & Contemporary Problems, Vol. 39, 1975.

Harvard Educational Review, Reprint Series No. 9, 1974.

American Journal of Orthopsychiatry, Vol. 52, July, 1982.

Columbia Human Rights Law Rev., Vol. 13, Fall-Wint. 1981–82 (U.S., England, Greece, Israel, Norway).

——————., Vol. 13, Spr.-Summ., 1981 (Australia, China, Columbia, Congo, Cuba, Czechoslovakia, Egypt).

Clearinghouse Review, Vol. 16, (Jan. 1983) (Third Annual Review of Poverty Law: 1981–82).

Children's Legal Rights. Vol. 2, Mar.-Apr. 1981 (Legal Issues for Children of the 80s).

Chi-Kent Law Rev., Vol. 57, 1981 (Symposium on Age Discrimination).

The Guardian, (National Assoc. of Counsel for Children, Denver, Co.) Vol. 5, Fall, 1983 (case index of all cases listed in their publication from 1978–83 from the U.S. and Can., alphabetically and by subject).

Chapter 2

The Family in Conflict I: Custody and Access*

Introduction

The child, as a biological and legal dependant, possesses a status which depends on the stability of the family unit. In the absence of any court order or parental agreement, the child's biological mother and father are presumed and recognized in law as the joint guardians or joint custodial parents of the child. That is, either parent, with or without the consent of the other, can exercise all of the rights and responsibilities associated with an adult who legally is in charge of a child.[1] In other words, the archaic presumption in favour of the father has been eradicated. The law assumes that a mother and father will both act with the necessary degree of cooperation and trust such that either parent, without verification from the other, can attend to the child's needs, free of any legally imposed structure by agreement or order of the court.

When the family unit breaks down, the disposition of the child by the parents or court is theoretically to be governed by the amorphous, presumably child-centered concept of the "best interests" of the child. In reality, the disposition is based less on what the child's best interests are and more on what the least detrimental alternative is.

The necessity of forming what amounts to another family unit for the child arises in four legal situations:

1) disputes between parents upon the event of a marital or cohabitation separation;

---

*This chapter utilizes existing law under the *Divorce Act* while reference is made to the *Divorce and Corollary Relief Act* (Bill C-47) (which has now passed first reading and will repeal its predecessor), when there is significant difference between present and proposed law.

[1]DesLaurier v. Jackson, [1934] S.C.R. 149, [1934] 1 D.L.R. 790; and note s. 20(1) of the *Children's Law Reform* Act which reads: "Except as otherwise provided in this Part, the father and the mother of a child are equally entitled to custody of the child."

In Ontario, the statutory devices for moving the child about can be summarized as follows:

Legal Parties	Statute	Decision-Making Forum
1. Married parents	*Children's Law Reform Act*	Supreme, District, Unified Family and Provincial Courts (Fam. Div.)
	Divorce Act*	Supreme Court
2. Unmarried parents	*Children's Law Reform Act*	Supreme, District, Unified Family and Provincial Courts (Fam. Div.)
3. Parents and the State	*Child and Family Services Act*, 1984*	Provincial Court (Fam. Div.)
	Courts of Justice Act, 1984	Supreme Court
4. Parent and Third Party (adoption)	*Children's Law Reform Act*	Supreme, District, Unified Family and Provincial Courts (Fam. Div.)
	Child and Family Services Act, 1984* Part VII: Adoption	Provincial Court (Fam. Div.)
5. The Child and the State	*Young Offenders Act*	Provincial Court (Fam. Div.)
	Provincial Offences Act	
	Training Schools Act	

*At the time of writing, the *Child and Family Services Act*, which will repeal the *Child Welfare Act*, has been passed but not proclaimed. The first reading of the *Divorce and Corollary Relief Act*, repealing the *Divorce Act*, occurred May 1, 1985.

2) disputes between a parent or both parents and a third party who has assumed ''parental'' care of the child, or who wishes to do so against the wishes of the parent;

3) disputes between a parent or parents and the state through its Children's Aid Society or child welfare superintendent, where the state is concerned that the child's welfare will be jeopardized if the status quo is maintained; and

4) disputes between the child and the state arising from the child's aberrant conduct, necessitating a temporary or permanent placement of the child outside of the home pursuant to mental health or criminal legislation.

The first two categories above, that is, custody and access between parents, is dealt with in this chapter. The third category will be discussed in Chapter 3, ''The Family in Conflict II: Child Protection and Adoption'', because the involvement of the state, as a party to the proceeding, changes the proceeding from a civil, private family dispute to what can be described as a quasi-criminal proceeding (despite its civil standard of proof and Rules of Procedure) with the potential for extremely severe consequences. The fourth category, also discussed in Chapter 3, is the placement of the child through the legal fiction of adoption, a category which must be considered separately since, unlike any other legal response, it represents the total dissolution of one family unit in favour of another. Unique within all of law, the adoption process amounts to a legal severence of a biological connection between one person and another on the assumption that such a drastic fiction is necessary to form a more viable, secure family unit for the dependent child. The fifth category will be discussed in Chapter 7, ''Crime and the Child'', although in many instances, the issues of ''where and with whom am I going to live'' will be the same for the child whether the precipitating event is criminal or civil in nature.

Custody by Contract

In the event of a family breakdown, it is obviously preferable that parents continue to act and plan on a basis of trust and cooperation with respect to their child. In fact, Ontario's *Family Law Reform Act* (hereinafter known as the *FLRA*) sanctions the right of parents to plan for the welfare of their children even before, and without regard to, the event of a family breakdown. A man and woman who are cohabiting but not married, or who are married and living together or intending to marry, may legally enter into a ''cohabitation agreement'' or ''marriage contract'' respectively, which outlines their respective rights and duties during cohabitation, in the event of separation or upon death. Such rights and duties can include child-support obligations and the direction of the child's education and moral training: ss. 51 and 52. However, such contracts cannot include a provision with respect to the custody of or access to a child in the event of separation or death. Parties who have cohabited in or outside of marriage may enter into an agreement which includes custody and access provisions only upon separation: s. 53. Presumably, the prohibition of such a provision in all but separation agreements represents the Legislature's concern that the changing custodial needs of the child, as well as the changing circumstances of each parent, require an assessment at the time of the precipitating event, rather than a pre-arranged resolution based on the circumstances at the time the contract was entered into. This approach is augmented by the necessary presumption that both parents are presumed to be equally responsible for the care of the child, militating against one or the other undertaking a greater share of such responsibility.

When entering into a child-custody contract, the parties need not assume that the custodial parent will have control of every aspect of the child's welfare. Ontario's new *Children's Law Reform Act* (hereinafter known as the *CLRA*) distinguishes the concept of "custodial parent", a role which encompasses the daily care of the child, from "incidents of custody,"[2] the responsibility for which can be assumed by either the custodial or non-custodial parent. The legislation declines to define "incidents of custody" but in practice they may include whatever the parties think appropriate for their own particular family dynamics. For example, while one parent may have custodial care, it may be more practical or better for the child if the non-custodial parent assumes the decision-making responsibility for the child's education.[3]

Joint Custody

Parties can also agree that both shall retain their full custodial powers by way of a joint custody provision which, in its simplest form, would mean that either parent would continue to make any and all arrangements related to the child's welfare, independent of notice to or consent of the other parent, as if the parties were cohabiting and had never separated. Often, in the face of the inevitable tension and strained communications characteristic of a separation, parties may agree on the principles of joint custody to assure the continued involvement of both parties, but they will reserve certain matters to the discretion of one parent only. For example, they may agree that the child will reside and be in the daily care of one parent but on all matters that affect major decisions related to the child's welfare, the consent of both parents will be necessary. The variations on the nature of the contract within the confines of a joint custody agreement are unlimited; there are even existing and workable joint custody agreements where one parent resides in Toronto and the other parent resides in Vancouver. In effect, there appears to be no legislative impediment to prevent parties from devising a contract which represents their family's wishes and needs, positively stating their intended, continued joint involvement as a principle of their separation and as a message to their child. (For further discussion regarding joint custody in the context of court proceedings, see below under "Custody by Court Order: Joint Custody".)

---

[2] Sections 21 and 28 of the *Children's Law Reform Act* provide as follows:

   s. 21 A parent of a child or any other person may apply to a court for an order respecting custody of or access to the child or determining any aspect of the incidents of custody of the child.

· · ·

   s. 28 The court to which an application is made under s. 21,
      (a) by order may grant the custody of or access to the child to one or more persons;
      (b) by order may determine any aspect of the incidents of the right to custody or access;
   The proposed *Divorce and Corollary Relief Act* also includes "incidents of custody".

[3] For a case in which a split in custodial decision-making was directed, see *Borel v. Borel*, summarized in (1981), 4 F.L.R.R. 68 (report of Commissioner to Supreme Court) in which the custody of two children, ages 5 and 3, was awarded to the mother but the father was granted the right to determine the child's education. See also *Donald v. Donald* (1980), 3 Sask. R. 202 (Q.B.) (mother has daily care and control, father has responsibility for education, guidance and other decisions, with permanent effect); *Charlton v. Charlton* (1980), 19 B.C.L.R. 42, 15 R.F.L. (2d) 220 (S.C.) (custody to mother, joint guardianship to both).

While Ontario legislation does not provide for same, it appears that in practice, parents may also enter into agreements with third parties whereby they delegate their custodial responsibilities for some period of time, or arguably indefinitely. These agreements are often necessary, primarily to allow a third party who is caring for the child on a temporary basis to attend to the child's medical or other special needs. In the absence of such an agreement, a hospital, doctor or teacher may very likely decline to accept the authority of the third party except in emergency situations. (Note that this does not apply to adoption, which must be conducted through a licensee or adoption agency.[4])

Whatever the agreement consists of, its terms are subject to the court's inherent jurisdiction to scrutinize any matters pertaining to children.[5] This has now been codified by s. 55(1) of the *FLRA* which allows the court to disregard any term of a domestic contract "respecting the support, education, moral training or custody of or access to a child."[6] The courts also exercise this superseding jurisdiction with respect to testamentary guardians.[7] On the other hand, a court may be used to enforce a custody agreement, even when the agreement was oral.[8]

Custody by Court Order

If the parents cannot agree on custody/access arrangements then either parent may apply at any time for a court order defining their respective custodial and access rights and incidents thereto: s. 21, *CLRA* (ss. 10, 11 of the *Divorce Act*). Unfortunately, the parents will have imposed on them a child-rearing regime that more often than not will be less accommodating, less flexible and less sensitive to the family's needs than that which could have been hammered out by private agreement. On the other hand, it is the minority of separating couples that can reach such an agreement. Typically, the court will award one parent custody, giving to that parent all of the duties, responsibilities and rights of a parent independent of the other, and providing the other with a varying degree of access. However, one can argue to divide up "incidents of custody" as allowed in the disposition section of the *CLRA* (s. 28) or s. 2(1) of the proposed *Divorce*

---

[4]The *Child Welfare Act*, s. 65; see the *Child and Family Services Act*, s. 135.

[5]*Clarke v. Clarke,* [1952] O.W.N. 671 (H.C.).

[6]See *Rosene v. Rosene* (1981), 22 R.F.L. (2d) 179 (B.C. C.A.); *Voegelin v. Voegelin* (1980), 15 R.F.L. (2d) 1 (Ont. Co. Ct.). For similar cases under the *Divorce Act*, see *Watkins v. Watkins* (1980), 25 Nfld. and P.E.I.R. 98, 68 A.P.R. 98, 14 R.F.L. (2d) 97 (Nfld. S.C.).

[7]Section 62 of the *CLRA* establishes the power of custodial parents to appoint someone to have custody or guardianship upon their deaths. Such an appointment will lapse if an application for court approval is not commenced within 90 days of its becoming effective. This section does not preclude any party from seeking custody through the courts. Despite this section, the courts retain an inherent jurisdiction to overrule it: *Kiehlbauch v. Franklin* (1979), 20 A.R. 31 (T.D.); *Re Doyle,* [1943] O.W.N. 119 (Surr. Ct.).

[8]See *Colter v. Colter* (1982), 38 O.R. (2d) 221 (S.C.) where an oral interim agreement was hammered out between the lawyers and parents, giving two children to the mother and two children to the father. Upon leaving the meeting, the mother changed her mind and phoned to repudiate. The court upheld the agreement, stating that (1) both parents were capable, and (2) s. 54(1) of the *Family Law Reform Act* requiring domestic contracts to be in writing did not bar the court's enforcement of an oral interim agreement witnessed by counsel. See also *Moldowan v. Moldowan* (1979), 1 Sask. R. 316, 13 R.F.L. (2d) 1, 2 Fam. L.Rev. 239 (C.A.) and *Sczesny v. Sczesny* (1981), 25 R.F.L. (2d) 240 (Sask. Q.B.) where the court held that the custody/access agreement as the status quo must remain in force until the final determination of the court on the matter.

and Corollary Relief Act which may or may not amount to joint custody in the view of the court.[9]

A parent cannot obtain exclusive legal custody except through a legal domestic contract or order of the court. In the absence of same, one parent cannot assume the role of the sole custodial parent by simply removing the child from the care of the other, except if the other expressly or implicitly consents or acquiesces to the arrangement, an exception which reflects the reality of many separation situations, but which lays the seed for more confusion usually leading to hurtful and expensive litigation. The operative section is s. 20(4) of the *CLRA*:

> s. 20(4) Where the parents of a child live separate and apart and the child lives with one of them with the consent, implied consent or acquiescence of the other of them, the right of the other to exercise the entitlement to custody and the incidents of custody, but not the entitlement to access, is suspended until a separation agreement or order otherwise provides.

It is still not clear from case law exactly what "acquiesce" means, or what "implied consent" includes, but it is clear that in the absence of an agreement, a party who removes a child from the other and who cannot prove the consent of the other will be ordered, unless there are exceptional circumstances related to the needs of the child, to return the child to the home where both parties were residing.[10] Some courts have attempted to set up an objective rule of thumb by suggesting that the time that must elapse before inactivity on the part of the non-custodial parent constitutes "implied consent" or "acquiescence" would be approximately three months, all other things being equal.[11]

Difficulties emerge when one attempts to integrate the legal system, rooted in rights of property and freedom from physical harm, with the infinitely more subtle and complex dynamics of a family under siege from within. The parents become involved in a nerve-wracking game of chess in which neither will leave the home, fearful that by doing so the other parent will be able to assume sole *de facto* custodial rights, solidifying a future court offensive based on "acquiescence" or "implied consent" of the parent who left.[12] Not surprisingly, the pawn in this chess game is the child. Eventually, one of several tie-breaking situations must result:

> 1) one party out of desperation or concern for the child will yield, allowing the other party to proclaim victory by default;

---

[9]See cases *supra*, note 3.

[10]*Wine v. Wine* (1976), 27 R.F.L. 129 (Ont. H.C.).

[11]*Re P. (G.E.) (an Infant),* [1964] 3 All E.R. 977 (C.A.).

[12]See *e.g. Peckford v. Peckford* (1980), 25 Nfld. and P.E.I.R. 106, 68 A.P.R. 106 (Nfld. T.D.); *Olson v. Olson* (1982), 51 N.S.R. (2d) 214, 102 A.P.R. 214 (Prov. Ct.); *Anderson v. Anderson* (1979), 21 Nfld. and P.E.I.R. 513, 56 A.P.R. 513 (Nfld. S.C.); *Briggs v. Briggs* (1979), 27 N.B.R. (2d) 88, 60 A.P.R. 60 (Q.B.). But see *Middaugh v. Middaugh* (1981), 32 O.R. (2d) 681, 122 D.L.R. (3d) 516, 22 R.F.L. (2d) 388 (C.A.). (After placing child with father for 14 months while mother re-establishes herself economically, interim custody until divorce hearing back with mother.)

2) one party will allege foul play on the part of the other and call upon the court to proclaim a constructive win; or

3) one party will cheat, *i.e.* remove the child without the consent or knowledge of the other.

At this point in time, the courts become involved, assuming the role of referee, and attempt to sort out exactly what happened in order to reach a fair decision. However, fairness from the perspective of the adult will not necessarily be the same as from the perspective of the best interests of the child. The dispute must therefore be resolved by integrating the adult expectations of "fair play" with the needs or best interests of the child, the protection of the latter being assigned to the judicial referee. It is this distinct dual quality of custody dispute resolution that invites so much foul play on the part of the adult parties who proclaim a "best interest" motivation to justify their conduct towards the other as a defensible means to an end.

Dynamics of Judicial Decision Making

Unfortunately, in crucial ways, the legal principles that have emerged from judicial decision making reinforce the playing of the game. For example:

1) The party who gains sole interim custody, in fact or in law, achieves a distinct advantage over his rival because the courts are reluctant to intervene with an arrangement that has survived a period of time without difficulty and upon which the child has established a sense of security, stability and consistency.[13] This principle encourages each adult to "grab" the child first and to base all actions on a fast win at any cost.

2) The interim proceeding that determines the care of the child under trial occurs many months before the trial, elevating its importance to the final result. Only on a rare occasion does the court decide the issue of interim custody on *viva voce* evidence, but instead relies on affidavit material. Weeks or months later, the transcripts of the cross-examinations may then be considered if interim custody is still at issue. The process deteriorates into one of written denunciation with no oral accountability before an adjudicator, aggravated by the rhetoric of both counsel.

3) Canadian courts will not impose joint custody against the will of either parent.[14]

4) The child is not usually a party to the proceeding and barring appointment from the judge in his discretion, the child will not be legally represented.[15] This encourages the parties to presume that each of them speaks for the child, knowing what he really wants and needs and to accuse the other of distorting the child's wishes or brain-washing him in order to bolster their own case. Except under the *Divorce Act*, nothing precludes the child from seeking party status in a custody proceeding through the

---

[13]*Jessop v. Jessop* (1976), 30 R.F.L. 21 (Ont. C.A.); *J. v. C.,* [1969] 1 All E.R. 788, at 824 (H.L.) and for status quo of interim custody situation, see *Papp v. Papp,* [1970] 1 O.R. 331 (C.A.).

[14]See *Kruger v. Kruger* (1979), 25 O.R. (2d) 673, 11 R.F.L. (2d) 52 (C.A.) and *Baker v. Baker* (1979), 23 O.R. (2d) 391, 8 R.F.L. (2d) 236 (C.A.).

[15]See *Rowe v. Rowe* (1976), 26 R.F.L. 91 (Ont. H.C.).

intervention of a litigation guardian. Section 21 of the *CLRA* states that a parent "or any other person" may make application. It may be that the denial of party status to the child under the *Divorce Act* requires review under the *Charter of Rights*.[16] However, the reality is that the child will be without funds to retain a solicitor.

5) The law continues to rely upon the adversarial process in custody dispute resolution. This means that the parties must actively prepare themselves for a battle as the court remains passive, awaiting the best and most devastating evidence that either can muster. The judge, bringing all of his biases and often with little family law background or mediating skills, becomes the individual who must be manipulated by the game players in the isolated and unreal world of the court room.

In the context of this decision-making paradigm, the chapter continues with a review of legal principles which have emerged from custody and access disputes.

Parties

Under Ontario's *CLRA*, the parties to a proceeding can include a parent of a child "or any other person" who might wish to apply to court for an order respecting custody of or access to a child, or an order determining any aspect of the incidents of custody of the child: ss. 21 and 63(3).[17] In fact, the latter section requires as parties

i) the mother and father;

ii) anyone who has demonstrated a settled intention to treat the child as his own;

iii) anyone who had actual care and upbringing of the child immediately before the application; and

iv) anyone else whose presence as a party "is necessary to determine the matters in issue."

The word "parent" is not defined in this piece of legislation, but under its predecessor, it has been interpreted to include any person who has demonstrated a settled intention to treat a child as a member of his or her own family. This interpretation would make sense in that it is the same as that under the *FLRA*, which delineates a parent's child support obligations and it reflects the required parties under s. 63(3). The Ontario Supreme Court determined under the repealed s. 35 of the *FLRA* that third parties who are not included under this extended definition of "parent" may nonetheless apply for custody under the phrase "or any other person", which was set out in s. 35 and is now incorporated in the operative s. 21 of the *CLRA*.[18] In contrast, one County Court

---

[16]The pre-*Charter* decision of *Mierins v. Mierins,* [1973] 1 O.R. 421 (S.C.) determined that a child is not a party under the *Divorce Act* and therefore there is no violation of his rights to representation pursuant to the *Canadian Bill of Rights* when the child is without counsel in a custody dispute.

[17]In one such application, an Indian band applied for custody under a similarly worded section in British Columbia. The court held that the band was not a "person" capable of being granted custody under the Act: *Re C. and V.C.* (1982), 40 B.C.L.R. 234 (Prov. Ct.).

[18]*Smith et al. v. Hunter and Sears* (1979), 15 R.F.L. (2d) 203 (Ont. H.C.).

decision held that "other persons" must be read in conjunction with the extended definition of "parent", such that if the applicants have not shown any prior intention to treat the child as their own, their application must be dismissed.[19] The reasoning of the former case would seem to be preferable to the latter in that once the child is before the court, the judge will have the option of making a decision that is appropriate to the child without the technical impediment of party status.[20] Under the *Divorce Act*, the parties who might apply for custody are limited to the petitioning and responding spouse although a Supreme Court hearing the divorce can rely on its inherent jurisdiction over a child's welfare to award custody to a non-party. It is suggested that to overcome the technical obstacle created by the *Divorce Act*, the application, for example, by a grandparent, could be brought before the divorce court by joining a proceeding commenced under provincial legislation, the effect of which would be supplementary to the federal jurisdiction rather than in conflict with it.[21]

Criteria:
General

The *Divorce Act* allows the court to make a custody order having regard to the parties' conduct and the conditions, means and other circumstances of each of them, to make an order providing for the "custody, care and upbringing of the children of the marriage": ss. 10, 11. Under ss. 16(5) and (6) of the proposed *Divorce and Corollary Relief Act*, "conduct" is omitted. Both interim and final orders are to be based on "best interests" ("condition, means, needs and other circumstances of the child") as well as "as much contact with each spouse as is appropriate in the circumstances". Although the latter guideline does not specifically direct the court to maximize contact with each parent, its specific inclusion would so indicate, especially given the section's margin title "Maximum contact". Ontario's custody legislation directs the court to find "on the basis of the best interests of the child" and includes seven criteria upon which to base "best interests" under s. 24(2) of the *CLRA*:

> s. 24(2) In determining the best interests of a child . . . a court shall consider all the needs and circumstances of the child including,
> - (a) the love, affection and emotional ties between the child and
>   - (i) each person entitled to or claiming custody of or access to the child,
>   - (ii) other members of the child's family who reside with the child, and
>   - (iii) persons involved in the care and upbringing of the child;
> - (b) the views and preferences of the child, where such views and preferences can reasonably be ascertained;

---

[19] *Re Smith et al. and C.A.S. for County of Kent* (1980), 29 O.R. (2d) 502 (Co. Ct.).
[20] *Re Squire* (1974), 16 R.F.L. 266 (B.C. S.C.).
[21] See *Re Fulford and Townshend* (1971), 5 R.F.L. 63 (Ont. C.A.) (*Infants Act*) and *Humphreys v. Humphreys* (1970), 4 R.F.L. 64 (N.S. S.C.) (variation of *nisi*) where awards of custody to third parties who were not "parties" in the legal sense were based on the inherent jurisdiction of the court to protect the welfare of the child.

    (c) the length of time the child has lived in a stable home environment;

    (d) the ability and willingness of each person applying for the custody of the child to provide the child with guidance and education, the necessaries of life and any special needs of the child;

    (e) any plans proposed for the care and upbringing of the child;

    (f) the permanence and stability of the family unit with which it is proposed that the child will live; and

    (g) the relationship by blood or through an adoption order between the child and each person who is a party to the application.

The section specifically forbids the court to take into account parental conduct unless it pertains to the person's ability to parent: s. 24(3).

Criteria: Interim   Whatever the wording of the governing legislation, ("best interests", *CLRA*; "fit and just", *Divorce Act*) the cardinal rule applied by a court on an interim application is the preservation of the status quo. As a result, unless there are some exceptional circumstances, the court will "leave well enough alone".[22] Exceptional circumstances might include a situation in which a child's welfare is at risk while in the care of the *de facto* custodial parent[23] or in which a child is in the care of the *de facto* custodial parent by reason of unlawful removal.[24] The evidence should be something of a persuasive and cogent nature to upset the status quo before trial. In a case in which one parent takes sole care and control of a child, the court will apparently consider the motivation and circumstances surrounding the relationship of the parties to determine whether that act is relevant to the custodial party's parenting ability. That is, the act of taking sole care in itself is not determinative of the issue of interim custody, the Ontario Court of Appeal noting that in most custody cases, one or the other must have taken *de facto* custody either prior to the commencement of the proceedings or after they had been instituted.[25]

Within the limits of reasonable predictability in family law, it is suggested that a mother who has been at home with an infant child as the daily custody

---

[22]See *Papp v. Papp, supra,* note 13; *Haskell v. Pinsonneault* (1981), 34 O.R. (2d) 571, 127 D.L.R. (3d) 641, 24 R.F.L. (2d) 352 (Co. Ct.) (child to remain with aunt and uncle rather than father on interim basis); *Re S.; N. v. N.* (1982), 42 N.B.R. (2d) 385, 110 A.P.R. 385 (Q.B.) (eight-year-old to stay with father, friends and school). This status quo doctrine also applies to parents who apply for variation in an interim order: *Labossiere v. Labossiere* (1982), 17 Man. R. (2d) 169 (C.A.); *Olinyk v. Olinyk* (1979), 1 Man. R. (2d) 209 (Q.B.); *Serruys v. Serruys* (1982), 29 R.F.L. (2d) 215, revg. (1982), 28 R.F.L. (2d) 452 (Ont. C.A.); *Moldowan, supra,* note 8; *Colter v. Colter, supra,* note 8. But see *Middaugh v. Middaugh, supra,* note 12 (after placing child with father for 14 months while mother re-establishes herself economically, interim custody back to mother).

[23]*Cf. Cropper v. Cropper* (1974), 16 R.F.L. 113 (Ont. C.A.), and *Hubert v. Hubert* (1976), 28 R.F.L. 273 (Ont. C.A.) with *Neil v. Neil* (1976), 28 R.F.L. 257 (Ont. C.A.) and *I.H. v. H.H.*, [1971] 3 O.R. 222 (S.C.). See also *W. v. W.* (1982), 28 R.F.L. (2d) 302 (Ont. Prov. Ct.) (onus of proof on party making allegations); *Cameron v. Cameron* (1979), 12 R.F.L. (2d) 394 (B.C.S.C.) (where conflicting allegations, court considered appointing psychiatrist for assessment).

[24]See *Sobanski v. Sobanski* (1973), 9 R.F.L. 318 (Ont. S.C.) and *Wine v. Wine, supra,* note 10.

[25]*Dyment v. Dyment,* [1969] 2 O.R. 248 (C.A.). But see *Curri v. Curri* (1981), 34 O.R. (2d) 429 (S.C.); *Sagrott v. Sagrott* (1979), 11 R.F.L. (2d) 395 (Ont. U.F.C.).

parent and who leaves the family home with the child as a result of unbearable tension, will retain her role as the daily custodial parent unless the court concludes that the mother's motivation in leaving the home, or the evidence presented by the mother, is simply an attempt to strengthen her custodial position on a hearing of the interim application.[26] When in doubt, the court might conclude that if the matter turns on the justification of this mother taking the child and leaving, the validity of the mother's actions should be left for determination at trial. It should be noted, that if *de facto* custody is the sole reason for awarding interim custody, the court is effectively making a custody decision that is unlikely to be disturbed at trial despite the irrelevancy of the criterion to the parenting abilities of either party.[27]

In assessing what circumstances will protect the welfare of the child on an interim application, a factor which remains paramount whether it be pursuant to the legislative language of "fit and just" or "best interests",[28] the court will consider the circumstances of care for the child during the cohabitation and as well, while not as a rule of law, it will also consider the age of the child, the assumption being that a child of infant years needs the care of a mother more than a father.[29] The values which the court brings to the making of this assessment may or may not be consistent with the changing roles of men and women in society. For example, in one decision the Motions Court, on an interim application, had decided that the wife's actions in willingly and voluntarily abandoning her traditional role of wife and mother of two young children and going into business were fatal to her claim of interim custody since the husband alone had been able to provide adequate support for the family without her contribution. The Master based this decision on the position that the children would have been better off with a mother rather than a paid "nanny" at home. Considering this to be "wilful misconduct" in breaking up the marriage, the Master granted interim custody of the two children, ages 4 and 6, to the husband. On appeal, the court concluded that the wife's actions did not amount to "wilful misconduct":

> The phrase "the traditional role of the wife" is an old ghost with an extraordinary capacity for returning to life. Of course, considerations of justice between the parents must yield to consideration for the welfare of the child. The wife should not be required to place herself in an intellectual and environmental straight-jacket; nor should she lose her right to equal

---

[26]See *e.g. Sobanski v. Sobanski, supra,* note 24; *Dyment v. Dyment, ibid.; Aquino v. Aquino,* [1971] 2 O.R. 463 (S.C.); *Lussier v. Lussier* (1977), 3 R.F.L. (2d) 335 (Ont. Div. Ct.). Where the method of removing the child raised issue with the fitness of the parent as custodial parent, see *Johnson v. Johnson,* [1971] 2 O.R. 516 (S.C.); affd [1972] 1 O.R. 212 (C.A.).

[27]See *Aquino v. Aquino, ibid.; Pitchers v. Pitchers* (1980), 21 A.R. 181, 31 A.R. 372 (Q.B.). But see *Haydukewich v. Haydukewich* (1981), 11 Sask. R. 61 (Q.B.) (father had son for two and a half years since separation; mother had applied for interim custody but status quo with father ordered. On factors other than status quo, mother awarded custody of child.)

[28]*Papp v. Papp, supra,* note 13.

[29]See *Johnson v. Johnson, supra,* note 26; *Jessop v. Jessop, supra,* note 13; *Burke v. Burke* (1980), 38 N S R (2d) 251, 69 A.P.R. 251 (T.D.) (tender years doctrine outweighed status quo).

treatment before the law merely because she does the things she has the right to do.[30]

Rejecting the values applied by the court of first instance, the Appellate Court then decided that all things being equal, it was in the best interests of the children to remain with their mother, at least on an interim basis, reversing the decision of the Master.

"Best Interests": Four Judicial Approaches

In the first edition of *Children and the Law*, the method of determining the "best interests" of children in the context of a custody dispute were said to break down into four distinct judiciary approaches. Using these approaches as a framework, the following discussion will review the present state of the law in an effort to lend some predictability to an inherently subjective and unreliable process.

The first approach is based on rebuttable judicial rules of thumb which may assist in or even dictate the final resolution of a custody battle. For example, judges in the past have been guided by the maxims that infant children as well as girls of any age are better off with their mother;[31] boys over the age of eight years belong with their father;[32] and children should not be separated from one another.[33] An example of a successful rebuttal to the tender years/female rule was the case in which a two-year-old daughter was awarded to her father. To achieve this, the court had to be convinced by the proffered evidence that the mother was unstable, using as an example, her intentions to marry an "irresponsible man." Once this rule of thumb was rebutted, and all other things being equal, there remained the influence of the old common law doctrine that the father was entitled to the custody of the children.[34] Other rules of thumb to

---

[30]*Tomlinson v. Tomlinson,* summarized in (1980), 3 F.L.R.R. 35 (Ont. S.C.). See also *Garro v. Garro* (1982), 16 Man. R. (2d) 15 (Q.B.) (mother working full-time and spending spare time on social life; custody to father).

[31]See *Bell v. Bell,* [1955] O.W.N. 341 (C.A.); *Philpott v. Philpott,* [1954] O.R. 120 (C.A.); *Re Murrin* (1981), 31 Nfld. and P.E.I.R. 230, 87 A.P.R. 230 (Nfld. T.D.) ("tender years" doctrine to apply in absence of strong evidence to contrary); *Mathews v. Mathews* (1980), 29 N.B.R. (2d) 280, 66 A.P.R. 280 (C.A.) (trial judge not putting too much emphasis on "tender years" doctrine); *Boser v. Boser* (1979), 4 Sask. R. 297 (Q.B.) ("tender years" doctrine deciding factor when both parents capable); *Francoeur v. Francoeur* (1979), 16 B.C.L.R. 332 (S.C.) (making welfare of child paramount consideration not altering rule that child of tender years normally with mother). But see *M.E.H. v. M.R.H.* (1981), 45 N.S.R. (2d) 629, 86 A.P.R. 629 (Fam. Ct.) for statement on out-datedness of "tender years" doctrine.

[32]*W. v. W. and C.,* [1968] 3 All E.R. 409 (C.A.); *Kerr v. Kerr* (1971), 5 N.S.R. (2d) 528 (N.S. S.C.).

[33]*Werely v. Werely* (1979), 14 R.F.L. (2d) 193 (Ont. H.C.) ("tender years" doctrine gives way to "non-separation of siblings" doctrine); *Mireault v. Mireault* (1981), 12 Man. R. (2d) 141, 25 R.F.L. (2d) 362 (C.A.). But see *McLean v. Barnfield* (1980), 23 A.R. 557 (Q.B.) (assessor recommending one of the two children needing to be with mother, two children not having close relationship. Court ordered daughter with mother and son with father).

[34]*Pollard v. Pollard* (1973), 14 R.F.L. 49, at 57 (N.B.C.A.). See also *Cotton v. Cotton* (1981), 12 Man. R. (2d) 161, 23 R.F.L. (2d) 141 (C.A.); *Fudge v. Fudge* (1979), 35 N.S.R. (2d) 526, 62 A.P.R. 526 (T.D.). For cases where the presumption of custody is to the mother where the child is illegitimate, see *Wong v. Graham* (1979), 1 Man. R. (2d) 365, 13 R.F.L. (2d) 139 (Prov. Ct.). But see *Pennell v. Pennell* (1981), 33 Nfld. and P.E.I.R. 23, 93 A.P.R. 23 (Nfld. T.D.) and *Power v.*

emerge have been that when a separated husband and wife are each planning to remarry step-mothers generally work out less satisfactorily than step-fathers, since the demands of infant children upon the former are heavier than on the latter;[35] and two-parent families are better than one-parent families.[36] One American decision advised that custody of a dark-skinned mulatto child born from a white parent and a black parent is better off with the black parent because the child would then be brought up "by his own people."[37] In the context of a custody dispute between parents and a third party, there existed the presumption that *prima facie*, the child belongs in the home of his parents unless circumstances dictate that the fundamental natural right of the parents to raise their children should be terminated.[38] This rule, again as a presumption, seems to have been rebutted if not replaced in Ontario under the general "best interests" test which makes the significance of the blood tie just one factor among many in assessing the welfare of the child.[39] (For further discussion of rules of thumb, see *supra* under "Criteria: Interim".)

With the advent of Ontario's new *CLRA*, the Legislature has reaffirmed that the sole guideline for awarding custody is the best interests of the child. However, s. 24(2) of that Act went further than its predecessor by delineating seven guidelines to assess "best interests" (noted above), which might be viewed as codifying some of the pre-existing rules of thumb. Note that they are not exclusive since the introductory words of the section direct the court to consider "all the needs and circumstances of the child. . . . " This would presumably make operative all previous rules of thumb which are not enumerated therein. However, there is no suggestion that any of these guidelines are so strong as to amount to rebuttable presumptions as has been the case in the past with some of the courts on some of the rules of thumb.

The second judicial approach to the assessment of "best interests" appears to be an attempt to allocate fault between the parents and to award custody according to the principles of justice within the matrimonial relationship itself. An English Court of Appeal summarized this approach as follows:

Crowe (1982), 52 N.S.R. (2d) 159, 106 A.P.R. 159 (Fam. Ct.) (illegitimate children must be treated on the same basis as legitimate children).

[35]*Bagg v. Bagg* (No. 2), [1961] Fam.L.R. 1130 (Aus.). *Re F., (An Infant)*, [1969] 2 All E.R. 766.

[36]*Murphy v. Murphy* (1978), 2 Fam. L. Rev. 299 (P.E.I. S.C.) (although mother's environment offered greater potential, the children would grow up in a one-parent family and by their being there, she would have little opportunity for re-marriage. The husband had a live-in housekeeper and was awarded custody).

[37]*Ward v. Ward* (1950), 216 P. 2d 755 (Wash.). But see *Fountaine v. Fountaine* (1956), 133 N.E. 2d 532 (Ill.).

[38]*Hepton v. Matt*, [1957] S.C.R. 606; *Gelfant v. Gelfant* (1980), 7 Man. R. (2d) 157, 20 R.F.L. (2d) 337 (C.A.). See also *Grant v. Grant* (1982), 25 R.F.L. (2d) 386 (B.C.C.A.); *Smith et al. v. Sears* (1979), 3 Fam. R. 121 (Ont. H.C.); *Re Ezekiel* (1980), 30 N.B.R. (2d) 343, 70 A.P.R. 343 (Q.B.); *Sasaki v. Sasaki* (1982), 134 D.L.R. (3d) 556, 27 R.F.L. (2d) 314, 19 R.F.L. (2d) 303 (Q.B.); *Dillman v. Dillman* (1980), 43 N.S.R. (2d) 230, 81 A.P.R. 230 (T.D.); *Forbes v. Forbes* (1982), 28 R.F.L. (2d) 124 (Sask. Q.B.).

[39]*Re Moores and Feldstein* (1973), 12 R.F.L. 273 (Ont. C.A.); *Re M.* (1981), 24 R.F.L. (2d) 276 (Nfld. T.D.).

It seems to me that a mother must realise that if she leaves and breaks up her home in this way, she cannot as of right demand to take the children from the father. If the mother in this case were to be entitled to the children, it would follow that every guilty mother (who is otherwise a good mother) would always be entitled to them, for no stronger case for the father could be found. He has a good home for the children. He is ready to forgive his wife and have her back. All that he wishes is for her to return. It is a matter of simple justice between them that he should have the care and control. Whilst the welfare of the children is the first and paramount consideration, the claims of justice cannot be overlooked.[40]

The application of the decision in this English Court of Appeal case in Canada has led to two distinguishable interpretations of the "fault allocation" approach. On the one hand, it has been held that while the interests of the child are of paramount concern, the conduct of the parents and their respective contribution to the breakup of the marriage must be considered as a separate factor of equal weight.[41] On the other hand, it has been held that while the conduct of the parents may be considered by the court, it does not amount to a separate factor but is relevant as information *only* as it may affect the court's paramount concern for the welfare of the child. Thus, where parties separate and the mother is found to be at fault, her conduct should be considered only as it relates to her ability to care for the child. The latter approach would appear to be existing law in Canada in view of later decisions by the Supreme Court of Canada.[42]

Ontario's *CLRA* codifies the latter approach under s. 24(3), stating that conduct is irrelevant except as it relates to the ability of a person to act as a parent of a child. Pursuant to this section, a decision of a trial judge was appealed and although upheld, the Appellate Court pointed out that contrary to the lower court's approach, adultery in itself may not be and should not be a factor of any significance in determining custody.[43] However, if the adulterous relationship had a disturbing and detrimental effect on the child, the court does not err by considering this as a factor in awarding custody to the father. The dissenting opinion of that Appellate Court, in concluding that a new trial was necessary, noted that the trial had been a "catharsis" for the embattled parents, with the "vast bulk of the 300 pages of the transcript" devoted solely to the marital

---

[40]*Re L. (Infants)*, [1962] 3 All E.R. 1, at 4 (C.A.).

[41]*Re Pittman and Pittman* (1972), 5 R.F.L. 376 (Ont. Surr. Ct.). See also *Re O'Leary* (1979), 27 N.B.R. (2d) 384, 60 A.P.R. 384 (Q.B.).

[42]*MacDonald v. MacDonald* (1975), 2 R.F.L. 42 (S.C.C.). See also *Re Moilliet* (1966), 58 D.L.R. (2d) 152 (B.C.C.A.); *Phillips v. Phillips* (1974), 14 R.F.L. 75, at 79 (N.S.C.A.); *Fullerton v. Fullerton* (1980), 31 N.B.R. (2d) 661, 75 A.P.R. 661 (C.A.). See also *Tomlinson v. Tomlinson, supra,* note 30 for this approach on an interim basis.

[43]*Cooney v. Cooney* (1982) 36 O.R. (2d) 137, 27 R.F.L. (2d) 136 (C.A.). See also *Gordon v. Gordon* (1980), 23 R.F.L. (2d) 266 (C.A.), delivered prior to the new legislation, in which the appellate court ordered a new trial due to the fact that the trial court relied on a Commissioner's Report which based his conclusion on the mother's moral character rather than the child's physical and emotional welfare.

battles, but that it told the trial judge little about the child who should have been "front stage, centre" in the minds of all the participants. The dissenting judge expressed concern that the trial judge's reasons did not indicate that he was aware that misconduct on the part of either of the parties is relevant on a custody issue only to the extent that it bears on their ability to be a good parent.

A third approach to the resolution of custody disputes involves the court quantifying the respective abilities of the parents, balancing their "assets" against their "liabilities", and awarding custody to the parent who scored the highest. Some of the previous rules of thumb (see above) are incorporated but become less presumptions and more simple variables[44] (except for those which are gradually becoming unacceptable in view of the changing roles of men and women in society).[45] In this context, the court has balanced such considerations as the suitability of living accommodation;[46] whether the wealth of the parents should be a factor, particularly when both parents are able to provide a comfortable and adequate home for the child;[47] whether the fact that a mother who sought a therapeutic abortion during the pregnancy of the subject child is to be used against her in terms of her ability to care for the child;[48] the kinds of employment and essentially, the amount of hours either parent will be able to spend with the children;[49] whether homosexuality in itself should be considered as a bar to a parent's right to custody or whether it should be considered along with all the other evidence in measuring the parent's potential to care for the child;[50] the intentions of either parent regarding the religious upbringing of a child;[51] which parent will better ensure and encourage contact with the other parent during access, all things being equal (this has clearly emerged as an important factor in determining a custody dispute, the courts considering the interest of the child to be inherently connected to a relationship with both parents, notwithstanding the separation);[52] which placement will allow all the children to

---

[44]See for example *Glasgow v. Glasgow* (1981), 44 N.S.R. (2d) 139, 83 A.P.R. 139 (Fam. Ct.) and *Ferjan v. Ferjan* (1980), 4 Man. R. (2d) 346, 19 R.F.L. (2d) 113 (C.A.) ("tender years" doctrine common sense but not law); *Rossignol v. Rossignol* (1981), 46 N.S.R. (2d) 458, 89 A.P.R. 458 (S.C. T.D.) ("tender years" outweighed by stability of status quo).

[45]For example, for court acknowledgment of out-datedness of "tender years" doctrine, see *M.E.H. v. M.R.H., supra,* note 31 and *Power v. Crowe* (1982), 52 N.S.R. (2d) 159, 106 A.P.R. 159 (Fam. Ct.).

[46]*Torresan v. Torresan* (1971), 6 R.F.L. 16 (B.C. S.C.).

[47]*Gauchi v. Gauchi* (1973), 9 R.F.L. 189 (Ont. S.C.); *Meikle v. Authenac* (1970), 3 R.F.L. 84 (Alta. C.A.).

[48]*Re Moores and Feldstein, supra,* note 39.

[49]*Re Pittman and Pittman, supra,* note 41; *Lagowski v. Lagowski* (1982), 28 R.F.L. (2d) 45 (Man. Q.B.); *McCalla v. McCalla* (1980), 5 Sask. R. 224 (Q.B.).

[50]*Case v. Case* (1975), 18 R.F.L. 132 (Sask. Q.B.); *Monette c. Sylvestre,* [1981] C.S. 731 (Que.); *B. v. B.* (1980), 16 R.F.L. (2d) 7 (Ont. Prov. Ct.); *Bernhardt v. Bernhardt* (1979), 10 R.F.L. (2d) 32 (Man. Q.B.); *Re Barkley and Barkley* (1980), 28 O.R. (2d) 136 (Prov. Ct.).

[51]*Re Agnew* (1975), 25 R.F.L. 10 (N.B. S.C.); *Pfeifer v. Pfeifer* (1982), 28 R.F.L. (2d) 236 (Sask. Q.B.) (custody to mother with stipulation that she expose son to father's religion).

[52]*Bradnam v. Bradnam,* summarized in (1983), 6 F.L.R.R. 186 (Ont. Co. Ct.); *Stanek v. Stanek* (1979), 7 Sask. R. 230 (Q.B.).

be together;[53] and, of course, all things being equal, the opportunity for stability and minimal disruption in the child's life.[54]

This third approach continues to be applied and effectively provides the court with a workable method of attempting to merge the claims of the parents with the child's best interests, given that the courts still cling to a passive, adjudicative role in which the decision is based on the selective evidence offered by each party. With the introduction of seven codified guidelines under the *CLRA* it is assumed that litigants will address themselves to these particular issues, providing the court with a more informed basis on which to make their balanced decision.[55]

The fourth approach, and arguably the preferable approach, incorporates the third approach but makes the *child*, and not the competing parental figures, the central figure or the "centrepiece"[56] of the decision-making process. In one such decision, the Australian Court of Appeal capsulized the concept when stating, with reference to an English Court of Appeal decision based on "matrimonial fault", that:

> Such language, it seems to me, only clouds the issue. The issue is not what is justice to the parents, but what is for the welfare of the child, and the welfare of the child can best be weighed by disregarding entirely any concept of the claim, just or unjust, on the part of the parents.[57]

Using this test, the courts treat the welfare of the child as the first and paramount consideration. It takes precedence even over the claims of an "unimpeachable parent and the justice of the case between the parents." For

---

[53]*Mullen v. Mullen* (1979), 24 A.R. 154 (Q.B.); *Re Hoekman* (1980), 31 Nfld. and P.E.I.R. 193, 87 A.P.R. 193 (Nfld. U.F.C.). See also note 33.

[54]*Jones v. Jones,* summarized in (1980) 3 F.L.R.R. 107 (Ont. Co. Ct.) (stability with father and live-in "nanny"); *Lapointe v. Pozzobon,* summarized in (1979), 2 F.L.R.R. 29 (Ont. Co. Ct.) (stability of father vs. mother); *Spencer v. Spencer* (1981), 20 R.F.L. (2d) 91 (B.C. C.A.). (uprooting children constituting grave risk to their feeling of security; custody to father); *Glauser v. Glauser* (1980), 9 Sask. R. 110 (Q.B.); *Ellert v. Ellert* (1982), 30 R.F.L. (2d) 257 (Sask. Q.B.) (tender years doctrine only one factor; plan which provides the best overall home environment most important); *DeCoste v. DeCoste* (1981), 44 N.S.R. (2d) 628, 83 A.P.R. 628 (S.C.) and *Lipscombe v. Parkinson* (1979), 1 F.L.R.A.C. 460 (Ont. U.F.C.) (status quo should remain even though siblings separated); *Brooks v. Brooks* (1982), 28 R.F.L. (2d) 168 (Sask. Q.B.) (great number of factors weighed; greater probability of stability with mother); *McPherson v. McPherson* (1982), 31 R.F.L. (2d) 380 (Sask. Q.B.) (maintain status quo because neither parent better than the other). But see *Holt v. Holt* (1981), 35 N.B.R. (2d) 459, 88 A.P.R. 459 (Q.B.) (child with father for four years. Court awards to mother based on better parenting style and apprehension of children about father's strictness); *Favel v. Favel* (1980), 3 Man. R. (2d) 258 (C.A.) (seven-year-old girl and five-year-old boy go to father who lives common law and can provide more stable home environment than mother who lives alone).

[55]For an example of a careful weighing process see *Re Barkley and Barkley, supra,* note 50, wherein the court, after its analysis of the effect of the mother's homosexuality on the child, concluded that "whatever significant risks remained in the area of [the child's] necessary adjustments to our 'homophobic' society, they are too esoteric and speculative for me to attach much weight to. I think they must give way to the more concrete indicia of 'best interests'."

[56]*Williams v. Williams* (1980), 15 R.F.L. (2d) 378 (Ont. Dist. Ct.).

[57]*Barnett v. Barnett* (1973), 21 Fam. L.R. 335, at 343 (Aus.); and see *Re Marriage of Watts,* [1976] 8 A.C.L.D. 384 (Aus.).

example, a father who was an Anglican clergyman and the curate of his Parish, and a mother who was a teacher of religion, suffered a marital breakdown as a result of the mother's adulterous conduct. On appeal by the father against an order granting custody of the children to the mother, the court observed:

> It seems to me that all experience shows that particularly serious minded people such as the mother in this case do not break up their marriages unless the relationship with their spouses have deteriorated severely indeed. So I hesitate to make moral judgments in this classic case. I do not find it particularly helpful.[58]

Similarly, where the mother's conduct was highly suspect, another court noted:

> If the interests of the children require a decision in favour of one parent, the perfectly proper interests and wishes of the other parent, unimpeachable or impeachable, must yield to the interests of the children. The phrase "unimpeachable parent" seems to exercise a certain fascination over judges and applicants from time to time. I think it is a most misleading phrase. It is hurtful to the other parent in whom it invariably creates an immediate resentment and a bitter sense of injustice, and, in my experience, it is a most potent stimulus for appeals to this court. I have never known, and still do not know, what it means. It cannot mean a parent who is above criticism because there is no such thing. It might mean a parent against whom no matrimonial offence has been proved. If so, it adds nothing to the record which is before the court and in any event is now outmoded. . . . The present case illustrates very aptly indeed how dangerous it is to make this kind of value judgment. Here the judge took the view that the father was the unimpeachable parent and, by necessary implication, and expressly, that the mother was the impeachable one because she had committed adultery with three men. Having come to that view, that the husband was unimpeachable and the wife impeachable, the judge's judgment followed to the conclusion which I have indicated [that the father should have custody of the children]. But it is quite impossible to decide whether a parent is unimpeachable or impeachable without an exhaustive investigation into the history of the married life.[59]

The dissenting opinion in a decision of the Saskatchewan Court of Appeal most closely reflects this fourth approach, the dissenting judge questioning the nature of the proceeding:

> From the standpoint of custody, the hearing of the petition was, in my respectful view, quite unsatisfactory. Virtually no evidence was directed to this issue. The parties primarily concerned themselves with adducing evidence to show whether, on the basis of the many marital battles engaged in by them, one or other of them should be favoured by the trial judge in his determination of the issue of cruelty.

---

[58] *Re K. (Minors)*, [1977] 2 W.L.R. 33 (C.A.).
[59] *S. (B.)(D.) v. S. (D.)(J.)*, [1977] 2 W.L.R. 44, at 49 (C.A.).

No one bothered to bring forward much information in respect of the two individuals who, of all the persons likely to be affected by these proceedings, least deserved to be ignored — the children. We know their names, sex and ages, but little else. Of what intelligence are they? What are their likes? Dislikes? Do they have any special inclinations (for the arts, sports, or the like) that should be nurtured? Any handicaps? Do they show signs of anxiety? What are their personalities? Characters? What is the health of each?. . . . In short, no evidence was led to establish the intellectual, moral, emotional or physical needs of each child. Apart from the speculation that these children are "ordinary" (whatever that means), there is nothing on which to base a reasoned objective conclusion as to what must be done for *this* and *that* child, as individuals and not as mere members of a general class, in order that the welfare and happiness of each may be assured and enhanced.

Nor was any direct evidence led to show which of the parents, by reason of training, disposition, character, . . . and such other pertinent factors . . . is best equipped to meet the needs of each individual child.[60]

This approach is to be distinguished from the third approach in that while the court would consider the same issues in both models, the court under the fourth approach would place itself in the position of the child and look outward from a subjective perspective based on the child's interests, rather than looking from the outside in (or down) at the actions and characteristics of all the family members, using assessment indicia that are just as likely to be irrelevant as relevant to the child's needs. This does not mean that the court is to be dictated to or persuaded by the child's wishes. Rather, that the court is attempting to look at the child's interests — to be distinguished from, but not exclusive of, the child's desires — by placing the child at the center of the examination. Using estate disputes as an analogy (another area where the court attempts to deal with the intangible), the court will put itself in the testator's (child's) shoes although the testator, being dead, is incapable of instructing the court as to the nature of his shoes. The court must then balance those conclusions against a sense of fairness to the contesting claimants. In the custody dispute, however, the court must not only determine what are the child's intentions or wishes, but also what suits this particular child best and accordingly consider which plan, if any, is most consistent with those conclusions.

The following observations solidify the conclusion that the fourth approach supersedes the other three in coming closest to the nebulous "best interests" criterion:

1) Because the approach places the child as a central figure, it encourages all parties and the court to understand more actively the child, and for this purpose, to seek assistance from other disciplines so as to make a comprehensive decision accommodating the child's perspective.

2) A decision-making process, premised on the child's needs alone, may rationally lead to alternative forums which allow a more comprehensive

---

[60]*Wakaluk v. Wakaluk* (1976), 25 R.F.L. 292, at 299 (Sask. C.A.).

examination of the child's needs than is possible in the courtroom. Lawyers and their clients might feel more inclined to avoid the courtroom structure since it is readily acknowledged that the traditional adversarial process does not lend itself to ascertaining a child's needs.

3) A decision-making process based on a concept of justice between the parents may have no real connection to the needs of a child. "Justice" *may* work to satisfy the parties as husband and wife (determining who is at fault for the marriage breakdown) but have little connection to the child's perceptions of the family situation. For example, whereas the law may consider that the deserting spouse is at fault for having left the matrimonial home, the child may come to a different conclusion, feeling that it is the "deserting spouse" who has been wrongfully deprived by the "deserted" spouse. The child's confusion is heightened by the fact that very often the spouse who is found to be at fault is depicted by the other party as a "bad mommy" or a "mean daddy." When the courts rely upon a process of "matrimonial justice" there is too great a risk that the court, the litigants and counsel will blur the essential distinction between the roles and duties of a husband and a wife and a parent and child.

4) A decision-making process rooted in presumptions of law is one governed by morality. However, morality in the context of the "family" is so complex and continuously changing that it is irresponsible for the court to rely upon it as a basis for decision-making in lieu of the more consistent and reliable approach premised solely on the particular child's needs.

It is clear that the difficulty with this fourth approach is that it necessarily requires a re-evaluation of the existing adversarial regime. Specifically, this approach suggests the following:

Court as Investigator

Court as Investigator

The court must play a more active role in obtaining information. As one decision of the Ontario Court of Appeal has noted, the court has to be sensitive to the fact that the litigating parties may not bring before the court all it needs in order to determine the actual best interests of the child. An investigative role for the court requires an acceptance of the assertion that a custody case is different from all other litigation.[61]

Joint Custody

Joint Custody

The court must be more responsive and flexible in its assessments and dispositions in attempting to fulfill the needs of the child. It is a truism that in the typical custody dispute, the child wishes and needs to continue a full and vital relationship with both parents. A more active attempt to serve the needs of that typical child may require a more aggressive application of the law to suit those

---

[61]*Gordon v. Gordon, supra,* note 43.

interests. In an Ontario Court of Appeal case in which the majority rejected the imposition of joint custody on the parties, the dissenting opinion stated:

> It is perhaps timely for courts in Canada to shed their "healthy cynicism" and reflect in their orders a greater appreciation of the hurt inflicted upon a child by the severance of its relationship with one of its parents. While purporting to award custody on the basis of a child's best interests, our courts have tended to overlook that in some circumstances, it may be in the child's best interests not to choose between the parents but to do everything possible to maintain the child's relationship with both parents. We accept now, I believe, that men and women who fall short as spouses might nevertheless excel as parents. We have also become increasingly aware over the last number of years that the context of a divorce action is the worst possible context in which to form an assessment of the spouses as people, let alone as parents.
>
> In my view, it is the responsibility of a court in a custody matter to assess, preferably with professional assistance, the ability of the parents to cooperate in the upbringing of their children and, in the light of that assessment, to choose from the range of options open to it, the one which will best serve the children's short and long-term interests. This is of paramount importance in a case where the trial judge finds that both parents exhibit sterling parental qualities and that their relationship between parent and children discloses a high degree of love and affection on both sides.[62]
>
> And what if occasional resort has to be made to the courts when the parents cannot agree on a major matter affecting the child? Is this to be the determinative consideration? It seems to me to be a modest price to pay in order to preserve a child's confidence in the love of his parents, and with it, his own sense of security and self esteem.[63]

To date in Ontario, and notwithstanding the language of provincial custody legislation that establishes jurisdiction to award joint custody orders, the case law is clear that joint custody cannot be imposed by order of court unless the parties are in agreement with it.[64] The proposed *Divorce and Corollary Relief Act* includes s. 16(3), specifically giving jurisdiction to award joint custody. Specifically, the parties must

---

[62]*Kruger v. Kruger* (1979), 25 O.R. (2d) 673, 11 R.F.L. (2d) 52, at 69 (C.A.), *per* Wilson J.A.
[63]*Ibid.*, at p. 73 (R.F.L.).
[64]For cases in other jurisdictions in which joint custody was ordered despite varying degrees of dissension between parents see: *Parker v. Parker* (1975), 20 R.F.L. 232 (Man. C.A.); *Miller v. Miller* (1974), 17 R.F.L. 92 (Man. C.A.); *Babyak v. Babyak* (1980), 7 Man. R. (2d) 98 (Q.B.); *Ramsay v. Ramsay* (1979), 1 F.L.R.A.C. 333 (P.E.I. S.C.); *McCabe v. McCabe* (1978), 11 R.F.L. (2d) 260 (P.E.I. S.C.); *Beard v. Beard* (1979), 10 R.F.L. (2d) 371 (B.C. S.C.) (parents living in Canada and New Zealand); *Charmasson v. Charmasson* (1982), 27 R.F.L. (2d) 241 (Ont. C.A.) (parents living in Canada and France); *Richard v. Richard* (1981), 35 N.B.R. (2d) 383, 88 A.P.R. 383 (C.A.) (trial judge ordered joint custody to be shared equally despite pre-trial joint custody agreement which gave three-quarters of the physical custody time to mother. On appeal, a pre-trial arrangement restored based on psychologist's evidence at trial); *Compeau v. Compeau*

1) accept that the other is a person with whom he or she can share, on an equal basis, control over and responsibility for the child, which together they as parents must assume in making important decisions relating to the child's care;

2) accept that the child must physically reside with one or the other of them and that the child must know that it has one home where it can look for guidance and admonition; and

3) accept that generous access by the other parent is an essential part of the agreement that could operate in such a way that it would not ultimately reduce to ruins the whole arrangement.[65]

The very concepts of "custody" and "access" represent more a property analysis of the child's welfare, than a child-centered assessment of "best interests".[66] Arguably, s. 28 of the *Children's Law Reform Act*, allowing the court to make orders for "incidents of custody" separate from "custody", gives Ontario courts the jurisdiction to institute imaginative and more appropriate arrangements which blur the distinction between the rigid concepts of "custody" and "access", arrangements which may or may not be labelled "joint custody".[67] The proposed *Divorce and Corollary Relief Act* also defines custody to include "incidents" thereof as well as s. 16(4) which gives wide discretion to impose conditions and restrictions. One court noted the following:

Custody is a bundle of rights or a number of incidents or rights which can be broken down into specific aspects. One of those aspects is the right to determine education. Both counsel, in their argument, address me on the possibility of Mr. Borel being granted the right to determine the children's education should his wife be granted custody. That is exactly what I intend to do. In doing so, I am not doing it to benefit Mr. Borel, to throw him a bone so he has something to console himself with, but because of what I view is a very real possibility of a positive contribution that he can make to his daughters' lives.[68]

(1979), 2 Fam. L. Rev. 284 (Prov. Ct.) (imposed joint custody as in the best interests of the child despite that neither parent was seeking it).

For cases parallelling Ontario's position see *Brown v. Brown* (1978), 2 R.F.L. (2d) 165 (Sask. Q.B.); *Zwicker v. Morine* (1980), 38 N.S.R. (2d) 236, 69 A.P.R. 236, 110 D.L.R. (3d) 336, 16 R.F.L. (2d) 293 (C.A.); *Silver v. Silver* (1979), 35 N.S.R. (2d) 88, 62 A.P.R. 88, 104 D.L.R. (3d) 689 (*sub nom. Re Silver*) (S.C. T.D.); *Chouinaid v. Chouinaid* (1982), 31 R.F.L. (2d) 6 (Sask. Q.B.); *Fontaine v. Fontaine* (1980), 18 R.F.L. (2d) 235 (Man. C.A.); *Carruthers v. Carruthers* (1982), 30 R.F.L. (2d) 215 (N.S. S.C. T.D.).

[65]*Kruger v. Kruger, supra,* note 62. See also *Baker v. Baker* (1979), 23 O.R. (2d) 391, 8 R.F.L. (2d) 236 (C.A.); *Gee v. Gee* (1979), 27 O.R. (2d) 675, 107 D.L.R. (3d) 423, 13 R.F.L. (2d) 31 (H.C.); *Fitzsimmons v. Fitzsimmons* (1978), 1 F.L.R.A.C. 164 (Ont. Prov. Ct.).

[66]See *e.g.,* Derdeyne, A.P. "Child Custody Contests in Historical Perspective" in (December, 1976), 133 *The American Journal of Psychiatry*, 1369.

[67]See *Borel v. Borel,* summarized in (1981), 4 F.L.R.R. 68. See also *Donald v. Donald* (1980), 3 Sask. R. 202 (Q.B.); *Charlton v. Charlton* (1980), 19 B.C.L.R. 42, 15 R.F.L. (2d) 220 (S.C.C.).

[68]*Borel v. Borel, ibid.* (custody of two children awarded to mother but father granted the right to determine child's education).

Non-Partisan Assessments/Supervision

The court needs the help of non-partisan professional assessment services in order to understand and properly assess the interests and needs of the child. It also needs supervisory services outside of the courtroom in order to assess the impact of its decision and to assist in implementing the direction of the court in cooperation with the parties and their lawyers.[69]

Listening to the Child

Upon reaching a reasonable age, the child must be heard and the court must therefore struggle with the best method to accommodate this aspect of the hearing. At the same time, one must remember that a child's testimony from the witness box or a private interview between child and judge in chambers both have their significant drawbacks.[70] (For more detailed discussion, see below under "Methods of Conflict Resolution: Listening to the Child.")

Alternate Models of Dispute Resolutions

In many cases, the essence of the battle is the difference in lifestyles and parenting styles between competing parents rather than the fact that one is better than the other. In other words, no real harm would come from either lifestyle or parenting style; the harm comes from the adversarial process itself. Consequently, adversarial and judicial processes should be replaced with alternate models for dispute resolution.[71] (For further discussion, see below under "Methods of Conflict Resolution.")

The courts have made every effort to make sure that access is exercised between the child and the non-custodial parent due to the child's obvious need and desire to maintain a relationship with this parent. This objective is at one and the same time necessary to the child's well-being as well as completely antithetical to the desires of the warring parents. Because of this contradiction, the courts have fashioned access in the form of a "right" that belongs to the child,[72] to be denied only when grave circumstances render it not to be in the best

---

[69]See *Vogt v. Vogt,* summarized in (1980), 2 F.L.R.R. 125 (Ont. U.F.C.).

[70]*Stevenson v. Florant,* [1925] 4 D.L.R. 530 (S.C.C.) affd [1926] 4 D.L.R. 897 (P.C.). And see *Re S. (Infants),* [1967] 1 All E.R. 202, where the court noted that it must carefully evaluate the significance of the child's wishes as information which is relevant to its decision, since the child may have been unfairly influenced by one of his parents, and his wishes may not reflect "an independent exercise of his own will"; *Taberner v. Taberner* (1971), 5 R.F.L. 14 (Ont. S.C.) where the court was concerned that to allow a child to be heard in open court might allow the child to feel he is making the decision, and conclude unrealistically that he is responsible for the decision of the court, if it is what he wanted, or that he has been betrayed or disappointed, if it is against his desires.

[71]See for example: Wallerstein, J.S., Kelly, J.B. "DIVORCE COUNSELLING: A Community Service for Families in the Midst of Divorce," in (January, 1977), 47(1) *American Journal of Orthopsychiatry* 4; Mnookin, R.H., Kornhauser, L. "Bargaining in the Shadow of the Law: The Case of Divorce" in (1979), 88 *Yale Law Journal* 950–56; Coogler, O.J. "Changing the Lawyer's Role in Matrimonial Practice," in (1977), 15 *Conciliation Courts Review* 1–8.

[72]*M. v. M. (Child: Access),* [1973] 2 All E.R. 81 (D.C.); appld in *Weiss v. Kopel* (1980), 18 R.F.L. (2d) 289 (Ont. Prov. Ct.).

interests of the child.[73] The proposed *Divorce and Corollary Relief Act* includes s. 16(6) which impliedly directs the court to maximize contact with each spouse. Access restrictions can also be imposed.[74]

Based on this access right, and in order to minimize interparental friction, judicial rules and guidelines have evolved to flesh out the meaning and implications of access. In its simplest form, access means that the non-custodial parent shall visit the child, including the making of appropriate arrangements for the visit.[75] Because access is for the benefit of the child, it should be exercised so as to create a minimum interruption in the child's regular activities. In this

[73]For cases where access denied in best interests of children see *Re Cascanette and Cascanette* (1982), 136 D.L.R. (3d) 679 (Ont. Prov. Ct.) (father denied all access due to psychiatrist's evidence that father's hostility to ex-spouse and refusal to compromise access demands could result in serious harm to child); *Goodfellow v. Goodfellow* (1982), 17 Sask. R. 198 (Q.B.) (history of extreme cruelty); *Caron v. Green (Caron)* (1983), 55 N.S.R. (2d) 624, 114 A.P.R. 624, 31 R.F.L. (2d) 430 (Fam. Ct.) (continual disregard of access restrictions, harming relationship between custodial parent and child); *Tobert v. Tobert* (1982), 40 A.R. 605 (Q.B.) (mental illness having detrimental affect on child); *Barker v. Duczek* (1980), 12 Man. R. (2d) 358 (Q.B.) (conflicting approaches to child-rearing, access parent being too permissive); *Plume v. Plume* (1981), 25 R.F.L. (2d) 420 (Ont. H.C.) (no contact or support payments since birth, father subsequently applying for access. Court denied access, holding that access benefits do not attach when no relationship between father and child); *Lachance v. Cloutier* (1982), 18 Alta. L.R. (2d) 328, 36 A.R. 124 (Fam. Ct.) (five and a half year common law relationship, hostility between parties after separation. Court denied access holding that, in Alberta, higher onus on natural father than on legal father to establish that access is in best interest of child); *Malainey v. Malainey* (1980), 3 Sask. R. 386 (Q.B.) (child's fears and anxiety of father's mental illness outweighs access rights); *Boileau v. Boileau* (1979), 13 R.F.L. (2d) 275 (Ont. Div. Ct.) (do not need physical harm to deny access; can also do so on basis of best interests). But see *St. Hilaire c. Menard* (1982), 31 R.F.L. (2d) 373 (C.S. Que.) (father unknown to child and not paying support; mother applying to deprive him of all parental rights and to change name. Court refused); *Gulash v. Gulash* (1981), 25 R.F.L. (2d) 212 (Sask. C.A.) (murder conviction and fact of being jailed not sufficient in itself to deny access; court orders hearing to determine child's best interests).

[74]See *Renwick v. Renwick* (1982), 16 Sask. R. 429 (Q.B.) (refrain from exposing child to casual nudity); *Howard v. Howard* (1982), 41 N.B.R. (2d) 171, 107 A.P.R. 171 (Q.B.) (not while drinking alcohol); *Seaman v. Seaman* (1981), 24 R.F.L. (2d) 433 (Ont. Co. Ct.) (not while spending night with girlfriend); *Rettger v. Rettger* (1980), 7 Sask. R. 437 (Q.B.) (access parent neglecting and physically abusing children; access limited to custodial residence only); *Thatcher v. Thatcher* (1981), 20 R.F.L. (2d) 75 (Sask. Q.B.) (flaunting access restrictions; directs supervised access); *Dodds v. Dodds* (1979), 28 Nfld. and P.E.I.R. 66, 79 A.P.R. 66 (P.E.I. S.C.) (lengthy visits disturbing child; court ordered daily visits between 9 a.m. and 6 p.m. despite fact that mother lived in Quebec and father lived in P.E.I.). But see *Lea v. Lea* (1983), 33 R.F.L. (2d) 173 (Q.B.) (court would *not* grant application to restrict access to visits when wife not accompanied by boyfriend); *J. v. R.* (1982), 27 R.F.L. (2d) 380 (Que. S.C.) (court strikes out clause in separation agreement barring homosexual mother from exercising access in presence of her lover; no evidence of impropriety, clause discriminating on basis of sexual orientation); *Knight v. Knight* (1981), 7 Sask. R. 321 (Q.B.) (child given six months in custody of mother before father allowed access, to give period of stability after leaving father's custody); *MacKintosh v. MacKintosh* (1980), 21 R.F.L. (2d) 113 (B.C. S.C.) (custody with restriction of not taking child out of jurisdiction).

[75]See s. 20(5), *CLRA*: "The entitlement to access to a child includes the right to visit with and be visited by the child and the same right as a parent to make inquiries and to be given information as to the health, education and welfare of the child." See also *Callender v. Callender* (1973), 11 R.F.L. 206 (B.C. S.C.); *McCutcheon v. McCutcheon* (1982), 41 N.B.R. (2d) 263, 107 A.P.R. 263, 29 R.F.L. (2d) 11 (Q.B.) (access includes taking child to place of choice unless otherwise restricted); *Glasgow v. Glasgow (No. 2)* (1982), 51 N.S.R. (2d) 13, 102 A.P.R. 13 (Fam. Ct.) (access limited to rights permitting contact with child, not interference with child's upbringing)

context only, the non-custodial parent should make arrangements to attend the hockey game or the ballet lesson with the child.[76] On the other hand, the custodial parent should not create obstacles to these access visits, for example, by encouraging the child to develop a closer relationship with his step-parent,[77] or by moving with the child if its effect is to interrupt the access.[78] Generally, where a custody/access agreement is involved, the courts tend to decide that the more specified and structured the access provision in an agreement is, the more likely it is that the parties assumed close proximity as a basis for entering into the agreement in the first place. If the agreement left it at "reasonable access" with very little else, the court will not so find.[79] It seems that one could just as easily conclude that the non-specified access was based on a mutual trust that the other would do nothing to prevent the exercise of access by the other party such as removing themselves from the jurisdiction.

If the child does not want to visit with the non-custodial parent, it becomes difficult to force such access in light of its being the right of and in the interest of the child. Accordingly, the courts have responded by suggesting, apparently as a bottom-line test, that the custodial parent is not obliged to physically force the child out of the door and into the arms of the waiting parent.[80] At the same time

---

[76]See *Legge v. Legge* (1980), 25 Nfld. and P.E.I.R. 95, 68 A.P.R. 95 (Nfld. T.D.) (access every third weekend so children can play with friends in neighbourhood on other weekends).

[77]*Penny v. Penny* (1973), 8 R.F.L. 247 (Sask. Q.B.). See also *Wheatley v. Flynn* (1982), 30 R.F.L. (2d) 263 (Ont. Prov. Ct.).

[78]*Frey v. Frey* (1980), 8 Sask. R. 87 (Q.B.).

[79]*E.g.,* see *Burgoyne v. Burgoyne* (1980), 38 N.S.R. (2d) 181, 69 A.P.R. 181 (T.D.); *Garrett v. Garrett* (1982), 36 Nfld. and P.E.I.R. 479, 101 A.P.R. 479 (P.E.I. S.C.) (court refused to recognize material change in circumstance after wife took children from P.E.I. to Ontario while continuing access visits for children in P.E.I.); *MacDonald v. MacDonald* (1981), 22 R.F.L. (2d) 463 (Man. C.A.) (custodial parent removing children from Winnipeg to Nova Scotia; no travel costs awarded to access parent who makes only $400 per month); *Korpesho v. Korpesho* (1982), 19 Man. R. (2d) 142, 31 R.F.L. (2d) 449 (C.A.), revg 19 Man. R. (2d) 145, 31 R.F.L. (2d) 140, [1983] C.C.L. 4452 (Q.B.) (court varied original award which restricted removal of child from city; new step-parent changing jobs and best interests of child in keeping new family together). For a full review of authorities see *Coulter v. Coulter,* summarized in (1984), 6 F.L.R.R. 166 (Ont. S.C.).

[80]*Singer v. Singer* (1974), 17 R.F.L. 18 (Ont. S.C.). See also *Loewen v. Loewen* (1982), 29 R.F.L. (2d) 25 (B.C. S.C.) (court suspending access until improvement in relationship between child and non-custodial parent; considering child's wishes); *Wood v. Wood* (1981), 12 Man. R. (2d) 265 (Q.B.) (children fearing and distrusting past behaviour of access parent due to his past mental illness. Father now under psychiatric treatment and never posed physical threat. Access ordered despite unwillingness of children, with help of mediator; mother to cooperate and assist); *Sigurdson v. Sigurdson* (1980), 7 Sask. R. 422 (U.F.C.) (evidence of abusive behaviour in past, teenagers refusing while custodial parent encouraging access. Court refused access; children best able to decide); *G. v. G.* (1980), 21 R.F.L. (2d) 372 (*sub nom. Grant v. Grant*), 31 Nfld. and P.E.I.R. 308, 87 A.P.R. 308 (P.E.I. S.C.) (previous mental and physical illness, child reluctant to see parent. Court adjourned matter for three months to allow child and applicant to undergo counselling. Custodial parent under legal obligation to encourage access visits); *Roy v. Roy* (1983), 32 R.F.L. (2d) 38 (Man. C.A.) (access previously denied due to mental illness; mother now stable. Court orders access despite children's reluctance (aged 15, 13, 10 and 8 years). Although natural reaction, it should not be overemphasized in the circumstances.)

however, the courts will view this development with great suspicion of the custodial parent, given the common assumption that most children want to see both of their parents. The court may decide that the custodial parent may have been directly or indirectly influencing or "brainwashing" the child against the non-custodial parent. If the court is so convinced then, with increasingly less patience, it may suspend child-support payments to the custodial parent until access occurs, or find the custodial parent in contempt, possibly with fines or incarceration, but more likely with a suspended sentence on the understanding that the parent will purge his or her contempt by ensuring that access occurs.[81] Unfortunately, this indirect and rather blunt instrument of pressure on the custodial parent frequently translates into pressure on the child. Each parent may seek to win the child to their side and to have the child perceive that parent as martyred and persecuted by the court and the other parent *because* of his love for the child. In other words, each parent pressures the child to rescue him. The child is now understanding less and less and becomes highly distressed. The courts, more in exasperation than judicious calm, threaten to change the child's custody, or even threaten to remove the child from both parents' custody altogether. But in the end, the court must return to the "best interests" test. The child's need for security rises to the fore, overriding all other considerations, so that the court is just as likely to suspend access indefinitely, reinstating support payments, despite the legitimate claims of the deprived non-custodial parent.[82]

As a postscript, the deprived parent is not permitted even the recourse of the wronged litigant in the normal civil suit in that he is prevented from seeking damages based on a claim of interference in his undisputed entitlement to a parent/child relationship.[83] Without any means of exacting accountability for the original objective of a continued relationship with the child, the situation sometimes precipitates desperate self-help actions.

Enforcement of Custody Orders: Intra-Jurisdictional
Given the conflict-ridden world of child custody described above, enforcement of custody orders becomes a necessary adjunct to the courts duties, as the parties move farther and farther away from cooperative parenting. When the custodial parent must yield up the child to a frustrated and hostile non-custodial parent, cautionary procedures may be necessary. The courts may:

1) permit access but stipulate that the child may not leave the court's jurisdiction;[84] direct that the visiting parent surrender his or her passport;[85] suspend a legal claim by the non-custodial parent until the child is

---

[81]See *Kett v. Kett* (1976), 28 R.F.L. 1 (Ont. H.C.); *Cillis v. Cillis* (1980), 20 R.F.L. (2d) 208 (Ont. H.C.); affd (1981), 23 R.F.L. (2d) 76 (Ont. Div. Ct.).

[82]See *El-Sohemy v. El-Sohemy* (1980), 17 R.F.L. (2d) 1 (Ont. S.C.); *Re Stroud and Stroud* (1974), 4 O.R. (2d) 567, 18 R.F.L. 237 (*sub nom. Stroud v. Stroud*) (S.C.); *Mann v. Mann*, summarized in (1981), 4 F.L.R.R. 84 (Ont. S.C.).

[83]*Schrenk v. Schrenk and Duke* (1981), 32 O.R. (2d) 122 (H.C.); affd (1982), 36 O.R. (2d) 480 (C.A.).

[84]*Ishaky v. Ishaky* (1978), 7 R.F.L. (2d) 138 (Ont. C.A.); *Strothman v. Strothman* (1979), 5 Man. R. (2d) 202 (Q.B.).

[85]*Ishaky v. Ishaky, ibid.* See also s. 38(3), para. 4, *CLRA* for statutory jurisdiction.

returned;[86] or, require that the visiting parent post a bond, with or without sureties,[87] or enter into a recognizance;[88]

2) permit access but only on the condition that it is subject to supervision;[89]

3) permit the non-custodial parent to visit the children but never all of the children at one time. This cautionary measure presumably acts as a deterrent for the unlawful removal of the children from the jurisdiction;[90]

4) deny access when the visiting parent has removed the children previously, since the threat of a repeated removal would be stressful to the children.[91]

Section 16(4) of the proposed *Divorce and Corollary Relief Act* gives the judge wide discretion to impose conditions or restrictions.

If all of these precautionary measures fail and the non-custodial parent has taken the children without divulging their whereabouts, the following measures are available:

Contempt of Court

1) A parent in contempt can purge it by returning the children. One court ordered the father's share of the matrimonial assets frozen until his contempt was purged.[92] Note that a lower court, normally prevented from citing for contempt outside the court room, is empowered under s. 39(1) of the *CLRA* to "punish by fine or imprisonment, or both, any wilful contempt of or resistance to its process or orders" in respect of custody or access. The fine is not to exceed $1,000.00 and imprisonment is to be no longer than 90 days. Query whether this section is not vulnerable to a challenge of being unconstitutional, given the findings of the Supreme Court of Canada regarding the jurisdiction of lower provincial courts.[93]

---

[86]*Sagrott v. Sagrott* (1979), 11 R.F.L. (2d) 395 (Ont. U.F.C.); *Cillis v. Cillis, supra*, note 81.

[87]*MacDonald v. Finkelman* (1976), 26 R.F.L. 302 (Ont. S.C.) and see s. 38(3), para. 3, *CLRA* for statutory jurisdiction.

[88]*Re Vogel*, summarized in (1981), 10 A.C.W.S. 223 (B.C. S.C.).

[89]See *Re Dulong and Klaus*, summarized in (1980), 3 A.C.W.S. 87 (B.C. S.C.); *Mintz v. Mintz* (1979), 33 N.S.R. (2d) 585, 57 A.P.R. 585, 103 D.L.R. (3d) 182, 2 Fam. L. Rev. 133 (*sub nom. Re Mintz*) (S.C. T.D.). See also s. 35 of the *CLRA* that enables a court to direct supervision of access or custody on consent of the supervising person, Children's Aid Society or other body.

[90]*Re Chaudhry and Chaudhry* (1983), 21 A.C.W.S. (2d) 408 (B.C. S.C.).

[91]*Bellos v. Bellos*, summarized in (1983), 17 A.C.W.S. (2d) 478 (Ont. S.C.). See also *Moglin v. Moglin* (1980), 1 Sask. R. 337 (Q.B.) (court considers effects of mother's custody application after she had taken the child to England). But see *Mintz v. Mintz, supra*, note 89 (court, after an attempted kidnapping, simply imposed supervised access).

[92]See *Hanney v. Hanney* (1979), 3 Fam. L. Rev. 52 (Ont. H.C.); *Genua v. Genua* (1979), 12 R.F.L. (2d) 85 (Ont. Prov. Ct.) (court held that, for a contempt finding, evidence must be clear and unequivocal and that non-compliance must be wilful. Because of intense emotions involved, ordinary court procedure should be modified; court should be slow to act. Contempt proceeding must not become an extension of the dispute which led to the breakdown of the family unit); *Hayes v. Hayes* (1981), 43 N.S.R. (2d) 349, 81 A.P.R. 349 (T.D.) (denial of access contrary to order not contempt when father argumentative and abusive in front of children and failing to pay support for children); *Cillis v. Cillis, supra*, note 81 (custodial parent denies access despite court order, husband seeking contempt citation. Court stays proceedings, ordering assessment to determine best interests. Insufficient evidence to make meaningful order with respect to future relationship between parties and children.)

[93]*Reference Re s. 6 of Family Relations Act, 1978; A.-G. Ontario v. A.-G. Canada,* [1982] 1 S.C.R. 62, 36 B.C.L.R. 1, [1982] 3 W.W.R. 1, 131 D.L.R. (3d) 257, 40 N.R. 206, 26 R.F.L. (2d) 113.

Restraining
Order

2) Under s. 36 of the *CLRA*, the court, including a provincial court,[94] can issue a restraining order against anyone "molesting, annoying or harassing" the child or the parent who has legal custody.

Disclosure of
Records

3) Section 40(1) of the *CLRA* permits the court to direct that a person or public body provide the court with such particulars of the address of the parent having unauthorized care of the child as may be in the records of the person or body. The information is to be given to the court, which may then give the particulars to the applicant parent. This application is available if it appears to the court that a party applying for custody, access or enforcement of same needs to know the whereabouts of the respondent parent or of the person having unauthorized care of the child. Section 40(2) of the Act stipulates that such information shall not be released when its purpose is simply to enable the applicant to identify or obtain particulars as to the identity of the person who has custody of the child, rather than to learn or confirm the whereabouts of the proposed respondent or unauthorized person for the enforcement of a custody or access order. Section 40(3) stipulates that the giving of this information is not to be deemed as a contravention of any Act, Regulation or common law rule of confidentiality, and s. 40(4) binds the provincial Crown. (Note Ontario's proposed *Support and Custody Orders Enforcement Act, 1985* which will create an agency to undertake, without fee, the enforcement of support and custody (but not access) orders or agreements by use of similar information-release sections or by court proceedings with the agency as applicant.) In one case, the officials at the Ontario Health Insurance Plan, the Registrar of Motor Vehicles, and the Ministries of Revenue and Community and Social Services were all ordered to provide the applicant with the particulars of the address of her husband, when she was seeking an order to enforce an interim custody order under the *Divorce Act*.[95] In another case, the Ontario Court of Appeal upheld a high court decision declaring that the section speaks to "records", to be distinguished from knowledge, and "records" means a written record kept by the agency or person in the course of its operation as a trade, business or public agency. The Appellate Court further concluded that if a person against whom an order is made sets out an affidavit declaring that he or she does not have those records, this is sufficient unless further information is brought to the court's attention that raises issue with the deposition, in which case, the court could explore the matter further.[96]

There have been a number of cases dealing with similar "information release" sections as they relate to the enforcement of support which will be helpful in interpreting s. 40(1). In one decision, the issue of solicitor-client confidentiality arose in this context. The court dismissed an application to set aside an order directing the solicitor to disclose the address of his client, stating that there existed a civil wrong to be redressed, that is, the failure to make support payments resulting in an application for disclosure of the

[94]*Re Bonde and Bonde* (1983), 19 A.C.W.S. (2d) 329 (Ont. Dist. Ct.).

[95]*Re Fish and Fish* (1978), 20 O.R. (2d) 782 (U.F.C.) (enforcement of custody order).

[96]*Robertson v. Robertson* (1982), 36 O.R. (2d) 658, 25 R.F.L. (2d) 103 (C.A.) (enforcement of custody order).

respondent's address.[97] The confidentiality of information was also tested in an Ontario Court of Appeal decision in which it was determined that the prohibition in s. 241 of the *Income Tax Act* against disclosure of information by Revenue Canada was absolute and a court, relying upon a similar provision for disclosure under domestic support legislation, cannot rely upon its inherent jurisdiction to order disclosure of information from Revenue Canada. (Note the proposed federal *Family Orders Assistance Act* which will provide for release of information from the records of the Departments of Health and Welfare and Employment and Immigration to assist in the enforcement of support, custody and access orders.) In the same decision, the court also determined that the decision of the trial judge requiring Bell Canada to disclose telephone numbers in order to assist the wife in locating the husband for the purpose of enforcing a custody order was not permissible. The court was concerned that to release such information might invite the disclosure of confidential information far beyond the whereabouts of the respondent, noting that the release of information about telephone calls is certainly more than the disclosure of an address.[98] Finally, in a 1979 decision of Ontario's High Court, it was held that the information disclosure section did not override the secrecy provisions in the *Real Estate and Business Brokers Act*.[99]

It remains to be seen whether the interests of the child in a custody dispute will have a different effect on the court's interpretation of "information release" sections than do the child's interests in the enforcement of support payments.

Examinations

4) One may examine any party or person in aid of execution or enforcement of judgment. Section 60.18(6) of Ontario's Rules of Civil Procedure provide that:

Where any difficulty arises concerning the enforcement of an order, the court may,

(a) make an order for the examination of any person who the court is satisfied may have knowledge of the matters set out in subrule (2); and

(b) make such order for the examination of any other person as is just.

Sub-section (b) may allow a party to pursue the whereabouts of an unauthorized person having care of the child. There is some question as to whether the procedure is available in cases other than for the enforcement of judgments for the recovery of money.[100] It is clear, in any event, that prior to relying upon this rule, all other efforts must have been exhausted.

---

[97]*Matson v. Matson,* summarized in (1980), 5 F.L.R.R. 127 (Ont. S.C.) (enforcement of support order).

[98]*Glover v. Ministry of National Revenue,* [1981] 2 S.C.R. 561n, 130 D.L.R. (3d) 383n, 43 N.R. 271, 25 R.F.L. (2d) 335; *Glover v. Bell Canada,* [1981] 2 S.C.R. 563n, 130 D.L.R. (3d) 382n, 42 N.R. 472n, 25 R.F.L. (2d) 334n, affg (*sub nom. Glover v. Glover (No. 2)*) (1980), 29 O.R. (2d) 401, 113 D.L.R. (3d) 174, 42 N.R. 475, 18 C.P.C. 107 (*sub nom. Glover v. Glover*) 18 R.F.L. (2d) 126.

[99]*Kowalski v. Spylo,* summarized in (1979), 2 F.L.R.R. 25 (Ont. S.C.) (enforcement of support order).

[100]See *C.I.B.C. v. Sutton* (1981), 34 O.R. (2d) 482 (C.A.).

*Police
Involvement*

5) Prior to the enactment of the *CLRA*, it was held that a court, relying upon its inherent jurisdiction, did not have the authority to direct the involvement of the police, to be distinguished from the sheriff, without notice to the police.[101] Section 37(2) of the *CLRA* meets this problem by giving to the court clear authority to direct the sheriff or the police, or both, having jurisdiction in any area where it appears to the court that the child may be, to locate, apprehend, and deliver the child to the person named in the order. Such an order may be made without notice (presumably to the police or to any other party), if the court is satisfied that it is necessary that the action be taken without delay. The Legislature has imposed some limitations on this broad authority. First s. 37(7) limits the time period during which the order is operative to six months unless the court is satisfied that a longer period of time is necessary in the circumstances. Secondly, s. 36(6) stipulates that the powers of the police or sheriff to enter and search any place where either has reasonable and probable grounds for believing that the child may be, are limited to the hours between 6 a.m. and 9 p.m. unless the court in its order authorizes entry and search at another time. (See below for role of *Criminal Code*.)

*Prerogative
Writ*

6) The extraordinary remedy of *habeas corpus* is available in seeking to enforce a custody order. In a Newfoundland Appellate Court decision, it was held that once a mother registered her order giving her custody under the *Divorce Act* in Newfoundland, she could apply by writ of *habeas corpus* to direct the uncle with whom the child was residing to return the child in conformance with the order.[102] Note that the court may decline to grant a *habeas corpus* application where, for example, there are alternative remedies available to the applicant, as is the case under Ontario legislation where any person can now apply for custody, or for the enforcement of custody orders without resort to such an extraordinary remedy.

*Enforcement of
Custody Orders:
Inter-Jurisdictional*

An order of custody, whether interim or final, if made within the context of divorce proceedings, may be registered in any province or territory throughout Canada. This is based on s. 14 of the *Divorce Act* which stipulates that any order of custody has legal effect throughout Canada, and s. 15 which provides that once the order is registered in another superior court in another province or territory, then it may be enforced as an order of that court or in such other manner as is provided by that province's or territory's Rules of Practice or Regulations. There is no such registration process for extra-provincial orders made pursuant to provincial legislation or under a foreign jurisdiction. However, even if the order were capable of being registered, there is no automatic right of enforcement since each superior court of every jurisdiction in Canada retains an inherent jurisdiction over the welfare of the children brought before it. At least three Canadian cases have asserted this inherent jurisdiction to override an order under the *Divorce Act*

---

[101]*Leponiemi v. Leponiemi* (1982), 31 O.R. (2d) 667 (S.C.); revd 35 O.R. (2d) 440, 26 R.F.L. (2d) 320 (C.A.).

[102]*Re Hutchings* (1976), 24 R.F.L. 328 (Nfld. C.A.). Note that the court will not entertain a *habeus corpus* application when the child is not physically present in jurisdiction: *Kovacs v. Graham* (1981), 16 Alta. L.R. (2d) 396, 33 A.R. 43, 23 R.F.L. (2d) 201 (Q.B.).

emanating from a jurisdiction other than its own.[103] In light of the possibility of successful forum shopping, inter-spousal abductions and kidnappings do not in themselves prevent the abductor from having a new day in a new court.

In an attempt to respond comprehensively to the increasing inclination of parties to use self-help, Ontario includes provisions in the *CLRA* which attempt to codify a process for recognition and enforcement of extra-jurisdictional orders. The objectives of such legislation is, as one judge described it, to ensure that "swift and easy modes of travel do not make it a simple matter for a disgruntled or emotional parent to take the law into his own hands and province-hop across the country, deliberately ignoring legitimate court orders."[104] The codified objectives under s. 19(b), (c) and (d) are as follows:

> S. 19(b) to recognize that the concurrent exercise of jurisdiction by judicial tribunals of more than one province, territory or state in respect of the custody of the same child ought to be avoided, and to make provision so that the courts of Ontario will, unless there are exceptional circumstances, refrain from exercising or decline jurisdiction in cases where it is more appropriate for the matter to be determined by a tribunal having jurisdiction in another place with which the child has a closer connection;
>
> (c) to discourage the abduction of children as an alternative to the determination of custody rights by due process; and
>
> (d) to provide for the more effective enforcement of custody and access orders and for the recognition and enforcement of custody and access orders made outside Ontario.

Inherent Jurisdiction

The problem of competing and/or conflicting jurisdictions dealing with custody of the same child frequently arises. At least two factors in Canadian law contribute to this confusion: inherent jurisdiction of superior courts and the test of "residence" with all of its exceptions. In the first place, the Supreme Court in every province is charged with an inherent and overriding jurisdiction regarding the welfare of the child. As a result, each of the respective Supreme Courts feel compelled to render an independent judgment concerning the best interests of the child. Cases have been decided on the basis of each fact situation and have varied results. The courts have:

> 1) directed that a child be returned and delivered up to the custodial parent,[105]
>
> 2) directed that the "kidnapping" parent return and deliver up the child, unless the kidnapping parent initiates proceedings in the jurisdiction of the child's ordinary residence. If proceedings are so commenced, the child may remain in the kidnapping parent's temporary and protective custody pending an order from the court of original jurisdiction;[106]

---

[103]See *Re Hutchings, ibid.; Ramsay v. Ramsay* (1976), 13 O.R. (2d) 85 (C.A.); *Re Abramsen,* [1977] 3 W.W.R. 764 (B.C. S.C.).

[104]*Re Tomyn* unreported, June 16, 1977 (Ont. S.C.).

[105]*Re Lougrhan* (1973), 9 R.F.L. 255 (Ont. C.A.); *Munz v. Munz* (1974), 15 R.F.L. 123 (Alta. C.A.); *Leatherdale v. Ferguson* (1964), 50 D.L.R. (2d) 182 (Man. C.A.).

[106]*Cochrane v. Cochrane* (1975), 20 R.F.L. 264 (Ont. C.A.).

3) granted custody to the "kidnapping" parent, in spite of an order existing in another jurisdiction, on the basis of the child's interests;[107]

4) assumed that jurisdiction exists to consider only the granting of an order for temporary or protective custody.[108]

Legislation in some provinces has also extended inherent jurisdiction to the lower courts by allowing them to supersede extra-jurisdictional custody orders when "serious harm" would result if the child were returned to the original jurisdiction.[109]

"Residence" Test and Its Exceptions

The meaning of a child's "residence" is unclear at law and since it is this finding of residency which will determine which court has jurisdiction to hear the matter,[110] the lack of clarity becomes a significant problem. Generally, it is the court of the child's ordinary residence that has jurisdiction. "Ordinary residence" cannot be changed by taking the child from the home without the consent or acquiescence of the custodial parent, whether or not there is a formal order or agreement. Indeed, in an attempt to assist in a clear definition of "ordinary residence", an English Court has suggested that there can be no acquiescence or consent by the custodial parent to the kidnapping or abducting of a child, leading to a change in the child's residence, until at least three months have elapsed from the date of the child's removal without action by the original custodial parent.[111] Nevertheless, because of an overriding concern for the child's interests, courts have assumed jurisdiction where the child was only physically present in that court's jurisdiction, demanding protective care through the adult party.[112] From the same motivation, courts have also assumed that the issue of the child's ordinary residence is a question of fact based on any particular moment in time.[113] Either interpretation allows an otherwise "foreign" court wide latitude to intervene.

In response to this situation, the Ontario Court of Appeal has listed five factors to take into consideration in determining where a custody hearing should be held:[114]

1) If the matter has already been before the court, then what is the court of "primary and original jurisdiction?"

2) If an order is outstanding, then from what jurisdiction was the order issued?

3) In what jurisdiction has the child predominantly resided?

---

[107]*McKee v. McKee,* [1951] A.C. 352 (P.C.).

[108]*Re Abramsen, supra,* note 103.

[109]For examples of a provincial legislature using "serious harm" as a reason for not enforcing extra-provincial custody orders see: Saskatchewan, the *Extra-Provincial Custody Orders Enforcement Act,* R.S.S. 1978, c. E-18; Nova Scotia, the *Reciprocal Enforcement of Custody Orders Act,* S.N.S. 1976, c. 15.

[110]See *e.g. Cochrane v. Cochrane, supra,* note 106.

[111]*Re P. (G.E.),* [1964] 3 All E.R. 977 (C.A.). For cases dealing with "ordinary residence" see *Williams v. Williams* (1979), 34 N.S.R. (2d) 271, 59 A.P.R. 271 (S.C. T.D.); *Olinyk v. Olinyk, supra,* note 22: *Mudd v. Mudd* (1980), 18 C.P.C. 72 (Ont. S.C.).

[112]*Nielson v. Nielson* (1971), 5 R.F.L. 313 (Ont. S.C.).

[113]*Vachon v. Vachon* (1975), 22 R.F.L. 392 (Ont. S.C.).

[114]*Cochrane v. Cochrane, supra,* note 106.

4) What is the forum of convenience for the resolution of the issue?

5) How did the children come before the court's jurisdiction, taking into account the equity of compelling the original custodial parent to come to the new jurisdiction for a hearing?

The Legislature's response is an attempt to codify and thereby clarify the case law, although it is unclear whether it also rationalizes the case law with the s. 19 objective of stemming the tide of inter-spousal kidnappings. Pursuant to the *CLRA*, a court in which an application for custody is brought shall only exercise its jurisdiction if the child is found to be "habitually resident" in Ontario *or* if the circumstances meet a number of specific requirements: ss. 22(1), 23. A child is "habitually resident" in a place where he resided (i) with both parents, (ii) with one parent by consent or court order, or (iii) with another person on a permanent basis for a significant period of time, whichever of the three last occurred: s. 22(2). Habitual residence may not be altered by the removal or withholding of the child by the non-custodial parent unless there has been acquiescence or undue delay in commencing due process by the custodial party: s. 22(3). However, in recognition of the possibility that in some cases the court may have to exercise its jurisdiction over a child not habitually resident, s. 22(1)(b) provides that the court may do so if satisfied that *all* of the following criteria apply:

1) the child is physically present[115] in Ontario at the commencement of the application for the order;

2) substantial evidence concerning best interests of the child is available in Ontario;

3) no application for custody or access is pending before an extra-provincial tribunal in another place where the child is habitually resident;[116]

4) no extra-provincial custody or access order has been recognized by an Ontario court;

5) the child has a real and substantial connection[117] with Ontario; and

6) on the balance of convenience, it is appropriate for jurisdiction to be exercised in Ontario.[118]

---

[115]For cases concerning "physically present" see *Kovacs v. Graham* (1981), 23 R.F.L. (2d) 201 (Alta. Q.B.); *Bazant v. Bazant* (1979), 7 Sask. R. 375 (U.F.C.): *West v. West*, [1981] 3 W.W.R. 101 (Alta. Prov. Ct.); *Re Taylor and Taylor* (1979), 100 D.L.R. (3d) 108, 10 R.F.L. (2d) 91 (*sub nom. Taylor v. Taylor*) (Man. Q.B.); *Olinyk v. Olinyk, supra,* note 22 (found no jurisdiction); *Dieno v. Dieno* (1979), 4 Sask. R. 228 (U.F.C.) (found no jurisdiction); *Mudd v. Mudd, supra,* note 111 (took jurisdiction); *Russo v. Bridgeland* (1982), 37 O.R. (2d) 618 (U.F.C.) (even though not physically present or even "ordinarily resident", court took jurisdiction because only existing custody order issued out of Ontario despite the fact that applicant father not custodial parent and custodial parent lived in Texas with child).

[116]For an example of this criteria in another jurisdiction, see *Vogt v. Vogt* (1982), 139 D.L.R. (3d) 398 (B.C. C.A.).

[117]For cases on "real and substantial connection" see *Hayes v. Hayes* (1981), 43 N.S.R. (2d) 349, 81 A.P.R. 349 (T.D.); *R. v. Miller* (1982), 36 O.R. (2d) 387 (Co. Ct.); *McArdle v. Riley* (1982), 28 R.F.L. (2d) 428 (B.C. C.A.); *Frappier v. Frappier* (1982), 21 Sask. R. 118 (Q.B.); *Labrecque v. Labrecque,* [1981] 2 W.W.R. 383 (Sask. Q.B.).

[118]For an example of this criterion in another jurisdiction see *Boal v. Scott* (1981), 12 Sask. R. 292 (Q.B.).

Even if this test is not satisfied for a child who is not habitually resident in Ontario, s. 23 provides the court with authority to invoke its jurisdiction in cases of "serious harm" if:

    (a) the child is physically present in Ontario; *and*

    (b) the court is satisfied that the child would, on the balance of probabilities, suffer serious harm[119] if,

        (i) the child remains in the custody of the person legally entitled to custody of the child,

        (ii) the child is returned to the custody of the person legally entitled to custody of the child, or

        (iii) the child is removed from Ontario.

A court may decline to exercise jurisdiction where it is of the opinion that it is more appropriate for jurisdiction to be exercised outside of Ontario: s. 25.

As a "safety net" precaution, s. 41 of the Act codifies the common law "inherent jurisdiction" by enabling the court, when it has decided to decline jurisdiction (ss. 25, 43) or considers itself to have no jurisdiction, to do any one or more of the following:

1. Make such interim order of custody or access as it considers to be in the best interests of the child.

2. Stay the application subject to,

    i. the condition that a party to the application promptly commence a similar proceeding before an extra-provincial tribunal, or

    ii. such other conditions as the court considers appropriate.

3. Order a party to return the child to such place as the court considers appropriate and, in the discretion of the court, order payment of reasonable travel costs and other expenses of the child and of any parties to or witnesses at the hearing of the application.

Extra-Provincial Orders   If there is an outstanding extra-provincial order, s. 42 of the Act directs the court to recognize the order unless it is satisfied:

    (a) that the respondent was not given reasonable notice of the commencement of the proceeding in which the order was made;

    (b) that the respondent was not given an opportunity to be heard by the extra-provincial tribunal before the order was made;

    (c) that the law of the place in which the order was made did not require the extra-provincial tribunal to have regard for the best interests of the child;

    (d) that the order of the extra-provincial tribunal is contrary to public policy in Ontario; or

    (e) that, in accordance with section 22, the extra-provincial tribunal would not have had jurisdiction if it were a court in Ontario.

Furthermore, the court under s. 43 can supersede an extra-provincial order not only when any of the aforesaid factors are applicable, but also if the court is

---

[119]Note that "serious harm", an undefined concept, need only be proved on a balance of probabilities: *O. v. O.* (1980), 17 R.F.L. (2d) 336 (Ont H.C.).

satisfied that there has "been a material change in circumstances that affects or is likely to affect the best interests of the child" and,

(a) the child is habitually resident[120] in Ontario at the commencement of the application for the order; or

(b) although the child is not habitually resident in Ontario, the court is satisfied

    (i) that the child is physically present in Ontario at the commencement of the application for the order,

    (ii) that the child no longer has a real and substantial connection with the place where the extra-provincial order was made,

    (iii) that substantial evidence concerning the best interests of the child is available in Ontario,

    (iv) that the child has a real and substantial connection with Ontario, and

    (v) that, on the balance of convenience, it is appropriate for jurisdiction to be exercised in Ontario.

Even when these two exemptions to the recognition of foreign orders is inapplicable, s. 44 of the Act enables the court to supersede an extra-provincial order if the court is satisfied, on a "balance of probabilities" test, that the child would suffer serious harm if removed from Ontario or returned to the person having legal custody pursuant to the extra-jurisdictional order. This exemption finds its parallel in the legislation of most of Canada's other provinces.[121]

(Note that the Hague Convention is also applicable to the enforcement of certain extra-provincial custody orders in Ontario. For discussion, see below under "Hague Convention.")

Judicial Application

It is apparent that the new legislation achieves nothing more than the codifying of case law and with it, the problems that arise when courts in different jurisdictions cling to the power of independent decision-making, even in the face of an extra-jurisdictional order. It is not clear what "serious harm" means. The "balance of probabilities" test, a less than strict standard of proof, coupled with the vagueness of the phrase "serious harm" effectively enables any absconding parent to come before a second court even in the face of a previously adverse order and re-assert a claim based on an even more elaborately woven tale, warning of dire consequences should the child be returned. And now, under the *CLRA*, the lower courts as well as the superior courts in Ontario have what amounts to a *parens patriae* jurisdiction to consider themselves seized of a custody dispute. These difficulties emerge all too clearly in two decisions of the Ontario Court of Appeal which were determined prior to the enactment of the amending legislation although they could very easily come within the provisions of the new legislation.

In the first case,[122] the wife was born in Canada and married her husband in

---

[120]For a discussion of residence and definition of "habitual residence", see in body under "Enforcement of Custody/Access Orders: Inter-jurisdictional: Residence and Standing."

[121]See *supra,* note 109.

[122]*Charmasson v. Charmasson* (1981), 34 O.R. (2d) 498, 131 D.L.R. (2d) 74, 25 C.R.C. 45, 25 R.F.L. (2d) 41; affd. (1982), 27 R.F.L. (2d) 241 (C.A.).

1969 in France where the parties resided. In 1974, a child was born in France. In 1980, a court in France granted an order of "non-reconciliation", the effect of which authorized the parties to obtain a divorce, awarding custody of the child to the father. That order of custody became void upon the parties' reconciliation. On March 27, 1981, the wife left the matrimonial home in France with the child and returned to Ontario where she obtained an *ex parte* custody order. When the husband finally appeared in Ontario, launching custody proceedings under the now repealed s. 35 of the *FLRA*, the trial judge declined to assume jurisdiction and ordered that the child be returned to the father. The wife appealed successfully; the Ontario Court of Appeal dealt with the jurisdiction issue as follows:

> Luc has been in Ontario for 8 months and while this may seem to be a relatively brief period of time, it is a period of tremendous growth in the life of a young child. For the purposes of determining custody, these changes will be more accurately observed from within Ontario.
>
> In my view the Ontario court is the forum conveniens. Luc has established personal, educational and language ties in Ontario and it would be in the best interest of his total development not to uproot him once again in order to send him back to the respondent in France for determination of the custody issue.
>
> In determining that the respondent should be given custody of Luc, the French court, no doubt, fully examined the merits of the custody issue. However, the inquiry [was] . . . a full two years ago. It cannot be said that the factors which the French court considered necessarily obtain today necessitating the return of the child to that jurisdiction for a re-hearing of the custody question. Of course, any court in Ontario hearing the issue on the merits would give due regard to the voided order of the French court.
>
> It was submitted by counsel for the respondent that the appellant, by removing the child from his home, family and friends and school before the end of the term without warning to the father, was acting in a way which cannot be countenanced by the court and which must be regarded as contrary to the child's best interests. In my opinion, this aspect of the wife's behavior is irrelevant for the purposes of jurisdiction and may go to the fitness of the mother as a custodial parent. Likewise, the allegations and counter-allegations of unfitness, sworn to in the affidavits filed in this matter, are considerations for the trial judge determining the issue of custody.[123]

In the second case,[124] two children, ages 6 and 4, were the subject of a custody determination in Texas after a trial by a judge and jury at the election of the wife. The parents had originally moved from Ontario to Texas and the mother had initially commenced proceedings in Ontario, which were adjourned *sine die* in light of her election to pursue her remedies in Texas. The six-week trial in Texas, with each of the parties and the children represented, resulted in an order in December, 1981, giving the father custody. A subsequent hearing in May,

---

[123]*Ibid.*, at p. 48.
[124]*Re Solnik and Solnik*, summarized in (1982), 5 F.L.R.R. 143 (Ont. C.A.).

1982 before a judge alone provided the mother with extended access for a period of six weeks during the summer. Hiding in a secluded estate in Quebec, the mother did not return the children to the father, and their whereabouts were unknown to the father at the time. The father obtained an order in Texas terminating access rights and commenced an action for damages for kidnapping which resulted in a judgment in excess of 1.5 million dollars. Criminal proceedings in Texas against the mother as a result of her abduction were also outstanding. Finally, the father attended a Unified Family Court in Ontario, believing the mother would return to the place of her family's residence in Hamilton. He obtained from the Hamilton court (where the mother had originally commenced an application) an order dated August 27, 1982, ordering the children to be delivered up to the police officers for the purpose of their return to their father. The Court of Appeal set aside this order on November 5, 1982, concluding that a short adjournment should have been permitted to the mother's counsel, who was unavailable as a result of a summer holiday, so that a proper inquiry could be made into whether or not it was in the children's best interests to be returned to the father. It was also noted that counsel for the mother, who appeared before the court on August 27th requesting the adjournment until the mother's new counsel returned from his holiday, had some difficulty getting instructions since the mother was still secreted with the children at the estate in Quebec.

The order of the Court of Appeal remitted the enforcement proceedings back to the Unified Family Court "for the receiving of evidence and hearing of submissions on behalf of the parties, by way of enquiry as to whether it is in the best interests of the children that the said application be allowed" with the qualification that the enquiry "is to be limited to any new facts which have arisen since the date of the Texas court order affecting the welfare of the children, and is not to be a re-trial of any matters already litigated in the Texas court." Not surprisingly, the mother re-asserted her claim for custody. In the face of the mother's claim for custody and with the apparent problem of attempting to satisfy the "best interests of the children" while at the same time imposing limitations on the evidence that could be heard, as directed by the Court of Appeal, the court hearing the matter allowed all evidence to be considered. In the course of a lengthy trial, the court effectively re-tried the issue. The father was again granted custody.

Returning to the original objective of stemming the kidnapping tide, based on these two cases one should ask whether or not it has become too easy, and therefore attractive, to establish a new "habitual residence" through self-help, regardless of existing court orders, *i.e.* legal abduction. Based on these cases, the absconding parent can precipitate yet another substantive review of the issue, with or without a change of circumstances, since the child can be established in Ontario to the satisfaction of the court by the time the other parent is able to seek legal redress, which can invariably be delayed. Secondly, one should ask how it is that a parent can claim a "best interest" exemption to escape an extra-provincial order and at the same time maintain that the original jurisdiction should not be seized of the matter. If there is a situation of "serious harm," Ontario's courts have the jurisdiction to direct that a child be returned to a neutral third party in the original jurisdiction until the matter is fully heard by the courts. At the very least, the absconding parent should be required, when applying to Ontario courts, to bring the action in the context of showing "serious harm" rather than re-litigating the issue of custody all over again. The cardinal problem is that every court feels that it must undertake a scrutiny of the facts of the situation, notwithstanding an existing extra-provincial order.[125] So long as this tendency represents prevailing traditional thought, it will encourage parties to do exactly what the legislation intended to avoid.

Criminal Code   Recent amendments to the *Criminal Code* attempt to supplement provincial legislation dealing with enforcement of extra-jurisdictional custody orders. The Act clarifies that an abduction can occur even in the absence of an existing custody order, although in those situations, the proceedings may not be commenced without the consent of the Attorney-General.[126]

The relevant provisions in ss. 250.1 and 250.2 are as follows:

ABDUCTION IN CONTRAVENTION OF CANADIAN CUSTODY ORDER

s. 250.1 Every one who, being the parent, guardian or person having the lawful care or charge of a person under the age of fourteen years, takes, entices away, conceals, detains, receives or harbours that person in contravention of the custody provisions of a custody order in relation to that person made by a court anywhere in Canada with intent to deprive a parent or guardian or any other person who has the lawful care or charge of that person of the possession of that person is guilty of

    (a) an indictable offence and is liable to imprisonment for 10 years; or

    (b) an offence punishable on summary conviction. . . .

ABDUCTION WHERE NO CANADIAN CUSTODY ORDER

s. 250.2(1) Every one who, being the parent, guardian or person having the lawful care or charge of a person under the age of 14 years, takes, entices away, conceals, detains, receives or harbours that person, in relation to whom no custody order has been made by a court anywhere in Canada, with intent to deprive a parent or guardian, or any other person who has the lawful care or charge of that person, of the possession of that person, is guilty of

    (a) an indictable offence and is liable to imprisonment for 10 years; or

---

[125]For cases in which the courts seized jurisdiction, see: *Re Hutchings, supra,* note 102; *Munz v. Munz, supra,* note 105; *Leatherdale v. Ferguson, supra,* note 105; *Re Abramsen, supra,* note 103; *Clement v. Clement* (1982), 29 R.F.L. (2d) 29 (Man. C.A.); *Grewal v. Grewal* (1982), 29 R.F.L. (2d) 23 (Sask. Q.B.); *Pockett v. Pockett* (1982), 19 Sask. R. 263, 30 R.F.L. (2d) 126 (Q.B.); *Goldin v. Goldin* (1979), 25 O.R. (2d) 629, 104 D.L.R. (3d) 76, 10 R.F.L. (2d) 193 (H.C.); *Labrecque v. Labrecque, supra,* note 117. For cases in which courts refused to exercise jurisdiction in the face of self-help measures where there was an existing court order in another jurisdiction see: *Propperl v. Propperl* (1981), 14 Man. R. (2d) 145, 26 R.F.L. (2d) 106 (C.A.); *Angeloni v. Angeloni* (1983), 32 R.F.L. (2d) 453 (B.C. S.C.); *Dieno v. Dieno, supra,* note 115; *Saulnier v. Saulnier* (1980), 17 C.P.C. 303, 3 Fam. L. Rev. 214; revd. 3 Fam. L. Rev. 215 (Ont. H.C.); *O. v. O.* (1980), 30 O.R. (2d) 588, 117 D.L.R. (3d) 159, 17 R.F.L. (2d) 336, 19 C.P.C. 276 (H.C.); *Beairsto v. Beairsto* (1982), 30 R.F.L. (2d) 459 (Alta. C.A.); *Sczesny v. Sczesny* (1981), 25 R.F.L. (2d) 240 (Sask. Q.B.).

[126]*R. v. Kosowan,* 6 Man. R. (2d) 71, [1980] 6 W.W.R. 674, 54 C.C.C. (2d) 571 (Co. Ct.) where no existing custody order, not constituting kidnapping).

(b) an offence punishable on summary conviction.

(2) No proceedings may be commenced under subsection (1) without the consent of the Attorney-General or counsel instructed by him for that purpose. . . .

The amendments presumably nullify the "colour of right" defence that has been used successfully in the past by abducting parents.[127] Under the present wording of the *Code*, the only defences available to the abducting parent are that he or she can establish that the taking of the child was done with the consent of the other parent having the lawful possession, care or charge of the child[128] (s. 250.3) or that it "was necessary to protect the young person from danger or imminent harm": s. 250.4. Further, it is specifically stated that it is no defence to show that the young person "consented to or suggested any conduct of the accused": s. 250.5.

It remains to be seen how willing Canada's Attorneys-General will be to invoke these amending provisions. Traditionally, the courts have been reluctant to invoke the use of the criminal law in the context of domestic proceedings and, in particular, domestic custody disputes.[129] It is submitted that, at least from the perspective of the child, the criminal law provides the most rational and sensible response to the sudden upheaval of one person from the life he has been living by another person. Furthermore, whether the basis is "best interests" or "serious harm" as under Ontario's *CLRA* and legislation in most other provinces, or whether it is expressed as "a great risk that his or her return would expose the child to physical or psychological harm or otherwise place the child in an intolerable situation" as set out in the provisions of the Hague Convention (see below), the effect is the same: namely that there is always an argument available to an abducting parent to rationalize the infringement of another person's freedom and rights (*i.e.* those of the child) based on their perception of that person's "best interests." The wording of the criminal law seems to show less tolerance for the position that an abduction of a child can be excused on this basis.[130]

The Hague Convention

The Hague Convention on the Civil Aspects of International Child Abduction was the result of a conference in November, 1979 involving delegates from 22 countries. The purpose of the meeting was to develop a practical

---

[127]See *e.g. R. v. Austin* (1957), 120 C.C.C. 118 (B.C. C.A.) and for cases where convictions have been registered prior to the amendments to the *Criminal Code*, see *R. v. Watts* (1902), 5 C.C.C. 246 (Ont. H.C.); *R. v. Kehoe* (1974), 21 C.C.C. (2d) 544 (Ont. Prov. Ct.); *Re Lorenz* (1905), 9 C.C.C. 158 (Que. K.B.); *R. v. Hamilton* (1910), 17 C.C.C. 410 (Ont. C.A.); *R. v. Falvo* (1972), 11 C.C.C. (2d) 378 (Man. Co. Ct.).

[128]See *e.g. R. v. Enkirch*, [1983] 1 W.W.R. 530 (Alta. C.A.); *R. v. Bigelow* (1982), 37 O.R. (2d) 304, 28 R.F.L. (2d) 1 (C.A.). See also *Publicover v. R.* (1982), 120 D.L.R. (3d) 310 (Fed. T.D.) where the mother sought assistance from the Minister of National Defence to recover her child whom the non-custodial father had taken to Germany. The court found there to be no jurisdiction to do so.

[129]See *Cummings v. R.* (1915), 26 C.C.C. 304 (Que. C.A.).

[130]But see *R. v. Miller, supra*, note 117 in which the charge was dismissed. The mother had a Nova Scotia custody order and had sent the children to live with the grandparents in Ontario. The father took the children. The court held that the Nova Scotia custody order had application only in Nova Scotia and that under the Ontario legislation, both parents were equally entitled.

response to an increasingly international problem. The convention's intent appears to be the return of the parties to the situation which existed before the child's unlawful removal, thereby permitting them to assert their claims in the original jurisdiction. This reflects much the same objective as that set out in s. 19 of the *CLRA*. In October, 1980, the Convention was adopted by the Hague Conference and came into force once it had been ratified by three states. It was ratified by Canada and, as a "federal state" with more than one system of law, by the independently contracting "states" of Ontario, New Brunswick, Manitoba and British Columbia as well as France, Portugal and Switzerland. Belgium, Greece and the United States have signed the Convention, but have not ratified it. It is important to note that the Convention applies only between contracting states with the one exception of states which are within the same federal jurisdiction. In other words, the Convention does not apply between provinces of Canada, but does apply between a province and another contracting state outside of Canada.[131]

The Convention is annexed as a schedule under s. 47 of the *CLRA* and when there is a conflict between the Act and the Convention, the Convention prevails: s. 47(9). For example, the *CLRA* exemption to enforcement of extra-provincial orders is based on a "serious harm" test while the Hague Convention's exemption is based on whether there is a ". . . grave risk that the child's return would expose him to physical or psychological harm, or otherwise place the child in an intolerable situation. . . ." Some courts may interpret the latter test more stringently than the former. The application of the Convention can be summarized as follows:

1) A Central Authority in each state (in Ontario, the Attorney-General) is the recipient of information concerning the unlawful removal or retention of a child as a result of a breach of custody rights: Article 8.

2) On the receipt of an application from a Central Authority of a contracting state, or from an individual of a Contracting State who allegedly has been deprived of lawful care of his child, to have the child returned, the Attorney-General is obliged to take all appropriate measures "to obtain the voluntary return of the child": Articles 9 and 10.

3) If the child has resided in the contracting state for less than a year from the date unlawful removal or retention commenced, then a judicial or administrative authority shall order the return of the child forthwith unless under Article 13(a) and (b):

   (a) the person, institution or other body having the care of the person of the child was not actually exercising the custody rights at the time of removal or retention, or had consented to or subsequently acquiesced in the removal or retention, or

   (b) there is a grave risk that his or her return would expose the child to physical or psychological harm or otherwise place the child in an intolerable situation.

---

[131]If an enforcement problem arises with respect to the Hague Convention and the solicitor is uncertain as to whether the state is a contracting state, one can contact the Department of Justice for the information and specifically, Mrs. Christine Verdon at (613) 995-6426.

According to this Article, the judicial or administrative authority may also refuse to order the return of the child if it finds that the child objects to being returned and has attained an age and degree of maturity at which it is appropriate to take account of its views.

4) If the child has resided for more than a year in Ontario, allegedly wrongfully, then the child should also be ordered returned unless it is demonstrated that the child is now settled in its new environment: Article 12.

5) The judicial or administrative authorities, in considering the circumstances, may consider the information relating to the child as provided by the Attorney-General, and the Attorney-General is obliged, after six weeks from notification, to explain to the applicant or the Central Authority of the requesting state, if so requested, the reasons, if any, for the delay in the return of the child: Article 11.

6) A court in Ontario cannot make an order with respect to the child's custody if an application has been lodged with the Attorney-General within a reasonable time after notice has been provided by the applicant or Central Authority of the requesting state, until there has been *first* a determination that the child is *not* to be returned in accordance with the Convention: Article 16; and, should an order of custody be obtained in Ontario prior to notice and application for the return of the child, that fact ''shall not be a ground for refusing to return a child . . . but the judicial or administrative authorities of the requested State may take account of the reasons for that decision in applying this Convention.'': Article 17. Nothing in the Convention prevents a court from returning the child at any time prior to the application of the Convention and in accordance with its internal law.

7) Presumably then, a person having allegedly unlawful care of a child would be subject to preliminary investigation by the Attorney-General and in the event there is a refusal to return the child voluntarily, the Attorney-General would initiate proceedings before an administrative or judicial authority for an order directing the return of the child: Article 7.

The Convention repeatedly uses the phrase ''judicial or administrative authorities'' in referring to the decision-making process. This then raises the question of whether the Attorney-General, as the Central Authority, may act not only as a designated party to the proceeding in the event of a court proceeding, but also as an administrative authority with the power of decision, arguably immune from review. For example, Article 20 provides that where adherence to the Convention would dictate the child's return, that action can be refused ''if this would not be permitted by the fundamental principles of the requested state relating to the protection of human rights and fundamental freedoms.'' Does the Attorney-General have the discretion to refuse to initiate proceedings as the Central Authority because a decision has been made as an administrative authority that Article 20 applies? Conversely, does the Attorney-General have the discretion to rely upon the Convention and the enforcement remedies of the Act to apprehend a child and have him returned as a decision not only of the Attorney-General as the Central Authority, but as an administrative authority? It is submitted that the reference to ''administrative authority'' in the Convention cannot refer to the Attorney-General and therefore must be a reference to include those states where domestic disputes are subject to administrative tribunals. Otherwise the Attorney-General, as the Central Authority, would be in a situation of conflict, wearing the hats of investigator and decision maker. Clearly, where there is a dispute between the Central Authority and the individual with whom the child resides, the matter must come before a court as defined in the Act for a resolution, the parties being the Central Authority and/or applicant and the respondent individual caring for the child. Section 47(5) of the incorporating legislation, the *CLRA*, must carry some meaning.

Unfortunately, the Convention seems to leave open the question of the merits of enforcing an order of a foreign jurisdiction. Specifically Article 20, as noted above, allows the child not to be returned if the Court decides that by so doing, the child's human rights and fundamental freedoms may be violated. In the "explanatory report" of the Convention, the following is stated with respect to Article 20:

> It is difficult to foresee how and in what circumstances this provision will be relied upon by the courts in refusing to return the child. All the delegations agreed, however, that such a ground for refusal should be allowed to intervene only exceptionally, and in rare circumstances.
>
> Article 20, adopted by the Commission in the final days of its work, represents the compromise reached by the delegations following a long debate on the exception of "ordre public". The Commission had previously adopted, by a majority of only one vote, a provision on public policy allowing Contracting States, by making a reservation, to oppose the return of the child where this would be considered incompatable with the fundamental principles of the requested State relating to family and children. This clause, which was far too broad, (it opened the door to consideration of the merits of custody rights), risked seriously compromising the success of the Convention. Such a clause could almost be construed to recognize that an abduction could be compatable with the interests of the child — something that was difficult to accept in a Convention whose prime object was to prevent wrongful removals involving the use of force. In addition, the reservation mechanism did not ensure reciprocity between the Contracting States, something which is essential in a Convention of this type.
>
> Aware, moreover, that the absence of any clause on public policy in the Convention might prevent certain member states of the conference from ratifying it, the Commission finally adopted Article 20 which, although couched in very general language, can be expected to be relied on only in very rare cases.

Methods of Conflict Resolution

Given the difficulties surrounding custody disputes as outlined throughout this chapter, the courts have tried gradually to move away from formal, adversarial, legalistic dispute resolution. As noted by one study which focused on the characteristics of the Ontario Supreme Court bench, the judges are inclined to depart from their usual role when involved in custody proceedings.

Court-Initiated Settlements

Although custody cases are difficult to try, the vast majority of cases filed never reach the point of decision. The main reason for this is that all but one of the judges interviewed stated that they make serious attempts to make the parties settle their disputes out of court. One judge admitted that he even goes so far as seeing the disputing parents in his rooms, and to browbeat them into making a settlement. The majority explore with the counsel the possibility of a settlement as they feel that it is in the child's interests to keep the case out of court, if at all possible. Counsel are usually equally anxious to avoid litigation in this field and bring pressure to bear on their clients to settle, wherever possible. This formidable combination of judge and counsel insisting on a settlement usually produces the desired result.[132]

The downside to this approach, which is very familiar to family practitioners, is that settlements arrived at under pressure from lawyers and judges, without professional intervention and counselling, may result in simmering discontent between the parents and future upheavals for the child.

Listening to the Child

In an attempt to short-circuit the court process, judges may also depart from their usual role by initiating the involvement of the child, at least to the extent of meeting the child and listening to his wishes. Section 65 of the *CLRA* directs the court, where possible, to "take into consideration the views and preferences of the child to the extent that [he] is able to express them." It goes on to authorize a recorded interview of the child by the court where the child may have his own lawyer present. The courts have held that the purpose of the judge hearing the wishes of the child is not necessarily to give effect thereto, but to put the judge in a better position to decide what is in the best interests of the child.[133] On the other hand, a court is sometimes reluctant to listen to a child because of the possibility that the child will feel that he is making the decision or that his wishes are being rejected.[134] Courts will also listen to and often give effect to the wishes of children who are in the older age brackets.[135]

The ability of a judge to assess competently the wishes of a child has been

---

[132] Adrian Bradbrook, "An Emperical Study of the Attitudes of the Judges of the Supreme Court of Ontario Regarding the Workings of the Present Child Custody Adjudication Laws" (1972), 49 Can. Bar Rev. 556, at 560.

[133] *Stevenson v. Florant,* [1925] 4 D.L.R. 530 (S.C.C.); affd. [1926] 4 D.L.R. 897 (P.C.); *Saxon v. Saxon* (1975), 17 R.F.L. 257 (B.C. S.C.); *Wakaluk v. Wakaluk* (1976), 25 R.F.L. 292, at 304–05 (Sask. C.A.). See generally *Peckford v. Peckford* (1980), 25 Nfld. and P.E.I.R. 106, 68 A.P.R. 106 (Nfld. T.D.); *Russell v. Terrelonge* (1978), 1 F.L.R.A.C. 198 (Ont. Prov. Ct.); *Schellenberg v. Schellenberg* (1979), 7 Sask. R. 203 (Q.B.); *Patton v. Patton* (1978), 1 F.L.R.A.C. 212 (Ont. Co. Ct.). For cases in which wishes of children did not in themselves amount to a material change in circumstances see *Jandrisch v. Jandrisch* (1980), 3 Man. R. (2d) 135, 16 R.F.L. (2d) 239; revg. (1979), 3 Man. R. (2d) 150 (C.A.); *Goguen v. Goguen* (1981), 38 N.B.R. (2d) 299, 100 A.P.R. 299 (Q.B.); *Brooks v. Brooks* (1978), 19 A.R. 318 (T.D.).

[134] *Taberner v. Taberner* (1971), 5 R.F.L. 14 (Ont. S.C.).

[135] *Loewen v. Loewen* (1982), 29 R.F.L. (2d) 25 (B.C. S.C.). (14 yrs. old); *Kelsey v. Kelsey* (1982), 39 N.B.R. (2d) 166, 103 A.P.R. 166 (Q.B.) (13 yrs. old); *Mullen v. Mullen* (1979), 24 A.R. 154 (Q.B.) (13 yrs. old); *Cain v. Cain* (1983), 33 R.F.L. (2d) 353 (Sask. Q.B.) (14 yrs. old); *Dauvergne v. Dauvergne* (1980), 38 N.S.R. (2d) 77, 69 A.P.R. 77 (T.D.) (15 yrs. and 11 yrs.); *Kiehlbauch v. Franklin* (1979), 20 A.R. 31 (T.D.) (9 and 8 yrs. old). But for cases where the older child's wishes were not followed see *Stanek v. Stanek* (1979), 7 Sask. R. 230 (Q.B.) (15 yrs. old); *Goguen v. Goguen, supra,* note 133 (13 yrs. old); *Peckford v. Peckford, supra,* note 133 (12 yrs. old); *Thatcher v. Thatcher* (1980), 7 Sask. R. 95, 16 R.F.L. (2d) 263 (Q.B.) (11 yrs. old).

the subject of much legal and non-legal consideration. In particular, one judge of the Saskatchewan Court of Appeal, in his dissenting opinion, noted these limitations:

> If the trial judge should decide to allow a child to express his wishes, the judge should then decide upon the procedure he should use in the particular instance for the expression of those wishes. A certain procedure may be appropriate for one case but not another. To call the child as a witness and ask direct questions to establish his preferences is a procedure that should be discouraged. It is generally, but not always, inappropriate. In the present case, the learned trial judge was right, in my respectful view, to decline to hear the children as witnesses, even though they were represented by independent counsel.
>
> The procedure involving a judge speaking to a child, informally, in his chambers, also is not a particularly satisfactory one. To expect a child in such a short period and abnormal atmosphere (from the child's point of view) to choose between parents, and to expect to obtain from that child an accurate insight into the reasons for the child's feelings and preferences is ordinarily to expect too much. (I refrain from commenting upon the desirability of this procedure for the purpose of finding out first-hand something about the child's character and personality as opposed to his opinions and preferences respecting the parent he wished to live with.)
>
> A procedure involving a trained and competent third party, independent of the parents, charged with the responsibility of ascertaining the child's opinions and preferences using such techniques as are most likely to yield genuine feelings and wishes, and be least harmful to the child, over such period of time as may be necessary, and thereafter reporting to the court, by giving testimony or otherwise, is the procedure to be looked upon with the most favour.[136]

In a Manitoba Court of Appeal case,[137] it was held that an *in camera* interview with the judge must be restricted to the ascertainment of the child's wishes. If the judge wished to probe the motivations behind the wishes, he had to do so in open court. (For further discussion on this issue, see Chapter 6, "The Child in the Court Room".)

Child Representation

Another response to the difficulties inherent in the traditional adversarial model has been to expand it to involve counsel on behalf of the child. The use of such representation was approved in a 1977 decision of the Ontario High Court where the court recognized the growing public support for the view that children are entitled to independent representation in custody cases "at least where it is clear that their true interests would not be served by an adversarial contest between parents or other parties. An important recommendation for such independent representation should not be allowed to languish unacted upon, as was the case in these proceedings for a period of well over six months."[138] The

---

[136]*Wakaluk v. Wakaluk* (1976), 25 R.F.L. 292, at 304 (Sask. C.A.).

[137]*Jandrisch v. Jandrisch* (1980), 3 Man. R. (2d) 135, 16 R.F.L. (2d) 239, revg (1979), 3 Man. R. (2d) 150 (C.A.).

[138]*More v. Primeau* (1978), 2 R.F.L. (2d) 254, at 260–61 (Ont. H.C.).

only specific provision in the *CLRA* dealing with this issue is s. 65(4) which now provides that the child is entitled to be advised by and to have counsel, if any, present during any interview the child may have directly with the judge. However, if the child somehow manages to become an applicant under s. 21, he will presumably be entitled to counsel like any other party to the proceedings.

In one particular decision which directed that the child have counsel, the comments of the Supreme Court judge also illustrate the frustration and the resentment of many judges in their role as arbitrator of custody disputes. On appeal from an interim custody order, the court stated:

> I think it is most unfortunate that parents who have a falling out, for whatever reason, and permit the strong feelings which each has against the other to affect the lives of their children, are able to resort to the normal type of litigation for the purpose of resolving their inability to do what is best for their children. I just cannot accept that either counsel in this case need any pleadings in order to determine what the issues are between the parties. At this moment in time, they are simply custody and access. Furthermore, I cannot believe that either of the parties fully recognize and understand the extent of the inroad which an action can have not only on their own lives but on the life of their child. I will not accept that having the differences now outstanding between the parties dealt with by a trial and subsequent report by the Official Referee at Ottawa will not permit the parents every right that they should have to ensure that this Court decides that which is in the best interest and welfare of the child. I have to think that, as in too many of these cases, the parents are only really interested in themselves and resort to the child or children as instruments through which they can attack each other. As I have said before, and as I said on several occasions throughout the course of the hearing here, it is as though the parents and their respective lawyers become involved in a game or contest which, although it has as its professed object the interests and welfare of their children, turns into a grudge battle with everything in sight being thrown towards the other. The children are simply relegated to the sidelines to watch and wait the outcome.
>
> Under all of the circumstances, I am not satisfied that the parties will do only that which promotes the best interest and welfare of their child. I realize that the age of the child is such that she is still of tender years. If she were older, the tug-of-war would undoubtedly have a greater effect on her. Nevertheless, I am going to appoint the Official Guardian to represent the interests and welfare of the child. . . .[139]

(For further discussion on this issue, see Chapter 6, "Child in the Court Room".)

Assessment

Despite the good intentions behind the nomination of counsel for the child, there are also drawbacks to the involvement of a third legal counsel. Although he may make the court aware of the individual whose interests are primarily at stake in the proceedings, he is still part of that legal fraternity fulfilling an unavoidably adversarial role in the context of a classic legal model of dispute resolution.

---

[139]*Van Vlasselaer v. Van Vlasselaer,* summarized in (1980), 3 F.L.R.R. 64 (Ont. S.C.).

There have been a few cases where the Superior Courts, recognizing the need for non-legal assistance, have invoked their "inherent jurisdiction" to appoint a non-legal professional to assess the situation and to report back to the court if it appears necessary "to arrive at a just and proper decision in the best interests of the child."[140] Such a move usually occurs after the parties have exhausted the legal process and, very likely, have exhausted the court. The assessor's report may assist or rescue the court in rendering a decision in these most difficult cases, but it is clear that it is now too late to rescue a harmonious relationship between spouses so that the child can enjoy and be secure in his contacts with both parents.

In response to the growing recognition that the courts require non-legal professional assistance, s. 30 of the *CLRA* provides the court with the jurisdiction to "appoint a person who has technical or professional skill to assess and report to the court on the needs of the child and the ability and willingness of the parties or any of them to satisfy the needs of the child."[141] If one of the parties refuses to partake in the assessment, "the court may draw such inferences in respect of the ability and willingness of any person to satisfy the needs of the child as the court considers appropriate": s. 30(6). The appointment of an assessor can be made at any time once there is an application before the court for either custody or access. (Alternatively, the court may request the Official Guardian to make a report with respect to custody, support and education of the child: s. 32.)

The filing of an assessor's report with the court does not necessarily mean the end of the dispute. The legislation makes it clear that the courts must still retain their overriding jurisdiction to decide what is best for the child, presumably based on the assumption that the court, with its procedural safeguards, is in a better position to make a fair and just decision on such a major decision than is a professional assessor whose process and methods of decision making are circumvented only by his own personal methods and abilities of discovering the least detrimental solution as well as the professional ethics of the organization to which he belongs.[142] Anything less would be a delegation of decision-making power which has been entrusted to the courts. In addition, s. 30(15) states that the appointment of an assessor does not prevent any party or counsel for the child from submitting other expert evidence as to the needs of the child and the ability and willingness of the parties to satisfy the needs of the child. Unfortunately, this may invite a parade of professionals attending at court,

---

[140]See *e.g. El-Sohemy v. El-Sohemy* (1980), 17 R.F.L. (2d) 1 (Ont. S.C.); *Cillis v. Cillis* (1980), 20 R.F.L. (2d) 208 (Ont. S.C.); affd (1981), 23 R.F.L. (2d) 76 (Ont. Div. Ct.).

[141]For cases under s. 30, see *Hampel v. Hampel* (1983), 31 R.F.L. (2d) 462 (Ont. Dist. Ct.) (court-appointed assessor due to parties raising serious deficiencies against one another and despite one party opposing assessment).

[142]For cases disputing an assessment, see generally *Gazdeczka v. Gazdeczka* (1982), 30 R.F.L. (2d) 428, affg on other grounds (1981), 28 B.C.L.R. 69 (B.C. C.A.) (Appellate Court dismissing claim that report inadequate after review of same); *O'Neill v. O'Neill* (1980), 17 R.F.L. (2d) 344 (Ont. Surr. Ct.) (court refuses to require Official Guardian to attend custody hearing, despite dispute of his report by one of the parties without "strong reasons" for doing so); *Grills v. Grills* (1982), 38 A.R. 475 (Fam. Ct.) (court overruled assessor's report stating that it was only part of the evidence to be considered).

each giving their own viewpoint as to what is best for the child such that "best interests" become less a function of what a mother and father believe, but more a melting pot of parental, professional and legal opinions strained through the value system of the presiding judge. The following cases represent instances in which courts have overruled the conclusions of assessors:

1) The assessor recommended joint custody as the best method of fulfilling the needs of the child. The court declined to accept the recommendation, citing conflicts between the parents at court which, given the state of Ontario law, prevents a judge from ordering same.[143]

2) The court found that the assessor's opinion was not sensitive enough to the wishes of the child which were lost in the process.[144]

3) The court was faced with opinions from four different professionals: a school psychologist who noted that both parents were good parents with no clear recommendation as to which parent should have custody; a psychiatrist recommending joint custody; a child welfare consultant strongly recommending that custody be awarded to the mother as the boy was at risk of developing emotional problems; and, a clinical psychologist recommending custody to the mother, with reasonable access to the father. In such situations the court, even more, is called upon to assess the assessors. In the instant case for example, the court noted that the child welfare consultant had not even seen the father prior to giving her opinion.[145]

Mediation

Even more encouraging is s. 31 of the *CLRA* which permits the court, at the request of the parties and with their consent, to approve mediation and appoint someone as mediator. This allows the parties recourse to an alternative and more appropriate model of dispute resolution with the approval of the court, but without usurping the court's overriding responsibility and power to determine the issue if called upon. Section 31(2) requires that the court, in appointing a mediator, have the consent of the proposed mediator and have his or her agreement to file a report with the court within the period of time specified by the court. Section 31(4) requires that before entering into mediation, the parties must decide whether the mediation is to be "open" or "closed". In the latter, the mediator would file a report that sets out only that an agreement was or was not reached by the parties. In the former, the mediator would have the mandate to file a full report on the process including anything that he considers relevant to the matter in mediation and presumably would be relevant to the court if agreement was not reached. If the parties agree on "closed" mediation, s. 31(7) confirms that evidence of anything said or of any admission or communication made in the course of the mediation is not admissible in any proceeding, except with the consent of all parties to the proceeding.

It is unfortunate that the legislation does not go a step further to require that mediation be mandatory although some professionals quite rightly note that

---

[143]*Marples v. Marples,* summarized in (1983), 5 F.L.R.R. 158 (Ont. S.C.). But see *Richard v. Richard* (1981), 35 N.B.R. (2d) 383, 88 A.P.R. 383 (C.A.) (Appellate Court restored a pre-trial inter-spousal agreement on the basis of the psychologist's evidence at trial despite the trial judge having substituted another custody arrangement by court order).

hostile parties to mediation can lead to poor or unsuccessful mediation. It is arguable that the superior courts' inherent *parens patriae* jurisdiction would allow it to stay proceedings until the parties had mediated the matter.[146] This interpretation is strengthened by the above-quoted Saskatchewan Appeal Court's dissenting decision which relied on its jurisdiction to refuse to hear the child in a witness box or to see the child in chambers and the above-noted Ontario Supreme Court's decision to stay proceedings in order to appoint counsel for the child. Instead of returning to the very process about which the court's complain by appointing a third legal counsel, could not an alternative model of mediation be ordered as an expansion on the jurisdiction to order an assessment?

"Incidents of Custody"

Ontario judges have the jurisdiction under s. 28 not only to make classic custody/access orders but also to fashion new arrangements suited to particular parents by dividing up the child care responsibilities as "incidents of custody". (The proposed *Divorce and Corollary Relief Act* also includes "incidents of custody" under s. 2(1)). This can sometimes mitigate the win-lose battles which often characterize the polarized concepts of "custody" and "access". Such a division may amount to "joint custody" in which case Ontario law dictates that it may not be imposed on unwilling parties. Nevertheless, an arrangement which falls short of joint custody can ensure more substantial participation of the non-custodial parent in the life of his or her children than the narrowly confined Sunday access visit. (See also *supra* under "Custody by Court Order: Joint Custody".)

Custody

Disputes and the Charter of Rights

It has become trite to say that the *Canadian Charter of Rights and Freedoms*, pursuant to s. 32 thereunder, is applicable only to state action and not private disputes.[147] Although it may also be automatic to classify custody disputes as private, it arguably becomes a grey area when the state enacts legislation which, in itself or through court enforcement, deprives the child of any power to participate in the determination of what must amount to his fundamental rights and freedoms. One commentator made the distinction that common law is outside the *Charter* while statute law, as an action of Parliament or the Legislature, is caught by the *Charter*.[148] Since most provinces have codified what has traditionally been the realm of common law, *i.e.* the ubiquitous *parens patriae* jurisdiction, the argument that the *Charter* may be applicable in certain instances becomes somewhat stronger. Nevertheless, it remains to be seen whether the *Charter* will further children's interests if the context of custody dispute resolution continues to be the adversarial legal model.

---

[144]*Tapley v. Tapley*, summarized in (1983), 5 F.L.R.R. 173 (Ont. U.F.C.).

[145]*Moss v. Colodny*, summarized in (1982), 4 F.L.R.R. 109 (Ont. U.F.C.).

[146]See *Proctor v. Proctor*, 14 R.F.L. (2d) 385 (Ont. Div. Ct.) (s. 18(6) of the *Judicature Act* [new s. 119 of the *Courts of Justice Act, 1984*] gives the court ample power to stay any proceeding where it is in the interests of justice to do so; court stayed proceeding for six weeks for physical and psychological assessment of wife).

[147]See *e.g.* K. Swinton, "Application of the Canadian Charter of Rights and Freedoms", in W.S. Tarnopolsky and G.A. Beaudoin, *The Canadian Charter of Rights and Freedoms* (Toronto: Carswell Company Limited, 1982), at pp. 44–49.

[148]See P.W. Hogg, "A Comparison of the Canadian Charter of Rights and Freedoms with the Canadian Bill of Rights", in *ibid.*, at pp. 7–8.

An American Appellate Court dealt with a constitutional argument on behalf of a ten-year-old child in a custody matter.[149] The latter asserted that his rights were being violated by an American court enforcing, under the *Unified Child Custody Jurisdiction Act*, a Swedish decree giving custody to the mother. The child was born in Sweden but since his father was an American citizen, he qualified for American citizenship. In its decision, the court noted, among other things, that the child's rights to equal protection and due process are not violated when decisions are dealt with in state court custody proceedings which are essentially private matters. The court went on to note that the constitutional rights of a child could not be equated with those of an adult: the right to travel or stay in the United States is not absolute for children, paralleling decisions in immigration cases where *de facto* deportation of children resulted from the deportation of the parents.[150] However, a New Jersey Superior Court decision suggests that a child does enjoy certain constitutional rights in custody disputes.[151] The New Jersey Legislature had enacted a statute protecting the confidentiality of intra-familial communications. The court found the applicable sections to be unconstitutional in custody proceedings on the basis that, by permitting a parent to invoke the legislatively created privilege, it would hamper a child's due process rights to introduce material evidence relevant to the determination of what custodial arrangement is in his best interests and welfare. The judge arrived at this conclusion despite the Legislature's motivation in enacting such legislation, *i.e.* that the privilege would encourage parties of a troubled marriage to seek qualified help, knowing that whatever information passed among the parties and counsellors would never be revealed. The judge stated:

> Yet, it is inconceivable to us that in promulgating this Act and, more particularly, the privilege, the Legislature took into consideration the best interests and welfare of the children of the marriage especially as might affect proper, and indeed, safe custodial placement.

Drawing a close parallel would be s. 31 of Ontario's *CLRA* providing for a "closed" mediation. Expanding the principle, one might challenge the lack of party status, discretionary representation of children and even the voluntariness of mediation, all codified under the same Act.

---

[149]*Schleiffer v. Meyers* (1981), 644 F. 2d 656 (C.A.).

[150]For a Canadian example based on different reasoning, see *Denis Manon v. R.,* [1976] 1 F.C. 499 (C.A.), in which it was held that the deportation of the mother, resulting in the *de facto* deportation of the child in her custody, did not offend the child's rights under s. 2 of the *Canadian Bill of Rights*. In dismissing the appeal, the court held that the child's leaving the country would not be a direct and unavoidable result of the application of the law of Canada but simply of the mother's decision to take the child with her. (For discussion of immigration issues, see Chapter 9: "The Child as Immigrant.")

[151]*M. v. K.* (1982), 452 A. 2d 704 (N.J.S.C.).

Chapter 2: Readings

American Bar Association, *Alternative Means of Family Dispute Resolution* (1982).

Anton, A.E., "Hague Convention on International Child Abduction" (June, 81), 30 *Int. and Comp. L.Q.* 537.

Basile, R., "Lesbian Mothers I" (1974), 2 *Women's Rights L. Rept.* 3.

Bates, F. "Custody Disputes Between Parents and Non-Parents: Recent Developments in Australia and Canada" (1981), 11 *Man. L.J.* 303.

"*Bezio v. Patenaude:* The 'Coming Out' Custody Controversy of Lesbian Mothers in Court" (1981), 16 *New England Law Rev.* 331.

Bradbrook, A.J., "An Empirical Study of the Attitudes of the Judges of the Supreme Court of Ontario Regarding the Working of the Present Child Custody Adjudication Laws" (1971), 49 *Can. Bar Rev.* 557.

_____., "The Relevance of Psychological and Psychiatric Studies to the Future Development of the Law Governing the Settlement of Inter-Parental Child Custody Disputes" (1972), 11 *J. Fam. L.* 55.

_____., "The Role of Judicial Discretion in Child Custody Adjudication in Ontario" (1971), 21 *U. of T.L.J.* 402.

"Civil Rights of a Minor U.S. Citizen Were Not Violated by an Indiana Court's Recognition and Enforcement of a Swedish Custody Decree Requiring the Child's Return to his Mother in Sweden", (January, 1982) 20 *J. Fam. L.* 351.

Coombs, R.M. "Custody Conflicts in the Courts: Judicial Resolution of the Old and New Questions Raised by Interstate Child Custody Cases"; Bruch, C.S. "Interstate Child Custody Law and *Eicke:* A Reply to Professor Coombs", (Fall, 1982) 16 *Fam. L.Q.* 251.

"Custody and Maintenance: The Role of Provincial Legislation for Divorced Families" (1980), 3 *Can. J. Fam. L.* 403.

Devine, J.R. "A Child's Right to Independent Counsel in Custody Proceedings" (1975), 6 *Seaton Hall L. Rev.* 303.

Eekelaar, J.M. "International Child Abduction by Parents" (Summer, 1982) 32 *U. of T. L.J.* 281.

Foster, H. and Skoloff, G. (eds.) *Custody Litigation: New Directions* (N.Y.: Harcourt Brace Jovanovich, 1981).

Goldstein, J., Freud, A., Solnit, A., *Before the Best Interests of the Child* (N.Y.: Free Press, 1979) and *Beyond the Best Interests of the Child* (N.Y.: Free Press, 1973).

Green, R., "Sexual Identity of 37 Children Raised by Homosexual or Trans-sexual Parents" (1978), 135 *Amer. J. of Psychiatry* 692.

Harris, B., "Lesbian Mother-Child Custody: Legal and Psychiatric Aspects" (1977), 5 *Bulletin Am. Acad. of Psych. and Law* 75.

Hoff, P.M., *Interstate and International Child Custody Disputes: A Collection of Materials*, 3rd Ed. (Child Custody Project, American Bar Association, 1982).

_____., "Child Snatching: Getting Relief Through Net Tort Remedies" (Fall, 1982), 5 *The Family Advocate* (ABA) (No. 2).

Hoff, P.M., Schulman, J., Volenik, A. and O'Daniel, J., *Interstate Child Custody Disputes and Parental Kidnapping: Policy, Practice and Law* (Legal Services Corporation — American Bar Association, 1982).

Ingraham, C., "Protection of the Rights of Minors and Children in Divorce Cases" (1967), 53 *Women's Law J.* 48.

Inker, "Expanding the Rights of Children in Custody and Adoption Cases" (1971), 11 *J. Fam. L.* 129.

"Joint Custody: Whose Need Does it Serve?" (1982), 5 *Family Law Advocate* (No. 2) (special issue on joint custody).

Journal of Orthopsychiatry, Vol. 51 (1981) (special issue on homosexual parents and their children).

Justice (British Section of the International Commission of Jurists), *Parental Rights and Duties and Custody Suits* (Chairman: Gerald Godfrey) (London: Stevens, 1975).

Katz, S., *Child Snatching The Legal Response to the Abduction of Children* (American Bar Association, 1981).

Kay, H.H. and Phillips, I., "Poverty and the Law of Child Custody" (1966), 54 *Calif. L. Rev.* 717.

Lemon, N.K., "Joint Custody as a Statutory Presumption: California's New Civil Code Ss. 4600 and 4600.5" (Spring, 81), 11 *Golden Gate U.L. Rev.* 485.

Mangrum, R.C., "Exclusive Reliance on Best Interests May be Unconstitutional: Religion as a Factor in Child Custody Cases" (1981–82), 15 *Creighton L. Rev.* 25.

Mnookin, R.H., "Child Custody Adjudication: Judicial Functions in the Face of Indeterminacy" (1975), 39 *Law and Contemp. Prob.* 226.

Morin, S. and Schultz, S., "The Gay Movement and the Rights of Children" (1978), 34 *J. of Social Issues* 137.

Note, "Custody and Homosexual Parents" (1974), 2 *Women's Rights L. Rept.* 19.

"Parental Kidnapping Prevention Act: Analysis and Impact on Uniform Child Custody Jurisdiction" (1981), 27 *N.Y. L. Sch. L. Rev.* 553.

Payne, J.D., "Behaviourial Science and Legal Analysis of Access to the Child in the Post-separation/Divorce Family", (1981), 13 *Ottawa L. Rev.* 215.

Polikoff, N.D., "Why Are Mothers Losing: A Brief Analysis of Criteria Used in Child Custody Determinations" (Spring, 1982) 7 *Women's Rights L. Rep.* 235.

——————., "Gender and Child Custody Determinations: Expanding the Myths", in Diamond (ed.) *Families, Politics and Public Policy* (U.S., 1983).

Rees, R., "A Comparison of Children of Lesbian and Single Heterosexual Mothers on Three Measures of Socialization", *Dissertatin Abstracts International* (1979).

Report of the New York State Law Revision Commission on Joint Custody in New York State (1982) (available from the National Center on Women and Family Law, 799 Broadway, Room 402, New York, 10003).

"Residence Restrictions on Custodial Parents: Implications for the Right to Travel" (Winter, 1980), 12 *Rutgers L.J.* 341.

Schulman and Pitt, "Second Thoughts on Joint Custody: Analysis of Legislation and its Impact for Women and Children" *Women's Law Forum* (1982), 12 *Golden Gate Univ. L. Rev.* 538 (includes state-by-state legislation summary).

Sheppard, A.T., "Unspoken Premises in Custody Litigation" (Spring, 1982), 7 *Womens Rights L. Rep.* 229.

Special issue on conflicts of law and child snatching (1981), 3 *The Family Advocate (ABA)* (No. 4).

Steinman, S., "The Experience of Children in a Joint Custody Arrangement: A Report of a Study" (1981), 51 *American Journal of Orthopsychiatry* (No. 3).

ten Broek, J., "California's Dual System of Family Law: Its Origin, Development and Present Status: Part I and Part II" (poverty and family law) (1964 and 1965), 16 and 17 *Stanford L. Rev.* 257 and 614.

"Tender Years Presumption in Child Custody Cases Held Unconstitutional and Gender-based Discrimination" (1981–82), 12 *Cumb. L. Rev.* 513.

"Termination of Parental Rights: Should Non-Payment of Child Support Be Enough?" (May, 1982) 67 *Iowa L. Rev.* 827.

Weiler, K.M. *et al;* "Re Moores and Feldstein: A Case Comment and Discussion of Custody Principles" (1974), 12 *Osgoode Hall L.J.* [207]

Weinhaus, S., "Substantive Rights of the Unwed Father: The Boundaries Are Defined" (May, 1981), 19 *J. Fam. L.* 445.

Weitzman, L. and Dixon, R., "Child Custody Awards: Legal Standards and Empirical Patterns for Child Custody, Support and Visitation After Divorce" (1979), 12 *U.C.D. L. Rev.* 473.

White House Conference on Children, Report (Washington, D.C.: G.P.O., 1970).

Wilcox, M.K., "A Child's Due Process Right to Counsel in Divorce Custody Proceedings" (1976), 27 *Hastings L.J.* 917.

Zaharoff, H.G., "Access to Children: Towards a Model Statute for Third Parties" (Summer, 1981), 15 *Fam. L.Q.* 165.

Chapter 3

The Family in Conflict II: Child Protection and Adoption

Child Protection: Introduction

Child Protection

This chapter will review Ontario's existing child welfare law under the *Child Welfare Act* (hereinafter known as the *CWA*) as well as the province's proposed new legislation entitled the *Child and Family Services Act, 1984* (hereinafter known as the *CFSA*), from the moment of state intervention to the disposition in the legal proceeding. Since this manuscript was submitted for publication coincidentally with the passing (but not proclamation) of the *CFSA*, and since existing case law will provide a foundation for the interpretation of the amending legislation, the chapter will provide a comparative analysis of both Acts. (A Table of Concordance is included at the end of the chapter.) A proclamation date of July 1, 1985 was originally set for the legislation (*CFSA*) which received Royal Assent on December 14, 1984. The new regulations are presently being developed and should be consulted as a complement to this chapter.

Although the discussion focuses on Ontario's child protection legislation, many other jurisdictions in Canada exhibit legal approaches and systemic dynamics which are similar and sometimes identical to those of Ontario and therefore, a consideration of existing law and reforming changes should still be of benefit to those in other jurisdictions. In addition, cross-references are made to cases outside of Ontario.

Provincial child welfare laws establish a system of state intervention into the privacy of the family in circumstances where the caretakers are unable or unwilling to provide a minimum standard of care. Historically, this minimum standard related only to the physical well-being of the child. Latterly, society has come to recognize that the standard must also apply to the emotional well-being of the child, although it is a less discernable concept.[1]

The involvement of the state as a party to the legal proceeding, a proceeding which is designed to provide authorization for state intervention, if necessary, distinguishes the child welfare process from the domestic custody dispute. A child welfare proceeding represents the manifestation of public responsibility towards children who are inherently powerless as a class, balancing the interest of the community in responsible parenting with the privacy rights of the parents to raise their children as they see fit. In recent times, and only in some jurisdictions, there has emerged a third party to the proceeding: the child. In these jurisdictions, the concept of the child's rights intertwines with adult efforts to secure the child's best interests.

The hearing itself is civil in nature, both in procedure and in terms of the necessary evidentiary burden. The latter is the usual "balance of probabilities" although, typical of the inconsistency in this area of the law, there are varying juridical opinions on the degree of proof that is required within the parameters of the civil proceeding, depending on the nature of the relief pursued by the state.[2] In one case, the court held that the removal of children from their home falls more within the realm of criminal than civil proceedings and consequently, within a civil standard of proof, a high preponderance of evidence should be required.[3] This approach to the evidentiary burden as well as to procedures would seem to be most just, given the potential of state removal of children from a family, and as shall become evident, the wide discretion of the court to determine the extremely complicated issues before it.

Pressures which lead to a removal order with all of its future implications are extremely complex and diverse.[4] It is not simply a question of deciding which

---

[1]See *e.g.* Ontario's *CFSA*, s. 37(2)(f) which will, upon proclamation, define "child in need of protection" to include a child who has "suffered emotional harm demonstrated by severe i) anxiety, ii) depression, iii) withdrawal or iv) self-destructive or agressive behaviour", and the parents are not consenting to treatment to remedy or alleviate the harm.

[2]See *e.g. Re Milner* (1975), 23 R.F.L. 86 (N.S.S.C.); *CAS of Winnipeg v. Bouvette* (1975), 24 R.F.L. 350 (Man. C.A.); *Blyth v. Blyth*, [1966] 1 All E.R. 524 (H.L.).

[3]*Re S.V.'s Infant* (1963), 43 W.W.R. 374 (B.C. Co. Ct.).

[4]See R. Landau, "Status Offences: Inequality Before the Law" (1981), 39 *U. of T. L. Rev.* 149, at 166 citing P. Hepworth, *Foster Care and Adoption in Canada* (Ottawa: The Canadian Council on Social Development, 1980), at pp. 55–73. In British Columbia (the only province with a detailed statistical breakdown), admission on the basis of physical abuse is minor (2.8%) compared to the 27 other categories. The amorphous "parent failure/neglect" cases amounted to 42.8% of the admissions, the author stating that "the proportion of children admitted to care for neglect or similar reasons are approximately the same in other provinces." Other categories in the B.C. statistics included desertion or abandonment; emotional disturbances needing treatment; one or both parents deceased; mental or physical illness of parents; adoption process; "awaiting permanent plan"; physical handicap; mental retardation; delinquent behaviour (*Juvenile Delinquents Act*); transient, unmarried mother; parental failure to provide needed medical treatment or prevention; parent(s) in prison; inability of family to provide needed education and training; lack of housing for family; behaviour of child. The small percentage of physical abuse cases was echoed in Ontario's statistics: Ontario Ministry of Community and Social Services, Research and Planning Branch, *Report No. 3: Child Abuse in Ontario* (1973), p. 62.

In the United States, R. Mnookin found that "despite a paucity of data, it appears that removal over parental objections takes place most often where the court determines that the parents' supervision and guidance of the child are inadequate, where the mother is thought to be

of two parents are better able to care for a child. The judge in a child welfare proceeding must make a far more difficult assessment of whether the quality of parenting has fallen below a nebulous community standard such that the child would be better off in the foster parent/group home stream, which is a potentially devastating stream in itself. Consciously or unconsciously, the judge reacts to political, sociological, psychological and/or psychoanalytic theories and values of the role and standard of parenting within the context of his own particular background and diverse community. The literature over the years has offered theories and some guidance to define and explain the causes of neglect and abuse and to offer methods of prevention and cures. Depending on the beliefs, perceptions and professional background of the authority, the focus may be on the pathology of the individual caretaker; the physical/psychological needs of the child; the child's well-being when he becomes a foster child; the socio-economic background of the agency workers or judges; the lack of resources of the Children's Aid Societies; or societal cause-and-effect analysis, with or without an economic context.

In practice, because of the amorphous ''best interest'' test necessarily resulting in an absence of clear, reliable, consistent standards as judicial guidelines, the determining factor in the final decision invariably becomes the background, values and perceptions of the Children's Aid Society worker (on whom judges often rely totally) and of the single judge. For example, in one northern Ontario case, the judge ordered that four children be made Crown wards less than six months after removal from their home.[5] In his decision, the judge revealed as his underlying reasons his concern, if not resentment, towards parents living on welfare:

> Mr. D said that never would he work with anybody from the Children's Aid Society, although he is quite ready to accept money from the system when it would please him. He is certainly ready to accept a pension for food for his wife and his children, to disengage himself of the obligation he has to support his wife and his child. The situation we have today is clearly and solely the result of the position that Mr. D took to try to take advantage of the system. . . . if there is a promise that Mr. and Mrs. D will not accept any financial help from the government, since he can work and he does work when it pleases him to do so, the girls will be returned to Mr. D. He has 60 days to file that promise with the court.[6]

---

emotionally ill, or where the child has behaviour problems.'': ''Foster care: In Whose Best Interests?'', *The Rights of Children* (Cambridge: Harvard Educational Review, Reprint Series No. 9, 1974), p. 158 at p. 168. See also M. Garrison, ''Why Terminate Parental Rights'', (1983), 35 *Stanford L. Rev.* 423, at 427 *n.* 20:

[One study] determined that the [admissions] were due to mental illness of the child-caring person (21.9%), neglect or abuse (14.6%), child behaviour problems (11.7%), physical illness of the child-caring person (10.9%), abandonment (10.7%), a parent's unwillingness or inability to continue care (10.1%), a parent's unwillingness or inability to assume care (8.8%), other family problems (9.1%) and parental deaths (2.2%).

[5]*Re D.,* unreported, Nov. 25, 1981 (Ont. Prov. Ct.), *per* Robson J. Leave to appeal to C.A. from Div. Ct. (Sept. 10/84) refused, Nov. 26/84.

[6]*Ibid.,* at p. 143 of the transcript of proceedings

On another level, the shapelessness of "best interests" as a test for removing children from their home permits standards to slide up and down the child-care spectrum, depending on the values and interests of the government of the day. Legislative reform varies significantly between the provinces, and over a few decades, within any one province, reflecting the full theoretical spectrum. On one end is the theory of "radical non-intervention", that is, the state should only intervene as a last recourse. Without de-emphasizing the seriousness of the problem of child abuse and neglect in society, the approach recognizes that fostering, group homes and even adoption do not often provide better alternatives than the family unit from which the child was taken. It parallels the position of Canadian and U.S. commentators who have come to their conclusions based on extensive research on the problems of children in care, and who advocate focussing the state's resources on systemic prevention, working with the child in the family. On the other end of the spectrum is the "child-saver" approach which puts the child under state care at any possibility of risk. And the pendulum swings anywhere in between. The preventive "radical non-intervention" approach is expensive, complex and often impolitic to the press and public. Removal is a clean, simple way of dealing with the problem and protects all the agents of the state from taking responsibility for the omnipresent, unpredictable possibility that this child might be *the* child who will suffer severe neglect if left with the family. The dynamic parallels that of the parole system in which one parolee who commits a serious offence brings down community wrath on all parolees and the Parole Board accordingly becomes extremely gun-shy when the next application is put before it.

Obviously, the one who suffers the most in the entire process is the child. Ironically, continuing the criminal law parallel, although it is the adults who are charged and found guilty, it is the victim, the child, whose major rights and freedoms are affected. Where a finding of parental neglect and state wardship is made, it is the child and not the parent who is displaced from his home and family and placed in an environment that may be even more deleterious than the home environment. Moreover, the more unwilling or negligent the "offender" (the parent) is towards the child's rehabilitation, the more drastic and far-reaching the result for the victim.

The real consequences to the child, over and above the severing of ties from the biological family, can be described with reference to the following observations:

1) In rendering disposition under child welfare legislation, the court may direct that a person under 16 is to be subject to guardianship by the state, temporarily or permanently. As a "ward" of the state, a person under 16 may be placed in a foster home, a secure locked or lockable treatment or custodial center.[7]

---

[7]Consider the decision of *Re Jacey Ann B. and C.A.S. of the City of Belleville*, summarized in (1984), 7 F.L.R.R. 66 in which an Ontario Provincial Court judge refused the request of the Children's Aid Society for the detention of a 14-year-old girl because the proposed detention facility was a place designated for the "open custody" of convicted young offenders under the federal *Young Offenders Act*. The court indicated that it had "considerable difficulty in concluding

2) From 1959 to 1972, the proportion of children in care in Canada steadily rose, stabilizing in the late 1970s. Their general age distribution became older over the same time, with fewer infants due mainly to the high turnover of infants for adoption. In 1976-77, 57.2 per cent of these children were living in foster homes, 20.8 per cent were in "institutional services" (more than 9 beds), 8 per cent were in adoption homes and 2.4 per cent were in group homes (1 to 9 beds).[8] The recently introduced *Young Offenders Act* should put greater pressure on child-care facilities, having raised the applicable age from 16 to 18 in all provinces.

3) According to one Canadian study, persons under 16 in foster homes pursuant to a temporary order of state guardianship average four different homes, while persons under 16 subject to a permanent state guardianship order were sent, on the average, to eight different homes.[9] U.S. studies show for those children in foster homes that 38 per cent had moved once or twice and 18 per cent had moved more than twice;[10] in addition, 48 per cent spend more than two and a half years in care.[11] Availability of appropriate facilities and quality of care has also been the subject of much criticism both in Canada and the U.S. While in foster care, many lose contact with their natural parents both because of the moves and because the agencies do not tend to put a high priority on encouraging parental contact and involvement: statistics show that instability and lack of any parental figure characterizes foster care in the U.S. today.[12] Can Canada's experience be significantly different?

4) Several provincial statutes allow "neglected" children to be held in receiving homes used for delinquent children or a training school while awaiting their hearing. Receiving or "observation" homes in Ontario have ranged from locked institutions to locked holding units, lockable homes or open homes. One of the *punishments* available as a disposition under the old *Juvenile Delinquents Act* and the new *Young Offenders Act* is that of being placed in a foster home, a lockable or locked treatment or custodial centre; the most severe punishment is training school. Is it any wonder that neglected children who find themselves removed from the family and sent to these institutions perceive themselves as criminal or are labelled by others as criminal.[13]

---

that a residence housing post-adjudication offenders is a place of safety for a 14-year-old girl." Under the *CFSA*, once proclaimed, the following sections will be applicable: ss. 57(2), (6) and 59 (general custodial rights of a Society) and s. 96 (locking up restricted to "extraordinary measures") and Part VI (Extraordinary Measures), s. 113(1) which permits locked or "secure" treatment if the child 1) has a "mental disorder" ("a substantial disorder of emotional processes, thought or cognition which grossly impairs a person's capacity to make reasoned judgments") or 2) has or has attempted or has threatened to cause harm to himself or another.

[8]P. Hepworth, *supra*, note 4, at pp. 75–93.

[9]National Council of Welfare on the Child Welfare System in Canada, *In the Best Interests of the Child*, (December, 1979), at p. 17 as referred to in R. Landau, *supra*, note 4, at p. 161.

[10]M. Garrison, *supra*, note 4, at p. 423 *n*.

[11]*Ibid.*, at p. 426 *n*.

[12]*Ibid.*, at pp. 423–24.

[13]See generally Landau, *supra*, note 4, at pp. 159–66.

5) At Arrell Observation Home for Children in Ontario from January 1, 1976 to December 31, 1976, there were 374 admissions for "children in need of protection." "Arrell is a locked door institution; the outer door is always locked. The inner doors can be locked between units; out-going mail is censored; and there are physical searches on admission."[14] In Manitoba in 1976 and 1977, the Manitoba Youth Centre (a closed custody institution which holds juveniles awaiting a court hearing, dispositions, etc.) admitted 1,353 and 1,311 children respectively under the *Child Welfare Act*.[15]

6) In 1973 in Canada, of 3,561 juveniles committed to training school, 24.7 per cent were committed for child welfare protection. Some provinces allow the child welfare administrator or superintendent to place a ward in a suitable place, including a training school, without a hearing. For the years ending March 31, 1976 and 1977 in Nova Scotia, 57 and 24 children respectively were admitted to training school under the province's *Child Welfare Act*. For the year ending March 31, 1977, 15 girls were admitted to the Nova Scotia School for Girls for offences against property and persons, 27 for education and truancy offences, and 43 for immorality, unmanageability, vagrancy and as children in need of protection. In the same year 173 boys were admitted for offences against property and persons, 11 for truancy and education offences, and 26 for immorality, unmanageability, vagrancy and as children in need of protection. "[Having reviewed several sets of statistics as well as those available from Alberta, Manitoba and Nova Scotia], it is clear that a large number of children were being committed to training school without having been convicted of any crime."[16]

In light of the potential for such severe, sometimes quasi-criminal consequences, one might well question the limited legal rights which are attached to the child in child welfare proceedings in most jurisdictions in Canada. Traditionally the argument has been that the fewer "legal technicalities" and the less complicated the procedure, the better society is able to respond to the "real issue" of the child's best interest on the untested assumption that state intervention is based on an accurate and sophisticated assessment of the possibilities of the home situation and can and will provide better alternatives for the child. It will remain to be seen how the *Charter of Rights* will effect the child welfare proceeding, having regard to the effect of the Constitution on child welfare law in the United States.[17] Given the absence of clear and consistent procedural and judicial guidelines, perhaps the courts will be inclined to replace the rubber stamp "best interests" defence with a more rational, empirical "reasonable limits" test under s. 1 of the *Charter* which will be rooted in the realities of the fostering/group home stream.

The steps of increasing state involvement under Ontario's child welfare legislation will form the framework of discussion for the remainder of the chapter.

---

[14]*Ibid*., at p. 160.

[15]*Ibid*., at p. 163.

[16]*Ibid*., at pp. 162–63.

[17]See J. Wilson, "Age Discrimination — Childhood", in *Equality Rights in Canada*, eds. A Bayefsky, M. Eberts (Toronto: Carswell Co. Ltd. forthcoming).

Delegation of State Protection Responsibilities: CAS and Private Citizen

Children's Aid Society

Ministerial Supervision of Societies

In Ontario, the state's power and responsibility for the detection and protection of neglected children is delegated under its child welfare legislation to self-governing, non-profit corporations known as Children's Aid Societies (hereinafter known simply as Societies), which are located throughout the districts or counties of the province. Although under the *CWA*, the Minister of Community and Social Services plays mainly a passive supervisory role (ss. 2(2), 3 and 17), upon proclamation, the *CFSA* will reflect what appears to be a legislative intention that the Ministry play a more active supervisory role as well as descending into the arena of providing direct services.[18] However, it should always be remembered that the real determinant of power lies in the ability to commandeer resources, a decision of the provincial government and specifically the Ministry of Community and Social Services.[19]

Statutory Functions of Societies

Each Society appoints a local director who is responsible to that Society's volunteer, community-based board of directors. (To avoid confusion it should be noted that a ''Director'' differs from a ''director'', the former being the Ministry's agent for the province and the latter being the chief staff person of a local Society.) The statutory functions of the Society under the *CWA* include:

a) investigating allegations or evidence that children may be in need of protection;

b) protecting children when necessary;

c) providing guidance, counselling and other services to families for

---

[18]Section 17 of the *CWA* allows the Lieutenant-Governor to displace a Society's board, appointing his own board of directors if in his opinion the Society is unable to perform its duties. Under the *CFSA*, the ''revocation and takeover'' powers will be more specific and broader. Sections 22–24 will allow the Minister specified gradations of intervention from the removal of one person from a Society's board to the direct operation of the Society. They will also provide for specific notice and hearing procedures. See also the discussion in the text of this chapter on the system of review procedures which the *CFSA* will introduce. They will include a new investigative level on behalf of the Minister entitled ''Program Supervisors'' who have absolute powers of entry and investigation of any agency or Society funded by the Minister. (See in body of chapter under ''Best Interests Disposition: Review/Termination of Order''.) See also the new ''Powers of the Director'', under s. 73 of the *CFSA*.

The Minister has taken over only one Children's Aid Society under s. 17, *CWA* in recent history, that being the Kenora Children's Aid Society. Grave concerns were raised at that time over the lack of due process. The *CFSA* will codify the required method of so proceeding and set out specific circumstances (which are extremely broad) in which the Ministry may institute its revocation and takeover powers (s. 22(1)):

1) The Society is not providing services in accordance with the legislation;
2) Someone in the Society has contravened a section of the Act or Regulation;
3) Approval of Society and premises would have been denied if it were being applied for in the first instance; or
4) The Society is not able or fails to perform its statutory duties.

The *CFSA* will also include new sections which permit the Minister to provide services or purchase services directly for children and their families, seemingly indicating the Ministry's desire to play a more active role in child care in the province: ss. 7, 8, 10, 22, 24 and 30(2), *CFSA*.

[19]See ss. 8–15 of the *CWA*; ss. 19–20 of the *CFSA*.

protecting children or for the prevention of circumstances which may lead to child protection proceedings;

d) providing care for children assigned or committed to its care under this or any other Act;

e) supervising children assigned to it under this or any Act;

f) placing children for adoption;

g) assisting parents of children born or likely to be born outside of marriage and their children; and

h) any other duties given to it by this or any other Act.[20]

The purposes of the Society under the *CFSA* will be substantially the same except that it will no longer be a function of the Society to assist the parents and the children in out-of-wedlock situations: s. 15(3), *CFSA*.

A Children's Aid Society can find itself in a position of conflict based on the above-listed responsibilities. For example, on the one hand its goal is to make every effort to keep a family together through supervision and assistance to the family in up-grading their level of child care, often with insufficient resources. On the other hand, the Societies run an expensive, institutionalized group home/foster care system set up as substitutional care-givers creating a subtle force in the opposite direction of the first goal. This is reinforced by the Society's responsibility for placing children for adoption which includes the receiving of thousands of requests from desperate couples and the Society's continual search for a good match of an available child with a prospective parent. The conflict is magnified in the situation of the 17-year-old girl who is about to give birth to a child born outside of marriage and who must make up her very vulnerable mind, with the assistance of a Society worker, as to whether or not to give up her baby.

Statutory Powers of Societies

A local director and any person designated by the board of directors have all the powers delegated to them under the *CWA*, as well as the powers of a school attendance counsellor under the *Education Act*, a police officer and an officer within the meaning of s. 10 of the *Public Authorities Protection Act*. All of these powers allow the Society's agent to cause an investigation to be made into all matters affecting children, including searches and apprehension of children, while being protected against possible liability in carrying out their duties: s. 4(2), *CWA*. The *CFSA* will not incorporate such powers from other legislation, but instead it will enable a child protection worker, as designated by the board of directors, to take specific steps with or without a warrant towards apprehension, with the statutory protection that no legal proceeding shall be instituted in consequence of his or her action unless the act is done maliciously or without reasonable grounds: ss. 37(1)(b) and 40(16), *CFSA*.

Private Citizens

Reporting Abuse by Private Citizens

In conjunction with the Children's Aid Society, the state, under its child welfare legislation, enlists the assistance of other persons in the community, effectively imposing a "good samaritan" liability on private citizens in matters pertaining to child protection. Section 49(1) of the *CWA* requires that every

---

[20]Section 6(2)(a)-(h) of the *CWA*.

person ". . .who has information of the abandonment, desertion or need for protection of a child or the affliction of abuse upon a child" report the information forthwith to a Children's Aid Society. The statute also ensures that their anonymity will be protected: s. 52(3), *CWA*.[21] "Abandonment" is not defined under the *CWA* although s. 48(1) of the *CWA* establishes the circumstances under which a person can be charged with "leaving" his child. "Desertion" again is not defined. "Need of protection" has an extensive definition under s. 19(1)(b) of the *CWA* (discussed below under "Finding Child 'In Need of Protection' ") and includes the ground of "desertion." And finally, "abuse" is defined under s. 47 of the *CWA* to include a condition of physical harm, malnutrition or mental ill-health of a degree that if not immediately remedied could seriously impair growth and development, or result in permanent injury or death; or sexual molestation.[22]

Section 49(2) and (3) of the *CWA* extend a reporting responsibility to professionals which specifically supersedes any obligation of confidentiality (with the exception of the lawyer/client relationship: s. 49(4), *CWA*) if the professional "has reasonable grounds to suspect, in the course of his or her professional or official duties that a child has suffered or is suffering from abuse that may have been caused or committed by a person who has or has had charge of the child". Note that this duty covers only a sub-section of the circumstances described under s. 49(1) of the *CWA*.

To obtain a conviction against the professional under the *CWA*, the evidence must show:

1) that the person committing the abuse has or has had charge of the child, and
2) the court must be persuaded on the evidence that is presented that the class of professionals to which the defendant belongs can be expected to exercise a standard of care which would have given the defendant "reasonable grounds to suspect" abuse in the circumstances of the case. That is, there is a distinction between a standard of care that would give rise to reasonable grounds to suspect abuse in the case of a pediatrician as opposed to a school teacher or public health nurse.[23]

Upon proclamation, the *CFSA* will include expanded provisions for professional reporting, first with respect to the definition of "abuse" and secondly with respect to who must report and when. Under this Act, the professional must again have "reasonable grounds to suspect . . . in the course of his or her professional or official duties": s. 68(3), *CFSA*. But the definition of "abuse" (the entire clause "to suffer abuse" will be defined) has been

---

[21]See also *Re Infant* (1981), 32 B.C.L.R. 20 (S.C.) in which parents' application to compel the disclosure of complainant's identity was refused based on the statutory protection.

[22]Note that s. 68(2) of the *CFSA* will define the duty in more precise terms: "A person who believes on reasonable grounds that a child is or may be in need of protection" with "in need of protection" being defined under s. 37(2) of the *CFSA*.

[23]*R. v. Stachula* (1984), 40 R.F.L. (2d) 184 (Ont. Prov. Ct.), and see *R. v. Cook* (1983), 37 R.F.L. (2d) 93 (Ont. Prov. Ct.).

expanded.[24] Further, s. 68(4) will elaborate on what the term ''professional'' can include, although note that it is not restricted to the list provided.[25] Also the professional will be required to report when he suspects that the child ''is or may be suffering or may have suffered'' abuse which will relieve him from the more onerous test under the *CWA* of reporting if the child ''has suffered or is suffering abuse.'' Note that although the words ''abuse . . . by a person who has or has had charge of the child'' will no longer be in the operative s. 68(3) of the *CFSA*, the enumerated definition of ''to suffer abuse'' will include these or similar words, depending upon the type of abuse.

A final note: under the *CFSA*, it will specifically spell out in s. 68(8) that the duty of professionals to report does not supersede the confidentiality of a solicitor-client relationship, but in every other case a solicitor is bound to report in the same manner as anyone else: s. 68(4)(d), *CFSA*. Although the parallel provision in the *CWA* does not achieve the same degree of specificity, the same responsibilities on the solicitor exist thereunder.[26]

Child Abuse Register

The ''information'' reported to Societies under s. 49 of the *CWA* and its parallel s. 68(2) of the *CFSA*, may be recorded in Ontario's Child Abuse Register: s. 52(3), *CWA*/ s. 71(5), *CFSA*. The information reported to Societies must also be reported to the Director for entry into the Register but only after verification: s. 52(2), *CWA*/ s. 71(3), *CFSA*. One presumes that only the verified information would have gone into the Register: the *CWA* does not so specify while the *CFSA* will so specify: s. 71(5), *CFSA*. Notice of the entry of a person's name in the Register must be sent to that person, informing him of the entry and his right to inspect the Register: s. 52(8) and (12), *CWA*/ s. 72(2), *CFSA*. The *CFSA* will extend this right of inspection to the child although he will not be included in the notice provision: ss. 71(11), 72(2), *CFSA*. Given the extent of loss of privacy and the possible repercussions to a person who is so registered, the legislation provides the registered person with a right to an administrative

---

[24]''To suffer abuse'' will be defined under s. 68(1) and 37(2) of the *CFSA* as follows:

s. 68(1) In this section and in ss. 69, 70 and 71, ''to suffer abuse'', when used in reference to a child, means to be in need of protection within the meaning of clause 37(2)(a) [physical harm inflicted], (c) [sexually molested or exploited], (e) [lack of necessary medical treatment], (f) [emotional harm suffered with no treatment rendered] or (h) [mental, emotional or developmental condition not being remedied].

[25]Under s. 68(4) of the *CFSA*:

s. 68(4) Subsection (3) applies to every person who performs professional or official duties with respect to a child, including,
  (a) a health care professional, including a physician, nurse, dentist, pharmacist and psychologist;
  (b) a teacher, school principle, social worker, family counsellor, priest, rabbi, clergyman, operator or employee of a day nursery and youth and recreation worker;
  (c) a peace officer and a coroner;
  (d) a solicitor; and
  (e) a service provider and an employee of a service provider.

[26]Section 68(8) of the *CFSA*: ''Nothing in this section abrogates any privilege that may exist between a solicitor and his or her client.''

hearing, subject to the *Statutory Powers Procedures Act*, for the purpose of deciding whether the request to expunge the registered person's name from the Register should be granted: ss. 12-20, *CWA*/ s. 72, *CFSA*.

Apart from some broad Ministry directives, it is not clear from the *CWA* or its Regulations or the *CFSA* as to what constitutes registerable information "verified in the manner determined by the Director." (Presumably, the Ministry will eventually fill this gap via the regulations of the *CFSA* which were unavailable at the time of writing: s. 199(d)-(g), *CFSA*.). In other words, it is not clear upon what basis the discretion will be exercised by the Director in deciding whether or not a person who is the subject of reported abuse will become a "registered person" in the Register. A Divisional Court decision offered a "bottom line" test in stating that there must be some credible evidence to indicate abuse and if a person is to be identified as an alleged abuser, some credible evidence to point to his or her responsibility for the alleged abuse. In the absence of such evidence, a registration cannot be supported. In deciding this issue, the court observed that with respect to the procedure upon application by a person for the expunging of his or her name:

> The principle issue before the Director on a s. 52(14) [*CWA*] hearing is whether the information in the register with respect to a registered person should or should not be in the register. He must decide on the evidence whether there is a sufficient basis for the allegation of child abuse and the identification of the alleged abuser. Once a registration is challenged the onus is on the children's aid society, which by reporting information to the Director purports to have verified it, to uphold the registration and that onus remains with the society throughout the proceedings. The Director's determination must be made on the totality of the evidence adduced before him. Having regard to the purpose and object of the registry and the social policy underlying the Act, the burden of proof, in my view, should not be too onerous. In establishing a central child abuse registry and providing for notice and expungement proceedings, the legislature ought, on the one hand, to protect the civil rights of individuals and, on the other, to protect and safeguard children in the province from abuse. The nature of the information entered is limited and is confidential save as is specifically provided in the Act. It is recognized that the register is an important monitoring device and provides invaluable assistance to those responsible for dealing with the difficult and highly emotional problems relating to child abuse. To permit the registry to achieve its purposes, entries should not be limited to cases in which abuse has been established by the standards of proof applicable to criminal or civil actions. In my view, the interests concerned and the public interest will be served if the burden of proof in s. 52(14) [*CWA*] hearings is satisfied by credible evidence supporting the information in the register. If credible evidence is adduced it remains for the Director to determine in light of the circumstances of the request before him whether the information should remain in the register. In the absence of credible evidence, the name must be expunged.[27]

---

[27] *Re Ridley and C.A.S. of Hastings*, summarized in (1981), 8 A.C.W.S. (2d) 296 (Ont. Div. Ct.).

The vagueness in the legislation, the wording of which will remain the same in the *CFSA*, becomes a matter of concern when one considers the uses made of this otherwise confidential information:

1) A Children's Aid Society that receives information concerning the abuse of a child is obliged to inquire of the Director whether the person referred to in their information has been previously identified in the Register: *CWA*, R.R.O. 1980, Reg. 97, s. 8(1) (hereinafter cited as O. Reg. 97/80, s. 8(1)). One presumes that a second reporting will lead to much more rigorous consequences than a first.

2) The Official Guardian may obtain information from the Register, and that information is admissible in evidence in a proceeding by the child, through the Official Guardian, against that person for damages by reason of the infliction of abuse upon the child: s. 51, 52(5), *CWA*/ ss. 77(2), 71(7)(b), *CFSA*.

3) A coroner, a legally qualified medical practitioner or police officer authorized in writing and directed by a coroner for the purposes of an investigation or inquest under the *Coroner's Act* may inspect or remove the information maintained in the Register and may disclose or transmit that information "only in accordance with authority vested in the person": s. 52(5), *CWA*/ s. 71(7)(a), *CFSA*.

4) Persons on the staff of the Ministry, of a Children's Aid Society or of a child protection agency outside of Ontario and anyone who is or may be providing services or treatment to a "registered person" (which definition will not include the subject child: s. 71(1)(c), *CFSA*), may inspect, remove and disclose information subject to the approval of the Director and any conditions he may wish to impose: s. 52(6), *CWA*/ s. 71(8), *CFSA*.

5) A person who is engaged in research may inspect the information and use it for purely academic purposes as long as the use does not identify the registered person: s. 52(7), *CWA*/ s. 71(10), *CFSA*.

6) A legally qualified medical practitioner approved by the Director may inspect the information: s. 52(9), *CWA*/ s. 71(12), *CFSA*.

Voluntary Agreements for State Assistance

Ontario's child welfare legislation authorizes parents to enter voluntarily into an agreement with a Society or with a Ministry for the provision of services, supervision, care or custody of their child without recourse to the courts. There are three basic types of agreements: general temporary care; "special needs" temporary care; and a "homemaker" agreement. Although the parents' guardianship rights are retained (*i.e.* rights over the child's property), custodial rights (*i.e.* rights over the care and control of the person) are delegated by this agreement in varying degrees depending on the terms of the agreement.[28] Case

---

[28]See prescribed Form 2 "Agreement for Custody and Care" pursuant to *CWA*, O. Reg. 96/80, s. 24(1). *Cf.* with s. 29(8) of the *CFSA* which will set out what a temporary agreement should include:

1) A statement by all parties that the child's care and custody are transferred to the Society;
2) A statement by all parties that the child's placement is voluntary;
3) A statement by the parent that he or she is temporarily unable to care for the child adequately

law indicates that the traditional prerequisites for the valid execution and enforcement of a contract are applicable in the instance of these contracts such that an agreement may be set aside if it is entered into under duress, coercion, or specifically under the threat of the Society's apprehension of the child.[29]

General
Temporary Care
Agreements

The temporary care agreement allows the parent[30] who is temporarily unable, for whatever reason, to care for the child, to place him in the short-term care and custody of a Children's Aid Society: s. 25(1), *CWA*/ s. 29, *CFSA*.[31] The Society has discretion as to whether to enter into such an agreement and is under a duty first to "consider what assistance to the child is possible while the child is in the care of his or her parent": s. 25(5) *CWA*.[32] Any one agreement cannot be for a period greater than six months, and although an agreement may be extended, it cannot be extended for any period or periods which in total are greater than 12 months (s. 25(1)(2), *CWA*/ s. 29(5), *CFSA*), or any combination of temporary care and wardship periods greater than 24 months (s. 25(3) *CWA*/ s. 29(6), *CFSA*), nor can any agreement or extension thereof be in effect beyond the child's 18th birthday: s. 25(10), *CWA*/ s. 32, *CFSA*.

The terms of the agreement are prescribed by Regulation (*CWA*, O. Reg. 96/80, s. 24 and Form 2) and include an undertaking that the parent will work with the Society and visit the child regularly. The parties may also agree to include any other term or condition that is not prescribed by and not inconsistent with the Regulations or Act. Under the *CWA*, if the child is 12 years or older he must give his consent to the agreement, if he is so capable: s. 25(8)(9), *CWA*. Incapacity, for the purposes of this section, must have been assessed within the last two years: *CWA*, O. Reg. 96/80, s. 25. The *CFSA*, on the other hand will

and has discussed with the Society alternatives to residential placement of the child;

4) An undertaking by the parent to maintain contact with the child and be involved in the child's care;

5) If it is not possible for the parent to maintain contact with the child and be involved in the child's care, the person's designation of another named person who is willing to do so;

6) The name of the individual who is the primary contact between the Society and the parent; and

7) Such other provisions as prescribed.

(Note s. 198(b) of the *CFSA*, which will permit regulations to be made "prescribing provisions" for temporary care agreements. The new regulations were unavailable at the time of writing.)

[29]*Ex parte D.*, [1971] 1 O.R. 311, 5 R.F.L. 119 (H.C.).

[30]"Parent" is extensively defined under s. 19(1)(e) and 92 of the *CWA*. Under s. 29(1), *CFSA* it will simply state that any person who has custody of a child and is temporarily unable to care adequately for him may enter into a temporary care agreement, rather than restricting it to a "parent."

[31]It has been held that a parent being unable to make adequate provision for his child is a necessary prerequisite without which the agreement will be set aside. In this case, the Family Court had made an order that the child be returned to his parents subject to supervision and the parents subsequently placed the child in the care of a Soceity pursuant to a temporary agreement. The court directed the agreement to be set aside, noting that such an agreement is available only where the parents are unable to make adequate provisions for a child, a state of affairs directly contrary to that found to be existing by the family court originally: *M.M. v. B.M.* (1981), 37 O.R. (2d) 120 (Co. Ct.); affd. 37 O.R. (2d) 716 *n* (C.A.).

[32]Under s. 29(4) of the *CFSA*, the Society will not be able to make a temporary care agreement unless (1) it has determined that an appropriate residential placement that is likely to benefit the child is available; and (2) it is satisfied that no less restrictive course of action, such as care in the child's own home, is appropriate.

make the same child a necessary party to the agreement rather than simply requiring his consent (s. 29(2), *CFSA*) while incapacity to participate will have to have been assessed within the previous *one* year: s. 29(3), *CFSA*. Finally, under the *CWA*, a person 16 years of age or older may, independent of his or her parent, enter into such an agreement, but again, the agreement may not extend beyond the person's 18th birthday: s. 25(11), *CWA*. However, under the *CFSA*, *no* temporary care agreement may be made with respect to anyone who is 16 years of age or older: s. 29(2)(a), *CFSA*. If the agreement was made before the 16th birthday, it may not extend beyond the 18th birthday: s. 32, *CFSA*.[33]

"Special Needs" Agreements

A "special needs" agreement is similar to a temporary care agreement in that the parent voluntarily surrenders care and custody of the child to the Society, but it differs on three points:

i) the inability of the parent to care for the child must be due to the child's "special needs": s/25(4), *CWA*/ s. 30, *CFSA*;

ii) there are no statutorily-prescribed time limitations with respect to the agreement so that the parties may enter into the agreement for such period or periods of time as is agreeable to them: s. 25(4), *CWA*/ s. 30(3), *CFSA*; and

iii) the agreement may be made with a Society or directly with the Minister: s. 25(4), *CWA*/ s. 30(1) and (2), *CFSA*.

"Special needs" is defined in the Regulations of the *CWA* as "needs related to or created by physical, mental, emotional, behavioural or other handicaps of children": *CWA*, O. Reg. 96/80, s. 13. Upon proclamation, it will be defined under s. 26(d) of the *CFSA* as a need that is "related to or caused by a behavioural, developmental, emotional, physical, mental or other handicap." (Note also s. 198(e) permitting the Ministry to further define "special need" under the *CFSA* regulations. The new regulations were unavailable at the time of writing.)

In practice, these agreements are distinguishable from the temporary agreements because they are usually for long-term placement. Since placement with an agency or Society may be unnecessary and detrimental to the child in many cases, the *CFSA* will provide the jurisdiction for a Society or the Ministry to enter into "special needs" agreements for *services* to the child, presumably while he remains at home, as well as care and custody if necessary: s. 30(1), *CFSA*. Under the *CWA*, as in the case of the temporary agreement, the consent of the child who is 12 years of age or older is required for this type of agreement to be valid except where the consent cannot be given because of the child's developmental handicaps.[34] However, the *CFSA* will require no such consent from a child under 16 years unless the service provided is that of counselling: s. 28, *CFSA*. For those who are 16 and 17 years old, an agreement may be made directly between the child and the Society or Ministry, but he or she must not be in the care of his or her parent: s. 31, *CFSA*. As with temporary agreements, all

---

[33]It appears that s. 10(4) of the *CFSA* will permit the Ministry to deliver direct services to a person over 16 years of age "as if those persons were children."

[34]Section 25(8) and (9) of the *CWA*.

"special needs" agreements under the *CFSA* will expire on the child's 18th birthday (s. 32, *CFSA*) subject to the Ministry's possible exemption under s. 10(4) of the *CFSA*.

"Homemaker"
Arrangements

The "homemaker" place, as a voluntary agreement between parent and Society, is not specifically contemplated by either Act. There is provision for a "homemaker" (a person approved by the Society, who lives in the child's home to care for the child: s. 23(1), *CWA*/ s. 74, *CFSA*) to be placed in a home when the Society finds a child "who . . . is unable to care for himself" *and* "has been left on the premises without competent care or supervision" *and* the person in charge of the child is unavailable or is unable to consent to the placement of a homemaker: s. 74(2), *CFSA*. (The working of the *CWA* is more vague and denotes "temporary" circumstances specifically: s. 23(2), *CWA*.) By implication, the placement is a form of apprehension: s. 27(1), *CWA*/ s. 42(1), *CFSA*, she may enter and live on the premises and carry on normal housekeeping activities "as are reasonably necessary for the care of any child on the premises and exercise reasonable control and discipline over any such child": s. 74(3), *CFSA*/ s. 23(3), *CWA*. Insofar as the number of "homemakers" placed appears to be a function of the discretion of the Director or the local director, Societies will vary in their practice of making such a service available. Given a Society's mandate to canvass all possibilities of assistance to maintain the child in his or her own home (s. 25(5), *CWA*/ s. 29(4)(b), *CFSA*), it provides a strong argument for the placement of a homemaker if it is appropriate, and if the family circumstances are known. Upon proclamation, the *CFSA* will make this alternative to care more of a possibility under the section which allows a Society or the Ministry to render services short of taking the child into care: s. 29(4)(b), *CFSA*. To bolster this approach, one need only refer to s. 1(b), and (c) of the *CFSA* which outlines the purposes of the Act including:

> s. 1(b) to recognize that while parents often need help in caring for their children, that help should give support to the autonomy and integrity of the family unit; . . .
>
> (c) to recognize that the least restrictive or disruptive course of action that is available and is appropriate in a particular case to help a child or family should be followed.

Review of
Voluntary
Placement

Under the *CWA* there is no mechanism whereby the placement of the child is subject to mandatory review as to its appropriateness. The kind of placement and the over-seeing of the child's progress is within the control and discretion of the local Society.[35] Under the *CFSA*, a new independent supervisory level (entitled a

---

[35]Form 2, *CWA*, O. Reg. 96/80:

  2. Society responsibilities.

    During the period of this agreement, THE SOCIETY WILL:

    (*a*) provide food, shelter, clothing, health and dental care for the child;

    (*b*) provide the following services for the child. . .;

    (*c*) provide the following services to the parents. . .;

    (*d*) keep the parents informed of the child's progress;

    (*e*) notify the parents as soon as possible of any emergency involving the child or any absence of the child from Society care; and

    (*f*) work with the parents and the child to plan for the return of the child to the parents.

"Residential Placement Advisory Committee") will be introduced upon the Act's proclamation for children in residential care (excluding foster care or secure treatment) pursuant to an agreement or court order: ss. 34-36, *CFSA*. The committee is to advise parents, children and societies of the availability and appropriateness of resources as well as to review each placement on a periodic basis or on request, and submit an advisory report to all parties concerned, including the Ministry.

Agreements and Consent to Treatment

By implication from the wording of the prescribed Form 2 under the *CWA*,[36] parents appear to retain their sole authority to consent to medical treatment for the child under these temporary agreements (except of course, in the case of emergency) unless they delegate it in writing to the Society. The *CFSA* will be more specific by stating in the body of the legislation that a temporary care agreement may provide that a Society is entitled to consent to medical treatment for the child where a parent's consent would otherwise be required: s. 29(7), *CFSA*.

Termination of Agreement

Where the parties are unable to come to an agreement and the Society is concerned that the child is at risk, it may take further steps by seeking intervention of the court. If the parties have entered into an agreement and subsequently experience differences of opinion, the *CWA* allows either party to terminate the agreement by giving at least 21 days notice in writing to the other parties, following which the agreement expires: s. 25(12), *CWA*. The notice period not only allows time for further negotiation but also time within which the Society can bring the child before the court if it believes that returning the child to its home will put him at risk. If there is no executed and valid agreement, a Society has no authority to hold a child in its care unless it decides to apprehend the child on the basis of a belief that he is in need of protection (discussed below under "Apprehension"), in which case they must proceed to court within five days through the mechanism of an apprehension: s. 27(1), *CWA*/ s. 42, *CFSA*. The *CFSA* will shorten the notice period for termination of a temporary care agreement from 21 to 5 days unless the parties otherwise agree to a longer period not to exceed 21 days (s. 33(2), *CFSA*), presumably so that this notice period will be the same as is usually available to a Society to apprehend and bring a child before the court where there is no voluntary agreement.

Commencing Child Protection Proceedings

Ontario's child welfare legislation provides two routes whereby a child who is suspected of being in need of protection can come before the Court as follows:

. . .

---

7. Placement
   THE PARENTS AGREE that the Society may place the Child with any person who in the opinion of the Society is qualified to provide care for the Child. The Society agrees to notify the parents if the Child is moved.

[36]Form 2, *CWA*, O. Reg. 96/80:

5. SPECIAL TREATMENT
THE PARENTS AUTHORIZE the Society to arrange for the following medical treatment for the Child [list specific medical, surgical, dental or psychiatric treatment].
The Parents understand that the Society may ask them to give their consent for treatment.

1) Commencement of Family Court protection proceedings while the child remains with the parents. Under the *CWA*, this is accomplished by obtaining an ''order to produce'', that is, a court order to require the person who has custody of the child to bring him before the court on a specified date. Upon proclamation of the *CFSA*, the Society will only need to file an application to commence proceedings while anyone else must still seek ''an order to produce''. This change reinforces the civil nature of the proceedings in which a Society need face no prerequisite burden of evidence before having the right to commence a civil proceeding.

2) ''Apprehension'' (discussed below) where designated persons take the child to a place of safety with or without warrant when the welfare of the child necessitates avoiding the delay of waiting for the commencement of protection proceedings.

Applicants

Section 21(1)(b) of the *CWA* permits a police officer or Society worker to ''apply to a court [Provincial Court (Fam. Div.) or a Unified Family Court] for an order requiring the person in whose charge the child is to produce the child before a court at a time and place named in the order.'' Under the *CFSA*, the parallel section will require only that an application be filed to commence proceedings, but will limit the use of this route to ''a Society'': s. 40(1), *CFSA*. Both the *CWA* and *CFSA* also have provisions whereby anyone else may bring a protection matter before the court by seeking ''an order to produce'' after having reported the matter to a Society with no results: s. 22(2), *CWA*/ s. 40(3), *CFSA*.[37] In these circumstances, the court must afford the Society an opportunity to be heard.[38]

In one case,[39] the court considered that while there is authority for a person other than a representative of the Society to apply for an ''order to produce'', this does not extend to enable the court to determine whether a child in the care of a Society is in need of protection or to make an order consequent upon such determination. Since the Provincial Court is a statutory court and nothing more, and the Act sets out limitations with respect to the nature of applications when children are in the care of a Society, s. 22(2), *CWA* cannot be relied upon to override those specific provisions. If this decision is correct, it suggests that a child who is in the care of a Society by way of temporary or Crown wardship, and therefore already found to be ''in need of protection,'' is immune from a subsequent finding from the Provincial Court, or from further intervention from that court. In such cases, relief may lie with a Superior Court which retains an

---

[37] As a prerequisite for seeking such an order, the *CWA* requires that the Society must have refused or failed within a reasonable time to apprehend the child or itself seek ''an order to produce''. The *CFSA* will simply require that a Society not have commenced proceedings, sought a warrant or apprehended the child. There will no longer need to be a specific refusal to act by the Society or a reasonable passage of time after notification of the Society during which it has not acted.

[38] See *Re Sturgeon and Sturgeon* (1974), 15 R.F.L. 100, at 104 (Ont. Prov. Ct.), for explanation of procedures for bringing child before court.

[39] *W.K. and A.K. v. C.A.S. of Sarnia*, summarized in (1982), 5 F.L.R.R. 92 (Ont. Prov. Ct.) (declined jurisdiction). But see *Re M.G.* (1980), 18 R.F.L. (2d) 355 (B.C. Prov. Ct.) wherein a 16-year-old prostitute, who was a temporary ward of the Society was found in need of protection. The court held that the Superintendent of Child Welfare was in no different position than anyone else who had custody of the child.

inherent jurisdiction regarding the welfare of children. (''Applicants'' for apprehension are dealt with below under ''Apprehension''.)

Grounds for Commencement of Proceedings

The grounds upon which protection proceedings will be commenced vary with the applicant. Essentially, if it is anyone other than a Society applying, the court, before issuing an ''order to produce'', must be satisfied ''that there are reasonable and probable grounds to believe'' that a child is in need of protection: s. 22(2), *CWA*/ s. 40(3), *CFSA*. (Under the *CFSA*, the court will be required to make an additional finding that, on reasonable and probable grounds, the child ''cannot be protected adequately otherwise than by being brought before the court''.) If a Society is the applicant, the decision as to whether a child might be in need of protection rests with that Society, not the court. Interestingly, the *CFSA*, once proclaimed, will no longer specifically require a Society to have ''reasonable and probable grounds'' before commencing an action as does the *CWA*. This coincides with the change in the nature of commencing proceedings (bringing them even more into the fold of civil proceedings), since there will no longer be a necessity for a Society to seek a court order to produce which technically needs some underlying grounds to be proved by preliminary evidence before being issued. An order to produce, pursuant to the Regulations, is obtained *ex parte* but the person named in the order may, within seven days after the order comes to his or her attention apply to the court to have it varied or discharged: R.R.O. 810 (Prov. Ct. Rules) ss. 67(2) and 72(4). In a recent case, a Provincial Court concluded that an order to produce, obtain *ex parte* by a Society under the *CWA*, does not violate the *Charter of Rights* as constituting an unreasonable seizure, arbitrary detention or cruel and unusual treatment of the mother, nor does it violate the mother's right to life, liberty or security. The court also dismissed the argument that the Society's application for an order to produce constituted an abuse of process, reasoning that if there is a clear basis for considering the child as apparently in need of protection, it would be wrong to prevent the Society from intervening, no matter how strongly one feels that the Society delayed its actions inappropriately. The remedy, if there is one, would more appropriately be an order of costs against the Society.[40] This reasoning would also be applicable to a Society filing an application to commence proceedings under the *CFSA* but the named person will have to register his objections/defence in the context of the actual protection proceedings since there will be no order to set aside.

Apprehension

There are three apprehension routes under Ontario's child welfare legislation[41], ''apprehension'' meaning the taking of a child to a place of safety before he is brought before the court to determine whether he is in need of protection. As with the commencement of proceedings, there are also two classes of instigators: designated agents of the state and anyone else.

---

[40]*Re T and the Catholic C.A.S. of Metro. Toronto* (1984), 46 O.R. (2d) 347 (Prov. Ct.).

[41]See generally ss. 21–22, of the *CWA* and s. 40 of the *CFSA*. Note that one superior court has held that the province's Human Rights Code did not apply to apprehension because it did not amount to arrest and detention: *Re A.M.* (1980), 16 R.F.L. (2d) 37, 2 Fam. L. Rev. 302 (*sub nom. Re M.*) (Sask. C.A.).

1) Any person may apply to a court for an order directing a Society worker to search for the child and take the child to a place of safety until the matter can be brought to court: s. 22(2), *CWA*/ s. 40(3), *CFSA*. As with an "order to produce", notice must be given to the Society who has refused or who has not taken action and who must be heard on the matter. Again, the court must believe on reasonable and probable grounds that the child is in need of protection and that he cannot be protected adequately otherwise than by being brought before the court to issue this type of order.

2) A justice of the peace may issue an "apprehension" warrant where it appears on information before him that there are reasonable and probable grounds to believe that the child is in need of protection or that the child has left or been removed from the Society's care and custody: s. 22(1), *CWA*/ s. 40(2), *CFSA*.[42] Although there are no restrictions under the *CWA* as to who may lay the information, the *CFSA* will limit the use of the section to a "child protection worker" and it is this worker as well as a "peace officer" who will be able to seek and execute the warrant: ss. 40(2) and (17), *CFSA*. Note further that the *CFSA* will require the justice of the peace to determine first whether there is available to him any less restrictive course of action.

3) Under s. 21(1) and (2) of the *CWA*, a police officer or a Director or local director (or their agents) can take a child to a place of safety without court order or warrant if they believe on reasonable and probable grounds that the child was "apparently" in need of protection or if the child had left or been removed from the Society's care and custody.[43] Upon proclamation of the *CFSA*, a "child protection worker" or a "peace officer" may so act without warrant if there are reasonable and probable grounds to believe that the child is in need of protection, has left or been removed from a Society's care *and* there would be a substantial risk to the child's health and safety to wait for a court hearing: s. 40(6), (17), *CFSA*.

The *CFSA* will have one more category of apprehension in order to integrate with the new *Young Offenders Act* which now excludes persons under 12 years old from bearing criminal responsibility for their acts. Under s. 40(10) of the *CFSA*, a peace officer (and not a child protection worker) will be able to apprehend someone actually or apparently under 12 years of age who the officer believes on reasonable and probable grounds has committed an act in respect of which a person 12 years of age or older could be found guilty of an offence, a not unusual occurrence.[44] However, this type of apprehension will result only in the officer returning the child to his parent and will only trigger a protection proceeding if the child "cannot be returned" to the parent or person caring for

---

[42]The warrant is issued as Form 32 under O. Reg. 810/80 (Rules of the Provincial Court), s. 65.

[43]See *Minister of Social Services v. C.* (1982), 26 R.F.L. (2d) 417 (Sask. Q.B.), *Re Western Man. C.A.S. and Daniels* (1981), 14 Man. R. (2d) 192, 128 D.L.R. (3d) 751 (C.A.) for discussion of "reasonable and probable grounds." But note that in *Minister of Social Services v. C. id.,* it was also held that a protection hearing could proceed whether or not the apprehending officer had reasonable and probable grounds.

[44]See s. 72 of the *Young Offenders Act* and, in Ontario, s. 1 of the *Provincial Offences Amendment Act, 1983*.

the child within 12 hours. (Note also s. 75 of the *CFSA* which will apply the same limited apprehension powers to children loitering in a public place between midnight and 6:00 a.m.).

A person authorized to apprehend with or without warrant or order, has the authority to enter any premises in order to search for and remove a child, if need be by force, and if there is an order or warrant, it is not necessary to describe the child by name: ss. 21(3) and 22(4), *CWA*/ s. 40(4) and (5), *CFSA*. (Note also s. 199(a) of the *CFSA* which will authorize the Ministry to make regulations "governing the exercise of the powers of entry". Regulations for the new Act were unavailable at the time of writing.) However, these sections do not give the "apprehender" any power to search for evidence for subsequent court proceedings.[45] Although one of the functions of a Society is to investigate allegations or evidence that children may be in need of protection, it does not yield an implied authority to enter and search for evidence. Nevertheless, when such illegally obtained evidence was challenged under s. 8 of the *Charter of Rights* (right to be secure against unreasonable search or seizure), the court concluded that "illegal" may not amount to "unreasonable" in certain situations. The headnote of the judgement reads as follows:

> Whether or not a search is unreasonable depends upon the nature and purpose of the statute under which it was ostensibly conducted and the facts and the circumstances of the case. Where the statute is not a criminal statute dealing with the liberty of the subject, but a child welfare statute designed to protect those who are unable to protect themselves, a search not authorized by the statute may not be unreasonable if it was conducted to obtain credible and trustworthy evidence as to whether a child is in fact in need of protection.[46]

The evidence was also challenged under s. 24(2) of the *Charter* (exclusion of evidence that would bring the administration of justice into disrepute). The headnote reads:

> It would be rare indeed that evidence of the environment in which a child is being raised would be excluded from a proceeding to determine whether the child is in need of protection, even if it was obtained illegally and as a result of an unreasonable search. Having regard to the nature of child welfare legislation and to the rights of the child, the admission of such evidence could not ordinarily be said to bring the administration of justice into disrepute on the tests set out in *Rothman v. The Queen* (1981), 59 C.C.C. (2d) 30 (S.C.C.).[47]

In an earlier decision of the British Columbia Supreme Court, it was held that the illegality of the warrant does not vitiate the jurisdiction of the judge when there is a complaint on oath in writing, alleging that the children appearing before

---

[45]*Re W. and C.A.S. of Regional Municipality of York*, summarized in (1982), 17 A.C.W.S. (2d) 147 (Ont. Prov. Ct.).

[46]*Ibid.*

[47]*Ibid.*

the court have been apprehended and are in need of protection.[48] Other decisions have delineated certain expectations of the "apprehenders." Ontario's High Court has held[49] that if allegations of acts of violence against children have been made, they should be investigated on the spot with the parents before a warrant is secured and not afterwards. If a warrant is obtained, it should be exercised and should not be used as an instrument to extort a consent or agreement with respect to the placement of a child into care. If the child is in definite need, if there are fresh bruises or serious medical observations, then it is in the child's interests that he be taken away from conditions which produce a serious threat and new dangers. In this case, however, the court could find no such reason for removing the child from the home and found, in fact, that the greatest damage had been done by the very act of removing the child. The court expressed its concern over the potential abuse of super and normal powers entrusted to the Society:

> . . .[the powers] are not provided to make the task of the social worker easier, to be twisted to extort consent, to enter law-abiding homes and spirit children away, or to cut the bonds of blood or adoption, but only to protect children against abuse and to cope with the emergencies and challenges which the sufferings of children present to society and which cannot properly be dealt with unless we sacrifice in particular cases our ancient liberties and much that makes the future of children in our society worthwhile.[50]

Once apprehended, a child will be detained in a "place of safety" which is defined to include a foster home, hospital or any other designated place except a place of secure custody or detention: s. 37(1)(e), *CFSA*/ s. 19(1)(f), *CWA*. He must be

1) brought before the court within five days to determine whether he is in need of protection,
2) returned to the parent, or
3) be the subject of a voluntary temporary care agreement: s. 27(1), *CWA*/ s. 42(1), *CFSA*.

In addition, if the "place of safety" is an observation and detention home (*CWA*) or "place of open temporary detention" (*CFSA*)[51] the child must be brought before the court more expeditiously: "as soon as is practicable" under the *CWA*, "within 24 hours . . . or as soon thereafter as is practical" under the *CFSA*. The

---

[48]*Re Mairs* (1961), 30 C.C.C. 361 (B.C.S.C.).

[49]*Ex parte D.*, [1971] 1 O.R. 311, 5 R.F.L. 119 (H.C.).

[50]*Ibid.*, at p. 128 (R.F.L.).

[51]This type of "place of safety" will no longer be defined under the *CFSA* as an "observation and detention home under the *Provincial Courts Act*" but "a place of open temporary detention". This phrase is defined in a subsequent part of the Act (Part IV: Young Offenders, s. 84) as a place of temporary detention in which the Minister has established an open detention program for those who were convicted under the *Young Offenders Act* and the *Provincial Offences Act*. An open detention program will have less stringent restrictions on the liberty of the child than does a secure temporary detention program: ss. 85(2)(a) and (b), *CFSA*.

child may remain there no longer than 30 days in total after which he must be placed elsewhere: s. 27(2), *CWA*/ s. 42(2), *CFSA*. In one case where the matter did not come before the court within the prescribed period, the court ordered the child to be returned to the parents even though it agreed with the lower court that the child was in need of protection.[52]

During the period of apprehension, it has been held by one Provincial Court judge that the Society has the authority to provide consent for medical treatment of a child since the child has effectively been removed from the control of the parent.[53] The court seemed to rely for this conclusion on the fact that if a parent were to remove a child who has been so apprehended, they could be subject to a charge of attempting to interfere with the Society in its care of the child. It is submitted that such an infringement of parental rights would necessitate far more specific legislation, especially in light of the fact that the child is before a judge within five days of apprehension, who is then able to order the transfer of most parental rights to the Society under the wardship provisions of the Act. Naturally, any emergency situation can also be dealt with in the usual common law context or through an expedited court order: s. 34, *CWA*. This latter position will be further strengthened upon proclamation of the *CFSA* by specific provisions which will state that parents of a child in care retain their right to give or refuse consent to medical treatment subject to the court's disposition after a protection hearing: s. 102(b), *CFSA*. On the other hand, s. 40(8) of the *CFSA* will authorize a child protection worker under the apprehension sections to have a medical examination conducted on the child. Regarding a medical examination under the *CWA*, it is doubtful that evidence obtained in this manner would ever be excluded at a hearing.[54]

Pre-hearing Issues

Notice and Parties

Where a child has been apprehended, the matter must come before the court within five days (as noted above) pursuant to an application to the court for an order finding the child in need of protection.[55] Under family court rules, the application and notice of hearing to the parents need not be issued by the court prior to service, as long as they are filed at or before the hearing.[56] Under the *CWA*, notice is to be given to the parent (meaning every "parent": s. 92, *CWA*) or other person having actual custody of the child, including, where applicable, any foster parent who immediately prior to the hearing has been caring for the child on behalf of a Society for a continuous period of more than six months (s. 28(6), *CWA*) and to the child if over nine years old unless the court directs otherwise or, if under 10 years, only if the court decides that the hearing would

---

[52]*Candlish v. Ministry of Social Services* (1978), 5 R.F.L. (2d) 166 (Sask. Q.B.) (as an appeal). But see *Re Kowaliuk; C.A.S. of Winnipeg v. Brooklands* (1933), 41 Man. R. 463 (Man. C.A.) (by way of *habeas corpus*) which held that the time limitation is directory only and failure to comply with it does not deprive the judge of jurisdiction.

[53]*Re B. (L)*, summarized in (1982), 17 A.C.W.S. (2d) 41 (Ont. Prov. Ct.).

[54]See s. 28(3) and (4) of the *CWA* and *Re W. and C.A.S. of Regional Municipality of York, supra*, note 45.

[55]See *C.A.S. of Winnipeg v. Ostopowich* (1982), 18 Man. R. (2d) 69 (C.A.) in which a Society's application was granted to extend the time within which it might apply to have a child found in need of protection.

[56]O. Reg. 810/80 (Provincial Court Rules), ss. 11, 12 and 66.

be understandable and not injurious to the child: ss. 28(7), 33(b), *CWA*.[57] Unlike the *CWA*, s. 39(1) of the *CFSA* will specifically delineate who are to be parties to the proceeding and who should therefore receive notice and standing: the applicant, the Society, the child's parents (meaning every parent: s. 37(1)(d), *CFSA*) and, if applicable, a representative of the Indian band. In addition, s. 39(4) of the *CFSA* will provide that a child who is *12* years of age or over is also entitled to notice and to be present unless being present would be emotionally injurious with the same provision for children under 12 years as exists under the *CWA* for children under 10 years. Finally, s. 39(3) of the *CFSA* will provide that *anyone* (including a foster parent) who has cared for the child continuously for the past six months will also be entitled to notice as a party, to be present and to make submissions.

Section 28(6) of the *CWA* specifically prohibits the court from proceeding to hear or dispose of the matter until it is satisfied that all persons entitled have received reasonable notice of the hearing or that reasonable efforts have been made, in the opinion of the court, to cause such notification. Although there will be no such specific prohibition under the *CFSA*, once proclaimed, the act of making these persons parties to the proceeding effectively accomplishes the same thing. "Reasonable efforts" have been held to mean:

a) first, that an exhaustive investigation has been made to ascertain the whereabouts of the parents so that, if at all possible, personal service can be effected; and

b) secondly, if personal service cannot be effected, the mode of such substitutional service should include publication of a full and complete notice in a newspaper published in the locality where the parents reside or last resided.[58] It has also been held that the disjunctive "or" in the notice provision of the *CWA* reading "the parent or other person having actual custody of the child" is not a sufficient bar to the statutory entitlement of one parent to notice simply because notice has been given to the other or given to a person not being a parent who had actual custody of the child. This interpretation will also be applicable to s. 39(1), para. 3 of the *CFSA*, which will make "the child's parent" a party. In addition, see s. 92 of the *CWA* (s. 37(1)(d) of the *CFSA*) which deems "parent" to mean more than one if the circumstances warrant it. Both Acts speak clearly enough to make the want of notice a fatal defect, and notice must be given to both a parent and the person having actual custody of the child.[59]

Once the application is returned to court, if it appears to the judge that there has not been appropriate notice, the matter can be adjourned but not for a period

---

[57]See *Re C.A.S. of Metro. Toronto and C.* (1979), 25 O.R. (2d) 234, 11 R.F.L. (2d) 100 (*sub nom. Re C*) (Prov. Ct.) (biological father of child born out of wedlock entitled to notice as coming under general definition of parent under s. 19(1)(e) of the *CWA*.).

[58]*Re Pearson*, [1973] 4 W.W.R. 274, 10 R.F.L. 234 (B.C.S.C.).

[59]*C.A.S. of Metro. Toronto v. Lyttle*, [1973] S.C.R. 568. See also *Department of Health and Community Services v. B* (1981), 24 R.F.L. (2d) 289 (Man. Prov. Ct.). See also s. 39(1) and (3) of the *CFSA*.

in excess of 30 days unless all parties agree: s. 28(12), (13), *CWA*/ s. 47(1), *CFSA*. (The issue of where the child will stay, pending the next court date is dealt with below under "Show Cause Hearings".) If the judge believes that any such delay would endanger the health or safety of the child, he can dispense with notice requirements and proceed but his usual disposition alternatives are limited by the fact that he may not order Crown or Society wardship for a period greater than 30 days and notice requirements apply to any subsequent hearings: s. 28(10) and (11), *CWA*/ ss. 39(7) and 53(7), *CFSA*.

Child as Quasi-Party

The most significant change between present day child welfare legislation and its 1978 predecessor concerns the emerging status of the child as a quasi-party to the proceeding. (See generally Chapter 6 "The Child and the Courtroom"). The Legislature under the *CWA* has not made the child a party but it did "gift" to him the following qualified set of "natural justice" rights: (Note s. 39(6), *CFSA* which will state that certain children may participate as if they were a party.)

1) Right to notice of hearing: The *CWA* provides in various sections that a child who is 10 years of age or more, is entitled to notice unless the effect of the hearing would be injurious to the emotional health of the child in which case the court may direct that the child not be served with notice. Under 10 years, the child is not entitled to notice but will receive notice if the judge decides that the child is entitled to be present at the hearing. The *CFSA* will adopt the same approach but will change the watershed age from 10 to 12 years. (Protection hearing: s. 28(7), *CWA*/ s. 39(4), (5), *CFSA*; review hearing: ss. 32(7), 37(4) and 38(4), *CWA*/ s. 60(4)(a) and (6)(a), *CFSA*; access application: s. 35(5), *CWA*/ s. 54(4)(a), *CFSA*.).

2) Right to be present in court: Under the *CWA*, there is a presumption that a child 10 years of age or older is entitled to be present at any hearing unless the court is satisfied that the effect of the hearing or any part thereof would be injurious to the emotional health of the child. Conversely, it is presumed that a child under 10 years of age is not to be present at the hearing unless the court is satisfied that the hearing or any part thereof would be understandable to the child and not be injurious to his emotional health: s. 33, *CWA*. As with notice, the *CFSA*, upon proclamation, will adopt the same approach but will change the ages from 10 to 12 years: s. 39(4), *CFSA*. Case law on this issue has developed some of the following guidelines: whether or not the child is present in court, his counsel is entitled to notice of all proceedings;[60] this section creates a presumption, not an obligation to attend;[61] for the purpose of a motion to decide whether the child is or is not to attend, the child should be present in the building but not in the court room, unless all of the parties otherwise agree and if the judge decides to exclude the child, that child should always be in the building when requested by counsel, in order to facilitate direct contact with his lawyer, as this may be necessary during the course of the proceeding.[62]

[60]See *Re Stephen A.*, summarized in (1983), 6 F.L.R.R. 120 (Ont. Prov. Ct.).
[61]*Re Robert H.*, summarized in (1981), 5 F.L.R.R. 13 (Ont. Prov. Ct.).
[62]*Re Adrian S.*, summarized in (1982), 5 F.L.R.R. 25 (Ont. Prov. Ct.).

3) Right to disclosure of assessor's report: The *CWA* provides that a child 10 or more years of age is to be provided with a copy of the assessor's report unless the effect of all or any part of the contents would be injurious to the emotional health of the child, in which case the court can withhold all or part of the report from the child: s. 29(3), *CWA*. Again, the *CFSA* will adopt the same approach but will change the age to 12 years: s. 50(4) and (5), *CFSA*.

4) Right to representation: The legislation provides the child with the unqualified right to representation or the court may decide to appoint counsel for the child to protect his interests: s. 20, *CWA/* s. 38, *CFSA*.

5) Right to appeal: The *CWA* gives the child the right to appeal, but only through a "next friend" who would then instruct the child's counsel: s. 43(1)(c), *CWA*. It appears that the *CFSA* will allow the child to appeal without the intervention of a next friend and if the child has had legal counsel in the trial proceedings or is 12 years of age or over, he may participate in the appeal as if he were a party: ss. 39(6) and 65(1)(a), *CFSA*.

(For discussion on the issue of whether a child *en ventre sa mere* can participate as a party through a next friend, see below under "Finding a Child in need of Protection: General Principles".)

Consent Orders   Upon return of the application, all parties may be in agreement as to the route to take. In this case, the court can proceed with the application of the Society, finding the child in need of protection and making a disposition reflecting the terms of the parties' consent. If, however, the order sought is that of supervision or wardship, the parties must first agree before the judge on the facts on which the order is based and the hearing is held: R.R.O. 810, s. 70 (Provincial Court Rules, Family Division). Further, the courts are reluctant simply to approve a consent arrangement, one court concluding that an order under the *CWA* cannot be made until the evidence produced satisfies the judge that the terms of the consent agreement are "in the best interests of the child" as so directed by the Act.[63] Under ss. 37(2)(1) and 51 of the *CFSA*, where the parent is consenting to a removal order, the court will need the consent of the child if he is 12 years of age or older and must specifically ask whether services have been offered by the Society to the parent and child to enable the child to remain with the parents and whether all parties have consulted legal counsel so that the court can be satisfied that they, including the child, understand the nature and consequences of the consent. If the court disagrees with the proposed consent order, then counsel should be given the opportunity to consider their position and, if necessary, the matter should be adjourned to allow counsel to prepare.[64]

Adjournments and "Show Cause" Hearings   Upon return of the application, assuming that all notice requirements are fulfilled and that there is no agreement among parties, the matter will probably be

---

[63]*Re Y.*, summarized in (1981), 12 A.C.W.S. (2d) 293 (Ont. Prov. Ct.). And see *B. v. Director of Child Welfare and C.* (1982), 29 R.F.L. (2d) 40 (P.E.I.S.C.) in which mother appealed consent order of permanent wardship, arguing that consent not freely and voluntarily given because of post-partum depression. Court dismissed application holding that evidence at trial showing mother mentally competent to offer free and voluntary consent. See also *McLeod v. Minister of Social Services for Sask.* (1979), 12 R.F.L. (2d) 1 (Sask. C.A.) (no need for child to be adjudged in need of protection in consent order to commit under s. 13 of *Family Services Act.*).

[64]*Luciano v. Hopkins* (1982), 28 R.F.L. (2d) 441 (Ont. Co. Ct.).

adjourned but for no longer than 30 days, except with the consent of all parties: s. 28(12) and (13), *CWA*/ s. 47(1), *CFSA*.[65] Given the number of cases that will be heard by the court in any one day as well as the need for further investigation and preparation by all parties and the opportunity of a pre-trial conference, the next issue to be heard will probably be the ''show cause'' hearing to determine where the child will reside in the interim. Nothing precludes a request for an adjournment of the ''show cause'' hearing since the child's placement, pending the duration of adjournments and the hearing may be crucial to the final disposition, paralleling the importance of interim custody orders in private domestic orders. Under the *CWA*, the onus of proof rests on the applicant Society ''to show cause why the child should remain or should be placed in their temporary care and custody'': s. 28(12), *CWA*. Section 28(15) of the *CWA* provides that on a ''show cause'' hearing, the court ''may receive and base its decision upon evidence that the court considers credible and trustworthy in the circumstances.'' The meaning of this section is somewhat unclear, both from the wording and the practice standpoint. It appears that some courts have been proceeding on the basis of documentary evidence, such as doctors' reports and medical records, the submissions of counsel and affidavit material filed, hearing *viva voce* evidence only in the most unusual cases.[66] Some courts have heard the submissions of counsel only. Some courts have wanted to hear one ''key witness'' *viva voce*. It also appeared that in contrast to the affidavit material that is admissible at the main hearing, the contents in this hearing need not be restricted to matters within the personal knowledge of the deponent.[67] There is no authority defining what evidence would satisfy the court under the *CWA* that the child should remain in care although it is clear that an Appellate Court would be reluctant to interfere with the judge's discretion except in extreme or unusual circumstances.[68]

Once the Society has been successful in a ''show cause'' proceeding, it has been held that the application to find the child in need of protection must be returned to court and cannot simply be withdrawn.[69] Presumably this suggests that, regardless of what the parties have agreed upon among themselves, the court has been seized of the responsibility for the child and therefore must hear some evidence so that it may either grant or dismiss the application. Nevertheless, it appears that the Society can withdraw its request for a ''show cause'' hearing as well as a ''protection'' finding without the court's sanction, the distinction presumably being that the court has made no substantive findings in the latter case.[70]

---

[65]Under s. 47(1) of the *CFSA* an extended adjournment will require not only the continued consent of all parties present at the hearing but also of the person who will be caring for the children during the adjournment. It will not be granted if the court is aware that a party who is not present at the hearing objects to the longer adjournment.

[66]*C.A.S. of Hamilton-Wentworth v. O. and O.*, unreported, March 25, 1982 (Ont. U.F.C.), *per* Steinberg J.

[67]*Cf.* s. 28(15) of the *CWA* (show cause hearing) with s. 28(5) of the *CWA* (main hearing).

[68]*Re A.M.* (1980), 16 R.F.L. (2d) 37, 2 Fam. L. Rev. 302 (*sub nom. Re M.*) (Sask. C.A.).

[69]*Re J.H.*, summarized in (1983), 5 F.L.R.R. 153 (Ont. Prov. Ct.).

[70]*Re S.P.*, summarized in (1982), 5 F.L.R.R. 96 (Ont. Prov. Ct.).

Once proclaimed, the *CFSA* will effect some significant changes to existing adjournment and show cause procedures:

1) Under the *CWA*, there is no explicit test for the court to apply in considering an appropriate placement during an adjournment and prior to an "in need of protection" finding. The Society simply has to "show cause" and the evidence is to be credible and trustworthy. On the other hand s. 47(3) of the *CFSA*, will require that, before placing the child outside the family, the judge must first find "reasonable and probable grounds to believe that there is a substantial risk to the child's health or safety . . . and . . . cannot be protected adequately" by being returned to the parent, with or without supervision. Thus the judge will be required to make a preliminary "in need of protection" finding even before subsequent investigations or the main hearing have taken place to warrant the child being removed from the family unit.

2) Unlike the *CWA*, it is clear that the court under the *CFSA* will have authority to impose conditions including supervision if the child returns home: s. 47(2)(b), *CFSA*. This will avoid the problem of the court having only two options, that of Society care or returning the child to the home with no supervisory jurisdiction attaching. This polarity of choices under the *CWA* often forces the court to err on the safe side by continuing Society care until the hearing. Included under the *CFSA* will also be the new option of placing a child with a third party, subject to appropriate conditions. This opens up the opportunity of utilizing the extended family or others in the native community or the neighbourhood instead of the anonymous and strange state homes: s. 47(2)(c), *CFSA*.

3) The introductory wording of s. 28(12) of the *CWA* is: "A court may from time to time adjourn a hearing" with the stipulation that no adjournment could be for more than 30 days. The wording implies the authorizing of more than one, even a series, of such adjournments prior to the judge making a finding. The introductory wording of s. 47(1) of the *CFSA* is: "The court shall not adjourn a hearing for more than 30 days. . . ." This may suggest that a single adjournment only will be allowable or, at least, is desirable. However, a strict interpretation in this manner would be unlikely given the practical exigencies of the courts and court proceedings. Section 48 of the *CFSA* will at least reinforce the approach of minimizing the delay since it directs a judge to fix a date or make other appropriate directions, or presumably to bring about the earliest possible resolution of the matter, if a determination has not been made within three months from the first court appearance. This section will in itself be a significant improvement over the existing law when often the scheduling incompatabilities of all the lawyers, expert witnesses and available court dates result in the tyranny of the status quo over the eventual disposition, the status quo often being a placement outside the family before any finding of neglect has been made.

4) Upon its proclamation, s. 69 of the *CFSA* will direct each Society to establish a "review team" of professional assessors for its operations. The section will allow a Society to refer the case of the child "who may be

suffering or may have suffered abuse'' to the team to review the case and recommend how to proceed. Section 69(7), *CFSA* will require that a Society who has a child in its care who ''may have suffered abuse'' shall not return the child to the care of the person who had charge of the child at the time of the possible abuse until it has referred the case to the review team and considers their recommendations. This step then may become another pre-hearing procedure in the child welfare process in abuse circumstances.

Finding Child "In Need of Protection"

A child ''in need of protection'' is defined by a long list of clauses under the legislation. However, before examining each section separately, there are some general principles that can be summarized as follows:

General Principles

1) For a child to be found ''in need of protection'' there must be a significant departure from the standard of care that one would generally expect for a child of a given age. There is a minimum parental standard for all society, and a secondary standard must be established considering the age of the parent and the community in which the parent resides. A teenage parent cannot live up to the standard expected of a middle-aged parent. Similarly, different standards apply to parents of native ancestry who reside in a small rural community in the northern part of the province than would apply to white middle class parents living in an urban centre in the south. What is an acceptable standard for the former might be unacceptable for the latter.[71]

2) For a child to be found ''in need of protection'' it is not necessary for there to be neglect on the part of a parent or person in charge, but it is necessary that the child be found ''in need of protection'' within the meaning of one of the definitions provided by the *CWA*[72] The court cannot intervene simply on the basis of a ''best interests'' concern for the child. It must decide whether the evidence is sufficient to come under one or more of the definitions set out in the *CWA* and may look at all of the circumstances to accomplish this.[73] Similarly, parents should not be deprived of caring for their child simply because, on a nice balancing of material and social advantages, other persons can provide more.[74]

3) Following from the principles under paragraph (2), a child welfare hearing is a two-step process. The court first determines that a child is ''in need of protection'', then deals with the question of disposition. While the court was first to determine if the child was ''in need of protection'' under s. 19 of the *CWA* before it could make any dispositions under s. 30, *CWA*, it had been held that the court could hear evidence dealing with both the

---

[71]See *Re E.*, [1980] 4 W.W.R. 296, 17 R.F.L. (2d) 274 (*sub nom. Re ECDM*) (Sask. Prov. Ct.); *Mooswa v. Ministry of Commn. and Social Services* (1978), 30 R.F.L. 101 (Sask. Q.B.).

[72]*Re Brown* (1975), 9 O.R. (2d) 185 (Ont. Co. Ct.).

[73]*Re Milner* (1975), 13 N.S.R. (2d) 378 (S.C.); *Dauphin v. Director of Public Welfare* (1956), 64 Man. R. 142, 5 D.L.R. (2d) 274, 117 C.C.C. 45 (C.A.).

[74]*Re Aubichon* (1970), 4 R.F.L. 39 (Sask. Q.B.).

finding and the disposition at the same time.[75] Note, however, that upon proclamation of the *CFSA*, the judge will be forbidden to consider evidence relating only to disposition before the court has determined whether or not the child is in need of protection: s. 46(2), *CFSA*.

4) A person who has "charge" of a child, a term used frequently throughout the apprehension, "show cause" and "protection" sections of both the *CWA* and the *CFSA*, is the person who has the care and control of the child at the time of apprehension. The word "charge" does not necessarily mean custody of the child, since a parent could have legal custody but delegate the care and control of the child to a third person.[76] However, it has been held that a child being cared for in hospital is still in his or her mother's charge until apprehended.[77] If the child is already a Society ward, it is uncertain whether a court will find that it has the jurisdiction to proceed to determine whether the child is "in need of protection."[78]

5) The question of the child being "in need of protection" refers to a present situation of harm or risk of harm. Where children were being cared for properly at the time of trial and the only evidence as to lack of proper care was evidence of past incidents coupled with the possibility of lack of care if future incidents of self-destruction occurred, the appellate court concluded that the trial judge erred in law in directing himself that the "possibility" of future incidents was sufficient evidence upon which to make a finding that the children required protection.[79]

6) If evidence is not called on behalf of an allegedly unfit person, and that person does not testify at the hearing, it is unnecessary to prove unfitness as of the date of the hearing but only as of the date of apprehension. To hold otherwise would be to place too heavy a burden on the resources of the state, for it would be quite impossible for the Society to keep the alleged unfit person under constant surveillance from the date of apprehension to the date of hearing.[80]

7) For the court to find a child "in need of protection", it must have had evidence before it and in the absence of evidence, the judge will be found to have exceeded his jurisdiction and any order will be set aside.[81]

8) For a child to be found "in need of protection", the child must be under 16 years of age pursuant to the definition of "child": s. 19(1)(a), *CWA*/ s. 37(1)(a), *CFSA*. However, in accordance with that definition, once a child is found to be "in need of protection" before the age of 16 years, the

[75]*St. Pierre v. Roman C.C.A.S. of Essex County* (1976), 27 R.F.L. 266 (Ont. Div. Ct.). But see *D. v. C.A.S. of Kent* (1980), 18 R.F.L. (2d) 223 (Ont. Co. Ct.) in which the court held that the needs of the child vis-a-vis the appropriate disposition must be considered only after the heavy onus of proving the child in need of protection has been met. In particular, the fact that the proposed intervention by the Society was minimal did not diminish the heavy onus.

[76]*Re K.*, unreported, July 21, 1976 (Ont. Prov. Ct. Fam. Div.), *per* Steinberg J.

[77]*Re V. (T.A.N.N.)*, unreported, March 17, 1982 (Ont. Prov. Ct. Fam. Div.), *per* Fischer, J.

[78]*Supra*, note 39.

[79]*W. v. Catholic C.A.S. of Metro. Toronto*, summarized in (1981), 4 F.L.R.R. 123 (Ont. Co. Ct.).

[80]*Supt. of Child Welfare v. Desbiens* (1978), 8 R.F.L. (2d) 86 (B.C.S.C.).

[81]*Kociuba v. C.A.S. of Halton and Chuchmach* (1971), 18 R.F.L. 286 (Ont. H.C.); *Re W.R.R. and T.A.R.* (1980), 23 B.C.L.R. 264 (Co. Ct.).

child can be subject to a wardship or supervisory order and the matter can be brought back for review until the child is 18 years of age. Note that under the *CFSA*, the child need be under the age of 16 years only upon apprehension or when the proceeding commenced to give the court jurisdiction to find the child "in need of protection": s. 43(3), *CFSA*. If a child 16 years of age has withdrawn from the care of his or her guardian, whether it be the parent or the Society, the courts, acknowledging the little that can be provided without the child's cooperation, defer to the "emancipated" state of the child.[82] Section 27(1) of the *CFSA* will recognize this inevitability by requiring the 16 and 17-year-old's consent before service is provided to him unless otherwise ordered.

A finding of "in need of protection" could arguably extend to a child *en ventre sa mere*. In one such case, the court held that a protection finding could have been made in the latter months of an alcoholic mother's pregnancy because of the possibility of fetal alcohol syndrome.[83] Obviously, to extend the definition of a "child" to include an unborn child can have profound consequences on the issue of abortion. (See Chapter 7 "Crime and the Child: Abortion".) In one decision, a Nova Scotia Family Court granted an application for an order appointing a guardian *ad litem* for an unborn child in the course of an action commenced by the father for an injunction to prevent the mother from having an abortion. The Nova Scotia Family Court held that a child *en ventre sa mere* was a disabled child in need of protection of its life, health or emotional welfare and therefore should have the right to be heard in court through a guardian *ad litem*. An appeal by the mother to quash this decision was dismissed by the Nova Scotia Supreme Court.[84] On the other hand, in the same circumstances, an Ontario High Court decision held that a "next friend" or "guardian *ad litem*" can act only for a "person" and an unborn child is not a person.[85]

Statutory Grounds

Each of the sub-sections under the *CWA* which go to make up the definition of "in need of protection" are dealt with below. The wording of the *CWA* section is footnoted with the wording of the equivalent or similar section under the *CFSA*, to take effect upon proclamation.

Section 19(1)(b)(i): Parental consent[86]

(i) a child who is brought, with the consent of a person in whose charge the child is, before a court to be dealt with under this Part,

One Provincial Court judge held that, based on the wording of this section,

---

[82] *Re S.*, unreported, July 22, 1982 (Ont. Prov. Ct. Fam. Div.), *per* Fischer J.

[83] *Re C.A.S. of Kenora and L.*, summarized in (1981), 4 F.L.R.R. 87 (Ont. Prov. Ct.).

[84] *Re H.* (1979), 38 N.S.R. (2d) 432, 106 D.L.R. (3d) 435 (*sub nom., Re Simms and H.*) (Fam. Ct.). And see *Re L.*, summarized in (1981), 4 F.L.R.R. 87 (Ont. Prov. Ct.).

[85] *Medhurst v. Medhurst* (1984), 46 O.R. (2d) 263 (H.C.). And see *Dehler v. Ottawa Civic Hospital* (1980), 25 O.R. (2d) 748 (S.C.); aff'd 29 O.R. (2d) 677 (C.A.); leave to appeal to S.C.C. refused 36 N.R. 180.

[86] *CFSA*, s. 37(2)(1): "The child's parent is unable to care for the child and the child is brought before the court with the parents' consent and, where the child is 12 years of age or older, with the child's consent, to be dealt with under this Part."

he needed nothing more than the consent of the person in whose charge the child is, to find that child "in need of protection." Another provincial court judge, in an unreported decision, came to the opposite conclusion, determining that the consent of the parent is not enough for such a finding unless that consent is coupled with facts that show the child is clearly in need of protection and that a protection order is in the best interests of the child.[87] Under the *CFSA*, the wording will specifically set out two requirements, one being the consent and the other being that the parent is unable to care for the child, thereby requiring the judge to have some evidence before him of lack of parenting capacity. In addition, the new section will require the consent of the child over 11 years of age as well, although this is subject to the umbrella s. 4 of the *CFSA* dealing with capacity.

Section 19(1)(b)(ii): Desertion of child[88] (See also ss. 47 and 48 below)

(ii) a child who is deserted by the person in whose charge the child is,

Leaving a child with a Children's Aid Society is not necessarily evidence of abandonment, desertion or that the parent was unmindful of parental duties.[89] Desertion has been interpreted as requiring a wilful omission to take charge of the child.[90] But in a 1979 Provincial Court decision, it was given a constructive interpretation such that a mother created a state of "desertion" by being in prison and unable to care for her child.[91]

Under the *CFSA*, although the word "abandon" will be substituted for "desertion" under the equivalent s. 37(2)(i), both words have been used interchangeably by judges and both dictionary meanings require intent on the part of the person who is leaving the child on his own. However, unlike the parallel section in the *CWA*, the wording of the *CFSA* will continue on, describing three different sets of circumstances:

1) Death (incorporating part of s. 19(1)(b)(iii), *CWA* discussed below);

2) Unavailability of parent without making adequate care provisions for the child (incorporating the non-intentional circumstances of s. 48, *CWA* discussed below); and

3) Refusal or inability to accept return of child from "residential placement" (definition: s.3(1), para. 25, *CFSA*). (No parallel section in *CWA*.)

If one adopts the dictionary meaning of "to abandon", that is, to give up to another's control; give up possession; forsake (withdraw one's help or

---

[87]See respectively *Re Golka* (1973), 13 R.F.L. 167 (Ont. Prov. Ct.) and *Re Jennifer M.*, unreported, October 7, 1974 (Ont. Prov. Ct. Fam. Div.), *per* Thomson J., as cited in Hartrick and Lazor, *The Child Welfare Act Annotated* (Toronto: Carswell Co. Ltd., 1983), p. 28.

[88]*CFSA*, s. 37(2)(i): "The child has been abandoned, the child's parent has died or is unavailable to exercise his or her custodial rights over the child and has not made adequate provisions for the child's care and custody, or the child is in a residential placement and the parent refuses or is unable or unwilling to resume the child's care and custody."

[89]*Re Pearson*, [1973] 4 W.W.R. 274, 10 R.F.L. 234 (B.C.S.C.).

[90]*Re Davis* (1909), 18 O.L.R. 384 (H.C.).

[91]*Re C.A.S. of Kingston and H. and G.* (1979), 24 O.R. (2d) 146 (Ont. Prov. Ct.).

companionship from) then it appears that someone can abandon a child whether or not he arranged "adequate care provisions." However, by including the "unavailability" category which arguably is a neutral term incorporating wilful as well as nonwilful circumstances, it would appear by implication that abandonment amounts to the wilful leaving of the child without having made adequate care provisions.

Section 19(1)(b)(iii): Loss of parent or parenting[92]

> (iii) a child where the person, in whose charge the child is, cannot for any reason care properly for the child, or where that person has died and there is no suitable person to care for the child,

If a court is persuaded that a child should have been removed at the time of apprehension, the court can apply the present tense of the words "cannot for any reason care properly" to conclude, based on further evidence since the apprehension, that the child should be found in need of protection.[93] This would be true of the parallel *CFSA* provisions, all of which will either use a present tense relating to the state of the child and/or parental conduct or will use specific "future risk" sections based on past harm.

Low parental intelligence should not be taken as determinative in itself of a child's need of protection under this section. The question should be one of deciding whether, in light of their individual capabilities, the parents are able to meet their parental responsibilities. Even if the answer to that question is no, then the court should decide whether, given the proper assistance and intervention, the parents can be provided with the tools necessary to care adequately for their child.[94]

By the same token a state of poverty should not be the basis in itself for removing a child. Some American cases have turned down protection applications when it appears that the basis is poverty *per se* especially when there is no evidence that the parent was offered any assistance by the social agency to remedy the condition. In the absence of evidence indicating that "reasonable and appropriate efforts" were taken by the social agency to remedy the conditions leading to foster care, parents' rights cannot be terminated. Where there is poverty such that the parents are reduced to the "voluntary entrustment" of their child to a social agency, that in itself is not sufficient to terminate parental rights.[95] Consider in this light the Ontario Provincial Court case in which the judge would not return the children unless the father stopped taking welfare.[96]

The principle as enunciated by the American cases above will be implicit under the *CFSA*, once that act is proclaimed, since the state may not intervene

---

[92] *CFSA*, s. 37(2)(i), *supra*, note 88. See also ss. 37(2)(e), (f), (h) and (l), of the *CFSA*.

[93] *Re MacKinnon* (1975), 20 R.F.L. 57 (Ont. Prov. Ct.).

[94] *C.A.S. of Kingston v. Reeves* (1975), 23 R.F.L. 391 (Ont. Prov. Ct.); *Re Miller* (1980), 8 Sask. R. 166 (U.F.C.) (conditions of dirt and squalor with no hope of improvement).

[95] *Weaver v. Roanoake Department of Human Resource*, summarized in (1980), 6 Fam. L. Rep. 2474 (Virg. Sup. Ct.) and see *Richardson v. Henry County Department of Social Services* summarized in (1982), 8 Fam. L. Rep. 2563 (Va. Sup. Ct.).

[96] *Re D*, unreported, Nov. 25, 1981 (Ont. Prov. Ct.). Leave to appeal to C.A. from Div. Ct. (Sept. 10/84) refused, Nov. 26/84.

thereunder on the sole basis of parental status. There must be evidence that the parent's conduct has caused the physical or sexual harm or that the parent has refused or is unavailable or unable to consent to treatment or services that might remedy or alleviate the harmful situation. If the family's state of poverty was resulting in the impairment of a child's healthy development, then without the provision of supportive services, it could not be said that the parent was refusing same. Note also s. 53(2) and (3) of the *CFSA* which will require a judge to ask after and pursue services which can keep the child in the home before he can make any kind of removal order.

The clause at the end of s. 19(1)(b)(iii) of the *CWA* (which presumably modifies both the "dead parent" and "lack of care" clauses preceding it) suggests a notion of exhausting the possibility of the extended family before relying upon this sub-section as a basis for intervention. Therefore, where a parent could not care for the child, there needed to be evidence before the court as to whether or not there was a suitable person to care for the person while the mother is absent by reason of disability or death.[97] This judicial principle has been codified in the parallel section under the *CFSA* where evidence will be required of inadequate provision for the child's care and custody before determining that the parent is unavailable to exercise custodial rights over the child. Note, however, that the wording is "unavailability" and not "incapacity." It is arguable that the codification of the extended family approach may apply only in circumstances more restrictive than those when the parents "for any reason" cannot care for the child. For example, "unavailable" may be interpreted to imply a temporary state of affairs but not permanent circumstances such as mental incapacity. Once proclaimed, the *CFSA* will make this umbrella "lack of parenting" clause in itself no longer necessary since s. 37(2) of the *CFSA* will categorize neglect situations by enumerating all of the different types of detrimental effects which can possibly be suffered by children, *e.g.*, physical, sexual, emotional, and then modifies each effect with an all encompassing, causative "lack of parenting" clause such as "[the parent] does not [care properly] or refuses or is unavailable or unable to [care properly]." This change should presumably focus the court's assessment on the child's well-being rather than on the broad, undefinable, necessarily subjective assessment of "proper care" by the parent. In addition, it will make state intervention permissible only if parental conduct is causing the harm or is preventing or not contributing to the amelioration of the harm being suffered by the child. This change might also be said to correspond with the deletion by the new legislation of the existing categories of "unfit or improper place" (ss. (iv)) or "unfit or improper person" (ss. (v) (see below)).

Section 19(1)(b)(iv): Unfit or improper place[98]

(iv) a child who is living in an unfit or improper place,

In an American case, evidence of filth in the living conditions affecting the physical condition of the child resulted in a removal order. The mother's

---

[97]*Re C.A.S. of Kingston and H. and G., supra*, note 91.
[98]There is no equivalent section under the *CFSA*.

"immoral" conduct as a prostitute was considered a valid consideration but immoral conduct alone was insufficient for a finding in the absence of evidence of demonstrable effect on the child.[99]

There is no comparable section in the *CFSA* which isolates the place of child-rearing as a factor in itself for state intervention. If the child were at risk or had suffered physical or sexual harm because of the nature of the environment, then intervention will be warranted under s. 37(2)(a), (b), (c) and (d) of the *CFSA*. If the result of the environment was something less than physical or sexual harm or the risk of either, then it appears that state intervention will require evidence of the provision of some remedial steps or services which were refused by the parents, or to which they were unable or unavailable to consent.

Section 19(1)(b)(v): Unfit or improper person[100]

(v) a child found associating with an unfit or improper person,

One Ontario case held that if a mother herself is determined to be "a child in need of protection", she must necessarily be unable or unfit to care properly for her child.[101] In another Ontario decision, the court held that the present status of being a single parent, the previous status as a Crown ward and the fact of the pregnancy of the parent at the age of 15 years, did not in isolation warrant a finding of "in need of protection."[102] Again, the *CFSA* will include no comparable section since the grounds are based on the child suffering specific harm rather than a subjective (and sometimes biased) assessment by a judge of what makes up an unfit or improper person.

Section 19(1)(b)(vi): Begging[103]

(vi) a child found begging or receiving charity in a public place,

Upon proclamation of the *CFSA*, the act of seeking charity will not in itself be a factor for state intervention. However, such an act, if sanctioned by the parent, may constitute a form of abandonment. If done without the knowledge of the parent and without some evidence of physical, sexual or emotional harm, begging by itself would not appear to be grounds for state intervention.

Section 19(1)(b)(vii): Inability to control child

(vii) a child where the person in whose charge the child is is unable to control the child,

It has been held that the concept of "control" should be broadly interpreted. The phrase applies not only to the physical well-being of the child, but also to the ability to cause the child to obtain a proper education.[104] The broad phrase "unable to control" will be deleted under the *CFSA* and will be replaced by

---

[99]*Re M.B.*, summarized in (1980), 6 Fam. L.Rep. 2415 (S. Dak. Sup. Ct.).

[100]No equivalent section under *CFSA*.

[101]*Re Latta and Latta* (1973), 15 R.F.L. 94 (N.S. Prov. Ct.).

[102]*Re T.L.M.*, unreported, December 3, 1976 (Ont. Prov. Ct. Fam. Div.).

[103]No equivalent section under *CFSA*.

[104]*Re S. (a minor)*, [1977] 3 W.L.R. 575 (C.A.); *Re Jepson and Maw* (an infant) (1960), 32 W.W.R. 93 (B.C.S.C.).

specific manifestations such as self-destructive or aggressive behaviour, anxiety, depression or severe withdrawal, or injury to others or other people's property. In order to obtain a finding, these incidents must be coupled with a parent who does not provide or refuses or is unavailable or unable to consent to services or treatment required to remedy or alleviate the situation or harm.[105]

Section 19(1)(b)(viii): Habitual absence from school[106]

> (viii) a child who without sufficient cause is habitually absent from home or school,

Due to the fact that provincial education legislation provides quasi-criminal proceedings and remedies, this section is rarely invoked for this purpose alone and will be removed altogether under the *CFSA* as a basis for a finding of in need of protection.

Section 19(1)(b)(ix): Neglect/refusal of necessary medical treatment[107]

> (ix) a child where the person in whose charge the child is neglects or refuses to provide or obtain proper medical, surgical or other recognized remedial care or treatment necessary for the child's health or well-being, or refuses to permit such care or treatment to be supplied to the child when it is recommended by a legally qualified medical practitioner, or otherwise fails to protect the child adequately,

Although the courts do not recognize a child *en ventre sa mere* to be a person for the purposes of representation by a next friend or guardian *ad litem,* [108] it has been held that an unborn child is entitled to state protection when the mother refuses to have a blood transfusion based on her religious beliefs. In this American case, it was held that an appropriate order will be made to ensure that a doctor will have the legal right to administer a transfusion against the woman's will in the event that he determines it to be necessary to save the woman's life or the life of the child.[109]

Some would argue that the court's position on intervention when a child is *en ventre sa mere* is a contradiction to the law of abortion. The state can interfere to ensure the child's live birth in one case but not in the other. Others might argue that the state has a different legal mechanism to "interfere" in the case of abortion, that is, the *Criminal Code*. In other words, once the mother has decided to bear the child, the child protection provisions then become operative. Still others would argue that the decision to bear the child is a private decision for the woman alone to make without state interference.

---

[105]See *e.g. Re C.; Minister of Social Services v. C.* (1981), 49 N.S.R. (2d) 210, 96 A.P.R. 210 (Prov. Ct.).

[106]No equivalent section under *CFSA*.

[107]*CFSA*, s. 37(2)(e): "The child requires medical treatment to cure, prevent or alleviate physical harm or suffering and the child's parent or the person having charge of the child does not provide, or refuses or is unavailable or unable to consent to, the treatment."

[108]*Medhurst v. Medhurst,* (1984) 46 O.R. (2d) 263 (H.C.). But see *Re H,* (1979), 38 N.S.R. (2d) 432, 106 D.L.R. (3d) 435 (*sub nom. Re Simms and H.*) (Fam. Ct.).

[109]*Raleigh-Fitkin-Paul Morgan Memorial Hospital v. Anderson* (1964), 201 A. 2d 537 (N.J.S.C.) and see *Re C.A.S. of Kenora and L,* summarized in (1981), 4 F.L.R.R. 87 (Ont. Prov. Ct.); *Forsyth v. Children's Aid Society of Kingston,* [1963] 1 O.R. 49 (H.C.).

In a highly publicized British Columbia case, parents of a seven-year-old boy refused to give their consent to life-saving medical procedures because they wished to see their severely-retarded boy "die in peace." The Provincial Court did not find the child in need of protection, reasoning that the surgery constituted "extraordinary surgical intervention" as distinguished from "necessary medical attention." The Appellate Court overruled this decision and found the child in need of protection, concluding that it was not within the court's prerogative, or that of any parent to decide that the quality of a person's life was so low that it did not deserve continuance. The decision went on to state that to conclude otherwise might mean that one is to regard the life of a handicapped child as not only less valuable than the life of a normal child, but so much less valuable that it is not worth preserving.[110]

Finally, it has been held that freedom of "conscience and religion" guaranteed by s. 2 of the *Charter of Rights* is not in conflict with the court's responsibility to find the child in need of protection if the child's parents refuse to consent to a blood transfusion on religious grounds.[111]

The comparable section under the *CFSA* will restrict state intervention to circumstances in which the child "requires medical treatment to cure, prevent or alleviate physical harm or suffering." This wording appears to be more specific and restrictive than that of the *CWA* which sanctions intervention when the child is not being provided with "proper" medical treatment "necessary for the child's health and well-being". In addition, the word "physical", if taken to modify both "harm" and "suffering" under the *CFSA* section, will exlcude instances of emotional ill health covered by the words "health and well-being" under the *CWA* so that one must resort to s. 37(2)(f), (g) and (h) under the new legislation (discussed below) which deals specifically with the non-physical ill health of the child.

Section 19(1)(b)(x): Emotional rejection or deprivation of affection[112] (See s. 47 below)

> (x) a child whose emotional or mental development is endangered because of the emotional rejection or deprivation of affection by the person in whose charge the child is,

If there existed a lack of recognition of a child's emotional needs on the part of the parents, this may have been sufficient to find the child in need of protection even when there was no question that the child's physical needs were

---

[110]*Supt. of Family and Child Services and Dawson*, summarized in (1983), 19 A.C.W.S. (2d) 99 (B.C.S.C.).

[111]*Re D.* (1982), 22 Alta. L.R. (2d) 228, 30 R.F.L. (2d) 277 (Alta. Prov. Ct.). See also *Re Wintersgill and Ministry of Social Services* (1981), 131 D.L.R. (3d) 184, 25 R.F.L. (2d) 395 (*sub nom. Re J.W.*) (Sask. U.F.C.) in which a blood transfusion was ordered despite evidence of "alternative treatments" because they weren't "available practically."

[112]There will be no section under the *CFSA* which absolutely parallels this section. Section 37(2)(f) and (h) of the *CFSA* will both deal with mental emotional and developmental conditions which must be remedied, but they are not defined as being caused by the rejection of the parents, but simply state that there is a protection situation if the parents do not provide or consent to necessary services or treatment to remedy the harm.

being taken care of satisfactorily. Further, this section could be construed as preventative in nature, permitting the court to intervene before physical harm due to emotional rejection has occurred.[113] Nevertheless the application of this section is to be based on an existing situation and where a child has never been in the custody of his parent, it cannot be said that the child has been endangered because of their emotional rejection.[114]

Upon its proclamation, the *CFSA* will introduce three very specific sections to deal with non-physical ill health of children which can incorporate this section of the *CWA* as well as s. 19(1)(b)(ix) of the *CWA*. (The latter section deals with parents withholding their consent to treatment, the former with parents being the cause of ill health.) As has been pointed out above, the *CFSA* sections break down in terms of the type of ill health suffered rather than the type of parental conduct. For a protection finding under the *CFSA*, not only must the specific ill health be proved but also that the parents are not providing or are unavailable or unable to consent to appropriate services or treatment. The new s. 37(2)(f) will introduce more specific terminology than the wording in either of the two *CWA* sections which may lead judges to require clinical evidence as to (1) the emotional harm suffered through anxiety, depression, withdrawal or self-destructive or aggressive behaviour; (2) definition of terms, especially "withdrawal" and "aggressive behaviour" compared to other children; (3) demonstration that any of these symptoms are "severe" compared to other children; and (4) services or treatment which will "remedy or alleviate the harm", a phrase that could see professional pitted against professional. Note that s. 37(2)(g) of the *CFSA* contemplates the prevention of the type of harm defined under s. 37(2)(f) of the *CFSA*.

The new s. 37(2)(h) will partially revert to the basic terms of the *CWA's* s. 19(1)(b)(x), that is, "*mental* [or] *emotional* . . . condition that if not remedied could seriously impair the child's *development*," while also adding a third category: "developmental condition." The wording is forward-looking but can also cover existing conditions of impaired development, evidence of which will necessarily be of a professional, clinical nature.

Section 19(1)(b)(xi): Parental conduct endangering life/health/morals[115] (See also s. 47, below)

---

[113]*Dauphin v. Director of Public Welfare* (1956), 64 Man. R. 142, 5 D.L.R. (2d) 274, 117 C.C.C. 45 (C.A.); *Re T.H. and C.C.A.S. of Metro. Toronto* (1981), 35 O.R. (2d) 151 (Prov. Ct.). But see *Minister of Social Services v. C.* (1982), 26 R.F.L. (2d) 440 (Sask. Q.B.) where "negative and inappropriate" parenting "threatening child's emotional well-being" not considered sufficient for a protection finding since the only manifestation was the bad behaviour of the boy.

[114]*Re Golka, supra*, note 87.

[115]*CFSA*, s. 37(2)(a): "the child has suffered physical harm, inflicted by the person having charge of the child or caused by that person's failure to care and provide for or supervise and protect the child adequately." See also s. 37(2)(b) of the *CFSA*: risk of suffering physical harm described under s. 37(2)(a); *CFSA*, s. 37(2)(c): "The child has been sexually molested or sexually exploited, by the person having charge of the child or by another person where the person having charge of the child knows or should know of the possibility of sexual molestation or sexual exploitation and fails to protect the child"; see s. 37(2)(d) of the *CFSA*, which covers the risk that the child may be sexually molested or sexually exploited as described in s. 37(2)(c) of the *CFSA*. See also s. 75 of the *CFSA* which parallels s. 47 of the *CWA*, discussed in the text (under "infliction of abuse").

(xi) a child whose life, health or morals may be endangered by the conduct of the person in whose charge the child is,

While the wording of this section can include present or future conduct, its application must be based on evidence as to present conduct that indicates a likelihood of future incidents and not merely a possibility.[116] Some case examples are as follows: In an American case it was held that when a mother fails to keep a child away from a physically abusing father, the child may be found in need of protection with possible suspension of the mother's parental rights.[117] In an Alberta case it was held that children who are involved in a "cult" and thereby estranged from parents are persons whose life, health or morals may be endangered and they are thereby subject to a finding of "in need of protection."[118] *Dicta* in an Ontario case noted that a mother's excessive consumption of alcohol during pregnancy and the mother's neglect or refusal to obtain proper remedial care or treatment while pregnant when so recommended by a physician would subject that child to a finding under this section *en ventre sa mere* because of the chance of fetal alcohol syndrome at birth.[119]

The future-looking aspect of the *CWA* will be incorporated into the *CFSA* by s. 37(2)(b) and (d) which are "future risk" sections related to physical and sexual harm. Past harmful conduct could still be used to show the potential for future harm. In addition, the separate s. 37(2)(a) and (c) *CFSA*, will permit a protection finding based on past harmful conduct alone which incorporates s. 47 of the *CWA* (infliction of abuse), discussed below. Note that the parental conduct phrases in these particular sections relate only to whether they caused or permitted the past harm. Present or future willingness by parents to remedy the situation, perhaps through counselling, will apparently be irrelevant to a judge's finding. The new legislation will also eliminate any reference to endangered morals, preferring to categorize all non-physical harm in clinical rather than ethical terms. It will also remove any potential for state intervention on the basis of what the judge finds to be immoral parental conduct.

Section 47: Infliction of abuse[120]

---

[116]*W. v. C.A.S. of Metro. Toronto*, summarized in (1981), 4 F.L.R.R. 123 (Ont. Co. Ct.); *Supt. of Family and Child Services v. M. (B.)* (1982), 37 B.C.L.R. 32, 4 W.W.R. 272, 135 D.L.R. (3d) 330, 28 R.F.L. (2d) 278 (S.C.) (child born with drug addiction; court has jurisdiction to anticipate deprivation).

[117]*Re Dauge*, summarized in (1982), 9 Fam. L. Rep. 2165 (Kansas C.A.).

[118]*Re M. (L. and K.)* (1979), 6 R.F.L. (2d) 297 (Alta. Juv. Ct.).

[119]*Re C.A.S. of Kenora and L.*, summarized in (1981), 4 F.L.R.R. 87 (Ont. Prov. Ct.).

[120]*CFSA*, s. 75(1):

In this section, "abuse" means a state or condition of being physically harmed, sexually molested or sexually exploited.

(2): No person having charge of a child shall

(a) inflict abuse on the child: or

(b) by failing to care and provide for or supervise and protect the child adequately,

(i) permit the child to suffer abuse, or

(ii) permit the child to suffer from a mental, emotional or developmental condition that, if not remedied, could seriously impair the child's development.

s. 47(1) For the purposes of this section and ss. 49, 50, 51 and 52, [CWA], "abuse" means a condition of,

    (a) physical harm;

    (b) malnutrition or mental ill health of a degree that if not immediately remedied could seriously impair growth and development or result in permanent injury or death; or

    (c) sexual molestation.[121]

(2) No person having the care, custody, control or charge of a child shall abandon or desert the child or inflict abuse upon the child or permit the child to suffer abuse.

(3) A court may, in connection with any case arising under subsection (2), hold a hearing in respect of any child concerned and may proceed as though the child had been brought before the court as a child apparently in need of protection.

This section and its parallel under the *CFSA* create "infliction of abuse" as an offence under the Act, punishable on conviction to a fine of up to $2,000 or imprisonment of up to two years, or both: s. 94(2), *CWA*/ s. 81(2), *CFSA*. Although outside the formal definition of "in need of protection," this section describes circumstances, the existence of which gives the court jurisdiction to proceed "as though" the child were the subject of protection proceedings: s. 47(3), *CWA*/ s. 75(7), *CFSA*. "Abuse" has its own definition within the section which also applies to the subsequent reporting sections including the Child Abuse Register. (Note that the *CFSA* definition will be more specific than that of the *CWA*.) One Provincial Court judge, in discussing the relationship of this section with that of s. 19(1)(b) of the *CWA* (meaning of "child in need of protection") stated the following:

> . . . the wording . . . of s. 47 relates to the wording found in parts of both s. 1(1)(b) [definition of "best interests"] and s. 19(1)(b) [definition of "in need of protection"] . . .
>
> Whether or not a consideration of "abuse" constitutes a matter separate and apart from the investigation conducted in protection proceedings, it is clear that the act of "abuse" often forms the basis of an apprehension of a child, a protection application hearing, a consideration of that child's "best interests" and an order under s. 30 [supervisory or wardship orders].
>
> Therefore, for the purposes of consistency it makes sense to adopt a

---

CFSA, s. 77(1):

In this section, "to suffer abuse", when used in reference to a child, means to be in need of protection within the meaning of clause 37(2)(a) [physical harm inflicted], (c) [sexual harm inflicted], (e) [necessary medical treatment not provided], (f) [suffered emotional harm with no provision of necessary services or treatment] or (h) [no treatment for a mental, emotional or developmental condition].

[121]See *e.g. Re S.* (1980), 15 R.F.L. (2d) 167 (Alta. Prov. Ct.) in which the court attempted to distinguish between the physical touching and contact between adult and child which is a necessary part of communication of affection and concern and physical contact as a means of sexual arousal and satisfaction to the adult.

definition of ''abuse'' in s. 47 when that issue arises in a protection application, either before an order is made under s. 30 or upon subsequent status review applications.[122]

The decision goes on to delineate the type of evidence required. There must be tangible evidence of damage suffered by the child if physical abuse is alleged; proof of intention is not a prerequisite and proof of negligence will support a finding.

Section 48(1), (2) and (3): Leaving the child[123]

s. 48(1) No person having the care, custody, control or charge of a child shall leave the child without making reasonable provision, in the circumstances, for the supervision, care or safety of the child.

(2) A court may, in connection with any case arising under subsection (1) hold a hearing in respect of any child concerned and may proceed as though the child had been brought before the court as a child apparently in need of protection.

(3) Where a person is charged with contravening subsection (1), the onus of establishing that reasonable provision was made in the circumstances for the supervision, care or safety of the child where the child is under the age of ten years rests with the person charged.

Like the previous abuse section, this section and its parallel under the *CFSA* may be proceeded with as though the child were the subject of protection proceedings: s. 48(2), *CWA*/ s. 75(7), *CFSA*. Also, under both Acts, the offence is punishable on conviction to a fine of up to $1,000 or one year imprisonment, or both: s. 94(3), *CWA*/[124] s. 81(1)(f), *CFSA*. Under the *CWA*, for any subsequent offence, the fine rises to $2,000 and imprisonment of up to two years while the *CFSA* will delete any reference to subsequent offences.

Section 54: Child in public place

s. 54(1) Subject to subsection 53(2), no person under sixteen years of age shall engage in any trade or occupation in a place to which the public has access between the hours of 9 o'clock in the afternoon and 6 o'clock in the morning of the following day.

(2) No person under sixteen years of age shall loiter in any place to

---

[122]*Re S.* (1979), 10 R.F.L. (2d) 341, at 349–50 (Ont. Prov. Ct.).
[123]*CFSA*, s. 75(3):

No person having charge of a child less than 16 years of age shall leave the child without making provision for his or her supervision and care that is reasonable in the circumstances.

CFSA, s. 75(4):

Where a person is charged with contravening sub-section (3) and the child is less than 10 years of age, the onus of establishing that the person made provision for the child's supervision and care that was reasonable in the circumstances rests with the person.

[124]For a case under this section see *R. v. S. (B.A.)*, summarized in [1982] W.D.F.L. 825 (Ont. Prov. Ct.) in which the mother was convicted and given three months imprisonment. She had left her four-year old child unsupervised all night and the latter drowned while playing by the water.

which the public has access between the hours of 10 o'clock in the afternoon and 6 o'clock in the morning of the following day or be in any place of public resort or entertainment during such hours unless accompanied by the person's parent or an adult appointed by the parent or in the case of a child in the lawful care or custody of a society, an adult appointed by the society to accompany that person.

(3) A person found contravening any provision of this section may be warned by a police officer, and, if the warning is not regarded or if, after the warning, the person is again found contravening any provision of this section, the person may be taken by the police officer to the person's home or to a place of safety and where the person is taken to a place of safety, the person shall be brought before a court as if the person had been apprehended pursuant to section 21 or 22. R.S.O. 1980, c. 66, s. 54.

Again, this section may be proceeded under as a court application to find the child in need of protection if the police warning is ignored or if the act is repeated and the child is taken to a place of safety. Section s. 75(5) of the *CFSA*, while excluding any reference to "a trade or occupation", will include circumstances similar to the remaining subsections in which the authorities may seek to find a child in need of protection (although the hours will change):

s. 75(5) No person having charge of a child less than sixteen years of age shall permit the child to,
>   (a) loiter in a public place; or
>   (b) be in a place of public entertainment, unless accompanied by the person or by an individual eighteen years of age or older who is appointed by the person,
between the hours of midnight and 6 a.m.

(6) Where a child who is actually or apparently less than sixteen years of age is in a place to which the public has access, unaccompanied by a responsible adult, between the hours of midnight and 6 a.m., a peace officer may apprehend the child without a warrant and proceed as if the child had been apprehended under subsection 40 (10) (child under twelve).

(7) The court may, in connection with a case arising under subsection (2), (3) or (5), proceed under this Part as if an application had been made under subsection 40 (1) (child protection proceeding) in respect of the child.

Section 37(2)(j & k) of the *CFSA*: Child under 12 years committing criminal act

s. 37(2) A child is in need of protection where,

. . .

>   (j) the child is less than twelve years old and has killed or seriously injured another person or caused serious damage to another person's property, services or treatment are necessary to prevent a recurrence and the child's parent or the person having charge of the child does not provide, or refuses or is unavailable or unable to consent to, those services or treatment,

(k) the child is less than twelve years old and has on more than one occasion injured another person or caused loss or damage to another person's property, with the encouragement of the person having charge of the child or because of that person's failure or inability to supervise the child adequately;

The above two "in need of protection" classifications do not exist under the *CWA* but will be necessarily included under the *CFSA* in conjunction with the changes to the law of juvenile crime under the new *Young Offenders Act* which absolves persons under 12 years from criminal responsibility for their acts. Note however that the circumstances under which these sections can be invoked are narrow, presumably with the intention of triggering state interference only in the instance of parental inadequacy or inaction. The act itself must be an injury to a person or his property; once is enough in serious circumstances while more than once is necessary for less serious circumstances. In the more serious circumstances, one must presumably show a causative link between the "services or treatment" to be proposed by the state and the likelihood of a reoccurrence *and* the custodial parent not providing or refusing "or is unavailable or unable to consent to" such services. In the less serious circumstances the Legislature did not include the same "services or treatment" provisos but it did narrow the circumstances to those in which the custodial parent's action or inaction contributed to the commission of the act itself.

Evidence

It is the evidentiary rules (or lack thereof) of a child welfare proceeding which so distinguishes it from other judicial proceedings. This distinction reflects society's fear that the strict application of evidentiary rules ("hiding behind technicalities") may interfere with the presentation of all information relevant to a child's welfare. As one judge stated:

> Since the immediate health and/or life of a child may hang in the balance, the ordinary rules of evidence as to admissibility should be modified to reflect the gravity of the situation consistent with as fair a hearing as is possible. . . . [In considering] the balance of probabilities, if the balance does not tip either way, then the resulting doubt should be determined in favour of the safety of the child.[125]

---

[125]*Re S., supra*, note 122 at p. 350. But see *Re S.A.H. and A.E.R.A.H.; Supt. of Family and Child Service for B.C. v. A.H.* (1982), 30 R.F.L. (2d) 23 (B.C. Co. Ct.) (statements made by children out of court were inadmissible as hearsay); *Re Application by Director of Child Welfare; Re C.L.* (1982), 30 R.F.L. (2d) 416 (Alta. Fam. Ct.) (hearsay evidence to prove main issue at trial not to be used except in extreme cases where other evidence unavailable); *Re K.* (1982), 36 B.C.L.R. 269, 133 D.L.R. (3d) 509 (S.C.) (11-year-old girl alleging rape against father; Society not wanting her to testify in order to gain "protection finding"; appellate court confirmed the judge's decision to require the testimony considering girl's age, competence to testify, likelihood of lasting damage and whether other available source of evidence). See also *E.C. v. C.C.A.S. of Metro Toronto* (1982), 37 O.R. (2d) 82 (Co. Ct.) (transcript of protection hearing of another sibling found admissible as evidence of parental past conduct under s. 28(4) for present hearing; *Re M.R.* (1979), 14 R.F.L. (2d) 289 (Ont. Prov. Ct.) (C.A.S. records compellable and admissible when used by Society to determine parenting ability); *Re C.A.S. (Belleville) and M.* (1980), 28 O.R. (2d) 795 (Prov. Ct.) (where a Society shows, on balance of probability, possibility of abuse, school records admissible); *Re Clarke Institute of Psychiatry and C.C.A.S. of Metro Toronto* (1981), 31 O.R. (2d) 486, 119 D.L.R. (3d) 247, 20 C.P.C. 46 (H.C.) (hearing under *Mental Health Act* to

The effect of this approach in many ways is to turn a child welfare proceeding into an inquisitorial forum where the primary consideration of the court is the plan proposed for the care of the child.[126] Accordingly, an exhaustive search of alternative placements should be undertaken by the counsel representing the parent in an attempt to put before the court a plan that enables a family to maintain its control while at the same time safeguarding the needs and interests of the child. If the court is to err on the side of the child's safety and welfare, this places the rights and benefits stemming from the parent-child relationship as a secondary consideration. Technical arguments will be of little assistance in a child welfare proceeding when they are balanced against the needs of the child. The best "defence" to an application by the state is the development and preparation of a plan of "rehabilitation" that is as effective as the state's and which plan will not compromise the child's welfare, but permit the parents to maintain direct involvement with their child. (For further discussion, see below under "Best Interests: Possible Dispositions".) Although the *CFSA*, under s. 46(2), once proclaimed, will specifically codify the principle that disposition evidence is not to be heard until after the court makes the protection finding, it is probably a safe prediction that the dynamic described above will continue under the new Act, especially since this principle of the order of evidence has always been in existence under the common law.

Having stated the above, the discussion will now focus on various sections of the legislation which have implications for evidence produced at a protection hearing:

> 1) The court, *on its own initiative*, may summon any person to attend before the court and compel that person to give evidence and produce such records, writings, documents and things considered necessary: s. 28(2), *CWA*/ s. 45, *CFSA*. That is, the court on its own initiative can effectively "descend into the arena" although, in at least one case, the court has indicated that any practice by the court to call a witness on its own initiative, or to enquire why a witness is not called, should be extremely restricted.[127] As well, it has been held that even if the witness is there through the court's own initiative, this does not exclude the application of Ontario's *Evidence Act*. As such, if the court were to require the introduction of medical reports, it would have to be in accordance with the statutory conditions set out in the *Evidence Act*.[128]
>
> 2) Under s. 28(3), *CWA*, the court can hear any person with any evidence relevant to the welfare of the child. Presumably then, a person who appears in court and purports to have relevant information could be heard in the discretion of the court although neither the court nor any of the parties had

---

obtain psychiatric records on mother not required in order to gain their production under s. 50 of the *CWA*).

[126]But see *Luciano v. Hopkins* (1982), 28 R.F.L. (2d) 441 (Ont. Co. Ct.) where it was determined that the trial judge "descended into the arena" unduly and the Appellate Court sent it back for re-trial.

[127]*Ibid.*

[128]*Re Brady*, [1970] 2 O.R. 262 (Co. Ct.).

called him as witness. The wording also seems to suggest that the court could rely on this section to override any evidentiary technicality which is applicable in any other type of litigation in order to guarantee that it hears all information concerning the child. One case interpreted the words "may hear any person" to suggest that the court has the power not only to hear the person but upon their appearance with evidence relevant to the child, to consider them to be a party to the proceeding.[129] The *CFSA* will contain no parallel provision although it appears that s. 45 of that Act will be sufficient authority to hear any person or evidence that the court considers relevant. In addition, the Rules of the Provincial Court enable the court to give party status to a witness on its own initiative.[130]

3) If any restrictions remain upon the court's ability to gather information, s. 28(4) of the *CWA* (and the near identical s. 46(1) of the *CFSA*) acts as a catch-all clause:

28–(4) Notwithstanding any privilege or protection afforded under the *Evidence Act*, before making a decision that has the effect of placing a child in or returning a child to the care or custody of any person other than a society, the court may consider the past conduct of that person towards any child who is or has at any time been in the person's care, and any statement or report, whether oral or written, including any transcript, exhibit or finding in a prior proceeding, whether civil or criminal that the court considers relevant to such consideration and upon such proof as the court may require, is admissible in evidence.

Given that this section appears to override the evidentiary rules of "best evidence", hearsay, and similar fact, a number of courts were reluctant to interpret it as broadly as the wording suggests, noting that the exemption provided by this section can only apply when the court is considering a decision that has the effect of placing a child in or returning a child to the care of a person other than a Society.[131] In another decision, a judge attempted to read some restrictions into the section by concluding that the phrase "and any statement or report whether oral or written" must be taken to refer generally to written material such as medical reports or the reports of social workers. Otherwise, letters of friends, neighbours and relatives would open the door to having a child protection case tried by way of hearsay, personal letters and even gossip.[132] Further, the phrase "in the person's care" has been strictly interpreted so that the conduct of the respondents

---

[129]*Re E.W.Z.* (1975), 23 R.F.L. 82 (Ont. Prov. Ct.).

[130]O. Reg. 810/80 (Prov. Ct. Rules), s. 10:

s. 10 The court may order that any person whose presence as a party is necessary to determine the matters in issue shall be added as a party.

[131]*C.A.S. of Kawartha-Haliburton v. Deborah H.*, summarized in (1980), 3 F.L.R.R. 27 (Ont. Prov. Ct.); *C.A.S. of Metro. Toronto v. C.* (1981), 21 R.F.L. (2d) 426 (Ont. Prov. Ct.).

[132]*Re B.*, unreported, July 14, 1982 (Ont. Prov. Ct. Fam. Div.), *per* Karswick J.

towards a child to whom they had access but not custody was not admissible.[133] These decisions of courts of first instance, likely in response to the "radical legislative encouragement upon the law of evidence"[134] were effectively overruled in an Appellate County Court decision.[135] In that decision, the court concluded that the section is not limited to a decision, the effect of which is to place a child in or return a child to the care or custody of any person other than a Society, for to import that restriction into the sub-section would inhibit the court's ability to consider fully the past conduct of the mother, except when it is about to decide to return the child to her custody. This effect would undermine the very intention of the Legislature to allow the court to consider all material that can have an important bearing on the future welfare of a child. The court noted the opening words of the section which, in the court's opinion, clearly indicated the intention of the Legislature that privileges or protections which would otherwise operate are to be abrogated when the matter of child welfare is before a court. As well, the Appellate Court determined that the filing of a transcript of a previous hearing is admissible, even if the witnesses are available, since, if the Legislature had intended to restrict the reference to such material to cases where the primary evidence of earlier witnesses was not available, it would have said so. By this judgment, a transcript of any proceeding involving a parent and a child is admissible at a later hearing, with the observation that if the substance of the transcript is not hearsay evidence and was subject to the test of cross-examination, its trustworthiness is enhanced. Perhaps of some consolation to those who put some faith in the rules of evidence, one provincial court judge[136] excluded a crown "dope sheet" and a pre-sentence report from admission under this section despite the Appellate Court decision on the basis that this information was untrustworthy and unfair. The court was concerned that because a "dope sheet" is a statement of what the Crown wishes to prove in a criminal proceeding, it may or may not be substantiated by evidence. As well, the pre-sentence report contained "double and triple" hearsay. On the other hand, the court held that a transcript of the criminal proceedings involving a parent and a coroner's report should be admissible as being trustworthy evidence since they included sworn evidence as well as conclusions of the report and the coroner's jury and therefore, they could not be said to be unfair to any of the parties. The court concluded that s. 28(4) of the *CWA* provides the judge with a wide discretion in terms of what the court may or may not consider.

Any remaining obligations on the court to put some restrictions on the admissibility of evidence can be assessed in the examination of evidence of past conduct as follows:

(i) evidence of past conduct would presumably invite a *voir dire* in

---

[133]*Family and Children's Services of London and Middlsex v. C.*, unreported, September 3, 1982 (Prov. Ct. Fam. Div.), *per* Vogelsang J.

[134]*Ibid.*

[135]*E.C. v. C.C.A.S. of Metro. Toronto* (1982), 37 O.R. (2d) 82 (Co. Ct.).

[136]*Re D. (T.A.M.),* unreported, March 17, 1982 (Prov. Ct. Fam. Div.), *per* Fischer J.

which the court would have to weigh the admissibility of the intended evidence against its duty to conduct a fair hearing;

(ii) if the court decides to consider the past conduct of a person then it appears it has a discretion to decide what written or oral information is relevant; and

(iii) having decided to admit evidence of past conduct, and having determined the issue of relevancy, the court then has the discretion to impose such rules of proof as it considers necessary to conduct a fair hearing.

It is submitted that the court is obligated to exercise its discretion in this minimum manner notwithstanding the opening *non-obstante* clause of the above-noted section. Even with this approach, the section may invite a challenge under the *Charter of Rights* due to the vague and unpredictable effect of the language of the section which arguably infringes the parties' right not to have their liberty infringed, except as prescribed by law and in accordance with the principles of fundamental justice.[137] In practice, the effect of s. 28(4) of the *CWA* is to leave to the discretion of the court not simply the overwhelmingly complicated decision of deciding the child's best interests, but as well, the determination of the process for rendering that decision, the latter of which will be unknown to the parties until the hearing commences. No doubt the argument that all is fair in a child welfare proceeding will be sustained to some extent as a "reasonable limit" under s. 1 of the *Charter*, but it is submitted that in no case can "no limits" be defined as "reasonable limits" in a free and democratic society. In addition, the argument once more begs the question of whether any and all state actions are by definition "in the best interests of the child."

4) Section 28(5) of the *CWA* permits the court to hear affidavit evidence in a hearing but confines the contents therein to facts within the personal knowledge of the deponent. Accordingly, while s. 28(4) of the *CWA* overrides the protection of the *Evidence Act*, it is still subject to s. 28(5) of the *CWA* and, in fact, this kind of personal knowledge restriction, since it was contemplated by the Legislature to be necessary even in a child welfare proceeding, may arguably have been applicable to other than affidavit evidence which is in written form before the court. The issue will be circumvented by the removal of s. 28(5) under the *CFSA*.

5) Although the child welfare legislation provides the court with the power, on its own initiative, to direct that the child and/or parent attend for an assessment, this power is only to be exercised *after* the child has been found in need of protection to assist the court in determining the best disposition of the matter.

---

[137]*Charter of Rights*, s. 1 "only to such reasonable limits *prescribed by law* as can be demonstrably justified." See *e.g. Re Ont. Film and Video Appreciation Society and Ont. Bd. of Censors* (1983), 41 O.R. (2d) 583, 147 D.L.R. (3d) 58 (Div. Ct.) for the principle that "prescribed by law" requires that the limitation on the right have "legal force"; affd (1984), 45 O.R. (2d) 80, 5 D.L.R. (4th) 766 (C.A.). Leave to appeal to S.C.C. granted (1984), 55 N.R. 318*n*. A limitation simply left to administrative discretion cannot therefore be considered to be one "prescribed by law." *Charter of Rights*: s. 7, "Everyone has the right to life, liberty and security of the person and the right not to be deprived thereof except in accordance with the principles of fundamental justice."

6) As is true in any other litigation proceeding, s. 28(9) of the *CWA* insures that the court's right to receive evidence is not restricted because of an inaccurate notice or application made in writing. In its discretion, the court can amend such inaccuracies at any stage of the proceeding or call an adjournment if further notice is considered necessary. This section effectively codifies the general common law principle that the court should be permitted to determine the real issue between the parties in spite of errors or inaccuracies in the pleadings, as long as no injustice is done to a party.[138] Perhaps for that reason, no parallel section will be included under the *CFSA*. In addition, the same principle can be based on the Rules of the Provincial Court (Family Division).

7) Finally, a court can dispense with the statute's notice requirements if "delay might endanger the health or safety of the child" (s. 28(10), *CWA*/ s. 39(7), *CFSA*) although it is restricted in the kind of order it may make: s. 28(11), *CWA*/ s. 53(7), *CFSA*. For further discussion, see above under "Pre-hearing Procedures: Notice and Parties."

"Best Interests" Disposition

Once an "in need of protection" finding is rendered, the court must then make a disposition in the child's best interests. This amorphous phrase is given shape by the eight criteria enumerated under s. 1(1)(b) of the *CWA*, some or all of which the judge may, in his discretion, consider relevant in all the circumstances: s. 1(2), *CWA*. The *CFSA*, once proclaimed, will increase the number of "considerations" to 14: s. 37(3) and (4). The new additions, for the most part, appear to reinforce the importance of the original parent-child attachment. They will include (1) relationships by blood or through an adoption order; (2) the preservation of a child's cultural identity (note that if this identity is "Indian or native", the court *shall* take it into consideration: s. 37(4)); (3) the child's religious upbringing; (4) the risk to the child of being kept away from the parents; (5) and the degree of risk that justified the protection finding in the first place. Other "considerations" most of which will be continued from the *CWA*, include (1) the child's physical, mental and emotional needs and development; (2) the importance of a positive and secure family unit; (3) the merits of the Society's plan as compared to the merits of returning the child home; (4) the effect of delayed disposition; (5) and the risk of returning the child to the parent.

Possible Dispositions

Under s. 30 of the *CWA*, the judge can make one of three possible orders, while under s. 53 of the *CFSA*, once proclaimed, he will be able to make one of five possible orders or no order at all. Before making such an order, the court may also require that the parent and/or child attend an assessment by a professional designated by the court in order to assist it in making one of these orders: s. 29, *CWA*/ s. 50, *CFSA*. The court may:

1) order that the child be the subject of a supervisory order, with or without judicial terms and conditions (s. 30(4), *CWA*/ s. 53(8), *CFSA*), in which case the child can be placed with or returned to his parent or other person subject to the supervision of the local Society. The *CFSA* will require that this order be for a period of at least three months and not more than twelve

---

[138]*Re Milner* (1975), 23 R.F.L. 86 (N.S.S.C.).

months, while the *CWA* directs a minimum period of six months with a maximum of twelve months.

2) order that the child be the subject of a "temporary wardship order", that is, that he be made a ward of and committed to the care and custody of the local Society. Any single order of temporary Society wardship has no minimum period but cannot exceed 12 months.

3) order that the child be the subject of a "Crown wardship order", that is, that he be made a ward of the Crown in which case, the care of the child is delegated to the local Society for an indefinite period until terminated pursuant to other sections of the Act.

Note that all three orders automatically terminate upon the child marrying or reaching 18: s. 42, *CWA*/ s. 67, *CFSA*. In the case of a Crown ward, the wardship can continue with the consent of the director. Under the *CWA*, the conditions are specifically stated in the Act that such care should continue until the child is 21 years if the child is enrolled as a full-time student at an educational institution, or is mentally or physically incapacitated: s. 42, *CWA*.[139] However, the parallel section of the *CFSA* will specify no conditions, leaving it "in accordance with the regulations."

4) A notable addition to the dispositions available under the CFSA will be an order of Society wardship for a given period followed by the return of the child to the parents under the Society's supervision for an aggregate period not to exceed 12 months: s. 53(1), para. 4, *CFSA*. This section will provide the court with a maximum degree of authority to direct the Society as guardian in terms of the planning and treatment for the child while in care of the Society. Admittedly, the court generally has no power to impose conditions upon a Society once the child becomes a ward[140] with the exception under the *CFSA* of holding the Society to its original plan presented prior to the disposition under s. 52 of the *CFSA*: s. 60(8)(b), *CFSA*. However by stipulating the length of time the child is to remain in a Society's care, coupled with the ability of the court to impose conditions upon a Society in its supervisory capacity when the child is returned home, the court will be able to achieve a degree of direction and control of the child's re-integration into the family which is not presently available.

5) Another alternative for the judge under the *CFSA*, upon its proclamation, is to issue a restraining order "instead of or in addition to making an order under s. 53(1)": s. 76, *CFSA*. This order may restrain or prohibit a person's access to or contact with the child with any necessary directions for implementing same.

A final notable provision under the *CFSA* will be that if the judge, having found the child in need of protection, decides that no court order is necessary to protect the child in the future, he may make no order at all and send the child home: s. 53(9), *CFSA*.

---

[139]See *e.g. Re J*. (1981), 50 N.S.R. (2d) 104, 98 A.P.R. 104 (Fam. Ct.) wherein notice to parents of application to extend wardship past eighteenth birthday to further child's education was dispensed with.

[140]*Re A. (J.)*, unreported, June 30, 1982 (Ont. Prov. Ct. Fam. Div.), *per* Fischer J.

The first three potential dispositions are listed in order of their increasing severity for both the child and the parent. Under a supervisory order, the child remains in the home subject to conditions imposed by the judge whereas under a Society or Crown wardship order, the child is removed from the family unit in favour of a Society placement. Once a child is removed from the home, parental rights to make contact with or make decisions about the child are substantially reduced and are subject to conditions imposed by the Society. As noted above, even the court has no jurisdiction to direct the Society regarding the carrying out of its mandate including the nature and program of supervision, training or treatment to which the child will be exposed.[141] Further, under a Crown wardship order, the parent and the child may lose all rights to each other permanently, since such an order with no stipulation for access allows the Society to place the child for adoption at which point all review and access rights cease: s. 38(7), *CWA*/ s. 60(9) and 54(7), *CFSA*. (For further discussion on guardianship rights under a Society/Crown wardship order, see below under "The State as Guardian: Placements".)

Nothing in the *CWA* requires a judge to make the least severe order possible in the circumstances and that he should only resort to the more severe order after a less severe arrangement has been tried and has failed. The only statutory directions as to the exercise of discretion exists under s. 30 of the *CWA* where the judge is directed to choose the disposition which is "in the best interests of the child" (defined under s. 1(1)(b) of the *CWA*) and under s. 30(5) of the *CWA* in which the judge is directed to find out first whether any efforts have been made by the Society or anyone else to assist the child within the family unit. Most judges appear to have operated under the presumption that the onus is on the state to demonstrate the need of protection and justify the extent of intervention and that the onus increases as the Society seeks a more drastic solution, *i.e.* Crown wardship.[142] Accordingly, the standard of proof required in an application for supervision has been less strict than evidence required to justify removal of a child from a family. The latter is an entirely different matter and one involving more serious consequences.[143]

Upon its proclamation, the principle of choosing the least restrictive alternative will be clearly delineated under the *CFSA* which effectively codifies past judicial considerations. Before deciding which disposition is appropriate, the court will be obliged to:

---

[141]*E. v. C.A.S. of Metro. Toronto* (1977), 4 R.F.L. (2d) 45 (Ont. H.C.); *Re A. (J), ibid, N. v. Supt. of Family and Child Services* (1982), 27 R.F.L. (2d) 328 (B.C.S.C.). But see discussion on new supervisory and review procedures under *CFSA* in the body of the chapter under "Best Interests Disposition: Review/Termination of Order".

[142]*Hansen v. C.A.S. of Hamilton-Wentworth* (1976), 27 R.F.L. 289 (Ont. Div. Ct.).

[143]*Re C.C.A.S. and M.* (1982), 36 O.R. (2d) 451 (Ont. Prov. Ct.). But see *D. v. C.A.S. of Kent* (1980), 18 R.F.L. (2d) 223 (Ont. Co. Ct.) in which the County Court held that the heavy onus of proving a child to be in need of protection in no way diminishes because the disposition sought is minimal intervention.

1) consider the extent to which the Society or other persons or agencies assisted the family before intervention: s. 53(2), *CFSA*;[144]

2) consider, before making any order removing the child from the family, whether it is satisfied that less restrictive services, including non-society and non-residential assistance, have been attempted and failed, or been refused, or would be inadequate: s. 53(3), *CFSA*; or

3) consider, before making a Society or Crown wardship order, whether it is possible to place the child with a relative, neighbour or other member of the child's community or extended family subject to supervision and the third party's consent: s. 53(4), *CFSA*.[145] If the child is "Indian or native," the court *shall* place the child within his native community "unless there is a substantial reason for placing the child elsewhere": s. 53(5), *CFSA*.

4) consider before making a Crown wardship order whether the circumstances justifying the order are unlikely to change within a reasonably foreseeable time not exceeding 24 months: s. 53(6), *CFSA*;[146]

5) consider whether any disposition at all is required; a child found to be in need of protection may or may not need state intervention in the future and in the latter case may be returned to the parent without any further state intervention: s. 53(9), *CFSA*;

6) consider, if the child is before the court on consent of the parent and child (if over 11 years) asking for a removal order, whether services have been offered by the Society to the parent and child to enable the child to remain with the parents and whether all parties have consulted legal counsel so that the court can be satisfied that they, including the child, understand the nature and consequences of the consent: s. 51(a) and (b), *CFSA*;

7) consider, before making any disposition, a plan for the child's care prepared in writing by the Society, including:

> (a) a description of services to be provided to remedy the condition that gave rise to state intervention in the first place;
>
> (b) a statement of the criteria by which the Society can gauge when its involvement is no longer necessary,

---

[144]For a case which illustrates the problem with courts taking this factor into consideration, see *C.A.S. of Winnipeg v. M.* (1980), 13 R.F.L. (2d) 65, revg (1979), 12 R.F.L. (2d) 132 (Man. C.A.) in which the Society was granted permanent wardship despite the alleged inadequacy of assistance given to the parent. The court held that the determining factor was the best interests of the child and not the failure of the agency to put all of its resources at the parents' disposal.

[145]See *e.g. C.A.S. of Central Man. v. Goertzen* (1980), 17 Man. R. (2d) 167, 21 R.F.L. (2d) 46 (C.A.) in which the court denied the Society's application for permanent wardship, giving custody to the grandparents; *Re S.B. and M.B.* (1979), 39 N.S.R. (2d) 18, 71 A.P.R. 18 (Fam. Ct.); *Re C.* (1980), 14 R.F.L. (2d) 21 (Ont. Prov. Ct.).

[146]See *e.g. Minister of Social Services v. Ardell* (1982), 17 Sask. R. 217 (Q.B.) (retarded parent; predicting no change); *Winnipeg C.A.S. v. L. (K.J.M.)* (1982), 28 R.F.L. (2d) 177 (Man. C.A.) (law breaking, incarcerated parent; predicting no change); *Re C.C.A.S. and M.* (1982), 36 O.R. (2d) 451 (Prov. Ct.) (mother's history of explosive behaviour which led to first two children being removed now shows improvement; Crown wardship denied); *Re F.M.* (1979), 11 R.F.L. (2d) 12 (Ont. Prov. Ct.) (six-year-old who had been in foster homes two-thirds of his life returned to mother; advantages of maternal custody outweighed advantages of wardship).

(c) an estimate of the time required to achieve the purpose of the state's intervention;

(d) if the plan is to remove the child, an explanation of why the child cannot be adequately protected in the home and what past efforts have been made to do so and what future efforts will be made to maintain the child's contact with the parent, and

(e) if the plan is to remove the child permanently, a description of the arrangements made or being made for the child's long-term stable placement: s. 52, *CFSA*.

Defence Counsel's Plan

As noted above in the discussion on evidence and the protection finding, the court will tend to err on the side of safety for the child and treat as a secondary concern the rights and benefits stemming from the parent-child relationship. This will undoubtedly be true under the new legislation despite the well-intentioned pronouncements of "least restrictive alternative" woven throughout the *CFSA*. Accordingly, the parents' or child's counsel must research and develop a plan that permits the parents to maintain legal care of their child and to rely upon s. 1(1)(b)(v) of the *CWA* (s. 37(3), para. 8, *CFSA*) which obligates the court, in determining the child's best interests to consider the plans of both the state and the parent.[147] Counsel must devote more energy outside than inside the court room, not only to his own plan but to the assessment of the state's plan. For the latter, he should consider the following:

1) the nature of the state's proposed placement, both in the immediate future and over the subsequent months; counsel should be particularly concerned if a stable temporary placement is not available under this plan;

2) the age of other children in the new home proposed by the state, as well as the age, experience and expertise of those parents who would be caring for the child;

3) sufficient information about the professional resources which would be made available to the child and to the parents, in order to allow counsel or an

---

[147]The definition of "best interests" under s. 1(1)(b)(v) of the *CWA* includes:

"the merits of any plan proposed by the agency that would be caring for the child, compared with the merits of the child returning to or remaining with his or her parent."

See also s. 38(5) of the *CWA* (comparing plans before terminating access under a Crown wardship order).

Under the *CFSA*, parallel sections which will require the court to consider counsel's plan include s. 37(3) para. 8, under definition of "best interests":

The merits of a plan for the child's care proposed by a society, including a proposal that the child be placed for adoption or adopted, compared with the merits of the child remaining with or returning to a parent."

See also the *CFSA* ss. 52 (consideration of Society's plan before making disposition) and 53(3) (considerations before removing child from parents).

And see *Re Catholic C.A.S. and M., ibid.* in which the judge awarded costs against the Society because they sought Crown wardship where defence counsel convinced court to make only a supervisory order. Costs were awarded because the Society had conducted inadequate research of the facts. See also *Re P.M.* (1980), 16 R.F.L. (2d) 200, 3 Fam. L. Rev. 213 (P.E.I.S.C.) for another case in which costs were awarded against the Society.

independent professional to assess the likelihood of success of the state's rehabilitative plan as compared to that of the parents'. The same kind of information is needed on the educational resources contemplated under the state's plan. If the child has a learning disability, will there be an appropriate learning facility for the child?

4) the state's prognosis on the expected benefits of the plan so that counsel will have base-line parameters by which to measure future accountability upon a status review; and

5) the nature and extent of involvement by the parents during the period of separation under the state's plan in order to solidify access and decision-making rights under a court order.

Having this information will ensure that if the parents have not been successful in resisting the application of the state, they are nonetheless in a better position for review when the matter returns to court.

Assessments

The court is given the power, on its initiative, to direct that the child or other person (except the foster parent) in whose charge the child has been or may be placed, attend for an assessment before a qualified person within a specified time: s. 29, *CWA*/ s. 50, *CFSA*. Unlike the court-ordered assessment in a domestic dispute, the assessment in a child welfare proceeding is the "court's report." Under the Provincial Court Rules of Practice, it receives a special evidentiary status: all parties must receive a copy of the report and any party may summon the author as a witness and cross-examine that person, presumably as the court's witness.[148] Under the *CWA* section, it has been held that the court can order either the child or the parent to attend, and that an assessment should not be limited to cases where only the child *and* parent are directed to attend for the assessment.[149] The new wording of the *CFSA* will codify this judicial principle by using the disjunctive word "or" in lieu of "and": s. 50(1), *CFSA*.

Access

Whether the order is one of supervision, Society or Crown wardship, the court has the jurisdiction prior to an adoption placement in conjunction with any other order or upon special access application to make an order regarding access rights to the child by any person: s. 35, *CWA*/ s. 54, *CFSA*. Note that no application for access may be made after a child has been placed for adoption: s. 38(7), *CWA*/ s. 54(7)(b), *CFSA*. Under the *CWA*, the applicants are restricted to the parent, the person with whom the child was placed or to whom the child was returned, the child (if over 11 years), and the Society. Upon proclamation, the *CFSA* will expand the number of possible applicants to include the child without an age restriction, the Society and anyone else, including an Indian band or native community representative, if the child is "Indian or native": s. 54(2), *CFSA*. As usual, the order must be made "having regard to the best interests of the child . . . as the court considers appropriate." Under the *CWA*, if the court is

---

[148]See O. Reg. 810/80 (Prov. Ct. Rules), s. 71 and contrast with *Re Sawyer*, summarized in (1984), 6 F.L.R.R. 156 (Ont. Prov. Ct.) which concerns assessment and Rules of Practice in a domestic custody dispute. And see *Re P. (V.D.); Re L. (M.) v. C.C.A.S. of Metro. Toronto*, unreported, October 7, 1982 (Ont. Prov. Ct.), *per* Main J. for jurisdiction of the court on assessment on its own motion rather than awaiting an application by either party.

[149]*Re P. (V.D.); Re L. (M.) v. C.C.A.S. of Metro. Toronto, ibid.*

persuaded that the family cannot meet society's expectations of adequate parenting either now or in the future and the child would only benefit from permanent placement elsewhere, then the order will probably be one of Crown wardship without access since only that order enables the child, following the expiration of the 30 day appeal period (Rules of Civil Procedure: O. Reg. 560/84, r. 72.02(6)), to be placed by the Children's Aid Society for the purpose of adoption.[150] Upon that event, the parents lose all rights and remedies with respect to the child, and specifically the right to seek access or a review of Crown wardship, unless the placement in the particular home has broken down: s. 38(7) and (8), *CWA*/ s. 60(9) and 54(7), *CFSA*.[151] (For discussion of access and adoption, see below under "Finality of Adoption Order". For discussion of access and conflict of laws, see below under "Jurisdictional Conflicts".) Under the *CFSA*, the statutory guidelines will be more detailed and directive: if the order is supervisory or Society wardship, the judge *shall* grant access unless continued contact is not in the child's best interests: s. 55(1), *CFSA*. However, in recognition of the particularly harmful family situation which must have given rise to a Crown wardship order the *CFSA* will require that the judge *shall not* grant access under Crown wardship unless:

1) a permanent placement is not or cannot be planned and access will not jeopardize the child's chance for a future permanent placement;
2) the child is at least 12 years old and wishes to maintain contact with the person;
3) the person with whom the child is placed does not wish to adopt him; and
4) some other special circumstances justifying an access order: s. 55(2) *CFSA*.

---

[150]For discussion of "best interests" in this context, see *C. v. C.A.S. of Metro. Toronto* (1980), 20 R.F.L. (2d) 259 (Ont. Co. Ct.) (issue of adoptability can be raised to determine access). But see *Re T.M.E. and A.D.E.* (1980), 26 A.R. 243 (Q.B.) in which the court declined to grant Crown wardship, leaving the child in temporary wardship, since the sole effect of the order was to deprive the mother of status and right to access. This, despite the court's acknowledgment that the mother's regaining custody was not a "realistic possibility". For a similar decision in Ontario see *Re N.*, summarized in (1984), 7 F.L.R.R. 61 (Ont. U.F.C.). The court therein noted that (1) the child was adoptable, well-adjusted and had bonded well with the foster mother, (2) that separation from the foster mother would be a "major psychological trauma"; and (3) that there were emotional ties with the biological mother. Therefore, despite the usual practice of reversing long term foster care for non-adoptables, the "somewhat heretical" Crown wardship order with access to the biological mother suited the child best. See also *C.A.S. of Hamilton-Wentworth v. B.F.* (1981), 25 R.F.L. (2d) 455 (Ont. U.F.C.); *C.A.S. of Haldimand v. R.B.* (1981), 25 R.F.L. (2d) 56 (Ont. C.A.) for principles underlying the granting of access in a Crown wardship proceeding; *Minister of Social Services for Sask. v. W.M. and L.M.* (1983), 32 R.F.L. (2d) 337 (Sask. C.A.) (onus on party seeking to deprive parent of access while child a ward).

[151]See *Re L.G. and M.G.* (1982), 30 R.F.L. (2d) 103 (Ont. Prov. Ct.) and *Cromwell v. C.A.S. of Kent County* (1979), 1 F.L.R.A.C. 430 (Ont. Co. Ct.) for a jurisdictional discussion of domestic *Family Law Reform Act vs. the CWA* with respect to access. See also *S. v. Dept. of Social Services* (1982), 27 R.F.L. (2d) 220 (Sask. Q.B.) in which the Saskatchewan court allowed an access application under the province's *Infants Act* despite children having been taken into care in order to allow the parents to make use of the assessment provisions under the *Infants Act*.

In addition, the court *shall not* terminate access to a Crown ward unless the circumstances that justified the order under s. 55(2) in the first place no longer exist: s. 55(3), *CFSA*.

Appeal
Any decision, with the exception of an assessment order, is subject to appeal to the local district court: s. 43(1), *CWA*/ s. 65, *CFSA*.[152] However, Appellate Courts are traditionally reluctant to interfere with a trial judge's first hand assessment of the witnesses and usually will grant appeals only on a point of law[153] although even this is limited if the court feels that granting the appeal would not be in the best interests of the child. The appeal may be launched by a parent or other person in whose charge the child may have been at the time of the child's apprehension, a Director from the Ministry or a local director from a Society, or, under the *CFSA*, an Indian or native representative. In addition, the *CWA* gives the child the right to appeal, but only through a "next friend" who would then instruct the child's counsel: s. 43(1)(c), *CWA*. It appears that the *CFSA* will allow the child to appeal in certain circumstances and without the intervention of a next friend. For example, if the child was the applicant in a status review, if he had received notice of any proceedings or if he had legal counsel in the trial proceedings, he will be able to participate in the appeal as if he were a party under the *CFSA*: ss. 39(6) and 65(1)(a), *CFSA*.

Pending the appeal, the legislation makes provision for the interim custody of the child, directing that the execution of the lower court order is to be stayed for 10 days and if the child was in the care of the Society up until the order was made,[154] the child is to remain with the Society for the ten day period or until the Appellate Court makes an interim custody order pending the appeal decision, whichever is earlier: s. 43(2), *CWA*/ s. 65(3), *CFSA*. Both Acts also include the complementary provision authorizing the Appellate Court to make a temporary care order in the best interests of the child pending the outcome of the appeal and may vary it at any time: s. 43(4), *CWA*/ s. 65(4), *CFSA*. The net effect of these sections is as follows:

1) *Child in care; order for Society care appealed:* The child will remain in Society care pending disposition of the appeal subject to any interim order the appellate court may make in favour of a non-Society caretaker (usually the parent).

---

[152]Under the recently enacted *Courts of Justice Act, 1984*, the County and District Courts will all now be referred to as District Courts. And for a case in which application to extend time to appeal permanent wardship order was denied see *C.A.S. of Winnipeg v. Olson* (1982), 16 Man. R. (2d) 363 (C.A.). Court based decision on its conclusion that the appellate mother failed to show that intention to appeal was formulated while appeal open to her or that she had arguable appeal on the merits. For case where extension application granted see *Horley v. C.A.S. of London* (1981), 22 R.F.L. (2d) 204 (Ont. C.A.). For case where appeal of committal was heard on the merits even though the temporary wardship order had expired and the child was returned to the mother, see *Minister of Social Services v. Checkosis* (1981), 15 Sask. R. 292 (Q.B.).

[153]*Director of Child Welfare v. Arkinson* (1982), 14 Man. R. (2d) 318, 27 R.F.L. (2d) 225 (*sub nom. Director of Child Welfare v. A.* (Man. C.A.); *C.A.S. (Halifax) v. Talbot* (1981), 49 N.S.R. (2d) 695, 96 A.P.R. 695 (C.A.); *Re D.,* unreported, Nov. 25, 1981 (Ont. Prov. Ct.). Leave to appeal to C.A. drom Div. Ct. (Sept. 10/84) refused, Nov. 26, 1984. But see *Genereux v. Metro.Toronto C.C.A.S.*, unreported, May 16, 1985 (Ont. C.A.).

[154]*Sabir v. C.A.S. of Winnipeg* (1980), 21 R.F.L. (2d) 460 (Man. C.A.).

2) *Child not in care; order for Society care appealed:* The child does not have to be placed in Society care until 10 days after service of notice of appeal on the court, giving the caretaker time to seek an interim custody order in his favour from the Appellate Court if he so wishes.

3) *Child in care; order for non-Society care appealed:* The child will remain in care for the 10-day period at which time he will be placed with the non-Society caretaker pursuant to the order with its terms and conditions unless the Society has successfully sought an interim order from the Appellate Court for the child to remain in its care pending the outcome of the appeal.

4) *Child not in care; order for non-Society care appealed:* unless the Society successfully seeks an interim custody order, the child will remain with the non-Society caretaker named in the order subject to its terms and conditions which are triggered after the 10-day period until the disposition of the appeal (the assumption here being that the caretaker at the time the order was made is the same caretaker named in the order).

Finally note that s. 43(8) of the *CWA* specifically allows a party to seek leave of the Appellate Court to introduce evidence either *viva voce* or by affidavit, concerning matters which occurred not only subsequent to but also before the decision of the first instance. This is a departure from the "fresh evidence" rule in appellate practice and one court noted that this wide power reflected the remedial nature of the Act as it ensured that the court hearing the appeal from the trial will have the opportunity of considering all relevant evidence.[155] Under the *CFSA*, the power will be limited to evidence relating to events occurring only *after* the appealed decision: s. 65(6), *CFSA*. As well, the new Act will make no specific provision regarding the admissability of *viva voce* or affidavit evidence although presumably the Appellate Court will be able to hear the same kinds of evidence admissible in the lower court as long as it relates to events occurring after the lower court decision.

Jurisdictional Conflicts

The courts have made it clear that child welfare proceedings are paramount to any other type of proceeding in any other court, whether the latter be pursuant to statute or inherent jurisdiction. For example, prior custody orders granted in divorce proceedings have no standing in the face of a Crown wardship order.[156]

---

[155]*Re M. and C.A.S. of Metro. Toronto*, summarized in (1982), A.C.W.S. (2d) 146 (Ont. C.A.); *D. v. C.A.S. of Kent* (1980), 18 R.F.L. (2d) 233 (Ont. Co. Ct.); *P. (S) v. C.C.A.S.*, summarized in [1983] W.D.F.L. 670 (Ont. Co. Ct.) where counsel on behalf of the child was permitted to file further evidence given that the interests of the child must be paramount and the evidence was relevant. See also *Minister of Social Services (Sask.) v. Cook* (1979), 12 R.F.L. 185 (Sask. C.A.) (appeal court has full power to review additional evidence as well as transcript and to substitute decision that it considers appropriate); *Genereux v. Metro Toronto C.C.A.S., supra* note 153 (error of law not necessary for fresh evidence at appeal level).

[156]*C.A.S. of Ottawa-Carleton v. D.J.L.* (1980), 15 R.F.L. (2d) 102 (Ont. Prov. Ct.). But see *Beeching v. Eaton* (1979), 10 R.F.L. (2d) 129 (Sask. Q.B.). See also *Protection de la Jeunesse — 48*, [1982] T.J. 2015; *Re L.G. and M.G., supra,* note 152; *C.A.S. of Halifax v. McIlveen* (1980), 20 R.F.L. (2d) 302 (N.S. Prov. Ct.). For discussion of domestic *Family Law Reform Act* vs. the *CWA* with respect to access see *Cromwell v. C.A.S. of Kent County, supra*, note 151; *Re R.* (1978), 1 F.L.R.A.C. 160 (Ont. Prov. Ct.); *C.A.S. of Hamilton-Wentworth v. B.F.* (1981), 25 R.F.L. (2d) 455 (Ont. U.F.C.).

The courts wish to avoid making any order that may undermine or conflict with a child protection order.[157] As another example, if a mother succeeds in gaining custody in the High Court but the child is the subject of a protection application, the Family Court is compelled to proceed notwithstanding the order of the Superior Court. The child has become subject to specific proceedings with respect to his protection and the responsibility for providing that protection rests squarely on the Provincial Court. No conflict exists since the Superior Court order is only a decision between mother and father and has no bearing as between the Children's Aid Society and the mother regarding the welfare of the child.[158]

In some circumstances, this approach might invite a parent to seek custody via a child-protection proceeding to circumvent a domestic proceeding. For example, a parent residing in Alberta who is caught in the throws of an imminent domestic custody dispute might take the child to Ontario and persuade the Children's Aid Society of the need for a protection proceeding with a resulting placement with the *de facto* custodial parent. This would effectively freeze the Alberta proceedings. It is suggested that the Children's Aid Societies should be reluctant to intervene in any such situation unless it is prepared to initiate the appropriate steps to have the child returned immediately to the jurisdiction of the child's "habitual residence", if necessary with the assistance of the child welfare agency in that jurisdiction. Otherwise, the allegations of abuse, coupled with the paramountcy of child protection legislation may effectively undermine laws which have been instituted in an attempt to stem the inter-parental kidnapping trend.

With respect to geographical jurisdiction, generally the appropriate forum to commence child welfare proceedings or review proceedings thereunder is the jurisdiction in which the child is residing.[159]

Review/Termination of Order   An order (other than assessment) may return to court via two routes: expiry or elective review. Just prior to expiry of a supervision or Society wardship order (Crown wardship is for an indefinite period), the Society must bring the matter back "for a review of the child's status" and the court may, in the child's best interests, vary the conditions of the existing order, make a new order permitted by the original section or terminate the order: ss. 32 and 37, *CWA*/ s. 61(1), *CFSA*. An additional option which the *CFSA* will include is that the court may order that the original order terminate on a specified future date. It has been specifically held that there is no authority for the continued involvement of a

---

[157]*C.A.S. (Hastings) v. A.-G.; P.G. v. C.A.S. Hastings; P.R. v. C.A.S. Hastings*, unreported, March 18, 1981 (Prov. Ct. Fam. Div.), *per* Kirkland, J.

[158]*Re Fortowsky and Essex Catholic C.A.S.,* [1960] O.W.N. 235 (C.A.); *Re Hearnden,* [1972] 2 W.W.R. 440 (B.C.S.C.). See also *Supt. of Family and Child Services v. P.* (1982), 28 R.F.L. (2d) 405 (B.C.S.C.) in which British Columbia court where child residing not deprived of its child welfare jurisdiction just because parents living in Alberta.

[159]See *e.g. Re L.L.A.* (1981), 17 Alta. L. Rev. (2d) 205, 25 R.F.L. (2d) 208 (Prov. Ct.); *Supt. of Family and Child Services v. P.* (1982), 28 R.F.L. (2d) 405 (B.C.S.C.); *Re T.S.* (1982), 31 R.F.L. (2d) 135 (B.C. Prov. Ct.); *McArdle v. Riley* (1982), 28 R.F.L. (2d) 428 (B.C.C.A.) (English wardship order, parents take children to Canada; refuse enforcement because no real and substantial connection between children and England at time of order); *Re P.* (1982), 36 O.R. (2d) 324 (Prov. Ct.) (considerations re transferring proceedings to where mother resides.)

Society once an order has expired.[160] (Note that expiry by marriage or reaching 18 years of age does not trigger a review: s. 37(1), *CWA*/ s. 60(2)(b), *CFSA*.) Presumably, the court could also order an assessment to be conducted under s. 29, *CWA* (s. 50, *CFSA*) before making a final disposition. The wording of the *CWA* clearly makes this possible since it indicated that on review, a court could make any order permissible "under this Part": ss. 32, 37, 38, *CWA*. However, the wording of the *CFSA* will limit the possible court orders to those delineated under s. 53: s. 61(1), *CFSA*. Nevertheless, there will arguably be nothing prohibiting the court from ordering an assessment in order to make a final disposition under s. 61(1) of the *CFSA* especially since the newly included s. 61(3) outlines a long list of preliminary considerations to which a court must put its mind before making the disposition including "what is the least restrictive alternative that is in the child's best interests." Further to this, the opening words of the assessment section (s. 50, *CFSA*) will make it available "where a child has been found to be in need of protection" which arguably will not be limited to the original hearing but continue for the entire time that the child is subject to an order under this Part of the Act.

The elective review route gives the Society, the parents, whomever the child is placed with, the child (if 12 or more years of age) and the Director, varying rights to seek review of the child's status prior to expiry. Upon proclamation, the *CFSA* will also add a representative of an Indian band or native community to those who may seek review if the child is "Indian or native." The following is an outline of statutory rights of elective review: (For case law discussion of the judicial test to be applied on review, see below under "Judicial Test on Review.")

Supervisory Order Review: s. 32, *CWA*/ ss. 60, 61 *CFSA*

The Society may at any time after the order has been made bring it back to the court to "review the child's status" and the court is to be guided by the same "best interest" considerations and possible dispositions noted above under an expiry review: s. 32(1) and (4), *CWA*/ ss. 60(2)(a), 61(1), *CFSA*. Note that if the Society removes the child who is only under a supervision order, it must bring the matter to court within five days "for a review of the child's status": s. 32(2), *CWA*/ s. 60(2)(c), *CFSA*.

The parent, the person with whom the child is placed, the child (if 12 or more years of age) and the Indian/native representative (under the *CFSA*) may also bring it back to court under the same considerations but only after the expiration of six months: s. 32(4), *CWA*/ ss. 60(4) and (7), *CFSA*.[161] The *CFSA*

---

[160]*Bailey v. C.A.S. of Parry Sound* (1979), 9 R.F.L. (2d) 188 (Ont. H.C.). But see *Powder v. Director of Child Welfare* (1980), 26 A.R. 368, 112 D.L.R. (3d) 381, 18 R.F.L. (2d) 272 (Q.B.) wherein temporary wardship order had expired after which the Society was to return child under supervision; Society had applied to extend wardship but hearing not occurring until after expiry; Court held that Society could retain custody if in the child's best interests because still under duty to maintain supervision.

[161]Note that the six-month-limitation period runs from the time when the appeal from the final order is dismissed or abandoned or the time for appealing the final order has expired: *M.M. v. B.M. and C.A.S. of Metro. Toronto* (1982), 30 R.F.L. (2d) 111 (Ont. S.C.); apprd. in *D. v. Porcupine and District C.A.S.*, unreported, November 18, 1983 (Ont. C.A.).

will create an exception to this six month limit: the same person can seek review at any time without regard to the six-month limitation if he can convince the court that ''a major element of the plan for the child's care that the court applied in its decision is not being carried out'': s. 60(8), *CFSA*.

Society Wardship Review: s. 37, *CWA*/ ss. 60, 61, *CFSA*

Again, the Society at any time and the parent, child (12 or more years) or Indian/native representative (under the *CFSA*) after six months, may seek a review of the child's status under Society wardship. (*CFSA* exception to 6-month rule dismissed under Supervisory Order Review.) The court may terminate or make any further order permitted by the original section as is in the best interests of the child: s. 37(1) and (2), *CWA*/ ss. 60(2) (a), (4), 61(1), *CFSA*.(Jurisdiction to order an assessment is discussed above with respect to reviews triggered by the expiry.) However, the overriding restriction on the court is that no further order may have the effect of the child being in care for a continuous period of more than 24 months: s. 37(2), *CWA*/ s. 66, *CFSA*.[162] This restriction applies regardless of how the child came into care, including voluntary parental agreements. An exception to the restriction is if the review was necessarily adjourned and the date for continuation came after the expiry of 24 months in which case the order to be reviewed shall cintinue until another order can be made: s. 37(3), *CWA*/ s. 66(3)(b), *CFSA*. A second exception included only under the *CFSA* will be an extension when an appeal under the original order is not disposed of. One court noted that the 24-month restriction reflects the Legislatures realization that it is not in the best interests of a child to be left for more than 24 months in the indefinite and uncertain circumstances of temporary wardship. After that period of time, the society should be in a position to enter into permanent planning for the child, either by returning him home, assuming rehabilitation efforts on the part of the family have been successful, or by placing him as a ward of the Crown.[163]

Crown Wardship Review: ss. 38 and 39, *CWA*/ ss. 60, 61, *CFSA*

Again, the Society at any time and the parent,[164] and child (12 or more years) or Indian/native representative (under the *CFSA*) after the expiry of six months,[165] may seek a review of the child's status under this type of order. (*CFSA* exception to 6-month rule discussed under Supervisory Order Review.)

---

[162]See *Re M.* (1980), 20 R.F.L. (2d) 292 (P.E.I.S.C.) in which 24 months were exhausted and Society applied for extension. Judge denied extension and ordered Crown wardship based on his *parens patriae* jurisdiction.

[163]See *Re Charbonneau and the C.A.S. of Ottawa* (1976), 14 O.R. (2d) 432 (Ont. Div. Ct.).

[164]Upon proclamation, the *CFSA* will limit the parent's absolute right to seek review of a Crown wardship order in the case where the child has been living continuously with the same foster parents for the two years immediately preceding the application by requiring them to seek leave: s. 60(5). Given the stability and accompanying security which have been built up in these circumstances after what was usually a very harmful situation to have given rise to a Crown wardship order in the first place, the Legislature obviously felt justified in putting the onus on the parent to present at least a *prima facie* case which would normally require substantial rehabilitation on the parents' part before exposing the child to the uncertainty of a court hearing and the obvious anxiety surrounding the possibility of returning home to his parents.

The judge may, based on a "best interest" test, terminate the order or make any further order permitted under the original section as is "necessary" except that he may not make a Society wardship order. In other words, his choices are limited to the continuation of Crown wardship with its potential for adoption placement, with or without parental access, supervision of the child by the Society after being returned to the family unit,[166] or termination of any state intervention altogether upon re-uniting the family unit either immediately or, under the *CFSA*, at a future date: s. 38, *CWA*/ s. 61(1)(2), *CFSA*. (Jurisdiction to order an assessment is discussed above with respect to reviews triggered by expiry.)

In addition to the general "best interests" test, there is one further judicial guideline under a Crown wardship review which does not apply to the other reviews and which concerns access. This is due to the far reaching implications of refusing access under Crown wardship which effectively terminates parental involvement and paves the way for an adoption placement. The *CFSA* differs significantly from the *CWA* in the manner in which it deals with this issue. Under the *CWA*, if the judge is considering terminating or forbidding access he must first:

> . . . consider whether the benefit to the child of any plan proposed for the child, including plans for seeking an adoption placement for the child, outweighs the benefit to the child of maintaining the access rights [s. 38(5), *CWA*].

In contrast, upon proclamation of the *CFSA*, there will exist a presumption against access under a Crown wardship order as described above under "Access". Presumably, this corresponds with the tough guidelines under the *CFSA*, newly imposed, to prevent a court from ordering Crown wardship in the first place except where it is absolutely necessary. Once circumstances become so harmful that a judge will be justified in ordering Crown wardship under the guidelines of the new Act, the long-term possibilities of a child's placement will take precedence over the benefits of maintaining the parent-child link. It remains to be seen whether Ontario's Family Courts will change their disposition pattern in conjunction with the proclamation of the new Act.

The Director or his appointee is also required to review the status of all Crown wards who have been in care without review for 24 months: s. 39, *CWA*/ s. 62, *CFSA*. After such a review, the Director *may* direct the local Society to bring the matter before the court under s. 37, *CWA*/ s. 60(2), *CFSA* for a status review. Under the *CFSA*, he will also be able to "give any other direction that, in the Director's opinion, is in the child's best interests."

---

[165]Note that the six month period runs from the time when the appeal avenues are exhausted so that a parents' review application was held to be premature when they applied after April, 1982 for review of a wardship order which was confirmed in July, 1981 because their appeal to the Court of Appeal was not decided until April, 1982. Accordingly, the earliest they could apply was October, 1982: *M.M. v. B.M. and C.A.S. of Toronto, supra*, note 161.

[166]See *M.M. v. B.M.* (1981), 37 O.R. (2d) 120 (Co. Ct.) affd (1982) 37 O.R. (2d) 716 (C.A.) in which it was held that the trial judge lacked jurisdiction to order the immediate termination of Crown wardship coupled with a gradual reintroduction of the child into the family.

It is very important to note that no application for review by any party is permitted once the child has been "placed for adoption" (s. 38(7), *CWA*/ s. 60(9), *CFSA*)[167] which may occur at any time once Crown wardship has been ordered as long as the appeal time has run its course (30 days: Rules of Civil Procedure: O. Reg. 560/84, r. 72.02(6)) and access rights ordered under the child welfare legislation have been terminated: s. 38(8), *CWA*/ s. 134(2), *CFSA*. Note that if the placement has broken down such that the child is no longer living with the potential adoptive family, this review prohibition is no longer in effect. Corollary to this cessation of review rights is the cessation of all access rights "other than under an order made under this Act": s. 69(15), *CWA*/ s. 137(1), *CFSA*.

In addition to the review routes outlined above, the *CFSA* will, upon proclamation, introduce a system whereby children's services or placements can be reviewed by other than an internal Society review. (For an outline of the Society's internal responsibilities, see below under "The State as Guardian: Placements.") Under s. 98 of the *CFSA*, there will even be a provision for the Minister to set up an Office of Child and Family Service Advocacy to advocate on behalf of those who are receiving services. The following *CFSA* sections are presumably intended to make up a system of checks and balances which will allow families to exact accountability from their service providers. However, with one exception noted under paragraph 5 below, it should be remembered that the final decision stemming from all complaint and review procedures will rest with persons appointed by the Ministry or the Ministry itself which may give rise to bias or conflicts of interest for the particular review tribunal:

1) *Sections 6 and 177, CFSA:* A program supervisor from the Ministry may at any time inspect the facilities and the services provided through the Ministry, its service providers and Societies to ensure compliance with the Act and Regulations.

2) *Sections 22, 179 and 187, CFSA:* Revocation and takeover powers of the Ministry of "approved agencies" (s. 22); revoking licenses of residential care givers and adoption agencies other than Societies (s. 179); takeover of residential care (s. 187). These sections will expand the Ministry's powers relative to the corresponding sections 17 and 18 of the *CWA*. The Minister may exercise its s. 22 powers if:

(i) an "approved agency" including a Society is not providing services in accordance with the Act or Regulations or any particular condition imposed on it;

(ii) if present circumstances are such that approval of the agency would be refused if it were applying for accreditation in the first instance; or

---

[167]In one case, a parent succeeded in convincing the court that they were capable of looking after their children again, but one of the two children was already placed for adoption so only one child returned home: *Telfer v. Annapolis County Family and Children's Services* (1982), 50 N.S.R. (2d) 136, 98 A.P.R. 136, 26 R.F.L. (2d) 365 (*sub nom. Annapolis County Family and Children's Services v. T.*) (C.A.). See also *Horley v. C.A.S. of London* (1981) 22 R.F.L. (2d) 204 (Ont. C.A.) (not "placed for adoption" until placed in the adoptive home and residing there).

(iii) a Society is not able or fails to perform all or any of its functions: s. 22 *CFSA*.

3) *Section 23, CFSA:* If the Minister decides that an agency's activities are likely to cause harm to a person's health, safety or welfare, he will be able to order the activity to cease and "take such other action as the Minister deems to be in the best interests of the persons receiving the approved service".

4) *Section 34, CFSA:* Review by Residential Placement Advisory Committee. The committee, made up by the Ministry, will consist of other service providers, "others who demonstrate an informed concern for child welfare," a Ministry representative and anyone else the Ministry considers appropriate including an Indian or native representative. This committee shall review:

(i) a residential placement in an institution within 45 days of its inception if the placement is intended to or actually lasts 90 days or more and at least once a year thereafter;

(ii) every residential placement of a child over 11 years who objects to the placement; and

(iii) any existing or proposed residential placement that is referred to them by the Ministry.

A "residential placement" will not include a placement under the *Young Offenders Act* or *Provincial Offences Act* (Part IV), secure treatment (Part VI) or placement with a person who is neither a service provider nor a foster parent: s. 34(1), *CFSA*. Section 34(4) outlines the objectives of the review which will basically amount to an assessment of the availability and appropriateness of the placement for the particular child. The committee's recommendations will go to all parties concerned while a report of its findings and recommendations will go to the Minister and if the subject child is over 11 years and is dissatisfied with the recommendations or if they are not followed, he may apply to the Children's Services Review Board, again constituted by the Ministry (s. 190), "for a determination of where he or she should remain or be placed." It is interesting to note that this section will apparently provide no other person with this right to go to the Board and will effectively rule out this route if the child is under 12 years of age.

5) *Section 60(8), CFSA:* In addition to the usual review rights, this section will allow, in certain circumstances, a review application to be made to a court regarding a supervisory or wardship order without the usual restriction of having to wait six months from the last time it was before the court. For this section to apply, the court must first be satisfied "that a major element of the plan for the child's care that the court applied in its decision is not being carried out". Note that if the child is a Crown ward, this section applies only if access has been ordered.

6) *Section 62, CFSA:* This section corresponds with s. 39 of the *CWA* in requiring the Director to review the status of every Crown ward on a yearly basis if it has not been otherwise reviewed by the court within that period. Under the *CWA*, the Director may direct the Society to seek a review of status before a judge if he considers it necessary. Under the *CFSA*, the Director will have the same discretion but may also "give any other

direction that, in the Director's opinion, is in the child's best interests.''

7) *Section 63, CFSA:* The Minister may appoint a judge of the Supreme Court, District Court, Unified Family Court, Provincial Court (Family, Criminal or Civil Division) or Provincial Offences Court to investigate, under the jurisdiction of the *Public Inquiries Act*, a matter relating to a child in a Society's care or the administration of the Act generally (limited to Part III — Child Protection). The judge then makes a written report to the Minister. This section corresponds with s. 3 of the *CWA*.

8) *Section 64, CFSA:* Each Society will be required to establish a written complaint procedure for ''any person regarding services sought or received from a Society.'' If that person is not satisfied with the response from the Society's board of directors, he may ''have the matter reviewed by a Director.''

9) *Sections 105, 106 & 107, CFSA:* Each service provider who places children in residential placements or provides residential services to children will be required to establish a written complaint procedure in accordance with the regulations to hear complaints from the child or the child's parents, specifically about violations of a child's rights as delineated under Part V — Rights of Children. If the complainant is not satisfied with the results, he may request that the Minister appoint someone to conduct a further review, and the Minister shall so appoint. Upon receiving his report, the Minister may or may not decide to take action.

Judicial Test on Review

Perhaps the most contentious area of judicial concern in the child welfare arena has been the issue of the appropriate test to be applied upon a review of the child's status. One faction holds that while the language of the Act may require the court to apply a ''best interests'' test in deciding what further disposition, if any, is necessary, the court must be satisfied that the child remains a child ''in need of protection'' although the court need not re-try the issue of whether the child, at the time of the review should have been found in need of protection at the hearing of first instance.[168] The other faction maintains that at the time of the review, the only issue to be assessed is the best interests of the child as prescribed by the legislation and as defined by s. 1(1)(b) of the *CWA* (s. 37(3), *CFSA*).[169]

It is submitted that the issue is not so much which test to apply as it is that, due to the rehabilitative and remedial nature of child welfare legislation, the ''best interests'' standard in a child welfare proceeding should be different from that standard applied in a private inter-spousal custody dispute. Because there is a presumption in society and in the legislation that a child's ''best interests'' lie with the original family unit, the child should not be displaced permanently from this environment on the basis of an objective balancing of which party, the parents or the Society, can offer the better or more secure resources. To do so would suggest that the test of ''best interests'' is to be applied without regard to

---

[168]See *C.A.S. of Winnipeg v. Olson* (1980), 19 R.F.L. (2d) 384 (Man. C.A.); *Re R.M.H.* (1984), 40 R.F.L. (2d) 100 (Alta. C.A.); *Hansen v. C.A.S. of Hamilton-Wentworth* (1976), 27 R.F.L. 289 (Ont. Div. Ct.); *Re G.* (1976), 30 R.F.L. 224 (N.B.S.C.).

[169]*Petty v. Director of Child Welfare for Alta.* (1967), 61 D.L.R. (2d) 524 (Alta. C.A.); *M.M. v. B.M., supra* note 166: *C.C.A.S. v. J.* (1981), 24 R.F.L. (2d) 195 (Ont. U.F.C.).

the purpose and intent of the Act: namely, to preserve the integrity of the family and to utilize resources of the state to protect children within the family unit.

The definition of "best interests" under the *CWA* includes the "relevant considerations" of the child's "opportunity to enjoy a parent-child relationship and to be a wanted and needed member within a family structure": s. 1(1)(b)(ii), *CWA*. The parallel *CFSA* sub-section refers to "the importance of the child's development of a positive relationship with a parent and a secure place as a member of a family": s. 37(3), para. 5, *CFSA*. Although this can be used to argue the child's return to the family as well as Crown wardship with no access to make adoption possible, it should be coupled with s. 30(5) of the *CWA* (s. 53(2) of the *CFSA*) which directs the court prior to making any such order, to inquire as to any efforts which may have been made by the Society or any other person "to assist the child" before intervention under the Act. (Note also that the *CFSA* will include new "relevant considerations", discussed below, which may reinforce the original family's fight for the child.) Accordingly, any removal of a child from his home should be based on an assessment that the action is necessary because the child's level of care will not satisfy an acceptable minimum otherwise.[170] An Ontario Provincial Court judge observed that although the Act does not expressly require a new finding of "in need of protection" upon a review, it would be manifestly unjust simply to ask what order is in the best interests of the child: returning the child to his or her home or making the child a Crown ward with a view to adoption into a home at a higher socio-economic level and/or with greater stability. It is far too easy at this stage to find that it is "safer" to keep children in care and that the resources are better, hence it is in their best interests. The onus upon the Society — the particularly high onus where the application has switched to one of Crown wardship — cannot be forgotten: "One cannot imagine that the Legislature intended to create a system whereby evidence to support limited intervention in the lives of a family would be adduced and then used later to support a "best interests" decision not to return a child to his or her home."[171]

By way of contrast, in a Unified Family Court decision, the court noted that upon an application to review Crown wardship: ". . . it is not enough to have an unfit mother change sufficiently so that she would now be classified as a fit person to parent the child, but the court must be satisfied that it would be in the best interests of the child to revoke the Crown wardship. . . [The amended *CWA*] is an attempt to equate 'children's rights' (to a stable, secure and permanent home), with the heretofore emphasized 'parental rights' (*prima facie*, that the natural parents are entitled to custody)."[172]

The issue then is when, if ever, is the court entitled to assess the issue of best interests without regard to the underlying rehabilitative intent of the legislation. Should it occur once the child is found in need of protection? Should

---

[170]*Re Sarty* (1974), 19 R.F.L. 315 (N.S.S.C.).

[171]*Re P.V. and A.V.*, unreported, October 4, 1979 (Ont. Prov. Ct. Fam. Div.), *per* Nasmith J., as summarized in *Hartrick and Lazor supra*, note 87.

[172]*Frappier and C.A.S. of Hamilton-Wentworth*, summarized in (1980), 2 F.L.R.R. 114 (Ont. U.F.C.).

it occur when the child is made a Crown ward? It is submitted that as long as a parent is entitled to seek a status review, ''best interests'' should be interpreted in accordance with the remedial nature of the legislation, which is rehabilitating parents to a minimum standard of acceptable parenting so that the child can be reared in his original family unit. If the courts apply the ''best interests'' standard of the private custody dispute, as they do from time to time, then it tells parents that once their child is found ''in need of protection'', they must compete with the best resources that the state or eager adoptive parents have to offer. Given the newly extended rights of foster parents to be heard by the court when they have cared for the child for a period of six months, one more voice is added to this competitive dynamic. The competitive ''best interests'' standard also tells the parents that the period of time for rehabilitation represented by the length of the Society wardship order, presumably given to the parents as a time period in which they may improve their parenting circumstances, also represents the period of time during which a status quo in another family unit is gaining ground. Applying the ''best interests'' principles of an ordinary custody dispute, the court might too easily be inclined to rule in favour of the status quo and thereby avoid the risk of another change in the child's life and the possibility that the parent will not ''make good'' on their promise and efforts to date. One of the specific ''relevant considerations of best interests'' is the importance of continuity in the child's care: s. 1(1)(b), *CWA*/ s. 37(3), para. 7, *CFSA*. The danger lies in isolating this guideline from all others.[173]

Both the competitive nature of ''best interests'' and the looming danger of the ever-strengthening status quo must have an oppressive effect on the ability and willingness of the parents to rehabilitate themselves to meet minimum standards. It is suggested that this effect is repugnant to the clearly rehabilitative nature of the legislation. As well, this approach consists of an untested assumption: namely, that the child's long-term interests will also be satisfied by placement with persons other than those biological or psychological parents who had been caring for them, especially in the context of successful rehabilitative efforts on the latter's part. In recognizing the degree of chance involved, one judge held that a court cannot assume that adoption is a panacea and accordingly, without evidence, the court cannot infer that a child is suitable for adoption, that adoption is probable or that such adoption would be in the interests of the child.[174]

Due to the different judicial approaches to a status review, there are also differences of opinion as to the nature of the onus that exists upon an applicant seeking review. In a 1981 Provincial Court decision, the judge held that parents who wish to reverse a Crown wardship process are not subject to the same heavy legal responsibility as was the Society in obtaining a Crown wardship order, but need only meet and satisfy the ordinary civil standard of proof based upon a

---

[173]See *Re D.*, unreported, Nov. 25, 1981 (Ont. Prov. Ct.). Leave to appeal to C.A. from Div. Ct. (Sept. 10/84) refused, Nov. 26/84; *A.N.R. and S.C.R. v. L.J.W.* (1983), 36 R.F.L. (2d) 1, revsg. (1982), 19 Man. R. (2d) 186, 32 R.F.L. (2d) 153 (S.C.C.).

[174]*Re C.A.S. of Kingston and H.* (1979), 24 O.R. (2d) 146 (Ont. Prov. Ct.). See also *Re N.*, summarized in (1984), 7 F.L.R.R. 61 (Ont. U.F.C.).

balance of probabilities. The parents should in no way be placed in the position of having to compete with the resources of the state when attempting to reverse Crown wardship status. State intervention should only continue if the level of care in the former home remains at, or has fallen again below the accepted standards. The court considered that the protection of the integrity of a family unit forms a basis for the rationale behind the demanding civil onus which must be discharged by an applicant Children's Aid Society when Crown wardship is ordered, and this rationale must be built into a status review application.[175]

Upon its proclamation, the *CFSA* may be interpreted by the courts either to lean in the direction of requiring the continuation of "in need of protection" circumstances in a review context, or it may simply be used to justify both approaches noted above because it lists so many variables to be included in the court's decision. For example, the new legislation will include an extra subsection (s. 61(3), *CFSA*) which outlines the following eight specific considerations for the judge to take into account on a status review:

(a) whether the grounds on which the original order was made still exist;

(b) whether the plan for the child's care that the court applied in its decision is being carried out;

(c) what services have been provided or offered under this Act to the person who had charge of the child immediately before intervention under this Part;

(d) whether the person is satisfied with those services;

(e) whether the Society is satisfied that the person has cooperated with the Society and with any person or agency providing services;

(f) whether the person or the child requires further services;

(g) whether, where immediate termination of an order has been applied for but is not appropriate, a future date for termination of the order can be estimated; and

(h) what is the least restrictive alternative that is in the child's best interests.

Sub-section (a) will specifically direct the judge's attention prior to making a review order to whether the original grounds for state intervention still exist, thereby overruling those judges who refuse to consider this based on a narrow interpretation of "best interests". Sub-sections (c), (d), (e) and (f) will direct the judge's attention to the services and assistance provided to the parents, implying that rehabilitation is still a prime goal under supervisory and wardship orders. Finally, sub-section (h) uses the phrase which re-occurs throughout this piece of legislation — "the least restrictive alternative" — presumably implying that this type of alternative is the preferable alternative. Nevertheless, the review order itself under s. 61(1) of the *CFSA* will still be governed only by "the best interests of the child", defined under s. 37(3) of the *CFSA* on the basis of what is best for the child's health and development, not whether the parents received appropriate support from the Society. The parents' best defence will be to complain early on to the court under s. 60(8) of the *CFSA* or to the Society board of directors under

---

[175]*M. v. C.A.S. of Metro. Toronto*, summarized in (1981), 4 F.L.R.R. 30 (Ont. Prov. Ct.). See also *T.M.M. v. C.C.A.S.*, summarized in (1981), 4 F.L.R.R. 30 (Ont. Prov. Ct.).

s. 64 that the Society's rehabilitative plan which was the basis of the original order was not being carried out satisfactorily.

Looking at "best interests" alone under s. 37(3) of the *CFSA*, the importance of the original parent-child attachment will be reflected in some of the new "considerations" which are: (1) relationships by blood or through an adoption order; (2) the preservation of a child's cultural identity; (3) the child's religious upbringing; (4) the risk to the child in being kept away from the parents; (5) and the degree of risk that justified the protection finding in the first place. All of these considerations may discourage a court from comparision shopping for the best family unit for the child, giving the parents some hope that their rehabilitative efforts will mean something in a review hearing. On the other hand, other sub-sections, most of which were continued from the *CWA*, will also be contained in the "considerations" including: (1) the child's physical, mental and emotional needs and development; (2) the importance of a positive and secure family unit; (3) the merits of the Society's plan as compared to the merits of returning the child home; (4) the effect of delayed disposition; (5) and the risk of returning the child to the parent. These considerations encourage comparison shopping, although the final one does direct a judge, as under s. 61(3)(a) of the *CFSA*, to consider whether the "at risk" circumstances which led to a protection finding are still in existence. Note, however, in utilizing any of these "considerations" that it is in the judge's discretion to note only those "considerations" which he decides are relevant to all the circumstances: s. 1(2), *CWA*/ s. 37(3), *CFSA*. The only exception to this discretion occurs under the new Act, in which a court is *required* to take into account a child's "native or Indian" heritage: s. 37(4), *CFSA*.

It remains to be seen whether decisions after the proclamation of the *CFSA* will reflect a change due to the new guidelines or will simply make it easier to seek justification somewhere in the same guidelines. The tyranny of the status quo will undoubtedly remain strong. Rehabilitative success becomes progressively less important the longer the placement outside the home lasts. The only possible defence to this tendency is to challenge the assumption that a child's long term best interests lie in seeking continuity at all costs rather than some combination of stability while maintaining some degree of connection with the original parents. The well-known search by adopted children for their birth parents is a phenomenon which reflects this need to connect with origins. Perhaps the "final line of defence" lies in s. 1 of the *CFSA* which outlines the purposes of the legislation. On the one hand, it states that the paramount objective will be to promote the best interests of the child. On the other hand, it recognizes (1) the desirability of supporting the autonomy and integrity of the family unit coupled with the desirability of the least restrictive alternative; and (2) the need to respect a child's cultural and religious origins.

The Native Child

The *CWA* is silent with respect to child welfare services for native people. In fact it makes no reference to any cultural recognition in the servicing of families in a multi-cultural community. The *CFSA* will significantly improve on its predecessor in both respects but its most significant departure is in the structural change to the child welfare industry as it relates to native families. Many lobby groups have made the argument that Societies throughout Canada have shown only minimal recognition of the distinct culture, mores and problems of the native community in delivering services to the family, in assessing whether to remove the child from the family and in providing placements[176] and adoptions with non-native families. The Societies in areas of high concentration of native peoples have had an embarrassingly disproportionate number of native staff and service delivers.[177] One Society even refused to give the usual supportive services to the mother, preferring to go directly to permanent guardianship on the grounds that it was the federal government's responsibility to provide such resources.[178] The over-representation of native children removed from their families[179] and the high incidence of placements with white families[180] (especially those who are eager to adopt) has led some commentators to label the trend "cultural genocide."[181]

---

[176]Put in the form of a case illustration: the native child who is placed in a non-native foster home — his hair worn Indian style now cut short, the home and the reservation being hundreds of miles away — is predictably and understandably unlikely to participate in counselling or other services provided by a Society that has already alientated the parents. See Gloria Shephard, "A Canadian Native Program" and Marie Linklater, "Working with Native Families" in (1977), 9 *Family Involvement Journal* 1 and 31.

See also "Native Foster Children Denied Cultural Links by Children's Aid Societies", *Globe and Mail*, Sept. 24, 1984, p. 50. The article covers a panel discussion organized in Toronto by the Canadian Association in Support of Native Peoples. Some of the criticisms included a Society turning down native people who apply to be foster parents because they are measured by non-native values including a room for every child, a home with a set number of square feet of space, a certain income and a Christian faith.

[177]See *e.g.* Louis Cameron, "The Violence of Oppression", (1977), 9 *Family Involvement Journal* 23. See also "Native Foster Children Denied Cultural Links by Children's Aid Societies", *ibid*, wherein one Society worker stated that there exists no job designation for a worker to deal with natives, there is a low representation of native workers on staff and no use is made of native homemakers while white homemakers are sent to native homes, causing conflict instead of assisting.

[178]*Man. Director of Child Welfare v. B.*, [1979] 6 W.W.R. 229, [1981] 4 C.N.L.R. 62 (Man. Prov. Ct.). The court held that the Society's approach was "unfair, unjust, discriminatory and illegal" since s. 88 of the *Indian Act* provides for the general applicability to Indians of provincial legislation. Nevertheless, he granted the Society's application finding that the mother's parenting probably would not improve even with assistance.

[179]Using 1977 data, a Canadian study estimated that indigenous (native) children represented 39% of all children in foster care in the four western provinces of Canada. In Alberta, the proportion was 44%. In Saskatchewan, it was 51.5% and in Manitoba, the figure was 60%: Patrick Johnston, *The Child Welfare System and Indigenous Peoples of Canada: An Overview*, (Ottawa: Canadian Council on Social Development, 1981). Using 1980–81 data, Johnston in a later publication estimated the percentage of native children in care: British Columbia — 36.7%; Alberta — 43.7 to 41.6%; Saskatchewan — 63.8%; Manitoba — 56% (estimate); Ontario — 8.0% (with an estimate from one worker at the Kenora CAS of 85%): P. Johnston, *Native Children and the Child Welfare System* (Toronto: The Canadian Council on Social Development in Association with James Lorimer and Co., 1983).

[180]See *e.g.* Judge Edwin Kimelman, *Manitoba Inquiry into the Adoption and Placement of Indian and Métis Children*, (Winnipeg: Manitoba Government Printing Offices, 1984).

[181]*Ibid*. Judge Kimelman who used the phrase "cultural genocide" to describe the practice of placing native children in white homes, expecially focused on the fact that during the time period which he studied, 53% of the children were placed outside Manitoba, and went to the United States, and about 86% of these children were of native ancestry. One thousand Indian children from Manitoba were adopted in the United States from 1968 to 1982. See also a recent Supreme Court of Canada decision which approved the adoption of a seven-year-old native child by white parents despite a

Some courts have participated in the trend in applying a white, urban test of "in need of protection" to the native child living on the reserve. For example, in one case the native mother's lawyer made the argument that the child was being adequately cared for by the extended family in the native community based on the traditional custom of the community sharing the child-care responsibilities. The court of first instance denied the application for Crown wardship and instead granted three-month temporary guardianship to the Society, believing the mother would change. However, the Appellate Court overruled the lower court and granted Crown wardship stating:

> As indicated, the mother is a treaty Indian and a lot of time was spent explaining to the court Indian culture and the habits of native Indians with respect to their children, their custody and their exchange by various members of the family, as well as their nomadic habits. None of this background information explained the utter lack of care of these children on the part of this mother.[182]

Upon its proclamation, the changes to be effected by the *CFSA* will be structural and they will also give direction to the decision making of judges and service providers. They include the following:

1) A declaration of the Act's purposes including a statement of recognition of the distinct culture, heritage and tradition of the Indian and native community, including the concept of "the extended family" and the corollary duty upon the state to ensure that Indian and native people, wherever possible, be entitled to provide their own Child and Family Services: s. 1(f), *CFSA*.

2) Procedural protections to ensure the awareness and involvement of the native community in any child protection proceeding including the right of a representative, chosen by the child's band or native community,

(a) to have party status: s. 39(1), para. 4, *CFSA*;

(b) to have status to seek access to the child and status review: ss. 54(2)(b), 60(4)(d), 76(4)(f), *CFSA*;

(c) to have notice of any access or status review application by a Society or other party: ss. 54(4)(d) and 60(6)(e), *CFSA*;

(d) to appeal: s. 65(1)(e), *CFSA*; and

(e) to notice of placement for adoption of a native child: s. 134(3), *CFSA*.

3) The definition of "best interests" both with respect to child protection and adoption will include a specific obligation to consider the "importance, in recognition of the uniqueness of Indian and native culture, heritage and traditions, of preserving the child's cultural identity": s. 37(4), 53(5), 130(3), *CFSA*.

---

vigorous battle from the native mother supported by the native community. Madam Justice Wilson stated "In my view, when the test to be met is the best interests of the child, the significance of cultural background and heritage as opposed to bonding abates over time.": *A.N.R. and S.C.R. v. L.J.W.* (1983), 36 R.F.L. (2d) 1 (S.C.C.).

[182]*C.A.S. of Winnipeg v. Redwood* (1981), 19 R.F.L. (2d) 232 (Man. C.A.).

4) There will be a specific obligation on the court when it has decided to remove a native child and on a Society to consider whether it is possible to place the child with a member of his extended family, a member of the child's band or native community or another Indian or native family: ss. 53(5), 57(2)(d), *CFSA*.[183]

5) The *CFSA* will authorize the creation and operation of "Indian and Native Child and Family Services" (Part X of the Act) which basically will replace Society services for native children within a particular jurisdiction: ss. 191-96, *CFSA*. At the time of writing, the Minister had signed an agreement with the Nishnawbe Aski (a group fo 42 Indian bands north and west of the Great Lakes basin) to give the latter the power to provide their own child and family services. In so doing, Community and Social Services Minister Frank Drea stated:

> The ties that bind native communities are strong. It is not uncommon in the native culture for families to take into their midst and hearts less fortunate relatives. It is our intention to support that tradition of the extended family.[184]

It remains to be seen whether the government dollars will follow.

The State as Guardian: Duties and Responsibilities

When a child is made a temporary Society ward, the local Society assumes all the rights and responsibilities of a legal guardian for the purpose of the child's care, custody and control: s. 41, *CWA*/ s. 59(2), *CFSA*.[185] When a Crown wardship order is made, it is the Crown, rather than the Society, which theoretically assumes the role of legal guardian although the guardianship powers and duties are delegated to the local Society with the qualification that the Director retains the power to transfer the child to another Society or institution: s. 40, *CWA*/ s. 59(1), *CFSA*. This guardianship role is subject to restrictions which do not exist in the usual parent-child guardianship relationship. Nevertheless, the main responsibility of the Society — to decide upon and review the most appropriate placement for the child which is available — was, for the most part, unfettered under the *CWA*. The *CFSA*, on the other hand, will introduce a myriad of checks and balances for the duration of a Society or Crown wardship order.

Placements

The *CWA* and its regulations set out a limited number of requirements of a Society regarding a child's placement. Within 60 days of admission to care, the

---

[183]See *C.A.S. of Winnipeg v. Big Grassy Indian Band* (1982), 13 Man. R. (2d) 320 (C.A.) in which the band offered to be guardian rather than see the child placed in an adoptive home outside the native community. The court dismissed the band's application, determining that it was not a suitable guardian despite the existence of a successful program conducted by the Fort Frances C.A.S. in which neglected native children were raised by an extended family on the reserve.

[184]*Globe and Mail,* October 17, 1984, p. 5.

[185]See *Kingsbury v. Minister of Social Services for the Province of Sask*. (1982), 4 C.R.R. 151, 31 R.F.L. (2d) 334 (Sask. U.F.C.) wherein the powers of guardianship of Alberta Social Services were such that when its 13-year-old ward ran away to Saskatchewan, Saskatchewan's Minister was bound to return her to Alberta's Minister. The court also held that the child's mobility rights under s. 6(2)(a) of the Charter were reasonably limited by the guardian's rights to determine where the child shall live.

Society is required to prepare and record a plan for "the care, treatment, social adjustment and educational progress" of the child which then was to be reviewed by them every three months: *CWA*, O. Reg. 96/80, s. 21. The statute gives corollary power to the Society to place the child for any period of time in or remove the child from a foster home or other suitable place (not including an observation and detention home except with court order: *Provincial Courts Act*, O. Reg. 807/80, ss. 5 and 6) according to the needs of the child: s. 45(1) and (2), *CWA*. This can include a placement out of province if not in conflict with the judge's original order.[186] Where practicable, the child should have visited the new home 10 days prior to the placement and a social worker must re-assess a foster home yearly, and visit the child within seven days of placement, then 30 days, and then every three months thereafter: *CWA*, O. Reg. 97/80, ss. 5(2), (c) and 6.

Upon its proclamation, the *CFSA* will introduce specific, mandatory guidelines for the Society to follow in determining a child's placement. Under s. 57(2) and (5) the placement must:

(a) represent the leat restrictive alternative for the child;
(b) where possible, respect the religious faith, if any, in which the child is being raised;
(c) where possible, respect the child's linguistic and cultural heritage;
(d) where the child is an Indian or native person, be with a member of the child's extended family, a member of the child's band or native community, or another Indian or native family, if possible; and
(e) take into account the child's wishes, if they can be reasonably ascertained, and the wishes of any parent who is entitled to access to the child.

These guidelines will reinforce the enunciated purposes of the *CFSA* under s. 1(d), (e) and (f) which recognize that services should be provided taking into account a child's need for continuity and stability as well as differences among children including physical and mental developmental differences, religious, cultural and regional differences and, in particular, differences in culture, heritage and tradition, especially of the Indian or native child.

Other sections of the *CFSA* affecting a Society's or service provider's discretion in making placements and delivering services will include (note that many of these requirements will not affect foster parents who will be excluded from the definition of "service provider" under s. 3(1), para. 27):

1) services to be available in French "where appropriate": s. 2(1);
2) children and parents "where appropriate", will be heard and represented in decision-making and complaints: s. 2(2)(a);
3) decisions to be made based on clear, consistent criteria subject to procedural safeguards: s. 2(2)(b);
4) no placements except in accordance with the Act and Regulations: s. 14;
5) Society will be required to provide prescribed standard of services and follow prescribed procedures: s. 15(4);

---

[186]*J.A.C.* v. *C.A.S. of Ottawa-Carleton* (1981), 22 R.F.L. (2d) 124 (Ont. C.A.).

6) a child 16 years and over (unless subject to the *Young Offenders Act*) must first consent to services offered unless otherwise ordered by a court: s. 27(1)(3); (note that consents including capacity to consent will be affected by ss. 4 and 28);

7) for a child under 16 years, (unless subject to the *Young Offenders Act*) consent to residential placement will be a pre-requisite either from parent or, if child is a ward, from Society: s. 27(2)(3);

8) before placement, removal or transfer of a child in or from a residential placement, the child's wishes shall be taken into account if ascertainable: s. 27(6);

9) a child between 12 and 16 years may receive counselling on his own consent although child to be encouraged to include parent: s. 28;

10) child not to be placed or allowed to go outside of Ontario unless extraordinary circumstances with Director's consent: s. 57(4);

11) Society to ensure that the child is afforded all the rights referred to in Part V of the Act (Rights of Children): s. 57(5)(a);

12) wishes of parent if entitled to access and, if Crown ward, of foster parent (of at least two years), must be taken into account in Society's major decisions: s. 57(5)(b);

13) Society will not be able to remove a child from a foster parent (of at least two years) without first giving 10 days notice to foster parent (presumably to enable him to initiate a complaint hearing under s. 64): s. 57(7) and (8);

14) child in care will have the right to a plan of care designed to meet his particular needs (to be prepared within 30 days of admission to residential placement) and to participate in the development of that plan and in any changes made thereto: s. 101(1), s. 101(2)(a);

15) child in care will have a right to receive well-balanced, appropriate meals and good quality, appropriate clothing: s. 101(2)(b) and (c);

16) child in care will have the right to be consulted and express views regarding significant placement decisions "to the extent that it is practicable given the child's level of understanding": s. 103;

17) Parts IV (child comes into care under *Young Offenders Act* or *Provincial Offences Act*) and VI (secure treatment program) will specifically carve out ministerial jurisdiction and authority from that of Societies;

18) in order to ensure that the Society will adhere to all of the above restrictions and guidelines, a system of multi-level reviews and complaint procedures will be included throughout the Act (See above under "Best Interests Disposition: Review/Termination of Order".)

There is no written direction under the *CWA* that the recorded plan and the subsequent placement(s) must be the same as that which was offered to, accepted by and recorded by the court under s. 36 of the *CWA* as a basis for its order and although one assumes they will bear some resemblance, there is no supervisory jurisdiction vested in the courts.[187] An earlier Alberta Court of Appeal case did

---

[187]See *supra*, note 141.

impose some limitations by suggesting that the Society's power as guardian does not extend to placing the child outside of the jurisdiction of the court nor generally to keep the whereabouts of the child concealed for a time from the parents.[188] This decision illustrates that while the Provincial Court may not direct the Society as to the carrying out of its mandate, the Society, like any guardian, is subject to the overriding supervision of the superior court in the exercise of its inherent jurisdiction. There is certainly no clear language in the *CWA* which acts to deprive the Superior Court of this jurisdiction and accordingly, a person may seek the court's intervention on the grounds that the Society has not properly exercised its discretion.[189] However, it should be remembered that resorting to a Superior Court should not simply be another route to appeal a Provincial Court decision since this type of proceeding is specifically provided for under the *CWA*. The choice of the Superior Court route should be limited to situations in which the improper exercise of discretion on the part of the authorities is jeopardizing the welfare of the child and there is no immediate alternative recourse available under the Act. This latter pre-condition becomes even more important once the *CFSA* is proclaimed since there will be so many new and different review and complaint mechanisms regarding Society services and placements albeit within the Ministry itself.

Adoption

When a child is made a Crown ward, the Society must endeavour to secure the child's adoption having regard to his best interests: s. 68, *CWA*/ s. 134(1), *CFSA*. (See generally ''Adoption'' below.)

Access to Parents and Others

Aside from any existing court order regarding access, (see above under ''Access'') the Society, under ss. 46 and 95, *CWA* has the power to regulate or forbid all contact with the child by anyone including the parents. Nevertheless, s. 4 of the Regulations under the *CWA*, O. Reg. 97/80 specifically obligates the Society ''to maintain and encourage contact'' between the child and his family unless the Society decides it is not in the child's best interests.

Although the *CFSA*, upon its proclamation, will contain basically the same section, (s. 79) it will also include a section giving the child in care a right to visit in private with family members (unless he is a Crown ward in which case he is not so entitled unless ordered by the court) and with any advocate and as well, it directs that he will be able to send and receive mail in private unless the service provider determines that the mail must be read by him in the child's presence in his best interests: s. 99, *CFSA*.

Consent to Treatment

Although there is no specific mention in the *CWA* of who has the power to consent to medical treatment when the child is a ward, the Society, by right of its guardianship role assumes this authority.[190] (See blood transfusion cases discussed above under ''Finding Child in Need of Protection: Statutory Grounds''.) Note also the decision of a Provincial Court judge which held that a

---

[188]*Re Children's Protection Act; Triskow's Case*, [1918] 3 W.W.R. 512 (Alta. C.A.). See also *Johnson v. Director General of Social Welfare* (1976), 50 A.L.J.R. 562; *Dube v. Minister of Social Welfare and Rehabilitation* (1963), 42 W.W.R. 86 (Sask. C.A.); *J.A.C. v. C.A.S. of Ottawa-Carleton, supra*, note 186. (Society placing child outside province with mother defeats court-ordered access to both parents; order granted directing return of child to province).
[189]*Re T. (A.J.J.) (an infant)*, [1970] 2 All E.R. 865 (C.A.).
[190]*Re A. and C.A.S. of Metro. Toronto* (1982), 141 D.L.R. (3d) 111 (Ont. Prov. Ct.).

supervision order includes the right of social workers to examine children physically.[191] This differs from the circumstances under a voluntary agreement where, even though the child and parent may be receiving the same services as under a wardship order, the parent, by proceeding voluntarily, retains the right to consent to medical treatment (see above under ''Voluntary Agreements for State Assistance: Agreements and Consent to Treatment'').

The *CFSA*, on the other hand, will spell out who is to exercise the authority to give medical consents under wardship care. It directs that if the child is a Soceity ward, it will be the Society which exercises the authority unless the court orders otherwise, but the court shall not give the parents the authority if failure to consent was a ground for a protection finding in the first place: s. 58(1), (2), *CFSA*. Further, if a parent of a Society ward who has been granted the authority, refuses, is unavailable or is unable to consent and the court deems such consent to be in the child's best interests, the court will be able to authorize the Society to consent: s. 58(3), *CFSA*. If the child is a Crown ward, the Society will have the indisputable authority to give consent: s. 59(1), *CFSA*. If the child lies outside the jurisdiction of the above-noted sections, (*e.g.* supervisory order), the parent will retain the right to consent: s. 102(b), *CFSA*.

Education

Under Part V of the new Act (Children's Rights), the child will have a right to the appropriate medical and dental care as well as a right to have his wishes heard whenever significant medical decisions are being made about him ''to the extent that is practical given the child's level of understanding''; ss. 101(2)(d) and 103, *CFSA*. Under the *CWA*, the Society is obligated to ensure that the child under its care receives an education ''in accordance with the laws of Ontario and in keeping with the child's intellectual capacity'' as well as occupational training and ''total development such as a good parent would provide for his or her own child'': s. 45(1), *CWA*.

Upon proclamation, the *CFSA* will impose a duty on the Society to educate the child ensuring that it ''corresponds to his or her aptitudes and abilities'': s. 57(3), *CFSA*, In addition, the child in care will have a corollary right to receive this type of education ''in a community setting whenever possible'' and to participate in recreational and athletic activities that are ''appropriate for the child's aptitudes and interests in a community setting wherever possible'': ss. 101(2)(e) and (f), *CFSA*. It appears that unless the child is a Crown ward, the parent will retain the right ''to direct'' the child's education under the *CFSA* subject to the overlapping power of the court and the Society to ensure that the child receives services appropriate to his needs: s. 102(a), *CFSA*.[192] In addition, the child in care will have the right to be heard on any significant decision regarding his education ''to the extent that is practical given the child's level of understanding'': s. 103, *CFSA*.

Religion

As is true of Ontario's educational system, there are some denominational Children's Aid Societies in some parts of the province, specifically Catholic

---

[191]*R. v. Lips*, unreported, September 17, 1982 (Ont. Prov. Ct. Fam. Div.), per Dunn, J.

[192]But see *Re C.A.S. of Belleville and M.* (1980), 28 O.R. (2d) 795 (Prov. Ct.) wherein court held that the Society having temporary custody of children was the ''guardian'' under the *Education Act* for the purpose of consenting to release of school records.

Societies and, in the Municipality of Metropolitan Toronto, the Jewish Family and Child Services. The legislation directs that a Protestant child shall not be committed to the care of a Roman Catholic Children's Aid Society, institution or foster home, and the same prohibition holds true for Catholic children in a Protestant Society, institution or foster home: s. 44, *CWA*/ s. 82(3), *CFSA*. If a child is other than Catholic or Protestant, he is to be placed, if practicable, with a family of his or her own religious faith. Note that the court or Director is exempt from observing this restriction on placement if there is only one Society in the jurisdiction or if the restriction would unduly delay placement: ss. 44(5), (6), *CWA*/ s. 82(4), (5), *CFSA*. In addition, notwithstanding anything in the above-noted sections, the court may have regard to the wishes of the child: s. 44(7), *CWA*/ s. 82(2), *CFSA*.[193]

Determination of a child's religion under the *CWA* for the purpose of placement is governed by s. 44(1), (2) and (3) of the *CWA*. If a child is born outside marriage, he is deemed to have the religious faith of his mother, otherwise, he is deemed to have that of his father unless there was an agreement between the parents that he be brought up in the same religious faith as the child's mother. If there is ambiguity or if these sections do not apply to the particular circumstances, the court is to decide what is ''proper''. In addition to the child's wishes and views, these circumstances might include:[194]

1) the religion of the parents;
2) if separated, the religion of the custodial parent;
3) the extent to which the child has been accustomed to one or both religious faiths of his parents, and the extent to which one or both parents have attended to the child's religious education, and
4) the intentions of the parents in terms of religious education for the child and the effect of a determination of religion that results in the child's placement in a denominational residential setting.

Upon proclamation of the *CFSA*, any reference to the father's and mother's religion in or out of wedlock will be deleted. The court is to adopt whatever religion will be agreed upon ''by the child's parent'' but where there is no ascertainable agreement, the court may decide on the religion, if any, ''on the basis of the child's circumstances'': s. 82(1), *CFSA*. In addition, the parent will also retain the right under the *CFSA*, unless the child is a Crown ward, ''to direct'' the child's religious upbringing: s. 102, *CFSA*. As well, the child in care will have a right, subject to s. 102, to receive religious instruction of his choice (s. 100(b), *CFSA*) and to be heard regarding any significant decision made about his religious upbringing ''to the extent that it is practical given the child's level of understanding'': s. 103, *CFSA*.

Miscellaneous   Absent anything in the legislation, a wardship order does not affect a child's

---

[193]See *Re Brian O.*, summarized in (1980), 3 F.L.R.R. 153 (Ont. Prov. Ct.); *Re P.S.B.* (1978), 15 R.F.L. (2d) 199 (Ont. Prov. Ct.).
[194]*Re Brian O.*, *ibid*.

property or inheritance rights.[195] (See generally Chapter 5, ''Property and Civil Participation''.) The Society may launch a civil action on behalf of a ward in its care if it is of the opinion that the child has a right of recovery against anyone who afflicted abuse upon him: s. 51, *CWA*/ s. 77(2), *CFSA*.

The Director has the authority to consent to the issuance of a passport for a Crown ward under 16 and to that ward's travelling outside Canada: *CWA*, O. Reg. 96/80, s. 14.

Adoption

Adoption: Introduction

The process of adoption in Ontario, governed by its child welfare legislation, can occur via two distinct routes: under Crown wardship or by private adoption. Under the former, as described above under ''Child Protection,'' the child has been found ''in need of protection'' and has become the subject of a Crown wardship order with no access granted to the parents: s. 38(8)(d), *CWA*/ s. 134(2)(a), *CFSA*. The Crown is now the legal guardian and has the authority to consent to an adoption; the parents no longer play any role or have any legal rights in the process. The child is placed in an approved home for adoption (s. 65, *CWA*/ s. 134-37, *CFSA*) by the Society which is under a duty to secure adoption of all Crown wards: s. 68, *CWA*/ s. 134(1), *CFSA*.

In the private adoption, the parent(s) must give their consent: s. 69, *CWA*/ s. 131(2)(a), *CFSA*. Within the private adoption process, there are two different streams: the ''family'' adoption, that is, by a step-parent or relative (the former being the most frequent), and adoption by unrelated persons. The former stream is a private process which requires no state agent as supervisor (s. 65(4), *CWA*/ s. 135(8), *CFSA*) but does require a court order as described below. The latter stream under the *CWA* utilizes adoption agencies and licensees to supervise the process and to match adoptive parents with children. Adoption agencies are non-profit organizations which include every Society while private ''licensees'' are persons who have applied to the Ministry for a licence to place the child for adoption: ss. 60 to 64, *CWA*. Within this private adoption stream, it is the adoption agency or licensee which has the sole right to place a child under 18 years for the purpose of adoption: s. 65(1), *CWA*. Upon proclamation of the *CFSA*, the same approach will be utilized in a simplified form. The classification of ''adoption agency'' will no longer be used so that the supervising bodies will be Societies and licensees, the latter being limited to an individual or a non-profit agency: ss. 135(1), 176(4)(b), *CFSA*.

Regardless of whether the placement occurs under Crown wardship or privately, the parties must make application to the Provincial Court (Fam. Div.) for an adoption order (s. 71, *CWA*/ s. 140, *CFSA*) and the judge is governed by certain legislated restrictions: ss. 71-78, *CWA*/ ss. 140-47, *CFSA*. If all restrictions are satisfied, the judge still has discretion to grant or deny the order based on the best interests of the child: s. 76(b), *CWA*/ s. 140, *CFSA*.

---

[195]*Re Maureen S.*, unreported, April 25, 1977 (Ont. Prov. Ct. Fam. Div.), and see *Re Wood* (1971), 5 R.F.L. 25 (B.C.S.C.) where the court determined that an order for the temporary wardship of a child does not prevent a father from appointing the maternal grandparents as the guardians of the child by a deed of guardianship executed by the sole surviving parent.

If an adoption placement has dragged on for a year with no resulting adoption order, the Director is mandated to review the situation and has several routes open to him, including the return of the child to the original family unit: s. 69(11), *CWA*/ s. 139, *CFSA*.

Finality of Adoption Order

The significance of an adoption order cannot be over-emphasized, especially since, unless appealed within 30 days (for which no extension of time for serving the notice of making the appeal shall be granted), it is final, irrevocable and immune from judicial review by way of any extraordinary remedy: s. 83, *CWA*/s. 151, *CFSA*. The order represents the only process in law where a person's biological identity is transformed through a legal fiction. The child is to be treated as if he had been born to the adopting parent, sharing by blood all of that parent's kindred relationships: ss. 86(1) and (2), *CWA*/ s. 152(2), (3), *CFSA*.[196] Both the biological and adopting parents must consent before the child can gain information about his biological origins, even assuming the adopting parents have told the child that he is adopted. Differences in race, religion or culture are no bar to an adoption[197] and the far reaching effects remain the same. The broad "best interests" discretion in granting the order will be expanded under the *CFSA* to include "considerations" of the child's cultural or religious background and, in particular, if the child is native, the preservation of his cultural identity. However, these variables will not amount to barriers to adoption but simply factors, which in his own discretion, the judge may or may not consider relevant, (s. 130(2), *CFSA*) with the one exception; that is if the child is "Indian or native" his cultural origins *shall* be taken into account. (Note that the *CFSA*, unlike the *CWA*, will contain two different sets of "best interests" considerations, one for child protection proceedings and one for adoption).

The one chink in the wall between families is based on property rights which vested before the adoption order: s. 86(4), *CWA*/ s. 152(5), *CFSA*. As an extension of this exception, and due to the even more powerful legal fiction of federal-provincial jurisdiction, if a native child has been adopted by a non-native parent, it has been held that such an adoption is valid as long as the effect of the adoption is not inconsistent with the child's entitlement to be or to continue to be registered as a native, pursuant to the *Indian Act*. If there is a conflict between provincial adoption proceedings and the federal *Indian Act*, the provincial legislation will be nullified to the extent that it is inconsistent with the *Indian*

---

[196]See *Re Woods; Canada Permanent Trust Company v. Dearington*, (1982), 133 D.L.R. (3d) 751, 11 E.T.R. 104 (N.S.T.D.) (will made in 1923, child adopted in 1924 when law would not have included child as beneficiary under particular provisions of this will; death in 1980 when law would have done so; applicable laws when property to be transferred, *i.e.* 1980). Conversely, all support obligations from the original family ceases: *Wagstaff v. Wagstaff* (1981), 48 N.S.R. (2d) 466, 92 A.P.R. 466 (Prov. Ct.) (step-parent adoption: arrears prior to adoption only ordered to be paid).

[197]See *Re W.; W. v. R.; R. v. W.* (1982), 19 Man. R. (2d) 186, 32 R.F.L. (2d) 153 (C.A.) in which court refused to grant adoption order of native child by white parents despite six-year-old viewing foster parents as psychological parents and mother as relative stranger; child's cultural and religious heritage being relevant but not determinative factors; possibility of losing treaty status and as child aware of native origins, court not wanting to cut off all legal ties; child made ward with custody to foster parents.) The S.C.C. reversed this decision on a bonding/status quo argument due to the length of time involved; *supra,* note 181.

Act.[198] On this basis, it might be arguable that to deny the child knowledge of his biological origins, with or without the consent of the biological and adopting parents, and to remove any reference to the child's biological origins in his birth certificate[199] would be inconsistent with the child's entitlement to be registered as an Indian and to have the benefits of that registration at a later date.

The pretense created by the legal fiction of adoption becomes strained as children are increasingly adopted at a later age, after they have established a relationship with their parents or relatives. In England, an exception to the finality rule was allowed when the court was satisfied that contact with the natural parent(s) was or would be in the best interests of the child: ''At the right time and in the right manner contact between 'J.' and his father is likely to be for J's real and lasting benefit.''[200] In another English case, although grandparents were successful in adopting the illegitimate child of their daughter, the court wisely observed:

> The ostensible relationship of sisters between those who are, in fact, mother and child is unnatural, and its creation might sow the seeds of grievous unhappiness for them both, and, indeed, for the adopters themselves. . . . Let them never forget that [the grandparents] owe a continuing and inescapable duty to the young mother as well as to the child who will always be hers, however much my order may purport to make it theirs, and let them reconcile the claims on them with anxious care.[201]

On the other hand in a 1977 English decision, the court refused to grant a conditional adoption order which would allow the paternal grandparents to see and have communication with the child unless the proposed adoptive parents had accepted freely the terms of access in the adoption order and were willing to see them work. The court considered it a priority for the child's welfare that he be able to start life afresh in a new home.[202]

Unlike the English *Adoption Act*, Ontario's *CWA* lacks a clear statutory provision which permits access to a natural parent in conjunction with an adoption order although the broad language of s. 82 of the *CWA* (s. 148(1), (2), *CFSA*) (interim adoption orders) may permit the court to so order during a probationary period before granting a final adoption order. For adoptions involving a Society or licensee, *i.e.* not a ''family'' adoption, all outstanding access orders except those rendered under the child welfare legislation are terminated: s. 69(15), *CWA*/ s. 137(1), *CFSA*. Further, s. 154 of the *CFSA* will specifically state that once an adoption order has been made, no court shall make an access order in favour of a ''birth parent'' or his family ''under this Part.'' Accordingly, it appears that the status of birth parents or anyone else for that matter in applying for access under the *Children's Law Reform Act* will not be

---

[198]*Natural Parents v. Supt. of Child Welfare in Petitions for Adoption* (1976), 21 R.F.L. 267 (S.C.C.). See also *Re W., ibid.*

[199]See the *Vital Statistics Act*, but note s. 80(2)(d) of the *CWA* and s. 156(3)(d) of the *CFSA* which direct that a copy of the adoption order is to be sent to a Registrar under the *Indian Act*.

[200]*Re J.,* [1973] 2 All E.R. 410, at 417.

[201]*Re A.B. (an Infant),* [1949] 1 All E.R. 709, at 710.

[202]See *Re B., The Times,* March 25, 1977.

precluded by this new section. Although s. 152(2), of the *CFSA* will direct that upon the making of an adoption order, the child will no longer be the child of the biological parent "for all purposes of law", s. 21 of the *Children's Law Reform Act* allows "a parent or a child or any other person" to apply for an order respecting custody of or access to a child. A practical problem remains since the secrecy of the adoption process would prevent the birth parents (except those involved in a "family" adoption) from knowing where the children reside and what name they have acquired. A potential solution is to seek an injunction in the Superior Court to direct the relevant Society or licensee to inform the birth parents' solicitor of the requisite information perhaps on the understanding that it would not be revealed to the birth parents to preserve the secrecy of the adoption process. However, this would severely limit the case which the solicitor could present to the court.

One Ontario mother attempted to obtain access rights under domestic custody/access legislation. Her child was adopted in February, 1979 and the mother applied for access in March, 1979. The court would not hear the matter on its merits and on appeal, the Court of Appeal in dismissing her application noted that if the effect of an adoption order is final and irrevocable, wiping out "everything that went before", then domestic legislation must be reconciled with the adoption provisions in such a manner that the biological parent is no longer a "parent" within the meaning of domestic legislation and therefore there is no basis for her status in an application for access. The court also observed that an application for access to an adopted child, if permitted, would render the secrecy provisions of adoption orders "as naught and render them meaningless." If the applicant biological mother were to have her "day in court", notice would have to be given to the adopting parents and their presence would be necessary in the court room, the effect of which would be to ignore the rights and protections given to the child and the adoptive parents by the legislation which attempts to create a new family unit.[203] This decision apparently overrides previous decisions in Ontario which suggested that in certain situations, access to a biological parent is not incompatable with adoption.[204] Other jurisdictions in Canada have not been so rigid in this issue, at least with respect to step-parent adoptions.[205]

---

[203]See *G.W. v. M.J.* (1981), 34 O.R. (2d) 44, 24 R.F.L. (2d) 342 (C.A.); *Re W. and J.* (1981), 130 D.L.R. (3d) 418 (Ont. C.A.). See also *Sayer v. Minister of Social Services*, 14 Sask. R. 181 [1982] 3 W.W.R. 358 (*sub nom. S. v. Minister of Social Services*) (Q.B.) (s. 38 of *Family Services Act* precluding access order after committal and adoption placement; adoption order superseding existing custody/access orders and no such order to be made under *Infants Act*); *A.D.E. v. Family and Children's Services of King's County* (1981), 49 N.S.R. (2d) 43, 96 A.P.R. 43 (Co. Ct.) (Consent of parent coupled with filing of notice of proposed adoption ousts court's jurisdiction under *Infants Act*).

[204]See *Lyttle v. C.A.S. of Metro. Toronto* (1976), 24 R.F.L. 134 (Ont. S.C.); *Re B. and B.*, unreported, February 7, 1977 (Ont. Prov. Ct.); *C.A.S. v. Burns*, unreported, June 27, 1977 (Ont. Co. Ct.).

[205]See Manitoba: *Burton v. Zurba* (1982), 16 Man. R. (2d) 327 (Co. Ct.) (access application allowed in step-parent situation where child and biological father wanted to keep contact and mother not objecting); *A.F. v. B.F.* (1981), 8 Man. R. (2d) 303, 22 R.F.L. (2d) 12 (Co. Ct.) (step-parent); *Williams v. Hillier*, 13 Man. R. (2d) [1982] 2 W.W.R. 313, 131 D.L.R. (3d) 630, 26 R.F.L. (2d) 164 (C.A.) (step-parent: nothing in statute which requires that there be exceptional circumstances

Ontario's Appellate Court did leave open the question as to what occurs if the biological parent establishes a relationship with the child after the adoption order, suggesting that if that were to occur, the biological parent might then have the status to apply for access under domestic legislation.

The artificiality of adoption is severely strained in the case of a step-parent adoption in which the biological parents have divorced, the custodial parent has re-married and his or her spouse wishes to adopt the child. Such an adoption cannot take place without the consent of both biological parents unless the court decides to dispense with this necessity. (See below under "Consent of Parents".) Nevertheless, once an adoption order has been granted, the courts have exhibited some disagreement as to access rights previously acquired under other proceedings. It has been held in British Columbia that an order for adoption and the change of the child's surname does not affect or extinguish the access rights given to a parent under a *decree nisi* or *Infant's Act* application.[206] On the other hand, a different court in Manitoba has ruled that where there is such a step-parent adoption, it implicitly cancels out any legal or non-legal arrangements between a child and his former parents.[207] It would then follow from this decision that in a step-parent adoption, the only way that access between the biological "non-parent" and the child could continue would be through the goodwill of the biological parent who permits access to the biological non-parent, thereby giving rise to circumstances which may allow the non-parent to gain standing in a future access application.

Ontario's Legislature appears to recognize the special nature of "family" adoption by exempting them, in effect, from the provision which terminates all past access orders (except those made under child welfare legislation) since it only applies to those placements handled by a Society or agency/licensee: s. 69(15), *CWA*/ s. 137(1), *CFSA*. Further to this, the *CFSA*, once proclaimed, will require that the child reside with the applicant for at least two years in the case of "family" adoptions whereas all other adoptions only require a six-month placement period which may be abridged: s. 140(1)(c), *CFSA*. One assumes that this extended period, combined with ongoing access rights, will give the non-custodial birth parent and his family sufficient time either to forge relationships with the child or abandon them, thereby enabling the judge at the end of two years to better determine whether the drastic step of adoption is necessary. (Arguably, the custodial birth parent will not be precluded from

---

to grant access to biological parent); *G.M.Z. v. T.S.F.B.*, 4 Man. R. (2d) 390, [1981] 1 W.W.R. 152, 115 D.L.R. (3d) 706 (*sub nom. Re Z. and B.*) 18 R.F.L. (2d) 47 (C.A.) (adoption order overturned on appeal because trial judge did not consider whether the biological father should have access rights after step-parent adoption despite the fact that he had not exercised his existing access rights for five and a half years). British Columbia: *Re Female Child, B.C. Birth Registration No. 74-09-131763*, [1980] 2 W.W.R. 577, 17 B.C.L.R. 21 (S.C.) (B.C. adoption order may include specific access order for biological parent). Saskatchewan: *Re Spence and McKenna* (1981), 14 Sask. R. 166, 127 D.L.R. (3d) 761 (Q.B.) (step-parent: biological father having right under s. 3(1) *Infants Act* to make access application; need exceptional circumstances).

[206]*Kerr v. McWhannel* (1974), 16 R.F.L. 185 (B.C.C.A.) (decree *nisi*) and see *Re Toms*, [1950] 2 W.W.R. 863 (B.C.S.C.) (decree *nisi*).

[207]*Sobering v. Sergeant* (1970), 6 R.F.L. 51 (Man. C.A.) and see *R. v. County Court Judge; ex parte Sobering* (1969), 8 D.L.R. (3d) 576 (Man. C.A.).

reducing the placement period to six months by involving a licensee in the placement. This circumvention may be thwarted by the Minister refusing to issue a license in the case of ''family'' adoptions.)

It is unfortunate that, in present day society, when there is a high incidence of family units re-forming at least once, the courts and Legislature are inclined to limit psychological relationships through legal and fictional strait-jackets. It may be that the appropriate response is to limit adoption only to the clearest of cases where there is no possibility of the re-emergence of the biological spectre. As an alternative to adoption in the step-parent situation, the English courts have also considered the possibility of awarding joint custody to the parent and proposed step-parent in order to vest some rights in the new family unit, without denying what has come before.[208]

Suitability of Adopting Parents

Outside of the ''family'' adoption, the suitability of adopting parents is determined by the Society in the case of Crown wards and by the applicable adoption agency/licensee in all other cases. The process of determination is governed by ss. 65 and 66 of the *CWA* (s. 136, *CFSA*) with the major tool of assessment being the ''home study'' conducted by an appointee of the agency/licensee: s. 65(6), *CWA*/ s. 136(1), *CFSA*. Societies are also limited in their selection of parents by the conditions set out in the legislation which are discussed below under ''The Adoption Order: Statutory Restrictions on Adoption Order.'' The Society can also remove the child after he has been placed at any time up until the adoption order if it is considered in the child's best interests.[209] In addition, before an adoption order is rendered the Director (or local director if the child was placed by a Society) will file with the court prior to the hearing, a statement in writing indicating (1) whether or not it is in the best interests of the child that the proposed adoption proceed, and (2) confirming that the child has resided with the prospective adopting parents for six months or more or that there are reasons to dispense with this prerequisite: s. 75(1), *CWA*. Note that under the *CFSA*, a similar statement must be filed but if the placement was other than a Society/licensee placement, *i.e.* ''family'' adoption, the child must have resided with the applicant for two years with no discretion to shorten this period: ss. 140(1)(c), 143(1)(a), *CFSA*. The basis of the Director's statement must be an

---

[208]*Re S. (infants)*, [1977] 2 W.L.R. 919. See also *Stoodley v. Blunden* (1980), 17 R.F.L. (2d) 280 (N.S.C.A.) wherein court refused to dispense with father's consent in step-parent adoption because no benefit would arise solely from an adoption which could not be obtained by other legal means less drastic than that of severing the father's parental relationship with the child.

[209]See *e.g. Re W. and C.A.S. (Peel)* (1981), 132 D.L.R. (3d) 424 (Ont. H.C.) (Society removed child, declined to supply particulars of allegations against foster father. Court held that *prima facie* right in Society to remove child but father entitled to particulars and to respond; onus on father to show illegality of removal); *D.B. and P.B. v. Director of Child Welfare* (1982), 39 Nfld. and P.E.I.R. 246, 44 N.R. 602, 30 R.F.L. (2d) 438 (S.C.C.) (Society removed child from placement on unsupported allegations of mistreatment; Court of Appeal dismissed *habeas corpus* application; the S.C.C. granted adoption holding that 1) Court of Appeal had the jurisdiction to safeguard the child's interests by overturning decision of Society and 2) Society acted unfairly); *Galbraith v. Supt. of Family and Children's Services* (1981), 25 R.F.L. (2d) 244 (B.C.S.C.) (Adoptive parents separated during probationary period; child removed against adoptive mother's wishes; court deferred absolutely to discretion of Superintendent, holding that adoptive mother had acquired no rights and no capriciousness or bad faith on part of Superintendent.)

up-dated report by a field worker on the ''adjustment'' of the child in the home: s. 75(4), *CWA*/ s. 143(5), *CFSA*. As with the home study, the recommendations from the Director for proceeding with the adoption do not apply in the case of ''family'' adoptions although the court may order that the Director prepare and file a statement for such adoptions: s. 75(5), *CWA*/ s. 143(6), *CFSA*.

If the Director recommends against the adoption, his written opinion is to be filed with the court at least 30 days prior to the hearing and is to be served upon the applicant parties within seven days after so filing it: s. 75(2), *CWA*. Under the *CFSA*, it must be filed *and* served at least 30 days before the hearing: s. 143(4), *CFSA*. The court will consider the recommendations made by the Director but is not bound by them and may accordingly grant or dismiss the application, depending on what it decides is in the best interests of the child: s. 76(b), *CWA*/ s. 140(1)(2), *CFSA*. Previous legislation provided the Director with the sole authority to determine whether the applicants were suitable as adopting parents.[210]

Consent

No adoption order can be made in Ontario without the written consent:

1) of every ''parent'' which is broadly defined and includes anyone who has lawful custody: ss. 69(1)(2), *CWA*/ s. 131(1), (2), *CFSA*; and

2) of the child if over 6 years of age: s. 69(6), *CWA*/ ss. 4 and 131(6), *CFSA*.

3) under the *CWA*, consent of the spouse of the child, if married, is required: s. 69(6), *CWA*; this requirement will be omitted under the *CFSA*, upon its proclamation.

In Ontario, unlike some other jurisdictions, specific statutory rules govern the consent process, especially with respect to parental consent. The practical and legal implications of these rules are discussed throughout the rest of the chapter. Some of the rules are as follows:

1) Consent must be in writing and an affidavit of execution must be attached to every consent: s. 70, *CWA*/ ss. 131(2), (12), (13), *CFSA*. Upon proclamation of the *CFSA*, consent from a parent may not be given in ''non-family'' adoptions unless the Society or licensee has advised the parents of their specific rights as listed under s. 131(4) of the *CFSA* and has given the parents an opportunity to seek counselling and independent legal advice with respect to the consent: s. 131(4)(b), *CFSA*.

2) Consent is not invalid by reason of the person being under 18 years of age: s. 69(13), *CWA*/ s. 4(5), *CFSA*. However, such a consent from the child's parent is not valid unless the Official Guardian is satisfied that the consent ''is fully informed and reflects the person's true wishes'': s. 131(11), *CFSA*/ s. 69(13), *CWA*. In addition, the *CFSA* will also require that if a consent is required from the person being adopted, it shall not be given until that person has had an opportunity to obtain counselling and independent legal advice: s. 131(7), *CFSA*. Finally, the new Act's umbrella

---

[210]See *Re Lee and C.A.S. of Ontario County*, [1971] 1 O.R. 474, 15 D.L.R. (3d) 656 (H.C.).

consent section (s. 4, *CFSA*) will govern the validity of the minor's consent.

3) The "parental" consent can only be given after the child is seven days old (s. 69(2), *CWA*/ s. 131(3), *CFSA*) and can be cancelled in writing within 21 days after the consent is given: s. 69(2), *CWA*/ s. 131(8), *CFSA*. (But see discussion below for repercussions.)

4) If the placement has been arranged through a Society, after the 21 days have expired on a parental consent, the rights and responsibilities of the legal guardianship for the child vest in the Society until an adoption order is rendered: s. 69(3) and (14), *CWA*. However, the *CWA* is silent with respect to an adoption arranged through a private licensee, leaving a legal and practical hiatus. The gap will be filled under the *CFSA* which will vest these rights in a licensee as well as a Society: s. 131(5), *CFSA*.

5) If the "parent" wishes to withdraw his or her consent *after* the 21-day period, it can be made the subject of a court application but *only* if the child has not already been placed for adoption in a new home. In this court application, the judge may allow the withdrawal of consent if he is satisfied that it is in the best interests of the child to do so, in which case the parents would regain custody: s. 69(9) and (10), *CWA*/ s. 133, *CFSA*.

6) The court can dispense with any of the consents required under s. 69, *CWA* if it is in the best interests of the child and if the person who has not given consent has had notice of the proceeding or reasonable efforts have been made to do so: s. 69(7) and (8), *CWA*. In addition, it could dispense with the child's consent if "appropriate" in all the circumstances: s. 69(6), *CWA*. This is carried over into the *CFSA* under s. 132 except that the two grounds for dispensing with consent will not apply to the Society or to the child. Specifically in the child's case, a separate section under the *CFSA* will set out the grounds for dispensing with consent which are: causation of emotional harm to the child or lack of capacity to consent because of a developmental handicap: ss. 131(9), *CFSA*.

Parental Consent

If a child is a Crown ward, the "parental" consent is given by the Director: s. 69(5), *CWA*/ s. 131(2)(b), *CFSA*. In other words, the parents from whom the child was taken have lost all rights to the child (as discussed above under "Child Protection") and are also not entitled to notice of the proposed adoption: s. 69(16)(c), *CWA*/ s. 145(4)(c), *CFSA*.[211]

If the route is private adoption, the consent of "every person who is a parent" is required: s. 69(2), *CWA*/ s. 131(2)(a), *CFSA*. Based on the extensive definition of "parent" under s. 69(1) of the *CWA* (s. 131(1), *CFSA*) there can be more than two parents in some circumstances.[212] It automatically includes the mother (but not the father), anyone who has declared his parentage or is proven to be the father under the *Children's Law Reform Act* and anyone who has treated the child as a member of his family within the previous 12 months or who is, by

---

[211] See also *Re Riopel and Rolfes* (1979), 99 D.L.R. (3d) 710 (Sask. Q.B.) (parents of permanent ward not entitled to notice where all avenues of appeal exhausted).

[212] See *Re M.L.A.* (1979), 25 O.R. (2d) 779 (Prov. Ct.) (social worker's affidavit is insufficient evidence of existence of other parent; supplement with mother's affidavit or by evidence that mother's affidavit not obtainable).

court order or written agreement, liable to provide support or granted custody or access rights. The only differences between the *CWA* and the *CFSA* with respect to the definition of parent is that (1) "guardian appointed at law" will be omitted under the *CFSA* and (2) the *CFSA* definition will include anyone "having lawful custody of the child" while the *CWA* requires consent from both the parent *and* anyone having lawful custody or control of the child. Notice to and consent from a parent are prerequisites to an adoption order which are strictly adhered to unless the child is a Crown ward. The dispensing with parental consent or notice is not done lightly.[213] (See discussion below under "Consent: Dispensing with Consent".)

The consent rules listed above attempt to balance the triangular nature of the interests involved in an adoption order: those of the biological parent(s), the child and the adopting parents. To protect the biological parent, the Act prohibits the execution of a consent until a child is at least seven days of age, allowing some time for the biological parent(s) of a newborn to consider her decision after the trauma of birth has subsided somewhat: s. 69(2), *CWA*/ s. 131(3), *CFSA*.[214] Further, the consent must be executed in the presence of a Children's Aid Society representative who must fully inform the parent of his or her rights: s. 70, *CWA*. Upon proclamation, the *CFSA* will go a step further by stipulating that a parental consent cannot be given until a Society or licensee has advised the parent of a specified set of rights: s. 131(4), *CFSA*.[215] Finally, the parent can withdraw consent within 21 days, although this "right" is somewhat illusory as will be discussed below: s. 69(2), *CWA*/ s. 131(8), *CFSA*. In addition, the time period is applied rigidly such that even 1 day over and the parent is out of luck.[216]

In recognition of the interests of the prospective adopting parents who very quickly develop a deep attachment to the child, especially to a newborn, the Act provides a specific and brief period of time at the end of which the rights of

---

[213]*C.A.S. of Metro Toronto v. Lyttle*, [1973] S.C.R. 568, 34 D.L.R. (3d) 127, 10 R.F.L. 131; *S. v. Minister of Social Services* (1983), 33 R.F.L. (2d) 1 (Sask. C.A.) (failure to give mother notice renders adoption invalid insofar as it affects the mother); *Re M.L.A.* (1979), 25 O.R. (2d) 779 (Prov. Ct.) (biological father of child born out of wedlock "parent" under s. 69(1); natural parent's right is a significant factor to be considered as part of "all the circumstances of the case" under s. 69(1) of the *CWA*).

[214]For a case in which a mother failed in arguing that her consent to permanent wardship was invalid due to its not being freely and voluntarily given because of post-partum depression, see *B. v. Child Welfare, Director* (1982), 29 R.F.L. (2d) 40 (P.E.I.S.C.).

[215]Section 131(4) of the *CFSA* states:

    s. 131(4) (a) the society or licensee has advised the parent of his or her right,

        (i)   to withdraw the consent under subsection (8),

        (ii) to be informed, on his or her request, whether an adoption order has been made in respect of the child, and

        (iii) to participate in the voluntary disclosure register under s. 158; and

           (b) the society or licensee has given the partner an opportunity to seek counselling and independent legal advice with respect to the consent.

[216]See, *e.g. Minister of Social Services and T. v. F. and B.*, (1981), 9 Sask. R. 129, 124 D.L.R. (2d) 626 (*sub nom. Re. Minister of Social Services and Folster*) 22 R.F.L. (2d) 288 (C.A.); *Director of Child Welfare v. Y.*, [1981] 1 S.C.R. 625, 9 Man. R. (2d) 39, [1981] 6 W.W.R. 337, 122 D.L.R. (3d) 193, 37 N.R. 121, 22 R.F.L. (2d) 417 revg. [1981] 3 W.W.R. 668, 9 Man. R. (2d) 45, 121 D.L.R. (3d) 716.

biological parents are completely extinguished, that is, within 21 days from the date of consent as long as the child is placed for adoption: s. 69(2) and (10), *CWA*/ ss. 131(8), 133(2), *CFSA*. After 21 days, the prospective adopting parents can enjoy a sigh of relief, knowing all that remains is the process of approval by the court without the spectre of the biological parents trying to revive their rights. (The *CFSA* will institute an interesting change: under the *CWA*, once the 21 days expires and the child is placed *by a Society or Licensee*, the parent is barred from applying to the court to withdraw consent. Thus, "family" adoptions escape the bar to court action. Under the *CFSA*, no such exemption will be made.)

With less clarity, and arguably as an accident of deficient drafting, the Act seems to protect the child and his interests within the context of consent arrangements. If the 21-day period has passed and the child has still not been placed by an agency/licensee for adoption, the consent cannot be withdrawn without the approval of the court, having regard to the child's best interests. Secondly, and of much contention, it appears that s. 69(7) of the *CWA* (s. 132, *CFSA*) (judicial power to dispense with consent) may be available when the parent has executed a consent, revokes it within the 21 days, and expects the child to be returned, only to find that the adopting parents or the agency/licensee have applied to the court for an order dispensing with the parent's consent, potentially using the very fact of the giving of consent in the first place as evidence that the parent is unfit.[217] This ironic situation results from a statutory hiatus created by the dual operation of ss. 69(2) and (7) of the *CWA* (ss. 131(8) and 132, *CFSA*). The Ontario Supreme Court, exercising its inherent *parens patriae* jurisdiction, has filled this hiatus in at least one case by overruling the revocation of consent of the parent.[218] The situation of a parent being blocked from withdrawing his or her consent within 21 days is not an unlikely occurrence since the child is often removed from the hospital after five days of being born and immediately placed with the prospective adopting parents, with or without the required written consent. The adoptive parents have passed their home study by the agency or licensee months before and are anxiously awaiting the day that the child arrives. There is no statutory prerequisite that parental consent be signed prior to this placement so that the adopting parents, on the fifth day of life, are given *de facto* care of the child without any accompanying legal guardianship or custodial rights or judicial scrutiny of same — just a pre-arranged consensus among the parties. There is no maximum time requirement within which the mother must sign her consent as long as it is seven days after the birth so that a substantial length of time may pass before the required written consent is even signed, let alone revoked. It is inevitable that many adoptive parents will fight a

---

[217]See *Re Adoption Act and Child* (1981), 35 N.B.R. (2d) 126, 88 A.P.R. 126 (Q.B.) (unwed mother had given and withdrawn consent "repeatedly"; unstable person for that and several other reasons; court held that instability and inability to make up her mind re adoption amounted to abdication of parental rights, disentitling her from exercising those rights).

[218]*Re Baby R.*, unreported, June 7, 1984 (Ont. S.C.), *per* Montgomery, J., overriding revocation of consent and directing trial of an issue. In *Re Baby I.*, summarized in (1978), 3 F.L.R.R. 146 (Ont. H.C.) the *parens patriae* jurisdiction was invoked to fill in the gap where a mother having permitted the placement of her child for adoption, refused to sign the necessary consents and seven months later claimed back the child.

"legal" consent withdrawal, using the all-powerful status quo argument as being the equivalent of "best interests" and reinforcing it with the fact that time periods which may objectively seem short are subjectively much longer for an infant and therefore have more significance. The Legislature has made an effort under the *CFSA* to ameliorate the tug of war by requiring that the child be returned to the parent once consent is withdrawn within 21 days: s. 131(8), *CFSA*. However, although the parent may regain custody thereby reversing the all-important status quo, the adoptive parents will still be able to seek to dispense with the biological parent's consent under s. 132 of the *CFSA*.

In contrast, parallel legislation in Manitoba requires that once the child has been placed for the purpose of adoption, consent cannot be withdrawn regardless of how much time has passed since the consent was given.[219] It is submitted that in the absence of similar legislation in Ontario, the court should be cognizant of the clear understanding, based on the written forms and the counselling of the agency or licensee, which led to the consent in the first place. The forms clearly provide that if the biological parent changes her mind within 21 days, the child is to be returned to her care. Any interpretation of the legislation which permits the court to intervene and expose the parents to an investigation or hearing, effectively penalizes them for having committed the act of consenting itself, consenting in the full knowledge of and reliance on the supposedly absolute right to revoke the consent within 21 days. This right both to give consent and revoke it are also fully known and accepted by the adopting parents under a signed acknowledgment as "rules of the game" and they are all too eager to play by any rules in the beginning. The whole process of a court nullifying the right to withdraw consent, can be viewed as giving "lip service" to one set of rules in order to obtain the consent for the adopting parents and replacing it with another set of rules in order to secure the position of the adopting parents. In effect, the immutable contract principle of giving effect to the parties' intentions upon entering the agreement has become mutable. One may immediately respond that contract principles have no place in an assessment of a child's best interests, but if this were the case, then fairness to the biological parent demands that a contract context should not form part of the process at all as it does now. In any event, the Legislature has determined that "best interests" must not come before an "in need of protection" finding in deference to the deeply held right to the privacy of the family in a democratic society. Is it then possible that one moment of vulnerability where a parent, often a young, unmarried woman who has just given birth, gives an oral or written consent, can reverse this presumption, leaving the parent exposed to comparision shopping by the judge for a set of parents who can provide a "better" (often amounting to a higher socio-economic level) environment?[220] If the adopting parents fear for the well-being of the child on being returned to the mother (the strongest argument for a judge to dispense

---

[219]*Child Welfare Act*, S.M. 1974, c. 30, s. 87(1).

[220]See *e.g. Erhart v. Bowers* (1979), 13 R.F.L. (2d) 209 (B.C.S.C.) (mother's nomadic life-style and self-imposed poverty balanced against "stable, two-parent family"); *Re I.D.* (1982), 41 N.B.R. (2d) 71, 107 A.P.R. 71 (Q.B.) (mother confined to wheel chair, natural parents immature and unemployed while adopting home "suitable").

with consent), the option is always open to convince the Children's Aid Society or a judge that the child should be the subject of a protection hearing. The argument in reply may be that the bonding which has taken place between adopting parents and the child in those first few weeks or months now makes the quality of care given by the biological parents irrelevant. Nevertheless, this argument can be made in the context of a protection proceeding in arguing that the parent "cannot . . . care properly for the child" (s. 19(1)(b)(iii), *CWA*) or "substantial risk of emotional harm" (s. 37(2)(g), *CFSA*), but it is submitted that a bonding argument, which is a branch of the usual status quo argument, should not in itself be sufficient to block the return of the child (unless the time period is substantially longer than a few months and the child is still an infant) since there is no consensus among the experts that irreparable damage will be done to an infant if he must re-adjust to a new parent-child relationship. In this context, every effort should be made to streamline the court process so that the status quo will not simply be a function of a full court calender despite earlier efforts on the part of the biological parents to regain the child. The *CFSA* amendment directing the immediate return of the child upon withdrawal of consent is one such attempt at streamlining. It seems only fair that the child should be returned and/or assisted in the return by a Children's Aid Society prior to consideration of whether the child should be with the adopting parents.

Role of Adoption Agency/Licensee   The difficulties in the competing interests under Ontario's legislation is heightened by the role of the "licensee" who facilitates the "private" adoption. Under the *CWA*, adoption placements are handled only by an "adoption agency" (every Society automatically being an adoption agency) and licensees. The former is defined as a corporation having objects of a charitable nature which places children under 18 years of age for adoption: ss. 59 and 60, *CWA*. A licensee is simply defined as a person who is issued a licence under the Act for the placement of a child under 18 years for adoption: s. 60(5), *CWA*, O. Reg. 96/80, s. 29(a). Upon proclamation of the *CFSA*, matters will be simplified by empowering all Societies and licensees to handle placements, the latter being defined as "a person or non-profit agency" (s. 176(4)(b)) and will be governed by the general licensing provisions under Part IX of the *CFSA*. Grounds for refusal of a licence by the Director are limited to whether the corporation or person is competent and will make placements "in a responsible manner" and in accordance with the Act and Regulations: s. 61(1), *CWA*/ s. 178, *CFSA*.

A licensee has a more complex role than a Society in that he is "retained" by the adopting parents insofar as they will pay his or her fees as prescribed by the legislation, but at the same time the licensee also must work with the biological parents to facilitate the placement in the absence of anyone else and this carries potential for conflicts of interest to arise. Both the licensee and the Society must obtain information from the natural parents and often have the responsibility of arranging for the parents' attendance at the Society's offices in order to obtain their executed consent. They must also obtain some form of delegated authority from the parents for the child to be removed from their care or the hospital's care and placed in the care of the adopting parents, with or without having obtained a written consent, since custodial authority technically remains with the biological parents until all consents are given, and under the

CFSA, until the 21-day-grace period has expired: s. 69(3), *CWA*/ s. 131(5), *CFSA*. This is important since the child may require medical attention while in the care of the adopting parents and the parents may be unavailable or, as is more often the case, the adopting parents (who are instructing the licensee) may wish to have nothing to do with the biological parents. Conflicts arise particularly for the licensee when his role, as outlined above, results in his being the advisor to the biological parents while being retained by the adoptive parents. This situation is seriously aggravated when parents revoke their consent and look to the licensee, retained by the adopting parents, for the return of their child.[221]

Child's Consent   If the child to be adopted is seven years of age or more, his written consent must be given unless the court decides that the requirement is inappropriate: s. 69(6), *CWA*/ s. 131(6), *CFSA*. In addition, the *CFSA* will require that the child's consent not be given until he has had an opportunity to obtain counselling and independent legal advice with respect to the consent. (For further discussion, see below under "Representation of the Child".) The requirement of the child's consent under the *CWA* must be read in conjunction with s. 77 of the *CWA* which imposes an obligation on the court to inquire into the capacity of the child "to appreciate the nature of the application" and the court is to hear the child, where practicable. Upon proclamation of the *CFSA*, the judge will be charged with the more exacting task of making sure that everyone giving consent "understands the nature and effect of the adoption order" and particularly with respect to the child, he must conduct the same inquiry as under the *CWA* but also consider the child's views and wishes if ascertainable. It has been held under the *CWA* that a formal hearing on this issue is not required and that affidavit evidence is sufficient, setting out the information indicative of the child's capacity to appreciate the nature of the application.[222] In practice, the requirement in this section is usually met by a congratulatory acknowledgment from the bench to the child. It would appear that if this section is to have any meaning especially given the more precise wording of the *CFSA*, the court should be apprised of the background of the child, whether the child had any relationship or contact with the biological mother or father and if so, whether the child realizes that, without the consent of all parties, further contact will not occur. In other words, the judge should inquire as to whether the child actually appreciates the permanency of the proceeding. To assist in this inquiry, the *CFSA* will allow the judge to summon anyone to court whom he thinks necessary to do so on his own initiative: s. 146(1) and (2), *CFSA*. However, since the consents of opposing parties are usually dispensed with prior to any such investigation and the child appears with the adopting parent(s) on an uncontested basis, such an investigation is unlikely to occur. It may put the accompanying adopting parent(s) into an uncomfortable and conflicting position and turn what is generally seen as a celebratory event into a defensive, disruptive, and stressful situation. Perhaps the safest and most effective route is for the judge to talk to the child alone at a time separate from the hearing although it is somewhat illusory to expect a judge to determine with any

---

[221]*CWA*, O. Reg. 96/80, ss. 25–47 describes the responsibilities of the licensee and restrictions *vis-à-vis* fees for services rendered.

[222]*Re M.L.A.* (1979), 25 O.R. (2d) 779 (Prov. Ct.).

accuracy in the space of a short interview in his chambers, whether or not a young child appreciates the irrevocability of the order and the fiction of losing one origin and gaining another. It is difficult for an adult, let alone a child, to appreciate the implications of such concepts.

Dispensing With Consent

The first part of this section will deal with the issue of dispensing with parental consent, while the second will deal with that of the child's consent.

Given the profound implications of an adoption order, the courts are traditionally loathe to dispense with parental consent unless the parent(s)' previous conduct was tantamount to the abandonment of the child.[223] The exception is the case of the non-custodial putative father who does not seek custody but who refuses to consent (if the jurisdiction requires his consent) when the mother has decided to give the child up for adoption. The court's reluctance to dispense with consent is at its strongest when an adoption application is used to circumvent or supersede the usual custody/access process in the case of step-parent adoptions. In this case, a "best interests" test is relied upon to balance the objective of stabilizing a new family unit for the child[224] with maintaining biological, historical family links. For example, despite a disentitlement to access rights under a divorce order, a father continued to attempt to see his children and supported them until the mother remarried and continued sending them Christmas gifts. In this situation, the father successfully

---

[223]*Re Liffiton and Campbell* (1972), 7 R.F.L. 353 (Ont. C.A.); *Re Desmarais: Desmarais v. Casper*, [1969] 1 O.R. 700, at 704 (Ont. C.A.); *Re Sharp: Sharp v. Sharp* (1962), 40 W.W.R. 521, at 546 (B.C.C.A.); *Re Drummond (infants)* (1968), 1 D.L.R. (3d) 309 (B.C.S.C.); *Re S.* (1980), 15 R.F.L. (2d) 314 (B.C.S.C.): *A. and B.C.* (1979), 13 R.F.L. (2d) 59 (Que. Youth Ct.); *Director of Child Welfare, New Brunswick v. D.* (1981), 37 N.B.R. (2d) 334, 97 A.P.R. 334 (C.A.) (although wardship ordered, court still refused to dispense with mother's consent unless proof of abandonment, serious misconduct by moral turpitude or other important reasons; balanced rights of parent and best interests of children); *Re G. (A.)* (1982), 40 N.B.R. (2d) 33, 105 A.P.R. 33 (Q.B.) (step-parent: although father failing to meet maintenance obligations, not persistently neglecting or refusing to maintain; court refused to dispense with consent); *Steele v. Bruin* (1981), 35 A.R. 255 (Q.B.) (step-parent: father supporting but showing little love or affection in past; court refused to dispense with consent in absence of moral turpitude, misconduct or dereliction of parental duty); *N.C.R. (an infant), Re* (1981), 34 N.B.R. (2d) 361, 85 A.P.R. 361, 122 D.L.R. (3d) 548 (*sub nom. Re M. and R.*) (C.A.) (Although mother left children with applicants for six years during which time she visited only four times and contributed no money, court refused to dispense with consent in absence of moral turpitude or abdication of parental rights); *Lutz v. Legal Aid of Man.* (1982), 37 A.R. 351 (C.A.) (child with foster parents due to health problems because reserve did not have necessary facilities; court refuses to dispense with consent); *Re D.I.B.* (1980), 32 N.B.R. (2d) 227, 78 A.P.R. 227 (Q.B.) (although all six children wards of state due to health problems and old age of parents, not abandonment); *Re A.P.* (1982), 42 N.B.R. (2d) 515, 110 A.P.R. 515 (Q.B.) (alcoholic father deserted mother and child for 11 years; mother remarried; court refused to dispense with consent because of evidence that father had stopped drinking for five and a half years and unfair to deny parental relationship after rehabilitation); *E. v. L.* (1982), 29 R.F.L. (2d) 113 (B.C.C.A.) (new adoption hearing ordered since the trial judge didn't give biological father proper and full hearing on merits before dispensing with consent).

[224]*Re Adoption of Infant, Registration of Birth No. 71-07-001117* (1979), 16 B.C.L.R. 212 (S.C.) (although statute does not require putative father's consent, if it did it would be a "best interest" test). But see *Vessey v. Coyle* (1981), 25 R.F.L. (2d) 80 (P.E.I.S.C.) (putative father withholding consent out of genuine concern for child and not for vindictive reasons; must interpret consent provisions with abolishing concept of illegitimacy; court refused to dispense with consent even though mother wishing to give up child for adoption).

resisted an application to dispense with his consent under an adoption application. The court noted: "By his conduct, he has indicated that he continues to have a very real interest in the children and it may very well be that, at some future time, he may establish a very real relationship with them."[225] On the other hand, an application to dispense with the father's consent was granted where the father had not seen the child for five years since the separation, and the divorce judgment provided no access to the child.[226]

Recently, seizing upon the phrase "best interests" in s. 69(7) of the *CWA* and the codified definition of same in s. 1(1)(b) of the *CWA*, the courts in Ontario have shown an inclination to depart from the traditionally rigorous test which required evidence of "abandonment" and to apply instead simply a "best interests" consideration where the factor of natural or blood ties is only one of several considerations and is not to be given more weight than any of the other relevant considerations set out in s. 1(1)(b), *CWA*.[227] (Note that the *CFSA* will also direct that an adoption order be made based on the child's best interests although the definition for adoption purposes will be slightly different than for protection purposes: s. 130(2), (3) (adoption), s. 37(3) (protection), *CFSA*.) This approach was discussed above under "Parental Consent" specifically with respect to those parents who attempted to revoke their consent within the authorized 21-day period only to be blocked by a "best interests" test. Using this approach, courts apparently distinguish themselves from otherwise binding appellate decisions based on "abandonment" because of a codified expression of "best interests." It is submitted that this approach should be resisted as establishing any new precedent. As in the case of child welfare law, the expression of "best interests" however codified as a definition, must be applied having regard to the nature of the proceeding.[228] It would be entirely inconsistent for the court to invoke the "best interests" test that is routinely applied in a custody dispute to that of dispensing with consent for the purpose of adoption,

---

[225]*Smith v. Harvey* (1974), 19 R.F.L. 367 (Ont. C.A.). See also *Re Birth Registration Nos. 67-09-024376 and 70-09-010670* (1979), 14 R.F.L. (2d) 109 (B.C.S.C.) (consent of father not dispensed with when inability to see or support children due to circumstances not entirely father's fault.)

[226]*M. v. G.* (1974), 15 R.F.L. 159 (Ont. C.A.).

[227]*S. v. J.B. and M.E.A.; Re B.L.P.*, summarized in (1984), 6 F.L.R.R. 118 (Ont. Prov. Ct.); *Re Pennington* (1980), 40 N.S.R. (2d) 373, 73 A.P.R. 373 (Co. Ct.) (balance benefits to child of adoption creating "normal" family with benefits to child of maintaining bond with biological parent); *Re L.C.B.* (1980), 3 Man. R. (2d) 390 (Co. Ct.) (basis for deciding whether to dispense with biological mother's consent as "best interests"); *Ross v. Anderson* (1979), 3 Sask. R. 271, 10 R.F.L. (2d) 286 (C.A.) (step-parent: sole criterion under statute is best interests and therefore case law prior to enactment of legislation irrelevant); *W.A. v. W.B.* (1981), 34 O.R. (2d) 716, 23 R.F.L. (2d) 371 (*sub nom. Adams v. Andrews*) (Prov. Ct.) (step-parent: "best interests" sole criterion with parental rights being only one factor); *Re R.P.L.* (1978), 2 Fam. Law Rev. 142 (N.S. Co. Ct.) (step-parent: positive benefits of adoption to be considered); *W. v. C.* (1981), 35 O.R. (2d) 730 (Prov. Ct.) (step-parent: best interests test); *Re Kennedy* (1980), 45 N.S.R. (2d) 659, 86 A.P.R. 659 (Co. Ct.) (grandparent adoption with father in jail with history of drug/alcohol abuse; best interests test dispenses with father's consent); *Sterling v. Martin* (1982), 32 R.F.L. (2d) 124 (N.S.C.A.).

[228]See for support *H. v. M.* (1980), 18 R.F.L. (2d) 138 (Ont. Prov. Ct.) ("best interests" not the same test as in custody dispute; here, must include consideration of parental rights and dispense with consent only where abandonment or misconduct).

having regard to the profound and irreversible effect of the latter order. For the courts to apply the same "best interests" test to adoption as it uses for custody would invite a blurring of any distinction between the two orders and suggest to the remarried custodial parent who is experiencing some access difficulties that an adoption order would solve the problem by effectively eliminating the non-custodial biological parent from the child's life. This result is completely antithetical to the traditional principle underlying access, that is, that the child's best interests are served by maintaining contact with both biological parents unless such contact is harmful to him. Upon proclamation, the *CFSA* will give some support to the argument that blood relationships create a presumption in favour of access and therefore against adoption by specifically including the factor as one to consider in assessing "best interests" in an adoption context: s. 130(2), para. 6, *CFSA*. Nevertheless, it is still only one factor to consider and the judge has the preliminary discretion to determine whether it is a relevant factor in all the circumstances.

Under the *CWA*, the court can dispense with the child's consent if it is appropriate in all the circumstances: s. 69(6), *CWA*. An Ontario Provincial Court has noted that the wording "the consent would not be appropriate" suggests that the operative test is appropriateness rather than "best interests." It held that the onus was on the applicants to satisfy the court that the dispensing with consent is "appropriate" and that the onus is a substantial one, since the child has a right to know his true origins. The judge proceeded to dispense with the requirements since the 13-year-old boy was of the belief that the male applicant was his biological father, there was no way of finding his biological father and there was evidence that the child was particularly sensitive and would be "devastated" if he learned the truth.[229] In a British Columbia case, a 10-year-old child was the subject of adoption proceedings by his natural mother and stepfather. The court refused to dispense with the consent of the child, asserting that when the child grew older it would be quite possible that he would take exception to being deprived of his real name and of the parenthood of his natural father. The court, relying upon the statute which required the consent of a child 12 years of age or older, refused to grant the order of adoption until the child was old enough to express an opinion.[230] The *CFSA* attempts to clarify the test for dispensing with the child's consent by using more precise language. The court will be able to dispense with the child's consent if satisfied that (a) obtaining the consent would cause the child emotional harm; or (b) the child is not able to consent because of a developmental handicap: s. 131(9), *CFSA*. (See also s. 4 of the *CFSA*, with respect to the validity of consents by minors.)

Representation of the Child

Under the *CWA*, the court can appoint a person to act as a guardian *ad litem* of the child before or upon the hearing of the application if, in the opinion of the court, such appointment is required to protect the legal interests of the child in the proceedings: s. 71(6), *CWA*. The court can also make any order it deems appropriate with respect to paying the costs of the guardian. No similar provision

---

[229]*Re A.*, summarized in (1980), 3 F.L.R.R. 47 (Ont. Prov. Ct.); and see *Re Carter* (1976), 27 R.F.L. 159 (N.S.C.A.); *Re R.* (1978), 7 R.F.L. (2d) 344 (B.C.S.C.).
[230]*Re Midland* (1955), 14 W.W.R. 699 (B.C.S.C.).

will be included under the *CFSA* and the Rules of the Provincial Court, as they now stand, do not enable the court to give direction for representation of a minor, only a person of "unsound mind": O. Reg. 810/80, s. 57. However, s. 131(7) of the *CFSA* will provide that the consent of a child seven years of age or older shall not be given unless he has had the opportunity to obtain independent legal advice with respect to the consent. Given the Legislature's intention, as it appears, to involve the child in an understanding of the adoption process and given the nature and effect of an adoption order itself, the omission under the *CFSA* of providing for child representation is noteworthy. The legislation may represent the intention of the Legislature to carve out the adoption proceeding from that of an adversarial process, asking the court to descend into the arena by entrusting the representation of the child's interests and wishes to the judge. Recognizing that an adoption proceeding is more of an inquiry than a typical adversarial proceeding,[231] one court held that, *because* of this fact, it was essential to have some system available to protect the interests of the child "because a proposed adoption desired by the intending adopter and by the natural parent might nevertheless not be in the best interests of the child."[232]

The Adoption Order

The judge may not grant an order in certain specified circumstances which apply to each party in the adoption triangle.

Statutory Restrictions on Adoption Order

Biological Parents

If the judge has dispensed with the consent of a "parent" or refused to allow the "parent" to withdraw his or her consent, the judge may not make an adoption order until any appeal on the matter has been disposed of or the time for commencing the appeal (30 days: s. 84(5), *CWA*) has expired: s. 74(2), *CWA*/ s. 142, *CFSA*. In addition, the judge must satisfy himself that every person who has given a consent understands the nature and effect of the adoption order: s. 76(a), *CWA*/ s. 146(2)(a), *CFSA*.[233] Under the *CFSA*, the judge, in addition, will be required to be sure that the said person "understands and appreciates the special role of the adopting parents": s. 146(2)(b), *CFSA*. Further, the *CFSA* will require that the Society or licensee inform the parent of the implications of the consent which are specifically outlined in the Act as well as giving the parent(s) the opportunity to seek counselling and independent legal advice: s. 131(4), *CFSA*. For anyone giving their consent under 18 years, the Official Guardian must be satisfied that the consent is fully informed and reflects the person's true wishes: s. 69(13), *CWA*/ s. 131(11), *CFSA*.

Adopting Parents

No adoption order shall be granted if the applicant(s) is not a resident of Ontario: s. 72, *CWA*/ s. 140(5), *CFSA*. Under the *CWA*, no order can be granted

---

[231]*Re Raghbeer* (1977), 3 R.F.L. (2d) 42 (Ont. Co. Ct.).

[232]See *Re G. (T.J.)*, [1963] 1 All E.R. 20, at 29 (C.A.).

[233]Generally see *Re M.L.A., supra*, note 222 (if adoption application unopposed and all supporting documents in order, formal hearing not required; formal hearing is required if (1) opposed, (2) issues raised re notice/consent, (3) court feels child should be heard on issue of capacity to appreciate nature of proceedings, (4) documentary evidence incomplete or unsatisfactory).

(other than for a step-parent adoption) if the applicant(s) is under 18 years, unmarried, a widow, a widower, a divorced person or living apart from his or her spouse unless the court is satisfied that there are special circumstances that justify the order: s. 74(1), *CWA*.[234] On the other hand, the *CFSA* will delete any mention of "unmarried, widow, widower, divorced person or living apart from spouse" presumably in keeping with the general prohibition against discrimination under s. 15 of the *Charter of Rights*. However, the court will not be precluded from using these factors in determining "best interests" since considerations underlying that phrase will be left open-ended under the *CFSA*: s. 130(2), para. 10. The *CFSA* leaves only the specific direction that if the applicant is under 18 years, the court shall not make an adoption order except under special circumstances: s. 141 *CFSA*. However, one major new prerequisite under the *CFSA* will be that for adoptions which do not involve a Society or licensee, *i.e.* "family" adoptions, the court will apparently lack jurisdiction to make an order unless the child has resided with the applicant for at least two years: s. 140(1)(c), *CFSA*. Under the *CWA*, Society and licensee adoption placements are for a period of six months and the Director, in his discretion, can even approve a shorter period if it is in the best interests of the child: s. 75(1), *CWA*. But the *CWA* does not even require this six-month precaution for "family" adoptions. The *CFSA* will continue this approach for Society and licensee adoptions (s. 143(1)(a) and (6), *CFSA*) but will add the two-year requirement going to jurisdiction for all other adoptions.

Except in the case of a joint application by the husband and wife, no more than one person may adopt a child: s. 74(4), *CWA*/ s. 140(4), *CFSA*. Finally, no order will be granted if the spouse of the applicant does not submit a written consent (s. 74(5), *CWA*/ s. 131(10), *CFSA*). Under the *CWA*, this requirement can be dropped if the spouses are living separately. In the same circumstances under the *CFSA*, the applicant will presumably seek to dispense with his or her spouse's consent under the general dispensation section (s. 132, *CFSA*).

The Child

The child must be resident in Ontario: s. 72, *CWA*/ s. 140(5) *CFSA*. (For discussion of the meaning of "resident" in an adoption context, see below under "Adoption and Jurisdiction".) The child must also have been placed by a Society/agency/licensee (unless it is a "family" adoption) before the applicants have status to apply. The precautions surrounding consent which are equally applicable to the child are dealt with above under restrictions relating to the biological parents.

---

[234]See *e.g. K. (L.) v. K. (E.E.)*, [1982] 4 W.W.R. 614 (Man. Co. Ct.) (despite adoptive grandparents and agency agreeing on adoption, court refused to grant order; lacking jurisdiction since statute prohibited adoption by one person still married but separated from spouse); *Re A. and B.; Re X.* (1979), 13 R.F.L. (2d) 165 (Que. Youth Ct.) (adoptive wife died before completion of proceeding; even though remaining applicant is not of the same sex as child, application may be granted if the court feels he has, by his actions, already adopted the child before the death of his wife; since an adoption application is a personal action attaching to the person of the adopter, it is not transmissible and is therefore extinguished on death of applicant).

For the purpose of adoption, ''child'', under the *CWA*, means a person whether under 18 years of age or 18 years of age or older: s. 59(2), *CWA*. Nevertheless, if the person to be adopted is over 18, or is under 18 and married, no adoption order can be made unless special circumstances justify the order: s. 74(1)(c), *CWA*. Under the *CFSA*, while there will be no specific definition of ''child'' for Part VII (Adoption), the court will be able to make an adoption order for anyone under 16, or over 16 and still under parental control if it is in the best interests of the child: s. 140(1), *CFSA*. No mention is made under the new legislation of the case where the person to be adopted is under the age limit but married, although it does provide that a court *may* make an order for a person over the age limit with no specific instructions as to how to exercise that discretion: s. 140(3), *CFSA*.

It is not clear what special circumstances are required to justify the making of the order under s. 74(1) of the *CWA* or what special circumstances will be required under s. 141 of the *CFSA* (applicant less than 18 years). Presumably, due to the choice of phrase which differs from that of ''best interests'', the interests of the child may in fact not be the deciding factor. In one decision, the court held that ''special circumstances'' imports ''something over and beyond a satisfactory placement'', exceptional in character, quality or degree and which is of such a nature as to distinguish or set the application apart from the ordinary or usual, so as to satisfy the court that it is justified, in this case, in making a single parent order.[235] In another decision, the court considered the application of a spouse who was separated and living in a common law relationship with someone else. The court granted the application, concluding that since the spouse and partner both consented to the adoption and the partner had in fact helped act as a parent to the child for two and a half years, special circumstances existed to grant the order.[236] It is arguable that this judge used ''special circumstances'' as a substitute for ''best interests'' since he was obviously anxious to provide the child with a two-parent family. It is difficult to conceive of any case in which ''best interests'' and ''special circumstances'' would not be coincidental. As noted above, this ''special circumstances'' limitation under the *CFSA* will only apply to the case of an applicant who is under 18. Otherwise, it appears that the overall ''best interests'' test will apply: s. 140(1), *CFSA*.

''Best Interests'' and the Adoption Order

The Act requires that, before making an adoption order, the judge be satisfied that it is in the best interests of the child: s. 76(b), *CWA*/ s. 140(1), *CFSA*. As noted above, the *CFSA* will include a list of criteria to determine ''best interests'' which is exclusively for adoption purposes whereas the *CWA* has one set of criteria which applies both to child protection and adoption proceedings. A ''best interests'' approach is traditionally used so as not to create rigid guidelines and fetter the court's discretion since every case will turn on its own individual facts.[237] Some of the decisions include the following cases. An adoption

---

[235]*Re Robert and L.*, summarized in (1980), 5 A.C.W.S. (2d) 354 (Ont. Dist. Ct.), as summarized in Hartrick and Lezor, *The Child Welfare Act Annotated* (Toronto: Carswell Co. Ltd., 1983).

[236]*Re Shewraj* (1982), 37 O.R. (2d) 64 (Ont. Prov. Ct.).

[237]See for example *Re D.A.A.* (1980), 31 N.B.R. (2d) 676, 75 A.P.R. 676 (Q.B.) (common law spouse of deceased mother lost out in bid for adoption of six-year-old to maternal uncle and wife

application was refused for an eight-year-old girl who enjoyed access to her father under a divorce order and who was aware of his interest in her. The judge held that she should not be adopted, at least until she was of an age where she could make a decision for herself. Since the British Columbia statute required the child's consent upon reaching 12 years, the implication was that this was the age when the Legislature contemplated the she could make her own decision.[238] In another case, the court chose to allow the order but ensured that the child would be taken care of in accordance with accepted medical procedures by requiring the adopting parents, who were naturopaths, to file an undertaking to provide all appropriate medical treatment, including normal vaccinations and innoculations.[239] The proximity in ages between the applicants and the child has been held to be a factor to be considered but not to be a bar to adoption in certain circumstances. In this case, the judge observed the applicants and the 17-year-old child together, and although the difference in ages was 12 to 15 years, he was persuaded that it was in the best interests to grant the adoption.[240] (This issue has also been dealt with specifically in an immigration context in which siblings often apply to adopt one another. See below under Chapter 9 "The Child as Immigrant".) Finally, when a Canadian citizen is seeking to adopt a child who may be subject to deportation otherwise, the phrase "best interests of the child" must be read in the context of adoption rather than immigration, although it is clear that the latter is related to the former so far as the granting of an adoption may avoid a severence of the parent-child relationship by reason of it resulting in deportation.[241] (Again, for detailed discussion, see Chapter 9 "The Child as Immigrant".)

Adoption and Jurisdiction

For the court to have territorial jurisdiction in an adoption proceeding, the applicant or the child must reside within its jurisdiction at the time the application is filed: s. 71(1), *CWA/* s. 144(1), *CFSA*. However, for the court to have jurisdiction to make an adoption order, the child and the applicant parties must be resident in Ontario: s. 72, *CWA/* s. 140(5), *CFSA*. As discussed more fully in Chapter 9, "The Child as Immigrant", the courts are particularly concerned that the adoption process is not used simply in order that the person being adopted can gain landed status. Residence has been determined to require more than a mere presence in the province on a casual visit or while passing through. There must be a reasonable connection between the parties and Ontario, and the child must have lived in Ontario for a sufficient time to enable an effective investigation to

---

where best interests "marginally better served"); *Re W., supra* note 197 (six-year-old native child viewed white foster parents as psychological parents and mother relative stranger; adoption order refused by C.A.; child's cultural and religious heritage relevant but not determinative; possibility of losing status rights and since child aware of native origin, court not wanting to cut off all legal ties; made child a ward, with custody to foster parents); revd. *supra*, note 181 S.C.C. holding that importance of cultural background abates as bonding grows stronger over time.

[238]*Re Toms,* [1950] 2 W.W.R. 863 (B.C.S.C.).

[239]*Re Gainor* (1976), 23 R.F.L. 348 (Alta. Dist. Ct.).

[240]*Re S.* (1979), 6 R.F.L. (2d) 229 (Ont. Co. Ct.).

[241]See *Re Shewraj, supra*, note 236; *Re Keise*, summarized in (1982), 16 A.C.W.S. (2d) 372 (Ont. Prov. Ct.).

be made into the suitability of the adopting parents and whether the adoption order would be in the best interests of the child.[242]

An adoption effected according to the law of any other jurisdiction of Canada or of any other state or country has the same effect in Ontario as an adoption in Ontario: s. 87(1), *CWA*/ s. 153, *CFSA*. In addition, in the course of obtaining an adoption in a jurisdiction outside Ontario, all consents or declarations made in accordance with the laws of that jurisdiction have the same force and effect as if they were made in Ontario: s. 87(2), *CWA*/ s. 131(13), *CFSA*.[243] This section suggests that it is not necessary for a court in Ontario to look behind an adoption order from another jurisdiction to determine whether it is valid in Ontario under common law principles of private international law. However, it has been held that the section does not prohibit an Ontario court from inquiring into the circumstances surrounding the granting of a foreign adoption order, nor does it prohibit an Ontario court from granting an adoption order even though there is in existence a foreign adoption order where the granting of the order would be in the best interests of the child.[244]

There are several cases of interest involving native people who have undergone an adoption process in accordance with their own customs, albeit not in accordance with the law of their jurisdiction. In these circumstances, the courts have made declaratory orders confirming the adoption customs to be valid and recognized by the court as if they were legal orders of adoption.[245] (For discussion of statutory conflicts between domestic custody/access proceedings or access under child welfare proceedings and adoption proceedings, see above under "Finality of Adoption Order".)[246]

Surrogate
Parenting
Very recently, scientific advances have made it possible for a woman to act as a surrogate parent for couples who are having problems conceiving and/or carrying their baby to term. More common are arrangements whereby the surrogate parent is paid to conceive and carry her baby to term and then give it up to the payors for adoption. Due to the ever-narrowing "baby market", desperate would-be parents are availing themselves of the surrogate parent route. This has focused attention on s. 67 of the *CWA* (s. 159 of the *CFSA*), which prohibits payments in relation to an adoption or the giving of consent for an adoption, since surrogate parenting often involves the payment of substantial funds.

---

[242]See *Re Rai* (1980), 27 O.R. (2d) 425 (C.A.), and see Chapter 9 "The Child as Immigrant".

[243]See also *Paquette v. Galipeau* (1981), 22 R.F.L. (2d) 192 (S.C.C.) where parents consented in Ontario, child taken to live in Quebec where, in order to effectively withdraw consent, parents launched a *habaes corpus* application in Quebec Superior Court. Court refused, based on Quebec law.

[244]*Re A.R.* (1982), 139 D.L.R. (3d) 149, 30 R.F.L. (2d) 73 (Ont. Prov. Ct.).

[245]See *Re Wah-shee* (1976), 21 R.F.L. 156 (N.W.T.S.C.); *Re Deborah E4-789; Kitchoolaik v. Tucktoo* (1972), 8 R.F.L. 202 (N.W.T.C.A.). See also *John v. Supt. of Child Welfare* (1979), 10 R.F.L. (2d) 330 (B.C.S.C.) (*Adoption Act* provisions apply to authorize adoption of Indian child by non-Indian couple).

[246]See also *Re Broddy and Director of Vital Statistics* (1983), 23 Alta. L.R. (2d) 77, 31 R.F.L. (2d) 225 (C.A.) (provincial adoption legislation is valid even if incidentally affecting capacity to marry; however, provision deeming adopted children to be "natural" children of their adoptive parents invalid as being interpretive of federal legislation).

Under the *CWA*, it is not clear that any violation of the section occurs in the surrogate situation unless it can be shown that the purpose of the contract is for adoption, although the contract between the birth parents and the payor parents may be void as contrary to public policy.[247] Several American jurisdictions have come to varying conclusions regarding the validity of the contract and whether or not there is a violation of "payment prohibition" legislation.[248] Upon its proclamation, the *CFSA* will apparently fill the gap in the existing legislation by stipulating that the prohibition for payment will apply not only to the child's adoption, placement for adoption or consent concerning the adoption, but also to "negotiations or arrangements with a view to the child's adoption" which would appear to include the surrogate parenting situation.

The concept of payment for a child is, on its face, repugnant to our society although history shows us that adoption was (and some would argue still is) a process that evolved not so much from a concern for the "best interests of the child" as for the purpose of satisfying the needs of adults who are unable to give birth to a child and who are otherwise economically and socially capable of caring for a child.[249] In this context, it is important to temper wholesale condemnation of surrogate parenting with the fact that the present day adoption industry under state supervision, for the most part, involves the placement of a child from a single mother, who often is pressued to give up the child because of her limited economic and social prospects, to a set of parents with, in comparison, substantial financial means. Can society reconcile its approbation if not encouragement of low-income single mothers giving up their children to middle class parents with its automatic condemnation of payment for same?

Right to Knowledge of Origins

The issue of whether an adopted person should have a right to knowledge of his biological origins has recently been gaining a high profile in light of the development of continent-wide organizations of "parent-seekers." Access to this knowledge has historically been seen as directly conflicting with both the child's need for stability and security in the adoptive family and with the success of the adoption process itself, which is presumed to be dependent on assurances of secrecy to all parties. One judge, while recognizing the importance of knowing one's biological origins, summarized the need for complete severence of the past as follows:

> [T]he sense of security of the child in his new home ought not to be disturbed readily. He must continue to know that this is indeed his home; that he is entitled to demand the loyalty of his new parents and that he is obliged to

---

[247]For an extensive British study of the costs and benefits of surrogate parenting see M. Warnock, Chairperson, *Royal Commission on Human Fertilization and Embryology* (London: H.M.S.O., 1984).

[248]See *e.g. Kentucky v. Surrogate Parenting Association*, summarized in (1983), 10 F.L.R. 1107 (K. Cir. Ct.) (court refused to bar surrogate arrangements); *In Re R.K.S.*, summarized in (1984), 10 F.L.R. 1383 (Dist. of Col. Sup. Ct.) (court directs a detailed factual inquiry before a wife may be allowed to adopt her husband's child who was born to a surrogate mother).

[249]See *e.g.* M.D.A. Freeman, "Adoption — Existing Policies and Future Alternatives" (1979), 9 *Fam. Law* 142; Vivienne Ullrich, "The Politics of Adoption" (1979), 8 *New Zealand University Law Review*, 235–55.

give them his loyalty in return. That sense of security and loyalty would be diminished if the adopting parents felt that a natural parent could interfere with the affection of the child, or their authority over him. They might feel that they were custodians of the child, with less than ordinary parental rights and responsibilities. Another factor, of general public policy, which I think is almost conclusive with children's aid societies, is that prospective adopting parents would be more difficult to find if they were generally aware that natural parents might be permitted to regain contact with adopted children.[250]

In contrast to these strongly held assumptions, one should compare the experience of other jurisdictions which have legislation which does allow access to birth information for adult adoptees. A major study done in Scotland found that such access created no detrimental effects on the process as a whole and in fact was beneficial to the relationship between adoptee and adopting parents once the curiosity had been sated.[251]

Short of a final adoption order, the Legislature and courts are unhesitating in their acknowledgment of the importance of the child retaining some connection with or knowledge of his origins. One judge, in denying an application to dispense with the parents' consent in an adoption application, stated the following:

I should also like to add that in considering the best interests of the children, the Court ought not to lose sight of the rights of children. Until proved otherwise, I believe that a child has a right to the knowledge of the existence of his natural parents, to a normal association with those parents, and to the benefit of the love, understanding and guidance which may be developed in the intimate relationship between the child and its natural parents. No Court should deny a child those rights without serious reasons.[252]

One High Court decision did attempt to define circumstances in which access to an adopted child would be appropriate but the Court of Appeal overruled this decision determining that all rights of access are extinguished on adoption. The High Court had stated that each case should be decided on its own merits and in so concluding, noted the following with respect to the significance of knowledge of origins:

There can surely be no doubt that any child, knowing he has been adopted will be curious about his origins. I heard the evidence of witnesses who have had experience with adopted children. I accept the opinion that there is more than mere curiosity but a basic, if sometimes unexpressed, need for a child who knows he has been adopted, to get in touch with his natural parents. This need becomes most apparent during early adolescence. To know who his real parents are gives a child a sense of identity, and

---

[250]*Lyttle v. C.A.S. of Metro. Toronto* (1976), 24 R.F.L. 134, at 137 (Ont. H.C.).
[251]J. Triseliotis, *In Search of Their Origins* (London and Boston: Routledge and Kegan Paul, 1973).
[252]*Re Kennette and Munro*, [1973] 3 O.R. 156 at 167 (Co. Ct.).

assurance of belonging, and an awareness that he does not come from nowhere, but has his own place in history as the child of known parents. And, surely, this need ought to be satisfied more readily when, as here, the child was born of a union with some stability, lived with both natural parents for more than a year, and when one of the parents did not abandon him, but steadfastly tried to gain custody of him.[253]

In a British Columbia case the court permitted an adoption to proceed by dispensing with the mother's consent. In so doing, the court noted that while the adoption will provide the child with stability, security, love and affection, the biological mother can "be comforted by the fact that [her child] knows her and though he does not wish to see her now, it may be that he will wish to become re-acquainted with her in years to come when he has achieved maturity."[254]

Although the introduction of adoption legislation occurred in 1921 (*Adoption Act, 1921*, S.O. 1921, c. 55), a secrecy provision sealing the court record was not added until 1958 (S.O. 1958, c. 11, s. 3). Under this amendment, an order of the court or the written direction of the Director was necessary to open the sealed documents. This provision continues under present legislation (s. 80(1), *CWA*/ s. 156(2), *CFSA*) with the one significant qualification added in 1978 of the Voluntary Disclosure Registry: s. 81(6), *CWA*/ s. 158, *CFSA*. The *CWA* section basically provides that if both the biological parent and the adopted child register on their own separate initiatives with the Registry, and if the adopting parents consent, the Director is to release birth information to both the child and the biological parent. Note that this is basically a passive process on the part of the Ministry which the *CFSA* also adopts with some changes discussed below. This "matching" can occur only if:

1) the adoptee is 18 years of age or older: s. 81(2), *CWA*/ s. 158(4), *CFSA*;
2) the birth parent has registered his or her name with the Registry: s. 81(5), *CWA*/ s. 158(7)(a), *CFSA*;
3) the adult adoptee has registered his or her name with the Registry: s. 81(5), *CWA*/ s. 158(7)(a), *CFSA*;
4) the consent of the adopting parents with respect to the disclosure of such information has been obtained: s. 81(6)(b), *CWA*/ s. 158(7)(b)(i), *CFSA*; and
5) Where 1) to 4) above is satisfied, there is a reaffirmation from the adoptee and the biological parent(s) that they continue to agree to the disclosure of the information: s. 81(6)(c), *CWA*/ s. 158(7)(b)(ii), *CFSA*.

When all of these conditions are satisfied under the *CWA* (note the *CFSA* amendments discussed below), those documents that were used upon the application for the adoption order as well as any other information in the Voluntary Disclosure Registry will be released to a Children's Aid Society in the jurisdiction presumably where either of the parties resides, and that Society is

---

[253]*Lyttle v. C.A.S. of Metro. Toronto, supra* note 250, at pp. 136–37.
[254]*Re Adoption No. 64-09-925411* (1974), 18 R.F.L. 196, at 198 (B.C.).

then to provide the information to the adopted child and the biological parent, providing guidance and counselling where necessary: s. 81(6)(d) and (e) and (7), *CWA*/ s. 158(7)(c), (d), (11), (12), *CFSA*.

In a recent County Court case,[255] a mother of three children, born in 1928, applied for an order from the court under s. 80(1) of the *CWA* to open her sealed adoption order for her inspection. She had already exhausted her other recourse under that section with no success, that is, seeking the Director's authorization to release information in their files of an identifying or non-identifying nature. This was done in spite of the consent of her own adopting parents. In keeping with the passive policy of the Ministry, no offer was made by the Ministry to seek the consent of the third party in the triangle — the biological parent(s) — not even to determine whether or not the parent(s) were still alive. The County Court raised issue with the nature of the Voluntary Disclosure Registry noting that it applied only to situations in which all parties consented and therefore all parties would have to have known of the Registry's existence. In the circumstances of the case before it, the court noted that it was unlikely if not impossible to possess this knowledge because of the possibility that the biological parent(s) had died prior to the Registry's instigation. As well, the County Court judge challenged the fact that the Ministry officials appeared to have information about adoptees apart from that which was in the Voluntary Disclosure Registry, and were, on given occasions, releasing such information of an identifying or non-identifying nature without any clear or consistent guidelines. The unauthorized acts of discretion seemed to favour those adoptees who could support their requests with a psychiatric or psychological report evidencing compelling need. The applicant in this case, on the other hand, refused to couch her request in pathological terms, maintaining that knowledge of one's origins is a significant and deeply felt need for everybody. Despite the fact that the judge found the process to be less than adequate, he concluded that the applicant's reliance on her "natural curiosity about herself and her roots" is not sufficient for the court to exercise its discretion to order disclosure under s. 80(1) of the *CWA*. While noting that the section did not provide any guidance for the exercise of judicial discretion, the court concluded that its powers must be exercised cautiously "to avoid draining the Registry system of useful content" and for that reason, the opening *non-obstante* clause, "subject to subsection 81(6)" was included. Accordingly, an order for disclosure under s. 80 of the *CWA* should only be made under exceptional circumstances where strong equitable concerns dictate that the sole registry exception must be overridden. Such cases could involve medical consideration showing that the mental and physical health of the applicant required some kind of disclosure.[256] The decision went to the Court of Appeal and several *Charter of Rights* arguments were introduced at that level. The appeal was dismissed and, as was the case with similar American constitutional

---

[255]*Ferguson v. Director of Child Welfare* (1983), 40 O.R. (2d) 294, 142 D.L.R. (2d) 609 (Co. Ct.); affd (1984), 44 O.R. (2d) 78, 3 D.L.R. (4th) 178 (C.A.).

[256]See also *Re Adoption of B.A.* (1980), 17 R.F.L. (2d) 140 (Man. Co. Ct.) ("identity crisis" insufficient grounds); *Kelly v. Supt. of Child Welfare* (1980), 23 B.C.L.R. 299 (S.C.) (Must show psychological well-being at stake or that medical history of parent necessary for his occupation or health; possibility of gaining inheritance not good cause.)

challenges,[257] the *Charter* arguments were not considered to be relevant. The court did not accept that any right or freedom guaranteed by the *Charter* had been infringed or denied and therefore the s. 1 "reasonable limits" test was not applied. If it had been applicable, evidence as to the practice in other jurisdictions would have been relevant since various countries and states do provide for the automatic release of birth information to adopt adoptees. In England and Wales, information of an identifying nature can be released to adoptees upon reaching their eighteenth birthday; in Scotland, their seventeenth birthday; in Israel, their twenty-third birthday. Similar legislation is found in Finland, South Dakota, Kansas and Arkansas.[258] Ironically, as a result of the Ontario County Court decision which questions the right of the Ministry to have *any* information in its possession, there has been a tightening up of the release of information by such officials.

Upon its proclamation, the *CFSA* will partially respond to some of the concerns about vagueness and lack of guidelines raised in the County Court case by dispensing with not only the consent of a deceased biological parent of the adoptee but also the requirement that their names be in the Registry if either are deceased: ss. 158(10), *CFSA*. In addition, the consent of the adopting parent will no longer be required if he or she is deceased: s. 158(8)(a), *CFSA*. Further, it will allow the Director to release information from sealed records in addition to the "Registry" system on the same basis that was described in the County Court decision, that is, when it is necessary in the Director's opinion to protect a person's "health": s. 157(2)(d), *CFSA*.[259] In such instances, the information to be disclosed will be described as "of a prescribed class" and presumably the Regulations will clarify this phrase, especially with respect to whether the information will be of an identifying nature. However, it is submitted that the vague phrase "necessary to protect a person's health" left to the discretion of the Director, coupled with the lack of any due process procedures, will continue the unfairness, arbitrariness and potential for inconsistencies for the adoptee which now exist under the *CWA*.

---

[257]See *e.g. Mills v. Atlantic City Department of Vital Statistics et al.* (1977), 372 A. 2d, 646 (N. J. Sup. Ct.); In *Re Maples*, (1978), 563 S.W. 2d 760 (Miss. S.C.); *Alma Society Inc. v. Mellon* (1979), 601 F. 2d 1225 (U.S.C.A. 2d Cir.).

[258]See *e.g.* England: *The Children Act*, 1975, s. 26; Scotland: *The Adoption Act, 1958 (Scotland)*, Eliz. 11, 6–7, c. 5, s. 22(4); Israel: *Adoption of Children Law*, 5720, 1960, No. 45, s. 27(3).

[259]Ontario's new government may stay the implementation of this section until receipt of a commissioned report on the issue.

Appendix A: Table of Concordance

Child Welfare Act and *Child and Family Services Act* (Ontario)

This Table is designed to assist those who are familiar with the *Child Welfare Act* to find the corresponding or equivalent provisions in the new *Child and Family Services Act*, once it has been proclaimed. Many sections have the same or similar wording, while others have been deleted altogether. In the latter case, a dash is used to indicate as such. (Check the upcoming regulations to determine whether the omissions have been incorporated therein.) The first numbers under the *Child and Family Services Act* column represent those sections which most nearly correspond to the particular *Child Welfare Act* section, if they exist, while any additional numbers represent sections which deal with the same or similar subject matter.

Please note that this new Act, once proclaimed, will incorporate the following Acts which will then be repealed:

Child Welfare Act, R.S.O. 1980, c. 66
Children's Institutions Act, R.S.O. 1980, c. 67
Children's Residential Services Act, R.S.O. 1980, c. 71
Children's Mental Health Services Act, R.S.O. 1980, c. 69

In addition, the *Child and Family Services Act* will contain the following new major additions: Part IV (Young Offenders); Part V (Rights of Children); Part VI (Extraordinary Measures) (secure facilities, ''instrusive measures'' and psychotropic drugs); Part VIII (Confidentiality of and Access to Records); Part X (Indian and Native Child and Family Services).

Child Welfare Act	*Child and Family Services Act* (under proclamation)
1(1)(a)	19(4)
(b)	37(3), (4); 130(2), (3)
(c)	3(1) para. 11
(d)	3(1) para. 13
(e)	—
(f)	3(1) para. 17
(g)	3(1) para. 18
(h)	—
(i)	19(1)
(j)	3(1) para. 22; 15(1)
(k)	3(1) para. 24
(l)	3(1) para. 28
(2)	37(3); 130(2); 1

Child Welfare Act	Child and Family Services Act (under proclamation)
2(1)	5(1)
(2)	17
(3)	—
3	63
4(1)	16
(2)	—
5	40(7)
6(1)	3(1) para. 1; 15(2)
(2)	15(3)
(3)	15(4)
(4)	15(5)
7	18
8 (1–5)	19(4)
(6)	19(5)
9	19(4)
10	—
11	—
12	—
13(1)	19(2)
(2)	19(3)
(3)	19(6)
14	—
15	20
16	—
17–18	22–24
19(1)(a)	3(1) para. 6; 37(1)(a); 43(3)
(b)	37(2)
(c)	3(1) para. 12
(d)	3(1) para. 14
(e)	3(2); 37(1)(d)
(f)	37(1)(e)
(g)	—
(2)–(3)	44
(4)	38(5)

Child Welfare Act	Child and Family Services Act (under proclamation)
20(1)	38(1)
(2)	38(2), (3)
(3)	38(4)
21(1)(a)	40(6), (17), (10), (11), (12)
(b)	40(1)
(2)	40(6)(a)(ii), (13), (17)
(3)	40(5), (14), (15), (17)
(4)	—
22(1)	40(2), (17)
(2)	40(3)
(3)	40(5)
(4)	40(4)
23	74
24	—
25(1)	29(1), (5), (8)
(2)	29(5), (10)
(3)	29(6)
(4)	30; 26(d)
(5)	29(4)(b); 1(b)
(6)	4(5)
(7)	—
(8)	28; 29(2)(b); 31; 27(2), (4), (5), (6)
(9)	4
(10)	32
(11)	31; 29(2)(a); 10(4); 27(1)
(12), (13)	33(1), (2)
(14)	33(3), (4), (5)
(15)	33(3), (4)
26	78
27(1)	42(1)
(2)	42(2)
28(1)	43(1), (2)
(2), (3)	45
(4)	46(1), (2)
(5)	—
(6)	39(1), (2), (3)
(7)	39(4), (5)
(8)	39(3)
(9)	—

Child Welfare Act	Child and Family Services Act (under proclamation)
(10)	39(7)
(11)	53(7)
(12)	47
(13)	47(1); 48
(14)	47(6)
(15)	47(7)
(16)	60(10)
29(1)	50(1), (2)
(2)	50(3)
(3)	50(4), (5)
(4)	50(6), (8)
(5)	50(7)
30(1)	53(1), (6); 76
(2), (3)	Pt. IV
(4)	53(8)
(5)	53(2), (3), (4), (5), (9); 51; 52
31	56
32(1)	60(2), (4); 61(1), (3)
(2)	60(2)(c)
(3)	60(3); 44
(4)	60(4), (7), (8); 61(1), (3)
(5)	60(6)
(6)	60(3); 44
(7)	60(6)(a); 39(4), (5)
33	39(4), (5), (6)
34	—
35(1)	47(5); 54(2), (4)
(2)	54(5)
(3)	54(6)
(4)	54(1); 55
(5)	54(4)(a); 39(4), (5)
(6)	54(3), (4)
36	49
37(1)	60(2), (4); 61(1), (3); 66(1), (2)
(2)	60(4), (7), (8); 61(1), (2), (3)
(3)	66(3)
(4)	60(6)(a); 39(4), (5)
(5)	60(6)
(6)	60(10)

Child Welfare Act	Child and Family Services Act (under proclamation)
38(1)	60(4), (5), (7), (8); 61(1), (2), (3)
(2)	60(2), (6); 61(1), (2), (3)
(3)	60(6)(b)
(4)	60(6)(a); 39(4), (5)
(5)	55(2), (3)
(6)	60(6)
(7)	60(9); 54(7)
(8)	134(2)
(9)	60(10)
39	62
40(1)	59(1)
(2)	73
41	59(2)
42	67
43(1)	65(1), (2); 39(6)
(2)	65(3)
(3)	—
(4)	65(4)
(5)	—
(6)	66(3)
(7)	65(5)
(8)	65(6)
44(1), (2), (3)	82(1); 102; 100(b); 103
(4)	82(3)
(5)	82(4)
(6)	82(5)
(7)	82(2)
45(1)	57(2), (3), (4); 101(2)(e), (f); 102(a); 103
(2)	57(6), (7), (8), (9)
(3)	—
46	79; 99; 137(2)
47(1)	75; 77(1); 37(2)
(2)	75(2)
(3)	75(7)
48(1)	75(3)
(2)	75(7)
(3)	75(4)

Child Welfare Act	Child and Family Services Act (under proclamation)
49(1)	68(1), (2)
(2)	68(3), (4), (5)
(3)	68(7)
(4)	68(8)
50(1)	70(2), (3)
(2), (3)	70(4), (5), (6)
(4)	70(7)
51	77(2), (3)
52(1)	71(1)
(2)	71(2), (3); 68(6)
(3)	71(5)
(4)	71(6)
(5)	71(7), (9)
(6)	71(8), (9)
(7)	71(10)
(8)	71(11)
(9)	71(12)
(10)	71(13)
(11)	71(14)
(12)	72(2)
(13)	72(3)
(14)	72(4), (6), (10), (11)
(15)	72(7)
(16)	—
(17)	72(8)
(18)	72(5)
(19)	72(9)
(20)	—
(21)	72(12)
53	—
54(1)	—
(2)	75(5)
(3)	75(6), (7)
55	—
56	40(9); Pt. IV
57(1)	41(3)
(2)	41(4)
(3)	—
(4)	41(5), (6), (7)
(5)	41(6) P.2

Child Welfare Act	Child and Family Services Act (under proclamation)
(6)	41(6) P.3
(7)	41(8), (9), (10)
58	—
59(1)	130(1); 175(b)
(2)	140(1)
60(1)	176(2)
(2)	176(3), (4); 175(b)
(3)	176(5)
(4)	176(6)
(5)	176(2)
(6)	176(7)
(7)	—
61(1)	178
(2)	179
62(1)	3(1) P.5; 190
(2)	181(1)
(3)	181(2)
(4)	181(3)
(5)	180(1)
(6)	180(2)
(7)	180(3)
(8)	182(2)
63	180–185
64	183
65(1)	135(1), (3), (6)
(2)	135(4), (5)
(3)	135(3), (5); 134(3)
(4)	135(8)
(5)	135(5)
(6)	136(1)
(7)	136(2), (3)
(8)	136(5)
(9)	136(6)
(10)	—
66	138; 139
67	159
68	134(1)
69(1)	131(1)

Child Welfare Act	Child and Family Services Act (under proclamation)
(2)	131(2), (3), (4), (8)
(3), (4)	131(5)
(5)	131(2)(b)
(6)	4; 131(6), (7), (8), (9)
(7)	132
(8)	132(b)
(9)	133(1)
(10)	133(2)
(11)	139(2), (3)
(12)	—
(13)	4(5); 131(11)
(14)	137(2)
(15)	137(1); 154
(16)	145(4); 155
70	131(12)
71(1)	144(1)
(2)	145(1)
(3)	144(2)
(4)	—; 146(1)
(5)	145(3)
(6)	—
72	140(5)
73(1)	140(1)
(2)	140(1), (2)
74(1)(a)	141
(b)	—
(c)	140(3)
(2)	142
(3)	—
(4)	140(4)
(5)	131(10)
75(1)	143(1)
(2)	143(4)
(3)	143(2)
(4)	143(5)
(5)	143(6)
76	146(2); 140(1); 131(4); 130(2), (3)
77	146(3), (4)
78	147

Child Welfare Act	Child and Family Services Act (under proclamation)
79	—
80(1)	145(2); 156(2)
(2)	156(3)
81(1)	158(1)(b)
(2)	158(4)
(3)	158(5), (6)(a)
(4)	157
(5)	158(6)(b); 158(8)(a), (9), (10)
(6)	158(7), (8), (9), (10)
(7)	158(11), (12)
82(1)	148(1), (2)
(2)	148(3)
(3)	148(4)
(4)	148(5)
83	151; 154
84(1)	150(1)
(2)	150(3)
(3)	150(2)
(4)	150(6)
(5)	150(4)
85	149
86(1)	152(1), (2)
(2)	152(3)
(3)	152(4)
(4)	152(5)
(5)	152(6)
87(1)	153
(2)	131(13)
88	—
89(1)	197–206
(2)	197(4)
90	21
91	—
92	3(2)
93	—
94(1)(a)	80; 81(1)(j)

Child Welfare Act	Child and Family Services Act (under proclamation)
(b)	81(1)(a)
(c)	81(1)(e)
(d)	80(b); 81(1)(j)
(e)	81(1)(f)
(f)(i)	81(1)(i)
(ii)	81(1)(b)
(iii)	81(1)(c)
(iv)	81(1)(d)
(v)	—
(vi)	160(3)
(2)(a)	81(2)
(b)	160(1), (2)
(3)	81(1)(f)
(4)	—
(5)	160(4)
(6)	81(3)
95	83; 161

Chapter 3: Readings

Abbott, P., "Childhood, Family and the Bureaucratic Alternatives in America" (1983), 43 *Pub. Ad. Rev.* 89 (biblio).

American Bar Association, *Foster Children in the Courts* (1983).

American Public Welfare Association, *The Law of Adoption Records* (Washington, D.C.: American Public Welfare Association, 1980).

Bakan, David, *Child Abuse: A Bibliography* (Toronto: Canadian Council on Children and Youth, 1976).

Besharov, D.J., "Child Protection: Past Progress, Present Problems and Future Directions" (Summer, 1983), 17 *Fam. L.Q.* 151.

Besharov, D. et al., *The Abused and Neglected Child, Multi-Disciplinary Court Practice* (Practicing Law Institute, 1978).

Binetti, M.S., "The Child's Right to 'Life, Liberty and the Pursuit of Happiness': Suits by Children Against Parents for Abuse, Neglect and Abandonment" (Fall, 1981), 34 *Rutgers L. Rev.* 154.

Brophy, M., "Surrogate Mother Contract to Bear a Child" (January, 1982), 20 *J. Fam. L.* 263.

Bulkley, J. (ed.), *Child Sexual Abuse and the Law* (National Legal Resource Centre for Child Advocacy and Protection, American Bar Association, 1982).

Child Abuse and Neglect (prepared by the Tree Foundation of Canada for the Solicitor General of Canada and the Ministry of National Health and Welfare, 1981).

Child Sexual Abuse: Incest, Assault and Exploitation (National Center on Child Abuse and Neglect, U.S. Dept. of Health and Human Services, 1981).

Children Without Homes (Children's Defence Fund, 1978).

Colvin, M., "Children Locked Up in Care — New Legislation" (Great Britain), (June, 1983), *L.A.G. Bull* 72.

Committee on Record Disclosure to Adoptees, Ont. Ministry of Community and Social Services, *Report* (Toronto: Queen's Printer, 1976).

"Constitutional Limitations on State Invervention in Prenatal Care", (June, 1981), 67 *Va. L. Rev.* 1051.

Cruickshank, D., "Alternatives to the Judicial Process: Court Avoidance in Child Neglect Cases" (1978), 12 *U.B.C. L. Rev.* (No. 2) 248.

Davidson, A., "Periodic Judicial Review of Children in Foster Care: Issues Related to Effective Implementation", (May, 1981), 32 *Juv. and Fam. Ct. J.* 61.

Davies, B., "Implementing the *Indian Child Welfare Act*", (July, 1982), 16 *Clearinghouse Rev.* 179.

English, A., "Child Abuse in the Foster Care System", (February, 1982), 15 *Clearinghouse Rev.* 851.

English, A., "Is There a Private Right of Action Under the *Adoption Assistance and Child Welfare Act* of 1980?" (February, 1983), 16 *Clearinghouse Rev.* 870.

Erickson, N.S., "Preventing Foster Care Placement: Supportive Services in the Home" (August, 1981), 19 *J. Fam. L.* 569.

"Fair Preponderance of Evidence Standard of Proof Prescribed by New York Statute in Parental Rights Termination Proceeding Violates Due Process: Case Note" (August, 1982), 20 *J. Fam. L.* 765.

Fanshel, D. and Shinn, E.B., *Children in Foster Care: A Longitudinal Study* (N.Y.: Columbia University Press, 1978).

Freeman, M.D.A., "Adoption — Existing Policies and Future Alternatives" (1979), 9 *Fam. Law* 142.

Freeman, M.D.A., "Parents, Child-rearing and the State: Who Knows Best?" (Great Britain) (1980), 130 *New L.J.* 1144–46.

Freeman, M.D.A., "The Legal Battlefield of Care: Children in Care" (Great Britain) (1982), 3 *Curr. Leg. Prob.* 117.

Garrison, M., "Why Terminate Parental Rights" (1983), 35 *Stanford Law Review* 423.

Goldstein, J., Freud, A. and Solnit, A.J., *Beyond the Best Interests of the Child* (N.Y.: Free Press, 1973) and *Before the Best Interests of the Child* (N.Y.: Free Press, 1979).

Golubock, C., "Current Status of Federal 1980 Foster Care Reforms" (Children's Defence Fund), (July, 1983), 17 *Clearinghouse Rev.* 294.

Grec, M., "Child Neglect: Fair Preponderance or Clear and Convincing Evidence" (U.S. S. Ct. Review), (Spring, 1983), 10 *Ohio N.U.L. Rev.* 405.

Guerrero, M.P., "*Indian Child Welfare Act of 1978:* A Response to the Threat to Indian Culture Caused by Foster and Adoptive Placement" (Summer, 1980), 7 *Am. Indian L. Rev.* 51.

Hardin, M. *et al.* (eds), *Foster Care Project* (National Legal Resource Centre for Child Advocacy and Protection, American Bar Association) (Boston: Butterworth Legal Publishers, 1983).

Hepworth, Philip H., *Foster Care and Adoption in Canada* (Ottawa: Canadian Council on Social Development, 1980).

Institute of Judicial Administration, American Bar Association, *Standards Relating to Abuse and Neglect* (Ballinger, 1981).

Isaacson, L.B., "Child Abuse Reporting and Statutes — The Case for Holding Physicians Civilly Liable for Failing to Report" (1975), 12 *San Diego L. Rev.* 743.

Jenkins, S. and Norman, E., *Filial Deprivation and Foster Care* (N.Y.: Columbia University Press, 1972).

Johnston, I.D., "Child Abuse and Neglect. Part I: Standards and Pre-adjudication Procedures for State Intrusion in the Family. Part II: The Adjudication Process and Standards and Procedures for Initial Disposition", (June and December, 1981) 9 *N.Z. U.L. Rev.* 217 (June) and 355 (December).

Johnston, P., *Native Children and the Child Welfare System* (Toronto: Canadian Council on Social Development in Association with James Lorimer & Co., 1983).

Kenniston, K. for the Carnegie Council on Children, *All Our Children: The American Family Under Pressure* (N.Y., 1977).

Kleinfeld, A.J., "The Balance of Power Among Infants, Their Parents and the State: Part I and II" (1970-71), 4 and 5 *Family Law Quarterly* 320(4) and 64(5).

Klibanoff, E.B., "Genealogical Information in Adoption: The Adoptee's Quest and the Law" (1977), 2 *Family Law Quarterly* (No. 2).

Lange, D.J., "Child Abuse and Ontario's New Reporting Register", (Fall, 1980), 4 *Legal/Med. Q.* 175.

Light, R.J. *"Abused and Neglected Children in America: A Study of Alternative Policies"* (*Harvard Educational Review*, November, 1973).

Manitoba Inquiry into the Adoption and Placement of Indian and Métis Children (Chairperson: Judge Edwin Kimelman) (Winnipeg: Queen's Printer, 1984).

Mnookin, R.H., "Foster Care: In Whose Best Interests?", *The Rights of Children* (Cambridge: Harvard Educational Review, Report Series No. 9, 1974), at pp. 29–48.

Musewicz, J., "The Failure of Foster Care: Federal Statutory Reform and the Child's Right to Permanence" (includes text of Model Foster Care Review Statute), (May, 1981), 54 *S. Cal. L. Rev.* 633.

National Centre on Child Abuse and Neglect, *Sexual Abuse of Children: Selected Readings* (National Centre on Child Abuse and Neglect, U.S. Dept. of Health and Human Services, 1980).

National Council on Welfare, *In the Best Interests of the Child* (Ottawa: Minister of Supply and Services, 1979).

O'Donnell, F.C., "The Four-sided Triangle: A Comparative Study of the Confidentiality of Adoption Records" (Ontario, Quebec) (May, 1983), 21 *U.W. Ont. L. Rev.* 129.

"Parental Rights of the Mentally Retarded: The Advisability and Constitutionality of the Treatment of Retarded Parents in N.Y. State" (1981), 16 *Colum. J.L. and Soc. Pbms.* 521.

Parliamentary Standing Committee on Health, Welfare and Social Affairs, *Child Abuse and Neglect: Report* (Ottawa: Queen's Printer, 1976).

Phillips, M.H. *et al.*, *Factors Associated with Placement Decisions in Child Welfare* (N.Y.: Child Welfare League of America, 1971).

Riddle, J.S., "Dependency and Neglect Proceedings: Rejecting Requirement that Court Apply Strict Scrutiny: *In Re Lester*, 417 A. 2d 877 (1980)" (May, 1981), 15 *Suffolk U.L. Rev.* 739.

Royal Commission on Family and Children's Law, *Report: The Protection of Children*, No. 5, Part 5 (Berger Commission) (Victoria: Queen's Printer, 1975).

Schlesinger, B., *Child Abuse in Canada* (Toronto: Faculty of Education, University of Toronto, 1977).

Shapiro, R.S., "Medical Treatment of Defective Newborns: An Answer to the 'Baby Doe' Dilemma" (Winter, 1983), 20 *Harv. J. on Legis.* 137.

"Surrogate Motherhood in California: Legislative Proposals" (March, 1981), 18 *San Diego L. Rev.* 341.

"Surrogate Mothers: The Legal Issues" (Fall, 1981), 7 *Am. J.L. and Med.* 323.

Tartanella, P., "Sealed Adoption Records and the Constitutional Right of Privacy of the Natural Parent", (Spring, 1982), 34 *Rutgers L. Rev.* 451.

Task Force on Child Abuse, *Report* (Toronto: Queen's Printer, 1978).

Tator, J. and Wilde, K., "Child Abuse and the Courts: An Analysis of Selected Factors in the Judicial Processing of Child Abuse Cases" (1980), 3 *Can. J. Fam. Law* 165.

Triseliotis, J., *In Search of Origins: The Experiences of Adopted People* (London: Routledge and Kegan Paul, 1973).

"$225,000 Award Reinstated Against Child Welfare Agency: Liability for Abuse of Foster Child" (June 10, 1983), 189 *N.Y.L.J.* p. 3, col. 1.

Unruh, M.C., "Adoptees' Equal Protection Rights" (Symposium: New Directions in Family Law), (August, 1981), 28 *U.C.L.A. L. Rev.* 1314.

Vornholt, R.P., "Application of the Vagueness Doctrine to Statutes Terminating Parental Rights" (April, 1980), 336 *Duke L.J.* 336.

Wald, M., "State Intervention on Behalf of 'Neglected' Children: Standards for Removal of Children from their Homes, Monitoring the States of Children in Foster Care, and Termination of Parental Rights" (1976), 28 *Stanford L. Rev.* 625.

Weiler, K. and Catton, K., "The Unborn Child in Canadian Law" (1976), 14 *Osgoode Hall L.J.* 643.

Chapter 4

Financial Support*

Introduction

Section 197 of the *Criminal Code* imposes a criminal liability for the failure of parents to provide necessaries of life to a child in their charge. The wording originally read, "everyone who is under a legal duty . . . to provide necessaries". Because the *Poor Laws of England* were not enforced in Ontario and because, at common law, a parent had no civil obligation to maintain his child, this original section was of little effect. As a result, Ontario enacted, in 1937, the *Children's Maintenance Act* which remained in effect until the 1970s and which established a parental duty of support enforceable by quasi-criminal proceedings. Sections 1 and 2 of that Act, as amended by the *Age of Majority and Accountability Act*, read:

> 1. Every parent shall maintain and educate his child or children under the age of sixteen years or who is or are sixteen or seventeen years of age and in full time attendance at an educational institution, regard being had to his station in life and means and to the ability of the child or children to maintain himself or themselves.

> 2. Every parent who fails without lawful excuse to comply with s. 1 is guilty of an offence and on summary conviction is liable to imprisonment for a term of not more than three months.

Section 3 of the *Children's Maintenance Act* qualified the extent of duty upon a parent by providing that "nothing in the Act shall be construed as compelling any special remedial treatment of a child contrary to the objection of the parent, guardian or person acting *in loco parentis*." With this qualification, and given the *Criminal Code* test of "necessaries of life", the courts were

---

*This chapter is primarily based on existing law under the *Divorce Act* and Ontario's *Family Law Reform Act* while reference is made to the *Divorce and Corollary Relief Act* (Bill C-47) and to Ontario's *Family Law Act, 1985* (Bill 1) (each of which repeals its predecessor and both of which have passed first reading) when there is significant difference between present and proposed law.

obliged from time to time to decide what was necessary for the child as distinguished from, perhaps, what might be of assistance or benefit for the child. In this regard, the courts considered necessaries of life to include:

i) medical treatment;[1]
ii) articles of clothing, household equipment, food and medicines;[2]
iii) education and training for trade;[3]
iv) solicitors' fees for the purpose for example, of preparing a marriage settlement.[4]

The tools for assessing the behaviour of children have become more sophisticated with time and with this a better understanding of the causal connection between destructive conduct by a child and environmental factors has developed. With this new knowledge came judicial scrutiny of the narrow limits suggested by the phrase "necessaries of life." In 1965, the Ontario Court of Appeal considered expenses for treatment, other than medical treatment, not to create a liability upon a parent since a cost of that type could not be said to be a "necessary of life".[5] A Provincial Family Court judge distinguished the ruling of the Appellate Court by holding that the exemption from liability under s. 3 of the *Children's Maintenance Act* referred only to "special" or "remedial" treatment. If the expense related to treatment *per se, i.e.,* treatment that was considered a necessary of life in all the circumstances (a psychological assessment in this case), then the parent was liable for payment.[6]

With the repeal of the *Children's Maintenance Act*, the civil liability to provide support for a child is no longer based on a standard of "necessaries of life". The obligation is now a function of the parents' ability to pay and the needs of the child. In dollar terms, there is no effective limit. Section 16 of the *Family Law Reform Act* (hereafter known as the *FLRA*) creates the obligation for child support (no change under Ontario's proposed *Family Law Act*):

s. 16(1) Every parent has an obligation, to the extent the parent is capable of doing so, to provide support, in accordance with need, for his or her child who is unmarried and is under the age of 18 years.

(2) Obligation under sub-section (1) does not extend to a child who, being of the age of 16 years or over, has withdrawn from parental control.

Using this standard, the Ontario Court of Appeal has recently determined that private school costs for a severely learning-disabled child for whom appropriate education was otherwise unavailable, constituted an expense for which a parent was now responsible.[7] This case arose under the *Juvenile*

---

[1] *Owen Sound General and Marine Hospital v. Mann,* [1953] O.R. 643, [1953] 3 D.L.R. 417 (H.C.); *R. v. Lewis* (1903), 6 O.L.R. 132, 7 C.C.C. 261 (C.A.).

[2] *Robert Simpson Co. Ltd. v. Twible; T. Eaton Co. v. Twible* (1973), 1 O.R. (2d) 629, 14 R.F.L. 44 (Co. Ct.).

[3] *Walter v. Everard,* [1891] 2 Q.B. 369 (C.A.).

[4] *Helps v. Clayton* (1864) 144 E.R. 222.

[5] *Re Landry,* [1965] 2 O.R. 614, [1965] 4 C.C.C. 291 (C.A.).

[6] *Re Taha* (1976), 28 R.F.L. 352 (Ont. Prov. Ct.).

[7] *Re Regional Municipality of Peel and A* (1982), 35 O.R. (2d) 260, 131 D.L.R. (3d) 297, 26 R.F.L. (2d) 351, 64 C.C.C. (2d) 289, revsg (1980) 30 O.R. (2d) 452, 120 D.L.R. (3d) 260, 56 C.C.C. (2d) 540, (C.A.).

Delinquents Act which created an obligation upon a parent for the costs of supporting a child adjudged to be a delinquent and subject to care and control outside the home. With the repeal of that statute, the obligation upon parents for the support of their children is now solely a function of provincial legislation which varies depending upon the jurisdiction. (For a discussion of subsection (2) "withdrawal from parental control", see below, under "Conduct of the Child".)

The issue of whether a breach of the support legislation creates a standard for civil liability based on negligence remains unresolved in Canadian jurisprudence.[8]

Marriage Breakdown

The great preponderance of child support issues that has been dealt with by the courts is within the context of a marriage breakdown. The single family unit becomes two, but the income usually does not increase, at least in the short run, to ease the financial strain of supporting two households. Each province has legislation providing for child support specifically on separation. Sections 16(1), 18(1) and 18(5) of Ontario's *Family Law Reform Act* establish the jurisdiction, obligate both parents jointly and delineate sixteen criteria to act as guidelines for the judge which are as follows:

s. 18(5)(a) the assets and means of the dependant and of the respondent and any benefit or loss of benefit under a pension plan or annuity;

(b) the capacity of the dependant to provide for his or her own support;

(c) the capacity of the respondent to provide support;

(d) the age and the physical or mental health of the dependant and of the respondent;

(e) the length of time the dependant and respondent cohabited;

(f) the needs of the dependant, in determining which the court may have regard to the accustomed standard of living while the parties resided together;

(g) the measures available for the dependant to become financially independent and the length of time and costs involved to enable the dependant to take such measures;

(h) the legal obligation of the respondent to provide support for any other person;

(i) the desirability of the dependant or respondent remaining at home to care for a child;

(j) a contribution by the dependant to the realization of the career potential of the respondent;

(k) where the dependant is a child, his or her aptitude for and reasonable prospects of obtaining an education;

(l) where the dependant is a spouse, the effect on his or her earning capacity of the responsibilities assumed during cohabitation;

---

[8]See *R. v. Kirkpatrick; ex parte Gutsch,* [1959] O.R. 539 (H.C.); *Kuseta v. Kuseta* (1972), 7 R.F.L. 89 (Ont. C.A.). In *Beauchamp v. Beauchamp* unreported April 28, 1977 (Ont. C.A.) the court refused to strike a claim for support based on a breach of the standard delineated by the then *Children's Maintenance Act* when one of the parties argued that it disclosed no reasonable cause of action.

(m) where the dependant is a spouse, whether the dependant has undertaken the care of a child who is of the age of 18 years or over and unable by reason of illness, disability or other cause to withdraw from the charge of his or her parents;

(n) where the dependant is a spouse, whether the dependant has undertaken to assist in the continuation of a program of education for a child who is of the age of 18 years or over and unable for that reason to withdraw from the charge of his or her parents;

(o) where the dependant is a spouse, any housekeeping, child care or other domestic services performed by the spouse for the family, in the same way as if the spouse were devoting the time spent in performing that service in remunerative employment and were contributing the earnings therefrom to the support of the family; and

(p) any other legal right of the dependant to support other than out of public money.

Ontario's proposed *Family Law Act* under s. 33(9) adds a child's need for a stable environment to (k) and restricts (e) to spousal support considerations. Section 33(7) of the proposed Act further delineates apportioning guidelines for child support: enforce joint parental obligations; give priority to the biological or adoptive parent over other "parents" as defined in the Act; and apportion according to capacity to pay. Section 33(8) does the same for spousal support: recognize economic consequences of spousal contribution; share the economic burden of child support equitably; provision to enable financial independence; and relieve financial hardship.

Section 11(1) of the *Divorce Act* directs the court to award "reasonable" child support "if it thinks it fit and just to do so having regard to the conduct of the parties and the condition, means and other circumstances of each of them." The proposed *Divorce and Corollary Relief Act* omits conduct, retains "condition, means and other circumstances" and adds needs, length of cohabitation, spousal function, economic advantages and disadvantages of separation, eventual spousal self-sufficiency and joint apportionment based on ability to pay: s. 15(5)(6)(7).

General Standard of Support

The general standard for child support orders has been developed in case law (codified by s. 18(5)(f) above) as depending on the accustomed standard of living while the family was together, a standard which is arguably reinforced by the "stable environment" clause in the proposed *Family Law Act*: s. 33(9)(k)(ii).[9] Some suggest that if dollars are more limited upon the event of a family breakdown, then the standard to which the child was accustomed during

---

[9]*Paras v. Paras,* [1971] 1 O.R. 130, 14 D.L.R. (3d) 546, 2 R.F.L. 328, (C.A.) (divorce); appld in *Giles v. Giles* (1980), 15 R.F.L. (2d) 286 (Ont. C.A.) (divorce) and in *Phyllis v. Phyllis* (1976), 14 O.R. (2d) 771, 74 D.L.R. (3d) 593, 24 R.F.L. 103, (C.A.) (divorce).

the cohabitation of his parents should have priority over the rights of either spouse to enjoy the same standard.[10]

In practice, children very often are not the beneficiaries of the foregoing judicial interpretation for some of the following reasons:

1) In the typical domestic dispute, children are not represented or, if represented, the advocacy focuses on custody, access and other non-monetary matters. As well, children are not parties to the domestic dispute unless they have launched an application or sought party status which rarely occurs. The financial security of the child depends on the advocacy of the parents, and to a much lesser extent, if at all, on the protective jurisdiction of the court.[11] In this context, note the 6-year limitation for support applications and the 2-year limitation for agreement enforcement in Ontario's proposed *Family Law Act*: s. 50.

2) In this scenario, support for the child becomes a bargaining item. The economic needs of the child can often be as negotiable as the vacation budget for wife or husband. Very often, the extent of the support obligation is compromised by the bargaining surrounding the disputed issue of access.

3) As support for the child is but one of a number of issues that are resolved in a "package settlement", a court will be reluctant to exercise its protective jurisdiction in setting aside the provision affecting child support for fear of scotching the settlement and perhaps perpetrating the often greater evil of extensive, hurtful, costly litigation.

4) Section 18(5)(f) uses the past tense, *i.e.* the standard of living to which the child *was* accustomed. The case law, however, refers as well to the standard which the child would have enjoyed had the family stayed together.[12] The distinction is significant. Too often a warring spouse, fatigued with battle scars, distances himself as much as possible from "that part of his life." Intentionally or unintentionally, he may minimize the standard of living that the parents had intended for the child.

5) Reinforcing the point under paragraph 4 above, the courts generally see themselves as the passive arbitrators of any dispute, whether it is domestic or otherwise. In this capacity, courts resolve the issues by assessing the evidence of an event that has occurred, rendering an award that returns the injured party to his pre-injury status or, if this is not possible, compensating him financially. In child support issues, there is no pre-injury static status to be considered. The court must assess the present needs of the child and the

[10]*Paras v. Paras, ibid.* See also *Phyllis v. Phyllis, ibid; Zwicker v. Morine* (1980), 38 N.S.R. (2d) 236, 69 A.P.R. 236, 110 D.L.R. (3d) 336, 16 R.F.L. (2d) 293 (C.A.) (divorce); *Johnson v. Johnson* (1982), 27 R.F.L. (2d) 10 (B.C.S.C.) (divorce); *Dyck v. Dyck* (1973), 11 R.F.L. 56 (Sask. Q.B.) (divorce); *Singer v. Singer* (1973), 13 R.F.L. 373 (Ont. S.C.); *Atwood v. Atwood,* [1968] 3 All E.R. 385 (divorce); *Patton v. Patton* (1982), 27 R.F.L. (2d) (N.S.S.C.).

[11]See *Dawe v. Dawe*, summarized in (1979), 2 F.L.R.R. 10 (Ont. Prov. Ct.) where the custodial mother did not request child support at the divorce and waited 10 years before finally seeking support. The court held that the father had settled into a new life with a new family, and reduced the quantum accordingly. Also see *Schwartz v. Brown* (1979), 10 R.F.L. (2d) 171 (Ont. Prov. Ct.) wherein the same circumstances prevailed and the court refused to order any support against the father.

[12]*Phyllis v. Phyllis, supra* note 9.

present ability of the parents to meet those needs, always with the proviso that the parties may return to court if circumstances change. The court is loathe to play any more of an active role, especially if it smacks of "crystal ball forecasting." However, this position may under-estimate the availability of usable information before it to assess, with high probability, the future needs of the children. Indeed, s. 18(5)(k) of the *FLRA* includes such a future-looking guideline which states: "where the dependant is a child, his or her aptitude for and reasonable prospects of obtaining an education." Many parents have already accustomed their children to a certain standard of living by the time the matter is before the court. In many situations, sufficient financial security or wealth exists that the court could impose a future obligation taking into account the likely needs of the children as they age, without too much risk to the parties, particularly if the matter can always be brought back to the court in the event of a material change of circumstances. Based on present standards, examples of foreseeable expenses as the children grow older include cost of living adjustments (see Appendix), private school, camp or orthodontory expenses. By the court's refusal to venture very far into these deep waters, it effectively penalizes the dependent spouse, who is forced to return to court periodically. Due to this costly, tiring and frequently humiliating process, the parties will often reach an unsatisfactory compromise out of court on the child's financial needs. Fortunately, the proposed *Family Law Act* has entrenched the most predictable of these future expenses by specifically allowing the court to include a COLA clause in the order (ss. 34(6)(7) and 38) while putting the onus on the payor spouse why he cannot afford it. (See Appendix for drafting information).

6) Courts are generally not attuned to the real costs of raising children, most judges being successful career men or women, and they are unaccustomed to adding up and budgeting for the real day-to-day costs of children's goods and services, especially in a long term inflationary context.

It is submitted that the language of federal and provincial legislation provides the court with ample authority to do what it deems appropriate in terms of the child's full financial security. Nevertheless, to highlight the practical exigencies involved in modifying "the accustomed standard of living" test in child support disputes, the following principles gleaned from Ontario cases are noteworthy:

1) It has been held that there is no jurisdiction to impose as part of an order of child support any automatic cost of living adjustment. To do so runs counter to the court's duties to assess the ability of the payor prior to any application for variation.[13] (Note the proposed change discussed under (5), above.)

2) To justify an exceptional cost for the child, irrespective of any joint parental intentions prior to the breakdown, it has been held that proof of

---

[13]See *Kadziora v. Kadziora*, summarized in (1983), 5 F.L.R.R. 156 (Ont. C.A.). See also *Armel v. Armel* (1974), 17 R.F.L. 71 (Ont. S.C.) for a decision which refused to take inflation into account in a variation application.

need must be forthcoming to justify an opportunity that otherwise is available through the public sector (in this case, private schooling).[14] However, another court, in the context of the *Divorce Act*, found that there is increased obligations on spouses once legal proceedings have been commenced. While the marriage existed, the father may not have had to support the child through university. However, it was held that once a decree *nisi* is granted, new obligations devolve upon him under s. 11.[15]

3) Support to a custodial mother for a child can be suspended or revoked if the father is prevented from exercising access.[16] The amount of child support can be reduced prospectively where a mother has agreed to foresake claims for child support in consideration for no access by the father.[17] If the custodial spouse moves such that it is more expensive for the non-custodial spouse to exercise access, the latter may deduct the cost of exercising that access from the regular monthly maintenance payments.[18] (For fuller discussion, see below under "Custody/Access Affecting Support".)

4) The equal obligation upon parents for the support of their children can result in a reduced amount of needed child-support dollars where the court injects a notional figure representative of the non-working parent's potential.[19]

5) In the absence of evidence of ability to adjust debt payments, long standing debt obligations may have priority over the obligation to support one's child.[20]

The above-noted cases arguably represent occasions where the courts have given more weight to the rights of the adults than the financial needs of the child. Dependent spouses of financially comfortable families will often obtain a support award far in excess of that payable for the child. It will include amounts not only for running their household, but also for vacation, grooming, entertainment, recreation, often without any proof of need greater than that which flows from the standard of living that the parties enjoyed during the cohabitation. In the absence of party status or representation, the child must be content with a standard which is largely subsumed by the dependent spouse without any assurance that the amount payable will be used fairly for the child. Consequently, as will be seen in the discussion of enforcement of support orders, the older child is often caught in the middle, seeking support from both parents, each one referring the child to the other for want of funds, and each one purporting to rely upon the court order.

---

[14]*Trahan v. Castelli*, summarized in (1979), 2 F.L.R.R. 71 (Ont. Prov. Ct.).

[15]*Crump v. Crump* (1970), 2 R.F.L. 314 (Alta. S.C.); affd 2 R.F.L. 388 (Alta. C.A.).

[16]*Cillis v. Cillis* (1980), 20 R.F.L. (2d) 208 (Ont. S.C.); affd 23 R.F.L. (2d) 76 (Ont. Div. Ct.). But see *Wright v. Wright* (1973), 1 O.R. (2d) 337, 40 D.L.R. (3d) 321, 12 R.F.L. 200 (C.A.) where it was held that a parent cannot avoid payment of child maintenance because of an inability to exercise a right of access.

[17]*Dawe v. Dawe, supra,* note 11.

[18]*Page v. Page* (1980), 31 O.R. (2d) 136, 118 D.L.R. (3d) 57, 19 R.F.L. (2d) 135 (C.A.).

[19]See *Re Lafond* (1979), 23 O.R. (2d) 437 (Co. Ct.).

[20]See *Re Makkinga and Makkinga (No. 2)* (1980), 28 O.R. (2d) 249 (Dist. Ct.) (supersedes *Re Makkinga and Makkinga* (1979), 25 O.R. (2d) 86 (Dist. Ct.) due to procedural defect of first appeal). But see *Younghusband v. Younghusband* (1982), 27 R.F.L. (2d) 453 (Sask. Q.B.).

As a partial response to these kinds of difficulties, recognizing the problems that are attendant on the child's state of dependency on one of the two warring parents, the following devices might be considered:

1) Apply to the court to sever the issues in order that the custody/access battle is determined first. All courts of record have the required jurisdiction to control their process, including the severing of issues to be tried. This will permit the court to focus on the child's economic needs without acquiescing to obvious and not so obvious "trade-offs" which often form part of a judgment that attempts to be palatable to both parties for the sake of a peaceful future. Severing will also ensure that proceedings which directly affect the emotional welfare of a child not be delayed. Sections 26 and 63(4) of Ontario's *Children's Law Reform Act* attempt to respond to this concern by directing that where an application for custody or access has not been heard within six months from the date of commencement of proceedings, the clerk is to list the application for the court, at which time a date for the hearing is to be fixed. The sections allow the court to sever the issues where it is in the child's best interests to determine the custody/access matter first. (See also s. 47 of Ontario's proposed *Family Law Act*.)

2) Agreements or orders of support that facilitate payment of the child's "exceptional" expenses directly to third party creditors not only ensure payment but also minimize future hostilities between the parents. They also quell the resentment of non-custodial parents who begin to see themselves as nothing more than a bank for the ex-spouse. Payments issued directly to third parties for such expenses as camp, orthodontory or private school can be arranged without losing the tax benefits of periodic support payments. (For discussion, see below under "Income Tax and Children".)

3) To offset the real effect of cost of living, it is suggested that the parties consider an arrangement that includes, in addition to other monthly payments, a periodic yearly payment equal to the increase as calculated by the cost of living index (see Appendix), which, at the election of the payor could be paid in one lump sum or over the ensuing 12 months. It is submitted that such payments would qualify as periodic support payments within the meaning of the *Income Tax Act*. (Again, see below under "Income Tax".)

4) In order to thwart the tendency of some non-custodial spouses to resist all support claims because they come from a "greedy, embittered, lazy" ex-spouse, one might consider applying for the appointment of an *amicus curiae*, litigation guardian or counsel for the child under the Rules of Civil Procedure or the Superior Court's inherent jurisdiction. This also relieves the custodial spouse of what might be considered as a conflict of interest situation in which one must advocate for oneself as well as the child for a portion of the same financial pie. Arguably, counsel for the child could isolate from the inter-spousal bargaining process, the true financial needs of the child and the ability of the parties to pay, leaving the court to make a more well-informed and less biased compromise for all family members.

Quantum   One cannot discuss a standard of support separate from quantum of support since availability of financial resources makes each dependent on the other. The court in *Paras v. Paras* gave clear acknowledgment to this self-evident reality:

Since ordinarily no fault can be alleged against the children which would disentitle them to support, the objective of maintenance should be, as far as possible, to continue the availability to the children of the same standard of living as that which they would have enjoyed had the family break-up not occurred. To state that as the *desideratum* is not to be oblivious to the fact that in the vast majority of cases, after the physical separation of the parents, the resources of the parents would be inadequate to do so and at the same time to allow to each of the parents a continuation of his or her former standard of living. In my view, the objective of maintaining the children in the interim has priority over the right of either parent to continue to enjoy the same standard of living to which he or she was accustomed when living together.

However, if the responsibility for the children is that of the parents jointly, neither one can justifiably expect to escape the impact of the children's maintenance. Ideally, the problem could be solved by arriving at a sum which would be adequate to care for, support and educate the children, dividing the sum in proportion to the respective incomes and resources of the parents, and directing the payment of the appropriate proportion by the parent not having physical custody.[21]

Section 18(5) of Ontario's *Family Law Reform Act* sets out a non-exhaustive list of variables which the court should take into account in determining a support order, basically reflecting a joint financial responsibility of both spouses for raising the children, which is linked with each spouse's ability to pay. Section 18(5)(c), "the capacity of the respondent to provide support", suggests a relative assessment. This section is comparable to the repealed *Deserted Wives and Children's Maintenance Act* wherein the court looked not only at a minimum standard but considered the adequacy of the payments in view of the father's ability to pay.[22] However, one Saskatchewan court held that insufficient income was no excuse and that the father was under a duty to seek employment that would earn the necessary income.[23] Note that the apportioning guidelines under s. 33(7) of Ontario's proposed *Family Law Act*, listed above under Marriage Breakdown, reinforce this approach.

Exceptional expenses for the child over and above the basic formula might include those found under s. 18(5)(d) (age and physical/mental health) or s. 18(5)(k) (the child's aptitude/reasonable prospects for education).

In assessing quantum where the court found the wife not to be entitled to support for herself, one court noted the following:

Those children have the right to be maintained at a standard of living commensurate with the ability of their parents to do so. They should not suffer as a result of being in either party's care. Two possibilities at least are

---

[21]*Paras v. Paras, supra,* note 9 and see re-affirmation of *Paras* decision by C.A. in *Giles v. Giles, supra,* note 9. But see *Allen v. Allen* (1981), 24 R.F.L. (2d) 152 (Ont. Co. Ct.) where the approach was to leave each parent with the same net disposable income.

[22]*Jeffery v. Jeffery* (1975), 21 R.F.L. 246 (Ont. Prov. Ct.). See also *Hubick v. Hubick* (1972), 5 R.F.L. 240 (Sask. C.A.) (prov. support application).

[23]*Sigurdson v. Sigurdson* (1980), 7 Sask. R. 422 (U.F.C.). See also *C. v. C. (No. 2)* (1979), 11 R.F.L. (2d) 364 (Ont. Co. Ct.).

indicated on the question of determining the quantum of maintenance. One is simply to look at the requirements of Mrs. Borel as to her overall needs, and then ask Mr. Borel to make-up the shortfall. That is a simple yet, in my opinion, unfair approach because it does exactly what I have always said I would not do, that is, it provides maintenance for Mrs. Borel indirectly when I would not award it to her directly. I think it is far more appropriate to look at the needs of the children and determine what those needs will mean in actual dollars, or do one's best to estimate that, and from there, determine who should pay what.[24]

It is not completely clear whether, in practical terms, these different approaches give rise to different dollar amounts. It is arguable that whether one allocates a notional amount representative of the expense of the child in the cost of rent or mortgage payments, etc., or whether one considers a portion, if not all, of the shortfall in the custodial parent's budget as representative of the child's costs, the amount will likely be the same. It is probably better for all concerned to accept the reality that every dollar paid to the custodial parent will not be directly used for the child's needs. At the same time, it should also be accepted that the custodial parent's time, effort and energy in caring for the child on an on-going basis can never be compensated for in dollars.[25] Indeed, one court held that the custodial parent's entire share of child support was satisfied by her care of the child so that the father was held responsible for the financial part.[26]

Judicial Intervention in Inter-Spousal Agreements

Despite the above observations that the court is a passive arbitrator, there are circumstances in which the judge will interfere. Under both the *Divorce Act* and the *Family Law Reform Act*, the court possesses an overriding jurisdiction to ensure that a child's standard of support is not jeopardized by an agreement between the parents. For example, a separation agreement which absolved a husband from supporting his child after divorce where he would otherwise have been able to do so is of no legal effect and does not affect the court in its responsibility to protect the rights of the child. As in the case of a court order for child support, subsequent conduct by a parent and its relationship to any support agreement by the parents cannot fetter the discretion of the court to properly re-assess the children's needs.[27] Moreover, if the court fears the wife will not enforce any order made for the support of the child, the money can be ordered to be paid into court to the credit of the child upon notice to the Official Guardian.[28] If a wife receives property from her husband in consideration of her waiving all maintenance claims for herself and her children, present and future, and subsequently the wife claims maintenance in a divorce action, the plaintiff husband must be taken to have known that any waiver of maintenance by the wife for the benefit of the child was ineffective.[29] If both spouses apply for a consent

---

[24]*Borel v. Borel*, summarized in (1981), 4 F.L.R.R. 68 (Ont. S.C.) (divorce). See also *Giles v. Giles*, *supra* note 9.

[25]See *Nielsen v. Nielsen* (1980), 16 R.F.L. (2d) 203 (Ont. Co. Ct.).

[26]*Phillips v. Phillips* (1981), 24 R.F.L. (2d) 139 (Ont. Co. Ct.).

[27]*Sands v. Sands* (1975), 24 R.F.L. 276 (Ont. C.A.).

[28]*Hansford v. Hansford*, [1973] 1 O.R. 116, 30 D.L.R. (3d) 392, 9 R.F.L. 233, at 235 (S.C.).

[29]*Krueger v. Taubner* (1975), 17 R.F.L. 267 (Man. C.A.).

order regarding child support, the court must still require evidence of parental means and child's needs and cannot delegate this discretion to the parents.[30]

These decisions are reflected in s. 55(1) of the *Family Law Reform Act*, which deals with domestic contracts, and more specifically in s. 18(4), covering support arrangements (ss. 56(1) and 33(4) of the proposed *Family Law Act*):

> s. 55(1) In the determination of any matter respecting the support, education, moral training or custody of or access to a child, the court may disregard any provision of a domestic contract pertaining thereto where, in the opinion of the court, to do so is in the best interests of the child.
>
> s. 18(4) The court may set aside a provision for support in a domestic contract or paternity agreement and may determine and order support in an application under subsection (1) notwithstanding that the contract or agreement contains an express provision excluding the application of this section,
>
> > (a) where the provision for support or the waiver of the right to support results in circumstances that are unconscionable;
> >
> > (b) where the provision for support is to a spouse who qualifies for an allowance for support out of public money; or
> >
> > (c) where there has been default in the payment of support under the contract or agreement.

It appears that s. 18(4) is only available upon an application for support. That is, it is not open for the payor spouse to apply under this section for relief unless the issue for support is already before the court.[31] Regarding s. 55, a court relied thereon when two parents entered into an agreement reciting that they had only one child when in fact they had two children applying the extended definition of "child" and "parent" in the Act. Although the parties accepted the agreement in settlement of all claims for child support, the terms were found to disregard the best interests of the child.[32]

Under the *Divorce Act*, jurisdiction for court intervention is found under s. 9(1)(e) (s. 11(1)(a), *Divorce and Corollary Relief Act* as yet unpassed):

> s. 9(1) On a petition for divorce it is the duty of the court
>
> . . .
>
> > (e) where a decree is sought under s. 4 to refuse the decree if there are children of the marriage and the granting of the decree would prejudicially affect the making of reasonable arrangements for maintenance.

If no relief for custody or maintenance has been claimed, the court is under a duty imposed by this section to ensure a fair and just settlement of the maintenance issue and may make an order in respect of custody and maintenance

---

[30]*Re Stevenson and Stevenson* (1979), 23 O.R. (2d) 539 (Prov. Ct.).

[31]*Porter v. Porter* (1979), 23 O.R. (2d) 492, 8 R.F.L. (2d) 349 (S.C.).

[32]*Barlow v. Barlow* (1978), 8 R.F.L. (2d) 6 (Ont. Prov. Ct.). See also *Boyd v. Boyd* (1980), 1 F.L.R.A.C. 649 (Ont. Prov. Ct.). But see *Stevenson v. Stevenson, supra,* note 30 where the court declined to intervene even in the face of the agreement's inadequacy because the contract provided for a specific "out-of-court" means for variation which should first be exhausted.

so that the divorce decree may be granted.[33] If necessary, the court will refuse to grant a decree. In one case, a husband had made an agreement with his wife to provide her with four pounds per week for the support of their child, forcing the wife to live on social security. The court refused to certify the divorce under the British *Matrimonial Causes Act* as it was not satisfied with the arrangement for the child's welfare, maintaining that four pounds per week for a wife and child was inadequate.[34] Query why the duty of the court in this respect appears to be limited to divorce proceedings commenced under s. 4 of the *Divorce Act* (marriage breakdown) and not under s. 3 (matrimonial offences).

Nothing in either the provincial or federal statutes eliminates attacks on the validity of a domestic agreement based on common law principles of duress, coercion, undue influence or the more recent phenomenon of failure to fully disclose. In fact, Ontario's proposed *Family Law Act* codifies this under s. 56(4). The courts have enunciated a clear duty upon contracting parties to fully disclose, the failure of which can constitute misrepresentation. Unlike non-domestic contracts, the courts may view innocent silence or failure to volunteer information, even when no request for same has been made, as violating the duty to disclose and jeopardizing the validity of the contract.[35] In light of the wording of s. 55 of the *Family Law Reform Act*, this protection would extend not only to the contracting adult party but also to the non-participating infant beneficiary of the contract.

Newly-Defined "Parent"

The *Divorce Act* defines "child" to whom an obligation of support exists as "any person to whom the husband and wife stand *in loco parentis* and any person of whom either the husband or the wife is the parent and to whom the other of them stands *in loco parentis*": s. 2 The burden of proof is on the applicant.[36] *In loco parentis*, as a common law principle, has always been available as grounds of support by way of a general Writ of Summons issued in the High Court under an equitable rather than statutory jurisdiction.[37] (The proposed *Divorce and Corollary Relief Act* substitutes the literal translation "in the place of parents.") Ontario did not adopt *in loco parentis* but instead attaches liability to a person who has, on a balance of probabilities,[38] "demonstrated a settled intention" to treat a child as a member of his family. Section s. 1(a) and (e) of the *Family Law Reform Act*, (s. 1(1) of the proposed *Family Law Act*) define "child" and "parent" respectively:

> s. 1(a) "child" means a child born within or outside marriage, subject to ss. 86 and 87 of the *Child Welfare Act* (which relate to the effect of adoption) [now the *Child and Family Services Act*], *and includes a person whom the parent has demonstrated a settled intention to treat as a child of*

---

[33]*Davies v. Davies* (1969), 3 D.L.R. (3d) 381 (N.W.T. Ter. Ct.). But see *Bair v. Bair* (1982), 27 R.F.L. (2d) 309 (Ont. U.F.C.).

[34]*Dennett v. Dennett, The Times*, March 24, 1977 (C.A.).

[35]*Couzens v. Couzens* (1981), 34 O.R. (2d) 87, 126 D.L.R. (3d) 577, 24 R.F.L. (2d) 243 (C.A.); *Hood v. Hood*, summarized in (1981), 4 F.L.R.R. 81 (Ont. S.C.).

[36]*Bouchard v. Bouchard* (1972), 29 D.L.R. (3d) 706, 9 R.F.L. 372 (Ont. S.C.).

[37]*Stone v. Carr* (1799), 170 E.R. 517.

[38]*Kowalchuk v. Lafrancois*, summarized in (1981), 3 F.L.R.R. 213 (Ont. Co. Ct.).

his or her family, but does not include a child placed in a foster home for consideration by a person having lawful custody. [emphasis added][39]

. . .

(e) "parent" means the father or mother of a child, and includes *a person who has demonstrated a settled intention to treat a child as a child of his or her family,* but does not include a person in whose home a child was placed as a foster child for consideration by a person having lawful custody. [emphasis added]

The standard of *in loco parentis* has been measured by the following indicators in the case of *Re O'Neil and Rideout*:

(1) Did the person provide a large part of the financial support necessary for the child's maintenance? This is a *sine qua non*.
(2) Did the person intend to "step into the father's [mother's] shoes?"
(3) Was the relationship between the person and the child a continuing one with the idea of permanency?
(4) If the child were living with and supported by its own father (mother), has the inference that such father (mother) has not been replaced by the other person, been overturned?
(5) Has the person, at the time pertinent to the action, terminated his position of *in loco parentis*?[40]

All of the above indicators can equally be applied to an assessment of the "settled intention" standard. However, this latter standard is arguably broader than that of the *Divorce Act*. For example, it has been held that a child is not a "child" as defined in the *Divorce Act* if a husband discovers at trial that the person whom he thought throughout the marriage to be lawful issue was, in fact, "illegitimate." In this situation, an *in loco parentis* relationship cannot exist because the relationship depends on an intention by the person to place himself in a position towards the child ordinarily occupied by the father, which intention must be based on the belief that someone else is the father.[41] On the other hand, the language of the *Family Law Reform Act* would seemingly catch this situation since it appears to make the subjective intentions of the payor less significant than the objective assessment of a presentation of family with the complementary definitions of "parent" and "child."[42] Indeed, the definitions in the *Family Law Reform Act* seem to be closer to the English legislation where "child of the family" was held to include a child of an undisclosed adultery.[43] The defining section in the English legislation covered, *inter alia*, "any other child . . . who has been treated by both those parties as a child of their family."

---

[39]Children who have been made wards of the state have been held to be "children of the marriage" in the context of a support proceeding under the *Divorce Act*. See *Martens v. Martens* (1981), 31 O.R. (2d) 313 (U.F.C.).

[40]*Re O'Neil and Rideout* (1975), 22 R.F.L. 107 (Ont. Surr. Ct.). For other divorce cases dealing with *in loco parentis*, see also *Bouchard v. Bouchard, supra,* note 36 (second husband and child of a previous marriage) and *Wasylenki v. Wasylenki* (1970), 12 D.L.R. (3d) 534, 2 R.F.L. 324 (Sask. Q.B.).

[41]*Aksugyuk v. Aksugyuk* (1975), 17 R.F.L. 224, at 277 (N.W.T.S.C.).

[42]See *Christmas v. Christmas* (1980), 3 Fam. L. Rev. 306 (Ont. Prov. Ct.) for proposition that once a settled intention has been demonstrated, it cannot be revoked.

[43]*W. v. W.* (1971), 10 R.F.L. 351 (Eng., Assizes).

Ontario cases, since the introduction of the *Family Law Reform Act*, seem to reflect a divergence of opinion as to the meaning of the ''settled intention'' test. The case of highest authority, a County Court decision on appeal from a Provincial Court, concludes that while the wording in the two statutes is different, the effect is the same. That is, a person who has demonstrated a settled intention to treat a child as a member of his or her family is the same as a person who has assumed an *in loco parentis* relationship to a child.[44] In this case, common law spouses had cohabited almost three years during which time only the ''husband'' contributed to the support of the family which included a child brought into their relationship by the common-law wife from her previous marriage. However, since their separation, the ''husband'' had paid nothing. The court found a situation of financial dependency to exist but observed that the test of ''settled intention'' or ''*in loco parentis*'' required something more in the way of fulfilling other parental duties and responsibilities.[45] Further, the burden of showing same rests with the applicant and is based on the words ''demonstrated'' and ''settled.'' Nevertheless, it has also been held that financial support is the essence of the *FLRA/in loco parentis* test.[46] In another case, a Provincial Court presumably distinguished the two concepts by specifically eliminating from the ''settled intention'' test the indicator from *Re O'Neil and Rideout* involving any reference to the intentions of the respondent at the time of the hearing. In other words, the revocation by an alleged parent of a prior ''settled intention'' is irrelevant. Nevertheless, the court considered the test to be the same notwithstanding this apparent distinction, relying on earlier common law in support of the elimination of the question of intention at the time of the hearing.[47] Another decision of the Provincial Court concluded that, due to the choice of new wording, the Legislature intended a new and different standard from that of *in loco parentis*.[48]

If there is a difference between the two concepts, then the more liberal objective approach of the provincial court decisions would appear to be preferable. The high frequency in today's society of reconstituted, serial families through remarriage or common law requires a flexible liability test to ensure that the child does not face an uncertain financial future. To base parental liability on a person's intention to replace the child's ''own mother or father'' is regressive, unpredictable and implicitly suggests that a child is a chattel with only one owner.[49] Further, it is inconsistent with the wording of the provincial statute

---

[44]*Re MacDonald* (1979), 24 O.R. (2d) 84, 97 D.L.R. (3d) 763 (Ont. Co. Ct.); and see *Bair v. Bair* (1982), 27 R.F.L. (2d) 309 (Ont. U.F.C.); *Waters v. Nicholls* (1979), 12 R.F.L. (2d) 342 (Ont. Prov. Ct.).

[45]See e.g., *Robinson v. Robinson* (1981), 28 R.F.L. (2d) 347 (Sask. Q.B.); *Olmstead v. Olmstead* (1981), 25 R.F.L. (2d) 67 (N.B.Q.B.); *Barham v. Barham* (1979), 1 F.L.R.A.C. 481 (Ont. Prov. Ct.) (65 days is too short to demonstrate settled intention). For a decision based on similar considerations under the *Divorce Act* see *Rathwell v. Rathwell* (1981), 10 Sask. 407, 21 R.F.L. (2d) 301 (Q.B.).

[46]*Waters v. Nicholls, supra,* note 44.

[47]*Barlow v. Barlow, supra,* note 32.

[48]*Christmas v. Christmas, supra,* note 42.

[49]For adoption of this objective approach see *Riopelle v. Daniel* (1982), 36 O.R. (2d) 335 (Prov. Ct. F.D.); *Christmas v. Christmas, supra* note 42. But see *Bair v. Bair, supra,* note 44.

which appears to expand the number of potential parenting figures for a child, recognizing that children are increasingly exposed to more than one set of psychological parents. It would also be inconsistent to find a person to be a parent in a custody dispute as a result of the dynamics that have existed between the adult and the child not a parent in a child-support dispute because of the emphasis in the latter on the adult's perceptions to the exclusion of the child's expectations. Finally, an approach that focuses on the factors in *Re O'Neil and Rideout* appears to invite increased "fault-oriented" litigation, something that presumably has been abandoned by the new legislation with respect to child support.[50] An emphasis on the subjective position of the alleged parent means judicial hearings that pretend to be capable of dissecting the dynamics of human relationship via rules of evidence. At best, a court of law can look at the fact of the relationships, the length of it, the presentation of the persons as a family within the community, the presence or absence of any agreement or understanding between the adult cohabitants, the understanding between the cohabitants and the child's non-custodial parent, the surname adopted by the child, the title used by the child in referring to the alleged parent be it "Mom" or "Uncle", and the presence or absence of direct financial contribution for the support of the child as aids to assessing whether or not there existed a parent-child relationship. These are facts that are readily available without the court inviting a "crystal ball" analysis of the "real" intentions of the alleged parent *vs*. the "real" understanding or perceptions of the children or other parent involved. If someone has developed a parental role in a very short time, he is protected by the court's adjustment of quantum and duration of support under s. 18(5)(e) (the length of time the child and the non-related person cohabited) and 18(5)(p) (the child's right to support from the biological parent). Note that Ontario's proposed *Family Law Act*, while limiting "duration of cohabitation" to spousal support considerations, includes ss. 33(5) and (7) which rank the biological or adoptive parent obligation before that of other "parents" as defined under the Act.

There is nothing in the provincial legislation that precludes the possibility of a child having more than one non-custodial parent with an obligation to pay support.[51] For example, in the case where a child's standard of living has substantially increased due to his mother's now defunct common law relationship, an applicant mother might argue that while she has always received support from the child's father, her divorced husband, she is entitled to an amount from her former common law spouse that reflects the difference in the two standards of living. This possibility is accentuated by the above-mentioned s. 18(5)(p), which suggests that the fact that the child may be entitled to support from another person goes to the question of quantum, not entitlement. Nevertheless, it has been held to be a prerequisite to seek support from the biological father first "in order to determine an orderly approach to the financial

---

[50]*C. v. C. (No. 2), supra,* note 23. See also *Sigurdson v. Sigurdson, supra,* note 23.

[51]See *Meservia v. Silvaggio* (1980), 20 R.F.L. (2d) 328 (B.C. Co. Ct.) wherein a person who was not the natural father stood *in loco parentis* to the children after a seven year common law relationship. He was found to be responsible for more than nominal support after the mother remarried again.

responsibilities'' between several sets of ''parents'' as defined by the legislation.[52] Yet, another court decided not to order the father to pay any child support once the mother had moved in with another man and both were working.[53] As noted above, the proposed *Family Law Act* codifies the former approach.

Finally, insofar as s. 18(5) may create a liability on a third party for child support, the *FLRA* does not permit a respondent to seek indemnity, contribution or any other claim over and against that third party. An order granting leave to issue a third party notice for this purpose was set aside on appeal.[54] Under s. 33(5) of the proposed *Family Law Act* a third party may now be added.

Parties to Applications for Child Support

A significant distinction between the federal *Divorce Act* and provincial domestic legislation is the question of who may be an applicant party in a child-support action. Under the *Divorce Act* (and the proposed *Divorce and Corollary Relief Act*), the court may act only upon an application by the husband or wife. Under s. 18(2) of Ontario's *Family Law Reform Act*, application may be brought by the dependent child himself, a parent of the dependant or by the Ministry of Community and Social Services or a municipality:

> if the Ministry or municipality is providing a benefit under the *Family Benefits Act* or assistance under the *General Welfare Assistance Act* in respect of the support of the dependant.

(Ontario's proposed *Family Law Act* adds an Indian band to the list and expands the circumstances which permit standing: s. 33(3).)

Note that ''parent'', as defined in s. 1(e) includes a third party who treats the child as a member of the family except where that party is a foster parent for consideration. If a dependent child makes an application, the court may order the money to be paid to a person or agency for the benefit of the child: s. 19(1)(e). Section 18(3)(a) and (b) theoretically eliminate difficulties that prevented government agencies from using High Court or Family Court proceedings to compel a spouse to support a dependant on assistance. However, Ontario's experience seems to be that it is infrequently invoked by the Ministry. Nevertheless, at least one court has itself brought the agency in as a third party.[55]

Section 2(4) of the *Family Law Reform Act* reads:

> s. 2(4) A minor who is a spouse has capacity to commence, conduct and defend a proceeding under this Act without the intervention of a next friend or guardian *ad litem* and give any consent required or authorized by this Act.

Relying upon that section it was argued before an Appellate Court that the common law rights of an infant were abrogated, such that a minor who is not a spouse has no capacity to commence or conduct a proceeding under the Act. The

---

[52]*Petrie v. Petrie* (1980), 18 C.P.C. 78, 20 R.F.L. (2d) 40 (Ont. S.C.).

[53]*Wilton v. Wilton* (1982), 30 R.F.L. (2d) 170 (Man. Q.B.); varied 36 R.F.L. (2d) 55 (Man. C.A.). See also *Lysne v. Wing* (1983), 33 R.F.L. (2d) 444 (B.C. Co. Ct.): revd in part 29 R.F.L. (2d) 102 (B.C. C.A.).

[54]*Stere v. Stere* (1980), 30 O.R. (2d) 200, 116 D.L.R. (3d) 703, 19 R.F.L. (2d) 434 (S.C.).

[55]*Butson v. LaCombe*, summarized in (1984), 7 F.L.R.R. 37 (Ont. U.F.C.).

argument was rejected, the court concluding that to deprive a child of such a substantive right requires clear statutory language, not simply negative intent.[56] Ontario's proposed *Family Law Act* removes the section altogether.

Conduct of the Parents

Ontario's *Family Law Reform Act* (s. 18(6)) and the proposed *Divorce and Corollary Relief Act* (s. 15(5)), make spousal conduct irrelevant to child support. Nevertheless, there are two exceptional decisions, both with respect to divorce proceedings, that appear to relate the conduct of the parents to the determination of a child's support. They may also have an impact on an order under the *Family Law Reform Act* having regard to the introductory wording of s. 18(5): ". . . the court shall consider all the circumstances of the parties." In one case, a wife was found responsible for the breakdown of the marriage by refusing to take blood tests confirming the male respondent to be the father of the alleged children of the marriage. On this basis, as well as recognizing the ability of the petitioner mother to support herself and the children, the court made no order for support against the respondent husband.[57] In a second situation, ". . . the wife took the risk of a pregnancy without the husband's consent before their marriage took place." Two and one-half months after the marriage, the wife left her husband. Five years later, when the wife sought relief from the father for support, the court considered, *inter alia*, the conduct of the wife in respect of the pregnancy, concluding that it was the wife's prime responsibility to support the child. The court declined to make any order unless the child suffered from want of support from the wife or was in distressed circumstances.[58]

While one court has refused to impose a blanket prohibition under the *Family Law Reform Act* on any consideration relating to parental conduct as it affects child support,[59] it seems safe to conclude that the issue of how one parent treated the other has been rendered irrelevant to the financial needs of the child. An attempt was made to relate the abusive conduct of a parent to an argument for increased child support pursuant to the aforementioned s. 18(6), but this was properly rejected, the court noting that to accept such an approach would result in an improper interpretation of that section.[60] It would seem appropriate for one to view the two cases which suggest that conduct is relevant, as anomalies to the usual and appropriate consideration of this criterion as it relates to child support.

Conduct of the Child: Withdrawal from Parents

Section 16(2) of the *Family Law Reform Act* provides an exemption from the obligation of child support if the child is 16 years of age or over and "has withdrawn from parental control." (Divorce legislation arguably subsumes this exemption under "other circumstances".) This phrase opens up an issue that is analogous to "constructive desertion" in spousal support claims. However, given the apparent intention of the legislation to minimize fault as an aspect of entitlement to support, the courts have properly taken a very narrow and limited approach to this potential defence. It would also be regressive for the child to

---

[56]*Re Haskell and Letourneau* (1979), 25 O.R. (2d) 139, 100 D.L.R. (3d) 329 (Co. Ct.). See also *Sloat v. Sloat* (1981), 25 R.F.L. (2d) 378 (B.C.S.C.) for a decision in which the child was accepted as applicant under the *Divorce Act*.

[57]*Allan v. Allan* (1973), 42 D.L.R. (3d) 766 (Man. Q.B.).

[58]*Little v. Little* (1974), 15 R.F.L. 377 (B.C.S.C.).

[59]*Zarate v. Calero*, summarized in (1984), 6 F.L.R.R. 172 (Ont. Prov. Ct.).

[60]*Crawley v. Crawley*, summarized in (1979), 2 F.L.R.R. 59 (Ont. Co. Ct.) and see *supra*, note 50.

have to prove his "constructive desertion" case when principles surrounding that legal notion seem to have been abandoned by the provincial legislation regarding spouses. Accordingly, the courts have limited the defence to the "clearest of cases of a free and voluntary withdrawal from reasonable parental control."[61] The court will have regard to the tendency of many children of this age to undergo a phase of parental-control difficulties, the effect of which should not be punitive because of this section.[62] Nevertheless, parents can expect to exercise reasonable control over a 16- to 18-year old and if the child, based on that control alone, decides to leave, the courts will find a free and voluntary withdrawal.[63] It has also been held that once having left, the parent does not have to take the child back.[64]

One judgment suggests that the defence must meet an even higher standard if the child suffers from various known emotional difficulties requiring psychiatric treatment. Otherwise, the section would allow the parent to reject financial responsibility for a child simply because of his behavioural problems. In such situations, if a parent wishes to rely upon this defence, he or she must lead evidence that all reasonable efforts to deal with the child have been taken.[65] It is suggested that short of intervention by the state through the Children's Aid Society, no parent should be entitled to this defence in the case of a child who is emotionally disturbed. The Legislature could not have intended a fault-finding inquiry for children, having eradicated it from inter-spousal proceedings. Emotional disturbance to the point of requiring treatment should be sufficient in itself to show that the child is not freely and voluntarily withdrawing from parental care.

Duration of Support

An application for child support under Ontario's *Family Law Reform Act* can be commenced once a child is born, but not before,[66] although the court may then include in its award the cost of pre-natal care and the birth: s. 19(1)(h). Under the same legislation, support cannot be awarded for a child upon his reaching the age of majority, *i.e.* 18 years, either through continuing periodic payments or through a lump sum payment, the effect of which would permit monies as support to be made available to the child after his 18th birthday: s. 16(1).[67] Also, note the discussion above wherein a parent may be relieved of his or her child support obligations if the child, being 16 years or over, voluntarily withdraws from parental control.

---

[61]*Re Haskell and Letourneau, supra*, note 56; *Dolabaille v. Carrington* (1981), 32 O.R. (2d) 442, 21 R.F.L. (2d) 207 (Prov. Ct.); *H. v. C. et al.* (1982), 27 R.F.L. (2d) 28 (Ont. Prov. Ct.).

[62]*H. v. C. et al., ibid.,* at 31.

[63]*Distefano v. Harolltunian* unreported, July 13, 1984 (Ont. Prov. Ct.).

[64]*Leroux v. Leroux* (1982), 31 R.F.L. (2d) 105 (Ont. Prov. Ct.).

[65]*H. v. C. et al., supra,* note 61, at p. 33.

[66]*Swanson v. Coombe* (1982), 26 R.F.L. (2d) 416 (Ont. Prov. Ct.).

[67]See also *Dolabaille v. Carrington (No. 2)* (1981), 34 O.R. (2d) 641 (Prov. Ct.). But see conflicting decision of *Younger v. Younger*, summarized in (1984), 7 F.L.R.R. 6 (Ont. S.C.) (decision under appeal) where court appears to award support for child over 18 years under the *Family Law Reform Act*.

The *Divorce Act* and the proposed *Divorce and Corollary Relief Act* read in part:

> s. 2. . . . "children of the marriage" means each child of a husband and wife who at the material time is
>> (a) under the age of 16 years, or
>> (b) 16 years of age or over, and under their charge but unable, by reason of illness, disability[68] or other cause, to withdraw himself from their charge or to provide himself with necessaries of life;

The *Family Law Reform Act*, under s. 18(5)(m) and (n) (s. 33(9)(l)(iii) and (iv) of the proposed *Family Law Act*, also specifically provides for increased support payments to the "dependent spouse if the child is 18 years or more and

> i) the child remains dependent due to "illness, disability or other cause",
> ii) the dependent spouse "has undertaken to assist in the continuation of a program of education" whereby the child remains dependent.

The prerequisite to such an award for child support is that there be a dependent spouse, absent which no award can be made. "Dependant" is defined as a "person to whom another has an obligation to provide support under this Part".: s. 14(a). It is difficult to justify the possible disparities which may be created between awards under a provincial order versus a decree *nisi* because the former only requires a dependency status on the part of one of the parents.

Under the *Divorce Act* it has been held that the meaning of the words "children of the marriage" is not restricted by a provincial *Age of Majority and Accountability Act*. An award may be made over the age of 18 years.[69] Note that the phrase "under their charge" from s. 2 of the *Divorce Act* does not require any court order — only the fact of a parent assuming the care and the maintenance of the child in his premises. If a 16-year-old lives by himself, "other considerations will have intruded to make this provision probably no longer applicable."[70] It might be that a child away at university, returning home to a parent, still is in the charge of that parent since that child's financial attachment has resided and continues to reside with the parent.

The contentious issue surrounds the scope of "by reason of illness, disability or other cause" in s. 2. The courts appear to give a broad interpretation to the phrase "or other cause" including not only conditions beyond the child's control (an interpretation based on reading the phrase "or other cause" *ejusdem generis* with the words "illness" and "disability") but also circumstances of volition on the part of the child such as his attendance at school. A child is "unable . . . to withdraw herself from the charge of a parent if that child is in regular attendance . . . in a secondary school, pursuing an education in the

---

[68]See *e.g. Haight v. Haight* (1982), 28 R.F.L. (2d) 392 (B.C.S.C.) where the child, while over 18, was declared a "child of the marriage" due to his learning disability, resulting in dependency.
[69]*Hillman v. Hillman*, [1973] 1 O.R. 317, 9 R.F.L. 392 (C.A.).
[70]*Tapson v. Tapson*, [1970] 1 O.R. 521, at 523, 8 D.L.R. (3d) 727, 2 R.F.L. 305 (C.A.).

ordinary course designed to fit her for years of life ahead.''[71] However, where a child had reached the age of 21 years and was attending university, the court held that ''child'' in the *Divorce Act* must be read in its ordinary sense and no obligation attaches in the situation of a healthy, able-bodied son or daughter, 21 years of age or over, who decides to extend his educational career indefinitely, particularly where the evidence shows a capacity to earn a sufficient amount to complete his course as well as the existence of capital assets.[72] On the other hand, the court has permitted a variation of maintenance under s. 11(2) of the *Divorce Act* on the basis of a change of circumstances, where the eldest child, age 18, began attending university and thereby added to the expense of his mother and himself. ''If his father was still at home, he would be spending more money on this boy to help him through and he should now do so.''[73] It was stated thusly in another case:

> It is to the credit of the respondent that he has supported all of his other children through university. One of them is a physician, another a teacher and the third has graduated from university and is about to enter into the study of medicine. In a family such as this, Janine, as the youngest child, has the right to expect her parents to help provide her with the same educational opportunities as those given to her brothers and sister. Indeed, in his testimony the respondent acknowledged a moral obligation to help Janine to achieve her educational goal. He denied a legal obligation and said that he could be depended upon not to ''renege'' on his obligation. In my opinion, Janine, despite her age, is a child of the marriage within the meaning of the Divorce Act as interpreted by *Jackson v. Jackson*, [1973] S.C.R. 205, 8 R.F.L. 172, [1972] 6 W.W.R. 419, 29 D.L.R. (3d) 641, and *Hillman v. Hillman*, [1973] 1 O.R. 317, 9 R.F.L. 392, 31 D.L.R. (3d) 44 (C.A.).[74]

The danger of imposing responsibility on a parent for a child attending school *ad infinitum* has been noted in at least one case.[75] The courts are inclined to temper awards in such cases by a general standard of what is fit and just in view of the circumstances of the case.[76] Accordingly, the court will consider the age of the child, his grades, ability to profit by further schooling, the child's academic records, the resulting employment opportunities from such education, the needs of the parent and even the state of the labour market and its effect on the child's potential to find employment.[77] In addition, any income earned by a

---

[71]*Tapson v. Tapson, ibid.* See also *Crump v. Crump* (1970), 2 R.F.L. 314 (Alta. S.C.); affd 2 R.F.L. 388 (Alta. C.A.); *Janzen v. Janzen* (1981), 21 R.F.L. (2d) 316 (B.C.C.A.) (university attendance).

[72]*Sweet v. Sweet* (1971), 4 R.F.L. 254 (Ont. H.C.).

[73]*Tobin v. Tobin* (1974), 19 R.F.L. 18, at 20 (Ont. S.C.).

[74]*Diotallevi v. Diotallevi* (1982), 27 R.F.L. (2d) 400, at 410 (Ont. S.C.) (divorce).

[75]See *Caryk v. Caryk* (1971), 6 R.F.L. 185 (B.C.S.C.); *Clark v. Clark*, [1971] 1 O.R. 674, 16 D.L.R. (3d) 376, 4 R.F.L. 27 (S.C.); *Jensen v. Jensen* (1971), 6 R.F.L. 328 (Ont. S.C.); *Madden v. Madden* (1970), 74 W.W.R. 304, 2 R.F.L. 319 (Man. Q.B.).

[76]See *Jackson v. Jackson*, [1973] S.C.R. 205, 8 R.F.L. 172; *Day v. Day*, [1975] 3 W.W.R. 563, 18 R.F.L. 56 (Alta. T.D.); *Wolch v. Wolch* (1982), 29 R.F.L. (2d) 212 (Man. Q.B.).

[77]See *Day v. Day, ibid.; Wasylenki v. Wasylenki* (1970), 12 D.L.R. (3d) 534, 2 R.F.L. 324 (Sask. Q.B.); *Jones v. Jones* (1970), 2 R.F.L. 393 (Sask. C.A.).

child attending university will be deducted in calculating the child's real expenses.[78] While s. 11 of the *Divorce Act* does not specifically consider a child's ability to assume some responsibility for partially supporting himself throughout university, it is submitted that it would be appropriate for the court to inject a notional figure where the evidence suggests the availability of employment or the clear abdication by the child of any attempt to seek employment. In a recent decision of the Supreme Court of Ontario, wherein a 21-year-old was awarded support, the decision read in part:

> I turn now to the claim for maintenance for Janine. She will be 21 years of age within a matter of days and has resided with her mother, the petitioner, since the separation of the parties. Janine is in full-time attendance at a university and has another two years to go until graduation. With the exception of the sum of $100 per month, paid by the respondent under the terms of an order for interim maintenance, her support has come from the petitioner. Her summer earnings last year amounted to the sum of $3,900 and, according to the evidence, there is a good reason to expect that she will be able to obtain a similar job with a similar salary in the summer of 1982. Her annual expenses as a full-time university student, of course, exceed her income, and if she is to be permitted to continue her education, it will be impossible for her to withdraw herself from the support of her parents. Although the budget submitted by the petitioner on behalf of Janine shows annual expenses totalling $10,866, I have come to the conclusion that a more realistic figure is in the neighbourhood of $8,000, with the result that her expenses exceed her income by the sum of approximately $4,000 per year.[79]

If the Court can find on the evidence that the parents expected some contribution from the child, then this factor could legitimately fall within the court's required consideration of the conduct of the parties, in terms of their expectations and attitudes.

Finally, in non-educational cases, *i.e.* where the child is working or unemployed, each case will turn on its facts. For example, one case held that the child was not entitled to support where he was unemployed and expected to receive unemployment insurance.[80] On the other hand, another court has ruled that a child who is no longer attending school and is living at home, searching for a job, is entitled to continued support. "There should be some reasonable allowance for a grace period between dependency and independence in terms of requiring any pre-existing support order to continue."[81]

Interim Awards of Child Support

Federal and provincial child support legislation usually provide for interim applications, recognizing that a contested matter may continue on interminably.

Section 10 of the *Divorce Act* provides:

---

[78]*Diotallevi v. Diotallevi, supra,* note 74.

[79]*Diotallevi v. Diotallevi, supra,* note 74, at p. 410.

[80]*Moore v. Moore* (1979), 2 Sask. R. 340 (Q.B.). See also *Murray v. Murray* (1982), 30 R.F.L. (2d) 222 (Sask. Q.B.).

[81]*Heddle v. Heddle,* summarized in (1984), 6 F.L.R.R. 169 (Ont. U.F.C.) (divorce: variation).

s. 10. Where a petition for divorce has been presented, the court having jurisdiction to grant relief in respect thereof may make such interim orders as it thinks fit and just. . .

> (b) for the maintenance of and the custody, care and upbringing of the children of the marriage pending the hearing and determination;

Section 19(3) of the *Family Law Reform Act* provides:

s. 19(3) Where an application is made under s. 18, the court may make such interim order as the court considers appropriate.

Note that the *Divorce Act* gives no authority for an interim lump sum award.[82] (The proposed *Divorce and Corollary Relief Act* substitutes "reasonable" for "fit and just" and permits lump sums.) Note further that Ontario's proposed *Family Law Act* substitutes the criteria for a final order rather than leaving it to what the court considers "appropriate": s. 34(3).

The test underlying an interim award is effectively the same as that under a final order insofar as the court's objective and priority is to minimize the disruption for the children in the face of a marital breakdown.[83] Sometimes the court will allocate resources in favour of the children, in some cases over the needs of a dependent spouse. Accordingly, if the children were attending a private school, for example, while the family was together, the court will take the view that this was intended by the parents and that it should not alter, at least until all of the matters are canvassed at trial.[84]

Note that under the *Divorce Act*[85] and the *Family Law Reform Act* (s. 19(1)(f)), the court can back-date any interim support order so that a dependent spouse, for instance, who attempts to negotiate on behalf of herself and the children, is not penalized in the event that a settlement is not reached.

Periodic/Lump Sum/Payments to Third Parties and Other Forms of Support Relief

Section 12 of the *Divorce Act* permits the court to order that support be paid into court. It may also be paid periodically or by lump sum (s. 11) to a spouse or trustee or administrator approved by the court, and the court may impose such terms, conditions or restrictions as it thinks fit and just when making any order under s. 10 or 11 of the Act. The proposed *Divorce and Corollary Relief Act* removes the trustee/administrator portion of the provision. Section 19(1)(b) of Ontario's *Family Law Reform Act* allows that a lump-sum payment for child support be paid or held in trust or, pursuant to s. 19(1)(e), that all or any of the monies be paid into court or to any other appropriate person or agency for the benefit of the child. In practical terms, Ontario's relief is much more comprehensive than that under a divorce order, creating an unfortunate disparity

---

[82]*Wierzbicki v. Wierzbicki*, summarized in (1982), 5 F.L.R.R. 78 (Ont. S.C.).

[83]One court based the test on the s. 16 general obligation of parents to support their children "to the extent the parent is capable of doing so in accordance with need," specifically disregarding s. 18(5) criteria: *Blackmore v. Blackmore* (1978), 28 O.R. (2d) 599, 7 R.F.L. (2d) 263 (S.C.).

[84]See *Welsh v. Welsh* (1980), 28 O.R. (2d) 255, 110 D.L.R. (3d) 88, 17 R.F.L. (2d) 318 (C.A.); *Parry v. Parry* (1980), 18 R.F.L. (2d) 259 (Man. C.A.); *Jarvis v. Jarvis* (1982), 27 R.F.L. (2d) 434 (Ont. H.C.).

[85]*Steinhubel v. Steinhubel*, [1970] 2 O.R. 683, 11 D.L.R. (3d) 669, 2 R.F.L. 317 (C.A.); and see *Dollabaille v. Carrington, supra*, note 61 for backdating under *FLRA* order.

which can significantly affect a child's financial security depending on which judicial proceedings the parents choose to pursue.

While under both statutes, a periodic and lump-sum award can be combined in one order[86] the *Divorce Act*, unlike the *FLRA*, does not permit a periodic award to be secured by placing a charge on property although one can secure property from which periodic payments are to come. (The proposed *Divorce and Corollary Relief Act* allows both simultaneously.) Under the *FLRA*, the court can make a periodic order and simultaneously order property to be secured in the event of default under the periodic order.[87] Section 19(1)(k) provides that any payment can be secured by a charge on property or otherwise. In addition, a child-support order can be framed as a transfer of property in trust for a child absolutely, for life or any number of years, a power which is not available to the court under the *Divorce Act*.[88]

The ability of the court under provincial legislation to order a lump-sum amount for child support is a change from previous legislation under which such power was omitted to Family Court affiliation proceedings. It has been held in the context of divorce proceedings that a lump-sum payment for child support should reflect the tests set out in the case of *Paras v. Paras*[89], that is, ". . . to continue the availability to the children of the same standard of living as that which they would have enjoyed had the family break-up not occurred." An order for lump-sum payment should not be on a compensatory basis. For example, the court should not take into account the number of years the wife had been taking care of the children on her own which would, in effect, be a retroactive allowance.[90] Nor should the court make a lump-sum award where it will harm a parent's earning power except in the most unusual circumstances.[91] It would seem that under the *Family Law Reform Act,* whether the application is from the child or the parent, the criteria set out in s. 18(5) and any other circumstances will govern the amount and the terms of payment. However, note that orders for lump-sum payments, transfer of property, irrevocable designation of insurance beneficiaries and securing of support payments cannot be made by the Provincial Court "except for the provision of necessaries or preventing the dependant from becoming a public charge."[92]

Lump-sum payments have been ordered as security where the history or

---

[86]*Raffin v. Raffin,* [1972] 1 O.R. 713, 22 D.L.R. (3d) 497, 5 R.F.L. 274 (C.A.).

[87]See *Nash v. Nash* (1974), 16 R.F.L. (2d) 295 (S.C.C.); *Van Zyderveld v. Van Zyderveld,* [1977] 1 S.C.R. 714, [1976] 4 W.W.R. 734, 68 D.L.R. (3d) 364, 23 R.F.L. 200. And see *Saracino v. Saracino* (1978), 22 O.R. (2d) 640, 8 R.F.L. (2d) 88 (C.A.) which holds that there is no jurisdiction under the *Family Law Reform Act* to vary maintenance granted under the *Divorce Act*.

[88]*Family Law Reform Act*, ss. 6(d), 19(1)(c). See also *Chadderton v. Chadderton,* [1973] 1 O.R. 560, 31 D.L.R. (3d) 656, 8 R.F.L. 374 (C.A.); *Sonntag v. Sonntag (No. 2)* (1975), 9 O.R. (2d) 318, 60 D.L.R. (3d) 246, 22 R.F.L. 98 (C.A.).

[89]*Paras v. Paras,* [1971] 1 O.R. 130, 14 D.L.R. (3d) 546, 2 R.F.L. 328 (C.A.).

[90]*Dart v. Dart* (1974), 14 R.F.L. 97 (Ont. S.C.).

[91]See *Zielke v. Zielke* (1982), 30 R.F.L. (2d) 113 (Alta. C.A.).

[92]*Family Law Reform Act,* s. 19(2). See also *Donheim v. Irwin* (1978), 6 R.F.L. (2d) 242 (Ont. Prov. Ct.) (provincial support application).

present circumstances[93] suggest difficulties with regular support payments or where the one-time payment will eliminate continued friction and mounting legal costs which have already consumed a large portion of the family's assets. In such situations, the court may direct the payment of monies into court if there is concern about the custodial parent's ability to manage the money.[94] Sometimes, if the custodial parent is applying for exclusive possession of the matrimonial home, the court will transfer the other spouse's interest in the home as lump-sum maintenance.[95] (For further discussion regarding matrimonial home see "Occupation of the Family Home" below.) If an applicant is seeking a lump-sum payment, then actuarial evidence should be presented to assist the court in arriving at a figure,[96] having regard to the accustomed standard of living, although the courts will award an amount without such evidence and make the calculation on the basis of the periodic award.[97] Note that a lump sum payment cannot result in effectively providing monies for a child who is 18 years of age or greater.[98] Nor can it result in a possibility that the child may die before the lump sum is used up, thereby creating an estate rather than providing maintenance.[99] And finally, a lump sum can be ordered in satisfaction of the payment of expenses for pre-natal care and birth[100] and in this manner, a mother acquired a home for herself and the children.[101]

If the payor spouse dies, the provincial legislation, unlike the federal statute, permits the order to be a debt on the payor's estate, and that the payor designate the dependent child as an irrevocable beneficiary to his estate. Ontario's proposed *Family Law Act* presumes that the order binds the estate unless stated otherwise: s. 34(5).

Competing Orders for Support

To avoid conflicting jurisdictional problems, s. 20 of the *Family Law Reform Act* provides:

> s. 20(1) Where an action for divorce is commenced under the *Divorce Act* (Canada), any application for support or custody under this Part that has not been determined is stayed except by leave of the court.
>
> (2) Where a marriage is terminated by a decree absolute of divorce or declared a nullity and the question of support was not judicially determined in the divorce or nullity proceedings, an order for support made under this Part continues in force according to its terms.

That is, an application for child support is stayed except by leave of the court when a divorce is commenced. Leave will likely be granted if the divorce

---

[93]See *Kivac v. Kivac* (1982), 28 R.F.L. (2d) 23 (Ont. Co. Ct.); *Lea v. Lea* (1983), 25 Sask. R. 168, 33 R.F.L. (2d) 173 (Q.B.).

[94]*Mann v. Mann*, summarized in (1982), 4 F.L.R.R. 84 (Ont. S.C.) (divorce: variation).

[95]See *e.g. Hoyer v. Hoyer* (1981), 24 R.F.L. (2d) 444 (B.C.S.C.); revd 30 R.F.L. (2d) 261 (B.C. C.A.); *Graves v. Graves* (1981), 23 R.F.L. (2d) 87 (P.E.I.S.C.); *Cormier v. Cormier* (1982), 31 R.F.L. (2d) 9 (N.B.Q.B.).

[96]*Lea v. Lea, supra,* note 93.

[97]*Rocha v. Rocha* (1981), 23 R.F.L. (2d) 366 (Ont. S.C.), (Prov. Ct. application).

[98]*Dolabaille v. Carrington (No. 2)* (1981), 34 O.R. (2d) 641 (Prov. Ct.) (Prov. support application).

[99]*Zielke v. Zielke, supra,* note 91.

[100]*Rosenthal v. Amar*, summarized in (1981), 4 F.L.R.R. 45 (Ont. S.C.) (support application).

[101]*Husted v. Husted* (1981), 23 R.F.L. (2d) 189 (Alta. Q.B.).

petition includes no claim for child support or if there is some urgency requiring an expeditious summary order available under the *Family Law Reform Act*.[102] Leave should also be granted if a child is a dependant for the purposes of the *Family Law Reform Act* and not a child of the marriage for the purposes of the *Divorce Act*. Note that for the purposes of s. 21(1) (review and variation), an order that "has been determined" includes a final or interim order.[103] Section 20(2) maintained the existing law by continuing a provincial child support order if it has not been determined in the divorce proceeding.[104] It has also been held that a decree *nisi* should include an existing agreement affecting a child's maintenance.[105] Ontario's proposed *Family Law Act* under s. 36(2) also permits the divorce court to determine and make an order for existing arrears under a provincial order.

Custody/Access Affecting Support
    The court may make an order of custody and/or access separate from an order of support: s. 35 of the *Family Law Reform Act* and ss. 10 and 11 of the *Divorce Act*. Since the standard of child support should not be the subject of bargaining, it has been held by the Ontario Court of Appeal that a parent cannot avoid payment for child maintenance because of an inability to exercise a right of access.[106] Nevertheless, the court's discretion to vary or rescind a support order is guided, under the *Divorce Act,* by the words "fit and just" in s. 11(2). (This will be changed under s. 17(3) of the proposed *Divorce and Corollary Relief Act* to "material change in the condition, means, needs and other circumstances. . ." Note also s. 17(5)(6) and (8) in this context.) In another Ontario decision, the phrase "fit and just" was interpreted to allow the court to order that child support be suspended until the wife made satisfactory arrangements to allow the husband to exercise access.[107] Although this may be a successful remedy for access difficulties, it does imply judicial sanction for linking access rights to maintenance payments. In so doing, the child's financial security becomes a function of the inevitable complications of the adult's "custody/access dance." One court allowed a non-custodial parent to deduct the cost of exercising access from his regular payments when the custodial spouse moved, making access more expensive.[108] Another court also linked the two orders to pressure a former wife to attend with the children a psychiatric assessment in a contested access dispute. The court concluded (prior to the amendments of the *Children's Law Reform Act* in October, 1982) that it had no authority to order an assessment but that it did have the power to stay all

---

[102]See *Re Tuz* (1975), 11 O.R. (2d) 617, 25 R.F.L. 87 (C.A.) and *Lakhani v. Lakhani* (1979), 22 O.R. (2d) 602, 10 R.F.L. (2d) 156 (S.C.); revd 23 O.R. (2d) 575 (H.C.).

[103]*Middaugh v. Middaugh* (1981), 34 O.R. (2d) 681, 122 D.L.R. (3d) 516, 22 R.F.L. (2d) 388 (C.A.); *McKay v. McKay* (1982), 30 R.F.L. (2d) 463 (Ont. S.C.).

[104]*Waite v. Waite* (1975), 25 R.F.L. 226 (Ont. Prov. Ct.); *Tomlinson v. Tomlinson* (1970), 4 R.F.L. 69 (Ont. Prov. Ct.); *Lefebvre v. Lefebvre* (1982), 38 O.R. (2d) 121 (Prov. Ct.); affd 38 O.R. (2d) 683, 30 R.F.L. (2d) 184 (Co. Ct.).

[105]*Stone v. Stone* (1973), 14 R.F.L. 143 (Ont. C.A.).

[106]*Wright v. Wright* (1973), 1 O.R. (2d) 337, 40 D.L.R. (3d) 321, 12 R.F.L. 200 (C.A.); *Doyle v. Doyle* (1982), 29 R.F.L. (2d) 45 (N.S. Fam. Ct.).

[107]*Kett v. Kett* (1976), 28 R.F.L. 1 (Ont. S.C.). See also *Glazebrook v. Glazebrook,* summarized in (1982), 4 F.L.R.R. 107 (Ont. U.F.C.).

[108]*Page v. Page* (1980), 31 O.R. (2d) 136, 118 D.L.R. (3d) 57, 19 R.F.L. (2d) 135 (C.A.).

proceedings and stay the obligation of the husband to provide child support until the assessment was completed.[109]

It is questionable whether the weapon of support payments is effective against continued access difficulties. It tends to reinforce the reaction of too many disgruntled fathers who may use or even aggravate access difficulties to avoid their support obligations. Secondly, no financial pressure by the courts will improve the interaction of two adults who are incompetent at parenting in a separation situation. Thirdly, it victimizes the children since they are the financial losers. Even if dollars are otherwise available, the financial issue becomes yet another focus of accusation and guilt which many warring parents will use to gain their child's loyalty. It seems more advisable for the court to re-assess the custody/access arrangement itself.

As a final note, a father with custody was ordered to make payments to defray a mother's access expenses.[110] Sections 10 and 11 of the *Divorce Act* and s. 18(5) of the *Family Law Reform Act* appear broad enough to encompass this order. The new divorce legislation, as yet unpassed, specifies consideration of economic hardship arising from the marriage breakdown (s. 15(6)(c)) as does Ontario's proposed *Family Law Act* (s. 33(8)(d)).

Variation of Support Orders

Sections 11(2) and 21(1) of the *Divorce Act* and *Family Law Reform Act* respectively read:

> s. 11(2) An order made pursuant to this section may be varied from time to time or rescinded by the court that made the order if it thinks it fit and just to do so having regard to the conduct of the parties since the making of the order or any change in a condition, means or other circumstances of either of them.

> (The proposed *Divorce and Corollary Relief Act* substitutes "material change in the condition, means, needs and other circumstances" of the spouse or child.)
>
> . . .

> s. 21(1) Where an order for support has been made or confirmed and where the court is satisfied that there has been a material change in the circumstances of the dependant or the respondent or evidence has become available that was not available on the previous hearing, the court may, upon the application of any person named in the order or referred to in subsection 18(3), discharge, vary or suspend any term of the order, prospectively or retroactively, relieve the respondent from the payment of part or all of the arrears of any interest due thereon and make such other order under section 19 as the court considers appropriate in the circumstances referred to in section 18.

> (The proposed *Family Law Act* makes no change but includes provision for filing domestic or paternity agreements with the court for variation/enforcement purposes: s. 35.)

A divorce court retains jurisdiction over a child's maintenance at any time after the decree *nisi*, even if it is silent as to child support. One court has suggested that proceedings should take the form of an application for variation under

---

[109]*Cillis v. Cillis* (1980), 20 R.F.L. (2d) 208 (Ont. S.C.); affd 23 R.F.L. (2d) 76 (Ont. Div. Ct.).
[110]*Bastien v. Bastien,* summarized in (1981), 3 F.L.R.R. 210 (L.J.S.C.O.); *Korol v. Korol* (1974), 18 R.F.L. 294 (Sask. Q.B.).

s. 11(2) of the *Divorce Act* rather than under provincial legislation which appears to apply under the *Family Law Reform Act*.[111] If the application to vary is made under the *Family Law Reform Act,* note s. 21(2) which requires it to be made to the original court or to a coordinate court in another part of Ontario. (This subsection will be removed under the proposed *Family Law Act*.)

A "material change in circumstances" warranting a variation in child support may refer to a change in finances, although it was noted that frustrated access may also be a ground. (See above discussion regarding "Custody/Access Affecting Support"). Remarriage is often cited as a ground since the *Family Law Reform Act* includes, as a factor in determining quantum, s. 18(5)(h), the legal obligation of a parent to provide support for any other person. However, it has also been held that children of the second union should not take priority over those of the first. All children have an equal claim to support from their father and the court, when determining the amount of maintenance to be paid, should permit and require a father to treat all of his children fairly and equally.[112] On the other hand, one court found that the effect of continued maintenance by the husband was to reduce welfare payments received by the wife and children of his first marriage. It was clear that the father could not support two family units so that monies paid to the prior family would have to be taken from his second family, necessitating outside support for his new family. In this situation, the second family was given priority.[113]

If the husband remarries, the court should consider the income of the second wife and if unemployed, her ability to be employed. In one case, the second wife married a man under an obligation to support the children of his first marriage, and the court felt that she could not reasonably expect the law to give her or her children's maintenance priority over her husband's children of his first marriage.[114] Conversely, if a wife remarries, saving herself rental, food and household expenses, there is a change in circumstances justifying a change in the quantum of maintenance to be paid by the wife's former husband.[115] On the other hand, in a recent Appellate Court decision the court concluded that the obligation of the father to support his children should continue "whatever the conduct of the mother and it is not relieved simply because the mother has remarried, whatever the responsibility of the new husband." In this case, the wife and husband had both remarried and the wife's second husband supported the children of the marriage and indicated at one time that he was prepared to adopt them.[116]

In this context, note the first obligation given to biological and adoptive parents under s. 33(7)(b) of Ontario's proposed *Family Law Act*.

---

[111]*Kravetsky v. Kravetsky* (1975), 20 R.F.L. 36 (Man. Q.B.); revd on other grounds 21 R.F.L. 211 (Man. C.A.). And see *Rinaldi v. Rinaldi* (1975), 21 R.F.L. 249 (Ont. Div. Ct.).

[112]*Re McKenna* (1974), 2 O.R. (2d) 571, 43 D.L.R. (3d) 515, 14 R.F.L. 153 (*sub nom. McKay v. McKay*) (H.C.).

[113]*Turner v. Turner* (1972), 8 R.F.L. 15 (Man. Q.B.). But see *Osborne v. Osborne* (1974), 14 R.F.L. 149 (Ont. S.C.).

[114]*Davis v. Colter* (1973), 12 R.F.L. 84 (Sask. Q.B.).

[115]*Impey v. Impey* (1973), 13 R.F.L. 240 (Sask. Q.B.).

[116]*Oxenham v. Oxenham* (1982), 35 O.R. (2d) 318, 26 R.F.L. (2d) 161 (Ont. C.A.). See as well *Turner v. Turner, supra,* note 113. *Osborne v. Osborne, supra,* note 113; *Denney v. Denney* (1972), 8 R.F.L. 220 (Sask. Q.B.); *Sands v. Sands* (1975), 21 R.F.L. 276 (Ont. C.A.)

Children Born Outside Marriage

Ontario's *Children's Law Reform Act,* enacted in 1977, abolished the common law distinction of "illegitimacy". Under s. 1 of that Act, a person is a child of his parents, and his status as a child is unaffected by the fact that he may have been born outside of marriage. Unless a contrary intention appears, all wills, documents, Acts and Regulations which include reference to a child or a person related by blood or marriage include a person regardless of the marital status of his parents thus ending the distinction in existing legislation: s. 2, *Children's Law Reform Act.* The *Family Law Reform Act,* in conjunction with the *Children's Law Reform Act* in Ontario replaced and expanded the kind of support relief that was previously available under Part III of the *Child Welfare Act* (R.S.O. 1970, c. 46) entitled "Protection of Children Born Out of Wedlock."

At common law, a child born outside marriage was regarded as *filius nullius*, "a son of nobody." He was deemed "illegitimate", a status which rendered him a child without rights or obligations in relation to his parents. He could not expect to inherit or receive support from his father or mother and neither parent had a right to custody or guardianship of the illegitimate child. Gradually, the harshness of the law was alleviated by a piecemeal approach to reform. Affiliation proceedings, first enacted as the *Children of Unmarried Parents Act*, and then incorporated as Part III of the 1970 *Child Welfare Act*, allowed the court to order that a putative father, once shown to be the father of the child, pay for the expenses of the child's birth and maintenance for his support to the age of 18 years. The *Legitimacy Act* (since repealed in 1977), first enacted in 1921 as the *Legitimation Act,* provided that if parents of any child born outside of marriage were to marry subsequent to the birth, the child was deemed to have been legitimate from the time of the birth. In some cases, various Acts would include the illegitimate child by specific reference to his status of illegitimacy. For example, the repealed *Workmen's Compensation Act,* R.S.O. 1970, c. 505, under its definition of "member of the family" provided that if the workman is the parent or grandparent of an "illegitimate child", such child is included, and that if the workman is an "illegitimate child", his parents and grandparents are also included. Besides the various legislative attempts to alleviate the inequitable consequences of "illegitimacy", the common law, for similar reasons, invoked the equitable jurisdiction of the High Court or relied on a presumption of legitimacy. By the latter device, a child born during lawful marriage was presumed to be legitimate, subject to clear, distinct and compelling evidence to the contrary.[117] A New York Family Court decision gives us an example of the court's determination to see that children were protected from the consequences of illegitimacy:

> In sum, the petition as proof of her shameless illicit love affair with the respondent is sufficiently clear and convincing to brand her as an adulteress, the respondent as a debaucher of her marriage and the husband as a pitiable

---

[117]*Comeau v. Gauthier* (1970), 3 R.F.L. 55 (Ont. Dist. Ct.); *Welstead v. Brown,* [1952] 1 S.C.R. 3, 102 C.C.C. 46; *Minaker v. Minaker* (1971), 4 R.F.L. 48 (Man. Q.B.); *Wikstrom v. Children's Aid Society of Winnipeg* (1955), 16 W.W.R. 577 (Man. C.A.); *Hiuser v. Hiuser,* [1962] O.W.N. 220 (C.A.).

cuckold, but it falls short of being entirely satisfactory to rebut the presumption of legitimacy where husband is potent and access is established.[118]

The presumption of legitimacy was held as ceasing to apply if the parties were judicially separated.[119] A voluntary separation was not sufficient.[120] The presumption was disproved by showing sterility before and during the period of gestation,[121] or by showing non-access by the husband at the relevant time.[122] In both cases, the court was forced to determine what constituted a normal gestation period.[123] Subsequently, the courts in England considered the ordering of blood tests which, though they would not prove paternity, might conclusively disprove paternity.[124] However, Part III of the *Child Welfare Act* did not provide the family courts with the power to order blood tests. The Ontario courts could, at most, draw an inference adverse to a party's case if the party refused to submit to blood tests.[125]

The putative father was able to bring an application for access and even for custody of his illegitimate child relying upon the High Court's inherent jurisdiction. Apparently, the High Court's equitable jurisdiction was considered sufficient to override the handicap of "illegitimacy" regarding questions of the child's custody or guardianship.[126] However, the same court that found jurisdiction regarding custody and access generally avoided invoking the same jurisdiction regarding child support unless a finding of paternity had been made against the respondent party, often resulting in the "illegitimate child" being inadequately supported for want of proof of paternity.[127]

Not all jurisdictions in Canada have dealt similarly with the status of "illegitimacy." New Brunswick, like Ontario, has abolished the concept of "illegitimacy" such that there exists no separate legislation for support or otherwise based on the status of birth outside of marriage. Prince Edward Island has unfortunately retained the status of the illegitimate child but with respect to support, all children are treated alike. British Columbia, Saskatchewan, Manitoba and Newfoundland try to do both. That is, they have retained the concept of "illegitimacy," and the procedure of an affiliation proceeding, but in the case of more permanent common law cohabitation arrangements, recourse for support of the child of that relationship can be had through the "ordinary" legislation as if the child were legitimate. Alberta has retained the notion of "illegitimacy" and relies primarily on the affiliation proceeding as a separate

---

[118]*Lee v. Stix* (1968), 286 N.Y.S. 2d 987, at 992.

[119]*Workun v. Nelson* (1958), 26 W.W.R. 600 (Alta. C.A.).

[120]*Re J.B.* (1967), 59 W.W.R. 358 (B.C. S.C.).

[121]*Himmelman v. Himmelman* (1959), 19 D.L.R. 291 (N.S. S.C.).

[122]*Henderson v. Northern Trusts Co.* (1952), 6 W.W.R. (N.S.) 337 (Sask. Q.B.).

[123]See also *Preston-Jones v. Preston-Jones,* [1951] 1 All E.R. 124 (H.L.); *Comeau v. Gauthier, supra,* note 117.

[124]*M. v. M.,* [1969] 2 All E.R. 243 (C.A.); *Re L.,* [1968] 1 All E.R. 20, 17 R.F.L. 374 (Eng. C.A.); *B.R.B. v. J.B.,* [1968] 2 All E.R. 1023.

[125]*Panaccione v. McNab* (1976), 28 R.F.L. 182 (Ont. Prov. Ct.). and see *Loewen v. Loewen* (1969), 2 R.F.L. 230 (B.C.S.C.).

[126]*Wood v. Wood* (1971), 5 R.F.L. 82 (Ont. S.C.).

[127]See *e.g. Mungal v. Jankie* (1974), 17 R.F.L. 84 (Ont. S.C.).

procedure for "illegitimate" children, although they may be covered by ordinary support legislation as if they were legitimate if the support award is incidental to a custody order.[128]

In contemporary society, the concept of "illegitimacy" has become outmoded, punitive and legally discriminatory. Ontario's Legislature has affirmed that there can be no basis for concluding that the needs and rights of a child are any less significant because he was born of unmarried parents. Whatever a judge may think about the kind of relationship between two parents, it has become irrelevant in the face of the needs of the "innocent" party, the child, which should be measured by the same standard and by the same proceedings as any other child. To require a separate judicial proceeding, let alone a separate status, through legislation only acts to reinforce the subtle and not so subtle prejudices of society that somehow "illegitimate" children have fewer rights. Abolishing the label is a first step to developing a different consciousness within the community and more significantly within the bench.

At present in Ontario, while the concept of illegitimacy has been abolished and while no separate proceeding for child support exists, it is naïve to expect that those judges who have presided under the old regime will apply a different standard now in assessing quantum. Although no data is available to prove the point, as a practical observation, children born outside of marriage still continue to receive fewer support dollars, which penalizes both the mother and the child. To some extent the difficulty may also be with the legislation. Under s. 18(5) of Ontario's *Family Law Reform Act*, a court may rely on the shortness or absence of cohabitation and the fact that there was no accustomed standard of living since in many instances, parents may not have cohabited, to conclude that a "bare necessities" standard is appropriate. Ontario's proposed *Family Law Act* has ameliorated the situation somewhat in limiting "duration of cohabitation" to spousal support considerations. As well, the court may not want the child-support award to be used to upgrade the single mother's standard of living which may be significantly less than the father's; and, of course, there is the unspoken tendency of the predominantly male bench to believe that the father should not be overly burdened by the folly of one event occasioned, after all, by the mother's seduction.

No court in Canada has carefully analyzed the approach to an award of financial support for a child born outside of marriage when there is no cohabitation to provide a bench-mark standard of living. For example, if the parties cohabited and if the financial situation of one of the parties improves following the separation, a further application for child-support variation can be made with the usual guidelines as to the existence of a second family who has an equal, but not greater claim. Will the quantum be the same in the case of parties who have not cohabited, one of whom is a 19-year-old mother on welfare and the other being a 38-year-old father, who is earning $60,000 per annum and supporting a wife and two children. It is submitted that s. 18(5) should be applied on the general basis of need and ability to pay without regard to the fact that the

---

[128]See W.H. Holland, *Unmarried Couples: Legal Aspects of Cohabitation* (Carswell: Toronto, 1982) for a full review of the different provincial statutes and approaches.

dependent child and father have never lived together and therefore without reference to the irrelevant measure of an accustomed standard of living. However, as in the case of any support order, regard should be had to the expected contribution of the mother either through her financial contribution, if employable or employed, or through her contribution as a mother at home. There should be no greater obligation to work on a mother of a child born outside of marriage than a mother of a child born inside marriage. It may be advisable, in certain jurisdictions, to consider an application through the child's next friend in order to demonstrate conceptually for the court that the money is for the child and that the determination of quantum should not be viewed as a battle between the mother and the father with all of its attendant assumptions and prejudices. If it became necessary, the money could even be paid to a trustee or into court.

Ontario's legislation makes changes to the prior affiliation proceedings, summarized as follows:

1) There is no longer any time limitation for the commencement of the support application;[129] at any time.[130] (Note the 6-year limitation period for all support applications under s. 50 of Ontario's proposed *Family Law Act*.)

2) The court that is competent to hear the child support application is also competent to make a prerequisite finding of parentage for the purpose *only* of the support proceedings.[131] As one case prior to the amendments suggested, it is no longer necessary to obtain a finding of paternity through an affiliation application before obtaining a support order.[132]

3) Unlike the repealed legislation, the court hearing the application has clear statutory authority to make a retroactive order thereby mitigating the detrimental effect on an award of adversarial tactical delays.[133]

4) Upon an application for variation, the *FLRA* eliminates any distinction between monies paid and payable such that a court can for example vary, discharge or suspend, prospectively or retroactively, a lump sum that is held in trust even though it has already been paid.[134]

---

[129]Note that on an interim application for support where paternity is in dispute, it has been held that there exists a heavy onus on the applicant before the court can consider making such an award: *Routley v. Dimitrieff* (1982), 36 O.R. (2d) 302 (S.C.); *Sweet v. Ferguson* (1981), 34 O.R. (2d) 745 (Prov. Ct.). Statements of financial information will also not be ordered on an interim basis: *Militello v. Hennessey* (1979), 1 F.L.R.A.C. 437 (Ont. S.C.) and the court file may be sealed: *B. v. P.* (1982), 35 O.R. (2d) 325 (Ont. S.C.). But where the putative father has been paying support voluntarily, he was ordered to continue on an interim application: *McTavish v. Meiklejohn* (1982), 27 R.F.L. (2d) 346 (Ont. Co. Ct.).

[130]*The Children's Law Reform Act,* Part 2 "Establishment of Parentage."

[131]*Sayer v. Rollin* (1980), 16 R.F.L. (2d) 289 (Ont. C.A.). Note the Ontario Supreme Court case of *Wiebe v. Quenneville* (1982), 30 R.F.L. (2d) 183 which would appear to have made a wrong finding that a declaration under the *Children's Law Reform Act* is a prerequisite to a support order under the *Family Law Reform Act*.

[132]*Mungal v. Janke, supra,* note 127.

[133]*Cf.* Part III (repealed) of the *Child Welfare Act*, R.S.O. 1970, c. 64 and the decision of *Hristesko v. Tufegdzich* (1976), 30 R.F.L. 136 (Ont. Prov. Ct.) with s. 19(1)(f) of the *Family Law Reform Act*.

[134]Compare Part III (repealed) of the *Child Welfare Act*, 1970 and the decision of *Ferrier v. Smith* (1974), 16 R.F.L. 223 (Ont. C.A.) with s. 21 of the *Family Law Reform Act*.

5) There now exists an appropriate mechanism for pre-trial discovery, a procedure for which there was no authority under the repealed legislation. Further, like any other application for child support, the parties must now prepare and file the appropriate statements of financial information.[135]

6) In determining parentage for the purpose of support there is no longer any statutory requirement that the applicant mother's evidence be corroborated by some other material evidence.[136]

7) Persons other than the mother of the child may apply for that child's support, including a child through a next friend. The operative provision of the *FLRA* does not limit who can be a party to a proceeding for support of a dependant child.[137]

8) There now exists statutory authority for the granting of leave for blood tests and the drawing of an adverse inference in the event that someone against whom leave has been granted, refuses to attend.[138] As well, in any proceeding the court need no longer meander through inconsistent case law on whether certain corroborative evidence gives rise to a presumption of paternity. The court must now apply a presumption of paternity in the following circumstances, except where the circumstances give rise to a presumption of paternity by more than one father in which case no presumption shall apply under s. 8(1) of *CLRA*.[139]

> s. 8(1) Unless the contrary is proven on a balance of probabilities, there is a presumption that a male person is, and he shall be recognized in law to be, the father of a child in any one of the following circumstances:
>> 1. The person is married to the mother of the child at the time of the birth of the child.[140]
>> 2. The person was married to the mother of the child by a marriage that was terminated by death or judgment of nullity within 300 days before the birth of the child or by divorce where the decree *nisi* was granted within 300 days before the birth of the child.

---

[135]See Rules governing procedures under *Family Law Reform Act* and *Children's Law Reform Act*. The latter proceeding is before a Unified Family Court or Supreme Court.

[136]See s. 59 of Part III (repealed) of the *Child Welfare Act,* 1970 and absence of such provision in the *Children's Law Reform Act*.

[137]See s. 18 of the *Family Law Reform Act,* the opening words "A court may, upon application. . . ." and see decisions of *Re Bagaric and Juric* (1980), 29 (2d) 491, 114 D.L.R. (3d) 509 (H.C.), and *Re Haskell and Letourneau* (1979), 25 O.R. (2d) 139, 100 D.L.R. (3d) 329 (Co. Ct.). Furthermore, note s. 4(1) of the *Children's Law Reform Act* and the opening words of the provision for an application for parentage: "*Any person having an interest* may apply to a court for a declaration. . . ." [emphasis added]

[138]The *Children's Law Reform Act*, s. 10.

[139]*Ibid.,* s. 8(3).

[140]See *G.J.R. v. B.A.R.* (1982), 29 R.F.L. (2d) 423 (N.S. Prov. Ct.) wherein this presumption was not overturned due to the fact of separation since there was evidence of access of the husband to the wife during separation. See also *Roberts v. Roberts* (1982), 54 N.S.R. (2d) 452, 112 A.P.R. 452 (N.S. Prov. Ct.): *Gareau v. Gareau*, 14 Sask. R. 138, [1981] 5 W.W.R. 450, 23 R.F.L. (2d) 307 (U.F.C.) where a child was born shortly after marriage and presumption not overturned; *Ministry of Comm. and Soc. Services v. Tolls* (1979), 12 R.F.L. (2d) 333 (Ont. Prov. Ct.) where a child conceived during separation while husband had access to wife and presumption overturned.

3. The person marries the mother of the child after the birth of the child and acknowledges that he is the natural father.

4. The person was cohabiting with the mother of the child in a relationship of some permanence at the time of the birth of the child or the child is born within 300 days after they cease to cohabit.

5. The person and the mother of the child have filed a statutory declaration under subsection 6(8) of the *Vital Statistics Act* or a request under subsection 6(5) of that Act, or either under a similar provision under the corresponding Act in another jurisdiction in Canada.

6. The person has been found or recognized in his lifetime by a court of competent jurisdiction in Canada to be the father of the child.

9) It should not be forgotten that if parentage cannot be proven, the alleged father may still be a "parent" under the extended definition of "parent" of the *Family Law Reform Act,* s. 1(e). (See above under "The Newly-Defined Parent".)

(For further discussion on disputed paternity, see below under "Declaration of Parentage".)

Declaration of Parentage

As noted above, a finding of parentage within the context of a support application is binding or applicable only for the purposes of those child-support proceedings. There also exists under the *Children's Law Reform Act* a statutory procedure for a "declaration of paternity" that is binding upon more than support proceedings; that is, it is presumably binding on all third parties, not simply the respondent father, for all purposes under the law. It is as follows:

s. 4(1) Any person having an interest may apply to a court for a declaration that a male person is recognized in law to be the father of a child or that a female person is the mother of a child.

(2) Where the court finds that a presumption of paternity exists under section 8 and unless it is established, on the balance of probabilities, that the presumed father is not the father of the child, the court shall make a declaratory order confirming that the paternity is recognized in law.

(3) Where the court finds on the balance of probabilities that the relationship of mother and child has been established, the court may make a declaratory order to that effect.

(4) Subject to sections 6 and 7, an order made under this section shall be recognized for all purposes.

s. 5(1) Where there is no person recognized in law under section 8 to be the father of a child, any person may apply to the court for a declaration that a male person is his or her father, or any male person may apply to the court for a declaration that a person is his child.

(2) An application shall not be made under sub-section (1) unless both the persons whose relationship is sought to be established are living.

(3) Where the court finds on the balance of probabilities that the

relationship of father and child has been established, the court may make a declaratory order to that effect and, subject to sections 6 and 7, the order shall be recognized for all purposes.

s. 6 Where a declaration has been made under section 4 or 5 and evidence becomes available that was not available at the previous hearing, the court may, upon application, discharge or vary the order and make such other orders or directions as are ancillary thereto.

To obtain a declaration, to be distinguished from a determination or finding within the context of a support proceeding, the application may only be brought before a Unified Family Court or Supreme Court: s. 3, *CLRA*. It may be said that the finding or determination constitutes an action *in personam* whereas a declaration flows from an action *in rem*, although not absolutely as the declaration can be rebutted at a future date. Were it to be an absolute discretion *in rem*, various difficulties might arise, as noted by the Ontario Law Reform Commission's *Report on Family Law, Part 3: Children:*

> The difficulties occasioned by the adversary system are obvious. A mother might bring an action to decide paternity for the purpose of obtaining maintenance for her child, and the father whom she names might be found, on the balance of probabilities, to be the actual father. If this judgment were to bind all the world, it would preclude the child from asserting paternity against some other person at a later time, although the child's interests might well be different from those of the mother and he would not have been heard. Similarly, a man who, for one reason or another, might wish to assert paternity and have a judicial decree to that effect would be estopped by the *in rem* judgment arising from a hearing of which he might not have had notice and at which he might not have had an opportunity to present a case.

Responding to its own observation, the Commission adds at p. 20:

> As an alternative, we propose that whenever a judicial decree of paternity is made, whether it is made in proceedings in which an immediate right involving the issue of paternity is being considered, or whether the decree is purely declaratory, obtains for the purpose of securing a future right, then this decree will operate as a presumption that the man named in the decree is the father for all other purposes. Since the decree would be only a presumption it would be open to rebuttal so that discovery of new evidence by the putative father disproving his paternity could later on operate to relieve him of his rights and obligations. Similarly, a man who discovered at some future time that he was the actual father and who wanted to assume parental responsibility could do so. Moreover, a child who wished to allege paternity against another man would not be precluded from doing so.[141]

The *Children's Law Reform Act* appears to achieve this objective by way of s. 6.

It may be unclear as to why one would want to seek a declaration under this Act since the vast majority of cases determining this issue are support cases which must be heard under the *Family Law Reform Act*. Indeed, a declaration

---

[141]Ontario Law Reform Commission, "Children," in *Report on Family Law, Part 3,* at p. 19.

with all of its underlying statutory evidentiary directives can be utilized for support proceedings where the alleged father disputes his parentage. Generally speaking, a declaration, as noted above, is the most all-encompassing determination of parentage under the law, including but not limited to support proceedings. Specifically, the declaratory route provides through Regulation (O. Reg. 99/80) for the registration of the finding of parentage as ordered or adjudged by the court. This is significant when one considers the duty upon the legal representative to canvas all potential claims against the estate by children born out of marriage. Section 23 of Ontario's *Estate's Administration Act* provides as follows:

s. 23(1) A personal representative shall make reasonable inquiries for persons who may be entitled by virtue of a relationship traced through a birth outside marriage.

(2) A personal representative is not liable for failing to distribute property to a person who is entitled by virtue of a relationship traced through a birth outside marriage where,

(a) he makes the inquiries referred to in subsection (1) and the entitlement of the person entitled was not known to the personal representative at the time of the distribution; and

(b) he makes such search of the records of the Registrar General relating to parentage as is available for the existence of persons who are entitled by virtue of a relationship traced through a birth outside marriage and the search fails to disclose the existence of such a person.

the property, or any property representing it, into the hands of any person other than a purchaser in good faith and for value, except that where there is no presumption or court finding of the parentage of a person born outside marriage until after the death of the deceased, a person entitled by virtue of a relationship traced through the birth is entitled to follow only property that is distributed after the personal representative has *actual* notice of an application to establish the parentage or of the facts giving rise to a presumption of parentage. [emphasis added.]

In the event that an application for a declaration is uncontested, the Rules of Civil Procedure suggest that default judgment may be granted although, in the face of any challenge, a trial of an issue will be directed.[142] In one case in which a trial of an issue was directed, judgment was granted on an uncontested basis after the respondent's pleadings had been struck. Although the respondent, through his solicitors, was provided with a notice of trial, neither he nor his solicitor attended. Thirteen months later, the respondent moved to set aside the judgment, arguing for the first time that he was not the father because the mother artificially inseminated herself. In the face of the results of the blood tests indicating a "99.93% likelihood" of his paternity, among other reasons, the application was dismissed.[143]

---

[142]See Rule 19.05 of Rules of Civil Procedure, March, 1984. See also *Gubins v. Stewart* (1982), 37 O.R. (2d) 427 (U.F.C.); *L. v. E.* (1982), 27 R.F.L. (2d) 267 (Alta. Q.B.); *Re M. and W.* (1979), 26 O.R. (2d) 266 (Div. Ct.); *Fox v. Dalzell* (1982), 28 R.F.L. (2d) 174 (Ont. Prov. Ct.).

[143]*Austin v. Lucas,* summarized in (1983), 6 F.L.R.R. 101 (Ont. S.C.).

It has been held that the principles of issue estoppel, cause of action estoppel, or arguably (but not considered) *res judicata* are not applicable where a previous affiliation proceeding under Part III (subsequently repealed) of the 1970 *Child Welfare Act* had been dismissed.[144] Further, no issue of retrospectivity is raised by the interpretation and application of the new legislation since it creates a new right. "It does not require the giving of a retrospective effect to the statute to hold. . ." that a child, the subject of a previously dismissed affiliation proceeding, is the child of her natural parents. The court also concluded that the limitation period defence under the repealed Part III of the 1970 *CWA* survived the *Family Law Reform Act*, 1978, given the presumption against the retrospective operation of any statute. However, that portion of the decision was subsequently struck by the Ontario Court of Appeal because it was not an issue properly before the court of first instance. In one other decision, and as *obiter* only, a Provincial Court judge suggested that a father of a child would have a limitation defence by reason of the repealed legislation which would survive and therefore could have no outstanding support obligations, the lower court apparently relying on the decision of the High Court prior to that portion of its reasons being struck by the appeal court.[145]

The issue is deserving of further comment, especially since some lower courts seem to have ruled differently (see below). It is clear that a major function of the declaration is to seek financial support for a child either through support proceedings or less frequently as an interest in an estate. In such proceedings, the competing interests include those of the father and his right to expect that a valid statutory defence will not be undone after the fact, and those of the child whose financial welfare usually receives high priority in relation to the putative parent. A consideration of the amending legislation, the *Children's Law Reform Act*, arguably suggests that the child's interest takes priority for the following reasons:

1) The rule against retrospectivity may not apply where, as in the case of this legislation, it can be said that it is a beneficial enactment, one that is not penal or prejudicial in nature.[146] Naturally, this argument succeeds only from the point of view of the child.

2) If the rule does apply, then there exists only a *presumption* against retrospective operation. Having regard to the legislation, it appears that the Legislature intended to rebut that presumption by enunciating in s. 1(1) of the *CLRA* that "*for all purposes of the law* of Ontario a person is the child of his or her natural parents and his or her status as their child is independent of whether the child is born within or outside marriage" [emphasis added]. Further to this, under ss. 2(1) and 2(2)(a), the Legislature eliminated the "illegitimacy" distinction in all Acts of the Legislature where there exists a

[144]*Re Bagaric and Juric* (1981), 34 O.R. (2d) 288, 130 D.L.R. (3d) 768, revg. 29 O.R. (2d) 491, 114 D.L.R. (3d) 509 (C.A.).

[145]*Dolabaille v. Carrington (No. 2)* (1981), 34 O.R. (2d) 641 (Prov. Ct.).

[146]See E.A. Driedger, "Status: Retrospective Reflections", (1978), 56 Can. Bar Rev. 264 and application of principle in *Sanderson v. Russell* (1979), 24 O.R. (2d) 429, 9 R.F.L. (2d) 81 (C.A.).

reference to persons described in terms of relationship by blood and this is to apply to any Act enacted before the amending legislation took effect (March 31, 1978). The Legislature specifically exempted from the scope of this retroactivity any Will, or instrument made before March 31, 1978. It seems reasonable to conclude that had the Legislature also wished to exempt any section of the repealed Part III of the 1970 *Child Welfare Act*, it would have said so.

3) An interpretation that perpetuates for children born before March 31, 1978 the distinction between "legitimacy" and "illegitimacy", denying all children born before March 31, 1978 the right to seek support from their father seems to nullify the purportedly universal remedy entrenched through the amending legislation[147].

In two cases, one from County Court on appeal and the other a decision of the Provincial Court, rulings have been made in favour of the child's interest. The County Court found the limitation under the repealed Part III of the 1970 *Child Welfare Act*, to be available only in proceedings already started before the Part was repealed and in this respect referred to s. 89 of the *Family Law Reform Act, 1978*, which seemed to protect the validity of actions, including affiliation proceedings, when commenced before the amending legislation came into effect.[148] The second Provincial Court case went even further on this issue. The hearing had occurred under the repealed legislation and the affiliation application had been dismissed. Nevertheless, the court considered that the new legislation gives new rights to children born out of wedlock which were not available when the previous matter was heard, and therefore those rights have not been the subject of adjudication and appear to be retroactive. Accordingly, the preliminary objection based on *res judicata* was overruled.[149] In support of the conclusion reached by the Provincial Court judge it is noteworthy that absent the right to commence a fresh application under the new legislation, there exists no relief under the *Family Law Reform Act* or the *Children's Law Reform Act* to open up a previously dismissed application based on new evidence derived from the now legislatively authorized blood tests.[150]

With the repeal of s. 59 of the 1970 *Child Welfare Act*, it is no longer necessary that the mother's evidence be corroborated by some other material evidence as to a condition of finding of paternity. Section 8 of the *Children's Law Reform Act* sets out the circumstances in which a male person is deemed to be the father of the child unless the contrary is proven on a balance of probabilities (see above under "Children Born outside Marriage"). Where the court finds that the presumption exists and the presumption is not rebutted it may, upon an application by any person having an interest, make an order declaring that the paternity is recognized in law: s. 4(2), *CLRA*. If no person can be presumed to be the father under s. 8, any person can seek a declaration that a

---

[147]Consider by analogy the decision in *Sanderson v. Russell ibid.*

[148]*Connelly v. Schiller* (1980), 20 R.F.L. (2d) 440 (Ont. Co. Ct.).

[149]*Bouchard v. Wheeler* (1981), 22 R.F.L. (2d) 104 (Ont. Prov. Ct.).

[150]See the *Children's Law Reform Act,* s. 6 which limits the re-opening of the matter to cases in which a declaration has been made.

male person is his or her father or the male person may apply to the court for a declaration that a person is his child: s. 5(1), *CLRA*. The court is to apply a balance of probabilities test in the case where no presumption exists: s. 5(3), *CLRA*. An application under s. 5(1) can only be made where the ''father'' and ''child'' are living: s. 5(2). There are no statutory presumptions concerning a female person alleged to be the mother of a child. Sections 4(1) and (3) provide that upon an application by any person having an interest, the court may apply a balance of probabilities test and make a declaratory order that a female person is the mother of a child.

While the *Children's Law Reform Act* provides that a balance of probability standard is to apply, it has been held under the repealed Part III of the 1970 *Child Welfare Act* with respect to proving paternity as a pre-condition for an affiliation order, that within the standards there are different degrees of proof depending on the gravity of the consequences. For example, where a father acknowledged a relationship with the mother over a long period of time with few birth control precautions, the ''consequences are not as grave to the putative father as they might be if in fact there was only one isolated act of intercourse''.[151]

Section 10 of the Ontario *Evidence Act* protects parties from answering any questions in proceedings commenced in consequence of adultery. For example, where a divorce action is started on the grounds of adultery, the accused party may claim the privilege of this section. It has been held that this privilege does not apply to a defendant putative father in affiliation proceedings. While the act of the defendant may be, in fact, adulterous, the affiliation proceedings could not be said to have been instituted in consequence of adultery.[152] Further, since the proceedings were civil in nature, it was held that there is nothing to prevent a defendant from giving evidence against himself since he was merely admitting to a civil liability.[153]

Note s. 9 of the *Children's Law Reform Act* which provides that a written acknowledgment of parentage that is admitted in evidence in any civil proceeding against the interests of the person making the acknowledgment is *prima facie* proof of the fact. In one Saskatchewan case, a putative father was estopped from contesting paternity proceedings when he had sworn he was the father in previous custody proceedings.[154] In another case, a defendant father had signed a declaration affirming his paternity for the purpose of birth registration and subsequently entered into a written paternity agreement with the child's mother for the purpose of support and, as well, paid, by oral agreement, an additional $550 per month for at least five months. Suddenly he stopped payments and denied paternity, alleging that all of the agreements were invalid because ''they

---

[151]*Robinson v. Mangoni* (1974), 17 R.F.L. 117, at 123 (Ont. Prov. Ct.). And see *Smith v. Smith,* [1952] 2 S.C.R. 312, [1952] D.L.R. 449.

[152]*Re Hollum,* [1960] O.W.N. 281 (H.C.).

[153]*Schmidt v. Hamilton,* [1946] 3 W.W.R. 610, [1947] 1 D.L.R. 301, 86 C.C.C. 385 (Man. C.A.). Note also the case of *Juric v. Ivankovic* (1982), 30 R.F.L. (2d) 456 (Alta. Q.B.) wherein the court rejected the argument that the putative father should not have to attend examinations for discovery in an affiliation proceeding since it would violate the right against self-incrimination under s. 11(c) of the *Charter of Rights.* The Court held that the section did not apply since the substantive aspects of the proceedings were civil in nature.

[154]See *Brochu v. Tanguay* (1982), 29 R.F.L. (2d) 462 (Sask. Q.B.).

were entered into by reason of extortion.'' The report of the Commissioner hearing the case was confirmed by the referring judge of the Supreme Court. On the issue of extortion, the Commissioner stated:

> Now the question to determine is whether the nature and extent of the threats of disclosure provides sufficient reason to set aside the Minutes of Settlement and the declaration of parentage. I do not believe that there is any question that a woman in the position of the plaintiff had at least the legal right to inform the world if she so desired as to her predicament. Has she, however, the right to use the threat of such disclosure as a lever to obtain funds, even if such funds are badly needed? No one has suggested or taken any legal steps to punish the lady by criminal charges of extortion. In my view, it is completely unprecedented to use a plea of extortion as a defence to a civil case. Neither I nor counsel have been able to find any Canadian law where this has been dealt with.

> The criminal offence of extortion is very close to the sin of blackmail. Lord Jewett in his well known dictionary of English law, (2nd ed.) at page 228, says this: "A person is guilty of blackmail if, with a view to gain for himself or another or with intent to cause loss to another he makes any unwarranted demands with menaces. For this purpose a demand with menaces was unwarranted unless the person making it does so in the belief (a) that he has reasonable grounds for making the demand, and (b) that the use of the menaces is a proper means of reinforcing the demand." In the Canadian Encyclopedia Digest, the language used is: "The words used must be such as would naturally and reasonably operate upon the mind of an ordinary person and put compulsion upon him to do as suggested rather than to pursue a course which he would otherwise have taken." If we applied this definition, assuming that there is any merit in raising extortion as a defence to a civil action, which I greatly doubt, can it seriously be argued that a competent successful businessman who is able to obtain and does receive competent, adequate legal advice, is going to sign documents containing important admissions and binding obligations, simply because of the continued vexatious, often rude, demands and threats made upon him by a woman obviously emotionally affected by the tragic turn of events? I do not so believe. In my view, the documents he signed are valid and enforceable and it is too late in the day to now deny paternity and shrug off the obligations he has already assumed. The effect of these documents combined with the relevant legislation is obvious.

> I would make two further comments. Counsel for the defendant in support of his claim of extortion has made much of the extravagant and even absurd claims advanced by the plaintiff in the issuance of a Writ against the defendant. I do not consider that argument as appropriate. There is nothing novel about over-inflated demands whether advanced by lawyers or by legal action. Again, a criminal charge of assault laid by the plaintiff against the defendant, later abandoned, may or may not have been justified. The evidence is unclear and in dispute and in my view has no relevance to the present issues.[155]

---

[155]*Trella v. Haid,* summarized in (1982), 5 F.L.R.R. 97 (Ont. S.C.).

The situation set out in s. 8(3) of the *Children's Law Reform Act* involving conflicting presumptions of paternity is similar to an English case in which a child was born within nine months of the termination of a marriage due to the death of the husband. The court initially recognized the deceased as the father of the child, relying upon a presumption of paternity arising from a calculated period of gestation prior to the death of the husband. The mother remarried upon the death of her first husband and before the birth of the child. As a result, a second presumption arose based on the circumstance that the second husband was married to the mother at the time of the birth of the child. (Both presumptions are codified in s. 8 of the *Children's Law Reform Act*.) The court held that there could not be two valid presumptions and ruled in favour of the first.[156] However, as a result of s. 8(3) of this Act, no male person in Ontario could be presumed and recognized in law to be the father of the child in these circumstances since the section effectively prevents the court from giving priority to one presumption over the other: ''No presumption shall be made as to paternity and no person is recognized in law to be the father.'' Therefore, an application under s. 5 (no person presumed to be the father), would be necessary since an application under s. 4 would seem to be doomed to failure. This section does not preclude a finding in the presence of satisfactory evidence.

In Ontario, to be distinguished for example from Nova Scotia,[157] there can be only one father for the purpose of a declaration or determination of paternity. That is clear from ss. 4, 5 and 8 of the *CLRA* which reflect the intention of the Legislature to impose a support obligation on only one male person by reason of his paternity. Accordingly, and predictably, once an intimate association with the mother is proven, the best if not only defence available to a putative father is to point a finger at an equally suspicious individual, persuading the court of the mother's ''promiscuity'', at least on one other occasion. If successful, this will give rise to the equally consistent possibility that the real father may not be the putative father.[158] Where the putative father raises this as a defence, he is required to produce the names of the ''other possibilities'' under examination for discovery.[159] In the absence of wording similar to that of the Nova Scotia legislation, the court would exceed its mandate in finding two men equally responsible for the support of the child by reason of the equality of probability of their paternity. This is not to say that if a finding is made that one male in particular is the biological parent, that another male cannot also be found to be a ''parent'' under the extended definition of the *Family Law Reform Act* as discussed previously.

Section 10 of the *Children's Law Reform Act* attempts to provide a codified procedure for the use of blood tests,[160] a procedure which only provides for

---

[156]*Re Overbury (deceased); Sheppard v. Matthews*, [1954] 3 All E.R. 308, at 310.

[157]See *Family Maintenance Act*, R.S.N.S. 1980, c. 6, s. 11(2): ''Where there are two or more possible fathers, a court may order each of them to make payments. . . .''

[158]See *e.g. Jonk v. Valleau*, summarized in (1982), 4 F.L.R.R. 114 (Ont. Prov. Ct.) and *Evans v. Hammond*, summarized in (1979), 1 F.L.R.R. 113 (Ont. Co. Ct.).

[159]*Kras v. Sardo* (1979), 26 O.R. (2d) 785, 12 R.F.L. (2d) 188 (U.F.C.).

[160]This procedure may apply to any proceeding where paternity is in dispute and is not limited to the *Children's Law Reform Act: Z. v. Z.* (1978), 20 O.R. (2d) 653, 2 R.F.L. (2d) 297 (Prov. Ct.).

judicial leave for the tests to be conducted and does not go so far as to order that anyone take the tests. It states:

s. 10(1) Upon the application of a party in a civil proceeding in which the court is called upon to determine the parentage of a child, the court may give the party leave to obtain blood tests of such persons as are named in the order granting leave and to submit the results in evidence.

(2) Leave under subsection (1) may be given subject to such terms and conditions as the court thinks proper.

(3) Where leave is given under subsection (1) and a person named therein refuses to submit to the blood test, the court may draw such inferences as it thinks appropriate.

(4) Where a person named in an order granting leave under subsection (1) is not capable of consenting to having a blood test taken, the consent shall be deemed to be sufficient,

    (a) where the person is a minor of the age of sixteen years or more, if the minor consents;

    (b) where the person is a minor under the age of sixteen years, if the person having the charge of the minor consents; and

    (c) where the person is without capacity for any reason other than minority, if the person having his charge consents and a legally qualified medical practitioner certifies that the giving of a blood sample would not be prejudicial to his proper care and treatment.

(Note that it has been held that this section is substantive in nature and cannot be invoked after an order has been given by the trial court and before an appeal has been heard.)[161]

This provision specifically confirms the Legislature's clear intention that children of any age are not immune from such proceedings.[162] As a point of interest, if s. 10(3) supports an interpretation that the court may draw an adverse inference against a minor under 16 if his parents refuse consent, then this may arguably be contrary to the rules of fundamental justice since a person may receive an adverse ruling based on the acts of others who purport to speak for him.

Judicial guidelines that have emerged with the codification of blood tests include the following:

1) In order for the court to grant leave, judicial discretion must be exercised requiring a consideration of evidence in support of the application for leave. Absence of evidence to support such a decision is an error on the record and

[161]*Evans and Martin v. Hammond, supra,* note 158.

[162]*Berg v. Walker* (1969), 70 W.W.R. 394 (B.C. S.C.) There existed a common law principle, codified in the Criminal Code and now eliminated under the recently enacted *Young Offenders Act,* that a boy under 14 years is incapable of having carnal knowledge. See *Berg v. Walker* for a case distinguishing civil from criminal proceedings.

may be summarily set aside.[163] The courts seem to disagree as to whether a *prima facie* case must emerge before leave is granted or whether it is for the court to decide, as long as it has some evidence before it and it turns its mind to the issue.[164] It is probably preferable to adopt the latter position in that it might be difficult to establish a *prima facie* case for the "one night stand" without the advantage of blood tests, thereby undermining the impact of the amending legislation.

2) The *CLRA* under s. 11, provides the Lieutenant Governor in Council with the authority to make Regulations with respect to:

   (a) the method of taking blood samples and the handling, transportation and storage thereof;

   (b) the conditions under which a blood sample may be tested;

   (c) designating persons or facilities or classes thereof who are authorized to conduct blood tests for the purposes of section 10;

   (d) prescribing procedures respecting the admission of reports of blood tests in evidence;

   (e) prescribing forms for the purpose of section 10 and this section and providing for their use.

No Regulations have, in fact, been introduced on these matters. In the absence of such directives, it would appear that the court is relying on s. 10(2), that is, leave given "subject to such terms and conditions as the court thinks proper." This then raises the adversarial issue of the nature and kind of testing to be performed and perhaps even the competency of the court to make any direction on these matters, given the apparent intention of the Legislature that these matters be dealt with outside the judicial forum. As a minimum, it would seem reasonable that the court should hear evidence on matters which are potentially the subject of ancillary Regulations. It should be noted in the interim, however, that s. 10(2) is *prima facie* subject to the Ontario *Evidence Act* and accordingly, a written report would be inadmissible where the author is not a doctor and the author is not available as a witness.[165]

3) A weak case for proving parentage can nonetheless succeed if the putative father refuses to submit to blood tests and provides no reason for his refusal other than that it was done on the recommendation of his legal counsel.[166] The legislation is silent as to what significance should be given to such an adverse inference and this may vary from court to court until the matter has been settled in Superior Court. There does, however, appear to be some judicial consensus that the court must draw something of an adverse inference simply to comply with the statute, although that may amount to very little. For example, one court accepted the explanation of the male defendant for refusing to participate, an explanation which amounted to his

---

[163]*J.R.D.* v. *L.K.S.* (1980), 20 R.F.L. (2d) 423 (Ont. Div. Ct.). See also *Re D. and S.* (1980), 30 O.R. (2d) 225, 118 D.L.R. (3d) 369 (Div. Ct.).

[164]For the former position, see *Rhan* v. *Pinsonneault* (1979), 27 O.R. (2d) 210 (Co. Ct.); for the latter position, see *Stewart* v. *Wilson,* summarized in (1984), 6 F.L.R.R. 141 (Ont. Co. Ct.).

[165]*Ferencz* v. *Meier*, summarized in (1982), 5 F.L.R.R. 38 (Ont. Prov. Ct.).

[166]*Sombach* v. *Duncan (No. 2)*, summarized in (1982), 5 F.L.R.R. 80 (Ont. Prov. Ct.).

non-belief in the accuracy of the tests and his refusal, due to the passage of time, to "dignify the accusation by submitting to such a test."[167] Given the nature and accuracy of this new scientific tool[168], it seems regressive to dilute the significance of the tests by setting up different degrees of an "adverse inference." It also seems inconsistent to accept passage of time as rebutting an adverse inference in the face of legislation which noticeably removes any statutory limitations for the commencement of such an action.

4) It has been held that the adult's privacy rights should be given some weight in the court's decision on the issue of leave, although in this case it was coupled with the child's best interests which would not be well served by unearthing the issue 13 years after his birth.[169] However, if the courts begin to find privacy rights out-weighing the child's rights based on a laches doctrine, then it is submitted that the courts are effectively applying a limitation period to an amending act, the *CLRA*, which specifically abolishes any such defence. The new legislation abandons the concept of the woman "catching the guilty rogue in time, if she can!" It is submitted that delay should only go to the question of reliability of the evidence, not to the question of whether to obtain the evidence in the first place. And in the case of blood tests, delay has no effect on its reliability as evidence.

The following excerpt from the decision of a Provincial Court, quoted with approval on appeal to County Court, capsulized a judicial argument against giving priority to the respondent father's "right of privacy":

> I do not believe that the privacy of the alleged father argument should be a factor in considering whether to grant leave. Privacy is a fabric that wears thin when litigants bring their disputes before a court of law. A litigant is obliged to answer questions on examination for discovery and on cross-examination. Once the Legislature enacted s. 10, I believe that public policy was set in this province, just as surely as it had been set by the federal government when Parliament enacted the finger-printing provisions in the *Identification of Criminals Act.*[170]

5) Finally, the discretion inherent in the granting of leave has been interpreted to require a consideration of the "interests of justice" as a concern equal to the best interests of the child. In this context, an Ontario Divisional Court, on appeal from a Supreme Court judge, refused leave for a second set of blood tests. A second set of special blood tests, able to be carried out only in the United States and in South Africa, might have reversed the negative results of the first set. The court held that to grant leave for this second set would result in "harsh and unreasonable terms" being

---

[167]*Rhan v. Pinsonneault, supra,* note 164.

[168]See N. Bryant, A.R.T., F.A.C.B.S., "Explanation of the Interpretation of Results Which Express the Likelihood of Paternity", *Family Law, 1983–84,* at p. 486, the Law Society of Upper Canada Bar Admission materials.

[169]*McCartney v. Amell* (1982), 35 O.R. (2d) 651 (Prov. Ct.). See also *J.R.D. v. L.K.S., supra,* note 163.

[170]*Stewart v. Wilson, supra,* note 164.

imposed on the alleged father who might lose the right to cross-examine the scientists who carried out the tests.[171] As a post script, it is suggested that the Divisional Court case turns on its own facts where the court seemed more concerned about the lack of natural justice due to the absence of ability to cross-examine, then with the general issue of how many sets of blood tests are covered by s. 10, although the court did interpret the section to refer to only one series of tests.

6) In addition to statutory directions for proving parentage, common law principles continue to apply although some modification will be necessary since most cases turn on the issue of what constitutes corroborative evidence. Under the amending legislation, the court need no longer have before it specific corroborative evidence. It must look to the totality of the evidence and apply a ''balance of probabilities'' test and hence, the following case references may be useful:

(i) If there is evidence of sexual relations with the putative father outside the period of gestation, the weight of such evidence diminishes as the date of the relations becomes more remote from the date of alleged conception.[172]

(ii) Evidence of a putative father's encouragement of an abortion is persuasive if coupled with the fact of his attendance with the mother at the doctor's office.[173]

(iii) Evidence that the putative father was associating with the mother on terms of close affection is persuasive if coupled with the lack of any evidence that the mother had been associating with other men.[174]

(iv) It is persuasive if there is evidence that the putative father accepted or admitted the mother's allegations of his paternity, either by word or conduct. Acceptance may be silent in circumstances where an explanation or denial is expected of him.[175]

(v) Letters written by the putative father indicating his paternity have constituted corroborative evidence, and the complainant mother has been found to be a competent witness to prove the putative father's handwriting.[176]

(vi) Evidence of a physical resemblance between the child and alleged father may be admissible, but the weight of such evidence is dependent on the circumstances. If the mother is a white Caucasion female with fair skin, blonde hair, blue eyes and has no distinguishing facial

---

[171]*Clarke v. Biggs* (1984), 37 R.F.L. (2d) 1 (Ont. Div. Ct.); *McCartney v. Amell, supra,* note 169, at p. 658.

[172]*Munroe v. Krause,* [1931] 2 W.W.R. 685, [1931] 4 D.L.R. 120, 56 C.C.C. 311 (Alta. C.A.); *Simpson v. Collinson,* [1964] 1 All E.R. 262 (C.A.).

[173]*Dunham v. Bradner* (1934), 62 C.C.C. 163 (B.C.C.A.).

[174]*Moore v. Hewitt,* [1947] 2 All E.R. 270, appld. in *Lewis v. Ragusa* (1973), 18 R.F.L. 366 (Ont. Prov. Ct.); and see *Re Chaskavich and Runzer,* 2 D.L.R. (3d) 617, [1969] 3 C.C.C. 213; affd 2 D.L.R. (3d) 619, [1969] 3 C.C.C. 216 (Sask. C.A.).

[175]*Luther v. Ryan* (1956), 115 C.C.C. 303 (Nfld. C.A.); *Bartley v. Gall,* [1925] 2 W.W.R. 669, [1925] 3 D.L.R. 585 (Man. C.A.).

[176]*Jeffery v. Johnson,* [1952] 1 All E.R. 450; *Walker v. Foster,* [1923] 4 D.L.R. 1204 (Ont. C.A.); *Workun v. Nelson* (1958), 16 D.L.R. (2d) 407, 26 W.W.R. 600 (Alta. C.A.).

features, and the putative father is the same, then the fact that the child resembles the putative father would have no value since the child could easily have inherited these characteristics from the mother. If there is a marked facial resemblance to the alleged father and the mother is an Indian with little resemblance to the child, the court may accept the resemblance as evidence in support of the applicant mother's case.[177] (vii) Evidence of admissions made by the putative father to a representative from a Children's Aid Society is persuasive. No caution is necessary prior to receiving statements from the putative father since affiliation proceedings are not criminal or quasi-criminal in nature.[178]

Support by Agreement

Under Ontario's *Family Law Reform Act*, a couple may enter into a domestic contract which, among other issues, deals with support of their children during the time the couple is living together, as well as after their separation. If the agreement is entered into before or during a marriage, outlining rights and obligations under the marriage, it is entitled a "marriage contract": s. 51, *FLRA*. If no marriage is contemplated, it is entitled a "cohabitation agreement": s. 52, *FLRA*. If the agreement is made after a couple have separated, it is entitled a "separation agreement": s. 53, *FLRA*. (For a discussion of clauses to include to avoid enforcement problems, see below under "Enforcement Problems".) Ontario's proposed *Family Law Act* will reinforce the usefulness of the domestic and paternity contracts by providing under s. 35 a variation and automatic enforcement mechanism for support and custody/access clauses.

A person under 18 has the capacity to enter into a marriage contract or a separation agreement but only if the terms of the agreement are approved by the court either before or after the agreement is made: s. 54(2), *FLRA*. Interestingly, the Legislature decided not to extend the same legal capacity to minors who are cohabiting outside of marriage, although the same minors are considered capable of entering into a separation agreement after cohabitation.

The *FLRA* allows a court to set aside any part of a domestic contract if it results in support arrangements which result in unconscionable circumstances (s. 18(4)(a))[179], or if, in the matter of a child's education, moral training or custody/access, the best interests of the child necessitate such an action (s. 55(1)).[180] Note that this section is not exclusive in that the usual common law remedies such as duress are still available. (For further discussion on this issue, see above "Judicial Intervention in Inter-spousal Agreements.") Note also that it

---

[177]*McLeod v. Hill*, [1976] 2 W.W.R. 593 (Sask. Prov. Ct.).

[178]*Re Power and Matchett*, [1953] O.W.N. 215 (H.C.); and see *R. v. Nottingham County Justice; ex parte Bostock*, [1970] 2 All E.R. 641.

[179]The courts have not developed judicial guidelines but instead base their assessment on each fact situation. However, see *Mance v. Mance* (1981), 22 R.F.L. (2d) 445 (Ont. Co. Ct.) for the principle that unconscionability can arise from a change in financial circumstances, even though the agreement itself was not unconscionable given the circumstances at the time it was signed.

[180]See for example *Boyd v. Boyd* (1980), 1 F.L.R.A.C. 649 (Ont. Prov. Ct.) wherein a non-custodial mother was ordered to pay support where it was shown that she was able, despite the fact that there was no obligation on her under the separation agreement. The father had need, and therefore the children's best interests necessitated the mother's payment of support. See also *Barlow v. Barlow* (1978), 8 R.F.L. (2d) 6 (Ont. Prov. Ct.).

has been held that a court may not summarily adopt the contents of a domestic contract as a support order under s. 2(8) of this Act.[181]

The *FLRA* also provides for "paternity agreements" which are contracts for the support of children of unwed parents who never cohabited. Section 58(1) reads:

> s. 58(1) Where a man and a woman who are not spouses enter into an agreement for,
>> (a) the payment of the expenses of pre-natal care and birth in respect of the child;
>> (b) support of a child; or
>> (c) burial expenses of the child or mother,
> on the application of a party to the agreement or a children's aid society made to a provincial court (family division) or the Unified Family Court, the court may incorporate the agreement in an order, and Part II applies to the order in the same manner as if it were an order for support made under that Part.

Unless within the agreement there is an admission as to paternity, the issue of whether the male person who enters into an agreement is, in fact, the father, is irrelevant.[182] Once the parties enter into such an agreement, the court, upon an application by a party to the agreement, may incorporate the agreement in an order. In so doing, Part II of the *Family Law Reform Act* applies to the order in the same manner as if it were an order for support. That is, once an agreement is confirmed by order, all the support remedies such as variation powers are available, even though the operative definition of "parent" pursuant to s. 16(1) may not have been satisfied. Further, a party may apply to the court under s. 18 seeking to set aside a provision for support in a paternity agreement and seeking a new support order if the provision for or waiver of support would result in circumstances that are unconscionable or where there has been default in the payment of support under the contract or agreement. This section provides the parties with this relief whether or not they had previously contracted to oust the court's jurisdiction by agreeing to exclude the application of s. 18(4).

"Paternity agreements" differ from "domestic contracts" under the *Family Law Reform Act* (and the proposed *Family Law Act*) as follows:

> 1) The terms of these agreements may not be set aside on the basis of the best interests of the child although the court may set aside the term of a paternity agreement, like a domestic contract, if the provision for or waiver of support results in circumstances that are unconscionable, or if the father defaults in his payments of support pursuant to the agreement.[183] On the face of it, this noticeable omission of a "best interest" criterion for intervention might suggest that the legislation contemplates two standards for judicial review of support arrangements, one that allows for unlimited power so as to

---

[181]*Solomon v. Solomon*, summarized in (1981), 4 F.L.R.R. 47 (Ont. Prov. Ct.); *Kirkhanan v. Kirkhanan* (1983), 44 O.R. (2d) 476 (H.C.).

[182]*Hrycewich v. Hegi* (1964), 50 W.W.R. 237 (Alta. Dist. Ct.).

[183]See *Family Law Reform Act*, s. 18(4).

secure nothing less than the child's "best interests" and the other which provides for something less than "best interests", but more than "unconscionability." Such a discriminatory interpretation should be resisted, based on the obvious intent and effort of the Legislature to eradicate the distinction under the *Children's Law Reform Act*. It is suggested that a "best interests" jurisdiction rests at least with the Supreme Court since it has been held that no agreement can oust the jurisdiction of the Supreme Court when the question of child maintenance is before it.[184]

2) For immediate relief, the Act permits application to a court to incorporate the terms of the agreement in an order: s. 58(1), *FLRA*. This section allows the Children's Aid Society to make the same application, although not a party to the contract. This broad presumption that the Children's Aid Society has a major interest in all children who are the subject of paternity agreements may represent a remnant from the repealed past where "illegitimacy" was associated with financial insecurity, resulting in state intervention. Finally, s. 35 of Ontario's proposed *Family Law Act* will provide a variation and automatic enforcement mechanism for domestic contracts and paternity agreements.

Enforcement Problems

Frequently, the most difficult support problem is enforcement, giving the lump sum award obvious advantages. Of some assistance will be the proposed release-of-information legislation which will provide information to locate those who are in breach of custody/access/support orders: the federal *Family Orders Enforcement Act* (access to Health and Welfare and Employment and Immigration records plus garnishee of federal payments) and Ontario's *Support and Custody Orders Enforcement Act* (access to both public and private records as well as automatic enforcement including garnisheeing, seizure and sale, registration on title and court proceedings). A major difficulty with child-support agreements or court orders based on Minutes of Settlement is the uncertainty of the language itself, particularly around the duration of the support obligation for an older child. Given the reluctance at least of Ontario courts to apply overriding rules to child support agreements, a number of practical suggestions are offered in an attempt to avoid future enforcement headaches as follows:

1) Parties may wish to mediate or arbitrate any subsequent difficulties in lieu of court proceedings; in the event of a change in circumstances, the agreement should clearly stipulate that pending the determination through mediation/arbitration, the obligation for child support shall remain as it is. The continuing obligation may be obvious but it appears in many cases that the payor party will rely upon the process of mediation/arbitration as a defence to their cessation or alteration of support payments and through time delays, attempt to evade their responsibility. As well, language that is clear in this regard might avoid the "catch-22" of seeking judicial enforcement only to find the proceedings stayed because the payor party has an application in the works for variation retroactively.

2) Regarding duration of support, spell out what the parties contemplate by the use of the words "child", "child of the marriage," and "dependant."

---

[184]*Re Green; Green v. Primeau* (1974), 15 R.F.L. 68, at 71 (Ont. S.C.).

Domestic agreements should have the advantage over court proceedings of providing the parties with some greater certainty of their mutual expectations. To limit the duration of child support for as long as the child is a "child of the marriage" simply invites a proceeding at a later date as to what the term means, with no assurance of the outcome.[185] Specify the maximum number of years for which support will be required and be clear as to whether a child is entitled to support or the same amount of support

(i)   if he is not living at home with either parent, or

(ii)   if he is working during the summers, or not working when he could be working in the opinion of one or both of the parties.

If the parties are reluctant, as often occurs, to negotiate an item so far into the future, then at least attempt to include the principles of entitlement, leaving quantum to be negotiated at a later date. Many parents are able to stipulate future principles of entitlement since they have already discussed their expectations for their child in terms of higher education as well as the child's responsibility to support himself. Also be sure to provide some grace period so that the day the child is not attending school is not the same day the support ends. It usually takes time for anyone to find a job.[186] Not all contingencies can be built into the agreement such as the meaning of "full-time attendance at a school", a standard prerequisite for continued support for a child of working age, *e.g.* whether it involves four, five or six credits.[187] It is also a common occurrence for a child of working age to cease attending school for a year and then return to school, creating no end of argument regarding support for that year as well as continuation of support. Without such a contingency provided for, the more expensive, frustrating and divisive remedy remains in the courts, since it retains its support jurisdiction as long as the child is dependent; the child himself can make an application to a Superior Court if no other relief is available.[188]

3) Where at all possible, quantify any child support obligation. Do not leave it to the court to decide what, for example, the parties contemplated as the maximum cost for camp or private school. The parties should put themselves in a position to quantify the maximum amount available for that purpose. No doubt in certain cases, it might be said that the unwritten number is more persuasive in terms of negotiation and enables the asking party to walk away from the table feeling that he or she got more for the child. If that is the case, which is doubtful, it is suggested that the gains are short-term and will be offset by later conflict at the cost of the child's relationship with both parents. If a "cost of living" clause is included in the agreement, then ensure that its calculation is clear enough that it can apply annually without recourse to a court for interpretation. It is suggested that there should be appended to the agreement an example of the calculation which, barring

---

[185]See *Ruttan v. Ruttan*, [1982] 1 S.C.R. 690, [1982] 4 W.W.R. 756, 27 R.F.L. (2d) 165; *Glassman v. Glassman* (1982), 38 O.R. (2d) 146, 29 R.F.L. (2d) 257 (Prov. Ct.); affd 42 O.R. (2d) 58, 35 R.F.L. (2d) 10 (Co. Ct.).

[186]*Heddle v. Heddle,* summarized in (1984), 6 F.L.R.R. 169 (Ont. U.F.C.) (divorce variation).

[187]*Flanagan v. Flanagan,* summarized in (1983), 6 F.L.R.R. 32 (Ont. Prov. Ct.).

[188]See *Downing v. Downing,* [1976] 3 All E.R. 474.

some change in the index that is used, will be applied each year to avoid confusion.[189] (See Appendix A at the end of this chapter for drafting.)

4) Ensure that the payments for the child are allocated as such and that the child support is not simply subsumed under an amount payable to the wife. There are obviously certain advantages for minimizing payments to a child in favour of a wife, if it is expected that the wife will shortly be disentitled to support by reason of her re-entry into the work force, re-marriage or cohabitation. The opposite is true when representing the wife. Nevertheless, it is often better to have the terms accurately represent financial needs of the child in the interests of future fulfillment by each party of their obligations.

5) Include a provision that enables the agreement to be summarily incorporated as a court order. While s. 2(8) of the *Family Law Reform Act* stipulates that any matter provided for in a domestic contract may be incorporated in an order under this Act, it has been held that the section cannot be invoked for the purpose of judgment by way of motion. This section has been held to be only procedural, simply enabling courts without inherent jurisdiction to incorporate incidental matters in a contract as an order of the court.[190] For a summary judgment to be granted in accordance with the terms of the contract, a specific term of the agreement confirming same must be evident.[191] Note the automatic enforcement provision under s. 35 of Ontario's proposed *Family Law Act* which requires only the filing of a domestic contract or paternity agreement.

6) Spell out in the agreement the effect of failure on the part of the payee to enforce the agreement. In the face of inconsistent case law on the issue of "hoarding" and the so-called "one year rule" regarding arrears, not to mention the expense of returning to court with or without costs, it may be preferable for the parties to address the matter of delay in the agreement. The contract could specify that in the event of non-compliance, failure to enforce within a given time shall be construed as acceptance of suspension of child support obligations for that period of time until a new agreement is made or until the court directs otherwise with respect to future payments. Although this forces the parties to face an unpleasant issue during negotiations, the tension that otherwise develops at a future date and is harboured by the payee without action on her part or his part will likely be more damaging and destructive for all family members in the long run. In this context, note the 2-year limitation period on applying for a support order after default of a contract under s. 50 of Ontario's proposed *Family Law Act*. In any event, it seems reasonable to expect the custodial parent to pursue available remedies in the event of non-payment, given a reasonable period of time to do so. Without such a provision, the remedy often pursued is denial of access which hurts everyone and usually entrenches both parties in their respective positions on the side of the angels.

Occupation of the Family Home

Prior to the enactment of the *Family Law Reform Act*, the child's interest in a continued secure residence was subject to a conflict between the rights of one

---

[189]See, *e.g.*, *Roberts v. Roberts*, summarized in (1982), 5 F.L.R.R. 23 (Ont. Prov. Ct.).

[190]*Solomon v. Solomon, supra*, note 181.

[191]*Kirkhanan v. Kirkhanan, supra*, note 181.

spouse's proprietary interest and the other spouse's (often the custodial parent) occupancy interest in the matrimonial home.[192] The Ontario Supreme Court stated:

> [W]hether a wife was justified in leaving the respondent or not, she does have custody of the four children and as of the 1st of September she must find a place for herself and the children to live in. There appears to be no financial hardship to the husband in finding alternative accommodation. However, there would be considerable financial and practical difficulty for the applicant [wife] to find temporary rental accommodation for herself and the four children until she is able to make permanent arrangements after the trial. . . The wife's difficulties far outweigh the inconvenience to the husband of moving at this time. Moreover, it is of considerable concern that the children be subjected to the minimum number of moves, and the minimum disturbance to the normal pattern of their lives.[193]

The *Family Law Reform Act* codifies this "best interest" by providing that even if a spouse has no proprietary interest in the home, a claim for exclusive possession may still be made "if in the opinion of the court, other provision for shelter is not adequate in the circumstances or it is in the best interests of the child to do so": s. 45(3), *FLRA*. (Section 25(3) of Ontario's proposed *Family Law Act* gives more detailed criteria including: the best interests of the child and the disruptive effect of the move on him; existing orders, contracts and the financial situation of each spouse; and availability of other suitable and affordable accommodation.) Note also:

1) s. 40, which provides that both spouses are equally entitled to any right of possession in the matrimonial home;

2) s. 42 which provides that a spouse may not sell, lease, mortgage or otherwise deal with the matrimonial home without the written consent of the other spouse, regardless of whether or not one spouse is the sole legal and beneficial owner of the home;

3) s. 43 which provides both spouses equally with the right of redemption or relief against forfeiture and to be entitled to any notice respecting the claim and its enforcement or realization.

Section 40(2) of the *FLRA* provides that, subject to court order, the right of both spouses to be equally entitled to any right of possession in the matrimonial home ceases upon the "spouse ceasing to be a spouse" but s. 45(1), giving the judge jurisdiction to order possession, applies to "spouses." On the face of it, possessory interests seem to be a function of the parents' marital status and may be secondary to the proprietary claims of the parents upon division of assets. The opening words of s. 45 are: "Notwithstanding the ownership of a matrimonial home and its contents, and notwithstanding section 40", the court may make a possessory order in favour of a spouse. This presumably gives the court an

---

[192]*Re Hutcheson*, [1950] O.R. 265, [1950] 2 D.L.R. 751 (C.A.); *Maskewycz v. Maskewycz* (1973), 13 R.F.L. 210 (Ont. C.A.); *Sawinski v. Sawinski* (1973), 14 R.F.L. 323 (Ont. Dist. Ct.); *MacDonald v. MacDonald* (1973), 13 R.F.L. 248 (Ont. C.A.); leave to appeal to Court of Appeal refused 13 R.F.L. 254; *Piscioni v. Piscioni* (1973), 10 R.F.L. 286 (Ont. S.C.).

[193]*LaPrairie v. LaPrairie* (1976), 29 R.F.L. 207 at 209–10 (Ont. H.C.).

overriding discretion in respect of the possession of the matrimonial home, regardless of the ownership of the home as determined under s. 4, and regardless of whether a spouse's right to possession may have ceased upon the divorce of the parties. However, in view of the definition of "spouse" in this Act, the overriding discretion provided by s. 45 appears to be available only when an application is commenced while the parents are married to each other since the order must be in favour of a "spouse." Consequently, unless the order is made while the parties are "spouses", a double standard may continue as far as the interests of the child are concerned. (Note however the discussion below regarding a possessory order classified as a support order.)

The courts have awarded exclusive possession under s. 45(3) to a custodial parent on a "best interests" test for some of the following reasons:

1) the children's ties to the community and their friends;[194]

2) the nature of the community as being ideal for the rearing of children;[195]

3) roots in a particular ethnic community and extended family nearby to provide assistance;[196]

4) the existence of a unique schooling opportunity such as the city's only French immersion program;[197]

5) the opportunity for the children to attend a school with an excellent reputation and the ability of the children to pursue their post-secondary education using their home as a base, and thereby avoiding high education costs;[198]

6) a large family should not be separated;[199]

7) to maintain as good accommodation for the custodial mother as the non-custodial father was able to provide when the children visited him;[200]

8) to avoid exposure to warring spouses in the throws of litigation;[201] or

9) to avoid exposure to alcoholic or dangerous parent.[202]

Note, however, that the mere fact of one spouse having custody of a child does not in itself constitute grounds for exclusive possession.[203]

Whatever the rationale, the decision is often based on what makes the most financial sense. In this context, it is often better not to move either because the cost of maintaining the home is reasonable and affordable to the custodial

---

[194]*Cicero v. Cicero,* summarized in (1978), 1 F.L.R.R. 34 (Ont. U.F.C.); *Tycholiz v. Tycholiz* (1981), 23 R.F.L. (2d) 31 (Man. C.A.).

[195]*Robertson v. Robertson* (1980), 3 F.L.R.R. 150 (Ont. U.F.C.).

[196]*Cicero v. Cicero, supra,* note 194.

[197]*Robertson v. Robertson, supra,* note 195.

[198]*Ashwell v. Ashwell,* summarized in (1984), 6 F.L.R.R. 132 (Ont. Co. Ct.).

[199]*Finley v. Finley,* summarized in (1979), 2 F.L.R.R. 35 (Ont. Dist. Ct.).

[200]*Langtvet v. Langtvet* (1978), 7 R.F.L. (2d) 224 (Ont. H.C.).

[201]*Korolchuk v. Korolchuk* (1982), 135 D.L.R. (3d) 184, 28 R.F.L. (2d) 216 (Sask. C.A.). But see *Barrett v. Barrett* (1982), 29 R.F.L. (2d) 13 (Ont. H.C.).

[202]*Campbell v. Campbell* (1979), 6 R.F.L. (2d) 392 (Ont. H.C.); *West v. West* (1982), 28 R.F.L. (2d) 375 (Ont. S.C.).

[203]*Campbell v. Campbell, ibid.*

parent[204] or, if the custodial parent is the breadwinner, because he can maintain it and the non-custodial parent will share in the appreciating equity. On the other hand, one court held that the house should be sold despite the plea of the wife and children to remain because it believed that, due to the husband's alcoholism and the inevitable unrealibility of support parents, the wife would be more financially secure if she received 70 per cent of the proceeds of the sale. The decision reads in part:

> I feel that having regard to the reasonably substantial equity in the matrimonial home, the applicant will be able to acquire, through her interest therein, other shelter which will be adequate for herself and the children, although not at a standard to which they have been accustomed. The respondent's share of the equity should enable him to re-establish himself in business, which he has a keen desire to do. Ordinarily, an equal division of the net proceeds of the sale of the matrimonial home is made. In the circumstances of this case, an equal division would not, in my view, be appropriate. The respondent has not paid anything to the applicant for the support of the children since the parties separated. The failure of the respondent to support the children was not by choice but by circumstances. It is clear from the evidence that the respondent loves the children and provided that his alcoholism is cured, the probabilities are that a good relationship with the children will be maintained. The respondent has no means at the present time to support the children and, indeed, may not be able to do so for some period of time. Only from the proceeds of the sale of the matrimonial home can the respondent contribute to the support of the children at this time. I consider that a sale of the matrimonial home is the only course that would be fair and equitable in the circumstances, and I so order it. Only through his interest in the proceeds of the sale of the matrimonial home can the respondent support his children, and I therefore consider the division of 70% thereof to the applicant and 30% to the respondent would be appropriate and fair and I so order it. In due course, if the husband's financial circumstances improve, it will be open to the applicant to bring an application for support. If such an application is brought, the contribution which the respondent is deemed to have made through an unequal division of the proceeds of sale of the matrimonial home will undoubtedly be taken into account.[205]

In some cases which deal with the high end of the income spectrum, the courts will order a sale of the house in order that the custodial spouse may purchase a second, less costly house. One such decision comes from the Ontario Supreme Court:

> Having regard to Jonathan's age, their wish he continue as a day pupil at Upper Canada College and that both his father and mother continue to play a significant and meaningful role in his upbringing and development, I

---

[204]See *e.g. Greenless v. Greenless* (1981), 23 R.F.L. (2d) 323 (B.C.C.A.).

[205]*Janssen v. Janssen,* summarized in (1981), 3 F.L.R.R. 198 (Ont. Co. Ct.). See also, *Cicero v. Cicero, supra,* note 194.

believe that he should have the stability that comes with his residing in a home as opposed to an apartment. Particularly, as his father, in the course of his duties and responsibilities as Chief Executive Officer, must travel a great deal. With the separation of his parents some sixteen months ago, and the necessity of his moving out of the home he has known and enjoyed and lived in for the past seven years, he should be afforded the stability of a residence until he completes at least his primary and secondary school education. I therefore direct that, out of the capital share on the sale of the matrimonial home the husband is entitled to receive, the sum of $100,000.00 shall be advanced to the wife, provided the same is used in the purchase of a home in which Jonathan shall reside with her.[206]

Note that a provincially appointed judge is without jurisdiction to order exclusive possession of a matrimonial home pursuant to s. 45 of the *FLRA*.[207] However, possession of a matrimonial home is also classified under the *FLRA* as support and the court, including a Provincial Court, is empowered to make as a support order, presumably as a more exacting and financially secure remedy, an order for exclusive possession. It is questionable whether in light of the effect of the order, there exists such jurisdiction but it has been specifically referred to in one decision as an order of support and therefore within the constitutional jurisdiction of the Provincial Court.[208] In addition, as an order of support, the court is able to make an order of exclusive possession in favour of an applicant who is an unmarried spouse with or without children.[209] In the same context, the only statutory basis for variation of an order for exclusive possession would be if it were classified as a support order. (Note that s. 34(2) of Ontario's proposed *Family Law Act* specifically prohibits the Provincial Court from making an exclusive possession order.)

Death of the Payor Parent

Under existing legislation unless specifically stated, an order or agreement for child support will not continue past the death of the payor spouse. Under s. 19(1)(i) of Ontario's *Family Law Reform Act*, the judge is allowed to include in the order that the ''obligation and liability for support continue after the death of the respondent and be a debt of his or her estate for such period as is fixed in the order.'' Under s. 34(5) of Ontario's proposed *Family Law Act* the order automatically binds the estate unless provided otherwise. There is no similar provision under Canada's *Divorce Act*. Even with the jurisdiction, these orders are not routinely granted as there apparently exists an underlying current of judicial thought that appropriate relief can be obtained, in the event of death, under provincial succession legislation as Ontario's *Succession Law Reform Act*.[210]

---

[206]*Rice v. Rice,* summarized in (1982), 5 F.L.R.R. 86 (Ont. S.C.).

[207]*Reference Re Section 6 of Family Relations Act, 1978; A.-G. Ont. v. A.-G. Can.* (1982), 26 R.F.L. (2d) 113 (S.C.C.).

[208]*Cipens v. Cipens* (1978), 21 O.R. (2d) 134, 90 D.L.R. (3d) 460, 7 R.F.L. (2d) 236 (U.F.C.).

[209]*Foong v. Foong,* summarized in (1980), 2 F.L.R.R. 96 (Ont. S.C.).

[210]*Norgard v. Norgard* (1978), 8 R.F.L. (2d) 268 (Ont. C.A.) (application to vary decree nisi).

Accordingly, it is suggested that whenever possible, an order or agreement for support should include a stipulation that it be binding upon the payor's estate. Not only does it eliminate future conflict and fluctuation in financial security, but also, and more importantly, the criteria to make an order under domestic support legislation is based primarily on the relative needs of the child having regard to the ability of the parent to provide support. It is not as clear whether support for the child in the context of "dependants' relief" has a similar focus.[211] Under s. 62(1)(a) of Part V of the *Succession Law Reform Act* entitled "Support of Dependants", the needs of the child compete not only with specified beneficiaries but also with other dependants based on the following criteria:

s. 62(1) . . . . the court,
  (a) shall inquire into and consider all the circumstances of the application, including:
    (i) the assets and means of the dependant,
    (ii) the capacity of the dependant to provide for his or her own support,
    (iii) the age and the physical and mental health of the dependant,
    (iv) the needs of the dependant, in determining which the court may have regard to the accustomed standard of living,
    (v) the measures available for the dependant to become financially independent, and the length of time and cost involved to enable the dependant to take such measures,
    (vi) the proximity and duration of the dependant's relationship with the deceased,*
    (vii) the contributions made by the dependant to the deceased's welfare, including indirect and non-financial contributions,*
    (viii) the contributions made by the dependant to the acquisition, maintenance and improvement of the deceased's property, business or occupation,*
    (ix) whether the dependant has a legal obligation to provide support for another person,*
    (x) where the dependant is a child, his or her aptitude for and reasonable prospects of obtaining an education,
    (xi) where the dependant is a child of the age of 16 years or more, his or her withdrawal from parental control,*
    (xii) where the dependant is the spouse of the deceased, a course of conduct by the spouse during the lifetime of the deceased that is an obvious and gross repudiation of the relationship,
    (xiii) the circumstances of the deceased at the time of death,
    (xiv) any agreement between the deceased and the dependant,*

---

[211]For a discussion on the competing claims and concerns regarding child support upon the payor's death, see R. Hull, and M.C. Cullity, *Probate Practice* (Toronto: Carswell, 1981), at pp. 126–52.

(xv) any previous distribution or division of property made by the deceased in favour of the dependant by gift or agreement or under court order, and*

(xvi) the claims that any other person may have as a dependant;

[* asterisks mark criteria not present under s. 18(5) of the *Family Law Reform Act*. Note that the equivalent of para. (xi) is found under s. 16(2) of the *FLRA*.]

While ''illegitimacy'' has been abolished as a concept and a status, it could be relevant insofar as the testator's rejection of the ''illegitimate'' child may be reflected in s. 62(1)(a)(vi). Such an interpretation would appear to be antithetical to the intent of the *Children's Law Reform Act* but this would appear to be irrelevant to the subjective assessment of a relationship between a father and child under this section.

To qualify for support under the *Succession Law Reform Act,* the child must come within the combined definitions of ss. 1(1)(a), 57(a), 57(d) and qualify under s. 58(1) and (3), that is, he must be a dependant for whom the deceased has not made adequate provision for proper support. The definition sections read:

s. 1(1) In this Act,

(a) ''child'' means a child born within or outside marriage, subject to sections 86 and 87 of the *Child Welfare Act* (which relate to the effect of adoption), and includes a child conceived before and born alive after the death of the parent;

. . .

s. 57 In this Part [Support of Dependants],

(a) ''child'' means a child as defined in s. 1(1)(a) and includes a grandchild and a person whom the deceased has demonstrated a settled intention to treat as a child of his family. . . .

. . .

(d) ''dependant'' means,

(i) the spouse or common law spouse of the deceased,

(ii) a parent of the deceased,

(iii) a child of the deceased, or

(iv) a brother or sister of the deceased,

to whom the deceased was providing support or was under a legal obligation to provide support immediately before his death;

. . .

s. 58(1) Where a deceased, whether testate or intestate, has not made *adequate provision for the proper support* of his dependants or any of them, the court, on application, may order that such provision as it considers *adequate* be made out of the estate of the deceased for the *proper support* of the dependants or any of them. [Emphasis added.]

(2) An application for an order for the support of a dependant may be made by the dependant or a parent of the dependant, or by,

(a) the Ministry of Community and Social Services in the name of the Minister;

(b) a municipal corporation, including a metropolitan, district or regional municipality but not including an area municipality thereof; or

(c) a Children's Aid Society, where the Ministry, municipality or society is providing an allowance or benefit in respect of the support of the dependant.

(3) The adequacy of provision for support under subsection (1) shall be determined as of the date of the hearing of the application.

It would appear that a child who was the subject of a lump sum order already paid into court under support legislation would remain a "dependant" under s. 57(d) since the deceased would arguably still be "providing support or . . . under a legal obligation to provide support." The same would be true if a child was the subject of a support order directed to be binding upon the deceased's estate. It is clear that in Ontario, if a child is 18 or more years of age or married, he would not be entitled to support under s. 16 of the *Family Law Reform Act* for want of standing as a dependant and the deceased would therefore be under no obligation to support him.

With regard to the apparent prerequisite finding of inadequate support under s. 58 of the *Succession Law Reform Act*, it would seem necessary for the court to make such an assessment by considering the child's needs not in a vacuum but in relation to the value of the estate and any claims thereon. It appears that the intentions of the testator are but one factor in considering the determination of what constitutes a "proper" support order. For example, the fact that under s. 58(2) of this Act an application can be made on behalf of a dependant by various welfare agencies suggests that whatever the intentions of the deceased, they are not determinative if the effect is to make the state responsible for support. The court can always consider the effect of prior support arrangements or orders in assessing what is "proper", although the court must look to present circumstances as dictated by s. 58(3) which could include the consideration of a substantially higher standard of living since the date of the original order of the domestic court and could include even future contingencies which can be predicted at the present time.[212] It is submitted that the adequacy of the original support order or arrangement should also be assessed in the context of the division of the estate's assets, especially with respect to the amounts devised to other dependants. The criteria under s. 62 could be utilized for the determination of what is "proper". thereby assessing simultaneously whether the present support is adequate and what amount of support, if any, should be forthcoming from the estate. The following is an excerpt from England's Court of Appeal:

> The first thing to be noticed is that the powers given to the Court only arise when any of the persons mentioned is left without adequate provision for his or her proper maintenance, which word will be used in this judgment where necessary as including education and advancement. The use of the word "proper" in this connection is of considerable importance. It connotes something different from the word "adequate." A small sum may be sufficient for the "adequate" maintenance of a child, for instance, but, having regard to the child's station in life and the fortune of his father, it may

---

[212]*Malychuk v. Malychuk; Traschuk v. Malychuk* (1978), 11 A.R. 372 (T.D.), cited in Hull and Cullity, *ibid.*, at p. 42 *n* 52.

be wholly insufficient for his "proper" maintenance. So, too, a sum may be quite insufficient for the "adequate" maintenance of a child and yet may be sufficient for his maintenance on a scale that is "proper" in all the circumstances. A father with a large family and a small fortune can often only afford to leave each of his children a sum insufficient for his "adequate" maintenance. Nevertheless, such sum cannot be described as not providing for his "proper" maintenance, taking into consideration "all the circumstances of the case" as the sub-section requires shall be done. In the next place, it is to be observed that, when the condition precedent to the exercise of the powers given by the subsection is shown to be fulfilled, those powers extend to make such provision as the Court thinks fit for "such" maintenance, that is to say, for proper maintenance. The task thus imposed upon the Court is obviously one of great difficulty. Upon what principles is the Court to act in determining what constitutes proper maintenance?

. . .

The amount to be provided is not to be measured solely by the need for maintenance. It would be so if the court were concerned merely with adequacy. But the Court has to consider what is proper maintenance, and therefore the property left by the testator has to be taken into consideration. So, too, in the case of children, a material consideration is their age. If a son is of mature, or nearly mature, age, his needs both for the present and the future can be estimated without much difficulty. In the case, however, of a son of tender age, although his immediate needs can be readily ascertained, it is extra-ordinarily difficult even to guess what his needs may be in the future. Where, therefore, the testator's estate is a large one the Court will be justified in such a case in making provisions to meet contingencies that might have to be disregarded where the estate is small.[213]

In protecting the interests of the child, it is obvious that any order, however nominal, is desirable. This safeguard would give the child the right to make future applications under the following criteria of s. 65 of the *Succession Law Reform Act*:

> s. 65 Where an order has been made under this Part [Support of Dependants], the court at any subsequent date may,
> > (a) inquire whether the dependant benefited by the order has become entitled to the benefit of any other provision for his support;
> > (b) inquire into the adequacy of the provision ordered; and
> > (c) discharge, vary or suspend the order, or make such other order as the court considers appropriate in the circumstances.

Two final notes: The court has the power to make an interim order for support of a dependent child "as it considers appropriate," which presumably may focus simply on the needs of the child. Secondly, any

---

[213]*Bosch v. Perpetual Trustee Company*, [1938] A.C. 463, at 476–78 (P.C.), cited by Hull and Cullity, *supra*, note 211 at 139. But see *Lukie v. Hegalson* (1976), 1 B.C.L.R. 1 (C.A.) which sees the assessment of adequate support as a prerequisite to applying the statute's criteria for quantum of support.

support order that the court may make can take a wide variety of forms under s. 63, depending on what the court deems "appropriate", including lump sum and periodic payments, trusts, transfers of specific property, securing property and payments to third parties.

Support Resources Outside the Family

In addition to parental support, various government resources exist to assist the indigent child or the child with special needs involving exceptional costs beyond the support abilities of the parents. The following are examples of such programs.

Family Benefits Act

The *Family Benefits Act* is administered through the provincial government and provides assistance to children indirectly through support of the family unit. That is, a child cannot be an individual applicant but must fall under the heading of "dependent child" which means:

s. 1(*f*) . . . a person residing in Ontario who is supported by his mother, dependent father or the person who stands *in loco parentis* to him and,

(i) who is under twenty-one years of age and attends an educational institution of a class defined by the Regulations and, if sixteen years of age or over, is making satisfactory progress with his studies, or

(ii) who is under 18 years of age and is not attending school because,

    a) he is of pre-school age, or

    b) he is unable to attend school by reason of mental or physical disability.

As policy, the Department will generally require a medical report from a qualified physician to substantiate any claim of "mental or physical disability", referred to in s. 1(f)(ii). However, a Department directive suggests that a written opinion of a school nurse or psychologist will suffice.

The Act also provides relief on the basis of a "single person" applicant. Section 1(1)(c) of O. Reg. 318/80, pursuant to the Act, defines single person to mean "an adult person who is a widow, widower, unmarried, deserted, separated or divorced and who is not living with another person as husband or wife." While "adult" is not defined in the Act, a reading of s. 7 which lists potential recipients of family benefit payments, and s. 2(5) of the Regulations, would seem to suggest that it is only upon reaching the age of 18 that a dependent child may apply as an independent "single person" applicant. The 18-year old individual will have to satisfy the Act's other conditions under s. 7 of the Act and s. 2(5) of O. Reg. 318/80, namely, to be found as a "person in need," to be receiving no support through other assistance Acts as so listed, and to be permanently unemployable.

Another potential recipient is a "disabled person," that is, one who has a major physical or mental impairment that is likely to continue for a prolonged period of time and who, as a result thereof, is severely limited in activities pertaining to normal living, as so verified by objective medical findings accepted by the Medical Advisory Board (see s. 20 of the Regulations). "Permanently unemployable person" means a person who is unable to engage in remunerative employment for a prolonged period of time as verified by objective medical findings accepted by the Medical Advisory Board (see s. 1(3)(c) of the

Regulations). While the definition of "disabled person" may overlap with the definition of "permanently unemployable person", it should be noted that a classification under the former heading will allow for more extensive benefits.

As a dependant, a child may suffer as a result of the Act's distinction between the mother and the father and their traditional roles within the family. Section 7(1)(d) provides that a mother with a dependent child will receive assistance for both herself and the child where she is, *inter alia*, a widow, a deserted wife, a divorcee, a mother of a child born out-of-wedlock or a wife whose husband is a patient in a sanitorium, hospital or similar institution, or whose husband has been in prison. Section 7(1)(e) provides that a father with a dependent child will receive assistance only when that father can be assessed as a "dependent father." "Dependent father" means a father who is permanently unemployable by reason of physical or mental disability and includes a father who is blind or otherwise disabled as defined by the Regulations: s. 1(g). Therefore, unless the father can satisfy the criteria of permanently unemployable, blind or disabled, the state will not provide assistance to the father either for himself or for his dependent children. Moreover, it is questionable in view of the lack of any clear statutory direction, just how cooperative or supportive the Department will be to a father desiring assistance for the cost of day care so that he can attempt to work while at the same time ensure that his children are properly supervised. There have been occasions in Ontario when s. 8 of the *Family Benefits Act* has been successfully invoked to seek entitlement for a father and his children on the basis of special circumstances. Perhaps this is an area for challenge under s. 15 of the *Charter of Rights* in the context of discrimination on the basis of sex.

Under s. 7(f) of the *Family Benefits Act*, a foster parent will be entitled to benefits for the support of a foster child. Naturally, foster parents are not eligible for an allowance on their own behalf unless they themselves are otherwise eligible, but it gives rise to the interesting situation in which benefits will be available to a dependent child when in the care of a foster parent, whether that "parent" is eligible or not, but possibly not to a dependent child living with his father unless that child's father is a "dependent father". "Foster parent" is not defined in the Act but since the definition of "dependent child" includes one who is "supported by a person who stands *in loco parentis*", the Act suggests that any person upon whom a child is dependent may qualify for support for the child.

Section 7(d)(ii) and (vii) of the Act respectively dictate that where a mother with a dependent child has been deserted by her husband, or support is needed for an illegitimate child, that support will not be forthcoming for a period of three months. Even when three months have passed, s. 8 of the Regulations may be invoked by the Director of the Family Benefits Branch to prevent any form of assistance being made available:

s. 8 Where the Director is not satisfied that an applicant or recipient is making reasonable efforts to obtain compensation or realize any financial resource that the applicant [or] recipient . . . may be entitled to or eligible for. . . . the Director may determine that the applicant [or] recipient is not eligible for benefit or he may reduce the amount of an allowance granted by the amount of the compensation, contribution or financial resource, as the case may be, that in his opinion is available to the applicant [or] recipient.

A directive from the Ministry suggests that unless the applicant mother actively pursues maintenance from the father of her child, or presents a valid reason to the district Director why such action cannot be pursued, the mother and child may receive less allowance or none at all. Note that ''desertion'' is not defined in the Act but it appears that the Ministry adopts the dictionary meaning such that ''desertion is the abandonment without consent or legal justification of a person and the duties and obligations connected therewith''. In this respect, reference should be made to the *Family Law Reform Act* which now permits the Ministry or the municipality in charge of family benefits or welfare to assume party status for an application for support where the dependent spouse or child is receiving public benefits: s. 18(3).[214] As well, s. 19(4) of the *FLRA* enables a dependant, the creditor of an order for support, to assign it to the municipality or Ministry. Regardless of these amendments, the Director apparently retains his discretion under s. 8 of the *Family Benefits Act* to disentitle the dependant and it is not likely that an assignment will act as a defence for the dependant to s. 8.[215]

If the non-custodial parent is on family benefits, it has been held that that parent should not be ordered to pay support, thereby providing public funds to be paid over to the dependant. This decision was based on the finding that the rights of the dependant are not subrogated through his parents under s. 18(5) of *FLRA*.[216]

Section 7(1)(d)(vi) of the *Family Benefits Act* provides relief to the mother with a dependent child ''who is divorced from the father of her dependent child and has not remarried.'' In order to qualify under this section, the applicant mother must be in possession of the decree *nisi* and decree absolute. If no maintenance has been provided under the decree *nisi*, the Director may rely upon his discretion, noted above, to demand appropriate legal action as a condition to entitlement or, if maintenance has been ordered but payments are in default, the Director may require that the mother take legal action against the father to enforce compliance with the order regardless of the Ministry's own status rights under the *Family Law Reform Act*.

Other qualifications under the *Family Benefits Act* unique to the support of children include:

1) Section 1(f)(i) which requires, under the definition of ''dependent child'', if the child is 16 years of age or over, that he is ''making satisfactory

---

[214]One case held that a court can award costs against the municipality if unsuccessful: *Re Stretch and the Corporation of the City of Kingston,* summarized in (1979), 1 F.L.R.R. 125 (Ont. Prov. Ct.).

[215]For cases dealing with assignments, variation of support orders and party status of Minister see: *Ministry of Comm. and Soc. Services v. Boucher* (1981), 22 R.F.L. (2d) 396 (Ont. U.F.C.); *Ministry of Comm. and Soc. Services v. Drysdale* (1983), 35 R.F.L. (2d) 158 (Ont. Prov. Ct.); *Ministry of Comm. and Soc. Services v. Fabian,* summarized in (1983), 6 F.L.R.R. 99 (Ont. Prov. Ct.); *Ministry of Comm. and Soc. Services v. Petzold,* summarized in (1981), 3 F.L.R.R. 229 (Ont. U.F.C.).

[216]*Rosenthal v. Amar,* summarized in (1981), 4 F.L.R.R. 45 (Ont. Prov. Ct.) (under appeal).

progress with his studies.'' As a general rule, satisfactory progress will be deemed to be regular attendance. The district office may make bi-annual checks in the months of February and October to confirm such progress.

2) Section 13(2) of the Regulations of the Act requires that the wages and salaries of dependent children be included as income. But if the money is confirmed by the recipient applicant as being used to further the child's academic education, an exemption from including such income within the income of the applicant is allowed. Casual earnings will be considered as any monthly earnings less the basic exemption for a single person.

3) This Act places restrictions on recipients who have accumulated certain amounts of capital. Property of the child will either make him no longer a claimable dependant or will be considered liquid assets available to the parent.[217] Monies held in trust for the child including funds paid into court are the property of the infant and are not ''liquid assets'' of the mother within the meaning of s. 1(1)(a) of the Act. The funds may remove the child from dependency status if they are payable at any time on application by the parent.[218] Payments received by way of compensation to a child for pain and suffering under the *Compensation for Victims of Crime Act* are not income as defined by the Regulations and therefore welfare payments should not be decreased by the amount of such payments.[219] Real property can be considered to be a ''liquid asset'' depending on all the circumstances including its potential for convertibility into cash.[220]

General Welfare Assistance Act

The *General Welfare Assistance Act* is a municipally administered welfare assistance plan which provides temporary immediate assistance and fills the three month hiatus under the *Family Benefits Act*. Children can obtain benefits under this Act via various provisions. Section 1(1)(c) and (a) of O. Reg. 441/80 under the *General Welfare Assistance Act* defines ''child'' as a person under 16 years of age and defines ''adult'' as a person 16 years of age or over. It allows for assistance under the following three exclusive categories:

s. 1(g) ''dependent child'' means a child who,
   (i) lives with a head of a family or a parent or a person *in loco parentis*,
   (ii) is wholly dependent upon the head of the family or a parent or person *in loco parentis* for support and maintenance, and
   (iii) is,
      A) of pre-school age,
      B) attending school,

[217]*Re Fawcett and Board of Review, Ministry of Comm. and Soc. Services* (1973), 1 O.R. (2d) 772, 15 R.F.L. 87 (C.A.). But see *Re Smith* (1973), 11 R.F.L. 388 (Ont. C.A.).

[218]*Re Fawcett and The Board of Review, Ministry of Comm. and Soc. Services, ibid.* See also *Re Man. Public Trustee and Man.* (1979), 105 D.L.R. (3d) 376 (Man. Q.B.).

[219]*Elliott v. A.-G. of Ont. and Minister of Comm. and Soc. Services* (1973), 2 O.R. 534, 34 D.L.R. (3d) 386, 9 R.F.L. 279 (C.A.).

[220]*Re Mahon* (1975), 21 R.F.L. 362 (Ont. S.C.).

. . .

    C) unable to attend school because of physical or mental disability, or

    D) [pursuant to Regulation] attending school on a part-time basis, or is excused from attending school.

. . .

s. 1(n) ''Single person'' means an unmarried adult, a widow, a widower or a separated or divorced person but does not include a person,

    (i) who is head of a family,

    (ii) who is an employable person under the age of 21 years living with either of his parents or with a person *in loco parentis*, or

    (iii) who is living with another person as husband or wife.

. . .

s. 1(i) ''Head of a family'' means a person who has charge of a household and has one or more dependants therein.

The second category, that of a single person, is further restricted by s. 6(4) of the Regulations which reads:

s. 6(4) An employable person under the age of eighteen years who is not the head of a family is not eligible for assistance unless the welfare administrator is satisfied that there are special circumstances that justify providing the assistance.

''Special circumstances'' is left undefined and is apparently in the sole discretion of the welfare administrator. It is questionable why a person between the ages of 16 and 18 years who is ''disabled'' mentally or physically or ''unemployable'' and ''in need'' should not be entitled to assistance as a single person in the same manner as in the case of any other adult.

In any event, note s. 8(6) of the Regulations of the Act which allows for emergency assistance notwithstanding the above-noted limitations. However, contributions from the provincial government for such emergency assistance will terminate after two weeks, straining the resources of the municipality and jeopardizing emergency entitlement beyond that period.

Other details of significance for children under the *General Welfare Assistance Act* include:

1) A dependent child includes a child who has been excused from school under Ontario's early school leaving provision, that is, O. Reg. 261/80 under the *Education Act* as long as he continues to live with the head of the family and be supported thereunder. But a child who leaves school altogether and is neither mentally nor physically disabled will not qualify as a dependent child. And in view of s. 6(4) of the Regulations, he may not receive benefits under the age of 18 as a single person applicant unless ''special circumstances'' exist. The legislation appears to have the ultimate effect of providing assistance for the child leaving home, not in school and unemployed but seeking employment only if he becomes a ''head of a family'' whereupon assistance will be made available to both himself and his dependants.

2) An employable single person will generally not obtain assistance when enrolled as a day student unless he attends a school under the *Education Act*, in which case an exemption allowance for assistance is available. (See ss. 6(3)(b) of the Regulations). In such cases, the welfare administrator will require a written statement from the school authorities supporting the desirability of the single person to continue school. Where a person is under 18 and is a "single person", there remains the additional burden of showing "special circumstances" which may preclude such an individual from "single person" relief, even where school authorities have supported continued education.

3) Unlike the effects of the *Family Benefits Act* in respect of a male "head of a family", the *General Welfare Act* does recognize that an unemployed but employable person who is head of a family might very well require assistance if it is shown that it is necessary for him to remain at home to provide care for the children if the household is without an adult capable of caring for the children and if alternative and adequate child care services are not available. (See Regulations, s. 3(d).) This eligibility in respect of a male "head of a family" is limited to six months whereupon the Director's approval is necessary.

4) Section 8(4) of the Regulations permits an application by a foster parent for general assistance on behalf of a foster child and barring any clear definition of "foster parent", it would include any person who stands *in loco parentis* to a child and upon whom the child is wholly dependent, rendering the situation one of caring for a "dependent child": O. Reg. 441/80, s. 1(g).

As with the *Family Benefits Act*, the *General Welfare Assistance Act* also sets limits on an applicant's capital assets (see above).

The Health Insurance Act

The *Health Insurance Act* provides insurance for health services performed by either a legally qualified medical physician (s. 1(k)) or a "practitioner", a person other than a physician who is lawfully entitled to render insured services in the place where they are rendered (s. 1(m)). Such practitioners include, for example, chiropractors or podiatrists, but do not include the services of a private social worker or psychologist. The following should be noted in respect of children under the *Health Insurance Act*:

1) "A child includes an adopted child, *de jure* or *de facto*, a stepchild and an illegitimate child": O. Reg. 452/80, s. 1(b).

2) "Dependant" is defined, *inter alia*, as:

"A child of an insured person who is dependent for support upon the insured person or upon the spouse of the insured person and who is
    (A) under the age of twenty-one years and unmarried, or
    (B) twenty-one years of age or over, mentally or physically infirm and dependent for support upon the insured person or upon the spouse of the insured person, before his twenty-first birthday, but does not include the spouse of any such child. [O. Reg. 452/80, s. 1(c)]

Every dependant of an insured person is an insured person: s. 11(2) of the Act.

3) Recipients of public assistance and their dependants are entitled to insured services without payment of any premium: O. Reg. 452/80, s. 28(1). Recipients of public assistance include children who are wards of the Children's Aid Society or in the care of the Children's Aid Society but not formally wards: O. Reg. 452/80, s. 1(k)(ii).

4) If a child is placed in a group home or a foster family situation by the court without connection to a Children's Aid Society, the unofficial "foster parents" are acting in the place of the natural parents. Accordingly, the child could be eligible for health insurance either under the foster parents' "family" status coverage, particularly if the relationship between the child and the foster parents is such that the child is an eligible dependant for income tax purposes, or alternatively, through continuation of his natural parents' family status insurance coverage. Where children are in a group home and the model of a foster parent is not applicable, the child will continue to receive health insurance coverage through his parents' family insurance status. Consequently, upon entry into such an agency, the health insurance number of the parents should be provided to the agency to protect the child's insurance coverage.

5) If a child is not dependent as defined, then a child of any age can apply for health insurance as a non-group subscriber, and if his income is below a certain level, he will receive full premium assistance: O. Reg. 452/80, s. 27;

6) A new born child of an insured person is entitled to insurance services during the three months following the date of birth without payment of any premium: O. Reg. 452/80, s. 25.

Vocational Rehabilitation Services Act

The *Vocational Rehabilitation Services Act* is designed to provide vocational rehabilitation programs that assist disabled persons to integrate themselves into the employment market. "Disabled person" is defined in s. 1(b) of this Act as meaning "a person who because of physical or mental impairment is incapable of pursuing regularly any substantially gainful occupation as determined by the Regulations." In one case, the Board refused an applicant who was mentally retarded, holding that facilities were available in the educational system. On appeal, the Divisional Court held that the Board erred in law in not considering whether the applicant was "a disabled person" within the meaning of the Act.[221]

A rehabilitation program can involve any number of services, including assessment services, rehabilitation counselling, tuition costs, books and training material, maintenance and travelling allowances to the extent necessary to provide for vocational rehabilitation services, medical, surgical or psychiatric treatment, costs for vocational tools, supplies, licences, or artificial limb devices.

Since a person under the age of 16 can, in Ontario, obtain part-time

---

[221]*Re Scott and Director of the Vocational Rehabilitation Services Branch of the Ministry of Comm. and Soc. Services for Ontario* (1978) 22 O.R. (2d) 52 (Div. Ct.).

employment and the definition of "disabled person" in the Act does not exclude an applicant who could obtain part-time employment, it is improper for a person to be refused vocational rehabilitation services solely on the ground that he is under 16 years and school attendance laws prevent him from obtaining full-time employment.[222] This case arose out of a situation of a learning-disabled child who, for want of a remedy through the educational system, applied for vocational rehabilitative assistance for special education costs. In a subsequent case, a court has more directly held that a person with a learning disability cannot be refused vocational rehabilitative assistance. It rejected the argument that the services sought are not vocational in nature but rather educational since they deal with raising the literary level of the applicant. The court held that the remedial education to be received constitutes "pre-vocational training" within the meaning of s. 5(d) of the Act:

s. 5 A rehabilitative program shall be established to provide

. . .

(d) for the payment of costs of assessment training, pre-vocational training, work adjustment training and personal adjustment training, including books and training materials.

The opportunity to make use of the program is not affected even if the ultimate goal is one which ordinarily is achieved by remedial attention within the educational system.[223] (For further discussion, see Chapter 8 "Education".)

If a person is a ward of a Children's Aid Society or resident of any institution, the Vocational Rehabilitation Services Branch has covered costs above that of residential living expenses if they could be related to raising that person's employment capacity.

Sections 14 and 15 of the Regulations under the Act established a Medical Advisory Board which assists the Director of the Vocational Rehabilitation Services Branch in determining eligibility of applicants for vocational rehabilitation services on the grounds of a physical or mental impairment and for the purpose of reviewing the progress of such cases and the advisability of continuing services to persons involved in a vocational rehabilitation program.

Section 5(e) of the Act provides for a maintenance allowance to an applicant to permit him to derive full benefit from the vocational rehabilitation program. The assessment of maintenance, both entitlement and quantum, will be based on a person's need, and in this regard the Act recognizes the needs of an applicant with a dependent child. "Dependent child" for the purpose of a maintenance allowance is defined as:

a child of a disabled person who is under 16 years of age or being 16 years or more, is in full-time attendance at an educational institution approved by the Director, or is by reason of mental or physical impairment unable to support himself, if . . . the child . . . is wholly supported by the disabled person,

[222]*Re Bruyn and Director of Vocational Rehabilitation Services Branch* (1975), 25 R.F.L. 159 (Ont. Div. Ct.).
[223]*Re Anderson and Director of Vocational Rehabilitation Services Branch* (1977), 15 O.R. (2d) 207 (Div. Ct.).

. . . ordinarily resides in Ontario, has an income of less than $1,300.00 per annum exclusive of support received from the disabled person . . . does not receive an allowance under the Act or under the *National Training Act* (Canada).

It has been held that the Board need educate a person only to the extent that he can become "regularly and substantially" gainfully employed but is not under a duty to fund further education to the person's ultimate potential.[224] In addition, note that while maintenance will be assessed relative to needs, other services under s. 5 which are included in a vocational rehabilitation program will be provided regardless of any assessment of one's needs. For example, tuition fees, artificial limb devices or the purchase of eyeglasses will all be provided as rehabilitation services rather than support services.

Sections 7(a) and (b) of the Act entrust to the Director of the Vocational Rehabilitation Services Branch the power to determine the eligibility of an applicant to receive vocational rehabilitation services and to suspend or cancel such services if the disabled person ceases to be eligible, fails to avail himself of the services authorized by him, is not benefiting from the program, is not making satisfactory progress towards rehabilitation, fails to provide information or fails to comply with any provision of the Act or the Regulations. The Director, in exercising his discretion, is assisted by a Medical Advisory Board.

The National Training Act

Related to the *Vocational Rehabilitation Services Act* is the *National Training Act* which is administered through the federal government's Ministry of Employment and Immigration. The Act comes as a result of an agreement between the federal and provincial governments wherein the federal government agreed to purchase from the provinces training services in order to enhance employment skills and opportunities for individuals. For example, through the Act, a person's tuition for a mechanics' course may be provided without charge as well as a training allowance relating to his family circumstances and living costs. Of specific interest to children is the definition of "adult" in the Act and its unwritten rule of application. "Adult" is defined as a person who is no longer required by law in the province in which he resides to attend school. He must not have attended school on a regular basis for any period of 12 months since he became an adult and the course must be suited to the applicant's needs and increase his earning and employment potential: s. 4. Although the definition and qualifying sections are different under this legislation than under the former statute, it appears that the application of the definition of "adult" continues not to apply to a child who is excused indefinitely from legal attendance by reason of the "early school leaving" policy such as exists in Ontario. Given the legal restrictions on people under 18 to participate in ordinary employment (see Chapter 5), the apparent refusal to make this training program available to those under an "early school leaving" program renders them effectively impotent in their attempt to locate an alternative work training program.

Day Nurseries Act

Day nursery services for dependent children are administered in Ontario

---

[224] *Re Mroszkowski and Director of Vocational Rehabilitation Services Branch* (1978), 20 O.R. (2d) 688 (Div. Ct.). (funded science degree but not subsequent law degree).

through the *Day Nurseries Act* which essentially establishes a licencing and funding structure for either day nurseries or for private home day care. A "day nursery" is defined in s. 1(d) of the Act as follows:

s. 1(d) "day nursery" means a premises that receives more than five children who are not of common parentage, primarily for the purpose of providing temporary care or guidance, or both temporary care and guidance, for a continuous period not exceeding twenty-four hours, where the children are,

> (i) under eighteen years of age in the case of a day nursery for children with a developmental handicap, and
> (ii) under ten years of age in all other cases,

but does not include,

> (iii) part of a public school, separate school, private school or a school for trainable retarded children under the *Education Act*,
> (iv) a place that is used for a program of recreation and that is supervised by a municipal recreation director who holds a certificate issued pursuant to s. 10 of the *Ministry of Culture and Recreation Act*, or
> (v) a children's mental health centre under the *Children's Mental Health Services Act*; [that will be replaced by the *Child and Family Services Act*]

s. 1(e) "developmental handicap" means a condition of mental impairment present or occurring during a person's formative years, that is associated with limitations in adaptive behaviour.

A "private home day care" is defined in s. 1(m) of the Act to mean:

s. 1(m) . . . the temporary care for reward of compensation of five children or less who are under ten years of age where such care is provided in a private residence other than the home of a parent or guardian of any such child for a continuous period not exceeding twenty-four hours;

Apparently, then, whatever the actual developmental stage of the child, a private home day care cannot care for a developmentally handicapped child who is 10 or more years of age.

The present Act has made amendments to the earlier *Day Nurseries Act*, R.S.O. 1970, c. 111 such that "private home day care", while not as regulated as the day nursery in terms of the needs of children, is now under some direction in terms of the safety of the building and the basic medical safety of the children. A private home day care agency now, like the day care nursery, cannot be operated without the authority of a licence issued by a Director under the legislation.

The Regulations under the *Day Nurseries Act* provide for financial assistance under s. 17 to "persons in need" defined under s. 1(e) to mean:

i) a person eligible for benefits under the *Family Benefits Act*,
ii) a person eligible for general assistance under the *General Welfare Assistance Act*, or

iii) a person who by reason of financial hardship, inability to obtain regular employment, lack of the principal family provider, illness, disability or old age, has available daily income, as determined by the Welfare Administrator in accordance with the prescribed Form, that is less than the per diem costs providing day nursery services or private home day care, as the case may be, to his dependent child or dependent children.

Income Tax and Children

Support Payments

Payments made for the support of a dependent child can be deducted from the income of the payor and added to the income of the recipient when certain conditions are met, conditions designed to ensure that any tax advantage is restricted to the dependant's support payments and that for every dollar deducted there is a corrollative dollar added. Amendments to the *Income Tax Act* in the last few years have:

1) expanded the categories of persons who can claim support for dependants as deductible payments in recognition of amendments to provincial domestic legislation, and

2) provided for more flexibility in the kinds of paying arrangements that can qualify as deductible support payments.

Further amendments of relevance to support arrangements may be forthcoming, given the proposals set out in the Federal Budget of February 14, 1984. At present, the Act as amended provides the following:

1) Spouses Living Apart

The payor and the payee, spouses or deemed spouses pursuant to the *Income Tax Act*, must be living apart at the time the payment is made *and* remain living apart throughout the remainder of the calendar year. This means that if the parties separate in January and reconcile and cohabit on December 15th of that year, then although all other conditions may have been satisfied, the payments for support cannot be deducted.

2) Payments Pursuant to Court Order/Written Agreement

The payment for child support must be made pursuant to a written separation agreement or order of a court of competent jurisdiction. Interim orders are included within this condition as well as interim domestic contracts, the purpose of which is to enable the parties to acquire the tax benefits without binding themselves on other issues or the question of "final" support. Revenue Canada considers the date the order is pronounced, not when it is entered, to be the commencement date for when payment has been made in accordance with an order.[225] Payments that are made prior to the order or agreement are not payments which are made pursuant to the order or agreement and are therefore not deductible. Subject to the recent Budget proposal, any order made retroactively will not provide the basis for deductible support payments because the wording of the tax

---

[225]*Brooks v. M.N.R.*, [1977] C.T.C. 2048, 77 D.T.C. 38 (T.R.B.). But see *Rodney v. M.N.R.*, [1975] C.T.C. 2143, 75 D.T.C. 113, 27 R.F.L. 246 (T.R.B.).

legislation points to the requirement of an order, decree or judgment *in existence at the time the payment is made* and throughout the remainder of the year. At the time the payment was made, there was no court determination.[226] The same applies to a written separation agreement that is to take effect at a date earlier than the date of its execution. The fact that the parties so agree will not bring the payments for that previous period of time within the Act.[227] However, under the recent Budget proposal, support payments made prior to the order or agreement in that year or preceding year will be deductible if the order or written agreement provides that the amounts are considered to have been paid and received pursuant to the order or agreement. Note that for unmarried spouses, the "retroactivity" of support payment deductions applies only with respect to orders, not written separation agreements.[228]

3) Specified Sum in Control of Payee Spouse

The payment must be an "allowance" for the maintenance of the child paid to a spouse or a deemed spouse in accordance with the *Income Tax Act*. An "allowance" means a *specified* sum of money which has been determined in advance of payment by the court or by the parties as being the required payment to be made. An allowance further connotes that the full control of the money is in the hands of the recipient, with no accounting by the payee to the payor with respect to the use of the money.[229] A specified sum of money as child support that is subject to automatic adjustment to account for cost of living increases will qualify even though the amounts payable are not capable of being specified at all relevant times.[230] Using this approach, it would appear that a provision for an annual automatic adjustment representing ordinary increases for camp or school fees would qualify, if all of the other conditions are met.

4) Payments to Third Parties

Amendments to the *Income Tax Act* in 1974 allowed payments made to a third party pursuant to an order or agreement made after May 6, 1974 for the benefit of the child, to qualify as deductible payments and to be included in the income of the custodial spouse. An order or agreement may provide that payments be made payable to a trustee, grandparent or into court, but the custodial spouse will be deemed to have received those payments and must therefore include them in his or her income. The fact that the payments are made to a third party does not in any way alleviate the requirement that

---

[226]*Bentley v. M.N.R.* (1954), 11 Tax A.B.C. 413; *Hobbs v. M.N.R.,* [1970] Tax A.B.C. 1187.

[227]*Milburn v. M.N.R.,* [1979] C.T.C. 2007 (T.R.B.).

[228]See Canadian Tax Reports, Special Report, April 25, 1984, No. 632, Extra Edition "Draft Income Tax Amendments Plus Technical Notes" at p. 17 and discussion of clause 15, notes on proposed amendments to s. 56.1 of the *Income Tax Act* and in particular the new s. 56.1(3).

[229]*R. v. Pascoe,* 63 D.L.R. (3d) 764 [1976] 1 F.C. 372, [1975] C.T.C. 656, 30 R.F.L. 1 (C.A.).

[230]See Revenue Canada Interpretation Bulletin IT 118R, August 30, 1976, para. 7.

the payments constitute an allowance as defined above.[231] The element of control or unfettered discretion by the recipient or delegate recipient is, however, still required subject to the recent Budget proposals discussed below. Consider three different ways of paying $1,500 per month in support:

i)   The husband agrees to pay to the wife the monthly sum of $1,500 and with her consent, $500 of this amount shall be paid directly to the private school where the children shall attend. The wife may at any time change this arrangement and require that the amount of $500 be paid to her directly.

ii) The husband agrees to pay John Doe, maternal grandfather, the monthly sum of $1,000 for the support of the children and with the consent of the wife, shall pay the additional monthly sum of $500 directly to the private school where the children shall attend. The wife may at any time change this arrangement and request that the $500 payable to the private school, be paid to her directly.

iii) A husband agrees to pay as periodic child support the monthly amount of $1,500, of which $500 shall be paid directly to the private school where the child shall attend.

Compare the examples for their tax implications:

(a) The payment to the private school would qualify as a deductible payment in examples (i) and (ii) as the wording of both is in accordance with the definition of an allowance;

(b) The payment for the support of the child made payable to the grandfather in example (ii) would qualify as a deductible payment because Revenue Canada considers that payments made to a third party (who is not a creditor) such as a trustee, the court or a relative, give that third party discretion which is deemed to be delegated by the recipient spouse. This discretion allows the third party to do with the money as he or she pleases and the custodial parent's consent or concurrence is not necessary.[232]

(c) The provision in (iii) will not qualify. The payment directly to a third party, even though a fixed pre-arranged amount, is not an allowance to the spouse because the recipient, or as in example (ii), the delegated recipient, has no discretion as to the use of the funds.[233]

The proposed amendments set out in the February 14, 1984 Budget will eliminate the need for such distinctions. The proposed amendments will permit any payment to any third party for any expenses related to the support of the child that otherwise would qualify as tax deductible, were it not for the fact of it being paid to a third party, as long as the agreement or order of the court stipulates that the relevant provisions of the *Income Tax Act* (ss. 60.1(1) or 56.1(2)) apply to such payments.

---

[231]*R. v. Bryce* (1982), 132 D.L.R. (3d) 635, [1982] C.T.C. 133, 82 D.T.C. 6126, 26 R.F.L. (2d) 457 (Fed. C.A.); leave to appeal to S.C.C. granted 42 N.R. 146 *n*.

[232]*Supra,* note 230, para. 14.

[233]See IT-188R, para. 14, Aug. 30, 1976, "Alimony and Maintenance."

5) Periodic Payments

The payment of support for a child must be on a periodic basis. Revenue Canada interprets this to mean that the payments should be made periodically, at fixed times not variable periods, and pursuant to some arranged obligation rather than as the result of the changing discretion of one or more individuals. Payments need not be weekly or monthly to qualify as ''periodic'' and an annual payment required by the court or by agreement is periodic if a series of such payments is to be made. It is important to ensure that the wording of the document distinguishes the payment of money as support and that of settlement installments. Use the words: ''as periodic support for the child, the monthly amount of $500, payable the 1st of each month commencing with the 1st day of January, 1984.'' This conveys the notion of an extended period and very clearly enunciates that there are regular payments for the one purpose of support.[234] When periodic payments are made for part of a year (for example, they are suspended during the month when the child is with the payor), they still qualify as deductible payments.[235] If a lump sum payment is made in place of several periodic payments to be made, but not yet due and owing under the document, that payment is not deductible because it is not considered to be periodic. A lump sum payment, however, paid in the taxation year, may be deducted if it is in satisfaction of periodic amounts due and owing for that year, but yet to be paid.[236] To confuse matters somewhat, it has been held that when a lump sum amount for child support is payable in installments, each of the payments will be deductible so long as it is clear that the payments are for support.[237] If, for example, the terms require interest to be payable on the unpaid amount, this would militate against deductibility.[238]

6) Outside Jurisdiction

In any agreement that involves one of the parties residing outside Canada, be very sure to consider the domestic tax laws of that jurisdiction. As one example, payments in many American states for child support are not deductible. Therefore, if the payor resides in New York state, there is no tax advantage to him or her; nevertheless, a Canadian recipient receiving these after-tax dollars may have to include the funds as income for his or her tax purposes. If the payor is a Canadian resident and the payee lives elsewhere, payments made to the recipient may be subject to withholding tax whether or not the recipient would be required to include such payments as income, unless such withholding tax is eliminated by treaty. Withholding tax will apply if the monies that the recipient receives would have been income in his or her hands in Canada, in order to achieve some balancing of the effect of

---

[234]*R. v. Pascoe, supra,* note 229.
[235]*Supra,* note 230, para. 12.
[236]*Supra,* note 230, para. 10.
[237]*Dorion v. M.N.R.,* 80 D.T.C. 1815; rvd 81 D.T.C. 5111 (Fed. Ct.).
[238]*Gagnon-Chartrand v. M.N.R.* (1983), 83 D.T.C. 77 (T.R.B.).

the deductibility of the payments by the payor spouse. A treaty ratified by the United States and Canada on August 15, 1984 takes effect for payments made on or after October 1, 1984. According to this treaty, maintenance or alimony payments as between separated spouses living in Canada and the United States are no longer subject to withholding taxes.[239]

7) Illegitimacy/Legitimacy

For the purpose of deductibility of child support payments, there is no distinction drawn between "illegitimate" and "legitimate" children, whether or not the parents cohabited,[240] in respect of orders or agreements made after December 11, 1979. This abolition of any distinction will also apply to orders or agreements rendered before December 12, 1979 if the parties agree, in writing, to make the payments deductible by the payor and added to the income of the recipient. The agreement will be applicable to the year in which it was made and thereafter.

8) Enforcement Costs

Note that the portion of a taxpayer's legal fees related to the enforcement or collection of child support when the entitlement has already been established through a valid separation agreement or order of the court, is deductible. It matters not through what legal means the child support order or agreement is enforced, be it in the Provincial Court under provincial enforcing legislation or through the various alternative remedies by writs of execution or in the superior courts. Revenue Canada will only permit a deduction for the enforcement or collection of child support, not the establishing of entitlement or quantum.[241]

9) Death of Payee Spouse

Finally, note that according to Revenue Canada's Bulletin IT-118R, August 30, 1976, payments made by the payor spouse will not be deductible from his or her taxable income after the death of the recipient spouse, even if the payments are made to the children or to the estate of the deceased spouse. Furthermore, if the payor spouse is entitled to such deductions, he will be precluded from making any flat rate dependent deductions which are restricted to "persons who wholly support a dependent person or a child." If a husband provides maintenance for the benefit of his children to the recipient spouse, then it is the recipient spouse who is said to "wholly support" the dependent persons and therefore the recipient spouse will benefit from the deduction: s. 109, *Income Tax Act*. However, in the instance where the recipient spouse has died and the agreement provides for

---

[239]The former treaty provided for a 15% withholding tax.

[240]The *Income Tax Act*, ss. 60 (c. 1), and 56(1) (c. 1).

[241]*Burgess v. M.N.R.*, [1979] C.T.C. 2374; rvd 125 D.L.R. (3d) 477, [1981] C.T.C. 258 (*sub nom. R. v. Burgess*), 81 D.T.C. 5192 (Fed. T.D.).

continued payments for the children, the payor spouse, while no longer able to deduct the payments from his taxable income, will then be able to avail himself of the s. 109 deduction.

Basic Dependent Deduction

Section 109(1)(d) permits a deduction from the income of a person upon whom a child is "wholly dependent . . . for support." The child need not be in the legal custody of the person. It is sufficient that the child is in the control of the supporting taxpayer in law or fact. The deduction is available for a child under the age of 21 years or 21 or more years if the child is in full-time attendance at a school or university, or if the child is mentally or physically infirm meaning that the child by reason of the infirmity is prevented from being gainfully employed during a considerable period of time. The "school" need not be an academically-oriented program and may include courses in commercial, technical, artistic or agricultural subjects. The amount of the deduction is different depending on whether the child is under or over 16 years of age. This amount varies from year to year in accordance with s. 117.1 which provides for an annual adjustment if indicated by upward changes in the Consumer Price Index.

If the taxpayer is not able to claim a marital spouse deduction, s. 109(1)(b) permits a deduction from the income of a person upon whom a child is "wholly dependent . . . for support," which is greater in amount than the deduction provided by s. (1)(d). This deduction is referred to as the "equivalent to married deduction". Unlike the requirements of s. (1)(d), the age of the child is irrelevant. The child must be wholly dependent upon the taxpayer and as is the case in all of the available deductions for children, the income of the child may be so great as to disqualify the taxpayer from taking advantage of the deduction.

There are certain features to the deduction format that can be summarized as follows:

1) Occasional payments made by a parent who is not housing his children have been held not to make those children "wholly dependent". For example, children in a foster home for whom the taxpayer makes occasional payments are not "wholly dependent".[242] "Partial support" is not enough; the support must be "complete in itself" to qualify the person as "wholly dependent".[243] A recent Interpretation Bulletin (IT-101R, September 26, 1984) appears to relax this rule by suggesting in paragraph 7 that if costs such as clothing, comforts or medical and hospital premiums are paid by the taxpayer and the child was supported by the taxpayer when out of the hospital, then the deduction would be available. Accordingly, it may now be that a parent who pays for his child's clothing and other comforts through a payment on a regular basis to an institution, mental health centre, Children's Aid Society or directly to the court, may be entitled to a deduction although to date this has not been the case.

2) The taxpayer may not claim both the deduction for a child and for maintenance payments. It appears that Revenue Canada will permit

---

[242]*Re Smoke and M.N.R.*, [1969] Tax A.B.C. 614.
[243]*Robertson v. M.N.R.*, [1968] Tax A.B.C. 207.

separated parents to arrange their affairs as they see fit so that while no duplication of claims is allowed, one parent will get the deductions available under s. (1)(b) or (d) and the other parent will claim the maintenance payments as deductions. In certain joint custody arrangements there is an exception to this rule and both parents may claim the same child for the deduction under s. 109(1)(d) but only if:

(i)   each parent has custody of the child during the year;

(ii) neither parent is claiming any support payments as a deduction;

(iii) neither parent is entitled to the "married equivalent deduction" under s. 109(1)(b). Only one parent can claim the "married equivalent deduction" in respect of the same child and if neither claims it, then it will be assumed that they could not agree who should claim it and therefore both have lost their entitlement to do so. If one parent re-marries during the year, then the other parent would be entitled to the deduction and apparently must take it. That is, the parent cannot forego the "married equivalent deduction" in order to continue the joint claim under s. 109(1)(d), as set out above. (Ref.: IT-191R, September 26, 1984, para. 36). The "married equivalent deduction" is not divisible.

3) For the purpose of the deductions under s. 109(1)(d), s. 109(3) stipulates that an "illegitimate child" is assumed to be wholly dependent on the mother and any other child wholly dependent upon the father unless the contrary is established. In spite of these outdated assumptions, especially in light of provincial legislation abolishing the status and repercussions of "illegitimacy", the Department appears to be ready to accept any arrangement between a mother and father provided that the child otherwise qualifies. The fact that the parents are unmarried does not interfere with (1) the availability of the "married equivalent deduction", for example, in respect of one of two children cared for by the custodial parent, (2) the availability of the "wholly dependent child" deduction in respect of another child, and (3) the availability of deductible maintenance payments by the non-custodial parent in exactly the same fashion as if the parents were married.

4) Finally, note that the expression "during the year", which is used throughout the section providing for such deductions, means "at any time in the year" rather than "throughout the whole of the year". For example, a dependent child reaching the age of 21 in a taxation year is under 21 years of age "during that year". (Ref.: IT-191R, September 26, 1984, para. 2)

Child Care Expenses

For 1983 and subsequent years, the maximum deduction for child care expenses is $8,000 at $2,000 for each eligible child with the total deduction not to exceed two-thirds of the taxpayer's earned income: s. 63, *Income Tax Act*. Child care expenses will normally be deductible only by the parent or supporting individual who has the lower earned income, regardless of whether the parents are married, their sexes or which of them actually paid the expense. This represents a radical departure from the former provisions of the Act which discriminated against male taxpayers in married and unmarried circumstances.

If the parents separate, different rules apply. If they separate for 90 days or more during the calendar year, each parent can claim his or her expenses provided they were incurred to enable that parent to earn income. Note however that if the parents separate for 90 or more days during the calendar year but reside together within the year or 60 days after year end, the higher income parent can claim expenses incurred to earn income for the period of the separation up to a maximum of $60 per child per week ($250 per week maximum) and with the maximum limits set out above, while the lower income parent can only claim the amount that his claim exceeds the other's claim, if any.

Educational Expenses

Student as Taxpayer

(i) Resident and Schooling in Canada

Section 60(f) allows a taxpayer enrolled at an educational institution in Canada and resident in Canada to deduct the cost of his fees from his taxable income. "Education institution" includes:

1) a university, college or other educational institution providing courses at a post-secondary school level;

2) a school operated by or on behalf of Her Majesty in Right of Canada or a province, a municipality in Canada or a municipal or public body performing a function of government in Canada;

3) a high school or secondary school providing courses towards a secondary school certificate or diploma that is a requirement for entrance to a college or university;

4) an institution certified by the Minister of Employment and Immigration to be an educational institution providing courses, other than courses designed for university credit, that furnish a person with skills for, or improve a person's skills in, an occupation.

(ii) Resident in Canada, Schooling Outside of Canada

If the taxpayer attends an educational institution outside of Canada and is resident in Canada, it is clear from s. 60(e) that such an educational institution is restricted to a university providing a course leading to a "degree," interpreted by the Department as a degree not lower than a Bachelor or an equivalent level. Under s. 60(g), if the taxpayer resides in Canada during the whole of the year near the boundary between Canada and the United States and attends an educational institution in the United States, "educational institution" would appear to include a university, college or other educational institution providing courses at the post-secondary school level. Note that expenses of a student who is resident in Canada and engaged in a correspondence course with an American "educational institution" would not qualify for deduction because s. 60(g) requires that the student commute to the U.S. institution before he will qualify.

(iii) Resident and Schooling Outside of Canada

If the taxpayer is attending school outside Canada and is resident outside

Canada, the deduction for tuition fees from income taxed in Canada is allowed only for full-time attendance of not less than 13 consecutive weeks. However, a deduction for tuition fees will not be denied simply because a student drops out after one term, or one year, or because a particular academic term falls short of being the full 13 weeks because of vacation break. Note that in respect of students residing and attending school outside of Canada, the Act requires full-time attendance if the student seeks a deduction for the educational expenses. This requirement does not apply in respect of students resident in Canada or resident outside of Canada but attending school in Canada. Consequently, fees paid for correspondence, night, summer or part-time courses will not qualify.

(iv) General Rules

If a student receives free tuition as an award, fees have not been "paid to the educational institution" and therefore no deduction is allowed, but neither is the value of the free tuition included in the student's income. Note that tuition paid out of academic awards such as prizes or fellowships may constitute "tuition paid" and the deduction may be available. For an award to constitute "tuition paid," it must fall within the wording of the relevant sections, namely, "tuition paid to the educational institution" or "tuition paid to the university." An award by the educational institution directly to the student will not satisfy the wording of "tuition paid to the university." An award out of the university's trust funds or income from trust funds may satisfy their requirements. If the tuition deduction is available, the student must include any such award in his income, subject to the annual exemption of $500 which may be deducted from the total of all such awards received in a year: s. 56(1)(n).

The Act does not define what constitutes allowable tuition fees but a department circular notes that whether or not they are set out separately, they will include tuition or academic fees, fees for admissions, fees for library and laboratory facilities, fees for examinations, any costs for a graduation certificate and costs for the re-reading of an examination paper to achieve a higher grade. Student membership fees that are specifically related to an academic program and its administration are also allowable but fees for social or athletic activities (even if compulsory), medical care, board and lodging and supplies or special equipment such as slide rule or microscope, are not deductible. However, if the cost of the books is included in the fees paid for a correspondence course, that cost would be included.

A student who makes a claim for tuition fees paid to an educational institution must attach to his income tax return a certificate provided by the educational institution to support his claim. A simple receipt may not be sufficient to support such a claim.

Reference can be made to Interpretation Bulletin IT-82R3 "Tuition Fees", February 20, 1984, which can be obtained from Revenue Canada.

Parent of Student as Taxpayer

The deduction for tuition fees under s. 60 of the Act can be claimed only by the student and not by a parent who actually paid the fees. The only full exception to this is when an employer pays tuition fees for an employee which are deductible as a business expense to the employer. Generally, the student would not be obliged to include this payment in his taxable income if the purpose of the course was for the benefit of the employer. A partial exception to this rule occurs under s. 110(1)(h) which allows a taxpayer who is a "supporting individual" to deduct the amount by which the student's education deduction exceeds that student's income for the year. For example, if a student's taxable income is $300 before deducting his education expense of $400, the student could claim a deduction of $300, while the excess $100.00 could be claimed by the "supporting individual". Section 110(9)(c) defines a "supporting individual" as "one who was during the year the student's spouse, parent, grandparent, brother or sister". This section provides that no more than one relative of the student may be a supporting individual for the year, and deems certain individuals to be the supporting individual in certain circumstances. Reference can be made to Interpretation Bulletin IT-224R3, "Education Deduction", May 22, 1984, which can be obtained from Revenue Canada.

Parents of students may also wish to make use of Registered Educational Savings Plans pursuant to s. 146.1. Under this section, any individual may enter into a contract referred to as an "Educational Savings Plan" with a promotor under which the individual or "subscriber" deposits funds in trust to accumulate income to be used for the post-secondary education of a named beneficiary. The promotor must have the plan registered with the Minister and having done so, neither the subscriber, the trust, nor the beneficiary is taxed on the income accumulating within the trust although funds deposited by the subscriber are not deductible. At the maturity date of the contract, the subscriber receives back all the amounts deposited less an enrollment fee. The income accumulates without tax consequences and is paid out to the student beneficiary or on his behalf as educational assistance payments, at which time the payments are included in the student's income for tax purposes. The advantage of the program is that it allows this accumulating income to escape immediate tax consequences and to be subject generally to a lower rate of tax in the hands of the student on payment out. The disadvantage is that the interest gained on the principal over the years will not be paid out to the student if the subject child decides not to attend a qualifying post-secondary institution. Instead, the interest will be paid out to other students. (The principal, of course, will then be taxable in the hands of the subscriber.) Included in Appendix B is an opinion report from a Toronto firm of chartered accountants which discusses in detail the mechanism of the Registered Education Savings Plan, including different varieties of such plans and an alternative to the plan through the creation of a family trust.

Family Allowance

Pursuant to s. 56(5) of the *Income Tax Act*, family allowance payments under the *Family Allowances Act* or any similar provincial allowance are included in income. Section 56(7) of the *Income Tax Act* defines the taxpayer who must include their family allowance as income as either:

1) a taxpayer who, in computing his income for the taxation year, has deducted an amount under s. 109 in respect of the child for whom a family allowance has been paid in the taxation year, or, where this is not applicable

2) a taxpayer to whom family allowance has been paid in respect of the child.

Accordingly, a father must include in his income any family allowance received in respect of his child if he has made a dependent deduction for that child for that year, even if it is the mother who has received and used the family allowance payment. However, if the child has not been claimed for the purpose of the s. 109 dependent deduction, then the parent who actually receives the family allowance payment must include the monies as income. Under the Regulations to the *Family Allowances Act*, the parent who is deemed to receive the payment is the female parent unless there is no female parent or unless the parents are separated and the male parent has *de facto* custody of the child. Thus, even if there is no separation agreement or court order, the separated father with whom the children are living is deemed to receive the family allowance payments and, to extend the example, unless the mother was claiming the children for the purpose of a s. 109 dependent deduction, it would be the father who would be obliged to include the payment as taxable income.[244]

In circumstances in which more than one taxpayer has claimed a personal deduction for a child under s. 109 of the *Income Tax Act*, as in the first year of separation or in the case of a joint custody arrangement, as described above, s. 56(8) of the *Income Tax Act* requires each tax-paying parent to include, in computing his income, a portion of the family allowance paid in respect of a child, calculated as follows:

$$\frac{\text{The personal deduction under s. 109 claimed by the taxpayer for the child}}{\text{The aggregate of the personal deductions under s. 109 claimed by each taxpayer for the child}} \times \begin{array}{l}\text{Total family or}\\\text{similar allowance}\\\text{paid in the year in}\\\text{respect of a child.}\end{array}$$

If the taxpayer lives in a province in which a deduction for the child in respect of whom an allowance is paid is not allowed, the allowance payments will not be included as income: s. 56(6). Quebec is the only province to which this subsection applies. The Quebec legislation does not permit any deduction for a dependent child who has not reached 16 years of age.

Note that the *Family Allowances Act* provides for payments in respect of a child who is wholly maintained by a department or agency of the government of Canada or by an agency or institution authorized under the law of the province to care, protect and have custody of children who are under 18 years of age: s. 9. These payments, referred to as "special allowances," are exempt from federal taxation: s. 12. Health and Welfare Canada will stop family allowance payments once the special allowances program is in effect. Where a parent simply endorses payment over to an organization, such as a Children's Aid Society or an individual, the family allowance payments may continue to be taxable income to

---

[244]See s. 9 of the Regulations to the *Family Allowance Act, 1973* in the Consolidated Regulations of Canada 1978, Vol. VI, c. 642.

the parent unless the agency has legal custody and requests a special allowance on its own behalf, in which case the parent will no longer be "wholly or substantially" maintaining the child.[245]

The definitions of "parent", "child" and "family" under the *Family Allowances Act* require that the child be "wholly or substantially maintained" by the parents: s. 2(1), *Family Allowances Act*. "Wholly or substantially maintained" is more precisely defined in s. 3(b) of the Regulations: C.R.C. 1978, vol. VI, c. 642, s. 3(b) (hereinafter cited as Regs.). "Wholly maintained" for an unmarried child (that is, a person resident in Canada and under the age of 18 years) means the provision of care, maintenance, education, training and advancement of the child who has no taxable income for that year or an amount less than a "self-supporting amount": Regs., s. 3(b). "Substantially maintained" for an unmarried child applies the same definition with the qualification that the supporting individual has contributed more than any other person to the child and no agency or institution has been awarded custody of the child: Regs., s. 3(d)(ii). A "married child" may still be eligible for family allowance depending on the income of his or her spouse: Regs., s. 3(c), (e). This means that children whose income exceeds the "self-supporting amount" as defined by the Regulations are ineligible for family allowances, and if ineligible for family allowance payments, are deemed to be ineligible for the child tax credit discussed below.[246]

Child Tax Credit   The child tax credit is a refundable credit administered through the federal income tax system. To obtain the credit each year, the claimant must file an income tax return together with a child credit schedule. The credit will be reduced by any balance of income tax, interest or penalty owing by the claimant.

The child tax credit is claimed by the parent entitled to receive the family allowance payment, not the parent who must report the family allowance payment as income for the purpose of the *Income Tax Act*. As noted above, the parent entitled to the family allowance payment is the female parent unless she does not have custody of the child. If the spouses are living separate and apart on December 31, it is not necessary to calculate entitlement to the child tax credit using the combined income of the parents. It will be calculated based on the income of the one parent entitled to the family allowance payment. For 1983 and subsequent years, there is no longer a distinction between married and unmarried parents. The income of unmarried parents as well as a parent and any other person who claims a personal deduction for the child must, like married persons, be combined in order to calculate entitlement to the child tax credit.[247]

---

[245]*Ibid.*, s. 3(d)(iv).

[246]*Ibid.*, s. 2(1) which defines "self-supporting amount" with respect to the income of a child in a taxation year as an amount which when multiplied by the number of months remaining in the year commencing with the month in which the child first receives that amount, is equal to the aggregate of:

(a) $150.00;

(b) the amount specified in s. 109(1)(c) of the Act as adjusted by s. 117.1 of the Act, and

(c) the amount specified in s. 110(1)(d) of the Act.

*For the child tax credit scheme see the Regulations under the *Income Tax Act*.

Appendix A: Drafting Provisions for Support and Inflation

by

Steven Wilson, B.A., LL.B., Mathews, Disdale and Clark, Toronto, 1984.

Cost of living clauses are designed automatically to link a payment determined at a given time with the increase in prices which may occur subsequent to that time: as prices rise, the payment automatically increases without further negotiation or resort to third-party assistance. The introduction of a cost of living clause may have a dramatic effect. In the example below, a payment of $500 per month in 1974 is fully tied to the rate of inflation, in this case, as measured by the Consumer Price Index. More precisely, it is tied to the Consumer Price Index, All-items (Not Seasonally Adjusted), 1981 equal to 100. By 1984, the $500 monthly payment has increased to $1,204.41.

CONSUMER PRICE INDEX FOR CANADA, ALL-ITEMS (NOT SEASONALLY ADJUSTED), 1981=100

	January CPI	Monthly Payment	Monthly Payment Adjusted by Jan. CPI	Difference in Monthly Payment
1974	49.9	$500.00	$500.00	
1975	55.9	500.00	560.12	$ 60.12
1976	61.2	500.00	613.23	113.23
1977	65.0	500.00	651.30	151.30
1978	70.8	500.00	709.42	209.42
1979	77.1	500.00	772.55	272.55
1980	84.5	500.00	846.69	346.69
1981	94.6	500.00	947.90	447.90
1982	105.4	500.00	1,056.11	556.11
1983	114.1	500.00	1,143.29	643.29
1984	120.2	500.00	1,204.41	704.41

Source: Steven Wilson, B.A., LL.B., Mathews, Dinsdale and Clark, Toronto, 1984.

A first consideration in the design of a cost of living clause is how to measure the rate of inflation. By far, the most widely used measurements of inflation in cost of living clauses is the Consumer Price Index, an index published by Statistics Canada to measure the change in consumer retail prices of a basket of goods and services. The components of this basket are based on data from family expenditure surveys and are adjusted every few years to reflect any change in consumer patterns.

Because the basket of goods and services is fixed for a few years, the use of the Consumer Price Index may show increases in prices of goods and services even though consumers generally no longer purchase some of these goods and services. A simple example will illustrate this point. If the price of butter rises sharply and the price of margarine does not, then consumers may switch from butter to margarine. The Consumer Price Index will register the increase in the price of butter (if butter is in the basket) even though consumers may not be purchasing butter. In labour disputes, cost of living clauses have been traditionally used. Paul Weiler, a respected arbitrator and the former Chairman of the British Columbia Labour Relations Board, has advocated using the GNE Price Deflation for Personal Consumption Expenditures as a "better measure of the actual impact on consumers of rising prices." (See *In the Matter of the Hospital Labour Disputes Arbitrations Act between 65 Participating Hospitals and CUPE*, unreported June 1st, 1981, Ont., Arbitration Chairman — Paul Weiler).

Whichever index is used, all parties drafting the clause should carefully define what index it is that they are applying. If the Consumer Price Index is to be used, then the parties should identify:

1) whether it is the Consumer Price Index for Canada or some city within Canada;
2) whether the data represents all items or a component of the index, example shelter, clothing and food;
3) whether the data are seasonally adjusted or not; and
4) what is the base period, *i.e.* 1981 equal to 100.

In drafting agreements in respect of domestic relations, cost of living clauses are constructed to provide the receiving spouse with some measure of protection against the declining value of the dollar. A threshold issue which the parties must resolve is the extent, if any, to which the receiving spouse is to be insulated from inflation. The paying spouse might well submit that there is no inherent right for anyone to keep abreast with inflation; if everyone were able to be insulated from inflation, then inflation would not be a problem. But inflation is a problem; everyone is not able to be insulated from inflation. Accordingly, the paying spouse might alternatively argue that the receiving spouse, like the paying spouse, should have no *automatic* right to "keep up to" inflation. Accordingly, the drafting of the clause would provide full protection against inflation only when the paying spouse's income increases faster than inflation and, by providing an increase less than inflation and equal to the increase in the paying spouse's income when the paying spouse's income does not increase as fast as inflation. This might otherwise be expressed as the paying spouse automatically provides an increase equal to the increase in the paying spouse's income up to but not in excess of the rate of inflation. This approach roughly marries two different determinants of a fair and equitable settlement, namely:

1) the ability of the paying spouse to pay, and
2) the right of the recipient spouse to continue to purchase the same bundle of goods and services as was determined at the outset.

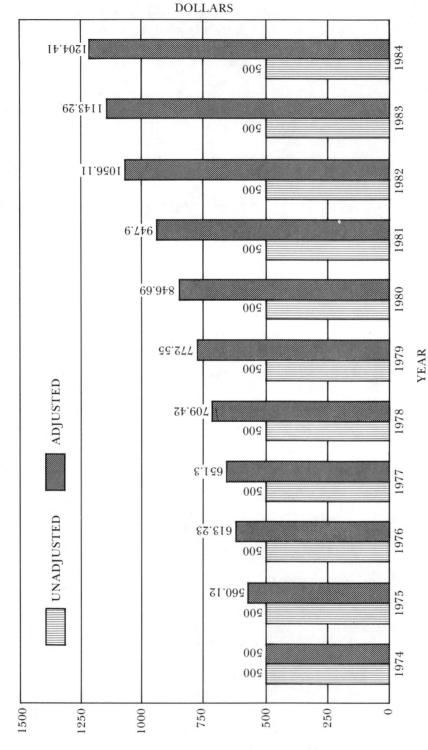

SUPPORT AND INFLATION

DOLLARS

UNADJUSTED   ADJUSTED

YEAR

Source: Steven Wilson, B.A., LL.B.; Mathews, Dinsdale and Clark, Toronto, 1984.

Appendix B

Compiled by Mintz & Partners, Chartered Accountants, Toronto

VOL. 2, *Mintz Matters* NO. II
APRIL, 1984

1. FINANCING YOUR CHILD'S EDUCATION

Most parents dream about their children obtaining some form of post-secondary school education, whether it be college or university. Dreams, by their nature, do not focus on cold, hard realities such as the rising cost of education, especially if your child will be attending school out of town.

Some take it for granted that their children will be able to obtain government student loans while others don't worry about the problem until high school graduation day. Government assistance cannot be counted on to finance the entire education cost and those who do not plan for the cost can find it a financial drain. In addition you may be passing up an opportunity for significant tax savings.

Registered Education Savings Plans ("RESP")

A RESP is a savings vehicle that allows a parent to contribute to a trust in which his children are the beneficiaries. Although the contributor does not get a tax deduction for his contributions, the income earned by the funds while in the trust will not be taxed until the money is withdrawn.

When the child is ready to attend college or university, the contributor will receive his original capital tax-free. The plan will then pay to the child the income earned by the plan on behalf of that child. The funds will be received by the child over the years he or she attends university and will be taxable in the year of receipt. Depending on the amount, the number of years over which it is paid, tuition fees etc, the child may pay no or very little tax on the funds. Thus the RESP can be used for income splitting with children.

Types of RESPs

There are three types of RESPs. The two older plans, University Scholarships of Canada ("USC") and the Canadian Scholarship Trust Foundation ("CST"), have operated for many years. The third plan, called the DSA Education Trust ("DSA"), is a recent addition.

The USC and CST plans require a separate plan for each child and the child cannot be older than 12 years when the plan is established. After the child reaches age 12, the beneficiary of the plan may not be changed. Payments must go to the named beneficiary or be forefeited.

The required contributions to these plans are fixed, based on the child's age on enrollment. The cost under one plan is about $9 per month if the child is enrolled at birth. If your child goes to university these plans will pay the child his proportionate share of the accumulated income. However, if he or she does not go to university or drops out, all or some portion of the accumulated income will be lost and paid to other students. Because of this forefeiture aspect there will be a larger pool of children funding the plan than receiving benefits, so that those who do qualify will receive an increased return. The low required contributions make these plans affordable and act to some extent as a means of forced savings.

The major disadvantage of these plans is that given the nominal contributions, there may not be sufficient accumulated income to pay the full cost of education, especially for a student attending college or university out of town. Moreover, the forfeiture aspect should also be a concern.

The DSA plan allows children to be enrolled at any age and allows the beneficiaries to be changed at any time. Each plan may have more than one beneficiary. The maximum contribution is $25,000 per beneficiary/contributor. Each parent could contribute $25,000 in respect of the same child. The original capital contribution may be withdrawn at any time without jeopardizing the plan. This allows one to invest the particular amount of capital necessary to produce a certain income payout.

The DSA plan is self-administered so contributors have full say in the making of investment decisions. The plan can invest in bonds (except Canada Savings Bonds), stock options and gold certificates. Commodity trading is prohibited.

As soon as the student is enrolled at college or university, he or she may be paid all or part of the plan's income. The USC and the CST plans do not permit the student to receive income until the second year of university. The first year is to be financed from the contributor's accumulated capital contributions.

The DSA plan may be used as a means of income splitting with children. In this regard it is superior to the USC and the CST plans as it allows for the capital amount to be varied, has low risk of forfeiture, and allows capital of significant size to be employed.

With the DSA plan, the tax bite to the student can be minimized by spreading the receipts from the plan over the years that the student is attending post-secondary school. Based on today's tax rates and exemptions, the student could earn about $6,000 annually from the RESP and pay no tax assuming he had no other source of income. Thus the use of the RESP diverts income from parent to child saving tax overall. The child will also have income against which his tuition fees can be deducted (parents cannot deduct for their children). Effectively, this makes the education costs tax-deductible.

If the student has other sources of income, he or she may end up paying some tax on the $6,000 of income from the RESP. However, it should be much less than the tax a parent would pay on receiving investment income and then giving the funds to the child. A top rate taxpayer would have to earn $12,000 of interest income in order to gift $6,000 to a child.

The Alternative — A Family Trust

A family trust is one of the best ways to split income with a minor child. A parent would make an interest-free loan to the trust, the trust would invest in income-producing assets and the income would be paid or allocated annually to children who are the beneficiaries. In this way, income that would normally be taxable to the parent will be taxed in the hands of the children annually. If you are a top rate taxpayer, and the child has no other income, the tax savings could be as much as 50% of the income paid to the child.

Instead of the child receiving all the income at the end of say four years, as is the case with the DSA plan, the family trust would allow the income to be taxable annually from inception of the trust. This may avoid placing the child in a taxable position during university as may occur with the DSA plan. Since the period of time over which income is taxable is far greater, larger amounts of funds can be loaned to the trust to generate income and the income splitting ability is greater accordingly.

Income from a RESP is taxed simply as ''other'' income. The $1,000 investment income deduction is not applicable, taxable dividends earned in the plan will not carry a dividend tax credit, and capital gains will effectively be fully taxed. This mitigates the advantages of having a self-administered fund. A family trust is not treated in this way. Rather, investment income will retain its character so that the beneficiary will be able to benefit from the above tax preferences.

The DSA plan has an advantage over a family trust in that no tax is payable on the income earned in the plan until it is paid to the beneficiary. Thus, where the child has other income, or the annual income earned in the plan is very large (say $20,000 per year or more), the tax deferral aspects of the RESP may be attractive.

Tuition fees paid for private schooling are deductible if the child is enrolled in secondary school. The RESP cannot be used to fund these tuition costs. A family trust, on the other hand, may be used to fund high school tuition fees effectively making such fees deductible. In some cases, private school tuition fees can exceed the cost of university education!

Conclusion

RESPs may be attractive in certain situations. For many families the DSA plan and a family trust will not be feasible because of the large initial capital required. Compared to a family trust, a RESP is certainly cheaper to establish and administer. However, persons with the capital and the inclination to consider a RESP such as the DSA plan should also give consideration to the alternative of establishing a family trust. When used in appropriate situations, a family trust can more than pay for its set-up costs within the first year of implementation. Overall the family trust may well be superior to the RESP, but this must be evaluated on a case by case basis.

Chapter 4: Readings:

Alberta Institute of Law Research and Reform, *Status of Children* (Edmonton: University of Alberta, 1976).

British Columbia Royal Commission on Family and Children's Law, No. 5, Part 2: "The Status of Children Born to Unmarried Parents"; Part 4: "Special Needs of Special Children" (Victoria: Queen's Printer, 1975).

Cassety, J. (ed.), *The Parental Child Support Obligation: Research, Practice and Social Policy* (Lexington, Mass.: Lexington Books, 1983).

Committee on One-Parent Families (Chairperson: Morris Finer), *Report* (Secretary of State for Social Services) (London: H.M.S.O., 1974).

Eden, P., "How Inflation Flaunts the Court's Orders" (1979), 1 *Fam. Adv.* 2.

Gamble, H. and Weeks, P., "Rights of a Child to Take Independent Action for Maintenance Under the *Family Law Act, 1975*", (Fall, 1982), 56 *A.L.J.* 68.

Holland, W.H., *Unmarried Couples: Legal Aspects of Cohabitation* (Toronto: Carswell, 1982).

Krause, H.D., *Child Support in America* (Charlottesville, Virginia: Michie Co., 1981).

McKee, E., *Too Little, Too Late: Services for Teenage Parents* (New York: Ford Foundation, 1982).

National Conference of State Legislatures, *In the Best Interests of the Child: A Guide to State Child Support and Paternity Laws* (available National Conference of State Legislatures, 1125 17th Street, Denver, Colorado, 80202).

National Council on Welfare, *One in a World of Two's: A Report on One-Parent Families in Canada* (Ottawa, 1976).

Ontario Law Reform Commission, *Report on Family Law, Part III: Children.*

Saskatchewan Law Reform Commission, *Children's Maintenance* (Saskatoon: Queen's Printer, 1976).

Sawhill, I., *Developing Normative Standards for Child Support and Alimony Payments* (1981) (unpublished paper available through The Urban Institute, 2100 M Street N.W., Washington, D.C., 20037) (economist looks at inequities).

Skoloff, G., "The Way We Were: A 46-Point Checklist to Use When Your Client's Former Standard of Living is in Question", (1979) 1 *Fam. Adv.* 18.

"Statutes Requiring Parents to Pay for Institutional Care of Retarded Kids Not Unconstitutional But May Be Entitled to Financial Relief" (May, 81), 19 *J. Fam. L.* 520.

Stenger, "Expanding Constitutional Rights of Illegitimate Children, '68–'80" (May, 81), 19 *J. Fam. L.* 407.

Weitzman, L., "The Economics of Divorce: Social and Economic Consequences of Property, Alimony and Child Support Awards", (1981), 28 *U.C.L.A. Rev.* 1181.

White, K. and Stone, R., ''A Study of Alimony and Child Support Rulings with Some Recommendations'' (1976), 10 *Fam. L.Q.* 75.

Yei, L., ''What Really Happens in Child Support Cases: An Empirical Study of the Establishment and Enforcement of Support Orders in the Denver District Court'' (1980), 57 *Denver Law Journal* 21.

Chapter 5

Property and Civil Participation

Legislation affecting children's civil rights and freedoms is unabashedly discriminatory, usually utilizing the watershed age of 18 years, at which point in time the child miraculously becomes an adult gaining the heady spate of concomitant rights and freedoms.[1] As this chapter will discuss, provincial and federal legislation creates a web of restrictions, the effect of which is to render the child relatively impotent as a participating citizen, reinforcing his role as a dependant in a family unit. A few exceptions have developed as children begin to have an increasingly larger effect in the market place as workers or as consumers or objects of consumption.

Employment A child who is legally able to work is legally entitled to his own wages. A parent, simply by reason of the status of parent, cannot recover the wages earned by the child.[2] The more important issue is the difficulties for the child in terms of his legal employability, legal ability to contract and legal right to deal with real and personal property.

The first hurdle facing the child choosing to work is the prohibitive restrictions found under educational legislation throughout Canada (see Appendix, Chapter 8) which require children under 15 or 16 to attend school although they do not prohibit the child from working after school, on weekends or on school holidays.[3] It also appears that legal employment could constitute a valid defence to a charge of truancy if such an opportunity could be shown to be

---

[1]Persons under the age of majority can be labelled infants, children or minors. The age of majority varies among the provinces between 18 years and 19 years and the *Indian Act* withholds specific majority rights until 21 years for status Indians.

[2]*Haas v. Nyholm,* [1923] 3 W.W.R. 921 (Sask. Dist. Ct.).

[3]See *Re Bruyn and Director of Vocational Rehabilitation Services* (1975), 25 R.F.L. (Ont. Div. Ct.) for authority re working outside school hours.

providing the child with "satisfactory instruction," a phrase which is usually not defined in education legislation. In addition, some provinces have legislation which allows pupils who are at least 14 years of age to leave school altogether in order to work. (See Appendix, Chapter 8). In Ontario, for example, upon the application of the child's parents, a school board is authorized to permit a pupil to enter the work force under some degree of undefined supervision. The child who is involved in such a program remains a "pupil" for the purposes of the school board, thereby ensuring that the board maintains jurisdiction not to mention provincial per capita funding. The program is presumably designed to provide an "educational experience in the work force" for the restless adolescent, although the degree of planning, supervision and "rubber stamping" varies from board to board.[4] (See generally Chapter 8, "Education".)

Assuming the child overcomes the first hurdle of legally being able to work, he must then confront the various federal and provincial employment laws that stand in the way of work opportunities. For example, in Ontario, persons under 16 are precluded from obtaining a game license (*The Game and Fish Act,* s. 42), from prospecting (*The Mining Act,* s. 19(1)) or from working in a logging camp (*Occupational Health and Safety Act,* O. Reg. 692/80, s. 4); under 15 years, he is precluded from working in a factory or office building (*Occupational Health and Safety Act,* O. Reg. 692/80, s. 4).

Adult Activities

If, through some wizardry, the child has sufficient wealth to participate in the affairs of society, one should consider the extent of the child's civil rights. The following is a survey of Ontario law, but it is generally reflective of other provinces' legislation.

Making a Will

Pursuant to s. 8 of Ontario's *Succession Law Reform Act,* a will made by a person who is under the age of 18 years is not valid unless at the time of making the will the person:

(a) is or has been married;

(b) is contemplating marriage and the will states that it is made in contemplation of marriage to a named person, except that such a will is not valid unless and until the marriage to the named person takes place;

(c) is a member of a component of the Canadian forces;

    (i) that is referred to in the *National Defence Act* (Canada) as a regular force or,

    (ii) while placed on active service under the *National Defence Act* (Canada); or

(d) is a mariner or seaman and at sea or in the course of a voyage.

Corporate Directors and Officers

Section 118 of the Ontario *Business Corporations Act*, 1982 states that a person may not be a director unless he is at least 18 years of age. However, it is possible for a child to be an officer of the corporation, except for the president who must be a director of the corporation.

Driving

Ontario's *Highway Traffic Act* states that a person must be 16 to obtain a driver's licence and no person under 16 may drive a motor-assisted vehicle on the

---

[4]See O. Reg. 261/80 in conjunction with ss. 10(7) and 20(2)(h) of the *Education Act*.

highway: ss. 23, 24. The *Motorized Snow Vehicles Act* states that no person under 16 may drive a motorized snow vehicle on a highway: s. 8.

Alcohol

Ontario's *Liquor License Act:* No person can sell or supply liquor to any person who apparently, if not actually, is under the age of 19 years: s. 44(1), (2). Similarly, no person under the age of 19 years can have, consume, purchase or attempt to purchase or otherwise obtain liquor: s. 44(3). No person under the age of 19 years can be on premises where liquor is sold: s. 44(5). If that person on the said premises is apparently under the age of 19, he can only be allowed on the premises if he shows a photocard prescribed by the Regulations proving he is over 18 (R.R.O. 1980, Reg. 581, 8(6a), as enacted by O. Reg. 534/82, s. 2(1)). As an offence by a liquor licence holder is one of strict liability[5], licence holders are increasingly insisting upon the production by the person of the prescribed identification card since, as long as there is no apparent inconsistency between the card and the person producing it, it is a valid defence to any charge: O. Reg. 534/82, s. 6a. A person under 19 years of age can be on prohibited premises if he is entertaining patrons and if the licence holder has received the written consent of the parent or guardian: O. Reg. 534/82, s. 10. A person under the age of 19 can also be supplied liquor by an adult if that adult is his parent or guardian and if the consumption takes place in a private residence: s. 44(7).

Tobacco

Under Ontario's *Minor's Protection Act* "No person shall either directly or indirectly sell, or give or furnish to a child under eighteen years of age cigarettes, cigars, or tobacco in any form": s. 1.

Attending Films

Ontario's *Theatres Act:* Children under 12 may not, unless accompanied by a person apparently 16 years or older, see a film after the hours of 7:30 p.m. on any day or during school hours. Children under 18 are not permitted to see a film classified as "restricted entertainment": ss. 19, 20. No person can show a film to any one apparently under 18 years if the film is classified as "restricted": R.R.O. 1980, Reg. 931, s. 19(1), as enacted by O. Reg. 438/81, s. 2. If the film is classified as "adult entertainment", no one under the age of 14 years can attend unless accompanied by a person at least 18 years of age: s. 19(2). Apparently, unlike the case of consuming liquor, there is no exemption for the showing of films in one's private residence.

Changing Your Name

Under Ontario's *Change of Name Act* a person must be at least 18 years of age to make an application for a change of name: s. 3. A parent cannot bring an application solely on his child's behalf for a change of the child's surname unless he also brings an application for a change of his own surname.[6] However, the court will require the consent of any person who is 14 years of age or over and

---

[5]*R. v. Boardman* (1979), 47 C.C.C. (2d) 334 (Ont. Co. Ct.).

[6]*Re Maakumpu* (1974), 22 R.F.L. 247 (Ont. Dist. Ct.). For further cases involving minors and change of name, see *Re Cormack and Howell* (1980), 29 O.R. (2d) 798 (Co. Ct.) (no jurisdiction under present Act to dispense with consent of natural unwed father); *Re Demers* (1981), 32 O.R. (2d) 351 (Dist. Ct.) (no jurisdiction under present Act to dispense with unwed father's consent so re-register under *Vital Statistics Act*); *Dubien v. Caya* (1982), 29 R.F.L. (2d) 139 (Ont. Dist. Ct.) (unwed father objecting, new husband consenting: application granted), *Re Phillips and Coughlin (No. 2)* (1980), 29 O.R. (2d) 507 (Co. Ct.) (first husband objecting while still demonstrating genuine interest in children; present husband consenting: order refused).

who is the subject of a change of name application by a parent. The consent must be in writing and the child is to attend at the hearing: s. 9(1).

Generally speaking, one parent will not be able to change the name of a child without the consent of the other parent unless the court decides that a parent's consent can be dispensed with because the parent, for example, has not contributed to the support of the applicant, cannot be found, or is incapable of giving consent or for any other reason: ss. 6(3) and 9(3). It has also been held that a court has jurisdiction under the *Divorce Act* (s. 12(b)) to restrain a parent from changing a child's surname if it is not in the child's best interest.[7]

Note that a change of name may be effected by mere reputation of the child and that it is not necessary in all cases to pursue a court application in order to call one's self or one's child by a different name. Accordingly, where there are persistent difficulties surrounding the change of name of a child because of lack of consent by a parent, it may be advisable to avoid such an application at that time and to call the child by the proposed name, allowing the child to develop an identity under that name. At a subsequent date, if necessary, the parent may still bring an application and with stronger grounds. In this respect, note s. 8(2) of O. Reg. 271/80 under the *Education Act* which allows a principal to record the surname by which the pupil is known in lieu of his legal surname in the child's record folder if the principal is satisfied that such name is gained by repute. Section 8(3) of the Regulations requires the principal to change the name of the pupil on the record folder when he is provided with a document indicating that a pupil's name has been changed as a result of adoption, marriage, or in accordance with the law of the province, state, or country in which the document was made. As well, note s. 13(1) of Reg. 271/80 which provides that a principal shall record the first names of the parents of the pupil on the record folder except where the surname of the parents differs from the surname of the pupil, in which case the surname of the parent shall be recorded. Where applicable, the full name of the guardian of the pupil will be recorded in the record folder: O. Reg. 271/80, s. 13(2). Where a parent or guardian of a pupil dies, the date of the death is recorded opposite the name of such person s. 13(3). Such folders are required by the Regulations to be kept in respect of each child enrolled as a pupil in the school. (See generally Chapter 8, "Education".)

Marriage   Under Ontario's *Marriage Act* "No person shall issue a licence to a minor, or solemnize the marriage of minor under the authority of the publication of banns, except where the minor is of the age of sixteen years or more and has the consent in writing of both parents in a form prescribed by the regulations": s. 5(2). The consent is not required for a child over the age of 16 years who is a widow, widower or divorced: s. 5(3). If one of the parents is dead or both parents are living apart, the required consent may be given by the parent having actual or legal custody of the child: s. 5(4). Where the parents of the child are dead or involuntary patients in a psychiatric facility or resident of a facility under the *Developmental Services Act,* the required consent may be given by a lawfully-

---

[7]*Comrie v. Comrie and Delorme* (1979), 13 R.F.L. (2d) 146, 5 Man. R. (2d) 297 (Q.B.); and see *Y. v. Y.,* [1973] 2 All E.R. 574, 14 R.F.L. 336; *Re T. (H.),* [1963] Ch. 238, [1962] 3 All E.R. 970; *Hoodekoff v. Hoodekoff* (1976), 25 R.F.L. 8 (B.C.S.C.).

appointed guardian or acknowledged guardian who has brought up, or who for the three years immediately preceding the intended marriage, has supported the child: s. 5(5). Where a person whose consent is required, as noted above, is not available or unreasonably or arbitrarily withholds his consent, the person in respect of whose marriage the consent is required may apply without the intervention of a next friend for an order dispensing with the consent and a judge of the Provincial or County Court hearing the application in a summary manner, may make an order dispensing with the required consent: s. 6. If a minor under 16, without parental consent, did obtain a licence and was married, the marriage will not automatically be found to be void under a court challenge.[8]

Human Rights

The *Ontario Human Rights Code, 1981* has no age limit as to the laying of a complaint and there have been cases where persons under 18 have complained of discrimination, for example, on the basis of sex, contrary to the Code. These cases have been investigated by the Ontario Human Rights Commission, according to its usual procedures. There are a number of sections in the Code which prohibit discrimination on the basis of age, but ''age'' is specifically defined in s. 26(a) to mean ''any age of 40 years or more and less than 65 years.'' The *Canadian Human Rights Act,* on the other hand, includes ''age'' as a category but does not define it, presumably leaving open the possibility of a challenge based on being under the age of majority. However, it specifically directs that it is not discriminatory to refuse or terminate employment if the person has not reached the minimum age prescribed by legislation: s. 14(b). Nor is it discrimination to discriminate on the basis of age in an area other than employment if it is ''in a manner prescribed by guidelines'' issued by the Canadian Human Rights Commission: s. 14(e). Finally, programs of ''positive discrimination'' to reduce the disadvantages and improve the opportunities of the enumerated groups do not amount to discrimination: s. 15(1). (For a discussion of age discrimination under the *Charter of Rights,* see Chapter 1.)

Voting

Under Ontario's *Election Act* a person must be 18 to vote: s. 10(1)(a). Under the *Legislative Assembly Act* a person must be 18 to become a member of the Legislative Assembly in Ontario: s. 6(1) and under the *Canada Election Act* a person must be 18 to vote and must be 18 to be a candidate for Parliament: s. 14(1)(a).

Consent to Treatment/ Counselling

An adult who provides medical or other professional assistance to a child is entering into a contract. Although the contract may be for a helping purpose, it still carries with it special liabilities due to the age of the client.

The problem facing the medical practitioner desiring to assist a child arises from the law of torts which protects individuals against nonconsenual physical contact by others. ''The application of force to the person of another without lawful justification amounts to the wrong of battery. This is so, however trivial the amount or nature of the force may be, and even though it neither does nor is intended nor is likely nor is able to do any manner of harm. Even to touch a person without his consent or some other lawful reason is actionable.''[9] The liability arising from a battery or assault upon a person may not be limited to

---

[8]*Legebokoff v. Legebokoff* (1982), 28 R.F.L. (2d) 159 (B.C.S.C.).
[9]Salmond, *The Law of Torts* (15th ed.) (London: Sweet and Maxwell, 1969), at p. 157.

surgical treatment but might include, for example, the prescription of a birth control pill, since within that action, there may be intention to bring a "material object into contact with another person" such as to constitute an application of force.[10] The torts of assault and battery may be actionable regardless of any harm that may have been caused and regardless of whether the person was angry or hostile. However, unless there are damages, no action will follow in practice or if an action does follow it may be dismissed as an abuse of the court's process.[11]

The application of force upon a person will incur no liability if it is lawful, and it is lawful when there is either adequate justification for the touching or consent by the person touched. For example, treatment of a child by a doctor will be justified when it is of an emergency nature even in the absence of consent.[12] The requisite consent in respect of the child is, under common law, the consent of the child's parent since anyone under the age of majority is presumed to be incapable of knowing the nature and consequences of the treatment. Such consent must also be specific as to acknowledging the particular terms and consequences of the treatment. A blanket consent form cannot be said to satisfy the requirement that the "consentor" understands the nature, purpose and expected consequences of the proposed treatment so as to be able to make a rational decision.[13]

In light of the more independent (and sexually active) role of teenagers in modern society, statute law and case law have made inroads on this presumption. For example, under O. Reg. 865/80 of the *Public Hospitals Act,* it states that a surgical operation may be performed on a patient or out-patient with the written consent of anyone who is sixteen years of age or over or of a married person: s. 50. Definitions of "patient" and "out-patient" restrict the application to persons received in a hospital for examination or treatment, and "hospital" is restricted to those institutions approved by the Act. The judiciary has also recognized that the common law and its rules with respect to age and legal capacity may have to keep pace with contemporary life styles. As noted by one Court of Appeal in England:

> . . . that case was decided in the year 1883. It reflects the attitude of a Victorian parent towards children. He expected unquestioning obedience to his commands. If a son disobeyed, his father would cut him off with 1 s. If a daughter had an illegitimate child, he would turn her out of the house. His power only ceased when the child became 21. I decline to accept a view so much out of date. The common law can, and should, keep pace with the times.[14]

In two significant Canadian cases, decided at a time when the age of

---

[10]See Wathan, *Medical Negligence* (London: Butterworth, 1957), at p. 165; Felming, *The Law of Torts* (2nd ed.) (Sydney: Law Book Co. of Australia, 1961), at p. 26.

[11]*Burk v. S., B. and K.* (1951), 4 W.W.R. (N.S.) 520 (B.C. S.C.).

[12]See *Public Hospitals Act,* O. Reg. 865/80, s. 50 and *Marshall v. Curry* (1933), 60 C.C.C. 136 (N.S.S.C.); *Mulloy v. Hop Sang,* [1935] 1 W.W.R. 714 (Alta. C.A.).

[13]*Halushka v. University of Saskatchewan* (1965), 53 D.L.R. (2d) 436 (Sask. C.A.); followed by *Zimmer v. Ringrose* (1978), 13 A.R. 181 (T.D.).

[14]*Hewer v. Bryant,* [1969] 3 All E.R. 578, at 582 (C.A.).

majority was not 18 but 25 years, the courts have held that persons under the age of 21 could consent to an operation if they were capable of fully appreciating the nature and consequences of a particular operation or particular treatment, if such an operation or treatment was for their benefit.[15] In both cases, the court suggested factors which might indicate the ability of a child to appreciate the nature and consequences of the treatment. Echoing the sentiments of the English Court of Appeal, the Canadian court noted:

> Although the common law imposes very strict limitations on the capacity of persons under 21 years of age to hold, or rather to divest themselves of, property or to enter into contracts concerning matters other than necessities, it would be ridiculous in this day and age, where the voting age is being reduced to 18 years, to state that a person of 20 years of age, who is obviously intelligent and is fully capable of understanding the possible consequences of a medical or surgical procedure as an adult, would, at law, be incapable of consenting thereto.[16]

In one American case, the Supreme Court of Kansas dismissed a battery suit against the hospital by a 17-year-old young woman who underwent a skin graft on her forearm and the repair of her injured finger. She had injured herself when her hand caught inadvertently in a door of the hospital room in which her mother had been placed following major surgery. The mother was in no condition to consent and the father, from whom the mother was divorced, was 200 miles away, his address unknown and not immediately available. The court denied recovery not on the basis of an "emergency" justification which might, in the circumstances, have been possible but because the 17-year-old "was mature enough to understand the nature and consequences and to knowingly consent to the beneficial procedure made necessary by the accident."[17]

Note that it is apparently crucial in the decisions of these cases that the treatment be found to be for the benefit of the child. For example, in a case in which a boy, aged 15, was permanently disfigured as a result of serving, without the consent of the mother, as a tissue donor for a severely burned cousin, the Appellate Court reversed the dismissal of the boy's suit, noting that the child had undergone a surgical operation for the benefit of another rather than for his own health needs.[18]

Based on these cases, a profile of the "emancipated" or "mature" minor emerges: someone who is for the most part between the ages of 16 and 18 years. The following factors are to be considered by the court in making the assessment of whether the particular person before the court is capable of understanding the nature and consequences of the treatment:

1) the maturity of the child;
2) whether the child is dependent upon his guardians or supporting himself;

---

[15]*Booth v. Toronto General Hospital* (1910), 17 O.W.R. 118 (K.B.); *Johnston v. Wellesley Hospital,* [1971] 2 O.R. 103 (H.C.).

[16]*Johnston v. Wellesley Hospital, ibid.,* at p. 108.

[17]*Younts v. St. Francis Hospital and School of Nursing Inc.* (1970), 205 Kan. 292 (S.C.).

3) whether the child is living outside the parental home or outside of parental influence;

4) the complexity of the treatment.

It might be arguable that these criteria could be applied to a child without regard to an arbitrary age limit. It would seem however that the onus upon a defendant to show the child to be capable of appreciating the consequences of the treatment is more demanding if the child is under 16 years.

It is often difficult for doctors to determine the limitations surrounding the capacity of the child as a patient to give his or her consent. This difficulty often arises in those situations where the young person, emancipated or not, wishes health assistance without the knowledge of the parent who, *prima facie,* should be informed in order to give the appropriate consent. Consider the not uncommon example of a 15-year-old girl who attends at a public health clinic and has an intra uterine device inserted by the doctor. First, the court, applying the foregoing criteria, will determine the ability of the child to consent independently to the treatment. On this finding, the court must then consider whether the treatment is beneficial to the child. If not, then even if the child has been found to have the capacity to consent, the doctor might be liable to a charge of assault. Such a situation has been considered by a Canadian court for a somewhat different purpose. A British Columbia Supreme Court dismissed an appeal from a ruling of the British Columbia Council of Physicians and Surgeons concerning a doctor who had been found guilty of "infamous or unprofessional conduct." The doctor had inserted a birth control device in a 15-year-old female patient without parental consent. On appeal, the doctor argued that the ethical rule of doctor-patient confidentiality should apply to the child's parents. The court responded by noting that in some circumstances the doctor's contentions might be true but that whether the conduct is professional or not in any particular situation is best decided by a medical inquiry committee as was done in the case against the doctor.[19]

Note that treating the child without parental consent may also give rise to a negligence suit, the argument being that the doctor has acted unreasonably in failing to obtain proper consent. Most consent to treatment problems arise as a result of admittedly intentional acts by the physician or hospital employees. But if a negligence suit is contemplated, it is important to note the limitation periods that often surround such actions against hospitals or physicians and that, unlike a suit based on assault and battery, injuries are a pre-requisite for the recovery of damages based on negligence.[20]

Counselling/ Therapy
Whereas there exists legislation governing the practice of medicine, there are many other types of professionals in the field of children — psychologists, social workers and child care workers — on whom the law does not appear to

---

[18]*Bonner v. Moran* (1941), 126 F. 2d 121, at 123 (D.C. C.A.).

[19]*Re D. and Council of College and Physicians and Surgeons of B.C.* (1970), 11 D.L.R. (3d) 570, at 578 (B.C. S.C.).

[20]*Mulloy v. Hop Sang, supra,* note 12; consd *Strachan v. Simpson,* [1979] 5 W.W.R. 315 (B.C. S.C.).

impose specific rules and regulations including the obligation to obtain consent unless the use of force such as physical restraint or holding is involved. Nevertheless, different kinds of liability may arise depending on the circumstances. The *Criminal Code* contains specific sections which may be relevant and if the child is under the supervision or care of a Children's Aid Society, the proposed *Child and Family Services Act* (now the *Child Welfare Act*) in Ontario will impose further restrictions on adults dealing with children.

Under the *Criminal Code:*

1) No one may entice away, conceal, detain, receive or harbour a child under 14 years of age with the intent to deprive a parent or person who has lawful custody of the possession of that child: s. 250. Accordingly, if a counsellor kept a child in a hostel or group home, knowing it was against the wishes of the parent, he could be liable under this section (which carries with it a possible penalty of 10 years imprisonment). Although the consent of the young person is no defence (s. 250.5) no one can be found guilty of the offence if the court is satisfied that the action was necessary "to protect the young person from danger of imminent harm": s. 250.4. Another similar section stipulates that no one may take or cause to be taken, without legal authority, an unmarried person under 16 years of age out of the possession of and against the will of the parent or person with lawful custody: s. 249. In both cases, there is no strict liability on a counsellor to inform the parents when the child comes to him for assistance. The substance of the offence is to intend to deprive the parent of possession of the child.[21]

There may be an instance where a child, effectively "living on the street," will be sheltered by a third party in circumstances which do not amount to an intention to deprive a parent of possession. It has been held that the phrase "takes or causes to be taken" requires some participation by the accused in the removal of the child either through physical involvement or inducement or enticement. The mere fact that the child is aware that he can find refuge with the accused does not constitute any inducement on the latter's part.[22] On the other hand, the Ontario Court of Appeal has determined that proof of the taking away does not require any element of persuasion and even if children involved took a very active, if not leading part in what occurred, a conviction will follow if it is proved that the taking was against the will of the parent.[23]

2) There is nothing in the role of a professional counsellor *per se* that absolves him from a possible charge of kidnapping (forcible confinement against the person's will: s. 247) or the civil liability for an action based on false imprisonment. Accordingly, the wise counsellor will ensure that the child has come of his own free will when seeking assistance.

---

[21]*R. v. Reid* (1967), 10 Crim.L.Q. 99; *R. v. Weinstein* (1916), 26 C.C.C. 50 (Que. Sess. Ct.); and see *R. v. Langevin and La Pensee* (1962), 133 C.C.C. 257 (Ont. C.A.); disapproving *R. v. Bebee* (1958), 120 C.C.C. 310 (Ont. C.A.); *R. v. Holmes* (1909), 16 C.C.C. 7 (Ont. C.A.).

[22]*R. v. Johnson* (1977), 37 C.C.C. (2d) 352 (Sask. Dist. Ct.).

[23]*R. v. Langevin and La Pensee, supra,* note 21.

3) If a child informs his counsellor about an offence or possible offence committed by the child, that counsellor is under the same duty to report as he would be had the client been an adult. The mere reception of such information would not form the basis for a charge of "contributing to juvenile delinquency" as provided in s. 33 of the now repealed *Juvenile Delinquents Act* (a section which no longer exists under the *Young Offenders Act*). It has also been held that evidence of passive acquiescence does not constitute aiding and abetting in the commission of a criminal offence.[24] And there is no obligation upon any person, let alone a professional, to be an informer or to report to the police any suspicions he may have concerning an offence.

Proposed *Child and Family Services Act* (now *Child Welfare Act*)

Section 79 of Ontario's proposed *Child and Family Services Act* creates an offence in respect of persons who interfere with children who are the subject of an order for society supervision or society or crown wardship under that Act. Specifically, interference means any action the effect of which is to:

(a) induce or attempt to induce the child to leave the care of the person with whom the child is placed by the court or by the Society;

(b) detain or harbour the child after the person or Society referred to in clause (a) requires that the child be returned;

(c) interfere with the child or remove or attempt to remove the child from any place; or,

(d) for the purpose of interfering with the child, visit or communicate with the person referred to in clause (a).

To sustain a conviction under this section in respect of detaining or harbouring a child, note that there first must be a demand made by a person authorized to require the child to be delivered up.

Confidentiality   A major issue which often accompanies the problems of young persons and consent is that of confidentiality. In fact, the latter issue may be more important to the patient than the treatment; that is, the consequences of ignoring the condition which brought the child to the professional originally may be less horrendous from the child's perspective than the consequences of his parents' knowing of the condition. From the point of view of the service provider, he should acquaint himself with the particular legislation or bureaucratic or professional policies which govern his practice regarding this issue.

If the young person is found to be capable of consenting in his own right, a medical doctor can proceed on the child's consent alone, but he should also inform his patient of his intent with respect to requesting the Ontario Health Insurance Plan not to audit the billings of this patient so that there is no possibility that they will spot check the services with the insured party, the

---

[24]*R. v. Salajko*, [1970] 1 C.C.C. 352 (Ont. C.A.); appld *R. v. Dunlop and Sylvester* (1979), 27 N.R. 153 (S.C.C.); *R. v. Sauve* (1979), 1 O.R. 824, 55 C.C.C. (2d) 149, 9 C.R.N.S. 145 (Ont. Prov. Ct.).

parents. Note that if the malady is venereal disease, the doctor will have no choice but to report it to the public health authorities as well as to the parents.

As discussed above, therapists and counsellors are under no obligation to report the fact that the child has been seeking their help as long as the assistance does not amount to a technical assault and battery of an "unemancipated" child or that it does not amount to an offence under the *Criminal Code* or the proposed *Child and Family Services Act* (specific sections outlined above).

Specificity of Treatment

As noted earlier, for consent to be valid, it must be specific as to the nature and consequences of the particular treatment proposed by the profession. The appropriate specificity of treatment is routinely conveyed to patients in the medical world but in therapeutic counselling, treatment can also take many forms of which the parent or child may not be made aware and which should be specifically alluded to in any consent. Some of these techniques include:

1) Time Out: This is a management technique involving the removal of a youngster from general program activities for a short period of time. It is designed to temper the frequency and/or the severity of specific inappropriate behaviour which is predictable in the child's conduct. Consequently, it is thought that this "conditioning" approach may have success.

2) Segregation: This involves the removal of a child from the mainstream of the program to a "place of safety" with a particular staff member who is assigned full time to the child and who remains in contact with the child to allow the opportunity for direct confrontation.

3) Holding: As the name suggests, this is the physical restraint of a child by one or more staff members. It is used to help a child express negative emotions safely or when adult intervention is needed to protect a child or others from the child's destructive impulses.

4) Physical Restraint: This technique is the restraining of a person by mechanical means, such as a straightjacket, rather than through staff holding. It is a technique which is crisis-oriented and is used to protect the child from self-mutilation, or others from his aggressive behaviour when alternative means of restraint are not feasible.

5) Medication: This technique generally refers to the use of injections rather than oral medication on an *ad hoc* basis to calm down an anxious or depressed youngster or to control "acting out" in a crisis situation. Administration of medication by injection can only be done by a duly qualified physician or by a registered nurse in certain situations.

If a child or parent intends to consent to any of the treatments noted above, it is advisable that the parties acknowledge, either by oral agreement or preferably within the written consent form itself, that:

1) the techniques noted above will be used only when lesser restraining methods have failed;

2) that the techniques will never be used simply to obtain compliance with adult requests;

3) that the techniques will never be used for the purpose of punishment;

4) that the management of drug medication ensures that no addiction will result.

Residential Commitment

In Ontario, a child may be voluntarily or involuntarily committed to a residential mental health facility under two different pieces of legislation: the proposed *Child and Family Services Act, 1984 (CFSA)*, Part VI (Extraordinary Measures) (for which there is no equivalent under the present *Child Welfare Act*), administered by the Ministry of Community and Social Services; and the *Mental Health Act,* administered by the Ministry of Health. The process, the facilities and the child's and parent's rights differ significantly depending upon which Act is invoked. Part VI of the *CFSA* with its extensive procedural safeguards applies to the mental health treatment of children (under 18 years) and can be invoked with certain restrictions by the child (if over 15 years of age), the parent, someone caring for the child, a Society who has custody of the child or a physician (if the child is over 15 years of age). The programs and facilities involved are those operated by or approved by the Ministry of Community and Social Services. The *Mental Health Act* sets out an overlapping jurisdiction in that it also can apply to the mental health treatment of children as well as adults and can be invoked, subject to its particular restrictions, by a physician who has examined the child as well as a justice of the peace or police officer. The facilities involved are "psychiatric facilities" as designated by the regulations and presumably may or may not include the same facilities designated by the *CFSA* in which case it is important to note that s. 4 of the *Mental Health Act* states that "where the provisions of any Act conflict with the provisions of this Act or the regulations, the provisions of this Act and the regulations prevail." Any such conflict may occur mostly with the procedures and grounds delineated for commitment and release. In addition, there may be some procedures during the stay of the child with which each Act deals differently although for the most part it appears that the extensive provisions under the proposed *CFSA* have no equivalent under the *Mental Health Act* and accordingly will be enforceable.

Under the *Child and Family Services Act, 1984,* there will be extremely detailed procedures regarding the exercise of a Society's power over a child in care. Chapter 3 canvasses this power under the subsection "The State as Guardian: Duties and Responsibilities" and included thereunder is a specific section on "Consent to Treatment." In addition, the subsection in that chapter entitled "Best Interests Disposition: Review/Termination of Order" outlines the system of multi-level review and complaint procedures which can be invoked by the parent and/or the child when the Society's care and treatment is disputed.

Of particular interest to this chapter are the provisions of the proposed *CFSA* which will govern "secure treatment", defined as "programs for the treatment of children with mental disorders, in which continuous restrictions are imposed on the liberty of the children" (Part VI: Extraordinary Measures, s. 109(1)); "secure isolation" (ss. 120–22); "instrusive procedures" including "mechanical means of controlling behaviour, aversive stimulation technique" or any other procedure labelled as "intrusive": (ss. 108(b), 124–25), and "psychotropic drugs" (s. 126). The Act only permits commitment to secure treatment on court order or in an emergency in which case it must come before the court within five days of admission although it has 45 days to dispose of the matter as well as 30 days for any adjournments: s. 110. The child must have legal representation (s. 110(5)) and the court may order an independent assessment to assist it in its decision: s. 112. The court may only order committal if it is satisfied that the child:

1) has a mental disorder;
2) has caused, attempted to cause or threatened to cause harm to himself or others;
3) secure treatment would be an effective remedy;
4) appropriate treatment is available at the recommended facility and
5) no less restrictive method of treatment is appropriate: s. 113(1).

The court must commit for a period of 180 days although, if the application was made by a Society, the child may be released in 60 days unless the parent consents to the full 180 days or unless the child is made a ward of the Society: s. 114. On application for extension, the court can add another 180 days if the specific criteria are met: s. 116.

Treatment by "secure isolation", "intrusive procedures" and/or "psychotropic drugs" are all governed by detailed provisions which dictate who may make such decisions, what restrictions are placed on the particular treatment, and in the case of psychotropic drugs, the fact that a child 16 years of age or over must first give a clearly informed and detailed consent except in emergencies over a 72-hour period: s. 126(1), (2), and (4). If the child is under 16, the child's parent or, if in care, the Society must give consent: s. 126(1)(b).

Under Ontario's *Mental Health Act,* any one can be committed by a physician's application, approved by the physician of the treatment facility, as an involuntary patient to a psychiatric facility if he is a danger to himself or others. Decisions as to treatment will be determined by the patient's in-house physician and the extensive rights, protections and review procedures outlined (at least on paper) under the proposed *Child and Family Services Act* have little or no parallel under the *Mental Health Act.* The Act sets up its own tribunal which reviews the involuntary patient's case at regular intervals, deciding whether to release or continue holding him. Ironically, if the person is under 18 and his parents or whoever has legal custody (including presumably a Children's Aid Society) consents to committal, his admission is termed "voluntary," no matter how strenuously the minor may oppose the admission or the specific treatment. His rights are even more restricted than that of someone over 18 due to the fact that the protections and review procedures available to the involuntary patient will not apply to this so-called voluntary or informal patient.

Parental Consent

Courts, using their *parens patriae* jurisdiction,[25] are reluctant to intervene in or usurp parental decision-making regarding the care and treatment of their

---

[25] See for example *Perepolkin v. Supt. of Child Welfare (No. 1)* (1957), 118 C.C.C. 263 (B.C.C.A.) and *Perepolkin v. Supt. of Child Welfare (No. 2)* (1957), 120 C.C.C. 67 (B.C. C.A.) in which *habeas corpus* was invoked to obtain the release of a child unlawfully in the care of the state.

*and
Judicial
Intervention*

children except in life-threatening situations.[26] Although one might now see some potential in challenging the situation under s. 15 of the *Charter* as denying the minor equal protection before and under the law based on age discrimination, it should be noted that the U.S. Supreme Court has already dismissed similar constitutional attacks.[27] From that U.S. decision comes the following:

> [T]he law's concept of the family rests on a presumption that parents possess what a child lacks in maturity, experience and capacity for judgment required for making life's difficult decisions. . . . Nonetheless, we have recognized that a state is not without constitutional control over parental discretion in dealing with children when their physical or mental health is jeopardized. . . . [However], simply because the decision of a parent is not agreeable to a child or because it involves risks does not automatically transfer the power to make that decision from the parents . . . to the state. . . . Most children, even in adolescence, simply are not able to make sound judgments concerning many decisions, including their need for medical care or treatment. Parents can and must make those judgments.[28]

However, a recent Ontario decision broke new ground in going behind parental decision making to judge for itself the capacity of the "child" to make his own decision although the "child" in this case was over 18 years of age.[29]

*Ability to
Contract*

Common law principles have the same limiting effect on the right of children to contract as statutory law has on the right of the child to seek employment with the exception that it is not illegal on the part of the adult party to enter into the contract. A child — in the case of contracts, meaning a person under the age of 18 — can enter into any contract if there exists an adult party who is prepared to assume the risk. With certain exceptions, the common law considers that contracts entered into by children are voidable, but only at the instance of the infant[30]. Certain contracts are voidable in the sense that they are valid and binding upon all parties unless the child repudiates them before, or within a reasonable time after, the attainment of his majority[31]. Other contracts are voidable in the sense that they are not binding upon the child unless ratified

---

[26]For Jehovah's Witness blood transfusion cases see *Forsyth v. C.A.S. of Kingston*, [1963] 1 O.R. 49, 35 D.L.R. (2d) 690 (H.C.); *Pentland v. Pentland* (1978), 20 O.R. (2d) 27, 86 D.L.R. (3d) 585, 5 R.F.L. (2d) 65 (H.C.). For a case in which the court ordered a life-saving operation when parents decided to cease such efforts on their profoundly retarded child see *Re Supt. of Fam. and Child Services and Dawson; Re Russell and Super. of Fam. and Child Service*, [1983] 3 W.W.R. 618 (B.C. S.C.). See also *Re S.D.* (1983), 42 B.C.L.R. 153 (Prov. Ct.). But see *Re D. (A Minor)*, [1976] 1 All E.R. 326 in which the court's jurisdiction was invoked to prevent the sterilization of an 11-year-old retarded child.

[27]*Parham v. J.R.* (1979), 99 S.C. 2493.

[28]*Ibid.*, at p. 2504–05.

[29]*Clark v. Clark* (1982), 40 O.R. (2d) 383 (Co. Ct.).

[30]*E.g.*, an infant having insufficient discretion to carry on a business or trade is not liable for goods supplied for this purpose: *Pyett v. Lampman*, 8 O.L.R. 149, [1923] 1 D.L.R. 249 (C.A.) (car purchase;) See also *R. v. Rash* (1923), 53 O.L.R. 245 (C.A.) where the infant even avoided a fraud conviction because the only creditors were those who supplied goods for the purpose of trade by an infant.

[31]*Wright v. Walker* (1923), 53 O.L.R. 553 (Ont. C.A.).

by him when he reaches his majority. (See below for more extensive discussion of ratification and repudiation.) In either case, the adult party to the contract is bound by its terms subject to the exceptions noted below. The mechanism of "voidability" allows a child to contract with an adult but ensures that there is no permanent or irrevocable liability on the child until he is an adult, whereupon he is assumed to have the ability to understand the consequences of entering into a contract. Accordingly, for example, specific performance cannot be enforced by either party because there is want of mutuality of enforceability[32]. Even if the child misrepresents himself as being over the age of majority, he may still not be bound by the contract[33].

These principles which create a presumption against the validity of a contract between children and adults represent a legal response to the concern of protecting persons of a minor age from the consequences of their inexperience in an adult world. However, the courts have made some exceptions to the voidability presumption in order to balance valid adult and corporate interests against these protective principles in fields where children are progressively becoming more active such as entertainment, sports and consumption of goods and services. On the other end of the spectrum, the courts have also carved out particular types of contracts which are so detrimental to the child's interests that they are void *ab initio*. The exceptions to the general rule of voidable contracts for children include:

Detrimental to Child's Interests

1) If a contract is found to be detrimental to the interests of the child, a court will find it to be void *ab initio* even if it is a contract for necessaries of life[34]. That is, it is invalid from the outset and neither of the parties can sue one another on the basis of its terms[35]. Such contracts might contain terms which put the child at a disadvantage as a party or which divest him of his rights. As an example, a contract for the purchase of land entered into by a child which contained a severe forfeiture clause for default in payments was seen as prejudicial to the child's interests. The court held that the contract was wholly void and the child was entitled to recover any payments made under the contract terms[36]. On the other hand, if a child has done work under a contract which is void by reason that its terms are prejudicial to his interests, he is entitled to the value of the labour and material he has provided[37].

---

[32]*Jackson v. Jessup* (1855), 5 Gr. 524 (C.A.); *Melville v. Stratherne* (1878), 26 Gr. 52.

[33]*Jewell v. Broad* (1909), 19 O.L.R. 1; affd 20 O.L.R. 176 (C.A.); *Confederation Life Assn. v. Kinnear* (1896), 23 O.A.R. 497; *R. v. Rash, supra,* note 30. But see cases where child may not avoid consequences of his fraud: *Wilbur v. Jones* (1881), 21 N.B.R. 4 (N.B. C.A.); *Re Shaver* (1871), 3 Chy. Chrs. 379; *Leary v. Rose* (1963), 10 Gr. 346; *R. Leslie Ltd. v. Sheill,* [1914] 3 K.B. 607 (C.A.) (bound to restore property). However, the misrepresentation must be explicit and cannot arise from mere inferences drawn simply from the child's conduct: *R. v. Rash, supra,* note 30 (engaging in a trade is not in itself a representation as to majority age).

[34]*Pyett v. Lampman, supra,* note 30 (car purchase). *International Accountants Society v. Montgomery,* [1935] O.W.N. 364 (C.A.) (correspondence course in accountancy).

[35]*Beam v. Beatty (No. 2)* (1902), 4 O.L.R. 554 (C.A.); *Butterfield v. Sibbitt and Nipissing Electric Supply Co.,* [1950] O.R. 504 (Dist. Ct.); *Re Staruch,* [1955] 5 D.L.R. 807 (Ont. S.C.).

[36]*Phillips v. Greater Ottawa Development Company* (1916), 38 O.L.R. 315, 33 D.L.R. 259 (C.A.).

[37]*Altobelli v. Wilson,* [1957] O.W.N. 207 (C.A.).

Conversely, where an infant has paid money under a contract, he is not compellable to complete the contract but neither can he recover the money unless he can show fraud[38].

Other examples include the following cases. A bond with a penalty was held to be void where it was to a child's prejudice[39]. A chattel mortgage containing the usual acceleration and repossession clauses was held to be prejudicial to the child and therefore void[40]. The fact that the rent payable was not the best rent that could be obtained was held not to be prejudicial to the child as to render it void[41]. A conditional sales agreement for the purchase of a motorcycle was not necessarily to the prejudice of the infant and therefore voidable only[42].

Necessaries of Life

2) Those contracts which are for necessaries are looked upon as *prima facie* binding upon the child if the contract is to the child's benefit. That is, the court will enforce the contract against the child immediately without the protection afforded in respect of a voidable contract. Section 3 of Ontario's *Sale of Goods Act* codifies the notion that a contract for necessaries with a child is an exception to the general rule of voidability. This section reads:

(i) Capacity to buy and sell is regulated by the general law concerning capacity to contract and to transfer and acquire property, but where necessaries are sold and delivered to a minor, . . . he shall pay a reasonable price therefor.

(ii) Necessaries in this section mean goods suitable to the conditions in life of the minor or other person and to his actual requirements at the time of the sale and delivery.

Under common law, necessaries have been held to be those things which the child requires for his living, health and education and any ancillary items a child would be expected to require in order to secure his necessaries. Note that the term ''necessaries'' is a relative expression to be construed with reference to the child's age, needs and standard of living[43]. In an action against the child based on a contract entered into for the purpose of necessaries, the onus is on the plaintiff to prove not only that the goods supplied were suitable to the condition in life of the child, but also that the child did not have the necessaries at the time of the sale and delivery[44]. As an example, where a child enters into a contract for the purchase of a house, an

---

[38]*Short v. Field* (1915), 32 O.L.R. 395 (C.A.); *Robinson v. Moffatt* (1915), 35 O.L.R. 9 (C.A.).

[39]*Beam v. Beatty (No. 2), supra,* note 35; *Phillips v. Greater Ottawa Development Company, supra,* note 36. But see *Doe d. Lemoine v. Vancott* (1837), 5 O.S. 486.

[40]*Ivan v. Hartley,* [1945] 4 D.L.R. 142 (Ont. H.C.).

[41]*Lipsett v. Perdue* (1889), 18 O.R. 577 (C.A.).

[42]*McBride v. Appleton,* [1946] O.R. 17 (C.A.).

[43]*Pyett v. Lampman,* note 30 (car purchase); *Wong v. Kim Yee* (1961), 34 W.W.R. 506 (Sask. Dist. Ct.): *Deziel v. Deziel,* [1953] 1 D.L.R. 651 (Ont. H.C.) (medical expenses).

[44]*Nash v. Inman* (1908), 2 K.B. 1 (C.A.).

item considered a "necessary," and the child signs a promissory note for its purchase, he will be liable under the promissory note to pay for the house[45]. Conversely, if a loan is made for something not considered to be a necessary, then the law will not require the child to repay the loan to the plaintiff[46].

Because the law considered that a child does not have sufficient maturity to carry on a business, services supplied to the child in the course of his business, while necessary for carrying on that business, are not considered a "necessary" to the child. Therefore, note that a contract for the purpose of supplying goods or services for a child's business is not binding upon the child[47].

In deciding the question of whether the contract is to the child's benefit, the facts of each case must be reviewed and presumably this requires a consideration of the mores of the particular society in which the child is living. That is, one should expect that the court would be less likely to find void a contract for necessaries entered into by a child of 16 years, totally independent of his family and living through independent means in the community, than that of a child of 17 years remaining at home in a dependent state. This position is reflected in s. 33(2) and (3) of Ontario's *Family Law Reform Act* which allow the adult plaintiffs to sue on a necessaries contract each parent who is still liable for the support of a child. If the parents of a child are no longer liable to provide necessaries for their child by reason of his withdrawal from their care, then although the child might still rely upon his minor status in challenging a contract's validity, the test as to whether it is beneficial to him should be applied less stringently to reflect the relatively early onset of an "adult" lifestyle.

Service or Employment Contracts

3) Contracts of service or employment, if beneficial to the child, will be seen as *prima facie* binding upon the child[48]. In determining whether the contract is for the benefit of the child, the court will look upon the terms of the contract, comparing them with the terms generally used by employers in the field of trade in which the child is to be engaged, and whether the terms of the contract will allow protection to the child, the opportunity for secure employment, the means for maintaining himself, and whether the contract provides fair compensation for the child's services[49]. A contract for service and employment is *prima facie* binding perhaps because where the contract is beneficial to the child, its effect is similar to providing the child with necessaries inasmuch as the contract will either afford the child the means to earn a living or to provide him with necessary instruction to this end. The contract must be clearly beneficial to the child and the onus to so prove will

---

[45]*Soon v. Watson* (1962), 33 D.L.R. (2d) 428 (B.C. S.C.); *Federal Life Assurance Co. v. Hewitt* (1907), 9 O.W.R. 857 (Co. Ct.); *Continental Life Insurance Co. v. Bowling* (1901), 21 C.L.T. 246 (Ont.).

[46]*Wong v. Kim Yee, supra,* note 43.

[47]*Pyett v. Lampman, supra,* note 30.

[48]*Roberts v. Gray,* [1913] 1 K.B. 520.

[49]*Leslie v. Fitzpatrick* (1877), 37 L.T. 461; *Fellows v. Wood* (1888), 9 L.T. 513.

be on the party asserting its validity[50]. It is for the court to construe the contract and to say whether, viewing it as a whole, it is for the benefit of the child. The mere fact that some provision may not be for the advantage of the child does not mean that the agreement is voidable in its entirety nor must "benefit" be limited to pecuniary benefit[51]. A recent case yields the example of a contract between a child and a junior hockey team which was found not to be beneficial to the child even though it did yield benefit, providing the child with the only means of entering into professional hockey. Indeed, that fact alone suggests that the bargaining position of the parties would be manifestly unequal, requiring the courts to be more than normally vigilant to protect the weaker party. The court further found that simply because an adult player signed the same contract as the child or because the child's father approved the contract does not *per se* make the contract beneficial to the child although each fact is evidence as to the overall issue of benefit of the agreement[52].

Note that a contract for apprenticeship and service is distinct from a contract of service and employment in that the former must comply with the *Apprenticeship and Tradesman's Qualifications Act*. According to the Act, an "apprentice" means a person who is at least 16 years of age and who has entered into a contract under which he is to receive, from or through his employer, training and instruction in a trade: s. 1(a). The contract of apprenticeship must be according to s. 14:

(a) for a period of at least two years;
(b) in the prescribed form;
(c) signed,
    (i)   by the employer,
    (ii) by the person to be apprenticed, and
    (iii) if the apprentice is under eighteen years of age, by a parent or guardian of the person to be apprenticed, but, if neither parent nor the guardian is willing to sign or is capable of signing, a judge of the county or district court of a county or district in which the employer carries on business may, upon the application of the person to be apprenticed and without the appointment of a next friend, dispense with the signature of either parent or of the guardian upon proof to the satisfaction of the judge that the contract is in the interest of the person to be apprenticed; and
(d) approved by the Director.

---

[50]*Toronto Marlboro Major Junior "A" Hockey Club v. Tonelli* (1975), 11 O.R. (2d) 664 (H.C.), and see also judgment in main action (1977) 18 O.R. (2d) 21, 81 D.L.R. (3d) 403 (H.C.); affd (1979), 23 O.R. (2d) 193 (C.A.).
[51]*Miller v. Smith & Co.*, [1925] 3 D.L.R. 251 (Sask. C.A.).
[52]*Toronto Marlboro Major Junior "A" Hockey Club v. Tonelli, supra,* note 50, at p. 212 (O.R.) (Court of Appeal judgment).

Section 16 of the Act states that every apprentice who is under 18 years of age shall perform and is entitled to the benefits of his contract of apprenticeship in accordance with the terms in the same manner and to the same extent as if he were of the full age of 18 years. That is, the contract is viewed as an "adult" contract and the rules noted above in respect to children entering into contracts are not applicable. Some contracts of apprenticeship and trade include: alignment and brake mechanic, autobody repair, carpenter, plumber, lather, or brick and stone mason. (See Regulations to the Act).

Public Policy Contracts

4) The status of void or voidable is sometimes set aside by statute. For example, Ontario's *Insurance Act* provides for anyone 16 years of age or older to enter into an enforceable life insurance contract as if he had full legal capacity to do so: s. 179. In the area of family law, Ontario's *Family Law Reform Act* now directs that a minor who has capacity to contract marriage also has capacity to enter into a marriage contract, separation agreement or paternity agreement that is approved by the court, whether the approval is given before or after the contract was entered into: ss. 54(2) and 58(3). Another example is the child who is a parent and wishes to place his or her child in the care of the Children's Aid Society by entering into an agreement. A child who is a parent is also able to place a child for the purpose of adoption by signing a consent. Under most provincial legislation, specific provisions ensure that these contracts, which otherwise might well be questioned because of the age of the parent, are valid and binding[53].

Child-Parent Contracts

5) Finally, there is the question of the validity of a contract between a child and his parent. This issue turns not only on the question of whether it is beneficial to the child, but also whether the parties as family members intended to create legally binding relations in the first place. A court must determine each case on the facts having regard to such factors as the age of the child at the time of the promise, the reason for the agreement, the degree of formality surrounding the mutual promises, the child's reliance on the promise and probably most significantly, the subject matter of the promise, with the likelihood that the greater the value of the promise, the more likely the parties, albeit parent and child, intended them to have effect[54].

Ratification/ Repudiation of Contract

If the contract entered into by the minor does not fall into any of the above exceptions, it is considered to be voidable as noted above; that is, the contract will only be enforceable upon the subsequent action or inaction of the infant. One of two types of "voidable" contracts is valid and binding upon the child unless he repudiates it before or within a reasonable time after reaching his majority. This is the case in most infant voidable contracts. When the contract is so repudiated, it is repudiated in its entirety[55]. Whether a "reasonable" time has

---

[53]See, *e.g.,* Ontario's *Child Welfare Act* at ss. 25(6) and 69(13) and its proposed replacement statute, the *Child and Family Services Act,* s. 4.

[54]See M.P. Furmston, *Cheshire and Fifoot's Law of Contract,* 9 ed. (London: Butterworth's, 1976), at pp. 104–07).

[55]*Henderson v. Minneapolis Steel and Machinery Co.,* [1931] 1 D.L.R. 570 (Alta. S.C.).

elapsed will depend on the circumstance of the situation[56]. In one case, three years was not considered reasonable[57]; in another, three months was considered reasonable[58]. The repudiation, whenever performed, must be a clear act; acquiescence by silence may not amount to such repudiation[59]. For example, a child who reaches his age of majority and then accepts a dividend as a shareholder will be held to have affirmed his contract of a share purchase, rather than to have repudiated it[60]. Whether a child was in possession of the shares of a company, he was subject to its obligations until he had repudiated the transaction. Therefore, a plea of "infancy" did not relieve him from liability to pay call on the shares if it was to be made before repudiation, but once he does repudiate the transaction, the interest acquired by him is at an end and with it, his liability for future calls[61].

If a child wishes to repudiate a contract from which he has already obtained some advantage, either he is estopped from doing so[62], or he must return to the other party a specific or equivalent value of that which he has received while a child[63]. Conversely, upon reaching his majority, a child cannot recover money which he has paid under a voidable contract unless he can show

   i)   that fraud has been practiced upon him[64]; or
   ii) that the contract was to his prejudice, and so not merely voidable, but void[65].

The other type of voidable contract is enforceable only if ratified after the infant reaches the age of majority. It is of a very specific nature and is codified in s. 7 of Ontario's *Statute of Frauds:*

> No action shall be maintained whereby to charge a person upon a promise made after full age to pay a debt contracted during minority or upon a ratification after full age of a promise or civil contract made during minority, unless the promise of ratification is made by a writing, signed by the party to be charged therewith or by his agent duly authorized to make the promise or ratification.

Interests in Property

Nothing precludes a child from owning land or personal property. The difficulty, however, is that as a result of the child's inability to contract as an

---

[56]*Edwards v. Carter*, [1893] A.C. 360 (H.L.); *Murray v. Dean* (1926), 30 O.W.N. 271 (H.C.); *Phillips v. Greater Ottawa Development Co., supra,* note 36 (2 years, 5 months after majority); *Hilliard v. Dillon,* [1955] O.W.N. 621 (necessity to act promptly).

[57]*Shepard v. Bruner* (1915), 24 D.L.R. 40 (Alta. C.A.).

[58]*Murray v. Dean, supra,* note 56.

[59]*Edwards v. Carter, supra,* note 56.

[60]*Re Prudential Life Insurance Co.; Re Patterson,* [1918] 1 W.W.R. 105 (Man. S.C.).

[61]*Cork and Bandon Ry. Co. v. Cazenove* (1847), 10 Q.B. 935.

[62]*McDonald v. Baxter* (1911), 46 N.S.R. 149 (N.S. C.A.).

[63]*Whalls v. Learn* (1888), 15 O.R. 481 (C.A.); *Louden Manufacturing Co. v. Milmine* (1907), 15 O.L.R. 53 (C.A.); *Butterfield v. Sibbitt and Nipissing Electric Supply Co., supra,* note 35; *Murray v. Dean, supra,* note 56; *Blackwell v. Farrow,* [1948] O.W.N. 7.

[64]*Short v. Field* (1915), 32 O.L.R. 395 (C.A.); *Robinson v. Moffatt* (1915), 35 O.L.R. 9 (C.A.).

[65]*Phillips v. Greater Ottawa Development Co.,* (1916), 38 O.L.R. 315, D.L.R. 259 (C.A.).

Guardian
of Property

adult, it is impractical for property to be held in the name of a child[66]. This does not mean that the child does not own a piano that has been gifted to him or the money in his bank account[67]. It means that in most instances, an adult third-party device is needed in order to accommodate the need for commercial transactions relating to any property, and this device is that of "guardianship." Parents, by the status of parenthood, are not automatically deemed in law to be the guardian of their child's property. Neither does legal custody of a child include the status of guardian to the child's property. Even an order of guardianship may be restricted to the guardianship of a child's person, to be distinguished from the child's property. Usually the child's property is managed and administered by his parents without any judicial appointment. As in other instances of domestic relations, the law is not invoked unless there is perceived to be a present or potential breakdown of relations. Where substantial monies or assets are concerned, a parent may request that he or she be appointed guardian and by adhering to the common law and statutory duties and rules, avoid any allegation at a later date of impropriety and accompanying liability.

In Ontario the recently enacted the *Children's Law Reform Act* has clarified the common law such that an appointment as guardian refers only to

---

[66]*E.g.*, an infant's deed has been held to be voidable as in any contract: *Mills v. Davis* (1860), 9 U.C.C.P. 510; *McKay v. McKinley*, [1933] O.W.N. 392. Transactions in real property in Ontario are subject to the following sub-sections:
Under the *Registry Act:*

s. 41(1) . . .A deed, conveyance, mortgage, assignment of mortgage, lease, assignment of lease, release, quit claim or discharge of mortgage shall not be registered unless there is . . . an affidavit . . . that each person, other than a corporation, making the instrument was of the full age of eighteen years at the time of execution of the instrument.

(4) A plan of subdivision shall not be registered unless the age of every person, other than a corporation, who executes the plan as an owner or who, as mortgagee consents to the registration of the plan, is proven . . . to be of the full age of eighteen years at the time of execution of the plan.

(10) Subsections (1) and (4) do not apply,

. . .

(c) to a minor who executes an instrument under the authority of a court of competent jurisdiction.

Under the *Land Titles Act:*

s. 76(1) Where a person who is not under a disability, might have made an application, given consent, or done an act, or been party to a proceeding under this Act, is a minor, . . . the guardian of the minor . . . may make such application, give such consent, do such act or be party to such proceeding as such person if free from disability might have made, given, done or been party to, and shall otherwise represent such person for the purposes of this Act.

(2) Where the minor has no guardian . . . or if a person yet unborn is interested, the Official Guardian shall act with like power or the land registrar may appoint a person with like power to act for the minor . . . or person yet unborn.

[67]Under s. 205 of the *Banks and Banking Law Revision Act:*

A bank may, without authority, aid, assistance or intervention of any other person or official being required,
(a) receive deposits from any person whatever his age, status, or condition in life, and whether such person is qualified by law to enter into ordinary contracts or not. . . .

guardianship of a child's property and custody refers to the care and control of the child in all other respects: s. 78. The guidelines that emerge from this legislation include:

1) For prescribed amounts, a guardian need not be appointed. A third party may safely pay to a married child or custodial adult an amount not exceeding $2,000 per annum for a total amount of $5,000 in respect of the same obligation. That payment, with a receipt, discharges the third party obligation as if the payment was made to an appointed guardian, although the parent or person who receives the money, if not the child, assumes all of the responsibilities of a guardian for its care and management: s. 52. The payor of any amount also has the choice of paying the money owed to the child into court in full satisfaction of the obligation[68]. Once paid into court, the money will be paid out pursuant to provincial Rules of Practice[69].

2) A parent or any person may apply for a judicial appointment of guardianship of the child's property. In deciding the appointment, the court will consider the ability of the applicant to manage the child's property, any plans proposed by the applicant and the views and preferences of the child, if they can be ascertained. The court may appoint more than one guardian, in which case the appointees are jointly responsible for the management and care of the property: ss. 48, 49 and 50.

3) In order for the child's property to be sold, encumbered or, if money, paid out, an order of the court is necessary if the guardian wishes to avoid what may be full liability if the transaction is subsequently found to be against the interest of the child: s. 60. The court may approve the transaction retroactively and in considering an order of approval, must be satisfied that the arrangements are necessary or proper for the child's support or education or will substantially benefit the child: s. 60(2)[70]. In making the order, the court may make directions which are necessary to the mechanics of any intended transaction such as authorizing the guardian to sign documents on behalf of the child. The only limitation upon the court is that with respect to land, it may not require or approve an alienation of the property that is contrary to the term of the instrument by which the child acquired his interest: s. 60(4).

4) A guardian must transfer all of the property to the child when he reaches the age of 18 years, and a married child under the age of 18 years may apply to the court for an order terminating the guardianship: ss. 54 and 57.

5) Upon appointing a guardian, the court must require the guardian to post a bond, with or without sureties, payable to the child in such amount as the court decides. The court does have the discretion to dispense with the posting of a bond where it has appointed a parent as the guardian: s. 56.

---

[68] Section 36(6) of Ontario's *Trustee Act* provides that where a child is entitled to money, the person by whom the money is payable may pay into the Supreme Court to the credit of the child and this is a sufficient discharge for the monies payable to the child.

[69] See Rule 73.03 of Ontario Rules of Civil Procedure.

[70] See *e.g. Re Wicks; Wicks v. Duffet* (1983), 34 R.F.L. (2d) 247 (Nfld. S.C.).

6) A guardian may, with the permission of the court, resign his office. As well, a guardian can be removed by court order for the same reasons that apply with respect to the removal of a trustee: ss. 58(1) and (2). Guardians may seek to pass their accounts, meaning to have their books related to the management of the estate approved by the court, and any interested person may require that the guardian pass his accounts: s. 53.

7) Finally, guardians are entitled to reasonable fees and expenses related to their responsibilities: s. 55.

Gifts

Perhaps it is of some consolation to children that they can receive a gift directly with no adult intermediaries. This may reflect the natural association of gifts with childhood. In fact, there is a presumption of intended gift from parent to child where there would be no such presumption between strangers[71]. However, there is a common law principle that property transferred to a child by a mother, as distinguished from a father, is not presumed to be a gift but rather to be held in trust by the child for the mother[72]. The distinction between parents is rooted in the common law which obligated only the father to support the child so that anything he transferred to his child was presumed to be with the intention of a gift in satisfaction of that obligation. In light of provincial legislation that now obligates both parents to support their children, it would make sense to dispense with this distinction and rely upon the single presumption in law in favour of the validity of any gift by the parent where the giving and taking is complete[73]. A gift to a child cannot be revoked and a gift to him for some particular purpose is a valid gift, even though the purpose fails[74].

A gift from a child is considered to be voidable, paralleling the protectionism of contract law. That is, the gift may be ratified after the child reaches his majority to guarantee the disposition to the donee. Ratification in this instance does not require any positive act. "The length of time may be sufficient, or just the fact that there was a fixed, deliberate and unbiased determination that the transaction [of giving] should not be impeached."[75] Still, the child will likely be able to repudiate the transaction even after a considerable period of time after attaining his majority if the donee has not been affected by any delay and the child, in giving the gift, has obviously been deprived of a real benefit.[76] As long as it can be shown that a parent has not unfairly influenced his child, gifts to parents from children are no different than gifts between adults[77]. The

---

[71]*Armstrong v. Armstrong* (1868), 14 Gr. 528, at 535–36; *Wilde v. Wilde* (1873), 20 Gr. 521. For rebuttal of the presumption see *Lattimer v. Lattimer* (1978), 18 O.R. (2d) 375 (H.C.).

[72]*Wispianska v. Kuzniar (Jopowicz)* (1978), 3 R.F.L. (2d) 6 (B.C. S.C.): *Lattimer v. Lattimer, supra,* note 71.

[73]*Royal Trust Co. v. Jones,* [1935] 1 W.W.R. 46 (B.C. S.C.).

[74]*Clark v. R.B. Bishop of St. John* (1937), 12 M.P.R. 183 (N.B. C.A.); *Smith v. Smith* (1836), 173 E.R. 178. See also *Olmstead v. Olmstead* (1981), 25 R.F.L. (2d) 67 & 74 (N.B. Q.B.) (gifts of bonds to children in wife's name; half the value exempted from matrimonial assets); *Foster v. Foster* (1978), 98 D.L.R. (3d) 390 (B.C. S.C.) (gift to child cannot be avoided simply because it was made to avoid legal debt liability).

[75]*Murray v. McKenzie* (1911), 23 O.L.R. 287 at 299 (C.A.).

[76]*Ibid.*

[77]*Royal Trust Co. v. Jones, supra,* note 73.

*Interest in
an Estate*

presumption of parental influence is recognized at law as long as the "dominion of the parent lasts". Therefore, in order to establish a valid gift by a child to the parent, it must be shown that the child, in giving, acted with independent advice or in some other way that might rebut the presumption[78].

Estate law, as it relates to children, has rigid rules additional to those governing children's property interests in general. In Ontario, they are found under the *Succession Law Reform Act,* ss. 15, 17 and 21 of the *Estates Administration Act,* (which apply to real property only) and the Rules of Practice. These rules structure the disposition of a child's interest where the deceased has died without a will and a child is a deemed beneficiary to the estate, or where there is a will but its terms create a hiatus with respect to disposing of property in which the child has an interest[79]. However, under s. 60(4) of the *Children's Law Reform Act,* the Supreme Court may not make directions contrary to the terms of a will, subject to orders of support for dependants. (See Chapter 4 for discussion of support orders involving estates.)

If the deceased leaves a will, then the provisions of the will govern with respect to the distribution of property subject to adequate provision for support of dependants. A will made after March 31st, 1978, when referring to children, includes all children of the deceased whether born of a married relationship or not, unless the will specifies otherwise, in which case the excluded child must bow to the wishes of the testator subject to his claim for adequate support: s. 2, *Children's Law Reform Act.* Wills made before March 31st, 1978, referring to children, are governed by the common law principles of interpretation.

If the deceased does not leave a will, ss. 45, 46 and 47 of the *Succession Law Reform Act* direct the disposition of the deceased's assets as follows:

1) the property will be divided equally among any surviving children subject to the rights of a surviving spouse, as outlined below;
2) the surviving spouse is entitled to a preferential share in the amount of $75,000 out of the net value of the estate in priority to any claim by a child;
3) if the person dies intestate as to some property and testate as to other property, the surviving spouse will be entitled out of the intestate property to the amount by which $75,000 exceeds the value of the testate property to which the spouse is entitled;
4) if the spouse is already entitled to property in the net amount of $75,000 from the testate property, then her preferential share claim is no longer applicable;
5) if the deceased is survived by a spouse and one child, the spouse is

---

[78]*Wright v. Vanderplank* (1856), 44 E.R. 340, 8 De.G.M. & G. 133.
[79]*Re LeBlanc* (1978), 18 O.R. (2d) 507, at 515 (C.A.):

[W]here in a will real property is devised to the executor and there is in the will a clearly expressed power of sale over real property and as a matter of interpretation that power extends to real property specifically devised to infants (minors), the executor may sell the specifically devised property without complying with s. 4 of the *Infants Act* [now s. 60, *Children's Law Reform Act,* providing for court approval of disposition of property in which minor has an interest].

entitled to one-half of the residue of the property after payment of the spouse's preferential share; if there is more than one child, the spouse is entitled to one-third of the said residue;

6) if a deceased child would have been entitled hereunder, then his issue takes on his behalf as if the child were alive.

The definition ''child'' or ''issue'' had been developed by the common law and amended by present-day legislation to reflect modern mores. For example, prior to the enactment of s. 2 of the *Children's Law Reform Act* and the *Succession Law Reform Act,* a child born out of wedlock could not share in an intestacy unless it was the mother who died and she left no children born in wedlock[80]. Note however that the definitions for the purpose of estate law do not extend as far as they do for support rights and obligations, that is, it does not include a child towards whom a person has demonstrated a settled intention to treat as a member of his family.

Some of the more basic rules of estate administration as it relates to children include:

1) If it is necessary for the personal representative to rely on the *Estates Administration Act* in order to have authority to sell the estate property, the Official Guardian must be notified if a child is a beneficiary of the estate. Notice is given to the Official Guardian in order that the child's interests will be protected, and the Notice is a prerequisite ot any action under the Act: Ont. Rules of Practice, Rule 67.01. The Official Guardian's approval is essential if there are children interested in the property, even though all of the other beneficiaries who are adults have approved the sale. Pursuant to s. 17(2) of the Act, the Official Guardian will approve the sale only if it is in the interest of the child and to the advantage of the estate and the persons beneficially entitled. In practice, the Official Guardian will not likely give his approval to such a conveyance on behalf of a child, in which case a court order must be obtained according to s. 17(5) of the Act.

2) If the purpose of selling the property under the Act is for paying debts of the deceased, the Official Guardian's approval on behalf of a child who is a beneficiary is not required: s. 17(1)[81].

3) If the only beneficiaries to an estate are children, the practice is for an application to be made to the Supreme Court under s. 60(4) of the *Children's Law Reform Act,* instead of the *Estates Administration Act.* The court will apply the same standard to the disposition of the property in which a child has an interest as it would have under the *Estates Administration Act.*

---

[80]See *Locke v. Yuers* (1982), 28 R.F.L. (2d) 209 (Sask. C.A.) (nephew born out of wedlock entitled to deceased father's share on intestacy); *Brown v. Brown* (1980), 19 B.C.L.R. 280 (B.C. S.C.) (parents married after conception but before birth; common law, not statutory law applies); *Belanger v. Pester,* 2 Man. R. (2d) 283, [1982] W.W.R. 155, 108 D.L.R. (3d) 84 (*sub nom.* Re Horinek) 6 E.T.R. 21 (Q.B.) (Bequest to grandchildren not extending to illegitimate children of testator's son).

[81]See also *Re Watson and Major,* [1943] O.W.N. 696 (H.C.); *Hilliard v. Dillon,* [1955] O.W.N. 621.

4) If a child, through his next friend, desires to sell land specifically devised to him, the court may exercise greater care because there is a possibility that the child might desire its use when coming of age or better be able to appreciate it even for sentimental value at that time.

5) If court approval is sought, the judge shall obtain a written or oral consent of the child if he or she is over 16 years of age: *Rules of Practice,* 67.03.

Aside from these few general principles, the reader is advised to contact the office of the Official Guardian or Public Trustee, having legal authority with respect to such matters in their jurisdiction.

Fatal Accidents and Civil Suits

The repeal of the *Fatal Accidents Act* through the introduction of Part V of the *Family Law Reform Act* represents a significant change in the notion of the monetary value of a family member. Primarily, the legislation finally recognized that damages may expressly include an amount to compensate for the loss of "guidance, care and companionship" that the claimant might reasonably have expected to receive from the injured or deceased person if the accident had not occurred. This becomes extremely important in the case of a child who has been injured or killed. Prior to the amending legislation, the wrong-doer was liable to compensate only the potential economic gain the child may have provided to his or her parents if the child had lived.

> Any lawyer who was advising his insurance client, prior to 1978 as to a reserve that should be set up on a file to meet the circumstances of the taking of a child's life would, knowing the inequities written into the *Fatal Accidents Act.* . . . simply multiply one or two hundred dollars by the age of the deceased infant and the total achieved would approximate the loss which could be proved[82].

In the same Ontario Supreme Court decision, the court notes the description of that state of the law which provoked another justice of the Supreme Court to write:

> It was said, in a kind of macabre gest that was a stain on our law, that it was better to kill a child than to injure one. This was a sickening situation, which embarrassed anyone who had anything to do with the law in this country. It was an affront to Canadians who expect their law to be the embodiment of national and civilized thought. Such low damage awards were barbaric, and did not reflect the prevailing views of our society which recognizes that children have a special value that transcends the pecuniary benefits they may some day bestow on their parents[83].

The relevant provisions in discussing the new basis for damages are ss. 60(1) and (2) of the *Family Law Reform Act:*

> s. 60(1) Where a person is injured or killed by the fault or neglect of another under circumstances where the person is entitled to recover damages, or

---

[82]*Reidy et al. v. McLeod et al.* (1984), 47 O.R. (2d) 313, at 316 (H.C.).

[83]*Ibid.* applg *Thornborrow v. MacKinnon; Kane et al. v. Murphy* (1981), 32 O.R. (2d) 740 (S.C.).

would have been entitled if not killed, the spouse, as defined in Part II, children, grandchildren, parents, grandparents, brothers and sisters of the person are entitled to recover their pecuniary loss resulting from the injury or death from the person from whom the person injured or killed is entitled to recover or would have been entitled if not killed, and to maintain an action for the purpose in a court of competent jurisdiction.

(2) The damages recoverable in a claim under subsection (1) may include,

    (a) actual out-of-pocket expenses reasonably incurred for the benefit of the injured person;

    (b) a reasonable allowance for travel expenses actually incurred in visiting the injured person during his treatment or recovery;

    (c) where, as a result of the injury, the claimant provides nursing, housekeeping or other services for the injured person, a reasonable allowance for loss of income or the value of the services; and

    (d) an amount to compensate for the loss of guidance, care and companionship that the claimant might reasonably have expected to receive from the injured person if the injury had not occurred.

Following are some of the judicial principles which have emerged:

1) The courts have concluded that s. 60(2) and the assessment of damages applies to a fatal and non-fatal accident[84] (codified in Ontario's proposed *Family Law Act*).

2) Pursuant to ss. 60(1), the legislation specifically expands the number of claimants to include a commonlaw spouse, a child born within or outside the marriage and the parent-child relationship reflected in the phrase "where the adult has demonstrated a settled intention to treat the child as a member of his or her family." In other words, the scope of the claimants with respect to damages parallels that of the child claimant with respect to support. This expanded scope was applied in one case where the "sister" of a 15-year-old deceased "brother" was not a blood sister but was raised with the deceased under letters of guardianship[85].

3) In assessing damages for loss of "guidance, care and companionship," a global figure should not be selected and then apportioned among the claimants. The value of the loss of guidance, care and companionship will vary with each claimant and with the facts of each case[86]. The quantum of damages will vary with the degree of guidance, care and companionship that has been lost, and apparently, the extent to which it will not be replaced. Where, in at least one case, the father remarried, the damages to which the child would have been entitled for loss of his mother's guidance, care and

[84]*Mason v. Peters* (1983), 39 O.R. (2d) 27 (C.A.); *Wessel v. Kinsman Club of Sault Ste. Marie (Ont.) Inc.* (1982), 37 O.R. (2d) 481 (H.C.); *Reidy et al. v. McLeod et al., supra,* note 82; *Thornborrow v. MacKinnon, supra,* note 83.

[85]*Wessel v. Kinsman Club of Sault Ste. Marie (Ont.) Inc., ibid.*

[86]*Re Hutcheson, Forbes and Luyben et al. v. Harcourt,* unreported, June 30, 1983 (Ont. C. A.), *per* Zuber, Goodman and Grange.

companionship was reduced because a stepmother had moved into the void so that the child was held not to be suffering any serious deprivation[87]. If both parents die, the quantum of damages will be significantly greater than twice the quantum representing the death of one parent and presumably the same would apply if all the children of a parent were killed at one time[88]. 4) The assessment of damages for loss of guidance, care and companionship, represent "imponderable elements of loss" and are essentially non-pecuniary in character. Once the purely pecuniary issues are dealt with, then guidance, care and companionship should be approached on a broad basis with the qualification that damages allowed for loss of care should not duplicate what has already been assessed as a strictly pecuniary loss. In addition, the courts must no longer award nominal damages, treating such claims as trivial, nor is it necessary to strain to characterize the loss of guidance and care of a parent as a pecuniary loss or relate it to a tangible monetary loss such as losing the benefit of being fed, clothed and properly sheltered by a parent[89]. For example, damages were awarded under s. 60(2)(d) for loss of guidance, care and companionship where the adult married child, age 23, had acquired a 100-acre farm of his own and was operating that farm in partnership with the 175-acre farm belonging to his father. The Appellate Court considered the loss of the guidance of his father, particularly in the case of the claimant as a young farmer, to be substantial, and coupling this factor with the loss of the companionship of both his parents who were killed, it assessed the damages at $10,000, increasing the amount from that of $1,000 as ordered by the trial judge[90]. In the same case, parents applied for damages for the loss of their child. The trial judge, apparently resisting the impact of the new legislation, assessed damages for the loss to both parents at $1. The Court of Appeal over-turned this assessment noting that the parents "lost a fine son who would have given them companionship and such care as they might have required from him as they grew older[91]".

The loss of guidance, care and companionship is not necessarily restricted to the nuclear family since every case will turn on the facts of the relationship of the claimant to the deceased. Accordingly, courts have awarded damages under s. 60(2)(d) to siblings and grandparents.

In light of the above guidelines, it is now encumbent upon the practitioner to consider very carefully the facts of the relationship between the deceased and his client. In addition, he should consider the relationship of the deceased to *all* other members of the family in light of the decision of the Ontario Supreme Court which held that all such members must be named and joined in the claim[92].

---

[87]*Kugelmass v. Natale et al.* (1982), 37 O.R. (2d) 357 (H.C.).

[88]*Trudel v. Canamerican Auto Lease and Rental Ltd.* (1975), 59 D.L.R. (3d) 344 (Ont. H.C.); apprvd and appld in *Re Hutcheson, Forbes and Luyben et al. v. Harcourt, supra,* note 86, at p. 20.

[89]*Hutcheson, Forbes and Luyben et al. v. Harcourt, supra,* note 86.

[90]*Ibid.*

[91]*Ibid.*

[92]*Donaldson et al. v. Piron et al.* (1984), 44 O.R. (2d) 487 (H.C.); but see *Campbell v. Carrier,* summarized (1980), 3 F.L.R.R. 138 (Ont. Dist. Ct.).

Section 62(1) of the Act does provide that where an action is commenced under s. 60, "the plaintiff shall, in his statement of claim, name and join the claim of any other person who is entitled to maintain an action under s. 60 in respect of the same injury or death and thereupon such person becomes a party to the action." Section 62(2) directs that the person who commences the action must file with the statement of claim, an affidavit stating "that to the best of his knowledge, information and belief the persons named in the statement of claim are the only persons who are entitled or claim to be entitled to damges under section 60." Section 63(2) of Ontario's proposed *Family Law Act* puts even more of an onus of specificity and effort on the applicant.

In one decision of the Ontario High Court[93], presently on appeal, the court exhaustively scrutinized the details of the differing relationships between the deceased 17-year-old child and that of his mother, sisters, brother and stepbrother to conclude, under the heading of damages for loss of "guidance, care and companionship," that the mother was to be entitled to damages of $65,000, the three sisters, $3,500, the one brother, $2,500, and the stepbrother, $15,000. Some of the factors that were considered significant by the trial judge were:

1) The nature of the companionship: On the evidence, the court gained the impression that since the husband had left home, the 17-year-old deceased child provided his mother with the companionship and advice a wife would normally seek from her husband. They also found there to be an exceptionally close bond between the deceased child and his stepbrother, with the former fulfilling a father role for the boy, involving him in most of his activities.

2) The effect of the loss: The court found a causative link between the death and the fact that the stepbrother's grades dropped in school, and that the mother had to seek medical assistance.

3) The activities and accomplishments of the deceased: In this respect, the court noted that the deceased took great pride in his cadet activities, had received the Duke of Edinburgh award, had been presented with a "fitness award" by the Lieutenant Governor, all of which led the court to conclude that the family lost those positive elements of the deceased's character which had already been specially recognized by those who observed him.

In the same decision, the court reviewed the relationship between another victim of the accident, who was also another 17-year-old child, and his family, in the same manner, awarding damages of $35,000 to the father, $50,000 to the mother, amounts varying from $2,000 to $10,000 to the siblings, and $2,500 to the child's grandmother.

There appears to be common criteria emerging from the cases with respect to the death of a child and the assessment of "loss of guidance, care and companionship" for damages, and these include:

1) Closeness of the family: The closer the family, the more likely the child

---

[93]*Reidy et al. v. McLeod et al., supra,* note 82.

would have attended to the care of the members of his family in the short and long term, and therefore the greater the loss.

2) The degree of responsibility which the child assumed within the family: The more responsibility the child took on within the family, the greater the likelihood of his future contribution, and therefore the greater the loss.

3) The qualities of the child *qua* child, his achievements and standing in his school and community: The more exceptional the child was in terms of his academic, extracurricular or vocational activities the more pride and joy he would have brought to the family and therefore, the greater the loss.

4) The role the child played in relation to the other members of the family: The more the child assumed the responsibilities attributable to a parent or a spousal figure, the more exceptional the child and therefore the greater the loss.

5) The extent of dependency between the child and the member of the family: The more dependent the member of the family upon the child because of illness, disability, age, common livelihoods or interests or other circumstances, the greater the loss.

Specific examples of cases in which a child was applying for damages under this section include:

1) Where the family was very close, an unmarried adult daughter, devoted to her father, who was a source of inspiration to her until his death at the age of 75 years; hence, the daughter was entitled to damages in the amount of $5,000.[94]

2) A granddaughter who was 12 years old when her grandmother died received more in damages than each of the adult children and more than any of the other grandchildren because at the time of death, she was enjoying the physical care of the deceased and, as a further consideration, being younger, she experienced a greater loss; therefore $5,000 was awarded as damages[95].

3) A father (who had two children, ages 8 and 12), suffered an accident which caused him to be permanently unemployable and to be a "very different person than he was." The children were held to be entitled to damages of $4,000 for the older and $5,000 for the younger, the court noting:

The deprivation suffered by these two boys is serious indeed. The language of the statute seeks to supply compensation to these boys as a result of the loss of the advantages of the guidance, care and companionship of their father. Such matters are precious indeed, and not easily replaced. Children can be damaged severely if they lose the benefit of their father's teaching, companionship and care, as occurred here. Though still alive, Mr. Kane is not the same man as a result of the injuries, and the quality of the boys' present and future life will suffer immeasurably because of that. They

---

[94]*Rayner et al. v. Patterson et al.*, summarized in (1982), 4 F.L.R.R. 118 (Ont. H.C.).
[95]*Fulcher et al. v. Near et al.* (1981), 35 O.R. (2d) 184 (S.C.).

will never have a normal relationship with their father, which they had before and which they would have continued to have until the day he died, if not for the accident. A substantial loss has been suffered by these boys, despite the gallant efforts of the mother to fill in the gap[96].

4) A 29-year-old daughter whose relationship with her late mother did not include, prior to the death, enjoyment of physical care or guidance, was found not to have suffered any significant loss of companionship and was awarded $1,000 in damages in compensation for the loss of companionship which she might reasonably have expected to receive from her mother in the future[97].

Children as Parties to Civil Proceedings

Litigation Guardian

In most cases, a minor cannot commence or defend a civil action on his own. The only exception in Ontario occurs under the *Small Claims Act* wherein a child can sue for wages up to $100 as if he were of full age. In all other proceedings, a child may only sue or be sued through the intervention of an adult, known as a litigation guardian in some jurisdictions or, in others, as a guardian *ad litem* (defendant) or next friend (plaintiff)[98].

If a private person, usually the parent, does not seek or is not granted the position of litigation guardian by the court, the office of the Official Guardian or Public Trustee (depending on the jurisdiction) will assume the role, or the court may appoint such an agency instead of a private next friend[99]. The litigation guardian is an officer of the court and is not a party to the proceedings, although he can be examined on discovery as if he were a party[100]. The intervention of a litigation guardian is a necessary procedure since the law considers the child incapable of bringing an action without the assistance of some adult person who will participate in the proceedings responsibly, whom the court may compel obedience to its orders and specifically, if plaintiff, may hold accountable for costs of the action. In Ontario, the new Rules of Civil Procedure, O. Reg. 560/84 under Rule 7, codifies the procedure with respect to the role and duties of a litigation guardian. Some of the sub-sections are as follows:

1) A court proceeding involving a minor shall be conducted by a litigation guardian unless otherwise provided by a court or statute: Rule 7.01.

2) Anyone other than the Official Guardian or Public Trustee must file an affidavit stating, among other things, that he has retained a solicitor, that he has no interest adverse to the child in the proceeding and that he is aware of his liability for costs: Rule 7.02(2).

---

[96]*Thornborrow v. Schmidt, supra,* note 83, at p. 756.

[97]*Fread v. Chislet* (1981), 32 O.R. (2d) 733 (H.C.).

[98]In a Nova Scotia Prov. Ct. case, the court held that it had the jurisdiction to appoint a guardian *ad litem* for an unborn child where the father was seeking an injunction to prevent the mother from having an abortion: *Re H.* (1979), 38 N.S.R. (2d) 432, 69 A.P.R. 432 (*sub nom. Re Simms and H.*), 106 D.L.R. (3d) 435 (Fam. Ct.). An Ontario superior court held the opposite: *Medhurst v. Medhurst* (1984), 46 O.R. (2d) 263 (H.C.).

[99]*Re Knoch* (1979), 9 R.F.L. (2d) 395 (Ont. S.C.).

[100]See *Re Whittal,* [1973] 3 All E.R. 35 (Ch. Div.).

3) A litigation guardian must be appointed by the court and if the child's interest is in an estate or trust, the Official Guardian is automatically appointed: Rule 7.03.

4) If no one applies or if the appointed litigation guardian is not acting in the interests of the child, the Official Guardian shall be appointed: Rule 7.04(a), and 7.06(2).

5) If a settlement is reached prior to commencing a proceeding, the court's approval must be given: Rule 7.08(3); with the child's consent if over 16: Rule 7.08(5)(c).

6) Detailed directions for paying money into court on behalf of a minor: Rule 73.02; or paying money out of court to a minor: Rule 73.03.

Case law has also yielded guidelines for the litigation guardian:

1) As is set out in Rule 7.08, the court will not approve a settlement entered into by the guardian unless satisfied that it is for the child's benefit[101] and such application for approval must be served on the Official Guardian, even if the Official Guardian is not the child's litigation guardian[102]. Case law prior to the new Rules of Civil Procedure and applicable in the absence of contrary legislative language confirms that the court will not force upon a litigation guardian a settlement of which the litigation guardian does not approve[103]. But if the litigation guardian refuses settlement recommended by his counsel and the court considers it reasonable, the court does have the jurisdiction to replace the litigation guardian with the Official Guardian[104].

2) While the new Rules are silent on this issue, case law suggests that a next friend cannot abandon either the conduct of his action or his financial responsibility without leave of the court. Just as the court will not approve a settlement which is not beneficial to the child, it will not approve a discontinuance of the action by the next friend unless it is also in the interests of the child[105]. In this respect, it is immaterial that the defendant would forego costs of the action instituted by the next friend on behalf of the child. However, the court has no power to compel the next friend to proceed against his will with the lawsuit and even if it had the power, it has been held that it should not exercise it in view of the risk of heavy expense and the next friend's reluctance to proceed with the action. While the court could remove the next friend, it cannot appoint another unless there is consent by the new agent[106].

---

[101]But see also *Schmidt v. Schroeder* (1982), 15 Sask. R. 230 (Q.B.), in which the court rejected the settlement since certain conditions fettered the court's discretion.

[102]See Rule 7.08(4) of the Rules of Civil Procedure and *Re Whittal, supra,* note 100; *Rhodes v. Swithenbank* (1889), 22 Q.B. 577.

[103]*Re Whittal, supra,* note 100.

[104]See Rule 7.06(2) and *Re Whittal, supra,* note 100; *Panzavecchia v. Piche,* [1972] 2 O.R. 811 (H.C.).

[105]*Vano v. Canadian Coloured Cotton Mills Co.* (1910), 21 O.L.R. 144.

[106]*Howe v. Vancouver* (1957), 9 D.L.R. (2d) 78 (B.C. S.C.); See also *Burris v. Burris* (1981), 45 N.S.R. (2d) 625 (S.C.).

3) The Official Guardian appears to have the continuing authority to resist an appointment where it results in a conflict of interest or for any other valid reason[107].

4) The litigation guardian is not the legal counsel to the person for whom he is appointed. The position of the litigation guardian may better be described as the legal personality or legal "ego" of the child[108]. One of the first duties of this individual is to retain a solicitor to act on behalf of the client: Rule 7.02.

5) If an action is brought on behalf of a partnership in the name of the partnership then the partners, although children, need not be represented by a litigation guardian[109].

6) Costs if next friend: He is in the same position as any other litigant, receiving or paying costs personally as between himself and the defendant[110]. If he fulfilled his role and responsibilities, he will be indemnified out of the infant's estate[111]. If he acted recklessly, he will be liable for his own costs[112].

7) Costs if guardian *ad litem:* If the minor defendant is unsuccessful, costs of the guardian *ad litem* can be ordered to be paid by the plaintiff and added to the amount of the plaintiff's judgment against the defendant[113].

8) Costs if Official Guardian/Public Trustee: It has been held that costs may be awarded to this public agency since it would be improper to charge them to taxpayers at large[114].

Children Suing Parents

As a final note in discussing children as litigants, reference should be made to the capacity of the child to litigate against a parent. In this respect, ss. 66 and 67 of Ontario's *Family Law Reform Act* now makes it clear that children and parents are not barred from launching civil actions against one another[115]. In several American states, such actions have been limited, if not defeated, by a

---

[107]*Starkman v. Starkman,* [1964] 2 O.R. 99 (H.C.).

[108]*Re Whittal, supra,* note 100 (the object of a litigation guardian is to supplement the want of capacity in judgment of the infant).

[109]*British Products Unlimited v. Tenenbaum,* [1949] O.W.N. 240 (H.C.); Rule 102, R.C.P.

[110]*Morris v. Wabash Ry.,* [1947] O.R. 877 (H.C.) (next friend entitled to recover out of infant's fund); *Smith v. Mason* (1897), 17 P.R. 444 (C.A.) (next friend liable for costs without prejudice to claim for indemnity for infants).

[111]*Graves v. Dufferin Paving Ltd.,* [1942] O.W.N. 76 (H.C.); revd on other grounds [1942] O.W.N. 498 (C.A.).

[112]*Mill v. Mill* (1884), 8 O.R. 370; *McAndrew v. LaFlamme* (1872), 19 Gr. 193 (where next friend charged with costs because he filed a bill for administration where the estate was small and the suit was not necessary in the minor's interest); *Hutchison v. Sargent* (1870), 17 Gr. 8 (next friend ordered to pay costs because suit instituted recklessly and without proper inquiry).

[113]*Petrie v. Speers Taxi Ltd.,* [1952] O.R. 731, [1952] O.W.N. 276, [1953] 1 D.L.R. 349 (C.A.); revg [1952] O.W.N. 186; appld *Rivard v. Toronto General Trusts Corpn.* (1953), 9 W.W.R. 370 (Man. Q.B.); *MacAulay v. Neville* (1870), 5 P.R. 235 (where an infant defendant appeared by solicitor instead of guardian *ad litem,* the solicitor was ordered to pay the costs).

[114]*P. v. Rolly's Transfer Co.* (1981), 20 C.P.C. 287 (Man. Q.B.).

[115]See also *Deziel v. Deziel,* [1953] 1 D.L.R. 651 (Ont. H.C.); *Young v. Rankin,* [1934] S.C. 499.

doctrine based on immunity of the family[116]. Ontario's Act went even further in allowing actions by persons for damages incurred before their birth, *en ventre sa mere*. This would be applicable to suits against third parties, but also could theoretically include suits against the mother by the child, as more and more is learned about the causal connection between ingesting substances such as heroin, alcohol, nicotine or even aspirin and unhealthy births[117].

Civil Liability

The counter-balancing side to a discussion of limitations on a child's right to participate in society must be a discussion of the limitations on his legal liability or responsibility for his own acts. If his ability to participate is restricted by reason of his minor status, with 18 years as the arbitrary cross-roads, then it would seem reasonable to assume that the degree of liability that attaches to the child's actions would similarly be distinguishable on the same basis of age classification: "kids will be kids" must have a legal parallel. As discussed below, this is only partly the case. The weakness in the law's rationale, whether related to the issue of participatory laws or the issue of legal liability, is that there appears to be little clinical or empirical data concerning a child's psychological or physical development that validates the various universally applied age levels or "age-stagism" principles[118]. In fact, the laws attributing rights and responsibilities to children less reflect some objective measure and more reflect the attitudes towards the family and the state of the economy which happen to prevail in a particular society at a particular time in its history[119]. And yet it is also true that the developmental growth of a child is, to a certain degree, a direct function of the expectations laid upon him by his contemporary society[120]. The law often fails to recognize this Catch-22 dynamic affecting a person's transition from child-like to adult-like capacity to participate.

In the area of civil liability, the issue becomes that of how to apply the

---

[116]*Chaffin v. Chaffin* (1964), 397 P. 2d. 771 (Oreg.); Contra *Peterson v. City and County of Honolulu* (1970), 462 P. 2d. 1007 (Hawaii); and see *Hoffman v. Tracy* (1965), 406 P. 2d. 323 (Wash.); *Tucker v. Tucker* (1964), 395 P. 2d. 67 (Okla.); *Emery v. Emery* (1955), 289 P. 2d. 218 (Calif.).

[117]See *e.g.*, *Re L.*, summarized in (1981), 4 F.L.R.R. 87 (Ont. Prov. Ct.) where the court considered the medical evidence of the existence of "fetal alcohol syndrome" to conclude that a child *en ventre sa mere* was "in need of protection" under provincial child welfare legislation.

[118]See *e.g.*, A. Skolnick, "The Limits of Childhood: Conceptions of Child Development and Social Context" (1975), 39 *Law Contemporary Problems* 38; G.B. Melton, G.P. Koocher, M.J. Saks (eds.), *Children's Competence to Consent*, Critical Issues in Social Justice Series (New York: Plenum Press, 1983); *Child Advocacy: Psychological Issues and Interventions*, 1983; "The Child and the Law", *Child Development and Social Policy: Review of Child Development Research* (Chicago: University of Chicago Press, 1973). The classic psychological text which has influenced courts more than most where children are concerned is *Beyond the Best Interests of the Child* wherein different age levels are discussed in relation to the court's handling of custody matters. See J. Goldstein, A. Freud, A.J. Solnit, *Beyond the Best Interests of the Child* (New York: Free Press, 1974). See also by the same authors, *Before the Best Interests of the Child* (New York: Free Press, 1979).

[119]See *e.g.*, P.K. Naherny and J. Rosario, "Morality, Science and the Use of the Child in History", *Schooling and the Rights of Children*, V.F. Houbrich and M.W. Apple, editors, (Berkeley, California: McCutchan Publishing Corporation, 1975), at pp. 5, 11, 13, 35 and *fn.* 29. See generally Philippe Aries, *Centuries of Childhood: A Social History of the Family* (New York: Random House, 1962): C.J. Ross, "Of Children and Liberty: A Historian's Views", *American Journal of Ortho-Psychiatry* (July, 1982), Vol. 52, No. 3.

[120]Skolnick, Arlene, *supra*, note 118.

concept of negligence with its "reasonable [adult] person" standards to a child's acts. Some general guidelines have emerged:

1) While all children are liable to be sued for wrongful acts[121], children under the age of six or seven years appear to be subject to the "tender years" doctrine and are therefore usually presumed to be incapable of negligence and therefore immune from liability for damages[122].

2) Children of six or seven years of age or more are presumed to be competent enough to be subject to a judicial review based on some combination of an objective and subjective standard. Objectively, did the child exercise a standard of care expected from a child of like age, intelligence and experience[123]? Subjectively, was the conduct negligent, given evidence of *this* child's "age, capacity, knowledge and experience[124]"?

3) Children old enough to try their hands at adult-like activities (to be distinguished from child-like activities such as playing hopscotch, hide and seek or playing with child-like toys) are attributed with adult-like "foreseeability" and therefore liability; having chosen to participate, they must pay the price of a standard of care applied to the reasonable person of at least 18 years of age[125].

---

[121]*MacBeth v. Curran,* [1948] O.R. 444 (H.C.); *Continental Guaranty Corp. v. Mark,* [1926] 3 W.W.R. 428 (B.C. C.A.).

[122]*Saper v. City of Calgary* (1979), 21 A.R. 577 (Alta. Q.B.): (under 6 years constitutes "tender years"); and see Wright and Linden, *Canadian Tort Law, Cases, Notes and Materials* (6th ed.) for the assertion that under the age of seven years constitutes "tender years" for the typical child. At p. 176 of the text, the authors argue that age itself is but one of the factors and that the test to determine the preliminary issue of the child's competence vis-a-vis negligence is a very subjective one. "All of the qualities and defects of the particular child and all of the opportunities or lack of them which he might have had to become aware of any particular peril or duty of care must be considered." Accordingly, a three-year-old child was found not to be liable for the tort of battery since the intention to cause harmful contact with another was lacking when the child dragged a baby from his pram: *Tillander v. Gosselin* (1966), 60 D.L.R. (2d) 18 (Ont. H.C.); affd 61 D.L.R. (2d) 192*n* (Ont. C.A.). Yet a five-year-old who had intended to slash his friend with a razor was found liable upon an action for battery because the child, while not understanding the gravity of his action, nevertheless had an intent: *Hart v. A.-G. for Tas. and Pascoe,* (Tas., unreported S.M.H. May 30, 1959) as cited in Fleming, *The Law of Torts* (4th Ed.), at p. 25. In *McEllistrum v. Etches,* [1956] S.C.R. 787 the court adopted the summary in Glenville Williams' text, *Joint Torts and Contributory Negligence* (1951), s. 89, p. 355 to find no particular age as the dividing line, only that:

> where the age is not such as to make a discussion of contributory negligence absurd, it is a question for the jury in each case whether the infant exercised the care to be expected from a child of like age, intelligence and experience. [at p. 793]

[123]*McEllistrum v. Etches, ibid.*

[124]*Oliver Blais Co. Ltd. v. Yachuk,* [1946] S.C.R.1, [1946]1 D.L.R. 5 at 16; revd [1949] A.C. 386, [1949] 2 W.W.R. 764, [1949] 3 D.L.R. 1 (P.C.). See also the dissenting opinion of Laskin C.J., in *Wade v. C.N.R.,* [1978] 1 S.C.R. 1064, at 1074–76 (Spent and Dickson JJ.); *Strehlke v. Camenzind,* 27 A.R. 256, [1980] 4 W.W.R. 464, 111 D.L.R. (3d) 319 (Alta. Q.B.).

[125]From Linden, *Canadian Negligence Law* (1972), at pp. 33–34 (as quoted in *Ryan v. Hickson* (1974), 7 O.R. (2d) 352 at p. 358 (H.C.):

> Special rules for children make sense, especially when they are plaintiffs; however, when a young person is engaged in an adult activity which is normally insured, the policy of protecting

Accordingly, a child who walks across an intersection in front of a city bus, holds up her hand and thereby causes an accident, is not responsible for the consequences of her act. As a five-year-old person, her absolute confidence that this manoeuvre would protect her from harm betrays a naïvete which one would expect from a child of "tender years" as opposed to a child in grade school[126]. However, a six-year-old child who, on his way to school, crossed at an intersection on an amber light, but did so in the path of a moving vehicle, was found to bear 10 per cent liability for the accident. The court took into account the child's age but attributed to him a degree of judgment to be expected even of a person of this age[127].

No special standards in assessing negligence attached to a minor in two different cases involving the operation of a snowmobile, one who was 14 years[128] and one who was 12 years[129]. This was mainly due to the fact that snowmobiling is classified as an adult activity because of the vehicle's power and possibility for harm. In the 12-year-old's case, the defendant was specifically found, "on the evidence," to have the capacity, knowledge and experience sufficient to become liable for damages occasioned by his negligence. In the 14-year-old's case, there appeared to be no consideration given to the question of capacity as it related to the child's negligence. On the other hand, an 11-year-old child driving a

---

the child from ruinous liability loses its force. Moreover, when rights of adulthood are granted, the responsibilities of maturity should also accompany them. In addition, the legitimate expectations of the community are different when a youth is operating a motor vehicle than when he is playing ball. As one American court suggested, juvenile conduct may be expected from children at play but "one cannot know whether the operator of an approaching automobile . . . is a minor or adult, and usually cannot protect himself against youthful imprudence even if warned". Consequently, there has been a movement toward holding children to the reasonable man standard when they engage in adult activities. A more lenient standard for young people in the operation of motor vehicles, for example, was thought to be "unrealistic" and "inimical to public safety". When a society permits young people of 15 or 16 . . . the privilege of operating a lethal weapon like an automobile on its highways, it should require of them the same caution it demands of all other drivers.

The principle is also enunciated in *Daniels v. Evans* (1966), 224 A. 2d 63, at p. 64 (New Hampshire) the court states:

We agree that minors are entitled to be judged by standards comensurate with their age, experience and wisdom when engaged in activities appropriate to their age, experience and wisdom. Hence, when children are walking, running, playing with toys, throwing balls, operating bicycles, sliding or engaged in other childhood activities, their conduct should be judged by the rule of what is reasonable conduct under the circumstances among which are the age, experience and stage of mental development of the minor involved.

However, the question is raised by the defendant in this case whether the standard of care applied to minors in such cases should prevail when the minor is engaged in activities normally undertaken by adults. . . . We are of the opinion that to apply to minors a more lenient standard in the operation of motor vehicles, whether an automobile or motorcycle, than that applied to adults, is unrealistic, contrary to the expressed legislative policy, and inimical to public safety".

[126]*Saper v. City of Calgary, supra,* note 122.

[127]*Steeves v. Sprague* (1978), 22 N.B.R. (2d) 423, 3 A.P.R. 423 (Q.B.).

[128]*Assiniboine School Division v. Hoffer* (1970), 16 D.L.R. (3d) 703 (Man. Q.B.); affd 21 D.L.R. (3d) 608 (Man. C.A.); affd 40 D.L.R. (3d) 480 (S.C.C.); *Ryan v. Hickson, supra,* note 125.

[129]*Ryan v. Hickson, ibid.*

dune-buggy at a high rate of speed — his vision obstructed by dust in the absence of light — who would have been unquestionably liable for damages if he were an adult, was found not to be responsible for the consequences of his actions as "it is expected of 11-year-old children that their excitement may lead them to act without proper attention and appreciation of possible danger"[130].

Although the above judgments may appear less than consistent, so too is the nature of childhood and hence the findings of capacity and liability in each case. Nevertheless, one must be wary regarding any assumptions which the judge may take judicial notice of as to the capabilities of any particular age level. To counter such biases, counsel may find it useful to have available for the court empirical evidence or professional opinion related to the particular environment of the subject child (*e.g.* rural/urban) in addition to evidence of the particular capabilities of the child in question.

Another problem is that different judges may give varying weight to the objective versus subjective test. It is submitted that the objective standard, supported by professional opinion, must be only a preliminary measure (less than a presumption) to be varied or negated by in depth evidence about the particular child as it relates to the actions of the child which are in dispute. The weight given to the subjective standard is justified by the fluid nature of childhood itself with its complex interaction of social, developmental and cognitive stages. The child is, in essence, a dependant of a family unit, developing through these stages and as such, the family's influence must be of primary significance rather than some abstract "reasonable child" measure.

Because the "adult-like" activity is often found to be so because of the degree of potential danger to others, the courts have resisted diminishing the standard of care expected because of age. Arguably, a wholesale imposition of an adult's standard of capacity and liability is the equivalent of making negligence for children a strict liability offence. It may be more fair to strike a degree of liability based on the capacity of the particular child to appreciate the nature and danger of the activity, as well as the degree of choice over his actions available to him in the context of family pressures. A 12-year-old's use of a rifle is decidedly the taking on of an adult activity, but his capacity to handle the weapon safely and foresee danger to others may be inextricably bound up in the expectations and role modelling of the father. One commentator paralleled the holding of a child to an adult standard of care in adult activities, to the holding of a lay adult to a professional standard of care in undertaking "professional" activities. The problem in this parallelism is that it assumes that the child had the same degree of choice, opportunity and knowledge as the adult in undertaking the activity and appreciating its consequences. This is rarely the case.

The American Law Institute *Restatement of Torts Second* states:

> It is impossible to lay down definite rules as to whether any child, or any class of children, should be able to appreciate and cope with the dangers of many situations. A child of 10 may, in one situation, have sufficient capacity to appreciate the risks involved in his conduct and to realize its unreasonable character, but in another situation he may lack the necessary

---

[130]*Christie v. Slevinsky and Western Union Insurance Co.* (1981), 12 M.V.R. 67 (Alta. Q.B.).

mental capacity or experience to do so; and in the case of another child of 10 of different mental capacity or experience, a different conclusion may be reached in the same situation.

This approach was taken in an Ontario case in which a child caused an explosion on private property:

> Was Randy negligent in removing the bung from the barrel and in putting a match in or close to the bung-hole? One must not apply the objective standard of care of the reasonable man but must rather look at the child, his background, knowledge and intelligence and then ask oneself whether this child, in these circumstances, was negligent. Randy comes from a broken home. . . . He failed grade 2. . . . His mother describes him as bright and described him as "a rough sort of boy who got into all sorts of scrapes." . . . . [T]he Hospital for Sick Children thought that he was of average intelligence. . . . He seemed bright enough to me in the witness-box. Clearly, a nine and a half-year old child of average intelligence would be guilty of negligence in crossing the street in the face of traffic against a red light. That child, even with the limitations imposed upon by his age, could and should be able to foresee the consequences of his action. But is the same true in this case? He certainly knew that he was not supposed to play with matches but continued to do so. Clearly, he would know that if he held a match too close to the flame he would burn his fingers and, I think, he should be expected to appreciate that if he held a match to paper or cloth, the paper or cloth would burn. The question of contributory negligence has given me considerable concern. I think it is a borderline case. I have come to the conclusion that Randy did not appreciate the risk of fire or explosion inherent in putting a match close or in the bung-hole of this barrel. The reasonable adult would appreciate this risk but I think it would place too high a standard on this boy to hold that he would appreciate the risk[131].

Parental Liability

The inherent dependency of a child gives rise to parental or third party liability for the child's acts. In many actions involving children, parents are joined as third parties either to share the liability or, in actions against children, to provide the only defendant with the financial resources or insurance coverage to satisfy judgment. Under existing law in an action for negligence against a parent, the injured party has to show that the parent failed to exercise reasonable care over his child which, if exercised, would have prevented the infliction of injury on others[132]. Under s. 70 of Ontario's proposed *Family Law Act*, the onus is reversed; the parent must show that he "exercised reasonable care and control of the child". The test of whether a parent has acted with reasonable care will centre on whether an adult would reasonably have been able to foresee the possibility of the danger arising from the child's conduct having regard, it appears, to the following factors:

---

[131]*Walker v. Sheffield Bronze Powder Co. Ltd.* (1977), 16 O.R. (2d) 101, at 108–09 (H.C.); see also *Strehlke v. Camenzind, supra,* note 124.
[132]*Smith v. Leurs* (1945), 70 C.L.R. 256 at 262.

1) Age: As the age of the child increases, so too do expectations that the child will conform to adult standards of behaviour; accordingly, the parental duty to supervise and control his activities diminishes[133]. However, the years just prior to adulthood can actually impose greater expectations on the parent. For example, fathers of two boys, 12 and 14 years, were found to be liable as a result of the negligence of their children in the operation of snowmobiles. It was the position of the court that fathers should be aware of the ordinary character of boys of 12 to 14 years, their general aptitude for mischief, their desire for excitement, and their lack of good and mature judgment[134].

2) The activity and its potential danger with its resulting degree of necessary supervision or prior instruction and warning: A 7-year-old boy's father is liable if he permits his child, without supervision and without warning, to pat a large and unfamilar German Shepherd dog[135]. A 13-year-old boy shoots his friend with a pellet gun which the parents knew to be readily accessible to the boy. The child is found negligent but so too is the father for failing to make the gun inaccessible and for failing to provide the instruction on its use[136]. On the other hand, if a father allows his son, who is 14 years old and well-trained in the use of firearms, to go out hunting game which results in a prairie fire, the father is not liable since he had instructed his child properly and acted reasonably on the basis of his son's maturity. The child was found to be solely liable[137].

3) Knowledge by the parent of prior acts or propensities of the child: Liability may attach to the parents, depending on whether they were aware that some peculiar trait existed in the child which, if not guarded against, could reasonably be foreseen to cause danger to others. Parents whose children have stolen a car during the night, causing damage to it during a police chase, may be found to be negligent. Even though the parents were found to have acted reasonably in not imposing a curfew on the children, the court considered whether one of the children, *to the knowledge of the parent*, had a propensity to steal, and barring evidence to that effect, noted that no special steps of care were therefore necessary to satisfy a reasonable standard of supervision or control[138].

---

[133]See *Sgro v. Verbeek* (1980), 111 D.L.R. (3d) 479 (Ont. S.C.).

[134]*Ryan et al. v. Hickson, supra,* note 125; and see *Lelarge v. Blakney* (1978), 92 D.L.R. (3d) 440 (N.B.C.A.).

[135]*Sgro v. Verbeek, supra,* note 133; See also *Hache v. Savoie* (1980), 31 N.B.R. (2d) 631, 75 A.P.R. 631 (Q.B.).

[136]*Floyd v. Bowers* (1978), 21 O.R. (2d) 204, 89 D.L.R. (3d) 559, 6 C.C.L.T. 65 (H.C.); varied on other grounds, 27 O.R. (2d) 487, 106 D.L.R. (3d) 702 (C.A.). See also *Moran v. Burroughs* (1912), 27 O.L.R. 539 (C.A.), wherein a 12-year-old boy shoots his friend with a rifle which the father knew to be in his possession. Father found negligent in failing to remove the gun immediately from his child.

[137]*Turner v. Snyder* (1906), 16 Man. R. 79: See also *Starr and McNulty v. Crone,* [1950] 2 W.W.R. 560 (B.C.S.C.); *Walmsley v. Hemenick,* [1954] 2 D.L.R. 232 (B.C.S.C.); *Ryan v. Hickson, supra,* note 133; *Delowsky v. Aiello* (1980), 119 D.L.R. (3d) 240 (B.C.S.C.); *Christie v. Slevinski, supra,* note 130.

[138]*Streifel v. Strotz* (1957), 11 D.L.R. (2d) 667 (B.C.S.C.); and see *Tillander v. Gosselin, supra,* note 122 in contrast to *Ellis v. D'Angelo* (1953), 253 P. 2d. 675 (Calif.).

Third Party
Liability

Third party liability of persons other than parents is based on the standard of care which any adult is expected to exercise in order to protect himself from the curiosity or improvident conduct of a typical child. Ontario recently introduced an *Occupier's Liability Act* which codifies the common law to a certain extent. It delineates two standards of care. The first is a general standard towards persons entering on the premises for whom the occupier must "take such care as in all the circumstances of the case is reasonable to see that [those persons]" are reasonably safe. The second, lesser standard, is owed towards those who "willingly assume risks" in entering onto the premises to whom the occupier must "not create a danger with the deliberate intent of doing harm . . . and not act with reckless disregard of the presence of the person. . . ." The Act goes on to specify that persons will be deemed to have willingly assumed all risks if they are trespassing on "rural premises", golf courses, rights-of way, unopened road allowances, private roads and recreational trails: s. 4(3) and (4).

Since there is no reference in the Act to special standards relating to children, previous common law cases should be useful in determining how the minority status affects the definition of "reasonable care." Depending on the age and capacity of the particular child, he may or may not be capable of "willingly assuming a risk" although this subjective test will not take him out of the strict liability circumstances of s. 4(3). Nevertheless, there may remain some degree of subjectivity in the "reckless disregard" test of the owner since the wording relates to "the presence of the [trespasser]" and is not a test in the abstract.

Traditionally, the common law had established the concept of occupier's liability based on the standard of care which decreased with the person's right to be on the property. A higher degree of care was owed by the occupier to a person who comes as a result of a contract or an invitation than to a person who enters merely as a licensee or as a trespasser[139]. However, because children were so often injured owing to nothing more than their "innocence," the courts found that the application of such a standard to children was too harsh. One way to circumvent the minimal protection owed to a trespasser was to find that a child who had been lured onto the private property was not a trespasser but, in fact, a licensee. As a licensee, the child would be owed a greater duty of care than were he a trespasser[140]. Implicit in this approach was the difficulty of determining what constitutes an allurement to a child[141].

In the 1977 Ontario case of *Walker v. Sheffield Bronze Powder Co. Ltd.*, it was held that the court should no longer concern itself with the distinction between trespasser and licensee and should apply ordinary negligence law.

---

[139]See *Willey v. Cambridge Leaseholds Limited* (1975), 48 D.L.R. (3d) 589 (P.E.I.S.C.); varied on other grounds, 57 D.L.R. (3d) 550 (P.E.I.C.A.); *Robert Addie and Sons, Colliers Ltd. v. Drumbreck*, [1929] A.C. 358 (H.L.).

[140]See *Ottawa v. Munroe*, [1954] S.C.R. 756; *Wallace v. Pettit* (1923), 55 O.L.R. 82 (C.A.); *Pianosi v. C.N.R.*, [1943] O.W.N. 766 (Ont. C.A.): *Jones v. Calgary; Jones v. Canadian Westinghouse Co. Ltd.* (1969), 67 W.W.R. 589 (Alta. S.C.).

[141]See *Riopelle v. Desjardins and Congregation of the Most Holy Redeemer*, [1950] O.R. 93: *Robinson v. Havelock* (1914), 32 O.L.R. 25 (C.A.); *Pedlar v. Toronto Power Co.* (1914), 30 O.L.R. 581 (C.A.).

I conclude from the authorities that, at least where we are dealing with children, we are no longer required to categorize the child as a trespasser or licensee or strain to find an allurement. We apply ordinary negligence law. The injury having occurred, we ask ourselves whether or not this sort of injury was foreseeable on the part of the occupier and whether, if it was foreseeable, he should have guarded against it. We must ask ourselves whether the precautions taken by the occupier to guard against the risk of injury were reasonable considering the use that he knew or should have known would be made of the property by people coming on the property without permission. An occupier is not required to take extravagant precautions. He must match the precautions to the risk. Unfortunately, too often, the occupier shelters behind a policy of insurance rather than a chain link fence. . . .

I have no doubt that the danger and injury were foreseeable. The occupier knew of the flammable and explosive nature of the contents of the stored barrels and should have foreseen the danger of injury. Furthermore, in my view, the precautions taken were inadequate. The only precaution was the direction to the employees to tighten the bungs with a bung wrench and store the barrels top to the wall. It was foreseeable that these instructions would not be strictly followed. It was foreseeable that children would play around the barrels and would try to investigate the contents[142].

Compare the results of this case to a majority decision of a 1977 Supreme Court of Canada case[143] in which the occupier, the Canadian National Railway, was not found to be negligent in the context of a "reasonable humanity" test, the majority holding that to find otherwise was to make the C.N.R. the insurer for all possible acts by potential plaintiffs. In this case, an eight-year-old boy, playing with friends on sand piles situated on a railway right-of-way that was 50 feet from the tracks, ran towards a slowly moving freight train in an attempt to board it. He fell beneath the cars and his leg was severed by the wheels. The accident was not discovered by the train crew until they reached the next station since the engine had already passed when the child ran out and the visibility from the caboose was restricted, due to its being pulled backwards. A final salient point is that agents of the C.N.R. knew that the children played frequently on the sand piles, but they were never chased away.

At the trial, the jury was asked:

"Q. 1   (a) Was there fault or negligence on the part of the Defendant Railway, its servants or agents which caused injury, loss or damage to the plaintiffs?

A.   Yes.

Q. 1   (b) If so, in what did such fault or negligence consist?

A.   (1) lack of fence and proper signs
     (2) lack of removal of sand or gravel from CN property

---

[142]*Walker v. Sheffield Bronze Powder Co. Ltd., supra,* note 131 at pp. 107–08. See also *Veinot v. Kerr-Addison Mines Ltd.,* [1975] 2 S.C.R. 111.

[143]*Wade v. C.N.R.,* [1978] 1 S.C.R. 1064.

(3) the making up of the cars originally

(4) CN being aware of conditions of property and aware of children playing in this area.

Q. 2 Was the Infant Plaintiff Peter Wade, a licensee or a trespasser in relation to the Defendant Railway at the time he was injured?

A. Licensee.

Q. 3 (a) Was the Infant Plaintiff, Peter Wade, enticed or allured to the defendant's premises by the presence of sand and gravel piles located thereon?

A. Yes.

Q. 3 (b) Was the Defendant's train an enticement or allurement to the Infant Plaintiff, Peter Wade, at the time he was injured?

A. Yes.

Q. 4 Was Peter Wade, at the time he was injured, a child of such an age, intelligence and experience as to understand and appreciate the risk of injury in attempting to board the defendant's train?

A. No.[144]

The provincial Appellate Court upheld the determination of negligence on the part of the railway company. In the Supreme Court of Canada, the majority decision found for the defendant, and, in particular, found that:

1) Regarding the lack of fence and proper signs: The duty cannot be that great as to require the company to erect a fence across the track at each public crossing so as to stop all persons from walking along the right-of-way. Fencing the right-of-way itself would not have stopped them, since they got to the site via the tracks.

2) Failure to remove the sand or gravel from the company's property: No duty upon the company arises out of the presence of piles of sand on a right-of-way, piles on which children have been seen to play in the past to the knowledge of the railway. Even if the sand piles constitute a playground, no duty should be imposed upon the railway to stop its trains or to post sentries.

3) The method in which the cars were made up: No duty exists upon the company to arrange its cars so as to give the crew in the caboose a perfect visibility at all times. The visibility must belong to the occupants of the locomotive, that of the occupants of the caboose being of minor importance.

4) Reasonable foreseeability: No occupier could have reasonably foreseen that a child playing on a pile of sand (some 50 feet from the track when the engine went by) would leave that place of safety, run towards the track and attempt to jump on the ladder of the box car. To find fault on the part of the company on this basis is tantamount to saying that a railway company is the insurer of all persons coming onto its land, a proposition which cannot be accepted. The train itself does not constitute an allurement unless there were particular features differentiating it from all other freight trains. Even if the

---

[144]*Ibid.*, at p. 1072.

train were an allurement, there were no reasonable and practicable measures to be taken by the defendant through the exercise of reasonable foresight, especially since no similar accidents had occurred. The fact that it was possible that an accident might occur is not the criterion. It must be sufficiently probable so that it would be included in the category of contingencies normally to be foreseen. The facts of this case were not sufficiently probable to render the C.N.R. liable[145].

The dissenting opinion of Laskin C.J. (Spence and Dickson JJ. concurring) maintained that the duty of care to take measures to prevent such an accident arose from the knowledge of the company through its agents that children played regularly on the sand piles which were in such close proximity to the trains. This position reflects much more that of the above-noted decision of *Walker v. Sheffield, Bronze Powder Co. Ltd.*

A final Supreme Court of Canada case[146] of note deals with the liability of those whose business it is to attract children. In this case, a 4-1/2-year-old child was struck by a car in the course of buying an ice cream from an ice cream vending truck. This time, reasonable foreseeability was considered in the context of a ''good neighbour'' doctrine: the ice cream vendors put themselves in such a relationship with their child patrons that they became the neighbours of all possible children and therefore must take reasonable care to avoid acts or omissions which ''you can reasonably foresee would be likely to injure your neighbour.'' The court, in applying this doctrine, concluded that it was inevitable that the defendant ice cream vending company would attract the patronage of young children, including those of pre-school age with little ability to comprehend danger and none to read a warning sign on the side of the truck. The failure to take proper steps to see that these children are not subjected to the dangers of traffic accidents was only to fail to do what anyone with the slightest common sense would have done. Except for one of the justices of the Supreme Court of Canada, no contributory negligence was found on the part of the parent in permitting her child to go out without supervision. In this case, the mother of four young children was on the phone speaking to her husband and was interrupted by the two youngest children and were crying for money to buy ice cream. The children in the neighbourhood had become accustomed to buying ice cream in this manner, if not from the identical vendor. The children had received strong instructions concerning the crossing of the street, ''to watch out for cars,'' such that it could not be said that the mother was contributorily negligent. The sole dissenter on the issue of the mother's contributory negligence could not accept that the standard of care of the ice cream merchant could be greater than that of a parent. He found that the duty of care resting on a parent does not come to an end because a third party comes into the picture[147].

Reviewing both Supreme Court of Canada cases, one asks what differentiates them such that the attraction of a slowly moving train, 50 feet from

[145]*Ibid.*, at pp. 1083–86.
[146]*Arnold v. Teno; J.B. Jackson Ltd. v. Teno,* [1978] 2 S.C.R. 288.
[147]*Ibid.,* per deGrandpre J.

what amounted to a children's playground, was found to be less foreseeable and required less rigorous duty of care than the attraction of an ice-cream truck on a residential street? Primarily, it appears that the intentional attraction of young children is the main different. Somewhat secondary factors appear to be: the ages of the children involved; public property *v.* private property; awareness of previous similar activity. In other words, the court went beyond a simple test of the reasonable person's foreseeability with accompanying reasonable precautions as described in the above-noted *Walker v. Sheffield, Bronze Powder Co. Ltd.*

Actions Ex Delicto

Before concluding this chapter, reference should be made to the matter of actions *ex delicto* involving children as one of the parties. An action *ex delicto* may refer to breaches of duty arising from a contract to be distinguished from actions *ex contractu* which would arise from a breach of promise set forth in the contract. As children are presumed to be exempt from binding contractual liability by law, so the law considers that a child will be liable only if the wrongful act is one that is unrelated to a contract. That is, the injured party cannot rely on an action in tort, *ex delicto*, to seek relief which, by the law of contract would not be available. In one such case, a rented car was damaged as a result of a child's negligence. The plaintiff could not recover damages on the basis of negligence since the driving of the car was within the purview of the contractual arrangement with the child. The plaintiff's remedy must be maintained in the contract and barring evidence to show that the agreement was for the child's benefit, that action may fail. However, the possible dismissal of his action based on the contract does not allow the plaintiff to proceed in negligence[148]. On the other hand, where a child sells goods which are in his possession under a lien agreement, he will be liable for damages for a tortious action based on conversion. The wrong doing committed is not contemplated by the contractual lien arrangements[149].

Other than the general statement noted above, it remains difficult to distinguish between arrangements where the remedy is rooted in the contract and those in which an action in tort may also be available. Note the following quote from a judgment where an action in detinue had succeeded against a child for the return of certain articles which he had borrowed from the injured party and which he had lent to a friend, without authority.

> [I]t seems to me that, when properly construed, the terms of the bailment of these articles to the infant appellant did not permit him to part with their possession at all. If it was the bargain that he might part with them, it was for the infant to establish that fact, and it seems to me that he has failed to do so. On that basis, the action of the appellant in parting with the goods was one which fell outside the contract altogether[150].

---

[148]*Dickson Brothers U-Drive Ltd. v. Sam Woo* (1957), 23 W.W.R. 485; affg 22 W.W.R. 143 (B.C.C.A.).

[149]*McCallum v. Urchak*, [1926] 1 W.W.R. 137 (Alta. C.A.); and see *R. Leslie Limited v. Sheill*, [1914] 3 K.B. 607 (C.A.).

[150]*Ballet v. Mingay*, [1943] 1 All E.R. 143, at 145 (C.A.).

Chapter 5: Readings

Alexander, E.R., "Tort Liability of Children and their Parents", in D. Mendes da Costa (ed.), *Studies in Canadian Family Law* (Toronto: Butterworth's, 1972).

Aries, Philippe, *Centuries of Childhood: A Social History of the Family* (N.Y.: Random House, 1962).

Barnett, L.D., "Child Exclusion Policies in Housing" (1978–79), 67 *Kentucky Law Journal* 967.

Beane, L., "Role of an Infant as a Member of a Partnership", (December, 1982) 87 *Com. L.J.* 622.

Bisset-Johnson, A., "Medical Consent and Minors." Paper delivered at conference on "Consent to Treatment and the Law", (Halifax, November, 1983).

Bowker, W.F., "Minors and Mental Incompetents: Consent to Experimentation, Gifts of Issue and Sterilization" (1981), 26 *McGill L.J.* 951.

British Columbia Law Reform Commission, *Report on Minors' Contracts* (Victoria: Queen's Printer, 1976).

British Columbia Royal Commission on Family and Children's Law, *Report #12: The Medical Consent of Minors* (Victoria: Queen's Printer, 1975).

Burt, "The Therapeutic Use and Abuse of State Power Over Adolescents" in Schoolar, J. (ed.), *Current Issues in Adolescent Psychiatry*, (1973).

Butler, K., "A Chance to be Heard: An Application of *Bellotti v. Baird* to the Civil Commitment of Minors" (1981), 32 *Hastings L.J.* 1285.

"Children May Recover for Loss of Companionship and Society of Father Tortiously Injured", (August, 1981) 19 *J. Fam. L.* 750.

Children's Competence to Consent (Critical Issues in Social Justice Series, 1983).

Citarella, K.C., "Civil Commitment of Children by Parents: *Parham v. J.R.*, 442 U.S. 584 (1979)" (Fall, 1980), 25 *N.Y.L. Sch. L. Rev.* 1001.

Clark, R.W., "Contracts for the Sale of Non-Necessary Goods: Vendor's Remedies Against Infant Purchaser" (1981), 7 *U. Tasmania L. Rev.* 85.

Clive, E., "What Has Happened to the Age of Minority?" (Scotland), (July, 1982), 27 *Jur. Rev.* 51.

Coens, T.A., "Child Labour Laws: A Viable Legacy for the 1980's" (October, 1982) 33 *Lab L.J.* 668.

Coleman, James S. et al., *Youth: Transition to Adulthood* (Report from Panel on Youth of the President's Science Advisory Committee) (Chicago: University of Chicago Press, 1974).

"Consent of Minors to Health Care," Institute of Law Research and Reform (Edmonton: University of Alberta, 1975).

Dickens, B.M., "The Modern Function and Limits of Parental Rights" (1981), 97 *L.Q. Rev.* 462.

Gaylin, W., "The 'Competence' of Children: No Longer All or None'', (March, 1982), 21 *J. of Am. Ac. of Child Psychiatry* (No. 2) 153.

Gosse, R., "Consent to Medical Treatment: A Minor Digression'', (1974), 9 *U.B.C. L. Rev.* 56.

Guggenheim, M., *The Rights of Young People: An A.C.L.U. Handbook* (1984).

Institute of Judicial Administration, American Bar Association, *Standards Relating to the Rights of Minors* (Ballinger, 1981).

Katz, S.N., Schroeder, W.A., Sidman, L.R., "Emancipating Our Children — Coming of Legal Age in America'', (1973) 7 *Fam. L.Q.* 3.

Kenney, A., Forrest, J.D. and Torres, A., "Storm Over Washington: The Parental Notification Proposal'' (1982), 28 *Family Planning Perspectives* (14) 185.

Kenny, T.J., "Should the Six Year Old Have the Vote?'' (1977), 2 *Journal of Pediatric Psychology* (No. 1).

Krever, H., "Minors and Consent for Medical Treatment'' in Dickens, B. (ed.) *Materials in Medical Jurisprudence* (University of Toronto, Faculty of Law, 1979).

Lewis, M., "Comments on Some Ethical, Legal and Clinical Issues Affecting Consent in Treatment, Organ Transplants and Research in Children'' (Summer, 1981), 20 *J. of Am. Ac. of Child Psychiatry* (No. 3) 581.

Mabbutt, F.R., "Juveniles, Mental Hospital Commitment and Civil Rights: The Case of *Parham v. J.R.,* 442 U.S. 584 (1979)'' (November, 1980), 19 *J. Fam. L.* 27.

Melton, G.B. "Toward 'Personhood' for Adolescents: Autonomy and Privacy as Values in Public Policy,'' (January, 1983), 38 *American Psychologist* 99.

Miller, D. and Burt, R.A., "Children's Rights on Entering Therapeutic Institutions'' (February, 1977), 134 *Am. J. of Psychiatry* 153.

Paul, E. and Pilpel, H., *Teenagers and Pregnancy: The Law in 1979* (1979), 11 *Family Planning Perspectives* 297.

Pettifor, "Working for Children: Ethical Issues Beyond Professional Guidelines'' (Alberta Mental Health Services, Calgary, 1979).

Pilpel, H., "Parental Consent Requirements and Privacy Rights of Minors: The Contraceptive Controversy'' (1975), 88 *Harv. Law Rev.* 1001.

Polier, "Professional Abuse of Children: Responsibility for the Delivery of Services'' (1975), 45 *Am. J. Orthopsychiatry* (No. 3) 357.

"Recognizing a Child's Action for Loss of Parental Consortium: Reconciling Cognate Actions With Workmen's Compensation Provisions: Case Note (July, 1981), 15 *Suffolk U.L. Rev.* 1082.

"Restrictions on the Abortion Rights of Minors: *Bellotti v. Baird,* 99 S. Ct. 3035 (1979)'' (Spring, 1980), 3 *Harv. Women L.J.* 119.

Roocher, G. (ed.), *Children's Rights and the Mental Health Professions* (N.Y.: Wiley-Interscience Publication, 1976) (Sponsored by the Society for the Psychological Study of Social Issues).

Rosenberg, N.S., "Sterilization of Mentally Retarded Adolescents'' (1980), 14 *Clearinghouse Review* (No. 5).

Siedelson, D.E., "Reasonable Expectation and Subjective Standards in

Negligence Law: The Minor, the Mentally Impaired and the Mentally Incompetent'' (November, 1981), 50 *Geo. Wash. L. Rev.* 17.

Simet, D.P., ''Power, Uncertainty and Choice: The Voluntary Commitment of Children: *Parham v. J.L.*'' (May, 1982), 20 *U.W. Ont. L. Rev.* 141.

Skegg, P.D.G., ''Consent to Medical Treatment in Minors'' (1973), 36 *Modern L. Rev.* 370.

Skolnick, A., ''The Limits of Childhood: Conceptions of Child Development and Social Context'' (1975), 39 *Law and Contemporary Problems* 38.

''Stability in Child-Parent Relations: Modifying Guardianship Law'' (May, 1981), 33 *Stan L. Rev.* 905.

Stern, D., Smith, S., Doolittle, F., ''How Children Used to Work'' (1975), 39 *Law and Contemporary Problems* 93.

Task Force on the Child as citizen, *Admittance Restricted: The Child as Citizen in Canada* (Ottawa: Canadian Council on Children and Youth, 1978).

Teitlebaum, L., ''The *Age Discrimination Act* and Youth'' (Symposium on Age Discrimination) (Fall, 1981), 57 *Chi-Kent L. Rev.* 969.

''The Child and the Law'', *Child Development and Social Policy: Review of Child Development Research* (Chicago: University of Chicago Press, 1973).

''The Impact of a Child's Due Process Victory on the California Mental Health System: Case Note'', (Mr 82), 70 *Calif. L. Rev.* 373.

Thomson, G., ''Minors and Medical Consent'' (Winter, 1981), 2 *Health L. Can.* 76.

''Torts and the Unborn'' (May, 1982), 33 *S.C.L. Rev.* 659 (special issue).

U.S. Dept. of Health and Human Services, *The Legal Status of Adolescents 1980* (1981).

Wadlington, ''Minors and Health Care: The Age of Consent'' (1973), 11 *Osgoode Hall L.J.* 115.

Weiler, K. and Catton, K., ''The Unborn Child in Canadian Law'' (1976), 14 *Osgoode Hall L.J.* 643.

Who Speaks for the Child: The Problems of Proxy Consent (Legal, philosophical and medical analysis of proxy consent) (Hastings Center Series in Ethics, 1982).

Chapter 6

The Child and the Courtroom

This chapter deals with several aspects of the child and the court room: the child as witness; the admissibility and weight of a child's testimony; when a child may be found in contempt of court; whether or not a child is allowed to be present during the proceedings; and finally, child representation.

The Child as Witness

Generally speaking, courts are reluctant to see a child appear as a witness, because the testimony may not be reliable (as dealt with below under "Testimony of Children") and because of the trauma which the child may undergo, especially if the proceedings are dealing with the mistreatment or the custody of that child. Nevertheless, certain proceedings revolve around the child such as custody/access, child welfare and criminal offences involving children so that their being called as a witness is sometimes unavoidable.

In civil custody/access proceedings, the child is competent and compellable as a witness, although the judge plays a protective role. For example, one court questioned the propriety of a child testifying in a custody dispute as follows:

> There is one matter of evidence to which I now wish to make special reference. . . . [C]ounsel stated he had instructions to call as a witness Michael, the 11-year-old boy now living with the father. I said that I could not prevent any witness being called, but that I strongly disapproved the involvement of children in the family disputes of their parents, unless it were impossible to prove necessary facts in any other way. Here it seemed to me that the evidence already adduced for the father was comprehensive, clear and full on the issues involved. The witness could be called, but I advised against it. I said that, if it were necessary in my judgment, I would see the children later.
>
> . . .
>
> The children were not called. I do not consider this to be a case in which I need interview the children.

In proceedings such as these where the welfare of the children and the future of the family is in the care of the Court, it seems not only reasonable but desirable and necessary that the judge should have some discretion to prevent the dispute between the parents from becoming, as it might here, a dispute on oath between children as to the parents' merits and conduct. In some cases that may be necessary. It goes against the grain of family life and uses the Court to set brother against brother. It should not be done where an impartial judgment, able to be fully informed otherwise, does not consider it necessary.[1]

As the court indicated in the decision above, one option in lieu of the child as witness is for the judge to interview the child privately. It is not improper for a trial judge to see children in a custody matter in his chambers if, through their counsel, both parties consent as long as the judge does not allow the comments of the children to be the sole basis upon which he writes his judgment, disregarding what is in their best interests.[2] However, where the judge sees the child in private, on consent of the parties, the information should be disclosed to the parties so that they might have an opportunity of contraverting it.[3] This reflects a concern by the court that for a custody proceeding to be fair and just, the parties must have an opportunity to meet the evidence upon which a decision will be made. However laudable and arguably necessary this open approach to chambers interviews may be, it goes some way to defeat one of the purposes of the interview being held in private which is to relieve the child of the misery of showing a preference for either parent in front of the other parent. In an English Court of Appeal decision, the court had promised the children that all of their wishes would be kept absolutely confidential. On appeal, the court stated:

It is, of course, often most desirable in matters of this sort that the judge hearing the case should see the children, and should see the children otherwise than in open court. One can well understand that in matters of this sort the children may be reluctant to express themselves freely and frankly when there is the possibility that what they say may be made known, and perhaps particularly made known to their parents. It is, of course, desirable in the highest degree that when children are seen in this way, not in open court, every possible step should be taken to insure that what they say should be said freely and frankly. Nevertheless in my judgment it is wrong that a judge should give a promise to a child such as was given in this case. . . Of course the concern of the court in these matters is the welfare of the children. It is certainly possible that when a judge sees the children in private something may emerge which requires further investigation as a matter of necessity for the benefit of the children themselves; and that may involve the necessity of a judge disclosing that which he has heard. How can he do that if he has made a promise to the children at the outset that nothing they say will be disclosed to anyone? Further, there is the position of this court. There is an appeal as of right from the judge's decision. This court has to arrive at a

---

[1] *Taberner v. Taberner* (1971), 5 R.F.L. 14, at 14–15 (Ont. S.C.).
[2] *Saxon v. Saxon* (1974), 17 R.F.L. 257 (B.C. S.C.).
[3] *Re Allan and Allan* (1958), 16 D.L.R. (2d) 172 (B.C. C.A.).

conclusion affecting the welfare of the children and decide whether the judge was right or wrong. How can this court discharge that task if something which may have been important in the judge's decision is something of which this court cannot make itself aware without breaking a solemn promise given by a judge to the person who supplied the information?[4]

In Ontario, the courts have interviewed children privately, in the presence of a court reporter. In one such situation, the court noted: "The parties do not ask for a transcript of what was said at that time until the final resolution of this matter, if ever."[5]

A Manitoba Court of Appeal recently considered this issue extensively.[6] Towards the end of the trial, the judge privately interviewed four children between the ages of 11 and 16 for approximately one and a half hours. There was no court reporter present and no record of the meeting was maintained. Neither the parents nor the Appellate Court had any idea of what transpired in the judge's chambers. However, after the interview with the children, the trial judge conducted his own examination and cross-examination of the mother for some 22 pages of transcript and it was clear from the transcript that these questions were prompted by the meeting with the children. The court then awarded custody to the father. On appeal, the Appellate Court reversed the decision, granting custody to the mother, and dealt with the issue of the interview as follows:

> Once again, if the purpose of such an interview is simply to ascertain the wishes of the children, that can be done in a private meeting with or without the consent of one or both counsel. There should always be a record of what is said in such a conference. A trial judge has a discretion to interview children in private, without counsel, but if the rights of the parties are subject to appeal it is important there be some record of what has been said in the interview. If it is not possible to have a verbatim transcript, it is possible at least to have a statement from the trial judge as to what was said.
>
> It is not proper, however, to go beyond the ascertainment of the wishes of the children. In the instant case, it became evident later in the proceedings that the children were asked, and gave their comments, on a range of topics extending well beyond their individual wishes. In effect, the children became private witnesses giving evidence in the cause to which only the trial judge is privy. I know of no basis in law for allowing such testimony as admissible evidence in the cause.
>
> If a judge feels it is necessary to go behind a child's expression of desire as to custody, and to determine why the child prefers one parent over the other, and into the subject of parental imperfections and frailties, the proper course is for the child to be called as a witness so that the evidence is in the open and it is subject to testing through cross-examination.[7]

---

[4]*H. v. H.*, [1974] 1 All E.R. 1145, at 1147–48 (C.A.).

[5]*Guy v. Guy* (1975), 22 R.F.L. 294 (Ont. S.C.); *Kralik v. Kralik* (1973), 12 R.F.L. 246 (S.C.); revd on other grounds, 4 O.R. (2d) 171 (C.A.).

[6]*Jandrisch v. Jandrisch* (1980), 16 R.F.L. 238 (Man. C.A.).

[7]*Ibid.,* at pp. 249–50.

Recent Ontario legislation responds directly to the difficulties of children as witnesses in custody disputes. Section 65 of the *Children's Law Reform Act* provides:

> s. 65(1) In considering an application under this Part [custody, access and guardianship], a court where possible shall take into consideration the views and preferences of the child to the extent that the child is able to express them.
>
> (2) The court may interview the child to determine the views and preferences of the child.
>
> (3) The interview shall be recorded.
>
> (4) The child is entitled to be advised by and to have his counsel, if any, present during the interview.

As in "private" custody disputes, there is nothing in child welfare legislation to render the child non-competent or non-compellable as a witness to a proceeding that affects himself or another child, although Ontario's legislation creates a presumption against the presence of a child in the courtroom if he is under the age of 10 years "unless the court is satisfied that the hearing or any part thereof would be understandable to the child and not be injurious to his emotional health": s. 33, *Child Welfare Act*. The new *Child and Family Services Act, 1984* will change the age from 10 to 12 years.[8] It should be noted, however, that this test applies simply to the child's presence in the court room to view the proceedings. Presumably one would apply a less broad exclusionary test to the witness question since the child as witness may be extremely important to a fair outcome of the hearing, whereas his mere presence goes more to the right of anyone to observe a hearing affecting his rights.

In one case, the child welfare legislation was invoked in an attempt to prevent a child from giving evidence as a witness in a criminal proceeding in which the child's father allegedly killed his mother. It was argued that to expose the child to such an experience rendered him "in need of protection" under the child welfare legislation. It was held that the circumstances did not warrant such a finding and even if they did, a finding of "in need of protection" does not immunize the child from the possibility of being subpoenaed to court as a witness.[9]

Testimony of Children

In order to ensure that testimony is reliable, the common law surrounded the admissibility of such testimony with various rules, one of which requires that the witness, before testifying, swear under oath to tell only the truth. This rule particularly affects the admissibility and weight given to a child's testimony since the witness must know the nature and meaning of an oath before taking it. As a result, in common law, when a child under the age of 14 years is called upon to testify, as a finding of fact, it is the responsibility of the court to inquire and determine whether the child has the necessary capacity to swear an oath. A child

---

[8] Section 39(4), *CFSA*.
[9] *Horncastle v. McDonald*, unreported, March 17, 1977, Ont. Prov. Ct. Fam. Div.

of 14 years of age or over is presumed to understand the nature of an oath and can be sworn without a preliminary inquiry into his capacity.[10]

This common law position with respect to the competence of children to testify in civil and criminal trials has been codified in various statutes including:

1) The *Canada Evidence Act:*

   s. 16(1) In any legal proceeding where a child of tender years is offered as a witness, and such child does not, in the opinion of the judge, justice or other presiding officer, understand the nature of an oath, the evidence of such child may be received, though not given upon oath, if, in the opinion of the judge, justice or other presiding officer, as the case may be, the child is possessed of sufficient intelligence to justify the reception of the evidence, and understands the duty of speaking the truth.

   (2) No case shall be decided upon such evidence alone, and it must be corroborated by some other material evidence.

2) The Ontario *Evidence Act:*

   Section 18 reproduces s. 16 of the Canada Evidence Act verbatim.

3) The *Criminal Code:*

   s. 586 No person shall be convicted of an offence upon the unsworn evidence of a child unless the evidence of the child is corroborated in a material particular by evidence that implicates the accused.

Note that a child of "tender years" is not defined in any of the above Acts, nor is a definition to be found in any statute including this term. Accordingly, the common law definition continues to apply such that "children of tender years" refers to persons under the age of 14 years.

It has been held that the determination of competency or capacity must be conducted before pre-trial examination for discovery and in the absence of such a determination, answers from a 9 and 11-year-old boy cannot be read in at trial.[11] Once there is a finding of competency with respect to the oath, the child will then be sworn and the evidence will be treated like all other testimonial evidence given under oath. Although a witness was only five years and nine months old, once he was found competent to take the oath it was the clear duty of the court to administer it.[12] An Appeal Court will not interfere with the trial judge's finding of competency or his conduct of the inquiry unless the examination has been abusive or there has not been any examination at all.[13] While the court will be under a duty to determine if the child is a competent witness, it has been held that a conviction will not be set aside where a 12-year-old gave evidence under oath without any preliminary finding of the child's capacity, neither party bringing the

[10]*Sankey v. R.* (1927), 48 C.C.C. 97 (S.C.C.); *R. v. Armstrong* (1959), 125 C.C.C. 56 (B.C.C.A.); *R. v. Dyer* (1972), 17 C.R.N.S. 207; leave to appeal to Supreme Court of Canada refused, 17 C.R.N.S. 233*n* (S.C.C.); *R. v. LeBrun* (1951), 100 C.C.C. 16 (Ont. C.A.); *R. v. Deol, Gill and Randev* (1981), 58 C.C.C. (2d) 524 (Alta. C.A.).

[11]*Strehlke v. Camenzind, Letourneau and Janor Contracting Ltd. (Third Party)*, [1980] 4 W.W.R. 464 (Alta. Q.B.).

[12]*Strachan v. McGinn*, [1936] 1 W.W.R. 412 (B.C.S.C.); *R. v. Brasier* (1779), 1 East P.C. 443.

[13]*R. v. Armstrong, supra,* note 10; *R. v. Pailleur* (1909), 20 O.L.R. 207 (C.A.); *R. v. Mulvihill* (1914), 22 C.C.C. 354 (B.C.C.A.); *R. v. Bannerman* (1966), 48 C.R. 110; affd. 50 C.R. 76 (S.C.C.); *R. v. Duguay,* [1966] 3 C.C.C. 266 (Sask. C.A.).

court's attention to any question concerning the age of the child.[14] The court distinguished its ruling from the Supreme Court of Canada decision of *Sankey v. R.*[15] on the basis that, unlike that case, neither party informed the court that the child was of tender years. As a result of this ruling, it may be that unless one counsel raises the issue of the child's "tender years", the evidence of the child on appeal will be considered competent testimony even where a finding of competency has not been rendered.[16] In those situations where an Appellate Court has concluded that a child should not have been sworn, the evidence will not then be treated as unsworn evidence, but will be completely disregarded.[17]

The capacity of the witness is to be determined as of the date when he gives evidence, rather than as of the age when he observed the incident. For example, in one case,[18] three witnesses, ages 17, 19 and 21 at the time of trial, were testifying about an incident which occurred some years ago when all three of them were of "tender years". The defence lawyer argued that their testimony should carry the same weight as the uncorroborated evidence of children. The Supreme Court of Canada disagreed:

> [I]t is quite clear that they were testifying as mature persons to what they had observed as children. But they were not testifying to a routine matter that happened 9 years before. If they were telling the truth, what they had seen must have made an indelible impression on their minds at the time and must have been something that they could never forget. Again, the trial judge had adequately instructed the jury, if any such instruction was needed, but these witnesses were mature witnesses testifying to something that had happened 9 years before. Questions of weight and credibility in these circumstances were entirely for the jury. It would, in my opinion, have been wrong for the trial judge to warn the jury that they must treat this evidence as though it had been given by children of immature years and to have warned them of the special risk in acting on the uncorroborated evidence of the young child, even when sworn. This would be a totally unwarranted and undesirable extension of the rules of practice. The need for this special warning disappears when the children give evidence as mature persons. It then becomes a matter of weight and credibility for the jury.[19]

The inquiry conducted by the trial judge is done by way of *voir dire* and can be conducted in any manner which will tend to disclose the child's capacity and understanding.[20] It is the exclusive prerogative of the judge to conduct the inquiry

---

[14]*R. v. McKevitt* (1936), 66 C.C.C. 70 (N.S.C.A.).

[15]*Sankey v. R., supra,* note 10.

[16]But see *R. v. Pawlyna* (1948), 91 C.C.C. 50 (Ont. C.A.); *R. v. Molnar* (1948), 90 C.C.C. 194 (Alta. C.A.).

[17]*R. v. LaRochelle* (1951), 102 C.C.C. 194 (N.S.C.A.); *R. v. Stone* (1960), 127 C.C.C. 359 (Ont. C.A.); *R. v. Hampton*, [1966] 4 C.C.C. 1 (B.C.C.A.); *R. v. Kowalski* (1962), 132 C.C.C. 324 (Man. C.A.).

[18]*R. v. Kendall* (1962), 132 C.C.C. 216 (S.C.C.).

[19]*Ibid.,* at pp. 220–21.

[20]*R. v. Armstrong, supra,* note 10; *R. v. Harris* (1919), 34 C.C.C. 129 (Sask. K.B.); *R. v. Fitzpatrick* (1929), 51 C.C.C. 146 (B.C.C.A.).

and determine the child's competency although he may ask counsel for assistance if he so desires.[21] Moreover, there is a positive duty on the part of counsel to instruct the child concerning the nature of an oath and the court may be adjourned to allow this to happen.[22] Leading questions are permissible.[23] An inquiry is always necessary since the court cannot make its finding as to the child's capacity to understand the oath by means of mere observation alone.[24]

"Understand the Nature of an Oath"

It has been difficult to distinguish between the two levels of capacity representing sworn and unsworn evidence as delineated by the *Canada Evidence Act* (above) since a fine line exists between respectively, an ability to appreciate the moral significance of an oath and simply understanding the duty of speaking the truth. Neither case law nor statute requires the judge to evaluate a child's appreciation of what may befall him if he should tell a lie. Instead, the early case of *R. v. Bannerman*[25] required from the child a "solemn assumption of a moral obligation before God to speak the truth." That is, the child need not understand the "spiritual retribution which follows the telling of a lie." The object of the law in requiring an oath is to get to the truth relative to the matters in dispute by "getting a hold" on the conscience of the witness. In this case, the child indicated that he knew it was wrong not to tell the truth but answered "No" in response to the question "Now, what would happen to you if you didn't tell the truth, do you know?" Counsel for the accused, on appeal, contended that while the child had understood the "nature" of the oath, he had not understood the "consequences" of the oath and therefore the inquiry into his capacity fell short of what was required by law. In reply, the court noted that any reference to "consequences" has been removed from the Canada *Evidence Act* and accordingly it was sufficient that the child understood the "nature" of an oath and not the "consequences."

The *Bannerman* decision restricted the reliance on the religious aspect of the oath to the obligation to tell the truth rather than to the possible consequences of not telling the truth. In two recent decisions of the Ontario Court of Appeal, the religious content of an oath was debated further. In the first case,[26] involving a 9-year-old, the court considered the following judicial inquiry at trial level as to the child's capacity:

Court:	How old are you, Sonia?
Sonia:	Nine
Court:	What do you do, do you go to school?
Sonia:	Yes
Court:	What grade are you in?
Sonia:	Four.

[21]*R. v. Lyons* (1889), 15 V.L.R. 15 (Aust. S.C.).

[22]*R. v. Armstrong, supra,* note 10; *R. v. Bannerman, supra,* note 13; *R. v. Brown* (1951), 99 C.C.C. 305 (N.B.C.A.).

[23]*R. v. Bannerman, supra,* note 13.

[24]*R. v. Lebrun, supra,* note 10; *R. v. Dumont* (1950), 98 C.C.C. 336 (N.B.C.A.); *R. v. LaRochelle, supra,* note 17; *R. v. Dunn* (1951), 99 C.C.C. 111 (B.C.S.C.).

[25]*R. v. Bannerman, supra,* note 13.

[26]*R. v. Budin* (1981), 58 C.C.C. (2d) 352 (Ont. C.A.).

Court:	Do you watch television?
Sonia:	Ya.
Court:	Have you ever seen anybody get in the stand and take an oath? Do you know what an oath is?
Sonia:	Ya, to promise.
Court:	To promise what? Promise to tell the truth?
Sonia:	Ya.
Court:	If I told you to take the Bible in your hand and you told me that you would tell the truth, would you do so?
Sonia:	(Witness indicating in the affirmative)
Court:	All right, do you know what would happen to you if you told a lie?
Sonia:	Yes.
Court:	What would happen?
Sonia:	You would get mad at my mother and father.
Court:	A little bit more than that. Could you be punished?
Sonia:	Yes.
Court:	I am satisfied that she understands.[27]

On the basis of this exchange, the Appellate Court set aside the conviction and directed a new trial. The court agreed with the *Bannerman* decision that a child need not understand the spiritual consequences of an oath but concluded that the statutory use of the word "oath" must be given its ordinary meaning, that is, a "solemn appeal to God (or to something sacred) in witness that a statement is true." Accordingly, the test must establish that the child believed in God or another Almighty, and that in giving the oath, the child is telling such Almighty that what he will say will be the truth.

The same court, in the later decision of *R. v. Fletcher*,[28] effectively overruled the first. The court approved the minority opinion in the earlier decision and relied on the English case of *R. v. Hayes*[29] in restricting the requirements of the oath to an understanding of the moral duty to tell the truth without reference to God or any Supreme Being. The court pointed out the folly of disallowing an intelligent child of 13 with a clear capacity to understand the moral obligation from testifying simply because the child does not believe in God.

If the *Fletcher* decision is determinative of this issue, then the distinction between the tests for sworn and unsworn evidence has become so fine that the most that can reliably be said is that the question will be a function of the particular child witness and the particular trial judge's views on children. Removing spiritual consequences and spiritual belief from the test leaves the judge to determine whether a particular child, having sufficient capacity to be heard, understands the concept of duty and duty to tell the truth as an obligation of secular social conduct. The Court of Appeal in *Fletcher* appeared to adopt as

---

[27]*Ibid.*, at pp. 356–57.

[28]*R. v. Fletcher* (1982), 1 C.C.C. (3d) 370 (Ont. C.A.).

[29]*R. v. Hayes*, [1977] 2 All E.R. 288 (C.A.), as cited in *R. v. Fletcher, ibid.*, at p. 378. And see *R. v. Horsburgh*, [1966] 3 C.C.C. 240 (Ont. C.A.).

adequate a line of inquiry which elicited answers as to age, school attendance and a moral obligation to tell the truth. The exercise of determining capacity to swear an oath becomes even more difficult (or some would say, futile) when one considers that since counsel has the duty to instruct the child concerning the nature of an oath, the child may simply be mimicking what the lawyer told him to say.

Affirmation
Because of the traditionally religious nature of an oath, s. 14 of the *Canada Evidence Act* and s. 18 of the *Ontario Evidence Act* allow a witness to affirm instead of swear an oath "where [he] objects on the grounds of conscientious scruples or is objected to as incompetent to take an oath." It has been held that a child who has been found incompetent to take the oath cannot make an affirmation under either Act:

> I cannot agree that infants and persons incompetent from want of intelligence are included in this section. If a witness is objected to for the want of rational intelligence, his evidence will still be inadmissible. In my opinion, this section was only intended to meet the case of persons commonly called atheists or persons without religious belief.[30]

In one case,[31] the Australian High Court suggested that analogous legislation allowing "affirmation" in lieu of swearing an oath applies to "any person" called as a witness and therefore children are included in its scope. The issue before the court involved the child's ability to be a conscientious objector to the swearing of an oath. The magistrate was satisfied with the intelligence of the child but questioned his maturity to understand the significance of the oath, not because the child has consciously rejected any belief in God, but because he appeared to lack knowledge of or belief in God and its relationship to the swearing of an oath. The Appeal Court upheld his decision to affirm. Under the Canada *Evidence Act* and the *Ontario Evidence Act,* the ability of a child to be a conscientious objector would be applicable to the first ground, that is, he "objects on the grounds of conscientious scruples." However the second ground, "is objected to as incompetent to take an oath" apparently requires no such subjective measure of the witness. However, it is unlikely that any court would use this phrase as a basis for admitting evidence as sworn if that evidence had also not met the test under *R. v. Fletcher* above.

"Sufficient Intelligence to be Heard"
Before a judge can admit even unsworn evidence, he must determine, pursuant to the evidence statutes, *above,* whether the child "is possessed of sufficient intelligence to justify the reception of the evidence and understands the duty to tell the truth." Perhaps this test is comparable to the common law test applicable to all witnesses that they must be able to interpret events properly.[32] (Note that an essential prerequisite to the admission of unsworn testimony is that the court first must inquire as to whether the child is capable of giving sworn evidence.[33] There are certain empirical truths about children that raise issue with

---

[30]*R. v. Lewis* (1887), Knox 8, at p. 10 (Aus.). And see *R. v. Budin, supra,* note 26, at p. 355.

[31]*Cheers v. Porter* (1931), 46 C.L.R. 521 (H.C. of Aust.).

[32]See Sopinka and Lederman, *The Law of Evidence in Civil Cases* (Toronto: Butterworths, 1974), at p. 450.

[33]*R. v. Bannerman, supra,* note 13; *Sankey v. R.* (1927), 48 C.C.C. 97 (S.C.C.).

their competency no matter how hard they try to please the judge, the lawyer who has met with them or the parent looking on expectantly in the courtroom. Consider the following exchanges from Jean Piaget's *The Child's Conception of the World:*

Gava
8-1/2 yrs. old

(The sun is alive because) it keeps coming back.
Does it know when the weather is fine?
Yes, because it can see it.
Has it eyes?
Of course! When it gets up it looks to see if it is bad weather and if it is, it goes off somewhere else where it's fine.
Does it know that it's called the sun?
Yes, it knows that we like it. It is very nice of it to make us warm.
Does it know its name?
I don't know. But sometimes it must hear us talking and then it will hear names and then it will know. (All this seems to be pure romancing, but as we shall see, Gava almost identifies the sun with God):
When your daddy was little, was there a sun then?
Yes, because the sun was born before people so that people would be able to live.
How did it start?
It was made in Heaven. It was a person who died and then went to Heaven. In Sunday School, he is called God.
Where did this person come from?
From inside the earth.
Where from?
I don't know how he was made.
How did that make the sun?
The person was very red and that made the light. Even in the morning before the sun is out, it is light all the same.
(In other words, this person (Jesus Christ) has set fire to Heaven, and this light made the sun. Gava is thinking probably of Christ's halo. He went on to tell us of a picture in which God was like the sun but with arms and legs!)

. . .

If you were to speak to the sun would it hear?
Yes, when you say your prayers.
Do you say your prayers to it?
Yes.
Who told you to do that?

At Sunday school I was told always to say my prayers to it.[34]

Roy
6 yrs. old

The moon has become a whole one.
How?
Because it's grown.
How does the moon grow?
Because it gets bigger.
How does that come about?
Because we get bigger. [Parce que nous on grandit].
What makes it get bigger?
It's the clouds.

. . .

What do they do?
They help it to grow.
How did the moon begin?
Because we began to be alive.
What did that do?
It made the moon get bigger.
Is the moon alive?
No. . . Yes.
Why?
Because we are alive.
How was it made?
Because we were made.[35]

Tag
6-1/2 yrs. old

Have you seen the clouds moving?
Yes.
Can you make them move yourself?
Yes, by walking.
What happens when you walk?
It makes them move.
What makes them move?
We do, because we walk and then they follow us.
What makes them follow us?
Because we walk.
How do you know that?
Because when you look up in the sky, they are moving.
Could you make them go the other way if you wanted to?
By turning round and walking back.
And what would the clouds do then?

---

[34]Jean Piaget, *The Child's Conception of the World* (London: Routledge and Kegan Paul PLC, 1973), at pp. 302–03.
[35]*Ibid.*, at pp. 289–90.

They'd go back.

Can you make anything else move from far away without touching it?

The moon.

How?

When you walk, it follows you. The stars too.

How?

When you move they follow too. The ones that are behind follow the moon.[36]

What is significant in these excerpts is not so much the dearth of scientific knowledge possessed by the children (which most adults suffer from), but the egocentricity of the children in the perceptions of events around them:

Just as the child makes his own truth, so he makes his own reality; he feels the resistance of matter no more than he feels the difficulty of giving proofs. He states without proof and he commands without limit.[37]

The superficiality of our approach to the child witness is accentuated by the continued reliance on the verbal questioning in the courtroom as the only method of obtaining information from a child. A cursory glance at disciplines more attuned to the child's developmental capacity offers alternatives.[38]

Young Offenders Act

The recently proclaimed *Young Offenders Act,* which constitutes a criminal code for persons between the ages of 12 and 17 years,[39] codifies the issues discussed above only for the purposes of that Act. The relevant ss. 60 and 61 of the Act deal with a "child" (a person apparently or actually under the age of 12 years) and a "young person" (a person between the ages of 12 and 17 years):

s. 60(1) In any proceedings under this Act where the evidence of a child or young person is taken, it shall be taken only after the youth court judge or the justice, as the case may be, has

(a) in all cases, if the witness is a child, and

(b) where he deems it necessary, if the witness is a young person, instructed the child or young person as to the duty of the witness to speak the truth and the consequences of failing to do so.

(2) The evidence of a child or young person shall be taken under solemn affirmation as follows:

I solemnly affirm that the evidence to be given by me shall be the truth, the whole truth, and nothing but the truth.

(3) Evidence of a child or a young person taken under solemn affirmation shall have the same effect as if taken under oath.

---

[36]*Ibid.,* at pp. 170–71.

[37]*Ibid.,* at p. 189.

[38]See *e.g.:* Kohlberg, L. "Development of Moral Character and Ideology" in *Review of Child Development Research,* Hoffman, M.L. and Hoffman, L.W. (New York: Russell Sage Foundation, 1964); Laing R.D., *Conversations with Adam and Natasha* (New York: Pantheon Books, 1977).

[39]Section 2 of the *Young Offenders Act* defines "young person" to include persons who are or appear to be between 12 and 17 years of age inclusively but the extension of the limiting age from 16 years to 18 years did not go into effect until April 1, 1985.

s. 61(1) The evidence of a child may not be received in any proceedings under this Act unless, in the opinion of the youth court judge or the justice, as the case may be, the child is possessed of sufficient intelligence to justify the reception of the evidence, and understands the duty of speaking the truth.

(2) No case shall be decided on the evidence of a child alone, but must be corroborated by some material evidence.

The apparent effect of these sections for proceedings under the *Young Offenders Act* will be:

1) To abolish any further juristic debates on the distinction between ''oath-ridden'' sworn and unsworn testimony. Now, all children ''solemnly affirm'' in a wholly secular context.

2) To preserve, with some modification, the presumption of ''tender years'' with respect to the child witness. The court must warn a child apparently or actually under the age of 12 years (as opposed to the common law cut-off age of 14 years) of the duty to speak the truth and the consequences of failing to do so, and must be satisfied, presumably by way of an inquiry, that ''the child is possessed of sufficient intelligence to justify the reception of evidence, and understands the duty of speaking the truth'' (which is the same wording as the federal and provincial *Evidence Acts*). Presumably, the youth court will utilize the inquiry method presently used in civil courts to determine intelligence and capacity and in particular, need only address the one (presumably lesser) test of determining whether the child understands the duty to speak the truth.

3) No inquiry is required of a person of or over the age of 12 years but the court has the authority, if it is concerned about such a witness, to warn him of the duty to speak the truth and the consequences of failing to do so. Nevertheless, it is suggested that this provision does not abolish the common law rule that permits any court to declare a witness of whatever age incompetent to testify if the person is shown to be suffering from an ailment rendering him incapable of interpreting observed events or of communicating properly.[40]

Corroboration   The distinction between sworn and unsworn testimony of children takes on significance in the course of a trial because of the statutory provision directing that no case can be decided and no one can be convicted of an offence based on the unsworn evidence of a child alone unless it is corroborated ''by some other material evidence'' in the former, or ''in a material particular by evidence that implicates the accused'' in the latter.[41] This principle is preserved and extended with respect to proceedings under the *Young Offenders Act* since, regardless of how mature or intelligent the child is, no testimony of children under 12 years can form the basis of a judge's decision without corroboration. No mention is

---

[40]See *supra*, note 32.

[41]The term ''by some other material evidence'' is from the *Canada Evidence Act*, s. 16(2); the *Ontario Evidence Act*, s. 18(2); the *Young Offenders Act*, s. 61(2). The term ''in a material particular by evidence that implicates the accused'' is from the *Criminal Code*, s. 586.

made of evidence from children of 12 years or more and therefore, presumably, a person *can* be convicted of an offence under the *Young Offenders Act* on the uncorroborated evidence of a 12-year-old which has only been affirmed since s. 60(3) of the Act attributes to "affirmed" evidence the effect of "sworn" evidence.

There is case authority to support a judge warning himself or a jury that convictions on the uncorroborated evidence of a child (including someone 12 or more years of age), even if the evidence is sworn, should be done only after weighing the evidence with extreme caution.[42] However, a recent Supreme Court of Canada decision effectively abolished all non-statutory corroborative requirements.[43] Given the clear wording of the Act, can it now be argued that such a warning is appropriate? The statute specifically deals with corroboration, limiting the requirement to those under 12 years old, and in addition deems affirmed evidence to have the same effect as if taken under oath.

If corroboration is required, the evidence that is necessary is that of independent testimony which implicates the accused, confirming not only the evidence that the crime was committed, but also that the accused committed it.[44] When the evidence of the young child requires corroboration, the unsworn testimony of another child which itself needs to be corroborated cannot be treated as supplying the requisite corroboration. That is, the unsworn evidence of one child cannot corroborate the unsworn evidence of another.[45] Finally, the evidence of an accomplice cannot corroborate the unsworn evidence of a child.[46]

Contempt of Court

A witness who is a child and who commits an act of contempt, such as refusing to testify, is not immune from a contempt charge. In criminal proceedings under the now repealed *Juvenile Delinquents Act*, certain jurisdictional difficulties existed because the Juvenile Court, where a "lower" Provincial Court, only had the authority to cite for contempt committed in the face of the court. It could deal with the contempt of a witness who refused to answer questions but it could not deal with the contempt of the individual outside of the court who, for example, made disparaging remarks about the court process to the media or refused to obey an order of the court. The gap was filled by the jurisdiction of a Superior Court since no offence was committed under the *Juvenile Delinquents Act* which would require the exclusive jurisdiction of the juvenile court.[47]

The new *Young Offenders Act* which replaced the *Juvenile Delinquents Act* has clarified this and other matters similarly arising from jurisdictional difficulties by way of s. 47.[48] The effect of this provision is as follows:

---

[42]*R. v. Kendall, supra,* note 18.

[43]*R. v. Vetrovee* (1982), 67 C.C.C. (2d) 1.

[44]See *R. v. Baskerville,* [1916] 2 K.B. 658 (C.A.); *R. v. Gemwill* (1924), 43 C.C.C. 360 (Ont. C.A.); *R. v. Silverstone* (1934), 61 C.C.C. 258 (Ont. C.A.); *Warkentin, Hanson and Brown v. R.* (1976), 30 C.C.C. (2d) 1 (S.C.C.).

[45]*R. v. Manser* (1934), 25 Cr. App. R. 18; *Re Paige and R.* (1948), 92 C.C.C. 32 (S.C.C.).

[46]*R. v. Bruce* (1971), 3 C.C.C. (2d) 416 (B.C.C.A.).

[47]*Vaillancourt v. R.* (1981), 120 D.L.R. (3d) 740 (S.C.C.).

[48]Section 47 of the *Young Offenders Act* reads:

(1) Every youth court has the same power, jurisdiction and authority to deal with and impose

1) In addition to the power of the Youth Court to punish for contempt in its face — a power which it already had as a court of record — it has the additional power of a Superior Court "to deal with and impose punishment for contempt." In other words, its contempt jurisdiction has expanded to include acts perpetrated outside of the courtroom: s. 47(1).

2) The Youth Court is the only court that can deal with contempt involving persons under the age of 18 years which emanate from proceedings before the Youth Court. It is also the only court that can now deal with contempt committed by a person under 18 years of age other than contempt in the face of the court, emanating from proceedings in any other court: s. 47(2).

3) The Youth Court now has concurrent jurisdiction with another court to deal with contempt committed by a person under 18 years, in the face of that other court: s. 47(3).[49]

4) A person under 18 years who is found in contempt may only receive a punishment(s) listed under s. 20 of the *Young Offenders Act*. No other form of punishment is permitted. Further, the young person can appeal a finding of and punishment for contempt, and the appeal will proceed as if it were an appeal from a conviction and/or sentence in a prosecution by indictment in ordinary court: s. 47(4) and (6).

Therefore, in any civil proceeding, even if a person under 18 years is found in contempt in the face of the court, the presiding judge must refer back to the provisions of the *Young Offenders Act* for the purposes of sentencing.

The Child's Presence in the Courtroom

Unless a judge rules under statutory jurisdiction that the proceedings before him are to be held *in camera*, anyone may attend a civil or criminal hearing including children. On the other hand, every judge has the inherent jurisdiction to

---

punishment for contempt against the court as may be exercised by the superior court of criminal jurisdiction of the province in which the court is situated.

(2) The youth court has exclusive jurisdiction in respect of every contempt of court committed by a young person against the youth court whether or not committed in the face of the court and every contempt of court committed by a young person against any other court otherwise than in the face of that court.

(3) The youth court has jurisdiction in respect of every contempt of court committed by a young person against any other court in the face of that court and every contempt of court committed by an adult against the youth court in the face of the youth court, but nothing in this subsection affects the power, jurisdiction or authority of any other court to deal with or impose punishment for contempt of court.

(4) Where a youth court or any other court finds a young person guilty of contempt of court, it may make any one of the dispositions set out in section 20, or any number thereof that are not inconsistent with each other, but no other disposition or sentence.

(5) Section 636 of the *Criminal Code* applies in respect of proceedings uner this section in youth court against adults, with such modifications as the circumstances require.

(6) A finding of guilt under this section for contempt of court or a disposition or sentence made in respect thereof may be appealed as if the finding were a conviction or the disposition or sentence were a sentence in a prosecution by indictment in ordinary court.

[49]Contrast the decision of *R. v. Marsden* (1977), 40 C.R.N.S. 11, 37 C.C.C. (2d) 107 (Que. S.C.) wherein the court held that a Superior Court has no jurisdiction over contempt committed in the face of a lower court.

control his own process for the proper administration of justice. This would include banning anyone from the courtroom who is causing a disturbance thereby interrupting or interfering with the proceedings which includes a restless child. A Superior Court may also rely on its inherent *parens patriae* jurisdiction to play a protective role in excluding a child in his own "best interests".

Child Welfare Proceedings

In most jurisdictions, the child welfare legislation has no specific provision concerning the presence of children in the courtroom. In Ontario, specific provisions codify the matter under s. 39(4) and (5) of the proposed *Child and Family Services Act* as follows:

> s. 39(4) A child twelve years of age or more who is the subject of a proceeding under this Part is entitled to receive notice of the proceeding and to be present at the hearing, unless the court is satisfied that being present at the hearing would cause the child emotional harm and orders that the child not receive notice of the proceedings and not be permitted to be present at the hearing.
>
> (5) A child less than twelve years of age who is the subject of a proceeding under this Part is not entitled to receive notice of the proceeding or to be present at the hearing unless the court is satisfied that the child,
>
> (a) is capable of understanding the hearing; and
>
> (b) will not suffer emotional harm by being present at the hearing,
> and orders that the child receive notice of the proceeding and be permitted to be present at the hearing.

Note that the *Child Welfare Act* has utilized essentially the same provisions but the watershed age is 10 years old: s. 33, *CWA*.

Case law on this section has developed some of the following guidelines:

1) whether or not the child is present in court, his counsel is entitled to a notice of all proceedings;[50]

2) this section creates a presumption, not an obligation to attend;[51]

3) for the purpose of a motion to decide whether the child is or is not to attend, the child should be present in the building but not in the courtroom unless all of the parties otherwise agree, and if the judge decides to exclude the child, that child should always be in the building when requested by counsel in order to facilitate the direct contact with his lawyer that may be necessary during the course of the proceeding;[52]

4) in deciding to dispense with the child's presence, one court found that the full participation in the hearing of the father, mother and Catholic Children's Aid Society was sufficient to protect the child's interest.[53]

---

[50]*Re Steven A.*, summarized in (1983), 6 F.L.R.R. 120 (Ont. Prov. Ct.).

[51]*Re Robert H.*, summarized in (1981), 5 F.L.R.R. 13 (Ont. Prov. Ct.).

[52]*Re Adrian S.*, summarized in (1982), 5 F.L.R.R. 25 (Ont. Prov. Ct.).

[53]*Re F.M.* (1979), 11 R.F.L. (2d) 120 (Ont. Prov. Ct.).

Young Offenders Proceedings

For children involved in proceedings under the *Young Offenders Act*, the following applies:

s. 39(1) Subject to subsection (2), where a court or justice before whom proceedings are carried out under this Act is of the opinion
    (a) that any evidence or information presented to the court or justice would be seriously injurious or seriously prejudicial to
        (i) the young person who is being dealt with in the proceedings;
        (ii) a child or young person who is a witness in the proceedings;
        (iii) a child or young person who is aggrieved by or the victim of the offence charged in the proceedings, or
    (b) that it would be in the interest of public morals, the maintenance of order or the proper administration of justice to exclude any or all members of the public from the court room,
the court or justice may exclude any person from all or part of the proceedings if the court or justice deems that person's presence to be unnecessary to the conduct of the proceedings.

(2) A court or justice may not, pursuant to sub-section (1), exclude from proceedings under this Act
    (a) the prosecutor;
    (b) the young person who is being dealt with in the proceedings, his parent, his counsel or any adult assisting him pursuant to sub-section 11(7);
    (c) the provincial director or his agent; or
    (d) the youth worker to whom the young person's case has been assigned.

(3) The Youth Court, after it has found a young person guilty of an offence, or the youth court or the review board, during a review of a disposition under ss. 28 to 33, may, in its discretion, exclude from the court or from a hearing of the review board, as the case may be, any person other than
    (a) the young person or his counsel;
    (b) the provincial director or his agent;
    (c) the youth worker to whom the young person's case has been assigned, and
    (d) the Attorney General or his agent,
when any information is being presented to the court or the review board the knowledge of which might, in the opinion of the court or review board, be seriously injurious or seriously prejudicial to the young person.

Note that s. 39(2) is distinguishable from s. 39(3) in that those who are immune to exclusion are more numerous in proceedings to determine guilt than to render a disposition.

As a converse of the above, s. 52(3) of the Act directs that s. 577(2) of the *Criminal Code* is applicable to the Youth Court proceedings which allow the court to permit a young person to be out of the courtroom during the whole or part of the trial on such conditions as the court deems appropriate. It is clear that for anyone to make this request on behalf of the accused young person, his approval or authority must be evident and without such authority a conviction will be quashed.[54]

The grounds for excluding the general public (including the media) under s. 39(1) presents some problems. Section 39(1)(b) of this Act which deals with "public morals, the maintenance of order or the proper administration of justice" is identical in wording to s. 442(1) of the *Criminal Code* as amended by s. 74 of the *Young Offenders Act* and case law under the *Criminal Code* section has held that discretion to exclude on this basis must be exercised cautiously.[55] For example, the fact that witnesses having to testify as to sexual behaviour may be embarrassed is not in itself sufficient to warrant exclusion of the public.[56] In the context of the *Young Offenders Act,* s. 39(1)(b) should be read in a manner which does not effectively duplicate the test under s. 39(1)(a) which focuses on the interests of the young person who is involved in some way with the proceedings. Presumably, s. 39(1)(b) is intended to maintain an orderly process within the courtroom and to protect the community at large from disruption. Of greater difficulty is the meaning of the test under s. 39(1)(a). From the use of "would" — to be distinguished from the word "might" in s. 39(3) — one can reasonably infer that the risk of harm under s. 39(1) must be probable or certain. Contrasting the words "injurious" with "prejudicial" suggests that the former refers to harm to the young person directly by his hearing the evidence whereas the latter refers to harm to the young person indirectly through others hearing the evidence. From the word "seriously" one must conclude that the harm, besides being probable or certain, must be substantial. It is also clear from recent case law that this section cannot be applied arbitrarily so as to create a blanket bar to public access on the presumption that every hearing involving juveniles should be heard *in camera.*[57] Accordingly, any judge or lawyer who wishes to invoke this section must necessarily consider evidence on the issue and give reasons for his decision in light of the facts of the particular case before the court.

Finally, the legislative objectives of s. 39 must be distinguished from those of s. 38, a section which provides for an absolute, non-discretionary ban on the publication of information which serves to identify the young persons or children involved in the proceedings. Since the latter section creates a basic protection of privacy of the young person and child in most circumstances, s. 39 should not be invoked for the same purpose. On the other hand, it is arguable that s. 38 is

---

[54]See *R. v. Page,* 64 W.W.R. 637, [1969] 1 C.C.C. 90 (B.C.C.A.).

[55]See *R. v. Warawuk,* [1978] 5 W.W.R. 389, 42 C.C.C. (2d) 121 (Alta. C.A.).

[56]*R. v. Quesnel* (1979), 51 C.C.C. (2d) 270 (Ont. C.A.).

[57]See *Re Southam Inc. and R. (No. 1)* (1983), 41 O.R. (2d) 113 (C.A.); *R. v. R.J.* (1982), 37 O.R. (2d) 173, 68 C.C.C. (2d) 285 (Prov. Ct. Fam. Div.); *Re Edmonton Journal and A.-G. for Alberta* (1983), 42 A.R. 383, 4 C.C.C. (3d) 59 (Q.B.). In *R. v. M.S.,* unreported, November 26, 1984 (Ont. Prov. Ct.) *per* Wang J., a 13-year-old was charged with murdering two children in the small town where the hearing was taking place. The judge refused defence counsel's application to exclude the public under s. 39(1)(a) on the basis that there had to be "strong and convincing evidence" to justify such an order where the "protection and rehabilitation of young people is a social value of super-ordinate importance" outweighing the general presumption that trials are to be public.

evidence of the Legislature's intention to absolutely shield the young person's identity from the public and press and in certain circumstances, such as hearings in a small community, the release of other information about the child through word of mouth or through the media may have the effect of identifying him thus justifying the invocation of s. 39. Nevertheless, it is submitted that regardless of this aspect, the s. 39(1) test must meet the standard of being "seriously injurious" or "seriously prejudicial" to the child and not simply to obtain privacy for its own sake.

Independent Representation for the Child

In Chapter 5, the role of the litigation guardian was discussed with regard to a child's property interests as well as the institutional role of the Office of the Official Guardian in Ontario and the Office of the Public Trustee in other provinces. However, this concept of providing someone whose role is to protect the child's interests has been limited to property rights, prompting the Ontario Law Reform Commission to comment as follows:

> It seems to us inconsistent, therefore, that so far in the development of the law in this province the right of a child to the protection of his own counsel in proceedings relating to his upbringing has not been established in any more than isolated instances. We believe that decisions concerning a child's physical and emotional welfare are as worthy of the state's special interests as those concerning his property rights, and that courts may be in the most informed position only when there has been an objective evaluation of a child's best interests by a person with qualifications who may present the child's case to a court.[58]

The model of the litigation guardian is based on the principle that he and not the child is the "legal entity" or "party" in the proceeding and it is his mandate to identify and protect the child's interests, which are to be distinguished from any notion of the child's wishes. The litigation guardian is not the child's lawyer but is the actual interested party who himself is represented by a lawyer. The child, as a "legal entity," is non-existent. The court need not concern itself with the wishes of the child, the assumption being that property matters cannot be comprehended by the young person and hence the adults must substitute their hard-earned wisdom and judgment. The fundamental concern for the court is the best interests of an individual who is legally handicapped and therefore requires a substitute legal personality as a protectorate.

The litigation guardian model is generally agreed to be inappropriate with respect to custody/access, child welfare and delinquency proceedings in Ontario. In criminal proceedings, by way of the repealed *Juvenile Delinquents Act,* which is now the *Young Offenders Act,* the minor is being accused of an offence for which, if convicted, he will be punished and as such, in our system of justice, he must have full party status, including the kind of independent representation that any adult receives. Further, no one under 12 years of age is the subject of such proceedings, and as such, the incapacity of the child gives way to the capacity of the teenager. In custody and child welfare proceedings, social scientists, and to a lesser extent, judges and lawyers, have come to understand that in order to know

---

[58]Ontario Law Reform Commission, *Report on Family Law: Part 3* (1973).

the child's "best interests" which is the goal in both proceedings, it is necessary to know the child and this includes his wishes as well as his needs. Accordingly, in custody and child welfare matters, there has been a gradual evolution toward legal representation of the child as a "legal entity" in his own right.[59]

Child Welfare Proceedings

Child Welfare Proceedings

More than any other Canadian jurisdiction, Ontario's *Child Welfare Act/Child and Family Services Act, 1984* makes every effort to ensure that a child has representation in all circumstances where it is necessary. Under s. 38 of the *Child and Family Services Act:*

s. 38(1) A child may have legal representation at any stage in a proceeding under this Part.

(2) Where a child does not have legal representation in a proceeding under this Part, the court,

    (a) shall, as soon as practicable after the commencement of the proceeding; and

    (b) may, at any later stage in the proceeding,

determine whether legal representation is desirable to protect the child's interests.

(3) Where the court determines that legal representation is desirable to protect a child's interests, the court shall direct that legal representation be provided for the child.

(4) Where,

    (a) the court is of the opinion that there is a difference of views between the child and a parent or a society, and the society proposes that the child be removed from a person's care or be made a society or Crown ward under paragraph 2 or 3 of subsection 53(1);

    (b) the child is in the society's care and,

        (i) no parent appears before the court, or

        (ii) it is alleged that the child is in need of protection within the meaning of clause 37(2)(a), (c), (f) or (h); or

    (c) the child is not permitted to be present at the hearing, legal representation shall be deemed to be desirable to protect the child's interests, unless the court is satisfied, taking into account the child's views and wishes if they can be reasonably ascertained, that the child's interests are otherwise adequately protected.

(5) Where a child's parent is less than eighteen years of age, the Official Guardian shall represent the parent in a proceeding under this Part unless the court orders otherwise.

---

[59]But see *Re R.A.M.; C.A.S. of Winnipeg v. A.M. and L.C.* (1984), 39 R.F.L. (2d) 23, revg 37 R.F.L. (2d) 113 (Man. C.A.) wherein the court held that the child needed a litigation guardian before he could proceed with any appeal in a child welfare proceeding notwithstanding that jurisdiction's child welfare legislation which provides the Provincial Court judge with the authority to appoint counsel to represent the interests of the child.

(The equivalent section under the *Child Welfare Act* is essentially the same: s. 20, *CWA*.) It has been held that once the child does have legal representation, counsel should have the same opportunity as any other trial lawyer to be fully prepared in taking a stand on the issues and specifically to cross-examine the parties.[60]

In Manitoba, where child welfare legislation does not provide for a child's right to retain counsel, the question of the nature and extent of the right to child representation in child welfare proceedings has emerged as a constitutional issue under the *Charter of Rights*. Under the Manitoba legislation, the child may have representation, but only if so ordered by the Child Welfare Court. In this particular case,[61] a 13-year-old child, who was in the care of a Children's Aid Society as a temporary ward, expressed a desire to live with his aunt. The child was unaware that he could put his wishes before the court and an order of permanent wardship was made at the hearing without any challenge. Subsequently, the child was belatedly informed of this right by counsel who represented him in delinquency proceedings. That lawyer then applied to be appointed as counsel to the child in the child welfare proceedings specifically for the purpose of launching an appeal of the permanent wardship order. A single judge of the Court of Appeal found that an order of permanent wardship affects this child's "liberty and security" under s. 7 of the *Charter*, and decided to appoint counsel for the child, noting that the child's right to be heard as an incident of the due process assurances of s. 7 of the *Charter* would be ineffective without a lawyer representing him. A secondary argument which also fortified the court's decision was the fact that it is taken for granted that a child has the capacity to retain and instruct counsel in juvenile proceedings, proceedings which could lead to the same kind of disposition provided for in child welfare proceedings, that is, committal to a Society. However, this decision was reversed by the full bench of the Court of Appeal which held that the child has no standing to take any procedural steps in protection proceedings and that it must be done through a next friend.

Whether the Legislature requires the appointment of counsel for the child or whether the child is able to retain counsel in his own right appears to be less problematic than the role which should be played by counsel for the child. The issue becomes relevant when the child is clearly capable of communicating with counsel and giving counsel a sense of his wishes which may or may not fall short of formal instructions. Specifically, does counsel advocate the child's wishes or what counsel perceives as the child's "best interests"? One judge described what she felt the role should be in the context of child welfare proceedings as follows:

> I am persuaded that essentially the role of the lawyer for the child is no different from the role of the lawyer for any other party; he or she is there to represent a client by protecting the client's interests and carrying out the client's instructions. At the same time, the lawyer is an officer of the Court and as such is obliged to represent these interests in accordance with well-defined standards of professional integrity.

---

[60]*Re M.* (1982), 29 C.P.C. 44 (Ont. Prov. Ct.).
[61]*Re R.A.M., supra,* note 59.

There is a tendency to assume that the quintessential legal representative for the child is, or should be, a paragon of legal, psychological, and sociological expertise. This is unrealistic. Lawyers generally have only legal skills, the proper utilization of which may undoubtedly involve some direct or indirect familiarity with or reliance upon other disciplines. Lawyers are called upon, in short, to exercise informed legal judgment. Lawyers for children can therefore be expected to do no more and no less than any other party's lawyer in the adversarial process. This is not to endorse the adversarial process in matters of family disputes. It is rather to acknowledge that it is through this process at present that these disputes are resolved. So long as the forum is the courtroom, the child's lawyer should represent his or her young client in a way which reflects equal participation with the other parties in this forum.

Representing a client in these cases usually involves executing a client's instructions and, without being misleading, attempting to show through the evidence that these instructions or wishes best match the child's needs. In other words, a mother who wishes custody of her child expects her lawyer to present her case in such a way that her wishes are shown to be in the best interests of the child. It is, in most cases, an articulation of the client's subjective assessment, rather than the lawyer's. It should be no different when the client is a child. Where, therefore, the child has expressed definite views, these views, rather than those of the child's lawyer, should determine what is conveyed to the Court. The child's advocate is the legal architect who constructs a case based on the client's views.

In its purest form, that means that the child's lawyer should present and implement a client's instructions to the best of his or her ability. And this, in turn, involves indicating to the Court the child's concerns, wishes and opinions. It involves, further, presenting to the Court accurate and complete evidence which is consistent with the child's position. And too, there is an obligation to ensure, in so far as this is possible given the age and circumstances of the child, that the opinions and wishes expressed by the child are freely given and without duress from any other party or person.

In child welfare proceedings, the Court is obliged at the disposition stage to make an order ''in the best interests of the child.'' Section 1(*b*)(vi) of the *Child Welfare Act, 1978* defines ''best interests of the child'' to include, among other things,

> (vi) the views and preferences of the child, where such views and preferences can reasonably be ascertained;

In other words, they are the views and wishes of the child, not those of his or her lawyer which should guide the Court in attempting to achieve a resolution which most closely coincides with the best interests of the child.

In many cases it is almost impossible to unerringly assess what is best for a child. Given this epistemological gap, why should the lawyer substitute his or her own opinion for that of the child. Consider too that a lawyer who formulates an opinion of the child's best interests is often making this judgment before the trial and therefore without the benefit of hearing all of the available evidence. Not even the most Solomonic of Judges would be expected to perform this feat.

In a trial it is for a Judge to determine ultimately what is in a given child's best interests. The bases for this determination include, among other evidence, the child's wishes. These wishes should, therefore, whenever possible, be articulated so that the Court has the benefit of knowing of all relevant factors and so that the child has an effective and meaningful role in the proceedings which affect him or her no less than any of the other parties.

There must undoubtedly be a degree of flexibility in a child's lawyer's role as articulator of his or her client's wishes. The child may be unable to instruct counsel. Or the child may be, as in this case, ambivalent about her wishes. Or the child may be too young. Although there should be no minimum age below which a child's wishes should be ignored — so long as the child is old enough to express them, they should be considered — I feel that where a child does not or cannot express wishes, the role of the child's lawyer should be to protect the client/child's interests. In the absence of clear instructions, protecting the client's interests can clearly involve presenting the lawyer's perception of what would best protect the child's interests. In this latter role of promulgating the infant client's best interests, the lawyer would attempt to guarantee that all the evidence the Court needs to make a disposition which accommodates the child's best interests is before the Court, is complete, and is accurate. There could in this kind of role be no inconsistency between what is perceived by the lawyer to be the child's best interests and the child's instructions. Where there is such conflict, the wishes of the child should prevail in guiding the lawyer.

In the case of a child who is capable of coherent expression the lawyer's role in representing the child's wishes does not preclude the lawyer from exploring with the child the merits or realities of the case, evaluating the practicalities of the child's position and even offering, where appropriate, suggestions about possible reasonable resolutions to the case. Offering advice is part of the lawyer's obligation to protect the client's interests. Obviously, however, given the vulnerability of most children to authority in general and given the shattered sensibilities in family disputes in particular, great sensitivity should be exercised during these exploratory sessions. The lawyer should be constantly conscious of his or her posture being an honest but not overwhelming one.[62]

While the above quote suggests that the role of counsel for the child is essentially no different from that of an adult, consider the following fact situations:

---

[62]*Re W.* (1980), 27 O.R. (2d) 314, at 316–18, 13 R.F.L. (2d) 381 (Prov. Ct.). But see *Re C.* (1980), 14 R.F.L. (2d) 21 (Ont. Prov. Ct.) in which the court held that the duty of counsel was to speak for the best interests of the child and not to take a strict adversarial role.

1) A 14-year-old street-wise girl who is a temporary ward of the Children's Aid Society runs away from the open mental health setting where she has been placed. She telephones her lawyer and indicates her refusal to return to the setting, complaining that she is always drugged and that she is not learning anything in any case. Her preference is to return home and try again with the help of counselling. Where is she? She will not tell counsel until he takes an oath of secrecy and only then discloses that she is staying with an older friend at her apartment. The Society is aware of counsel's involvement from prior proceedings and inquires as to his knowledge of the child's whereabouts. Counsel advises the Society that he has communicated with the child but cannot disclose her whereabouts. Does the solicitor-client privilege apply?

2) A 13-year-old girl confides in counsel that she has had sexual relations with her father. She has sought a lawyer's assistance because the social worker she is seeing feels obliged to report the matter to the child welfare authorities. She does not want to leave home, nor does she want anyone to know about the matter. Most importantly, she wants nothing bad to happen to her father; rather, she wants her dad to get help, but in total secrecy. Is it possible for the solicitor to act in accordance with the child's wishes, both in respect of reporting the incident to a local Society and of the up-coming custody proceedings, or do the circumstances require the lawyer to act contrary to the child's wishes in accordance with her interests, at least as perceived by the lawyer?

With the few exceptions noted above, the courts are generally reluctant to dictate to counsel the nature of their roles, leaving it to the determination of their governing bodies. In its *Report to the Law Society of Upper Canada* (May, 1981), the Professional Conduct Committee's Sub-committee on the Legal Representation of Children made these comments in the context of child representation and child welfare proceedings:

> We have been asked to consider whether the Rules of Professional Conduct should be changed to permit counsel representing children not to follow the instructions of the child if to depart from the instructions were, in counsel's opinion, in the child's "best interests". We were also asked to consider whether the Rule on solicitor/client privilege should be amended to permit disclosure when it would be in the "best interests" of the child.
>
> Your Sub-Committee does not recommend there be any changes to the present Rules of Professional Conduct. These Rules are applicable when there is a true solicitor/client relationship. They would not apply if the intent of s. 20 [of the *Child Welfare Act*] was to have a guardian-type of legal representation as is argued by the Official Guardian. When the child does not have the capacity to fully understand the consequences of the proceeding he is involved in then the relationship with his or her lawyer is not the normal solicitor/client relationship. But this is not a new problem. Our profession has confronted this problem historically in the many criminal cases in which infants have had the benefit of defence counsel. It is with a more mature child who can be said to have a capacity to instruct his counsel

that the problem arises. When there is concern that the child may be lacking in capacity to provide instructions, the appointment of a legal guardian may be necessary. If the child is mature and responsible enough to accept the consequences of his or her acts and decisions and understands fully the nature of the proceedings and can express a preference as to its resolution, the Committee tends to favour the traditional solicitor/client approach than the guardian-type of representation. Decisions as to the capacity of the child to properly instruct counsel must be determined by the individual lawyer in the particular circumstances. One of the factors that the lawyer would take into account in making this decision would be the ability of the child to accept rationally the advice he or she is receiving. If the child stubbornly, without reason, refuses to accept the advice of counsel, it may be that the child lacks the maturity to properly instruct counsel.

We have concluded that there should be no exception to the present Rule on solicitor/client privilege. The Rules now permit disclosure of confidential information to prevent a crime. Again, it would be up to the individual lawyer to decide if any breach of confidentiality is warranted in the circumstances. Obviously, the Rule only contemplates disclosure in extreme circumstances.

The lawyer, in such circumstances, would have to satisfy himself as to the ability of the child to give instructions. In the absence of capacity to give instructions, the lawyer is under a duty not to accept the instructions, and to advise the court that the infant, in his opinion, is incapable of giving instructions, at which point the Official Guardian should be notified by either the lawyer or the court.

Even where a child may lack the capacity to properly instruct counsel, in our view there is no place in a quasi-criminal [child welfare] proceeding for counsel representing a child to argue what is in his opinion the best interests of the child. Counsel should not be deciding whether training school would be "good" for the child. Without wishing to be placed in the role of a substantive arbiter of the law, the Sub-Committee concluded that s. 20 probably amounted to a recognition of the right of the child to counsel, and if counsel were, indeed, retained for the child, separate and independent from the provisions of s. 20, subsection 2, that counsel would unquestionably have a relationship with the child which was in accordance with the ordinary rules of conduct. His duty would be to the child, and only to the child, subject to his duty to the court. The relationship of solicitor and client would be established, and there would be a solicitor and client privilege with respect to communications between the child and the lawyer. The situation must be directly related to the retainer of a child in criminal proceedings.

. . .

The Sub-Committee feels that if the legislature of the Ministry of the Attorney General is of the view that some special circumstances exist in the case of infants requiring some special form of representation, that the legislature should be explicit in the wording of such legislation, and there should be no ambiguity whatsoever in such legislation. Particularly is this so where such legislation would, in the ordinary course, be entirely contrary to the traditional role of solicitor and client.

Contrast the Law Society of Upper Canada's position with that of British Columbia's child welfare legislation in which the legal "representative" for the child is based on a different model than that of the traditional solicitor-client relationship. Indeed, the legal representative is referred to as the "family advocate" and by legislation his responsibilities include:

> 1) collection and presentation of information to the court with the power to request that any person having relevant information prepare a written report, and
> 2) intervention at any stage in any proceedings concerning children including adoption, guardianship, custody, access, delinquency or child welfare in order to act as counsel *for the interests and welfare* of the child. [63]

The elementary distinction between the two models is the legislated role in British Columbia of legal counsel premised on the existence of an objective measure of a child's "best interests." In the Ontario model, reliance is placed on the traditional advocate's role which has always been flexible enough to adapt to the particular characteristics of the solicitor-client relationship as it varies with each area of practice. For example, the client approach of a family law lawyer is distinctly different from that of the corporate law lawyer based on the different origins, objectives and repercussions of the proceedings. The irrationality of the wronged spouse can often far outstrip that of a person of 13 or 14 years and the power remains with the solicitor in both cases to divest himself of a client who will not follow his advice. It is submitted that the "best interests" approach to the representation of the child amounts to redundancy and represents no practical change in the law since every proceeding affecting a child has its mechanisms for protecting that child's best interests such as the litigation guardian, the Official Guardian/Public Trustee and Children's Aid Societies. Note the following quote from an Ontario Divisional Court decision which appears to proceed on the assumption that representation must be "best interests" representation:

> It is our view that the *Child Welfare Act* from its commencement and through the entire Act is an Act designed for the welfare of the child. It is further our view that the Children's Aid Society is a Society appointed by the community to act in matters to protect the interests of children. To consider the appointment in this particular case of the Official Guardian to act on behalf of the child it seems to us that we would in effect have two parties acting on behalf of the child. [64]

Custody/Access Proceedings

Domestic Custody/Access Proceedings

In custody/access matters, positions such as that of the Law Society of Upper Canada on the nature of child representation (discussed above in the

---

[63] For British Columbia legislation, see s. 2 of the *Family Relations Act* and s. 6(2) of the *Family and Child Services Act*.

context of child welfare proceedings) remain applicable. The legislation in Ontario and other provinces is much less precise than legislation on child welfare or delinquency proceedings, but Ontario's Provincial Court Rules provide the court with the power to make such directions as it deems appropriate for the representation of the child[65] which can include the permitting of the child to seek private counsel or the appointment for the child of institutionalized counsel (in Ontario, the Official Guardian). The rule has not been tested but, unlike s. 20 of the *Child Welfare Act*/s. 38 of the *Child and Family Services Act, 1984,* the court is apparently free to define the role that it expects from counsel presumably depending upon the age of the child, an impression of his views or the stage of the proceedings. For example, if the conflict is at an early stage, the court may request the involvement of counsel for the child to facilitate family mediation and/or family assessment to ensure that in the event that the matter cannot be resolved out of court, there is full information before the court. This role can be seen as analogous to that of the *amicus curiae*, a role utilized in Alberta. It is clear in that jurisdiction that the *amicus curiae*, as a "friend of the court," is under no obligation to advance the wishes or instructions of the child whom he has been appointed to "represent" or, more accurately, protect. It is also clear that the court as the adjudicator is under no duty to abide by the recommendations of the *amicus curiae* although, for many reasons, judges will generally reach a decision consistent with the views of that office.[66] The *amicus curiae* role integrates into one creature, the litigation guardian and the lawyer, so that the "best interests" of a child are being protected through counsel rather than through someone who is the "legal entity" in the proceeding and who retains the lawyer. This type of role in custody proceedings has been endorsed in an Ontario Divisional Court decision:

> Based on my experience in this case, I doubt the desirability of having children represented by counsel or advised by "their own" (the children's term) solicitor as a practice. There may well be cases where in the circumstances a trial judge considers it desirable for the children to have separate representation at trial. If that is so, the Official Guardian would appear to be available and can be called upon at that point. Early involvement of solicitors for children can, I think, cause more harm than good.[67]

It would seem then, that where matters are pending before a High Court, counsel might be advised to invoke the discretion of the court under its *parens patriae*

---

[64]*Re Helmes* (1976), 13 O.R. (2d) 4 at 5.

[65]See Provincial Court Rules, under the *Provincial Courts Act,* R.R.O. 1980, Reg. 810, s. 36. See also *Letourneau v. Haskell* (1979), 25 O.R. (2d) 139 (Co. Ct.) wherein the court held that r. 8 of the Provincial Court Rules and r. 92 of the Rules of Practice are merely directive and not imperative. The court is not bound to give directions concerning the representation of children nor does s. 16 of the *Family Law Reform Act* abrogate the legal rights of infants with respect to capacity to commence or conduct a proceeding under the Act.

[66]As one rare example, see *Irmert v. Irmert* (1983), 36 R.F.L. (2d) 260 (Alta. Q.B.) wherein the court disagreed with the recommendation of the *amicus curiae* that two children, ages 7 and 10, be separated between the two parents.

[67]*Rowe v. Rowe* (1976), 26 R.F.L. 91, at p. 96 (Ont. H.C.).

jurisdiction, for an order appointing counsel as guardian *ad litem* prior to any legal action on behalf of the child as a client.

While this "best interests" role has been approved as appropriate for those children who are found to be incapable of instructing counsel or of expressing their wishes,[68] it is submitted that the role is detrimental for those children who are not of that group, both because the child is deceived into thinking that his interests, as he sees them, will be put before the adjudicator in this crucial decision about his life and because this crucial decision, which must be based on "best interests," cannot be made without knowing the child and his wishes. It is submitted that one cannot "know" a child (or anyone for that matter) by listening to an adult who presumes to be the incarnation of the child's personality as well as his legal counsel. In any case, there are other mechanisms at a judge's disposal besides turning a lawyer into an *amicus curiae* to make sure that all the information which the judge considers relevant to the child's best interests are before him. For example, a Superior Court already has the power to order the parties to participate in an assessment, with the assessor reporting back to the court.[69] Even if the domestic legislation does not include this type of mechanism, general mediation services are available in many communities.

To superimpose the model for protecting a child's property interests onto the role of a child's legal counsel in a custody proceeding also poses several inconsistencies. A child will very likely be incompetent to judge his best interests with respect to property since "best interests" are basically the equivalent of increasing or preserving wealth, an objective which only the adult, seasoned in the market place, can pursue effectively. In the context of family disintegration, on the other hand, there is no simple, objective equivalent for "best interests" and age as a measure of competency becomes far less relevant. Unlike the property or estate dispute, "in many cases, it is almost impossible to unerringly assess what is best for the child. Given this epistemological gap, why should the lawyer substitute his or her opinion for that of the child."[70] Secondly, the subject matter of a custody dispute, unlike an estate dispute, clearly involves the child subjectively as well as his relationship with his family as a continuing dynamic. The property dispute presents a still-life portrayal of one event for judicial scrutiny. The custody dispute presents a slice of family existence for a still-life judicial assessment. The latter necessitates the participation of the child since the court's responsibility is to listen to all versions of the truth.

---

[68]See decision of *D.B. and P.B. v. Director of Child Welfare for Newfoundland, N.K.J. and E.J.J. (Intervenors) and C.* (1982), 30 R.F.L. (2d) 438 (S.C.C.) and comments of Wilson J. concerning the assistance of the court-appointed legal counsel.

[69]See *Cillis v. Cillis* (1980), 20 R.F.L. (2d) 208 (Ont. H.C.); affd 23 R.F.L. (2d) 76 (Ont. Div. Ct.). *El-Sohemy v. El-Sohemy* (1980), 17 R.F.L. (2d) 1 (Ont. S.C.).

[70]*Re W., supra,* note 62, at p. 317.

Chapter 6: Readings

American Bar Association, *Advocating for Children in the Courts* (1979).

"Appointing Counsel for the Child in Actions to Terminate Parental Rights" (Mar., 1982), 70 *Calif. L. Rev.* 481.

British Columbia Royal Commission on Family and Children's Law, *Fourth Report: The Family, the Courts and the Community* (Victoria: Queen's Printer, 1975).

"Child Witness and the Nature of an Oath" (1981), 13 *Ottawa L. Rev.* 426.

Committee on the Representation of Children in the Provincial Court (Family Division), Ontario Ministry of the Attorney-General, *Report* (Toronto: Queen's Printer, 1977).

Devine, J.R., "A Child's Right to Independent Counsel in Custody Proceedings" (1975), 6 *Seaton Hall L. Rev.* 303.

Dootjes, I., Erickson, P. and Fox, R.G., "Defence Counsel in Juvenile Court: A Variety of Roles" (1972), 14 *Can. J. Crim. Corr.* 132.

Erickson, P., "Legalistic and Traditional Role Expectations for Defence Counsel in Juvenile Court" (1975), 17 *Can. J. Crim. Corr.* 78.

Feshbach, S. and Feshbach, N.D., *Child Advocacy and Family Privacy* (1976).

Flammang, C.J., "Interviewing Child Victims of Sex Offenders", in L. Schultz (ed.) (1980), *Sexual Victimology of Youth* 175.

Hirshberg, B.A., "Who Speaks for the Child and What Are His Rights? A Proposed Standard for Evaluation" (Winter, 1980) 4 *Law and Human Behaviour* 217.

Kagan, J., *Understanding Children: Behaviour, Motives and Thought* (N.Y. Harcourt, Brace and Jovanovich, 1971).

Kaplan, E.N., "Domestic Relations — Appointment of Counsel for the Child: Statutory Schemes and the New York Approach" (1972), 58 *Cornell L. Rev.* 177.

Knitzer, J.E., "Child Advocacy: A Perspective" (1976), 46 *American Journal of Ortho-psychiatry* (No. 2) 200.

Kohlberg, L., "Development of Moral Character and Ideology" in Hoffman et al. (eds.), *Review of Child Development Research* (N.Y.: Russell Sage Foundation, 1964).

Kreutzer, M.A., *An Interview Study of Children's Knowledge About Memory* (Society for Research in Child Development) (Chicago: University of Chicago Press, 1975).

Leon, J., "Recent Developments in Legal Representation of Children: A Growing Concern with the Concept of Capacity" (1978), *Can. J. of Fam. Law* (No. 3) 1.

MacDonald, W.E., "A Case for Independent Counsel to Represent Children in Custody Proceedings" (1972), 7 *New Eng. L. Rev.* 351.

McDermott, J.F. et al., "The Concept of Child Advocacy" (1973), 130 *Am. J. of Psychiatry* 1203.

Melton, G.B., "Children's Competency to Testify" (Spring, 1981), 5 *Law and Human Behaviour* 73.

Note, "Competency of Children as Witnesses" (1953), 39 *Va. L. Rev.* 358.

Note, "Parent-Child Incest: Proof at Trial Without Testimony in Court by the Victim" (1981), 15 *U. Mich. J.L. Ref.* 131.

Parker, J.Y., "Rights of Child Witnesses: Is the Court a Protector or Perpetrator?" (1981–82), 17 *New Eng. L. Rev.* 643.

Piaget, Jean, *The Child's Conception of the World* (St. Albans, Eng.: Granada Publishing Ltd., 1929).

Piaget, Jean, *The Moral Judgement of the Child* (Markham: Penguin Books, 1932).

Polow, J.J., "The Lawyer in the Adoption Process" (1972), 6 *Fam. L. Q.* 72.

Radin, M.E., "Role of the Lawyer for the Pre-school Child in Custody Litigation" (Winter, 1981), 9 *J. Psych. L.* 431.

Ramsey, S. H., "Representation of the Child in Protection Proceedings: The Determination of Decision-Making Capacity" (Fall, 1983), 17 *Fam. L. Q.* 287.

Report on Representation of Children in Provincial Court (Family Division) (Ministry of the Attorney-General, Ontario) (1977), 29 *R.F.L.* 134.

Representing the Minor (papers presented at Ontario Section of Canadian Bar Association, 1979).

Shore, M.F., "Legislation, Advocacy and the Rights of Children and Youth" (1979), 34 *American Psychologist* (No. 10) 1.

Stanton, A.M., "Child-parent Privilege for Confidential Communications: An Examination and Proposal", (Spring, 1982), 16 *Fam. L. Q.* 1.

Stapelton and Teitlebaum, *In Defence of Youth: A Study of the Role of Counsel in American Juvenile Courts* (N.Y.: Russell Sage, 1972).

Westman, J. C., *Child Advocacy: New Professional Roles for Helping Families* (N.Y.: Free Press, 1979).

Westman, J. (ed.), *Proceedings of the University of Wisconsin Conference on Child Advocacy* (Dept. of Continuing Medical Education) (Madison: U. of Wisconsin, 1976).

Chapter 7

Crime and the Child[1]

The *Young Offenders Act* (hereinafter referred to as the *YOA*) which was proclaimed on April 2nd, 1984, repeals the *Juvenile Delinquents Act*[2] (hereinafter referred to as the *JDA*), and it thereby has created a new Canadian juvenile justice system. The broad principles of s. 3 of the new Act give some indication of the Parliamentary intentions underlying the overhaul of the *JDA*. They basically amount to the position that although young persons should not be held accountable for their criminal acts (that is, through sentencing/disposition) in the same manner and to the same extent as the adult, they should bear some degree of criminal responsibility and should conversely be guaranteed the same rights and freedoms as the adult who is facing criminal proceedings. Generally, the approach is to incorporate all aspects of the *Criminal Code*, not just its summary procedures (s. 51, *YOA*),[3] with exceptions as carved out by the *YOA* to reflect its s. 3 principles which are uniquely applicable to young persons. Except where they are inconsistent with the *YOA*, any defence, evidentiary rule, onus of proof or presumption under the common law or *Criminal Code* are now available to young persons under the *YOA*. Section 51 removes any lingering doubt that criminal proceedings against young people are anything but criminal in nature and therefore require the application of procedures and protections characteristic

---

[1] Of assistance in compiling and updating this chapter was N. Bala and H. Lilles, *The Young Offenders Act Annotated,* a Report for the Solicitor-General of Canada, Policy Branch, November, 1982.

[2] Section 79 of the *YOA* sets out the transitional provisions relating to the repealed legislation.

[3] Section 51 of the *YOA* reads:

> s. 51 Except to the extent that they are inconsistent with or excluded by this Act, all the provisions of the *Criminal Code* apply, with such modifications as the circumstances require, in respect of offences alleged to have been committed by young persons.

Jurisdiction

of our criminal law system, to be distinguished from our mental health or child welfare systems.

The jurisdiction of the new Act covers youthful offenders between the ages of 12 and (effective April 1st, 1985) 17 years inclusively;[4] under 12 years of age, there is no criminal responsibility.[5] The definition of "young person" directs that the operative age for jurisdictional purposes is the age at the time the offence was allegedly committed, not at the time of trial. Further, the definition catches those who committed offences on their 12th birthday. The court and judge mandated to adjudicate this new criminal system are appropriately entitled the Youth Court and Youth Court judge and can be from any court level which the provincial legislature designates.[6] Any offences covered by the Act include only those created by federal legislation so that now, provinces must prosecute young persons for provincial offences under their own legislation.[7] This change eliminates the past inequality of young persons facing the same criminal process and disposition for minor provincial offences as for *Criminal Code* offences, while their adult counterparts were subject to provincial regulatory by-laws or quasi-criminal enforcement proceedings. Nevertheless, the unequal effect is continued to some extent since the definition of "offence" under s. 2(1) of the *YOA* does include the infringement of any federally-created regulation, rule, order, by-law or ordinance. The inclusion of these "offences" may make the provision vulnerable to the application of s. 15 of the *Charter of Rights* which guarantees that every individual is equal before and under the law, although the government's defence may lie in the s. 15(2) exemption for "affirmative action" laws. (See generally Chapter 1 "Introduction: Children's Rights".) Finally, a

---

[4]Section 2(1) of the *YOA* reads:

s. 2(1) . . . "Child" means a person who is or, in the absence of evidence to the contrary, appears to be under the age of 12 years.

. . .

"Young person" means a person who is or in the absence of evidence to the contrary, appears to be
(a) 12 years of age or more, but
(b) under 18 years of age or, in a province in respect of which a proclamation has been issued under subsection (2) prior to April 1, 1985, under sixteen or seventeen years, whichever age is specified by the proclamation
and, where the context requires, includes any person who is charged under this Act with having committed an offence while he was a young person or is found guilty of an offence under this Act.

[5]Section 72, *YOA*.

[6]See s. 2(1), *YOA* for definition of "Youth Court" and "Youth Court judge." There is no requirement that a Youth Court judge be appointed directly or individually. It is sufficient for a province to designate the jurisdiction of a Youth Court judge to a Provincial Court judge and where the provincial court judge sits under the *YOA*, he or she presides over a Youth Court. See *Re L. and R.* (1984), 13 C.C.C. (3d) 148 (B.C.S.C.); *Re R. and N.* (1984), 12 C.C.C. (3d) 350 (Ont. H.C.).

[7]Section 2(1), *YOA* reads:

. . . "Offence" means an offence created by an Act of Parliament or by any regulation, rule, order, by-law or ordinance made thereunder other than an ordinance of a Yukon Territory or the Northwest Territories.

In the province of Ontario, young persons, like adults, will now be prosecuted for provincial offences pursuant to the *Provincial Offences Act*, which provides for the application of the *Provincial Offences Act* to young persons with the specific qualification that the application of the quasi-criminal legislation is consistent with that of the *YOA*.

conviction under the *YOA* is no longer based on the amorphous, status offence of being a juvenile delinquent,[8] but on specific offences under specific pieces of federal legislation other than the *YOA*. In particular, the convicted young offender will be found guilty of a summary or indictable offence and no longer will there be any issue of whether the "offence" of "juvenile delinquency" is summary in nature.

General Procedure

For all offences covered by the Act including both summary and indictable offences, the *YOA* incorporates Part XXIV of the *Criminal Code*, that is, "Summary Convictions", as its procedural provisions except:

1) to the extent that they are not inconsistent with the *YOA*: s. 52, *YOA*;

2) the 6-month limitation period governing summary conviction offences does not apply under the *YOA*. The limitation period is a function of the particular offence committed: s. 5(2) *YOA*; and

3) the Youth Court, unlike the "summary conviction" court, is not governed by s. 744 of the *Criminal Code* (jurisdiction to order costs): s. 52(5) *YOA*.

All of this effectively means that a Youth Court will not proceed by way of indictment, preliminary trial or trial by jury. Every other aspect of the Youth Court proceedings must be carefully considered in light of specific provisions of the *YOA* which may modify, vary or add to the proceedings for adults under Part XXIV of the *Criminal Code,* presumably in order to satisfy the s. 3 principles of the *YOA* and specifically s. 3(1)(e) which declares that young persons have the right "to be heard in the course of, and to participate in, the process" and that they should have "special guarantees of their rights and freedoms."

The ensuing chapter reviews the provisions of the *YOA* in light of existing law from the moment of contact between the state and the child until the final disposition, with emphasis on issues particularly relevant to the representation of the young person.

Initial Contact

Representation

Under the repealed *JDA* and the *YOA*, initial contact between a police officer, often a specialized youth officer, and the young person frequently takes a diversionary form away from judicial proceedings, ranging from a simple warning to visiting the parents with the young person. Under the *YOA*, however, s. 11(1) presumably applies to such an encounter; that is, the young person has the right to retain and instruct counsel without delay "at any stage of proceedings against him and prior to and during any consideration of whether, instead of commencing or continuing judicial proceedings against him under this Act, to use alternative measures to deal with him."

---

[8]*A.-G. of B.C. v. Smith,* [1969] 1 C.C.C. 244 (S.C.C.). But note the decision of *Morris v. R.,* [1979] 1 S.C.R. 405, 91 D.L.R. (3d) 161, 43 C.C.C. (2d) 129, in which the Supreme Court of Canada laid to rest the myth that juvenile delinquency is the only offence committed. The court noted that the *JDA* created a special procedure; it did not create an offence. A young person charged or convicted with an offence was no different than an adult insofar as the offence means a violation of the *Criminal Code* or such other statute.

Although it is only with respect to arrest or detention[9] that there exists a statutory obligation on the officer to inform the young person of his rights to retain and instruct counsel (s. 11(2)), s. 3(1)(g) states that

> [Y]oung persons have the right, in every instance where they have rights or freedoms that may be affected by this Act, to be informed as to what those rights and freedoms are;

Further, this right has been held implicitly to necessitate a corollary duty on the officer to give the young person access to a telephone and a list of lawyers' names and phone numbers before there is any further discussion by way of investigation.[10] It is submitted that the wording of s. 11(2) is not exclusive in that the proclamation of a right, as under s. 11(1), must have been effected with the intention that it is to have universal effect and it is not to be limited to those young persons who are sufficiently street-wise and experienced to know of and demand compliance with the right. Reference should be had in this context to the U.S. Supreme Court decision of *Miranda v. Arizona*[11] in which the constitutional right "in all criminal prosecutions . . . to have the assistance of counsel" includes by implication the right to be clearly informed of that expressed right.

Section 11(1) appears to go even further than the protection provided by s. 10(b) of the *Charter of Rights* which provides everyone with the right, *on arrest or detention,* to retain and instruct counsel without delay and to be informed of that right; the right under the *YOA* is triggered not when reasonable grounds lead to an arrest or detention, but prior to or upon reasonable grounds leading to "any consideration" of whether to use diversionary "alternative measures." "Alternative measures" means "measures other than judicial proceedings . . . used to deal with a young person alleged to have committed an offence": s. 2(1), *YOA*. The ordinary dictionary meaning of "alleged" includes "affirmed, especially without proof; advanced as an argument." If the passive form "alleged" includes an investigative officer's reasonable suspicions, then even a simple warning may amount to an "alternative measure" let alone the "consideration" of an "alternative measure."

Statements

The right to retain and instruct counsel must be viewed in the context of s. 56 of the *YOA* which governs the admissibility of inculpatory statements made by young persons to the police, and in particular, to investigating officers. Section 56(2) outlines four prerequisite safeguards with which an officer must comply before a statement made to him is admissible in court against the young person. However, s. 56(3) exempts oral, spontaneous statements from these

---

[9]"Detention" as it is used in s. 10 of the *Charter of Rights* has been defined to mean some form of compulsory restraint by process of law, which has also been held to exclude detaining persons for breathalizer tests and customs searches. Hence, the questioning of a young person or the accompanying him to his home for the purpose of warning him and his family may not in itself constitute detention. See *R. v. Simmons* (1984), 11 W.C.B. 462 (Ont. C.A.); *R. v. Rahn* (1984), 11 W.C.B. 218 (Alta. C.A.); *R. v. Currie* (1983), 4 C.C.C. (3d) 217, 19 M.V.R. 15 (N.S.C.A.). But see *R. v. Therens* (1983), 5 C.C.C. (3d) 409, 33 C.R. (3d) 204, 20 M.V.R. 8 (Sask. C.A.), affg. 70 C.C.C. (2d) 468, 16 M.V.R. 285 (Sask. Prov. Ct.).

[10]See *Brownridge v. R.*, [1972] S.C.R. 926 at 952, 7 C.C.C. (2d) 417, 18 C.R.N.S. 308 (S.C.C.).

[11]*Miranda v. Arizona* (1966), 384 U.S. 436, 86 S. Ct. 1602.

prerequisites as long as they were made before the officer had had a "reasonable opportunity" to fulfill the requirements under s. 56(2), one of which is that the young person has been given a "reasonable opportunity" to consult with counsel. It appears that the time at which an officer must permit the young person to avail himself of the right of counsel, as discussed above, may in some circumstances be prior to and in other circumstances subsequent to the time represented by a "reasonable opportunity" to fulfill the requirements of s. 56(2). Query whether it will affect the admissibility of the spontaneous statement if prior to the statement the young person was not adequately informed or whether s. 56 is an exclusive statement of admissibility. In this context, note s. 56(1) which states that, subject to s. 56, "the law related to the admissibility of statements made by persons accused of committing offences applies in respect of young persons."

Since the phrase "spontaneous statement" is not defined under the Act, recourse can be had to the common law for same. The authors V. Bala and H. Lilles in their report entitled *The Young Offenders Act Annotated*,[12] use a 1932 Supreme Court of Canada case to describe its meaning as a statement to the police in response to a casual question, made voluntarily and without any inducement, before the accused is apprehended or warned and presumably not made in response to a direct question or as a result of interrogation.[13] If the officer complies with the time requirements under s. 11(1) within which the right to retain and instruct counsel must be given effect, as discussed above, it would arguably be the rare instance that a statement could be defined as "spontaneous" since the prompt presence of counsel would inhibit same. Since the time at which adults are instructed as to their right to counsel is much later than that of young persons, spontaneous statements from adults would be more reasonably expected. It is suggested that the s. 56(3) exemption could only apply where the investigating officer is not suspicious that the young person might have committed an offence. Any other interpretation would mean that the right to representation guaranteed to the young person under one section has no effect on the admissibility of culpable statements, which would probably not have been made had the s. 11(1) rights been given effect. It is submitted that this latter interpretation is inconsistent with s. 3(1)(e) which dictates that young persons should have "special guarantees" of their rights and freedoms and s. 3(2) which directs that the *YOA* should be liberally construed to give effect to the principles under s. 3(1). Indeed, it is suggested that the nature of childhood and its predictable inclination towards spontaneity requires a strict interpretation of s. 56(3) coupled with s. 11(1) if young persons are to have "special guarantees of their rights and freedoms."

Section 56(2) codifies the common law rules with respect to admissibility of incriminating statements made by children, the basic guidelines being that statements must be voluntary, that is to say, made without "fear of prejudice or hope of advantage exercised or held out by a person in authority".[14] In order to

---

[12]Bala and Lilles, *supra*, note 1.

[13]*Ibid.*, at pp. 385–86.

[14]*Ibrahim v. The Queen*, [1914] App. Ct. 599, at 609.

give effect to this rule when a child is making the statement, case law has developed more specific guidelines.[15]

s. 56(2) No oral or written statement given by a young person to a peace officer or other person who is, in law, a person in authority is admissible against the young person unless

(a) the statement was voluntary;

(b) the person to whom the statement was given has, before the statement was made, clearly explained to the young person, in language appropriate to his age and understanding, that

(i) the young person is under no obligation to give a statement,

(ii) any statement given by him may be used as evidence in proceedings against him,

(iii) the young person has the right to consult another person in accordance with paragraph (c), and

(iv) any statement made by the young person is required to be made in the presence of the person consulted, unless the young person desires otherwise;

(c) the young person has, before the statement was made, been given a reasonable opportunity to consult with counsel or a parent, or in the absence of a parent, an adult relative, any other appropriate adult chosen by the young person; and

(d) where the young person consults any person pursuant to paragraph (c), the young person has been given a reasonable opportunity to make the statement in the presence of that person.

Note that the young person may waive his rights under s. 56(2)(c) and (d) if he does so by written, signed statement: s. 56(4).

There are differing opinions as to when the "caution" under s. 56(2)(b) should be administered. In one recent discussion paper, it was stated that present case law imposes no obligation on the police to give the caution merely because of a suspicion and that there is no reason why a new standard should be adopted under the *YOA*.[16] Bala and Lilles suggest that the English Judges' rules should be

---

[15]See *R. v. Jacques* (1958), 29 C.R. 249 (Que. S.W.C.); *R. v. Yensen*, [1961] O.R. 703, 29 D.L.R. (2d) 314, 130 C.C.C. 353 (Ont. H.C.); *R. v. Wilson* (1970), 1 C.C.C. (2d) 14 (B.C.C.A.); *R. v. R. (No. 1)* (1972), 9 C.C.C. 274 (Ont. Prov. Ct.) where the court noted some of the distinct qualities of children to include: (i) reduced capacity to understand one's rights; (ii) reduced capacity to protect oneself in the adult world; and (iii) impact of authority suggesting to the child that he must answer all questions. See as well *Re J.P.B. and A.W.T.* (1976), 362 A. 2d 1183 (N.J.) where the question of voluntariness arose within the context of a therapy session. A defendant child made admissions regarding the commission of an offence in a group counselling session at a juvenile institution. This was in response to a direction from his supervisor to admit all prior anti-social activities including criminal acts. It was also understood that failure to cooperate in the group session would entail sanctions, including a transfer to a less desirable facility. In view of these facts, the juvenile's admissions were held inadmissible as evidence against him absent the "Miranda warning."

[16]Ferns, B.A., and J.C. Pearson, "Discussion Paper on the Young Offenders Act" (Law Society of Upper Canada and Canadian Bar Association, Ontario, May 24, 1984) citing *Dupuis v. R.* (1932), 104 C.C.C. 290 (S.C.C.); *R. v. Wolbaum*, [1965] 3 C.C.C. 191 (Sask. C.A.); *R. v. Draskovic* (1971), 5 C.C.C. (2d) 186 (Ont. C.A.).

followed such that s. 56(2) should be complied with "as soon as a police officer has evidence which would offer reasonable grounds for suspecting that a person has committed an offence."[17] And as suggested above, one cannot determine when the caution involving counsel should be administered without taking into account the implications of s. 11(1), that is, the right to retain and instruct counsel "prior to . . . any consideration of whether . . . to use alternative measures to deal with [the young person]."

Note that s. 56(2)(c) seems to allow the police to choose between counsel or a parent as the adult consultant. The child who therefore declines to consult with his parent, perhaps out of fear of parental repercussions, which may in some cases induce as much fear as the police, may be said to have been given his opportunity under that section. This section raises the question of whether "persons in authority" can include parents as well as the police. The test for determining whether a person is someone "in authority" has been held to be subjective.[18] Further, in one Ontario High Court decision, it was held that a parent who is present at the confession must be called by the Crown during the *voir dire*.[19] It is noteworthy that in its introductory title for s. 43 the *Criminal Code* also uses the phrase "persons in authority", which includes parents and teachers, when it creates the authority to assault a child for disciplinary purposes. Given that it is unreasonable to expect the police to inquire into the dynamics between child and parent, it would appear to be good practice for counsel to do so, as well as the judge himself, in determining admissibility, having regard to the "special guarantees" of the rights and freedoms under s. 3(1)(e). One author points out that anyone who makes a threat or inducement to an accused in the presence of a person in authority is himself considered to be a person in authority.[20] Given that it is not an uncommon experience for legal counsel, arriving at the police station, to confront a parent who has allied himself with the police, hoping the process will "teach the boy a lesson." The parent's presence in this situation as automatic satisfaction of the safeguards under s. 56(2) would seem less than just.[21]

The preliminary wording of s. 56(2)(b) requires the person in authority to explain the caution clearly "in language appropriate to [the young person's] age and understanding." Therefore, the Crown should be able to prove beyond a reasonable doubt that his agents met the subjective test that that particular child understood what was being said to him. (Presumably this test is also applicable to s. 56(4), which permits the young person to waive his rights to consult with or have his counsel or parent present.) This is particularly important for the child who is emotionally traumatized and reacts in a totally submissive manner without regard to the significance of what is being said, and who only wishes to take the path of least resistance. This section, if effectively implemented, can also offer

---

[17]Bala and Lilles, *supra*, note 1, at p. 386.

[18]*R. v. Rothman* (1981), 59 C.C.C. (2d) 30 (S.C.C.).

[19]*R. v. Midkoff* (1980), 3 Cdn. J. Fam. Law 306 (Ont. H.C.).

[20]P. McWilliams, *Canadian Criminal Evidence* (Toronto: Canada Law Book, 1974), at p. 248.

[21]See also Fox, "Confessions by Juveniles" (1962-63), 5 Cr. L.Q. 459, as cited in Ferns and Pearson, *supra*, at note 16 in which it is suggested that the presence of a parent at the interrogation of a juvenile may actually hinder the obtaining of a "true" statement.

protection to the learning-disabled child who, while hearing the words and acknowledging his understanding, is nevertheless unable to comprehend in so short a time an oral explanation without the use of specific modes of communication such as pictures.[22] In fact, the Crown may need to show that contact was made with the parent as to their child's particular ability to understand the significance of the proceedings, especially in light of the duty of the police to contact the parents as soon as possible upon arrest: s. 9(1), *YOA*.

Less frequently used is s. 56(5) which allows the court to refuse admission of any statement made by the young person under duress to another who is not, in law, a person in authority. It is a discretionary remedy only, it does not require a *voir dire* and the onus is upon the accused to satisfy the court of the duress. The *YOA* is silent with respect to what constitutes "duress" as is the *Criminal Code*, although it has been held under the latter that such a defence should succeed only in exceptional circumstances where there is a threat of physical harm.[23] Given the vulnerability of childhood as reflected in the "special guarantees" of s. 3, the narrow interpretation of "duress" should arguably be expanded to cover situations of other than a physical apprehension of harm. Although there is no presumption of influence arising from the parent/child relationship in the *Criminal Code*, note the presumption in civil law against the validity of a contract between a parent and child in recognition of the unequal balance of power between the bargaining parties. Perhaps the definition of "duress" might be expanded to include the apprehension of psychological as well as physical harm in the sense of the threat and withdrawal of love or exclusion from the family.

Detention and Bail

The effect of s. 7 of the *YOA* is to continue the provisions of the repealed *JDA* with respect to detention before trial, that is, that alleged young offenders are to be detained in facilities separate from those of adults. There are three exceptions to the statutory requirement:

1) if the young person is temporarily restrained after his arrest but prior to his detention, which would refer to situations where the young person is taken to the station in a police vehicle and "processed through" including fingerprinting and photographs: s. 7(2), *YOA*.

2) if a Youth Court judge (or, if not "reasonably available", a justice) determines "that the young person cannot, having regard to his own safety or the safety of others, be detained in a place of detention for young persons": s. 7(3)(a). This section appears to codify the wide interpretation given to an analogous provision of the repealed *JDA*, that is, that the court is to consider the safety of the accused child, the other people who are sharing

---

[22]See *e.g.*: H. Litsky J., *Childhood Experiences as Causes of Criminal Behaviour* (Ottawa: First National Conference of Learning Disabilities, October, 1977); R. Underwood, "Learning Disabilities as a Pre-disposing Cause of Criminality" in *Canadian Mental Health* (December, 1976); P.R.S. Koopman, "*Cognitive Disorders and Syntactical Deficiencies in the Inmate Propulations of Federal Penetentiaries in Canada*", Report to Solicitor-General of Canada (March, 1982).

[23]*R. v. Carker (No. 2)*, [1967] S.C.R. 114.

confinement with the accused child and the safety of the persons charged with the care and control of the accused child.[24]

3) if the Youth Court judge or justice determines that no separate place of detention for young persons is "available within a reasonable distance." This section is a reponse to the practical problem that in many jurisdictions, separate facilities for children simply do not exist: s. 7(3)(b).

In addition to the prohibition of mixing young persons with adults, the *YOA* has introduced another alternative for interim disposition under s. 7(4). This section allows a judge to place the young person with "a responsible person" on the following conditions:

1) the adult must be "willing and able to take care of and exercise control over" the person;

2) the young person is willing to be placed with the adult;

3) the adult undertakes in writing to take care of and to be responsible for the attendance of the young person at court. This form of relief is distinct from those available under the *Criminal Code's* bail provisions, incorporated into the *YOA* under s. 8, since it effectively relies on "constructive custody" rather than on a third person's surety or detention to ensure that the accused does not get into any more trouble and does appear at the trial. Providing this alternative is consistent with the principles of s. 3(1)(f) which state that the rights and freedoms of young persons include a right to "the least possible interference with freedom that is consistent with the protection of society".

The s. 7(4) alternative seems somewhat ambiguous in its nature since it is unclear whether it provides a form of release prior to the operation of the *Criminal Code* bail provisions, as incorporated by s. 8 of the *YOA*, or whether it simply gives the court one more alternative in the context of a bail hearing. The authors Balla and Lilles rely on the latter interpretation, pointing out that the provision "is not intended to be an alternative to release; rather, only following a finding by the youth court that the criteria for detention [presumably the show cause provisions under s. 457(7) of the Code] have been met" should a court place a child under s. 7(4) of the *YOA* "as an alternative to actual custody."[25] In other words, s. 7(4) is a form of release like any other conditional form of release under s. 457 of the *Criminal Code* which can be blocked only if the Crown can show cause under s. 457(7) why the young person should not be released.

On the other hand, one might argue that s. 457 of the *Code* is not triggered automatically on arrest, but that s. 7(4) can operate independently of the *Code's* release presumptions and "show cause" guidelines. If one assumes this

---

[24]*R. v. P.*, [1979] 2 W.W.R. 262, 8 R.F.L. (2d) 277 (Man. Q.B.).

[25]Bala and Lilles, *supra*, note 1 at 50. But see *R. v. L.G.*, unreported, April 25, 1984 (Alta. Prov. Ct.) *per* White A.C.J., where the court concludes that s. 7(4) of the *YOA* cannot be invoked in conjunction with s. 457 of the *Criminal Code* for the purpose of releasing a juvenile into the care of a parent. S. 457, dealing with judicial interim release, means release from custody and the relief under s. 7(4) is in itself a form of custody.

interpretation, then the section could only receive a more liberal application than that represented by s. 457 of the *Code* in keeping with s. 3(1)(e) ("special guarantees" of rights and freedoms), s. 3(1)(f) (least possible intervention with freedom consistent with protection of society) and s. 3(1)(h) (removal from parental responsibility only as a last resort). This section may, in fact, be used as an immediate measure on arrest to return the child to the parent without precluding a subsequent show cause hearing under s. 457 of the *Code*.[26]

As noted above, s. 8 of the *YOA* (in conjunction with ss. 51 and 52 of the *YOA*: general applicability of the *Criminal Code*) incorporates the bail provisions of the *Criminal Code* into proceedings under the *YOA* with some jurisdictional modifications as well as the possible alternative approach under s. 7(4), as discussed above. Some of the modifications include:

1) The application for release is to be heard by a Youth Court judge unless one is not reasonably available, in which case it shall be heard by a justice: s. 8(1);

2) If a justice has made the order under s. 8(1), it is subject to review by a Youth Court judge at any subsequent time upon application by either party, and the Youth Court is to hear the matter "as an original application" that is *de novo:* s. 8(2), *YOA*. Although ss. 457.5 and 457.6 of the *Code* provide review routes also, they can only be utilized if the original order was made by a Youth Court judge and not a justice: s. 8(7), *YOA*. Note that, in contrast to the *YOA* review route, the *Code's* review routes (a) limit the possible applicants (s. 457.5: the accused; s. 457.6: the Crown); (b) do not specifically provide that the review application should be heard "as an original application";[27] and (c) specifically outline the kind of evidence to be heard and the type of order which the judge may make.

3) When the original order is by a Youth Court judge and thus only reviewable under s. 457.5 and 457.6 of the *Code*, the review level is a Superior Court (Supreme or District) if the Youth Court judge was a Provincial Court judge. When the Youth Court judge is from a Superior Court level, then it must be reviewed by a judge of the Court of Appeal: s. 8(6).

4) If the young person is charged with one of the serious offences governed by s. 457.7 of the *Code*, then it is only the Youth Court judge that may release him from custody under that section and any appeal from that decision is to the Court of Appeal in accordance with s. 608.1 of the *Code:* s. 8(8) and (9).

Parental Notice/Court Appearance

Section 3(1)(h) of the *YOA* states that "parents have responsibility for the

---

[26]See *R. v. L.G., ibid.*

[27]Even in the absence of the express wording "as an original application", it has been held that a review by a judge of the justice's order under s. 457.5 of the *Code* is, in effect, a *de novo* hearing and is not an appeal based only on the record of proceedings before the justice. See *Re Powers and R.* (1972), 9 C.C.C. (2d) 533, 20 C.R.N.S. 23 (Ont. H.C.); *R. v. Sexton* (1976), 33 C.R.N.S. 307 (Nfld. Dist. Ct.); but see *R. v. O'Neill* (1973), 11 C.C.C. (2d) 240, 21 C.R.N.S. 107 (N.B.S.C.).

care and supervision of their children, and, for that reason, young persons should be removed from parental supervision either partly or entirely only when measures that provide for continuing parental supervision are inappropriate.'' To give effect to this principle, the Act creates some procedural guarantees for the involvement of parents of accused juvenile offenders. Section 9 requires that notice be served on a ''parent'' as defined by the Act subject to certain exemptions, and s. 10 permits the court to require the appearance of the parent before the court if his presence is necessary or in the best interests of the young person. The parent who is so ordered and fails to appear is subject to summary contempt proceedings as set out in the *Code*. Perhaps the most significant aspect of parental involvement so far as counsel for the young person is concerned, is its relation to s. 56(2)(c), that is, the prerequisite consultation with and presence of the parent or other adult for subsequent admission of inculpatory statements from the young person at trial.

The notice provisions apply to two classes of circumstances pursuant to s. 9(1) and (2):

1) when a young person has been arrested and detained pending his appearance in court;
2) when the young person has been issued an appearance notice or summons or has been released on giving his promise to appear or entering into recognizance.

In the first case, notice is to be given by the officer in charge at the time the young person is detained either orally or in writing, stating the place of detention and reasons for arrest. In the second case, notice of the summons, appearance etc. is to be given in writing by the person who issued the summons or appearance or by the officer in charge if the young person has been detained and then released as described above. In both cases, notice is to be given ''as soon as possible'' and should include the name of the young person, the charge with the time and place of appearance and a recital of the right to counsel: s. 9(6).

Note that failure to give notice generally does not invalidate the proceedings (s. 9(8)) except that failure to do so under class (2), noted above, does render subsequent proceedings invalid unless (a) the parent attends at court with the young person or (b) the judge dispenses with notice, ''having regard to the circumstances'' pursuant to s. 9(10)(b): s. 9, *YOA*. One author advises that in order to avoid technical foul-ups involving the notification prerequisites, the Crown might simply subpoena the parents and then rely on s. 9(10)(a), (parental presence in the court room) to validate the proceedings.[28]

Section 9(10)(a) states that, in the case of failure of notice, the judge may also adjourn the proceedings in order to give proper notice. However, s. 9 appears to be exclusive with respect to a class (2) notice, described above, in that proceedings would be void and therefore incapable of being adjourned if the test under either (a) or (b), described above, is not satisfied. Accordingly, s. 9(10)(a) would be applicable only to those accused groups of young persons who are being detained pending their court appearance.

---

[28]Ferns and Pearson, *supra*, note 16, at p. 43.

As a final precaution, the *YOA* provides under s. 9(3) that if the whereabouts of a parent are unknown or it appears that no parent is available for notification purposes, the notice is to be given to an adult relative or, if unavailable, another adult, both of whom must be known to the young person and "likely to assist him." In addition, note that the definition of "parent" under s. 2(1) of the Act includes anyone who is under a legal duty to provide for the young person *or* who has, in law or in fact, custody and control of the young person. Notification requirements would therefore be satisfied if served on a non-custodial parent who may have lost all contact or interest in the child, but who continues to be responsible for support payments until he is 21 years of age. In fact, because the wording of the definition does not appear to be exclusive, a parent in the usual sense of mother or father would arguably continue to be applicable and could therefore include parents who no longer take care of their 17-year-old who has left home and is no longer economically dependent on them. Their parent is no longer under a legal duty to provide for the child under domestic legislation, nor does he have custody or control over the child and yet his notification would be considered satisfactory, based on this interpretation despite the fact that he may not meet the condition imposed on the other adults, that is, that he is likely to assist the young person. A Children's Aid Society or training school, possessing the powers of the guardian with respect to a child under the age of 18 years, would qualify as a "parent" and notice upon the director or supervisor of the agency would satisfy the requirement. An individual who is neither the mother or the father of the child but with whom the young person resides and who exercises the "custody or control" in a parental fashion would qualify under the definition, whether or not that person has a duty to provide for the young person, because the clauses in the definition are disjunctive.

The Right to Counsel

As discussed above under "Initial contact: Representation", the right to counsel, meaning the opportunity for a child to retain and instruct his own lawyer, exists not only at any stage of the proceedings but also prior to and during any consideration by the state of "alternative measures" against the young person.[29] The Act defines "alternative measures" to include "measures other than judicial proceedings under this Act used to deal with the young person alleged to have committed an offence." Balla and Lilles advise that "alternative measures" include forms of diversion and specifically that of "police screening", that is, deciding not to institute a charge against a young person but instead, warning him and sending him home for parental discipline.[30] It has further been suggested earlier in the chapter that having given the child a right at this early stage of investigation, there is a concomitant duty upon the state to give effect to it so that as soon as the young person is isolated, questioned or

---

[29]Section 11(1), *YOA*:

s. 11(1) A young person has the right to retain and instruct counsel without delay at any stage of proceedings against him and prior to and during any consideration of whether, instead of commencing or continuing judicial proceedings against him under this Act, to use alternative measures to deal with him.

[30]Bala and Lilles, *supra,* note 1, at p. 21.

attracts any suspicion at all as an alleged offender, even for the purpose of a "contact" or "warning", the opportunity to consult with counsel should be made available. The broad wording of s. 11(1) of the *YOA* in addition to that of s. 10(b) of the *Charter of Rights* (right on arrest or detention to retain counsel) must add an even greater obligation upon the courts to protect the right of the child to counsel. Further, the fact that specific sections of the Act call for the repeated act of informing the young person of his right to counsel (s. 11(2), (3), and (9)) this in itself does not release the authorities from doing so at the early stage defined by s. 11(1) especially in light of s. 3(1)(g) (general right to be informed of all rights). Indeed, repetition at every stage of the proceeding is another form of instituting the "special guarantees" of the young person's rights and freedoms: s. 3(1)(e). (Stages include contact, arrest and detention, bail hearing, hearing for transfer to adult court, trial and review of disposition.)[31]

At a bail hearing, a s. 16 "transfer to adult court" hearing, at a trial or at a hearing for review of disposition, the duty to inform the young person of his right to counsel is fortified by the power of the court to order and implement counsel for the young person if he wishes a lawyer but has been unable to obtain one. If, for practical reasons, the young person's desire to have counsel has been blocked by problems of accessibility, lack of information, financial or even parental impediment, the court on its own initiative may refer the child to a counsel, which is funded by a legal aid program, if in existence, or refer the child to the Attorney-General of the Province who, upon such referral, *must* appoint counsel: s. 11(4), (5) and (6), *YOA*.[32] This prescription for affirmative implementation of the legal right of representation (one of the special guarantees of s. 3(1)(e)) distinguishes the criminal process for children from that of adults, the latter being restricted to a simple adjournment to allow the accused to retain counsel. Further, it is submitted that the availability of duty counsel, who "only meet the juveniles at court and have little or no time to prepare"[33] does not satisfy the intent of these sections. In a U.S. decision, a conviction was quashed where the young person was minimally represented:

> To "administer justice without respect to persons, and do equal right to the poor and to the rich" we must apply the same standard, whether counsel be court-appointed or privately retained. From the facts of this case it is plain

---

[31] See *R. v. K.S.* (1982), 8 W.C.B. 502 (Ont. Prov. Ct.) wherein it was held under s. 10(b) of the *Charter* that the duty on authorities to advise a person of his right to retain and instruct counsel was to be exercised with greater care with a juvenile than with an adult.

[32] In *R. v. Ronald H.*, unreported, June 29, 1984 (Alta. Prov. Ct.) *per* Fitch J., the court ruled that in determining whether counsel should be appointed under s. 11(4), financial circumstances are irrelevant. The court noted that the duty of a parent to provide "maintenance" under provincial domestic legislation does not include the duty to pay for legal counsel. Nevertheless, there should be some inquiry concerning the financial circumstances, however brief. But if the young person cannot obtain counsel privately, and the court is aware that legal aid programs will not be made available, then if the court directs an appointment of counsel, the provincial Attorney-General must make one available.

[33] Bala and Lilles, *supra*, note 1, at p. 83 citing the *Report on Representation of Children in Provincial Court (Family Division)* prepared for the Ministry of the Attorney-General, found at (1977), 29 R.F.L. 134.

that West's lawyer fell far short of this standard. West might just as well have had no lawyer. By his own admission West's attorney conferred with West for no more than an hour prior to trial, and perhaps for little more than five minutes. He conducted no investigation. At the trial he called no witnesses for the defense. After the prosecution presented its case, the defense moved for a directed verdict. When the court denied this motion, the defense immediately rested. We hold that . . . West's legal representation was so inadequate as to deny his constitutional rights.[34]

In one Ontario Court of Appeal decision, representation by duty counsel was considered to leave the accused undefended, the court noting, "It is true that duty counsel was there, but he was not the person who had been selected by the accused to represent him."[35]

Aside from s. 543(3) of the *Criminal Code*, wherein a court may appoint counsel in the face of the accused's "insanity", there is no authority for the court to appoint counsel where the accused does not wish a lawyer, regardless of the young person's apparent legal needs. The court does have the power under s. 11(7) of the *YOA* to permit an adult, meaning a person over the age of 17 years, to assist the accused at the young person's request although the court has some discretion to determine whether the particular adult is suitable. Care should be taken to avoid the use of this section as a common and equal substitute for the full exercise of the court's duties and powers to ensure legal representation under s. 11 of the *YOA*.

There appears to be no practical statutory repercussions against the Crown or the validity of the proceedings generally if the s. 11 requirements have not been fulfilled, although s. 56(2) does render a statement by a young person to the police inadmissible if an opportunity to consult with counsel has not been made available. Similarly, although recourse is available under s. 10(b) of the *Charter*, which guarantees the right to retain and instruct counsel on arrest or detention without delay and to be so informed, again such recourse results only in the inadmissibility of inculpatory statements if the opportunity has not been furnished to the accused.[36]

Transfer to Adult Court

Probably the most hard fought issue under the repealed *JDA* concerned the issue of transfers of alleged young offenders from the juvenile to the ordinary adult court. No doubt this is due to the sharp increase in the severity of the consequences of the latter. For example, the time limitation for a committal period of two or three years provided by s. 20 (discussed below) no longer applies. Further, there is no equivalent review process of dispositions (discussed below), which under the *YOA* includes an automatic year-end review and an earlier elective review of custodial dispositions and elective review of non-custodial dispositions. Finally, once moved to adult court, the young offender does not have the benefit of the declared principles set out in s. 3 of the

---

[34]*West v. State of Louisianna* (1973), 478 F. 2d 1026 (5th Cir.) at 1033, cited in Bala and Lilles, *supra*, note 1, at p. 84.

[35]*R. v. Butler* (1973), 11 C.C.C. (2d) 381 (Ont. C.A.). See also *Re R. and Speid* (1983), 43 O.R. (2d) 596, 3 D.L.R. (4th) 246, 8 C.C.C. (3d) 18 (C.A.) (*Charter* case on counsel of choice).

[36]See *R. v. Manninen* (1983), 43 O.R. (2d) 731, 3 D.L.R. (4th) 541, 8 C.C.C. (3d) 193 (C.A.).

YOA, the effect of which is to permit the application of the criminal law in a manner that is less arbitrary and more responsive to the individual needs of the young person, notwithstanding the gravity of the offence committed. A comparison of the case law under s. 9 of the repealed *JDA*[37] with the wording of s. 16 of the *YOA* reveals many differences, both substantive and procedural.

Substantive
Issues

The test for transfer applications under the repealed *JDA* required the court to be satisfied that "the good of the child and the interests of the community demanded it." The Ontario Court of Appeal considered this wording to mean there were two separate and equal issues to be determined and that the word "demand" imparted a requirement of urgency such that the transfer should have occurred if the crime was of a most serious nature and the criminal or other records of the juvenile supported no other recourse or solution. A child whose record suggested he was salvageable, that is, there seemed to be no evidence of incorrigibility, should have remained in the juvenile justice system.[38] However, in various situations, this rigorous test was modified to satisfy other competing interests. In one case, a juvenile was transferred where a co-accused, just a few months older than the juvenile, was to be tried in adult court, the reasoning being that due administration of justice must be served which includes the avoidance of different verdicts and punishments for the same offences.[39] In another case, the court had regard to the nature of the crime including the degree of pre-meditation, brutality and violence to make a transfer decision. It held that the act in itself can speak more to the offender's incorrigibility than any past criminal or other record. Accordingly, in the case of a violent and premeditated murder, that act can be so overwhelming that the separate requirement that the juvenile be incorrigible is implicit in the act without separate consideration.[40]

The language of s. 16 of the *YOA* still requires that both the interests of the community and the needs of the young person be considered: "if the court is of the opinion that, in the interest of society and having regard to the needs of the young person. . . ." (Note that the child must also be 14 years of age or more when he committed the offence to be subject to this transfer provision: s. 16(1).) Removing the word "demand" may suggest a less onerous test for the Crown, one that does not require a cumulative effect of "urgency" or "necessity by reason of no other recourse or solution." On the other hand, the test may be as onerous under the *YOA* as it was under the repealed legislation, notwithstanding the absence of the word "demand", by reason of s. 16(2) which specifically sets out all the factors which the court is obliged to consider:

s. 16(2)(a) the seriousness of the alleged offence and the circumstances in which it was allegedly committed;

(b) the age, maturity, character and background of the young person and any record or summary of previous findings of delinquency under the *Juvenile Delinquents Act* or previous findings of guilt under this or any other Act of Parliament or any regulation made thereunder;

---

[37]For a review of these cases see J. Wilson, *Children and the Law* (1st Ed., 1978), at pp. 204–06.

[38]*R. v. Mero* (1976), 30 C.C.C. (2d) 497 (Ont. C.A.).

[39]*R. v. Smith* (1975), 28 C.C.C. (2d) 368 (Man. C.A.).

[40]*R. v. Clements and DeGrandpre* (1983), 5 C.C.C. (3d) 308 (Ont. C.A.). Leave to appeal to S.C.C. dismissed (1983), 52 N.R. 395n.

(c) the adequacy of this Act, and the adequacy of the *Criminal Code* or other Act of Parliament that would apply in respect of the young person if an order were made under sub-section (1), to meet the circumstances of the case;

(d) the availability of treatment or correctional resources;

(e) any representations made to the court by or on behalf of the young person or by the Attorney General or his agent; and

(f) any other factors that the court considers relevant.

The cumulative effect of this criteria may simply amount to a codification of the existing case law.[41] Indeed, it is arguable that the test is even more onerous by reason of the application of those principles set out in s. 3 of the *YOA* and in particular s. 3(1)(a) (different standards of accountability between adult and young person), s. 3(1)(c) (developmental considerations in rendering disposition) and s. 3(1)(f) (least possible interference with freedom). Accordingly, notwithstanding the gravity of the offence, the court would be hardpressed to make an order transferring the young offender to the adult court in the face of compelling evidence as to the availability and appropriateness of treatment or correctional resources within the young offender correction system. Further to this, the catch-all criterion of s. 16(2)(f) ("any other factors that the court considers relevant") may broaden the test even more. For example, under the repealed legislation, a transfer order was quashed on appeal because the court based its decision on the "extraneous matter" of the refusal of the child charged with theft to name the receiver of the goods.[42] Although there must be some relevancy limitation on the s. 16(2)(f) criterion, this case under the repealed *JDA* may have been decided differently under the *YOA*.

Procedural Issues

The *YOA* now codifies a more consistent and reliable process for transfer applications than had evolved under the repealed *JDA*. Consider the following:

1) Only one application can be brought for transfer with respect to any one alleged offence: s. 16(6). The application must be made after the laying of the information and prior to adjudication: s. 16(1). It cannot be brought after disposition as appeared to be possible under s. 20(3) of the *JDA*.

2) The age of the person (minimum of 14 years) is determined as at the date of the offence: s. 16(1). No longer applicable is the case law under the repealed *JDA* that suggested the relevant time frame to be the date of the transfer hearing.

3) The alleged offence must be indictable, as was true under the *JDA*, but excluded from those indictable offences for which a transfer application can

---

[41] See the principles set out in *R. v. Mero, supra,* note 38. See also *R. v. B.R.C.*, (1984), 13 W.C.B. 193 (Alta. Prov. Ct.), wherein the court concluded that the considerations for transfer under the repealed *JDA* were not enumerated but built up in case law. Refusing to impart any significance to the different wording under the *YOA*, the court concluded that "Full consideration of s. 16(2) of the *YOA* would sufficiently cover my considerations for transfer under the *JDA*, particularly since s. 16(2) basically covers the criteria required for transfer under the *JDA*" [at p. 8].

[42] *R. v. N.* (1981), 58 C.C.C. (2d) 91, 44 N.S.R. (2d) 559 (N.S.S.C.).

be made are those referred to in s. 483 of the *Criminal Code* (''Magistrate's Jurisdiction'') including

(a) the following offences or attempts to commit same where the relevant value of the subject matter of the offence does not exceed $200

(i) theft, other than theft of cattle;

(ii) obtaining money or property by false pretenses;

(iii) unlawfully having in one's possession any property or proceeds therefrom knowingly obtained by the commission of an offence punishable by indictment;

(iv) having, by deceit, falsehood or other fraudulent means, defrauded anyone.

(b) the following offences

(i) keeping, being found in or permitting a gaming or betting house

(ii) involvement in betting, pool-selling, bookmaking, etc.

(iii) involvement in lotteries or games of chance

(iv) cheating at play

(v) keeping or found in a common bawdy house

(vi) driving while disqualified, or

(vii) fraud in collecting or paying fares.

Note that it has been held under the *JDA* that a hybrid offence, that is, one punishable by way of indictment or on summary conviction at the election of the Crown, constitutes an indictable offence unless the Crown elects otherwise and therefore, in the absence of electing otherwise, such an offence can form the basis for a transfer application.[43]

4) The ''applicants'' in transfer proceedings include the young person and the Attorney-General or his agent but not a private prosecutor. The young person may be seeking certain advantages of the adult court given the opportunity for preliminary inquiries or trial by jury. The language of s. 16(1) seems to clarify and reverse the effect of those decisions under the repealed *JDA* which suggested that the court had jurisdiction on its own to initiate the consideration of a transfer.[44]

5) Under the repealed *JDA*, both practice and case law suggested that all those persons who have a right to be present also have the right to call evidence, to cross-examine witnesses, to examine all of the documents which the court receives and to make submissions before the decision is made. Nevertheless, case law did suggest that the hearing was not strictly of a ''judicial nature. . . more of an administrative proceeding. . . The court is not bound to observe the strict rules of trial procedure, but must at least observe the rules of natural justice. . . The court may receive hearsay evidence at a hearing of this kind but, of course, cannot base its evidence solely upon it. . . .''[45] It appears, in spite of the serious consequences to the

---

[43]*R. v. K.J.H.* (1980), 5 Man. R. (2d) 14 (Q.B.), wherein the court relied on s. 27(1)(a) of the federal *Interpretation Act*. See also *R. v. B.* (1980), 8 C.C.C. (3d) 185 (B.C.C.A.), revg (1979), 51 C.C.C. (2d) 251 (B.C.S.C.).

[44]See *R. v. Metz*, [1977] 5 W.W.R. 374, 36 C.C.C. (2d) 22 (Man. C.A.).

[45]*R. v. F.J.Y.*, unreported, November 30, 1979 (Ont. Prov. Ct.), *per* Andrews C.J.; *R. v. Arbuckle*, [1967] 3 C.C.C. 380, 59 W.W.R. 605 (B.C.C.A.).

alleged young offender, that this description of the proceeding continues to apply under the *YOA*. For example, the court is obligated under s. 16(3) to consider a predisposition report compiled by the provincial director. While the author of the report will be subject to cross-examination in accordance with the provisions of s. 14, it is clear that the court will, by reason of the contents of such a report, necessarily consider hearsay evidence. Subject to this one codified exception, it is submitted that the characterization of the transfer hearing as less than judicial should be abandoned, having regard to the contrast in severity of consequences to the accused between the Youth Court and an adult court.

6) Section 16(9) to (13) provide for the review of a Youth Court's decision regarding a transfer application. The operative word is "review" which has been defined in reference to s. 608.1 of the *Criminal Code* (review by court of Appeal) to mean:

> [T]he review should take the general form of an ordinary appeal and not a hearing *de novo* or one in which either side has the *right* to submit additional material to the Court of Appeal. However, while no such *right* exists, the Court, as in appeals, can grant leave in the usual way and upon the usual grounds to a party to produce new evidence.[46]

The alleged young offender and the Crown both have the right to seek review by the "Superior Court" (the level will depend on the level of the Youth Court in each province) and that court will "in its discretion, confirm or reverse the decision of the Youth Court."[47] Insofar as the right of appeal ends with the Court of Appeal, it is interesting to note that in those provinces where a Superior Court is designated as the "youth court", there is only one opportunity for appeal or review of the decision, whereas in those provinces where a provincial court is designated as the "youth court", there exists a right of review and a further appeal from the decision of the reviewing court, with leave: s. 16(9), (10), (11).

Hearing

The determination of the child's guilt and the nature of the ingredients of the offence to be approved for a conviction is more a matter for a criminal law text than for this chapter, which is attempting to focus on the elements of the process which are unique to young persons, elements which arise before and after trial for the most part.

Predisposition and Assessment Reports

In order to assist the court in determining the most appropriate disposition after a finding of guilt, the *YOA* provides for two different court-directed information resources, either or both of which the judge may avail himself: the pre-disposition report and the medical or psychological report.

---

[46]*R. v. West*, [1973] 1 O.R. 211, at 217, 9 C.C.C. (2d) 369, 20 C.R.N.S. 15 (C.A.).

[47]See *R. v. Smith* (1973), 6 N.B.R. (2d) 494, 13 C.C.C. (2d) 374 (C.A.) for the principle that the duty of the court under s. 608.1 of the *Criminal Code* is to examine the record below and render the decision that "should have been made" by the judge below giving proper regard to his findings of fact in the inferences which he has drawn, a principle which likely will be applicable to review of decisions concerning transfer applications.

The predisposition report provides the court with an historical and descriptive background of the young person in the family and community, including whether or not the offender has previously been involved with the criminal law system and if so, the success of any previous dispositions. It is prepared by the "youth worker" (formerly the "probation officer"), as designated by the provincial director under s. 14.

The report is also to include the youth worker's own observations and conclusions on a number of issues including *inter alia*:

1) the results of an interview with the young person and if reasonably possible, with the parents: s. 14(2)(a);
2) the results of an interview with the victim: s. 14(2)(b);
3) the "maturity, character, behaviour and attitude of the young person and his willingness to make amends": s. 14(2)(c)(i);
4) the relationship between the young person and his parents and the degree of control and influence of the parents over the young person: s. 14(2)(c)(vi).[48]

The other items for consideration in the report are more factual in nature and less open to subjective interpretation by the youth worker.

Various principles have emerged from case law governing predisposition reports in the adult criminal system which may be applicable to the *YOA* proceedings:

1) The contents of the report should be properly substantiated and not be the subject of impression or speculation.[49]
2) The report on "behaviour" is not to include the statement that the offender is suspected of being involved in criminal activity which has not resulted in a criminal conviction.[50] However, this must be read within the context of s. 14(2)(c)(iv) which asks for the inclusion of a history of "alternative measures" used for the young person which are by definition measures to deal with someone who has not been tried or found guilty of any offence.
3) The fact of a prior conditional or absolute discharge should be included in a predisposition report.[51] This rule is consistent with s. 36(1)(e) which requires the court in rendering any disposition to consider any prior finding of guilt. However, as discussed below, no reference should be made in the predisposition report to the fact of any prior findings of guilt where the

---

[48]In *R. v. Shane B.*, unreported, June 15, 1984 (Alta. Prov. Ct.), *per* Fitch J., the court concluded that s. 14 of the *YOA* contemplates a predisposition report in respect of *each* charge under the Act unless there are special circumstances or the relevant dispositional information is available to the court from other sources. In the opinion of this court, the report is to include: the accused's version of the events; the "intelligence" of accused; reference to availability of community services; ability of accused to participate in fine option program; and probation officer's recommendations.

[49]*R. v. White* (1978), 16 Nfld. and P.E.I. 46 (Nfld. C.A.).

[50]*R. v. Morelli* (1977), 37 C.C.C. (2d) 392 (Ont. Prov. Ct.).

[51]*R. v. Ian*, [1975] 2 W.W.R. 747, 22 C.C.C. (2d) 184 (B.C.C.A.).

circumstances of s. 45 apply, that is, the young person's criminal records have been destroyed.

4) A predisposition report should fall short of recommending the form of punishment, respecting the fact that this matter lies exclusively within the "preserve of the judge and should remain outside the ambient of any probation officer's report unless his views are sought".[52]

5) Section 14(5) and (6) codify case law principles by ensuring that the accused has full knowledge of the contents of the report, as well as the opportunity to agree with, explain or dispute the contents. Further, if the court does not consider the matters to be important enough to require formal proof, they should be ignored as factors influencing the sentence.[53] Further, prejudicial statements which are denied should not be considered by the court in imposing a sentence if in the face of such denial the facts alleged in the prejudicial statements cannot be formally proven.[54] The report is filed at the request of and on behalf of the court and is neither evidence for the Crown nor the defence.

It is clear from the prescribed contents of the report that it will contain hearsay evidence. Case law under the repealed *JDA* suggests that after the adjudication, the ordinary laws with respect to the admissibility of evidence are relaxed such that strict compliance with the *Evidence Act* is not required at the disposition stage.[55] However, there is no indication in s. 14 or throughout the *YOA* that the proceedings at the stage of disposition should be any different than those in the adult criminal system. For example, notice of all of the contents and the right to cross-examine the author of the report are specifically guaranteed by ss. 14(5) and (6).

6) The discussions between the young offender and the youth worker are not privileged with the exception that inculpatory statements cannot be used against him in other civil or criminal proceedings except those under s. 16 (transfer to adult court), s. 20 (disposition), or ss. 28 to 32 (review of disposition): s. 14(10). This must be the case since these discussions clearly form the basis of the youth worker's advice to the court on the issue of disposition. What is less clear is whether such statements can be used against the young person in respect of another disposition arising from a different charge, in respect of a review of the present disposition, or in respect of an application for transfer to adult court arising from a different charge. Section 14(10) would suggest that in *any* subsequent disposition hearing or review of disposition hearing (except under s. 33 (review of disposition where failure to comply, discussed below) or in any application for transfer to an adult court arising from any charge, the statements made by the young person to

---

[52]*R. v. Silk* (1979), 20 Nfld. and P.E.I.R. 465 (Nfld. C.A.). But see *R. v. Shane B.*, *supra*, note 48, where the Youth Court judge stipulates that the youth worker should provide the court with his recommendations.

[53]See *R. v. Benson and Stevenson* (1951), 110 C.C.C. 247 (B.C.C.A.); *R. v. Carey* (1952), 102 C.C.C. 25 (Ont. C.A.); *R. v. Bezeau*, [1958] O.R. 617 (Ont. C.A.); *R. v. McGrath* (1962), 133 C.C.C. 57, at 62 (S.C.C.).

[54]*R. v. Silk*, *supra*, note 52.

[55]*Re P.*, [1973] 2 O.R. 818 (H.C.).

the youth worker could be used against him. Section 14(10) also suggests that any such statements could not be used to prove the commission of any offence arising from another charge since, except as cited above, all statements by the young person are inadmissible in any civil or criminal proceedings. Note that previous reports can be required by the court in rendering a further disposition: s. 14(8). It is noteworthy that the duties of the youth worker under s. 37 of the *YOA* no longer include the duty to represent "the interests of the child", which was true under the repealed *JDA*, suggesting that the youth worker is more properly recognized as an agent of the state or in the case of the predisposition report, an agent of the court.

Medical/
Psychological
Assessment

Section 13 of the *YOA* gives the court the power to order an assessment of the young person to assist it in making an appropriate disposition, reviewing a disposition, determining mental fitness to stand trial or determining whether the young person should be transferred to adult court: s. 13(1)(a), (b) and (c). The court may order such a report with the consent of the young person and prosecutor *or* where the court has "reasonable grounds to believe that the young person may be suffering from a physical or mental illness or disorder, a psychological disorder, an emotional disturbance, a learning disability or mental retardation" *and* if the judge thinks such a report would be helpful in his decision making: s. 13(1)(e), *YOA*. An assessment can be sought by the young person, the prosecutor or the court on its own initiative. The assessment is to be conducted by a "qualified person" which means a "person duly qualified by provincial law to practice medicine or psychiatry or to carry out psychological examinations or assessments, as the circumstances require or, where no such law exists, a person who is, in the opinion of the Youth Court, so qualified, and includes a person within a class or persons designated by the Lieutenant-Governor-in-Council of a province or his delegate: s. 13(11). For the purpose of the assessment, the young person can be remanded into custody for a period not exceeding eight days or, if satisfied that observation is required for a longer period to complete an examination or assessment, supported by evidence of at least one qualified person, he can be remanded for a longer period not exceeding 30 days: s. 13(3).

The extraordinary remedy of assessment should be implemented carefully with the same kind of procedural safeguards typical of any criminal proceeding. Its implications for the present proceedings as well as for concurrent or subsequent civil or criminal proceedings (inculpatory statements are not privileged as under a predisposition report) are very serious. Consider the following:

1) Section 13(1) provides for a discretionary order. The court must therefore act judicially and exercise its discretion in accordance with the evidence before it. No reasonable grounds can be said to exist in the absence of hearing evidence.[56]

2) In exercising its discretion, there appears to be a two-step process. First, the court must on reasonable grounds believe that the young person may be

---

[56]*R. v. J.M.*, unreported, June 28, 1984 (Ont. Prov. Ct.), *per* Bean J.

suffering from a "physical or mental illness or disorder, a psychological disorder, an emotional disturbance, a learning disability or mental retardation." Only after making this determination can the court then consider, again on evidence before it only, whether a "medical, psychological or psychiatric report in respect of the young person might be helpful in making any decision." The words "might be helpful" must be read in accordance with this two-step process if the court is to avoid concluding that in every case it might be helpful to find out more about a child, a conclusion that would result in the court exercising no discretion, reducing the process of assessment to a "fishing expedition" by the court, the Crown or defence counsel.

3) The application for an assessment by a party or by the court on its own motion must indicate the reasons for the request and specify the purpose for which it is requested in accordance with the provisions of s. 13(1)(a), (b) or (c). Specifically, the reason for the application should set out, for example, that the Crown is considering recommending a committal order to "open" or "secure" custody under s. 20(1)(k) or that the Crown is seeking an order of hospitalization under s. 20(1)(i). Without setting out in detail the purpose of the requested assessment, the court cannot make a reasonable decision as to whether the assessment will be helpful in making any decision, nor can the court properly conclude which of the various disciplines covered by the definition of "qualified person" would be appropriate to conduct the assessment.

4) In any application for assessment, the young person should be fully informed of the purpose and possible consequences of the assessment since anything said, or arguably not said, in the face of a court-directed assessment can have a prejudicial effect on the accused.[57] The young person should be advised in any consideration of a s. 13 order that the report prepared by the assessor forms part of the record of the case, and that statements made by him to the assessor can be self-incriminating. As well, the young person should be informed that his refusal to participate or his silence at the assessment may allow the court to draw an inference adverse to him.[58] Consider the following exerpt from a decision based on s. 543 of the *Criminal Code*:

> It is a serious matter to remand an accused person to a psychiatric institution for observation for 30 days even though he has been convicted of a serious offence, and particularly in the circumstances of the possible pending application under the dangerous offender section. If he is so remanded, he might well refuse to converse with anyone at the psychiatric institution and some adverse inferences might be drawn against him in those circumstances when it comes to the matter of sentence. It appears to me that what the trial Judge has effectively done,

---

[57]*R. v. Johnson*, 51 W.W.R. 280, [1965] 3 C.C.C. 42 (Man. C.A.); *Vaillancourt v. R.* (1975), 1 S.C.R. 13, 21 C.C.C. (2d) 65; *R. v. Sweeney (No. 2)* (1977), 16 O.R. (2d) 814, 35 C.C.C. (2d) 245 (C.A.).

[58]*R. v. Sweeney (No. 2)* (1977), 16 O.R. (2d) 814, 35 C.C.C. (2d) 245 (Ont. C.A.).

although inadvertently, amounts to a breach of the principle that no person is bound to incriminate himself; that is, having in mind the pending application by the Crown under the dangerous offender sections.[59]

In the absence of an order under s. 13, there is no authority for the Crown to have the child assessed without his consent and without the consent of his legal guardian. Furthermore, in the absence of any order and in the event such an assessment is conducted with the consent of the parties, it is suggested that the assessor may stand as a "person in authority" and accordingly, the appropriate warning must be given under s. 56 of the *YOA* for the consent to be admissible.

5) The order that follows the application, when granted, should similarly set out the reasons for directing an assessment and the nature of the assessment that the court requires. For example, a referral to a family court clinic and a qualified person therein for assessment without specificity as to what kind of assessment is to be carried out does not comply with the discretion that is to be exercised by the court; in effect, the same discretion is delegated to the clinic and fails, as well, to provide the young person with a full understanding of the reasons for the assessment and the consequences in failing to participate.

6) With respect to an order under s. 13(1)(a) (assessment involving an application for the transfer of the young offender to adult court), the court should not proceed with such extraordinary relief if no application for transfer has been brought and the court has simply been advised that the Crown is "considering" whether to bring such an application. As noted above, the assessment should not be used for the purpose of a "fishing expedition," in the sense that the Crown may or may not proceed with the s. 16 application, depending on the outcome of the psychiatric examination.[60] Further, an application under s. 13(1)(a) must, by reference to s. 16, be brought after the laying of the information and before a finding of guilt.[61]

7) An application under s. 13(1)(b) to assist in determining the unfitness of an applicant to stand trial by reason of insanity, requires the court to determine whether there is an issue as to his insanity or fitness to stand trial in the first place. Again, the court should not, at the risk of incrimination through psychiatric assessment, make an order without some preliminary conclusion that "fitness to stand trial" is an issue.[62]

8) An application under s. 13(1)(c) to assist in reviewing a disposition should be made only, given the definition of "disposition", after a finding that the young person is guilty.

Dispositions

The *YOA* is distinguished from the *Criminal Code* by its combination of statements regarding general principles, assessment techniques, more flexible

---

[59]*Re Chapelle and R.* (1980), 52 C.C.C. (2d) 32, at 37 and 38 (Ont. S.C.).
[60]*R. v. J.M., supra,* note 56.
[61]*Ibid.*
[62]*Ibid.*

sentencing remedies and a unique judicial process for the review of dispositions at a later date. The following paragraphs deal specifically with each possible sentencing alternative available to the judge as set out under s. 20. Note that the introductory s. 20(1) states that the court may make "any one of the following dispositions or any number thereof that are not inconsistent with each other":

Absolute Discharge

Absolute Discharge, s. 20(1)(a)

The court may grant an absolute discharge if it is "in the best interests of the young person and not contrary to the public interest." This wording is identical to that of s. 662.1 of the *Criminal Code* with the exception that the latter forbids an absolute discharge for offences with a minimum sentence or for offences punishable by 14 years of life imprisonment. Accordingly, case law under s. 662.1 of the *Code* can be useful under the *YOA* with the qualification that the test for the granting of an absolute discharge should arguably be less rigorous with respect to young offenders, especially since the *YOA*, unlike the *Criminal Code*, does not provide for suspended sentences or a conditional discharge. Section 3(1)(a) of the *YOA* stipulates, as a principle for the application of the statute, that young persons are not to be held accountable in the same manner or suffer the same consequences for their behaviour as adults. It is suggested that s. 3(1)(a) fills the gap created by the lack of a suspended sentence or conditional discharge provision in the *YOA* to the extent that an absolute discharge should be granted in any instance where the court, if operating under the *Criminal Code*, might have considered a conditional discharge or suspended sentence.

Fine

The Penalty of a Fine, s. 20(1)(b)

The court can impose a fine in an amount not exceeding $1,000, to be paid at such time or on such terms as the court may fix. Note that the section requires the court to "have regard to the present and future means of the young person to pay" before imposing a fine. Note further s. 20(8) and (9) of the Act, which effectively prevent automatic committal of a young person who fails to pay a fine as would occur with his adult counterpart. Rather, upon default, the young person may be subject to an application for review of disposition at which time the court may impose a custodial sentence for failing to pay the fine, but only if the young person has "wilfully failed or refused to comply"; this wording would not seem to apply where the young person has made all reasonable efforts to obtain the money through employment.[63] This acknowledgment of the limitations on a young person to earn money seems to be fortified by s. 21(2) which permits the young person to discharge the fine in whole or in part by earning credits for his work performed in a program established at the discretion of the province for that purpose.

---

[63]The same principle is applied to fines imposed upon young persons for violation of provincial offences. Consider amendments to the *Provincial Offences Act* ("Part V–8: Young Persons", s. 91(i)) [en. 1983, c. 80, s. 1].

*Compensation
Payment*

Payment of Monies as Compensation, s. 20(1)(c)

The court can fix an amount for payment by the young offender by way of compensation for: (a) loss of or damage to property; (b) loss of income or support; or (c) special damages for personal injury. All of these amounts must be readily ascertainable[64] and must have arisen from the commission of the offence. No order for general damages is permitted. As with the directed payment of a fine, the Youth Court is obliged by s. 21 to have regard to the present and future ability of the young person to pay. This section should be read in conjunction with s. 20(1)(f) which enables the court to direct the compensatory amount ordered to be paid be satisfied "in kind or by way of personal services at such time and on such terms as the court may fix" in which case consent of the person to be compensated is required: s. 21(6). In considering an order for compensation, the court may hear any representations from the victim and the victim is to receive notice of the terms of the order: s. 21(4) and (5). Note that an order under s. 20(1)(f) cannot be made unless the young person is a "suitable candidate" (s. 21(7)(a)), unless the carrying out of the order will not interfere with normal hours of work, or education (s. 21(7)(b)), and unless the services can be completed in 240 hours or less and within 12 months of the date of the order (s. 21(a)) with possibility of extension on review: ss. 21(8), 32(9).

Restitution

Restitution, s. 20(1)(d)

There is no payment of monies in an order of restitution. Restitution is designed to put the victim in the position in which he would have stood had the offence not occurred and therefore requires the return by the young offender of a piece of stolen property to the owner. It is conceivable that the court could direct an order of restitution and if certain repairs were needed on the item in order to restore its former state, the court could also order compensation for the necessary repairs. As in the case of an order for compensation, the court may consider representations by the victim and notice of the order is to be provided to the victim: s. 21(4) and (5). Note that s. 20(1)(e) is an extension of the principle of compensation and restitution. It applies to an innocent third party purchaser of the stolen property who can be compensated for the purchase price by the offender under this section if a restitution order has been made, again, having regard to the young person's ability to pay and again, the purchase price may be paid in kind with the consent of the third party: s. 20(1)(f), s. 21(6).

*Community
Service*

Community Service Performance, s. 20(1)(g)

The court can direct the young offender to "perform a community service." Such orders do not require the consent or even the willingness of the young offender, although the court must be persuaded, as with personal service orders, that he is a "suitable candidate" and that the order will not interfere with normal working and school hours: s. 21(7). That is, the court may conclude that the only way to import the message of a moral or ethical responsibility to the young

---

[64]For a common law basis for "readily ascertainable" see *R. v. Zelenski,* [1978] 2 S.C.R. 940, 86 D.L.R. (3d) 179.

offender is by requiring him to work without payment for a worthwhile or charitable community service. As is true with compensatory services, the court cannot make an order for community services unless there is evidence that it can be completed within 240 hours or less and within 12 months of the date of the order, with a possible extension upon review: s. 21(8), s. 32(9).

Prohibition,
Seizure or
Forfeiture

Orders of Prohibition, Seizure or Forfeiture, s. 20(1)(h)

This section incorporates within the *YOA* all the remedies that are available in various federal statutes for these purposes. For example, the forfeiture of a controlled drug may be made under the *Food and Drug Act* or seizure of obscene matter may be made under s. 160 of the *Criminal Code*. Where the court is impeded from making such an order because the legislation providing for prohibition, seizure or forfeiture is provincial, then it appears that the court could rely on the catch-all s. 20(1)(l) which permits the judge to impose ''such other reasonable and ancillary conditions as it deems advisable and in the best interests of the young person and the public.''

Treatment
Committal

Treatment Committals, s. 20(1)(i)

An order for committal to a mental health facility as a disposition can be made by the court only where:

1) there is a medical or psychological report prepared pursuant to s. 13 recommending treatment and the young offender suffers from a ''physical or mental illness or disorder, a psychological disorder, an emotional disturbance, a learning disability, or mental retardation'';
2) the young offender has consented: s. 22(1);
3) the parents of the young person have consented unless the court has dispensed with their consent if it appears that the parent is not available in the opinion of the court, or is not taking an active interest in the proceeding: s. 22(1) and (2); and
4) a mental health facility has consented to admit the young offender: s. 22(1).

The court is obligated to impose such conditions as it considers appropriate under s. 20(1)(i). Although this type of disposition is subject to s. 20(3) which imposes a maximum time period for dispositions of two-years' duration, it is submitted that the court should include in its order a definite period of time for committal, although the wording of this section does not require it as do the ordinary committal provisions for young persons. Although it is conceded that it is difficult to specify time periods when this kind of treatment is involved, the open-ended use of such a section is antithetical to the reforms instituted under the *YOA* which were meant to prevent the kind of indeterminate sentencing that was characteristic of dispositions under the repealed *JDA*. In this context, note s. 20(7) which prohibits any disposition with respect to a young offender, which results in a punishment that is greater than the maximum punishment that would be applicable to an adult who has committed the same offence.

An inhibiting factor with respect to this disposition is the prerequisite of the consent of the young person under s. 20(1)(i) and 22(1), which can be withdrawn at any time subsequent to admission to the mental health facility, in which case the matter would necessarily be the subject of a "review of disposition" application. This on-going consent requirement distinguishes committal under the *YOA* from civil committal, reflecting again the concern that dispositions affecting juvenile offenders should no longer be subject to the unfettered discretion of several levels of administrative decision makers. Note that parental consent is also required, which is consistent with s. 3(1)(h) (removal from parents as last resort), but that it may be dispensed with if the parent is not available or is not "taking an active interest in the proceedings": s. 22(1) and (2).

Probation

Orders of Probation, s. 20(1)(j)

The court may place the young person on probation for a specified period which cannot exceed two years. Any order of probation must include those conditions set out in s. 23(1) (peace bond, assurance of court appearances and notification to authorities of whereabouts), although it may also impose any of the additional, broadly worded conditions listed in under s. 23(2), providing the court with an almost unlimited opportunity to mold probation conditions to suit the circumstances and the particular young person. Two of these conditions require attention insofar as they are unique to the *YOA* and present certain difficulties with respect to the legal rights of the custodial parents. Section 23(2)(e) enables the court to direct that the young person reside with a parent or such other adult as the court considers appropriate, as long as the adult is willing to provide for the care and maintenance of the young offender. Section 23(2)(f) effectively permits the judge to delegate discretionary powers by ordering that the provincial director or his delegate "specify" the place of residence of the young person, presumably with unfettered discretion. Under both sections, the order affects the care and custody of the young offender, suspending the operation of any order for physical care or custody under federal divorce or provincial domestic or child-welfare legislation. However, as an order that technically affects only the residence of the child, it is submitted that the parents retain the residual rights of guardianship, including the right to consent to treatment, to direct the child's education and to exercise access. To hold otherwise would be to make a s. 23(2)(e) condition amount to a s. 20(1)(k) custody order and it is inconsistent with the principle s. 3(1)(h) which provides that the young person should "only" be removed from parental supervision *either partly or entirely* "when measures that provide for continuing parental supervision are inappropriate." It is suggested that an order of probation, while supplementing the parents' disciplinary powers, cannot be used in a manner that overrides the overall authority of the parents to raise and care for their child.

Custody
Committal

Committal to Custody, s. 20(1)(k)

In accordance with s. 3(1)(f) and (h), the principles of "least possible interference with freedom that is consistent with the protection of society" and removal from parental supervision only as a last resort, makes a custody committal the most radical disposition, only to be used when others fail, or are totally inappropriate. The judge, in making a custodial order, must designate whether it is to be "open" or "secure", the former referring to a community residential centre, a group home, a child care institution, or forest or wilderness camp, or any other like place or facility as designated by the province and the latter referring to a place also designated by the province "for the secure containment or restraint of young persons": s. 24(1) and (2).[65] The judge must also specify the time period which cannot exceed two years from the date of committal or three years if the offence is punishable by imprisonment for life: s. 20(1)(k). Before making such an order, the court must consider a predisposition report, as discussed above, in accordance with s. 14: s. 24(11).

The Act provides guidelines upon which the judge must rely in deciding between "open" and "secure" custody: s. 24(3), (4) and (5). They create two objective factors for consideration — age and the gravity of the offence — as well as the subjective assessment of the court as to whether secure custody is "necessary for the protection of society having regard to the seriousness of the offence and the circumstances in which it was committed, and having regard to the needs and circumstances of the young person": s. 24(5). It is clear that this subjective test is supplementary to and does not override the prerequisite elements of age and gravity of offences provided under s. 24(3) and (4). They are as follows:

1) If the accused was between the ages of 12 and 14 years at the time the offence was committed, he can only be committed to secure custody in one of the following fact situations:
   (a) the offence is punishable under the *Criminal Code* by life imprisonment;
   (b) the offence is punishable under the *Criminal Code* by five years imprisonment or more *and* the young person has been previously found guilty of an offence (under the *YOA* or by way of the *JDA*) similarly punishable; or
   (c) the offence is s. 132 of the *Criminal Code* (prison breach) or s. 133(1) of the *Criminal Code* (escape or being at large without excuse) or an attempt to commit same.

If some of these criteria are met, the court must still satisfy itself under s. 24(5), noted above, that secure custody is necessary for the protection of society.

---

[65]The "open" or "secure" custody facilities must be designated by the province and a judge cannot so designate. Similarly, a judge has no authority to order that a term of open custody be served at a specified place or facility. The court does have the authority and the only authority to determine whether the committal is "open" or "secure": *Re C.F.*, unreported, July 16, 1984 (Man. Q.B.), decision of Kroft J. See also s. 24(6) for the operative provision. With respect to Ontario law, see Parts IV and VI of the *Child and Family Services Act* for provisions regarding the custody of young persons who come into care with the Ministry of Community and Social Services under the *YOA* or the *Provincial Offences Act*. Note however that new Ontario legislation has made such young persons who are 16–17 years of age subject to the care and facilities of the Ministry of the Solicitor-General. Some commentators have suggested that the difference in treatment on the basis of age could be the subject of a s. 15 *Charter* challenge.

2) If the accused was between 14 and 18 years of age at the time the offence was committed, he can only be committed to secure custody in one of the following fact situations:

    (a) the offence is punishable under the *Criminal Code* by five years imprisonment or more;

    (b) the offence is under s. 132 of the *Criminal Code* (prison breach) or s. 133(1) of the *Criminal Code* (escape or being at large without excuse), or an attempt to commit same;

    (c) the offence is indictable *and* either in the previous 12 months the young person was found guilty of an offence punishable under the Criminal Code by five years or more or at any previous time he was committed to a secure facility.

Again, if any of the criteria are met, the court still must address itself to the test under s. 24(5).

Transfers within or between the secure and open custody settings can be made pursuant to s. 24 as long as the kind of custody imposed by the judge is not altered except by way of judicial review.[66] S. 24 also preserves the principle that young persons committed to custody shall be held separate and apart from convicted adults, but s. 24(14) permits the transfer of a young person, within the context of a "review of disposition" hearing, to a provincial correctional facility for adults when he has reached 18 years of age. Unlike a transfer of the hearing to the adult courts, the Act is clear in s. 24(14) that the provisions of the *YOA* continue to apply whether or not the person over the age of 17 years was transferred to an adult facility.

Catch-all Conditions

Imposition of Conditions, s. 20(1)(l)

The court is empowered to impose upon a young offender "such other reasonable and ancillary conditions as it deems advisable and in the best interests of the young person and the public." This section appears to codify a 1979 decision of the Supreme Court of Canada[67] in which it was held that any miscellaneous conditions cannot be imposed in isolation or independent of any other order under s. 20. Defence counsel could make imaginative use of this section in relation to his client's particular needs, relying on the s. 3(1) principles. For example, in relation to s. 3(1)(f) (least possible interference with freedom) and s. 3(1)(h) (continuing parental supervision), s. 20 might be invoked to utilize the services of a counsellor in lieu of an order of probation and thereby provide greater flexibility and effectiveness for the young offender and his family and avoid the involvement of yet another bureaucracy.

Principles of Sentencing

As already noted, the s. 3 "declaration of principles" codifies the legislative objectives with respect to the application of the *YOA*. Section 3(2) directs that the Act is to be "liberally construed" in accordance with these principles. Specifically with respect to sentencing, reference should be made to s. 3(1)(a), (b), (c), (f) and (h):

---

[66]*Ibid.*

[67]*A.-G. of Ont. and Viking Houses v. Regional Municipality of Peel*, [1979] 2 S.C.R. 1134, 104 D.L.R. (3d) 1, 49 C.C.C. (2d) 103.

s. 3(1)(a) [W]hile young persons should not in all instances be held accountable in the same manner or suffer the same consequences for their behaviour as adults, young persons who commit offences should nonetheless bear responsibility for their contraventions.

The doctrine of *doli incapax* as it relates to children and criminal acts has been effectively abolished by the *YOA* and replaced by an age level of 12 years, below which no child will be held criminally responsible for his acts. However, the principle enunciated above applied as a guideline for sentencing, albeit not for conviction, partly re-introduces the doctrine to some extent and in this respect, case law under the repealed doctrine may be of some assistance.[68]

s. 3(1)(b) [S]ociety must, although it has the responsibility to take reasonable measures to prevent criminal conduct by young persons, be afforded the necessary protection from illegal behaviour.

This principle supports both a rehabilitative approach to sentencing to prevent further and perhaps more serious criminal conduct and a custodial approach to prevent the person from further harming society. It is foreseeable that the Crown will be relying on the latter interpretation of the section in the face of defence counsel relying on ss. 3(1)(a), (c), (d), (f) and (h), all of which favour a liberal and rehabilitative approach to the offender.

s. 3(1)(c) [Y]oung persons who commit offences require supervision, discipline and control, but, because of their state of dependency and level of development and maturity, they also have special needs and require guidance and assistance.

This section seems to suggest that while the young person, like any other offender, needs to be disciplined and supervised, he is also at a malleable stage in his life wherein guidance, assistance and counselling can still "straighten him out." This objective can be coupled with the unique assessment provisions built into the Act to determine, for example, whether a learning disability may be at the root of the anti-social acts,[69] forming the basis for a rehabilitative plan which should suit the best interests of the young person as well as society. However, the

---

[68]Section 72 of the *YOA* repeals ss. 12 and 13 of the *Criminal Code*, 1983 which read:

s. 12. No person shall be convicted of an offence in respect of an act or omission on his part while he was under the age of seven years.
s. 13 No person shall be convicted of an offence in respect of an act or omission on his part while he was seven years or age or more, but under the age of fourteen years, unless he was competent to know the nature and consequences of his conduct and to appreciate that it was wrong.

Section 72 substitutes a new s. 12 of the *Criminal Code*, 1984 which now reads:

s. 12. No person shall be convicted of an offence in respect of an act or omission on his part while he was under the age of twelve years.

The bar to criminal prosecution of children under 12 years is also applied to provincial offences under the *Provincial Offences Act, supra,* note 7. See also J. Wilson, *supra*, note 37, at pp. 180–83 for discussion and review of cases concerning the doctrine of *doli incapax*.
[69]*Re T.O.A. and Regional Municipality of Peel* (1982), 35 O.R. (2d) 260 (C.A.).

principle does not go so far as to require the judge to go behind the simple availability of a youth facility to determine whether its program is appropriate.[70] Thus, defence counsel must not only have an alternative appropriate facility in readiness but also the professional evidence to support one over the other.

> s. 3(1)(d) [W]here it is not inconsistent with the protection of society, taking no measures or taking measures other than judicial proceedings under this Act should be considered for dealing with young persons who have committed offences.

Although the wording of this section may make the principle more applicable to diversionary schemes in place of any judicial proceedings leading to formal conviction, it is submitted that the absence of such diversionary schemes or "alternative measures" in many jurisdictions would make the absolute discharge the equivalent to "other than judicial proceedings." Factors which may convince the court in varying degrees to lean towards an absolute discharge include:

1) the actual appearance of the offender before the court;
2) the degree of remorse shown by the young person;
3) the age of the offender and the extent of prior criminal involvement;
4) the gravity of the offence;
5) any compensatory steps taken prior to the hearing;
6) the willing involvement of the family as a support resource;
7) the disciplinary measures already imposed or intended to be imposed by the parents and their impact on the young person; and
8) the short and long term effect upon the offender of the stigma arising from conviction and sentencing.

> s. 3(1)(f) [I]n the application of this Act, the rights and freedoms of young persons include a right to the least possible interference with freedom that is consistent with the protection of society, having regard to the needs of young persons and the interests of their families.

This is the clearest and strongest basis upon which defence counsel can build a plan based on the particular child's needs which will provide a more appropriate alternative outside of the juvenile penal system to the classic probation/custody disposition, as long as the court can be convinced that society will also be protected in the short and long term. However, one of the serious drawbacks of the *YOA* is the absence of any provision allowing the judge to commandeer funding for appropriate placements. Accordingly, while the court may be convinced of the appropriateness of counsel's plan, both for the young person and for society, budgetary and practical constraints such as the lack of resources or of available beds in appropriate resources may tie his hands. In practical terms, sentencing under the *YOA* may very likely result in different levels or tests of "appropriateness" depending on the family's income.

---

[70]The principle of appropriateness as a necessary ingredient to the committal of a young person to a facility was expressed in *Re Aline D.* (1975), 536 P. 2d 765 (Cal. S.C.).

Depending on all of the factors (see above under the discussion of s. 3(1)(d)) this section might also be relied upon to convince the court to do little or nothing at all in line with the "radical non-intervention" theorists/practitioners who have determined that often state intervention aggravates rather than eradicates the anti-social conduct of the young person.

s. 3(1)(h) [P]arents have responsibility for the care and supervision of their children, and, for that reason, young persons should be removed from parental supervision either partly or entirely only when measures that provide for continuing parental supervision are inappropriate.

This section codifies another version of "radical non-intervention" which acknowledges the parents and the family in many circumstances as being the most appropriate supervisory and disciplinary unit in society.

Finally, in discussing the principles of sentencing and the dispositions available to the court, reference should be made to those mandatory limitations on sentencing as prescribed by the legislation:

1) Maximum limitation of two years, s. 20(3): Subject to the following paragraphs, no disposition under s. 20, with the exception of s. 20(1)(h) (prohibition, seizure or forfeiture), shall continue for more than two years. If the court makes more than one disposition at the same time in respect of the same offence, with the exception of s. 20(1)(h) and (k) (custody), the combined duration of the dispositions cannot exceed two years. If the court makes more than one disposition at the same time or at different times in respect of different offences, then the maximum period is three years: s. 20(4).

2) Exception — three year limitation: Under s. 20(1)(k)(ii), if the young person is found guilty of an offence punishable under the *Criminal Code* by life imprisonment, duration of the disposition can last up to three years.

Under s. 20(4), where more than one disposition is made with respect to different offences, the "continuous combined duration of those dispositions shall not exceed three years." The phrase "continuous combined duration of those dispositions" appears to cover dispositions for several offences which are rendered at the same dispositional hearing, dispositions for several offences which are rendered at different dispositional hearings, or pursuant to s. 20(2), separate dispositions for separate offences, one of which comes into effect forthwith, while the other comes into effect at a future date. Accordingly, if a young offender has received, for example, a one-year custody and one-year probation disposition for a particular offence and he then commits another offence on being released from custody, the duration of the second disposition cannot exceed 12 months after the time in which the probation period would have ended. If the same offender should commit a third offence either within the time that his two dispositions are running or before the age of 18 years, the court is effectively barred from imposing a disposition under s. 20 of any duration. Obviously, in this situation, there are only two alternatives: an absolute discharge or a transfer under s. 16 to the adult court. Balla and Lilles suggest that the basis for the three-year maximum "is that any benefit a young person can receive from involvement with the juvenile correction system should occur within that period. Any need for an extension beyond the three year period would suggest that the young person has 'outgrown' the juvenile system and would be unlikely to benefit from further exposure to the dispositions provided in the *YOA*. . . ."[71]

3) Exception, s. 20(1)(h) (prohibition, seizure or forfeiture): An exception to the two and three year duration rule applies with respect to an order of prohibition, seizure or forfeiture presumably because the duration or limitation for same is limited by the specific legislation providing for the order and in those cases where there is a conflict, the incorporating legislation applies.

4) Postponement of disposition, s. 20(2): Under this section, a Youth Court now has the authority to postpone a disposition. For example, the judge may make an order of committal to open custody effective six months from the date of the order while imposing other dispositions to take effect immediately. The postponement of the committal order for a period of months during which the young offender must abide by other dispositions, contemplates something of a "conditional committal", since presumably the young offender could apply for a review of disposition with respect to the committal aspect of the sentence prior to its taking effect. (See below for discussion of review of dispositions.) However, as noted above, no combination of dispositions can continue to be in force longer than three years although the postponement time of any disposition would not be included in calculating the duration of a particular disposition.

5) Continuation of disposition into adulthood, s. 20(5): This section confirms that the disposition as ordered by the court is not altered by reason that the young offender attains the age of 18 years during the course of its duration. For example, if the offender turned 18 while under a custody disposition, he is not automatically transferred to an adult facility, although the provincial director may apply for same, but the court will only authorize the transfer if it is in the best interests of the young person and the public and in doing so, "the provision . . . of [the *YOA*] shall continue to apply" to that person: s. 24(14).

6) Equality of sentencing between young offenders and adults, s. 20(7): This provision stipulates that no disposition with respect to a young person can result in a punishment that is greater than the maximum punishment that would be applicable to an adult who has committed the same offence. While s. 20(9) stipulates that s. 722 of the *Criminal Code* (punishment for summary conviction offences) does not apply to the *YOA*, it would appear reasonable to conclude that the intention of s. 20(9) was to avoid fettering the Youth Court's discretion in making dispositions under s. 20 rather than to act as an exception to the very clearly-stated equality of sentencing principle enunciated in s. 20(7). This conclusion is also consistent with s. 15 of the *Charter of Rights* which guarantees equality before and under

---

[71] Bala and Lilles, *supra*, note 1, at p. 188.

APPEAL ROUTES

NATURE OF APPEAL	INCORPORATING PROVISION OF CRIMINAL CODE	PROVISION PARTICULARS
1. Summary Conviction: s. 27(1)(b), *YOA*		
(a) finding of guilt (defendant only) or order dismissing information (defendant and A.-G.)	s. 748(a)(i); s. 748(b)(i)	— appeal to superior court with criminal jurisdiction — appeal on questions of law, mixed fact and law, and facts alone[72] — appeal from first appellate court to Court of Appeal on question of law alone: s. 771(1)(a), *Code*
(b) disposition (deemed a sentence for appeal purposes) (defendant and A.-G.)	s. 748(a)(ii); s. 748(b)(ii)	— same basis of appeal as 1(a) above — Appeal from first appellate decision to Court of Appeal on question of law alone: s. 771(1)(a), *Code*
(c) stated case in respect of conviction, order, determination or other proceeding (defendant and A.-G.)	s. 762	— based on erroneous point of law or excess of jurisdiction — stated case appeal precludes a s. 748 appeal — Appeal to Superior Court of criminal jurisdiction; further appeal to Court of Appeal with leave, on question of law alone: s. 771, *Code*
2. Indictable offences: s. 27(1)(a), *YOA* acquittal or order dismissing information (deemed acquittal for appeal purposes) (defendants and A.-G.)	s. 603(1)(a); s. 605(1)(a)	— A.-G. limited to question of law alone: s. 605(1)(a), *Code* — defendant can appeal on question of law alone: s. 603(1)(a)(i), *Code*; with leave of the Court of Appeal or based on the certificate of the trial judge, on grounds

[72] *R. v. Antonelli* (1977), 38 C.C.C. (2d) 206 (B.C.C.A.).

involving question of facts alone or question of mixed law and facts: s. 603(1)(a)(ii), *Code*; on any ground of appeal not already mentioned that appears to the Court of Appeal to be a "sufficient ground of appeal", with leave of the Court of Appeal: s. 603(1)(a)(iii), *Code*
— no appeal to Supreme Court of Canada without leave within 21 days of Court of Appeal judgment (discretion to extend time); s. 27(5), *YOA*

(b) disposition (deemed a sentence for appeal purposes) (defendant and A.-G.)
    s. 603(1)(b);
    s. 605(1)(b)

3. Insanity:
(a) unfit to stand trial s. 13(7)(8)
— defendant   s. 603(2)(a)   — with leave of the Court of Appeal unless sentence is one fixed by law
— A.-G.   s. 605(3)

(b) not guilty by reason of,
— defendant   s. 603(2)(b)   — same rights of appeal as 2(a) above
    — appeal on question of law alone
— A.-G.   s. 605(1)(a)   — same rights of appeal as 2(a) above
    — appeal on question of law alone

the law. Whereas under the old *JDA* regime, some might have argued that a disposition is treatment, not punishment and therefore might fall under the s. 15(2) "affirmative action" provision of the *Charter*, this approach has been overridden by recent case law[73], coupled with the implicit acknowledgment of the *YOA* that the proceedings are in fact criminal and that the dispositions amount to punishment.

Appeals

The right of appeal is governed by s. 27 of the *YOA*. An appeal lies from a finding of guilt, an order dismissing an information or a disposition made under s. 20: s. 27(1). There is no appeal from reviews of disposition by the Youth Court under ss. 28 to 32 although a s. 33 determination *is* appealable. Unlike the *JDA*, the *YOA* provides for appeals as a right and young offenders are governed by the same procedure for appeals as their adult counterparts. Variation from province to province will occur both because of different provincial appeal rules (made under the authority of s. 438 of the *Criminal Code*) and because the appellate level will depend upon whether the Youth Court in a particular province is a Provincial, County, District or Superior Court. Note that by reason of s. 52 of the *YOA*, Part XXIII of the *Criminal Code* (remedies by way of *certiorari, habeas corpus, mandamus* and prohibition, would be applicable to any procedure under the *YOA*. Section 27(1) dictates that the manner of proceeding will depend on whether the offence was indictable or summary, thereby incorporating both the procedures of Part XVIII of the *Criminal Code* (appeals — indictable offences) and Part XXIV, s. 747 to 771 (appeals — summary convictions). Section 27(2) provides that, in the case of a hybrid offence, if no election has been made, it will proceed as a summary offence paralleling the adult process and overruling the opposite approach taken under the federal *Interpretation Act*. The preceding chart reflects the differing avenues and implications of appeal.

Temporary Release From Custody

With respect to any order for secure or open custody there exists under s. 35 of the *YOA* a "temporary release program" similar to that for adult offenders under the *Penitentiaries Act*, the *Prison and Reformatories Act,* and the *Parole Act*. This type of program is new to juvenile justice legislation although its effect is much the same as that which existed under the repealed *JDA* where equivalent programs were in operation under the jurisdiction of provincial authorities who administer juvenile correction programs. Under s. 35, the provincial director has a strictly administrative power to release a young offender on a one-time basis for a period not exceeding 15 days (s. 35(1)(a)) or on a more frequent or repeated basis amounting to day release (s. 35(1)(b)) but only as long as necessary "to attain the purpose for which the young person is released": s. 35(2). These purposes, specified under each of the two sub-sections, are broadly worded: for temporary release, permissible grounds are medical, compassionate, humanitarian, rehabilitative or for the purpose of re-integration into the community; on a more frequent basis, release is for educational or employment reasons. Under the

---

[73]See *R. v. W; R. v. L.* (1983), 41 O.R. (2d) 576, 147 D.L.R. (3d) 575n, 4 C.C.C. (3d) 575n (H.C.). But see *R. v. S.B.* (1983), 3 C.C.C. (3d) 390 (B.C.C.A.), revg 1 C.C.C. (3d) 73, [1983] 1 W.W.R. 512 (B.C.S.C.).

former, the young person could be released to attend a funeral, visit a close relative in the hospital or perform various services at home, especially if the family depended on him for economic reasons. The latter type of program could be utilized for normal educative or employment purposes, as well as for remedial programs or treatment available only in the private sector (as long as the family could afford it).

The temporary or day release can be revoked by the director apparently for any reason under s. 35(3), in which case the young person can be arrested without warrant and returned to custody: s. 35(4). In addition, a young person who is released and fails to comply with any term or condition of his release may also be arrested without warrant and returned to custody: s. 35(4). Further, it appears that a young person who is absent from custody without lawful excuse is subject to prosecution under s. 133 of the *Criminal Code* (or alternatively under the analogous section of the *YOA*: s. 33(1)). Cases under the *Code* section would suggest that the person must first have knowledge of the revocation of his temporary release before a charge under s. 133(1)(b) of the *Code* will succeed. As well, the Ontario Court of Appeal has noted with respect to this section that it is not every breach of a condition of temporary release that operates to deprive the inmate of a lawful excuse, but rather only a willful breach of a condition which shows an intention by the inmate to withdraw himself from the control in the sense of custody of the correctional authorities, even where the permit in itself provided that apparent breach of the conditions rendered it null and void and deemed the inmate to be unlawfully at large.[74] This decision could arguably be no less applicable to a charge under s. 33 of the *YOA*. (Note that the young person cannot be charged under both s. 133 of the *Code* and s. 33 of the *YOA*: s. 33(9).)

Arguably there is no restriction upon the provincial director with respect to the number of consecutive releases as long as they are ''to attain the purpose for which the young person is released.'' If the frequency and/or time periods were substantial, it may be more appropriate for the provincial director to invoke s. 29 of the *YOA*, discussed below, and recommend release of the young offender from custody and placement on probation. Failing this route, a number of consecutive releases might provide the basis for an application by the young offender himself for the review of his committal disposition even prior to the limitation of six months pursuant to s. 28, discussed below.

Review of Dispositions: Judicial

Unique to the young offenders' justice system and consistent with the s. 3 principles of the *YOA* (especially s. 3(1)(c), (f) and (h)), any disposition is subject to periodic judicial review in which the judge can confirm or vary the original disposition. In any such review, the *YOA* is clear in requiring:

1) notice of the application for review to all parties including the young offender, his parents and the Attorney-General or his agent: ss. 28(11), (12) and 32(5);

2) notice to the young person and to his parents of the right of the young person to legal counsel: ss. 28(13), 32(5), and 11(3)(d);

---

[74]*R. v. Seymour* (1980), 52 C.C.C. (2d) 305 (Ont. C.A.).

3) notice of and receipt of any written material prepared by the provincial director including the written material referred to in the *YOA* as the young person's "progress report" and the right to cross-examine same: ss. 28(7), (10) and 32(4);

4) the right of the young person to present evidence in support of his application for review of disposition or to reply to the evidence of such other party who applies for a review of disposition: ss. 28(17), 32(7);

5) the right not to be punished for the same offence, again consistent with s. 11(h) of the *Charter of Rights,* so that the young offender, upon a review of his disposition, cannot be subject to a more onerous disposition than that which was previously imposed: ss. 29(17) and 32(8).

Since an application for review of disposition neither adjudicates the original case as to guilt or innocence nor imposes a disposition any more onerous than the original, there is no right of appeal with one exception. In a s. 33 review (failure to comply with terms of disposition or escape from custody), an appeal lies as if the decision were an original disposition under s. 20 (s. 33(10)) since the review effectively amounts to a charge of committing a further offence,[75] and allows the judge to impose a more onerous disposition. Note finally that an application for review of disposition cannot be launched unless and until all proceedings by way of appeal have been completed: ss. 28(5) and 32(5).

There are two kinds of dispositional reviews by a Youth Court other than that under s. 33: Review of custodial and non-custodial dispositions.

Review of Custodial Dispositions

The provincial director is obligated to initiate a review of custodial dispositions before the Youth Court at the end of one year from the date of disposition, or if there is more than one disposition, then from the earliest disposition: s. 28(1), (2). In addition, the director, the young person, his parents and the Attorney-General have the right to seek a review after six months from the most recent disposition made in respect of an offence (or earlier with leave) as long as the application is based on one of the following grounds:

1) sufficient progress to justify a change in disposition;
2) circumstances that led to committal have changed materially;
3) new services or programs are available that were not available at time of disposition; or
4) "on such other grounds as the youth court considers appropriate": s. 28(3) and (4).

The court must first be satisfied that there are grounds for review under one of these four categories before proceeding with the review: s. 28(3). Presumably these are also to be the underlying criteria for the judge's decision on whether or not to vary the disposition.

Although there is no discretion as to whether or not to proceed under the mandatory year-end review, the Act is silent as to the criteria that the judges are to use in deciding whether to vary the disposition with the exception that it cannot be made more severe. Perhaps Youth Courts will have recourse to the s. 28(3)

---

[75]*R. v. S.B.,* unreported, April 10, 1984 (Ont. Prov. Ct.), *per* Hamlyn J.

criteria combined with a modified version of a parole board's guidelines. Note that under both types of review, the court is required to obtain from the director a "progress report on the performance" of the young person since the disposition took effect, to assist it in the decision: s. 28(7). Again, although there is no further guidelines enunciated as to what "progress" and "performance" pertains to, those under s. 28(3) may be helpful. Further, since there is no statutory prohibition, the report will probably be used in a s. 28(3) review to determine both whether to proceed and whether to vary the disposition.

Having conducted the review hearing, the court must make one of three orders under s. 28(17):

1) confirm the disposition;
2) vary "secure" custody downwards to "open" custody; or
3) vary custody downwards to probation for a period not exceeding the remainder of the period for which the young person was committed to custody.

Note that the court does not have jurisdiction to terminate a custodial disposition altogether, unlike reviews of non-custodial dispositions as discussed below.

Review of Non-custodial Disposition

Although there is no mandatory year-end review, the equivalent of a s. 28(3) review is provided under s. 32(1) wherein the young person, his parent, the Attorney-General or the provincial director may make application after six months from the date of disposition (or earlier with leave) and the Youth Court must proceed to review the disposition if it is satisfied that there are grounds under any of the following criteria:

1) material change in circumstances that led to disposition;
2) young person unable to comply with or is experiencing difficulty in complying with the terms of disposition;
3) the terms of disposition are "adversely affecting" the young person's opportunities to obtain services, education or employment; or
4) such other grounds as the court considers appropriate: s. 32(2).

As with a s. 28(3) review, the legislation appears to contemplate a two-step process whereby first, the court must be satisfied that there exists grounds for review under s. 32(2) and second, having been so satisfied, the court will then address the question of whether or not to vary the disposition, and if so, in what manner. For this review, however, a "progress report" is optional in the discretion of the court. After the hearing, the judge must make one of the three following orders:

1) confirm the disposition;
2) terminate the disposition and discharge the young person from any further obligation under the disposition; or
3) vary the disposition or make such new dispositions under s. 20, other than a custodial committal, for such period of time, not exceeding the remainder of the period of the earlier disposition, as the court deems appropriate in the circumstances of the case: s. 32(7).

General Review
Issues

A comparison and analysis of these two sections raises a number of issues:

1) To review a custodial disposition, it is technically the provincial director who must cause the young person to be brought before the court, either on the year-end basis or earlier, the latter being done on his own initiative or at the request of other parties. Notwithstanding the fact that the provincial director is in the position of the applicant, it seems reasonable to conclude that any onus would rest on the party who seeks a change in disposition. The language of the section recognizes the director as the nexus between the institution caring for the child and the court in terms of initiating the proceeding and nothing more should be implied from that procedural operation. In the case of non-custodial reviews where the young offender is generally not in any institution, the involvement of the provincial director as applicant is not necessary.

2) The procedure for leave applications under both sections is undefined both prior to and after six months. A two-step process is already suggested by the wording in ss. 28 or 32 insofar as the court must first be satisfied on one of the stipulated grounds before it will conduct a review. In the case of an application prior to six months, there is impliedly a more rigorous test to meet before proceeding to the second stage. It is likely that the court will lean heavily on the provincial director and his "progress report" in exercising its discretion to grant leave prior to the expiry of six months.

There seems to be no guarantee of a full hearing on the question of leave. In fact, the language of ss. 28(17) and 32(7) appears to have the effect of limiting the right of a full hearing to the review stage only. Except for the year-end mandatory review of a custody disposition, it is unclear whether the young person is entitled to be present and submit a full case in support of leave on one of the stipulated grounds. (Under a non-custodial review, the director is no longer an intermediary and therefore, presumably, the applicant, if the young person, would appear before the court.) Under a s. 28(3) review, (custodial review in the first six months), the provincial director *must* "cause the young person to be brought before the youth court" after six months if such a review is requested by any of the parties "*and*, where the youth court is satisfied that there are grounds for review" [emphasis added] the court shall so review. One assumes that the young person will at least have the right to be represented at this stage, although, other than this, it would appear to be up to the court as to the form which this leave hearing would take. On the other hand, prior to six months, the relevent wording under s. 28(3) is that the director shall "cause the young person to be brought before the Youth Court. . ., with leave of [the court], at any [time earlier than six months]. . . ." This arguably supports a process whereby the young person is not to appear in a leave application under six months although it seems inconceivable that the court would not require the presence of the person who applied for leave in the first place if, in fact, it was the young person or even his parents. The difficulty is that disputes between the parties are more likely to occur under the six-month limit where the young offender, for example, argues that a three-month commitment has resulted in sufficient progress to change the disposition, yet in these circumstances, the young offender has no clear right to full participation.

Having set up a review structure based essentially on leave hearings both prior to and after six months, providing anything less than a fair and full hearing is inconsistent with the principle enunciated under s. 3(1)(e) (special guarantees and right to be heard and participate in decision-making process). The obvious danger lies particularly in the custodial reviews under one year where the only mandatory applicant and evidence is the provincial director and his own "progress report" on the young person.

An alternative approach would be to have the leave application heard at the same time as the review and if leave is not granted, the application would be dismissed. However, this procedure might open up the possibility of frivolous applications, the effect of which would turn the courtroom into a monitoring device of the institution where the young offender resides, and thereby arguably defeat the opportunity of providing any effective rehabilitative treatment, not to mention tying up the court's time. A suggested middle approach which would enable the young person to be involved in the procedure in accordance with s. 3(1)(e) would involve written submissions from all interested participants (including the young offender) to be made available to all participants ahead of the hearing to give time for reply.

3) Aside from the procedural issues, the sections are not clear as to the substantive test to be applied on leave applications prior to the expiry of six months. The courts will probably be inclined to use an "exceptional circumstances" test for granting leave, once again reflecting concern that otherwise the opportunity to make early applications would lead to flood-like proportions. The young offender may quickly learn to manipulate the judicial process in resistance to secure treatment methods. It is suggested that to apply an "exceptional circumstances" test is not necessarily inconsistent with those principles set out in s. 3 which require the court to focus upon the special needs of young persons. Presumably, the court carefully considered the appropriate disposition originally and returning to court on other than an "exceptional circumstances" basis might, among other things, turn the court into a treatment centre or treatment supervisor.

4) "Sufficient progress" as a ground for a review of a disposition applies to a custodial but not non-custodial review: s. 28(4)(a). It may be that Parliament considered any disposition that was non-custodial to be premised upon its successful completion by the young offender such that the possibility of review midway through the disposition would be counter-productive. In any case, s. 32(2)(d) allows the court to review non-custodial dispositions "on such other grounds as the Youth Court considers appropriate." For example, a young offender who has consented to his admission to the hospital and has made substantial progress may rely upon this section and effectively argue the same ground as s. 28(4)(a).

5) Section 28(4)(c) provides as a ground for custodial review the availability of new services or programs that were not available at the time of the original disposition. It remains to be seen whether the courts will apply a

"due diligence" test to this ground analogous to the "fresh evidence" test on appeal in order to avoid "penal shopping." Consider the case of a young offender committed to a provincially-operated maximum-security setting against the wishes of his parents who are concerned that in such a facility the young offender will learn more, not less, about crime. The parents' counsel subsequently locates an alternative private resource and asks for a re-hearing, arguing that the private resource is more appropriate to the child's needs. If the program was available at the time of the disposition, then it may be argued that submissions concerning its appropriateness should have been made at the time of the original disposition and that the section contemplates only programs that were not previously in existence. This interpretation may be buttressed by the concern that to hold otherwise would be unmanageable and diminish the importance of the original disposition hearing since there always exists a private resource more appropriate to a young offender's needs than those available through the state's correctional system. Moreover to permit the argument means that the appropriateness of the resource is a function of the economic class of the young offender's family, resulting in a two-tier system of penal consequences.[76] This arguably inconsistent with s. 15 of the *Charter of Rights* which ensures equal treatment and equal benefit under the law although, one would have to argue discrimination on the basis of the unenumerated ground of income. Given the limited state resources, this inequality argument could arguably have the unfortunate practical consequence of depriving some young persons of appropriate and rehabilitative resources because others could not afford it. On the other hand, the discretion for making the original disposition is broad enough to allow such placements and every effort should have been made at that stage to seek out the most appropriate placement. In any case, especially if there has been "progress" on the part of the young person, alternative private resources could be put forward under the catch-all s. 28(4)(d) which allows the court to consider any other ground which it considers appropriate. It is nevertheless unfortunate that the court has no power to order the state through whatever level of government or bureaucracy that it chooses to provide the funds for a private resource when a particular program which is necessary and appropriate for the young person is not available through the state. This discretion of the court to commandeer private resources would be similar to the stated intent of Ontario's new education legislation (see Chapter 8: "Children and Education"), which theoretically permits educational authorities to use public funds to educate certain "special needs" students in private facilities when the appropriate program is not available under the public education system. It is difficult to differentiate between the right of the child to be educated in the manner which meets his

---

[76]*E.g., Elan One,* a residential facility in Maine, U.S.A., is and has been available for Canadian youths involved in the criminal justice system and who are appropriate candidates. *Elan* describes the appropriate candidate as ". . .a non-psychotic adolescent of normal or better intelligence, who exhibits uncontrolled repetitive acting-out behaviour." It costs $24,014 (U.S. dollars) per year, exclusive of personal and medical expenses to attend *Elan*. The opportunity available is therefore for the few.

particular needs versus the right of a child to participate in a program (which usually includes education) which meets his particular needs and both of which are intended to produce healthy, happy, self-fulfilled, responsible citizens of the state.

6) Section 32(7) enables the court, in reviewing a non-custodial disposition, to vary it or to make a new disposition under s. 20. Specifically with respect to the disposition of absolute discharge, the definition of which is apparently not changed by the *YOA*, a court would be precluded from varying, for example, an order for probation and substituting in lieu thereof an absolute discharge retroactively, the result of which would amount to the court undoing a conviction through a review of disposition.

Review of Disposition Where Failure to Comply

Section 33(1)(a) provides for a review of disposition in the event of a young offender's wilful failure or refusal to comply with a disposition or any term or condition thereof.[77] Section 33(1)(b), which provides for a review of disposition in the case of an escape or an attempted escape from custody, is an alternative option available to the Crown in lieu of proceedings under ss. 132 or 133 of the *Criminal Code*, ''prison breach'' and ''escape and being at large without lawful excuse'' respectively. For both grounds of review, the process is commenced by the laying of an information by the Attorney-General or the provincial director prior to the expiration of the disposition or within six months thereafter and the child will be ordered to appear. Although the section does not amount to an offence,[78] the process includes the issuing of information, a summons or warrant and an appeal from the resulting disposition of the court is conducted as if it were an appeal from an original disposition for a summary conviction offence. As well, while s. 33 does not create an offence, the ''offender'' is protected from the principle of ''double jeopardy'' insofar as proceedings under s. 33(1)(b) preclude the Crown from proceeding under ss. 132 or 133 of the *Criminal Code*: s. 33(9). Furthermore, it has been held that a young offender who is detained by reason of a review of disposition under s. 33(1)(a) is entitled to the right of a bail hearing in accordance with s. 457 of the *Criminal Code*.[79]

While not constituting an offence, this review provision is distinct from reviews under s. 28 and 32 in that it requires a criminal standard of proof before a

---

[77]This provision is necessarily included because s. 20(8) of the *YOA* precludes the operation of Part XX of the *Criminal Code* (punishments, fines, forfeitures, costs and restitution) except for s. 655(2) to (5) (restitution where no conviction), 662.1(2) (procedural), 683 (pardon), 685 (remission), 686 (royal prerogative for mercy) with modification. Accordingly, the *Criminal Code* consequences for failure to comply with sentencing, probationary and fine orders are not incorporated into the *YOA*.

[78]In *R. v. Dennis D.*, unreported, August 8, 1984 (Ont. Prov. Ct.), *per* Webster J., the court concluded that s. 33 does not create an offence nor does it permit arraignment or pleas. Furthermore, the language in s. 33(9) and (10) emphasizes the distinction between the ''review'' process of s. 33 from that of the ''prosecution.'' The opportunity for the young person to be heard under s. 33(6) suggests a process entirely different from a plea in response to a charge. The fact that the onus of proof is beyond reasonable doubt under s. 33 reviews does not indicate that the section creates an offence.

[79]*R. v. S.B.*, *supra*, note 75. The Crown's application for detention was dismissed where the child was the ward of a training school and at the time of the show cause hearing was in the custody of his guardian.

court can make any changes in the disposition: s. 33(6). Section 33 can also be distinguished from the other types of reviews because the young offender may receive a more severe disposition than was originally imposed: s. 33(6) and (7). While a progress report is mandatory in a s. 33 review (s. 33(2)), it is suggested that any statements made by the young offender to the youth worker should not be used in determining whether there was wilful refusal, failure to comply or escape, or attempt to escape from custody unless a proper warning was given pursuant to s. 56 since the young offender may be subject to a more severe disposition.[80] To reinforce this approach, note that s. 14(10) is incorporated into a s. 33 review (by way of s. 33(2) and 28(10)). This section directs that no statement made by the young person in the course of the preparation of the predisposition report "is admissible in evidence against him in any civil or criminal proceedings except in proceedings under section 16 [transfer to adult court] or 20 [dispositions] or sections 28 to 32 [reviews]." In fact, one could argue that such statements cannot be used in the determination of a different (and more severe) disposition under s. 33, a section which is not included in the s. 14(10) exemptions. Section 33(6) does not incorporate s. 20 but simply states that the court may "vary the disposition or make any new disposition listed in s. 20 that the court considers appropriate." On the other hand, one might also argue that since s. 33(2) incorporates the provisions relating to a predisposition report "with such modifications as the circumstances require", the use of inculpatory statements at the disposition stage under s. 33 might be one such circumstance. However, it is then difficult to understand why s. 14(10) did not specifically incorporate this exception as it did with other provisions.

Review of Dispositions: Administrative

There are two major levels of administrative review of dispositions: the director's decision to release the young person from custody onto probation and the "review board's" jurisdiction concurrent with the Youth Court's jurisdiction under ss. 28 and 29. Note that both of these routes deal only with custodial dispositions, leaving non-custodial dispositions entirely to the courts.

Under s. 29 of the *YOA*, the provincial director has the discretion to recommend that a young offender in custody be released and placed on probation "if he is satisfied that the needs of the young person and the needs of society would be better served" by such a change. He then must cause notice of his recommendation to be given to all the parties, including in his notice the reason for his recommendations and the recommended conditions are to be attached to the probation order. If none of the parties who receive notice seek a Youth Court review of the recommendation within 10 days of receipt of the notice, the Youth Court must *either* release the young person from custody and place him on probation with any conditions it considers advisable "having regard to" the director's recommendations *or* descend into the arena by making no direction at all "where the court deems it advisable" in which case the director may then seek a review hearing: s. 29(4). Given that the director's recommendation varies the disposition downwards, that is, in a less restrictive direction, a young person or his parents might apply for a review if they disagreed with the recommended conditions or the Attorney-General might apply to challenge the providence of

[80]Bala and Lilles, *supra*, note 1, at p. 269.

the director's decision. This section appears to set up a system of "checks and balances" on the administrative powers of the provincial penal authorities. (For discussion of the form the review would take, see below.)

The *YOA* creates a new creature under s. 30 known as a "review board", an administrative tribunal which a province may or may not establish in its discretion. With some modifications, the board is to carry out the same duties and functions of the Youth Court under s. 28 (custodial disposition review) and s. 29 (director's recommendation changing custody to probation), the main difference being that it cannot release a young person from custody and place him on probation (s. 30(1))[81] and that its decisions take effect 10 days after being handed down unless one of the parties seeks a review thereof in the Youth Court: s. 29(5). Although the board's jurisdiction and powers are in lieu of and not exclusive of the Youth Court, implying the necessity of natural justice procedures at the administrative level as well as compliance with the codified procedures under ss. 28 and 29, it is not clear whether any record of the proceedings is required, the board not being a "court of record." The board's proceedings are subject to s. 11 of the *YOA* (right to counsel) and, of course, the *Charter of Rights*, as a creature of federal statute, and therefore the s. 7 guarantee of principles of fundamental justice apply.

If the Youth Court does conduct a review of the board's decision, it is submitted that, absent consent of all parties, it should be conducted on a *de novo* basis. Had Parliament intended that the court sit on appeal only, it would presumably have used that term as opposed to "review."[82] In addition, although the court has the discretion to alter proceedings codified under ss. 28 and 29 in the context of this type of review "as circumstances require" (s. 31(2)), it is submitted that the natural justice protections should not be abandoned except with the consent of all parties. For example, all parties might consent to rely upon a particular transcript of the board hearing as sufficient representation of a particular witness's contribution, although this should not preclude cross-examination of the same witness for further clarification or for the eliciting of new evidence. In other words, the effect of the board's decision can mean no more than that of a recommendation to the court since, under s. 30(5), it is only binding if all parties choose to accept it. Accordingly, the parties should in no way be limited in their right to a full hearing before the Youth Court by reason of the institution of this "intermediary mediation process."

Privacy and

Once again in fulfillment of the s. 3 principles of the *YOA*, the

---

[81]If the board decides that a young person should be released from custody and placed on probation it must put this in the form of a recommendation to the youth court and if no application for review of the recommendation is made by any of the parties the court *shall* effectively follow the recommendation: s. 30(6), *YOA*.

[82]But see *R. v. West,* [1973] 1 O.R. 211, 9 C.C.C. (2d) 369, 20 C.R.N.S. 15 (C.A.), in which "review" was defined in reference to s. 608.1 of the *Criminal Code* (review by a Court of Appeal) to mean

The review should take the general form of an ordinary appeal and not a hearing *de novo* or one in which either side has the right to submit additional material to the court of appeal. However, while no such right exists, the court, as in appeals, can grant leave in the usual way and upon the usual grounds to a party to produce new evidence.

Criminal Records

consequences of having a criminal record are less severe for the young person than for his adult counterpart. Unlike the *Criminal Code*, the *YOA* attempts to limit the consequences in three areas:

1) destruction of criminal records;
2) deemed partial suspension of criminal records; and
3) maintaining general privacy of proceedings.

Destruction of Criminal Records

Destruction of Criminal Records: s. 45

This is an extensive provision which directs that all records kept on a particular young person in accordance with the *YOA* and "all copies, prints or negatives" shall be destroyed for two different classes of young persons. The destruction of records means that the young person is "deemed not to have committed any offence in respect of which records are required to be destroyed": s. 45(5). This is an exhaustive prescription which would be applicable to subsequent court proceedings as well as any employment or academic applications such that, were the young offender to be asked whether he had any prior convictions, the legal answer would be an unequivocal "no." Note also that s. 45(8) provides for the retroactive application of these rules to any records relating to an offence of delinquency under the *JDA*.

The word "records" is not defined in the *YOA* although it does specifically include fingerprints and photographs (ss. 45(1) and 44(4))[83] and a predisposition report or psychiatric assessment report: ss. 13(9) and 14(4). If the full intent of this section is to be given effect, the records should be deemed to include any form of recording whatsoever, including any testimony that is transcribed through any recording or other audio device, even if it is not reduced to a written form. The Act does specifically cover the organizations which keep the records which are affected by s. 45 (the relevant Youth Court, the police, the government and any relevant private organization): ss. 40 to 43. Further to this, and unlike the repealed *JDA*, these sections provide an exclusive list of those persons or organizations who may have access to the records, thereby making any destruction order more far-reaching and effective since it would be applicable to these persons or organizations (with the one exception of those using the information for research purposes: s. 45(3)).

---

[83]It has been held that s. 44 of the *YOA* dealing with fingerprinting of young persons applies to young persons charged with theft under $200, a hybrid offence under the *Criminal Code*. The court noted that although s. 2(1) of the *Identification of Criminals Act* restricts fingerprinting to persons in lawful custody, ss. 453.3 and 455.5 of the *Code* permits the requiring of a person under summons or appearance notice to attend for fingerprinting, and s. 51 of the *YOA* incorporates all of the provisions of the *Code* except where inconsistent with that legislation. The fact that there is no specific incorporation in s. 44 of ss. 453.3 and 455.5 of the *Criminal Code* does not mean that they are implicitly excluded by reason of s. 51, otherwise alleged young offenders would have to be kept in custody until fingerprinted, a result contrary to the *YOA*. Furthermore, as a hybrid offence, it is considered to be indictable within the meaning of s. 2 of the *Identification of Criminals Act*. The characterization of the offence arises from the categorization under the statute creating the offence and not the *YOA* which provides for the means of prosecuting it or enforcement: *Re M.H. and R.* (1984), 14 C.C.C. (3d) 210 (Alta. Q.B.), *per* Miller A.C.J.

The first class of young persons to which this relief is available is described under s. 45(1) as those who were charged with an offence and were acquitted or the charges were dismissed for any reason other than acquittal, withdrawn or stayed and no proceedings were taken against them for a period of three months.

The second class, described under s. 45(2), include:

1) Anyone who has not been charged with or found guilty of an offence under the *YOA* or any other federal Act or regulation, whether as a young person or as an adult,

    (a) for two years after all dispositions have expired *and* the person has been found guilty only of summary offences (not indictable) in the past: s. 45(2)(a)(i); or

    (b) for five years after all dispositions have expired *and* he has been convicted of any indictable offences in the past: s. 45(2)(a)(ii). Note that this would not include indictable offences for which the records were destroyed pursuant to s. 45.

2) Anyone under class (a) or (b) above who has been charged with an offence during the above-noted waiting periods but (i) who is eventually acquitted at trial or on appeal; (ii) no proceedings are taken against him for six months; or (iii) the charge is dismissed for any reason other than acquittal, withdrawn or stayed and no proceedings are taken against him for six months: s. 45(4).

3) Anyone who has, after becoming an adult, been granted a pardon under the *Criminal Records Act*: s. 45(2)(b).

Partial Suspension

Deemed Partial Suspension of Criminal Records

Short of destroying records, the *YOA* gives the young offender another relief in the form of a partial suspension of a conviction, that is, he is deemed not to have been found guilty or convicted, where the disposition arising from the offence was an absolute discharge or where it (or they) ceased to have any effect: s. 36(1)(a) and (b). The applicability of this partial suspension is necessarily limited to matters under federal jurisdiction and includes:

1) any disqualification from contracting with the Crown by reason of conviction under certain offences: s. 36(2);

2) any prejudice to the young offender in applying for employment in any work, undertaking or business that is within the legislative authority of the federal government: s. 36(3);

3) a disposition under an offence created by any Act of Parliament "for which a greater punishment is prescribed by reason of previous convictions." For example, s. 234(1)(b) of the *Criminal Code* provides that a conviction for a second offence of impaired driving requires a mandatory minimum of 14 days imprisonment. In effect, this young person would now be treated as a first offender: s. 36(5).

The suspension is partial in that the young offender is still subject to his record, regardless of s. 36, for the purposes of:

1) pleading *autrefois convict* in respect of any subsequent charge relating to the offence: s. 36(1)(c);

2) an application for a transfer to ordinary court under s. 16: s. 36(1)(d);

3) the determination of a bail application: s. 36(1)(e);

4) the determination of dispositions or sentences for any offences: s. 36(1)(e);

5) the National Parole Board or any provincial parole board considering the finding of guilt in determining an application for parole: s. 36(1)(f); and

6) any examination of a witness as to whether he has been convicted of an offence pursuant to s. 12 of the *Canada Evidence Act*: s. 36(1).[84] Note that it has been held that an absolute discharge is not a "conviction" for the purposes of the *Canada Evidence Act*.[85]

Privacy of Proceedings

Privacy of Proceedings

The *YOA* includes provisions which reflect the position that criminal proceedings involving young persons and children should be subject to a less exacting standard of public scrutiny than those of their adult counterparts. This is presumably based partly on the fact that the young person is considered to be particularly rehabilitatable and should therefore not carry a public stigma into his life in either the short or long term.[86] Section 38 retains the effect of those provisions under the old *JDA* which precludes the publication of any information, the result of which leads to the identification of the young offender. Section 39, which pertains to the exclusion of persons from the court room, appears to fill a gap created by recent decisions under the *JDA* which ruled sections of the *JDA* which contained an absolute prohibition of public access to the courtroom as unconstitutional, because they violated the guaranteed freedom of expression of the media pursuant to s. 2(b) of the *Charter*.[87] The Act purports to cure the constitutional problem of a "blanket prohibition" by requiring the

---

[84]In *Morris v. R.*, [1979] 1 S.C.R. 405, 91 D.L.R. (3d) 161, 43 C.C.C. (2d) 129, the Supreme Court held that an adult offender can be the subject of cross-examination under s. 12 of the *Canada Evidence Act* concerning delinquencies committed by the offender while a young person, if the offence which gave rise to a finding of juvenile delinquency would have been punishable under the *Criminal Code* if committed by an adult.

[85]See *R. v. Danson* (1982), 66 C.C.C. (2d) 369 (Ont. C.A.).

[86]See *Re Southam Inc. and R.* (1984), 48 O.R. (2d) 678, at 698–99, 16 C.C.C. (3d) 262 (H.C.), *per* J. Holland J.

In my view, based on the evidence which I heard from expert witnesses, the protection and rehabilitation of young people involved in the criminal justice system is a social value of the "superordinate importance" which justifies the abrogation of the fundamental freedom of expression, including freedom of the press, to the extent effected by s. 38(1) of the *YOA*. Section 38(1) is, in my view, a reasonable limitation on that freedom.

[87]See *Re Southam and R. (No. 1)*, (1983), 41 O.R. (2d) 113, 3 C.C.C. (3d) 515, 34 C.P.R. (3d) 27 (C.A.); *Re Edmonton Journal and A.-G. of Alberta* (1983), 4 C.C.C. (3d) 59, 146 D.L.R. (3d) 673, [1983] 3 W.W.R. 141 (*sub. nom. R. v. G.B.*) (Alta. Q.B.).

court to exercise a discretion on a case-by-case basis, which presumably amounts to a "reasonable limit" under s. 1 of the *Charter*.[88]

The discretion to exclude any person from all or part of the proceedings can be exercised if the court decides that:

1) any evidence or information presented to the court or justice would be seriously injurious or seriously prejudicial to a child or young person who is the alleged young offender, a witness or victim: s. 39(1)(a);

2) it would be in the interests of "public morals, the maintenance of order or the proper administration of justice": s. 39(1)(b).

This discretion does not extend to the exclusion of the prosecutor, the alleged young offender, his parent, his counsel or any adult assisting him, the provincial director or a relevant youth worker: s. 39(2). Note, however, that once proceedings reach the disposition stage, the list of persons who may not be excluded no longer includes the prosecutor or the parents and the criteria is limited to "information. . . the knowledge of which might. . . be seriously injurious or seriously prejudicial to the young person": s. 39(3). Perhaps the omission of parents and prosecutor contemplates information of a confidential nature, the effect of which might harm a parent/child relationship or might be prejudicial to the young person in the hands of the Crown at a later date.

Note that under s. 17, the privacy rules are different in the case of a hearing to transfer the young person from the Youth Court to the ordinary adult court. In that situation, the court *must* make an order if the young person is not represented or if represented, there is an application by the prosecutor or the young person, restricting the publication of "*any information* respecting the offence" in any newspaper or broadcast. The order expires (1) once the order for transfer is refused, or, if granted, is set aside on review and the time for all reviews against the decision has expired or the proceedings of such review have been completed (s. 17(1)(c)) *or*, (2) "the trial is ended, if the case is transferred to ordinary court": s. 17(1)(d). There appears to be some difficulty in the interpretation of this last phrase. If, as the wording on its face suggests, publication of any information respecting the offence is precluded until after the trial in adult court, then there is a conflict between s. 17(1)(d) which is an automatic ban with no judicial discretion and ss. 73 and 74 of the *YOA* which, in effect, provide that proceedings in an ordinary court after transfer are presumed to be open and subject to public reporting unless exclusion is ordered "in the interest of public morals, the maintenance of order or the proper administration of justice": s. 442(1), *Code*. Under s. 17, the only opportunity for an order not banning publicity is where the young person is represented by counsel and neither the young person nor the prosecutor requests a ban. The effect then is that the

---

[88]*Southam v. R., supra,* note 86, at 699. Further, with respect to s. 39(1)(a) of the *YOA*, the court observed:

Again, I hold that the interests of society in the protection and rehabilitation of young people involved in youth court proceedings is a value of such superordinate importance that it justifies the discretion given to a youth court judge under s. 39(1)(*a*). Section 39(1)(*a*) is, in my view, a reasonable limitation on freedom of expression, including freedom of the press.

community, through the media, is less informed about the young person who has committed the more serious offence, for which a transfer is warranted, than about less serious offences. This seems directly converse to what one would expect since the protection of the community is an objective which is paramount throughout the s. 3 principles of the *YOA*, and it would obviously be far more at risk with respect to the serious offences and the interests of the community in the proceedings must increase in direct proportion to the risks the community is undergoing.[89] A more reasonable interpretation of the word "trial" is that it refers to proceedings under s. 16 of the *YOA* (the hearing of the application for transfer).[90]

Crimes Against Children

This part of the chapter deals with offences under the *Criminal Code* in which the victim is exclusively a minor or in which the sentencing is affected by the minority of the victim.

Assault Causing Bodily Harm: s. 245.1

An accused, found guilty of assault causing bodily harm on his four-year-old daughter, received a suspended sentence and probation for three years. On appeal, the sentence was increased to one year in prison plus three years probation, the court having regard to the age of the victim:

> [T]he accused was present and permitted these grave injuries to be inflicted upon this defenseless little girl. There was also evidence of his active participation in the assault. Little children are entitled to look for protection to their parents or to those to whose care they are entrusted, and brutality of the kind involved in the present case cannot and will not be tolerated. In light of the injuries inflicted upon this unfortunate child the sentence imposed is entirely inadequate. Deterrence and the protection of those who cannot protect themselves is the important factor to be considered here.[91]

Abandonment: s. 200

Section 200 of the *Criminal Code* provides:

> s. 200 Every one who unlawfully abandons or exposes a child who is under the age of ten years, so that its life is or is likely to be endangered or its health is or is likely to be permanently injured, is guilty of an indictable offence and is liable to imprisonment for two years.

A conviction does not depend on the parent having the actual physical custody of the child for as soon as he knows that his child is in a situation of danger and

---

[89]See *R. v. M.L.*, unreported, February 26, 1985 (Ont. Prov. Ct.) *per* Wong, J. Even the test of "reasonable limits" as considered by Mr. Justice Holland in *Re Southam, supra,* note 86, would not seem to permit the application of this section in the manner apparently necessitated by s. 17(1)(d). Further, the reasoning of the Ontario Court of Appeal in *Re Southam (No. 1), supra,* note 87, with respect to provisions under the repealed *JDA*, would be applicable in considering a constitutional attack on s. 17 of the *YOA*.

[90]See Bala and Lilles, *supra,* note 1, at p. 159 in which the authors have come to an opposite conclusion regarding the interpretation of s. 17(1)(d) of the *YOA*.

[91]*R. v. Ardmore* (1972), 5 C.C.C. (2d) 536, at 538 (Ont. C.A.). And see *R. v. Watson,* [1968] 3 C.C.C. 11, at 14. In *R. v. Akilak* (1983), 43 A.R. 368 (N.W.T. Terr. Ct.) the court sentenced an older brother who had inflicted multiple burns to the groin and buttock area of his six-month old infant brother: "There can be no question but that small children, defenceless members of our society, rightly deserve the full protection that the law can provide and those who harm such members of our society will be severely and harshly dealt with." (at p. 370).

neglect, he has abandoned and exposed his child within the meaning of this section.[92]

Homicide,
Infanticide and
Concealment:
ss. 206, 216,
226, 227

Section 206 of the *Criminal Code* reads:

s. 206(1) A child becomes a human being within the meaning of this Act when it has completely proceeded, in a living state, from the body of its mother whether or not
    (a) it has breathed,
    (b) it has an independent circulation, or
    (c) the navel string is severed.
    (2) A person commits homicide when he causes injury to a child before or during its birth as a result of which the child dies after becoming a human being.

Section 216 reads:

s. 216 A female person commits infanticide when by a wilful act or omission she causes the death of her newly-born child, if at the time of the act or omission she is not fully recovered from the effects of giving birth to the child and by reason thereof or of the effect of lactation consequent on the birth of the child her mind is then disturbed.

Section 227 of the Code reads:

s. 227 Everyone who in any manner disposes of the dead body of a child, with intent to conceal the fact that its mother has been delivered of it, whether the child died before, during or after the birth, is guilty of an indictable offence and is liable to imprisonment for two years.

A charge of infanticide cannot be maintained where there is no evidence of a wilful act or omission by the accused mother, no evidence that she has fully recovered from the effect of giving birth and no evidence that by reason of giving birth to the child, the balance of her mind was not disturbed.[93] Note that the definition of "newly-born child" in s. 2 of the *Criminal Code* means "a person under the age of one year", overruling previous case law which held to the contrary.[94] If the person was one or more years of age, then presumably the mother would be subject to a charge of murder or manslaughter. In a 1977 decision of the Ontario Court of Appeal,[95] the court expressed concern over the fact that no appeal had been launched from a conviction where the mother had pleaded guilty to a charge of infanticide. Psychiatric evidence given at the time of sentencing, following her plea of guilty, indicated that at the time of the offence, she was in a state of post-partum depression which had reached the point where she did not realize the consequences of her act when she permitted her child to drop from her knees to the floor, expecting that it would simply quiet him. The mother, aged 24, had a strained relationship with her husband and evidence

---

[92]*R. v. White* (1871), L.R. 1 C.C.R. 311.
[93]*R. v. Jacobs* (1952), 105 C.C.C. 291 (Ont. Co. Ct.).
[94]*R. v. Marchello* (1951), 100 C.C.C. 137 (Ont. H.C.).
[95]*R. v. Szola* (1977), 33 C.C.C. (2d) 572 (Ont. C.A.).

indicated that she required further psychiatric care and that incarceration would be detrimental. Without disturbing the conviction, the Appellate Court varied the sentence of 12 months indefinite imprisonment, plus probation for two years (the offence carries a maximum punishment of five years imprisonment) to a conditional discharge with conditions including attendance for psychiatric assessment and treatment.

Section 226 of the *Criminal Code* reads:

> s. 226 A female person who, being pregnant and about to be delivered, with intent that the child shall not live or with intent to conceal the birth of the child, fails to make provision for reasonable assistance in respect of her delivery is, if the child is permanently injured as a result thereof or dies immediately before, during or in a short time after birth, as a result thereof, guilty of an indictable offence and is liable to imprisonment for five years.

Where the evidence indicated an intent to conceal and a failure to obtain assistance, the conviction was nevertheless quashed due to facts which made the section inapplicable. After the birth of the child, the accused mother, believing the child to be dead, placed the body in a chute which led to an incinerator. The baby was later discovered by the janitor but not before the child died as a result of burns. It was held that the death did not occur "as a result of the accused's failure to obtain assistance for her delivery" as per s. 226, but resulted from events having nothing to do with improper delivery. Furthermore, the child was born at nine o'clock in the morning and the time of death occurred at about five o'clock in the afternoon. The section specifically reads "if the child. . . dies immediately before, during or in a short time after birth". The court noted that "The lapse of time in itself. . . takes the case out of the ambit of this section."[96]

Abortion: s. 251

The inclusion of the offence of abortion in this chapter is obviously problematic since the alleged offence raises the profound and controversial issue of the status of the fetus, that is, whether it is a child or not a child. Nevertheless, by its very controversy, it is necessarily included and should also be seen in the context of child-protection proceedings and civil-injunction proceedings discussed elsewhere in the book.

Under s. 251 of the *Code*, the indictable offence of abortion can be committed by a third party who "uses any means for the purpose of carrying out [the] intention" to procure a miscarriage. The offence can also be committed by the pregnant woman who "uses any means or permits any means to be used for the purpose of carrying out her intention" to procure her own miscarriage. The third party is liable to life imprisonment while the pregnant mother is liable to imprisonment for two years.[97] Section 251(3) defines the "means" for the procurement of a miscarriage to include the administration of a drug or other noxious thing, the use of an instrument and manipulation of any kind. The British

---

[96]*R. v. Bryan* (1959), 123 C.C.C. 160, at 162 (Ont. C.A.).

[97]See *R. v. Parent* (1975), 24 C.C.C. (2d) 207 (Que. C.A.), wherein an accused, having impregnated a woman and introduced her to an abortionist with the intention that the latter induce a miscarriage, was liable to be convicted as a party either to the offence committed by the third party or committed by the pregnant woman.

Columbia Court of Appeal has held that the definition in this subsection is not all-inclusive and that the effect of the words "any means" in s. 251(1) and (2) is to include any and all other means.[98]

Section 251(4) of the *Code* sets out an exemption to the offence where the abortion has been approved by a therapeutic abortion committee in an accredited or approved hospital under the auspices of the provincial Minister of Health.

It has been held that s. 45 of the *Criminal Code* which precludes criminal liability for surgical operations performed "having regard to the state of health of the person", cannot apply so as to remove criminal liability for the offence of abortion; on the other hand, the common law defence of necessity preserved by s. 7(3) of the *Code* may apply.[99] The same decision held that the evidence for a successful defence of necessity must show "real and urgent medical need" and that it was therefore impossible for the accused to comply with the law. In a recent decision of the Ontario Supreme Court, the court held that s. 251 of the *Criminal Code* did not contravene ss. 2(a), 7 and 12 of the *Charter of Rights* by infringing upon the pregnant woman's "freedom of religion and conscience", right to "liberty and security of the person", and right "not to be subjected to cruel and unusual treatment or punishment."[100]

With the advent of more sophisticated pre-natal diagnostic techniques and causative analyses, the dilemma for the Legislatures and the courts may become one of attempting to reconcile the moral/legal question surrounding abortion with the increasing concern of child welfare authorities when a fetus, which the pregnant woman intends to carry to term, is in need of protection. Some apprehension cases have been based on the alcoholism of the pregnant woman which could have led to "fetal alcohol syndrome" in the newborn infant[101] and the refusal of a Jehovah's Witness to have a blood transfusion causing risk to the fetus.[102] In this context, standing has been granted to a private citizen to act as a "protector" of the fetus in challenging the constitutionality of abortion laws[103], although there has been mixed judicial response to the question of whether the father has standing to act as a next friend to a fetus in seeking an injunction to prevent an abortion; in effect, to the question of whether the fetus is a "person" to be protected.[104] Parallel developments have occurred in the civil area where children, through a next friend can sue third parties and even the mother for *in*

---

[98]*R. v. Smith* (1960), 128 C.C.C. 140 (B.C.C.A.).

[99]*Morgentaler v. R.* (1975), 20 C.C.C. (2d) 449 (S.C.C.).

[100]*R. v. Morgentaler et al.* (1984), 47 O.R. (2d) 353 H.C.J.; affd (1984), 48 O.R. (2d) 519 (C.A.). For an opposite conclusion see *Roe v. Wade* (1973), 410 U.S. 113; *Doe v. Bolton* (1973), 410 U.S. 179.

[101]*Re C.A.S. of Kenora and L.*, summarized in (1981), 4 F.L.R.R. 87 (Ont. Prov. Ct.).

[102]*Raleigh-Filkin-Paul Morgan Memorial Hospital v. Anderson* (1964), 201 A. 2d 537 (N.J.S.C.).

[103]See *Minister of Justice of Canada et al. v. Borowski*, [1981] 2 S.C.R. 575.

[104]See *Re H* (1979), 38 N.S.R. (2d) 432 (*sub nom. Re Simms and H*) 106 D.L.R. (3d) 435 (Fam. Ct.) wherein judge consented to appoint a guardian *ad litem*. For cases in which courts refused standing see *Medhurst v. Medhurst* (1984), 46 O.R. (2d) 263 (Ont. H.C.); *Dehler v. Ottawa Civic Hospital* (1980), 25 O.R. (2d) 748 (S.C.); affd (1981), 29 O.R. (2d) 677 (C.A.). Leave to appeal to S.C.C. refused 36 N.R. 180.

vitro damages which were manifested upon birth although, for such an action, the child must be born and exhibiting the damages before an action can lie.[105]

Neglecting to Provide Necessaries: s. 197

Section 197 of the *Criminal Code* provides:

s. 197(1) Every one is under a legal duty

(a) as a parent, foster parent, guardian or head of a family, to provide necessaries of life for a child under the age of sixteen years;

(b) as a married person, to provide necessaries of life to his spouse; and

(c) to provide necessaries of life to a person under his charge if that person

(i) is unable, by reason of detention, age, illness, sanity or other cause, to withdraw himself from that charge, and

(ii) is unable to provide himself with the necessaries of life.

(2) Every one commits an offence who, being under a legal duty within the meaning of sub-section (1), fails without lawful excuse, the proof of which lies upon him, to perform that duty, if

(a) with respect to a duty imposed by paragraph 1(a) or (b),

(i) the person to whom the duty is owed is in destitute or necessitous circumstances, or

(ii) the failure to perform the duty endangers the life of the person to whom the duty is owed, or causes or is likely to cause the health of that person to be endangered permanently; or

(b) with respect to a duty imposed by paragraph (1)(c), the failure to perform the duty endangers the life of the person to whom the duty is owed or causes or is likely to cause the health of that person to be injured permanently.

(3) Every one who commits an offence under subsection (2) is guilty of

(a) an indictable offence and is liable to imprisonment for two years; or

(b) an offence punishable on summary conviction.

(4) For the purpose of proceedings under this section,

(a) evidence that a person has cohabited with a person of the opposite sex or has in any way recognized that person as being his spouse is, in the absence of any evidence to the contrary, proof that they are lawfully married;

(b) evidence that a person has in any way recognized a child as being his child is, in the absence of any evidence to the contrary, proof that the child is his child;

(c) evidence that a person has left his spouse and has failed, for a period of any one month subsequent to the time of his so leaving, to make provision for the maintenance of his spouse or for the maintenance of any child of his under the age of sixteen years is, in the absence of any evidence to the contrary, proof that he has failed, without lawful excuse to provide necessaries of life for them; and

---

[105]See s. 66 of the *Ontario Family Law Reform Act* which overrules the common law in permitting children to bring proceedings against their parents.

(d) the fact that a spouse or child is receiving or has received necessaries of life from another person who is not under a legal duty to provide them is not a defence.

"Necessaries of life" has been defined to mean such necessaries as tend to preserve life, not necessaries in their ordinary legal sense, and may include medical aid.[106] Medical treatment tending to preserve life is a necessary of life and if it were established that the parent of a child, by denying treatment to the child, accelerated the child's death, then he could be convicted of the offence of criminal negligence causing death (s. 203) if the requisite reckless disregard for the child's life and safety was demonstrated.[107] More recently, an Ontario Provincial Court had defined necessaries of life under the repealed *JDA* to include "every day needs" as distinguished from luxuries and accordingly, a group home that provides its charges with shelter, clothing, pocket money, recreation, transportation, education, dry cleaning, parental attention and supervision is providing services that are "necessaries of life."[108]

An Ontario Provincial Court ruled that the essential elements of the offence under s. 197 are first, proof of a legal duty to provide the necessaries of life which are to be determined by the circumstances of the case and secondly, failure to perform the duty must be with respect to a person in destitute or necessitous circumstances or, in the alternative, the failure must endanger the life of the person to whom the duty is owed, or cause the health of that person to be permanently endangered. The court concluded that the offence was made out when the accused, a mother of a new-born infant, failed to keep medical appointments for the child, although the child was obviously malnourished for several weeks prior to his death. At death, the child was found to be severely undernourished and dehydrated and the accused was held to have been aware of medical facilities available to her and her child. Her lack of concern for the child was evidenced by cancellation of the appointment and by so doing, the mother denied the necessaries of life.[109] The fact that the dependant was in receipt of public assistance did not prevent the court from finding him or her "in destitute or necessitous circumstances."[110]

A belief that necessary medical treatment is against the teachings of the Bible is not an excuse.[111] The existence of a civil order for child support payments does not affect a parent's legal obligation to maintain his child and does not oust the jurisdiction of the Criminal Court to convict on this offence.[112] A husband or a father cannot escape the duty imposed under this section by relying upon a separation agreement which does not provide an adequate maintenance allowance. The relevant question to be asked is "Has the husband

[106]*R. v. Brooks* (1902), 5 C.C.C. 372 (B.C.S.C.).

[107]*R. v. Cyrenne and Cramb* (1981), 62 C.C.C. (2d) 238 (Ont. Dist. Ct.).

[108]*Re Taha* (1976), 28 R.F.L. 352 (Ont. Prov. Ct.).

[109]*R. v. Degg* (1981), 58 C.C.C. (2d) 387 (Ont. Prov. Ct.).

[110]*R. v. Wood* (1911), 19 C.C.C. 15 (Ont. C.A.); *R. v. Brown* (1941), 75 C.C.C. 285 (Sask. Dist. Ct.); *Cole v. Pendledon* (1896), 60 J.P. 359.

[111]*R. v. Brooks, supra,* note 106; *R. v. Cyrenne and Cramb, supra,* note 107 and see *R. v. Lewis* (1903), 7 C.C.C. 261 (Ont. C.A.).

[112]*Re Brooks* (1930), 54 C.C.C. 334 (Ont. S.C.).

provided the necessaries for his wife and children whether this be done pursuant to the provisions of a separation agreement or not?''[113] Section 197(4)(c) is consistent with case law that has held that a parent cannot, by leaving his wife and living apart from her and the children, divest himself of liability under this section. Indeed, the mere omission of the parent to pay any part of his earnings towards the support of the child may constitute wilful neglect.[114] This sub-section should be read in conjunction with s. 197(1)(a), the effect of which is to extend the liability beyond previous case law which held that no liability will attach, for example, to a step-father.[115] Also note that s. 197 is an included offence of s. 203 (criminal negligence causing death) but unlike s. 203, a condition of wanton or reckless disregard for the life of the child is not a prerequisite under s. 197.[116] Finally, s. 197(4)(d) nullifies the existing case law that held that the fact that a dependent wife was maintained comfortably by her father negated the existence of ''destitute or necessitous circumstances.''[117] The wording of this sub-section is meant to include the not infrequent situation where another person, not under a legal duty to provide necessaries of life, does so for a destitute child. Perhaps the only defence that is available is the accused's inability to support his wife or child separate and apart from his unwillingness.[118]

Corrupting Children: s. 168
With the repeal of the *JDA*, the s. 33 offence of ''contributing to juvenile delinquency'' no longer exists. Remaining is s. 168 of the *Code* as follows:

> s. 168(1) Every one who, in the home of a child, participates in adultery or sexual immorality or indulges in habitual drunkenness or any other form of vice, and thereby endangers the morals of the child or renders the home an unfit place for the child to be in, is guilty of an indictable offence and is liable to imprisonment for two years.
>
> (2) No proceedings for an offence under this section shall be commenced more than one year after the time when the offence was committed.
>
> (3) For the purposes of this section, ''child'' means a person who is or appears to be under the age of 18 years.
>
> (4) No proceedings shall be commenced under sub-section (1) without the consent of the Attorney-General, unless they are instituted by or at the instance of a recognized society for the protection of children or by an officer of the juvenile court.

Note that prosecution under this section is limited under s. 168(4) which prevents proceedings from being commenced without the consent of the Attorney-General unless they are instituted by or at the instance of a Children's Aid Society or its equivalent or by an officer of the juvenile court (presumably a ''youth worker'' as defined under s. 2 of the *YOA*). A mother of a child and her

---

[113]*R. v. Harenslak* (1937), 67 C.C.C. 267 (Alta. C.A.); *Brooks v. Blount,* [1923] 1 K.B. 257.

[114]*R. v. Connor,* [1908] K.B. 26. And see *Poole v. Stokes* (1914), 110 L.T. 1020.

[115]*R. v. Charron,* [1969] R.L. 125.

[116]*R. v. Deabay,* [1966] 2 C.C.C. 148 (N.B.C.A.).

[117]*R. v. McDonald* (1942), 78 C.C.C. 330 (Ont. C.A.).

[118]*R. v. Yuman* (1910), 17 C.C.C. 474, 22 O.L.R. 500 (C.A.).

common law husband were convicted under this section where they had photographed their 11-year-old child in sexually suggestive poses. The only intent required to be proved is the intent to do those acts which if found by the court to be sexually immoral, lead to the result that the morals of the child are endangered. The Crown need not prove that the accused intended such a result.[119]

Sexual Intercourse with Female Child: s. 146

Section 146 of the *Criminal Code* reads:

s. 146(1) Every male person who has sexual intercourse with a female person who

(a) is not his wife, and

(b) is under the age of fourteen years,

whether or not he believes that she is fourteen years of age or more, is guilty of an indictable offence and is liable to imprisonment for life.

(2) Every male person who has sexual intercourse with a female person who

(a) is not his wife,

(b) is of previously chaste character, and

(c) is fourteen years of age or more and is under the age of sixteen years,

whether or not he believes that she is 16 years of age or more, is guilty of an indictable offence and is liable to imprisonment for five years;

(3) Where an accused is charged with an offence under subsection (2), the court may find the accused not guilty if it is of the opinion that the evidence does not show that, as between the accused and the female person, the accused is more to blame than the female person.

It has been held that s. 146(1) does not violate the guarantee of fundamental justice under s. 7 of the *Charter of Rights* although the effect of the concluding words of the sub-section is to remove mistake as to age as a defence.[120] The defence available under sub-section (3) was considered where the victim testified that she engaged in intercourse because it was pleasurable and that sexual intercourse "just sort of happened."[121]

Incest: s. 150

Section 150 of the *Criminal Code* provides:

s. 150(1) Every one commits incest who, knowing that another person is by blood relationship his or her parent, child, brother, sister, grandparent or grandchild, as the case may be, has sexual intercourse with that person.

(2) Every one who commits incest is guilty of an indictable offence and is liable to imprisonment for fourteen years.

(3) Where a female person is convicted of an offence under this section and the court is satisfied that she committed the offence by reason only that she was under restraint, duress or fear of the person with whom she

---

[119]*R. v. E and F* (1981), 61 C.C.C. (2d) 287 (Ont. Co. Ct.).

[120]*R. v. Stevens* (1983), 3 C.C.C. (3d) 198, 145 D.L.R. (3d) 563 (Ont. C.A.). Leave to appeal to the S.C.C. granted June 6, 1983 (1983), 2 S.C.R. XIV.

[121]*R. v. Quesnel* (1979), 51 C.C.C. (2d) 270 (Ont. C.A.)

had sexual intercourse, the court is not required to impose any punishment upon her.

(4) In this section, "brother" and "sister", respectively, include half-brother and half-sister.

Proof of the relationship as set out in this section is an essential element of the crime.[122]

Seduction:
ss. 151 and 152

Section 151 and 152 of the *Criminal Code* read:

s. 151 Every male person who, being eighteen years of age or more, seduces a female person of previously chaste character who is sixteen years or more but less than eighteen years of age is guilty of an indictable offence and is liable to imprisonment for two years.

s. 152 Every male person, being twenty-one years of age or more, who, under promise of marriage, seduces an unmarried female person of previously chaste character who is less than twenty-one years of age is guilty of an indictable offence and is liable to imprisonment for two years.

To constitute seduction, the child must give her consent. That is to say, a girl cannot be seduced when, as a matter of fact, she has been raped. Furthermore, there is no seduction if the girl has not been enticed, induced or caused to surrender her virtue due to some art, influence, promise or deception.[123] A court has noted as *dicta* that "previously chaste character" does not necessarily imply that the female is physically a virgin. "It is not therefore an absolute physical intactness which is required to constitute 'chaste character'. . . . The Legislature is speaking of character, something that may be amended, not a masterial substance like glass. . . . I see no reason for holding that a previous act of illicit intercourse should disqualify a girl from the protection of the provision."[124] In this decision the court ruled that the promise of marriage must be absolute and not simply conditional in the event of a pregnancy in order to support a charge under s. 152. The court also found that where the complainant had sexual intercourse with the accused on a number of occasions in 1910, a charge of seduction under promise of marriage, based upon a similar act in 1911 cannot be sustained since the woman was found not to be of "previously chaste character".

Illicit Sexual
Intercourse:
s. 153(1)(a)

Section 153(1)(a) of the *Code* establishes an indictable offence against a male person who has illicit sexual intercourse with his step-daughter, foster daughter or female ward. It has been held that consent of a complainant is no defence to this charge.[125]

Procuring
Sexual
Intercourse:
s. 166

Section 166 of the *Criminal Code* provides:

Every one who, being the parent or guardian of a female person,

---

[122]*R. v. Schmidt or Smith* (1948), 90 C.C.C. 270 (Ont. C.A.); revd 92 C.C.C. 53 (S.C.C.).

[123]*R. v. Schemmer*, [1927] 3 W.W.R. 417 (Sask. Prov. Ct.); *R. v. Gasselle* (1934), 62 C.C.C. 295 (Sask. C.A.); *R. v. Moon*, [1910] 1 K.B. 18 (C.A.).

[124]*R. v. Comeau* (1912) 19 C.C.C. 350, at 355, 5 D.L.R. 250 (N.S.S.C.). And see *R. v. Johnston* (1948), 91 C.C.C. 59 (Ont. C.A.); *Magdall v. R.* (1920), 34 C.C.C. 244 (S.C.C.).

[125]*R. v. Williams* (1973), 12 C.C.C. (2d) 453, at 455 (Ont. C.A.).

> (a) procures her to have illicit sexual intercourse with a person other than the procurer, or
>
> (b) orders, is party to, permits or knowingly recieves the avails of, the defilement, seduction or prostitution of the female person,
>
> is guilty of an indictable offence and is liable to
>
> (c) imprisonment for fourteen years, if the female person is under the age of fourteen years, or
>
> (d) imprisonment for five years, if the female person is fourteen years of age or more.

Sexual Assault and Aggrevated Sexual Assault: ss. 150, 155, 157, 245.2, 246 and 246.3

Section 149(1) and 156 which created the offences of indecent assault on a female and male person respectively have been repealed and replaced by sections broken down by the severity of the sexual assault. In the context of the child as victim, note s. 246.1 and in particular, sub-section (2) therein:

> 246.1(1) Every one who commits a sexual assault is guilty of
>
> (a) an indictable offence and is liable to imprisonment for ten years, or
>
> (b) an offence punishable on summary conviction.
>
> (2) Where an accused is charged with an offence under sub-section (1) or section 246.2 or 246.3 in respect of a person under the age of fourteen years, it is not a defence that the complainant consented to the activity that forms the subject-matter of the charge unless the accused is less than three years older than the complainant.

The *Criminal Code* does not define "sexual assault" and the question of the sexual aspect of the assault will presumably be as much a determination of fact as was the question of "indecency" under the repealed s. 149(1) and offence of indecent assault.[126] In the case of a child under 14, a jury was directed in the case of a charge of indecent assault to conclude that if there was "touching which was in itself indecent, it was indecent assault however willing the child might have been". This direction may be applicable to the new sections with the one variation that the jury will have to decide whether the touching was of a "sexual" and not "indecent" nature.[127]

The acts of "buggery" and "beastiality" are retained as offences under s. 155 of the *Code* although it exempts any two persons, *each* of whom is under 21 years of age, if done in private, thus preserving the status of the child as a victim regardless of his willingness or consent. Furthermore, there exists the offence of "gross indecency" set out in s. 157. Unlike the offence of buggery, there is no absolute liability based on the victim's age and although consent is not a defence, it is considered along with all the other circumstances in determining whether what was done was an act of gross indecency.[128] The offence of gross indecency does not require the participation of the child, that is, through some sexual act on his part. For example, an adult masturbating in the presence of a young child was convicted of this offence.[129]

---

[126]See *R. v. Edgett* (1974), 6 C.R. 42 (N.B.C.A.); *R. v. Louie Chong* (1914), 23 C.C.C. 250 (Ont. C.A.).

[127]*R. v. Sutton*, The Times, May 4, 1977.

[128]*R. v. St. Pierre* (1974), 3 O.R. (2d) 642, 17 C.C.C. (2d) 489 (C.A.).

[129]*R. v. G.* (1982), 38 A.R. 48, 70 C.C.C. (2d) 24 (Q.B.).

If the accused himself is under the age of 18 years, note that s. 72 of the *YOA* provides that no one under the age of 12 years carries any criminal liability for his acts. Furthermore, s. 147 of the *Criminal Code* provides that no male person shall be deemed to commit an offence under s. 146 (sexual intercourse with female under 14) or 150 (incest) while he is under the age of 14 years. It has been held that an accused who was over this age may be convicted of rape as a party to the offence, notwithstanding that the actual perpetrator being 13 years of age is sheltered from prosecution by reason of this section.[130] Unlike the common law and the precursor to s. 147, this section no longer enacts a rule of physical and legal incapacity. Rather, it implicitly recognizes that the act of the person under 14 years of age is an offence for which he may be brought before the court, but it directs the court not to convict.

---

[130]*R. v. Cardinal* (1982), 3 C.C.C. (3d) (Alta. C.A.) affd [1984] 2 S.C.R. 523.

Chapter 7: Readings

Allard, H.A., "Diversion of Children from the Juvenile Courts" (1980), 3 *Can. J. Fam. L.* 439.

Bala, N. and Lilles, H., *The Young Offenders Act: Annotated* (Ottawa: Dept. of Solicitor-General, 1982).

Bazelon, D.L., "Racism, Classism and the Juvenile Process" (1970), 53 *Judicature* 373.

Berlin, M. and Allard, H., "Diversion of Children from the Juvenile Courts" (Fall, 1980), 3 *Can. J. Fam. L.* 439.

Besharov, D.J., *Juvenile Justice Advocacy: Practice in a Unique Court* (N.Y.: Practising Law Institute, 1974).

Binder, A., "Ad Populum: Argumentation in Criminology: Juvenile Diversion as Rhetoric" (includes bibliography), (April, 1984), 30 *Crime and Delinquency* 309.

Birkenmayer, A. *et al.*, *A Review of Alternatives to the Incarceration of the Youthful Offender* (Ontario, Ministry of Corrections, 1976).

Boyd, N., "Circularity of Punishment and Treatment: Some Notes on the Legal Response to Juvenile Delinquency" (1980), 3 *Can. J. Fam. L.* 419.

——————, "Cruelty of Benevolence: The Release of Delinquents from Ontario's Training Schools" (June, 1981), 19 *Osgoode Hall L.J.* 237.

Braithwaite, L., "Treatment Rhetoric versus Waiver of Fifth and Sixth Amendment Rights by Juvenile Suspects" (Winter, 1981), 72 *Crim. L.* 1867.

Brenner, S., "Disobedience and Juvenile Justice: Constitutional Ramifications of Childhood as a 'Moral' Concept", (May, 1983), 21 *J. Fam. L.* 457.

Clarke and Koch, "Juvenile Court: Therapy or Crime Control and Do Lawyers Make a Difference?" (Winter, 1980), 14 *Law and Society Rev.* 263.

Coates, R., "Deinstitutionalization and the Serious Juvenile Offender: Some Policy Considerations", (October, 1981), 27 *Crime and Delinquency* 477.

Coons, W., "Learning Disabilities and Criminality" (Canada), (July, 1982), 24 *Can. J. Criminology* 251.

Costello, J.C., Worthington, N.L., "Incarcerating Status Offenders: Attempts to Circumvent the Juvenile Justice and Delinquency Prevention Act" (Summer, 1981), 16 *Harv. Civil Rights L. Rev.* 41.

Dootjes, I., Erickson, P. and Fox, R.G., "Defence Counsel in Juvenile Court: A Variety of Roles" (1972), 14 *Can. J. Crim. Corr.* 132.

Dougherty, "The Crime of Incest Against the Minor Child and the States' Statutory Response" (1979), 17 *J. Fam. L.* 106.

Eastman, F., "Procedures and Due Process" (May, 1983), 34 *Juv. and Fam. Cts. J.* 29.

Erickson, P., "Legalistic and Traditional Role Expectations for Defence Counsel in Juvenile Court" (1975), 17 *Can. J. Crim. Corr.* 78.

"Evaluation Standards" (for Juvenile and Family Courts) (May, 1980), 31 *Juv. and Fam. Cts. J.* 3.

Ewaschuk, E.G., "Abduction of Children by Parents" (1979), 21 *Crim. L. Q.* 176.

"Federal Youth Corrections Act: Limiting the Right to Treatment — Case Note" (Fall, 1982), 16 *Suffolk U.L. Rev.* 836.

Fox, S., "Philosphy and the Principles of Punishment in the Juvenile Court" (1974), 8 *Fam. L.Q.* 373.

"Freedom of Speech and Association: Child Pornography and Unprotected Speech" (Supreme Court 1981 Term), (November, 1982) 96 *Harv. L. Rev.* 141.

Freeman, M.D.A., "Sentencing: 'Short, Sharp Shocks' — A Comment" (Great Britain), (January, 1980), 137 *New L.J.* 28.

Guernsey, C.E., "Accountability of the Juvenile Court", (May, 1983), 34 *Juv. and Fam. Cts. J.* 67.

Hackler, J., Paranjape, W., "Juvenile Justice Statistics: Mythmaking or Measure of System Response?" (includes bibliography), (April, 1983), *Can. J. Criminology* 209.

Hackler, J., Brockman, J., "Opinion-role Typologies for Cross-Cultural Comparisons of Juvenile Courts" (Canada), (November, 1980), 31 *Juv. and Fam. Cts. J.* 61.

Hagan, J., "The Legislation of Crime and Delinquency: A Review of Theory, Method and Research", (Spring, 1980), 14 *Law and Society Rev.* 60.

Hall, Hamperian, Pettibone and White (eds.), *Major Issues in Juvenile Justice Information and Training* (Academy for Contemporary Problems, 1981).

Institute for Judicial Administration, American Bar Association, *Standards for Juvenile Justice* (Ballinger, 1981).

Jonas, S., "Press Access to the Juvenile Courtroom: Juvenile Anonymity and the First Amendment", (Spring, 1982), 17 *Columb J.L. and Soc. Prob.* 287.

Kittrie, N., *The Right to be Different* (J. Hopkins Press, 1971).

Law Reform Commission of Canada, *Working Paper #7: Diversion* (Ottawa: Queen's Printer, 1976).

Lemert, E., *Instead of Court: Diversion in Juvenile Justice* (Centre for Studies of Crime and Delinquency, National Institute of Mental Health) (Washington, D.C.: U.S.G.P.O., 1971).

Lerman, P., "Child Welfare, the Private Sector and Community-based Corrections" (includes bibliography), (January, 1984), 30 *Crime and Delinquency* 5.

——————, *Community Treatment and Social Control: A Critical Analysis of Juvenile Correction Policy* (Chicago: U. of Chicago Press, 1975).

——————, "Trends and Issues in the Deinstitutionalization of Youths in Trouble", (July, 1980), 26 *Crime and Delinquency* 281.

Mackay, A.W., "The Charter of Rights and Freedoms: Its Implications for Young Offenders". Paper prepared for Continuing Legal Education Society of Nova Scotia Conference, Halifax, June 11, 1983.

Marks, R.D., "Juvenile Non-Criminal Misbehaviour and Equal Protection", (Winter, 1980), 13 *Fam. L. Q.* 461.

McLaughlin, E.J. and Whisenand, L.B., "Jury Trial, Public Trial and Free Press in Juvenile Proceedings: An Analysis and Comparison of the IJA-ABA Task Force and NAC Standards", (Fall, 1979), 44 *Brooklyn L. Rev.* 1.

McLeod, J., "*Doli Incapax:* The Forgotten Presumption in Juvenile Court Trials" (Canada), (June, 1980), 3 *Can. J. Fam. L.* 251.

Miller, A. and Ohlin, L., "The Politics of Secure Care in Youth Correctional Reform" (Massachusetts), (October, 1981), 27 *Crime and Delinquency* 449.

Moyer, S., *The Pre-Judicial Exercise of Discretion and Its Impact on Children: A Review of the Literature* (Toronto: Centre for Criminology, University of Toronto, 1975).

National Center on Institutions and Alternatives, *The Violent Juvenile Offender: A Selected Bibliography* (1979); *Deinstitutionalization of Juvenile Offenders: A Selected Bibliography* (1979).

National Institute of Law Enforcement and Criminal Justice, *Prosecution in the Juvenile Courts: Guidelines for the Future* (Washington, D.C.: U.S. Dept. of Justice, GPO, 1973).

National Juvenile Law Center, *An Introduction to Litigative Advocacy Under the Juvenile Justice and Delinquency Prevention Act of 1974* (2nd ed. 1981).

"Note, Transfer to Adult Court: Balancing the Good of the Child and the Interests of the Community" (Ontario), (Spring, 1981), 4 *Fam. L. Rev.* 50.

Olt, S.J., "*The Federal Youth Corrections Act*: Flaws in Equal Protection Analysis" (March, 1981), 19 *J. Fam. L.* 295.

Petersilia, J., "Juvenile Record Use in Adult Court Proceedings: A Survey of Prosecutors" (Winter, 1981), 72 *J. Crim. L.* 1745.

Pink, W., "Schools, Youth and Justice" (includes bibliography), (July, 1984), 30 *Crime and Delinquency* 439.

Reker, G., Coté, J., Peacock, E., "Juvenile Diversion: Conceptual Issues and Program Effectiveness" (January, 1980), 22 *Can. J. Criminology and Corr.* 36.

Reuterman, N., Hughes, T., "Developments in Juvenile Justice During the Decade of the 70's: Juvenile Detention Facilities", (July–August, 1984), 12 *J. Crim. Just.* 325.

Sarri, R., "Gender Issues in Juvenile Justice" (July, 1983), 29 *Crime and Delinquency* 381.

Schultz, L. (ed.), *Sexual Victimology of Youth* (1980).

Schur, E., *Radical Non-Intervention: Rethinking the Delinquency Problem* (Englewood Cliffs, N.J.: Prentice Hall, 1973).

Schwartz, I. and Krisberg, B., "Rethinking Juvenile Justice" (includes bibliography, statistics), (July, 1983), 29 *Crime and Delinquency* 333.

"Sex with Minor Female, Not Males, Doesn't Violate Equal Protection", (July, 1981), 9 *Am. J. Crim. L.* 235.

Shepherd, A., "Life With Gault", (Fall–Winter, 1980), 12 *Colum Human Rights L. Rev.* 273.

Stapelton, W.V. and Teitlebaum, L.E., *In Defence of Youth:A Study of the Role of Counsel in American Juvenile Courts* (N.Y.: Russell Sage, 1972).

"Status Offender Incarceration Decreases Partly Offset by Relabelling, Net Widening" (February 16, 1981), 12 *Crim. Just. Newsl.* 5.

"The Supreme Court, 1979 Term" (1980), 94 *Harvard Law Review* 75 (abortion decisions).

Time Out: A National Study of Juvenile Correctional Programs (University of Michigan, 1976).

Tweedie, I., "Police Cautioning of Juveniles: Two Styles Compared" (March, 1982), 1982 *Crim. L. Rev.* 168.

Underwood, R., "Learning Disabilities as a Pre-disposing Cause of Criminality", (December, 1976), *Can. Ment. Health*.

Zimmerman, J., Rich, W., Keilitz, I. and Broder, P., "Some Observations on the Link Between Learning Disabilities and Juvenile Delinquency", (January, 1981), 9 *J. Crim. Just.* 1.

Chapter 8

Children and Education[1]

An important context in which to discuss the legal rights of the child within the education system is to identify competing interests including: 1) the consumer-students, parents and minority groups, and whether or not they are constitutionally protected; 2) the service deliverer — the teachers and the principal; 3) and the funder/supervisor — the school board and the Ministry of Education. Note that it is only the student of all these parties who is under a legal duty to be part of the education system and the corollary rights which are attached to this one interest group should be assessed in that light. The discussion which ensues focuses on the legal rights and obligations of the child in relation to the other interest groups listed above from the simple duty of the state to provide accommodation and the student to avail himself thereof, to the obtaining of an education that is appropriate to each student's interests and abilities.

At common law, a child had no legal right to an education and there was no obligation on a parent to ensure that his child was educated. All rights or obligations related to education are therefore derived from statute and jurisdiction to legislate is primarily that of the province's.[2] Ontario's legislation and practice will form the basis for discussion in this chapter although on many issues, other provinces have similar legislation to that of Ontario's. (Hereinafter, all section numbers refer to Ontario's *Education Act* unless otherwise indicated.) In addition, as one commentator noted, Ontario's recent "special education" amendments to the Act "represent Canada's boldest education initiative".[3]

---

[1] Of assistance in compiling and updating this chapter was Wayne MacKay's text, *Education Law in Canada* (Toronto: Emond Montgomery Publications Ltd., 1984).

[2] *The Constitution Act*, 1867, s. 93(1). Note that education for Indian children on reserves is governed federally under the *Indian Act*, s. 114. In addition, see discussion in body of chapter on constitutionally guaranteed minority rights.

[3] See MacKay, *supra*, note 1, at p. 49.

Right to
Accommodation

Qualification

The minimum expression of the child's educational rights is his statutory entitlement "to attend school without payment of fee" if he is "qualified to be a resident pupil": s. 31. The "qualifying" phrase is defined under s. 32 (public schools) and s. 39 (secondary schools) basically to include two prerequisites: 1) the potential student must be between six years and 21 years of age; and 2) the school must be in the school section where either the potential student *and* his parent or guardian resides, or where either the student or parent/guardian is assessed for school taxes. Both the residence and/or tax assessment prerequisite link the right to attend with the payment by the parent of school taxes since every adult occupant or tenant of land (parent or not) is liable for the payment of school taxes for the particular section in which he resides: s. 125. As a corollary, in the instances where a student attends school in another section as of right under the Act, the board which received the parents' taxes on behalf of that child must pay a fee to that board which educates that child: s. 48. In essence then, the state and the parent have entered into a compulsory contract for educational services with consideration, which is supplemented by a portion of their general tax dollar. What these "educational services" amount to and whether the contract is legally enforceable is the subject of this chapter.

In Ontario, unlike other jurisdictions, the Roman Catholic or Protestant parent may elect to direct his education taxes levied for public schools to support either Roman Catholic or Protestant separate schools if they exist in the parents' school section; otherwise, the taxes will automatically be directed to the public school board.[4] If the parent so elects, the child is entitled to attend the Catholic or Protestant elementary school; neither the Legislature nor the courts have in the past recognized the right of publically-supported separate schooling past the grade 10 level although the Ontario government announced in July, 1983 its intention of doing so for the Catholic system in the near future, in gradual stages.

Under present legislation (August, 1985) a child of a parent who is not Roman Catholic may attend a separate school, but only in the discretion of the separate school board which may or may not charge a tuition fee which, in turn, may or may not be assumed by the public school board where the child is qualified to attend: ss. 46 and 31(2). Some Catholic school boards charge while others do not and there is no clear rule or guideline with respect to reimbursement from the public school board. Accordingly, in most instances, the non-Catholic parent who wishes his child to attend a separate school will effectively pay twice for his child's education. (For further discussion on the issue of denominational schools, see below under "Right to Accommodation: Denominational Schools.")

There are a few cases in which the potential student, in attempting to qualify in a particular jurisdiction, claimed that a particular adult was his guardian for the purposes of the *Education Act*. In this respect it should be noted that, pursuant to the *Children's Law Reform Act*, 1982, the definition of "guardian" under s. 1(1) para. 22 of the *Education Act* now means "a person who has lawful custody of a

---

[4]*The Education Act,* ss. 119 (Catholic) and 138 (Protestant). By way of contrast, see *Bintner v. Regina Public School Board* (1965), 55 D.L.R. (2d) 646 (Sask. C.A.) and *Renaud v. Tilburn North R.C. School Trustees,* [1933] O.R. 565 (C.A.).

child other than a parent of the child."[5] This amendment eliminates the unnecessary problems caused by the original definition which required a court order, which appoints a person as legal guardian, while retaining the necessary concept of legal custody. The few cases which now exist on the issue focus on the propriety of an applicant third party seeking a court order for guardianship or custody of a child (before the amendment) only for the purpose of avoiding the payment of school taxes or fees. As in the case of adoption applications to circumvent immigration hurdles, the courts will not grant a guardianship or custody order if the sole or primary reason for the application is to avoid the payment of school taxes or circumvent the lawful requirements of the *Education Act.*[6]

There are certain exceptions to the prerequisites to the right to qualify which can be summarized as follows:

Age

> 1) If a pupil has completed elementary school and has attended one or more secondary schools for a total of at least seven years, the board of the secondary school *may* charge a fee: s. 39(6).
>
> 2) If the board chooses to operate a kindergarten (five-years-old), a junior kindergarten (four-years-old) or a beginner's class (pre-kindergarten, or pre-grade one), the child who is otherwise qualified and resides in the school's attendance area has a right to attend at four or five years of age: s. 33.

Taxes/Jurisdiction

> 1) A student who is qualified to attend in one jurisdiction may attend school in another jurisdiction if it is more accessible (ss. 38, 40(1)(a)), if the school provides a subject(s) not provided at his present school (s. 40(1)(b), (c)), or if the school provides French-language instruction (s. 40(1)(d)). This right is subject to space being available.
>
> 2) If the student is 18 years of age and has been promoted to a secondary school, he has the right to attend a secondary school in other than the jurisdiction in which he resides subject to space being available: s. 39(5).
>
> 3) If the child is a ward of or in the care of a Children's Aid Society or training school, he will be permitted to attend without payment of fee an elementary or secondary school in the district in which he resides: s. 45.
>
> 4) If a child is solely supported by a single parent who resides in Ontario but is not assessed for school purposes in Ontario and if that parent places the child in a residence (other than one covered by the *Children's Residential Services Act*) which is assessed for tax purposes, the child shall be able to

---

[5]*The Children's Law Reform Amendment Act, (1982),* s. 20(1).
[6]See *Re Majid Novin-Kashany* (1980), 17 R.F.L. (2d) 240 (Ont. Surr. Ct.); *Re Liau (infants)* (1971), 5 R.F.L. 147 (Ont. Surr. Ct.); *Re Kovach and Srut et al.* (1984), 44 O.R. (2d) 699 (Ont. Prov. Ct.).

attend school in that school district without payment of fee as if he were a resident pupil: s. 43.

5) If a child resides with a parent or guardian whose residence is on tax exempt land (for example, a university campus), he is not qualified to attend unless he or his parent(s) pay school taxes (s. 44(1) or a fee (s. 41(2)), the latter being subject to the availability of space.

6) Notwithstanding the prerequisites of s. 31(1), s. 31(2) acts as a catch-all clause. If the potential student resides in the board's jurisdiction but is not qualified to attend under the Act without payment of fee, the board, in its discretion, may admit the person from year to year without the payment of fee.

If none of the exceptions are applicable, a non-qualified student has the right to attend upon payment of fee and subject to the availability of space: s. 46.

Nature of Right   The statutory right to accommodation which every jurisdiction in Canada provides is limited to just that, a right to be housed in a school (defined as a body of pupils) from Monday to Friday and from September 1 until the end of June. The right to receive quality education or a certain kind of education does not form part of this right and must be explicitly provided for by statute. The concept of compulsory education in a free and democratic society, if constitutionally sound, is only one side of the coin, the other side of which must be the child's right to an education, whether or not it is found in any statute. If education is a necessity of life as one court suggested,[7] and if it is a right which can be categorized as "deeply rooted in the traditions or conscience of this country"[8], surely it can be ranked as integral to the "life, liberty and security" guarantee under s. 7 of the *Charter of Rights*. This position has been adopted in decisions of the United States Supreme Court[9] and Professor Wayne MacKay, in his recent text, *Education Law in Canada*[10] observes with respect to Nova Scotia legislation:

> The compulsory-attendance provisions of the *Education Act* provide strong support for the argument that there are legal rights to education. If the state has the right to compel a child to attend school, surely a child has a corresponding right to claim some beneficial education from the school. Only if what is provided in the educational process is valuable and of real quality does it make sense to penalize students for non-attendance. Education must mean more than just sitting in the classroom if the state is to be justified in sending those who do not attend to a reformatory. Any other conclusion would indicate an abuse of state power.
>
> In the United States, education rights have been protected as one aspect of liberty under the Constitution. The same approach could be followed in Canada by relying on s. 7 of the *Charter*. Without a proper education, our child lacks both liberty and security of the person.[11]

---

[7]*Re T.O.A. and Regional Municipality of Peel* (1982), 35 O.R. (2d) 260 (C.A.).

[8]*R. v. Morgentaler et al.* (1984), 47 O.R. (2d) 353 (H.C.); affd 48 O.R. (2d) 519 (C.A.).

[9]*Goss et al. v. Lopez et al.* (1975), 419 U.S. 565 (U.S.S.C.); *Tinker v. Des Moines Independent Community School District* (1969), 393 U.S. 503 (U.S.S.C.); *Peter Mills et al. v. Board of Education of District of Columbia et al.* (1972), 348 F. Supp. 866 (U.S. D.C.).

[10]MacKay, *supra*, note 1.

[11]*Ibid.*, at 72.

(For a more detailed discussion on this issue, see below under "Equality Rights".)

The only overriding rights which a Legislature and the school system must yield to are entrenched constitutional rights, and in particular, in relation to accommodation, those affecting religion under s. 93(1) of the *British North America Act* (now *Constitution Act, 1867*) and s. 2 of the *Charter*, and language under s. 23 of the *Charter*. Both are discussed more fully below under "Denominational Schools" and "Minority Language Instruction."

The entitlement to accommodation is an indisputably legally enforceable right under all jurisdictions and it has been held to be a right that belongs to the child.[12] On the other hand, the right to choose how a child shall be educated essentially rests with the parent within the broad parameters of acceptability laid down by the Ministry of Education.[13] (For further discussion on this issue see below under "Duty to Attend: Statutory Exemptions".) Since public education is provided not merely for the benefit of the child or a parent, but for the ultimate interests of the state in producing a reasonable citizenry[14], the right of the child is, as stated above, complemented by corollary duties upon the parent, child and school board. As will be seen, the laws concerning truancy and parents' liability for children who have failed to attend school, as well as the behaviour expected from a child who attends school, exacts responsibility from both parents and children. With respect to the school board's responsibility, s. 149, para. 6 of the *Education Act* states:

> Every board shall provide instruction and adequate accommodation during each school year for the pupils who have a right to attend a school under the jurisdiction of the board.

A parent is entitled to damages for failure of the board to satisfy its duty to provide accommodation.[15] Although there may be some discretion as to what is "adequate" accommodation, the duty to provide it is absolute. In one case,[16] a board closed down a school because of the municipality's failure to contribute enough funds, thus depriving the resident children of schooling for the remainder of the year. In defence to a mandamus application against the board to keep the

---

[12]*Wilkinson v. Thomas*, [1928] 2 W.W.R. 700 (Sask. K.B.); *Campbell and Cosans v. United Kingdom* (1982), 4 E.H.R.R. 293, at 307.

[13]See also *Meyer v. Nebraska* (1923), 262 U.S. 390 and *Pierce v. Society of Sisters* (1925), 268 U.S. 510 for parental rights over education based on the Fourteenth Amendment liberty rights which include privacy of the family. In *Pierce*, the court noted:

> The fundamental theory of liberty upon which all governments in this Union repose excludes any general power of the State to standardize its children by forcing them to accept instruction from public teachers only. The child is not the mere creature of the State; those who nurture him and direct his destiny have the right, coupled with the high duty, to recognize and prepare him for added obligations. [at p. 535]

[14]*Ottawa R.C. Separate School Trustees v. Ottawa* (1915), 24 D.L.R. 497, at 500 (S.C.); affd 30 D.L.R. 770 (S.C.); revd [1917] A.C. 76, 32 D.L.R. 10 (P.C.); *Commonwealth v. Green* (1929), 168 N.E. 101 (Mass.).

[15]*Henchel v. Board of Medicine Hat School Division No. 4* (1950), 2 W.W.R. 369 (Alta. D.C.).

[16]*McLeod v. Board of Trustees of School District No. 20 (Salmon Arm)* (1952), 4 W.W.R. (N.S.) 385, 2 D.L.R. 562 (B.C.C.A.).

school open, the board stated that compliance with such an order would be impossible due to the lack of funds. On appeal, it was held that the paramount consideration is the interests of the children:

> [I]t would be creating a dangerous precedent, under these circumstances, to relieve the School Board from the absolute and imperative duty imposed upon it by statute to provide school accommodation for the children within its jurisdiction. To hold otherwise might very well encourage public and Governmental authorities to disregard prudent limitations upon their expenditures and then permit them to rely upon their own improvidence as an excuse for non-fulfillment of their statutory duties.[17]

While a School Board is under an obligation to accommodate children in a school within its jurisdiction, it is under no obligation to accommodate them in a particular school or maintain a particular school. An application for an injunction was sought to restrain a defendant board from implementing the exclusive use of the French language in a high school, thereby depriving the English-speaking students, who were in attendance from continued access to that particular school. The Appellate Court, in dismissing the appeal, stated:

> The Board is not under any obligation to maintain, in the sense of "to perpetuate", any particular school it establishes. "Maintain" in the Ontario Acts is not a direction to keep forever. It encompasses only authority and obligation to expend money upon the school and keep it in operation so long as the Board feels that it is desirable to do so for the provision of the educational needs of the pupils for whom it is responsible. "Maintain" in my view means the duty from year to year to keep up the operation of the school so long as the Board is of the opinion that such school should be operated as an appropriate means of discharging its duty to provide accommodation for its pupils. The direction to maintain is not inconsistent with discontinuing the operation of any particular school or class when it deems it can otherwise discharge the obligation imposed upon it to provide educational facilities for its pupils.[18]

The Appellate Court went on to indicate further that the only right that a pupil possesses is the right to attend a school in his district. That right is not infringed where the board decides to change or to close one school, provided that the board is prepared to admit and accommodate him in another — in this case, a school where English is used as the language of instruction.[19] Moreover, it has been held that a board's decision to close a particular school, as long as another school is available to the child is not a "statutory power of decision" within the meaning of s. 1(1)(d) of the *Statutory Powers Procedure Act* or s. 1(f) of the *Judicial Review Procedure Act*. It was further held that the right or privilege of parents to have their children attend a particular school is not a legal right or privilege and is

---

[17]*Ibid.*, at 563 (D.L.R.).

[18]*Crawford v. Ottawa Board of Education*, [1971] 2 O.R. 179, at 189 (C.A.). See also *Lapointe v. Board of School Trustees, School District No. 3 Hanson and Plourde; Goulette v. Board of School Trustees, School District No. 3*, (1979), 25 N.B.R. (2d) 91 (S.C.).

[19]*Crawford v. Ottawa Board of Education, ibid.*, at p. 190.

not subject to judicial review under the above statutes.[20] This principle has been somewhat refined as a result of the judicial development of a standard of "procedural fairness" for any administrative decision making such that while the school board is an autonomous body with wide powers of management and complete discretion in its fulfillment of obligations to accommodate children, this does not mean that the action of a board is unassailable. If a school board acts outside its statutory powers, interferes with the rights of others, acts in bad faith or with bias, or perhaps even unfairly, its actions may be questioned and the court may intervene.[21]

Transportation

Unlike other jurisdictions, the *Education Act* in Ontario uses permissive language with respect to the board's responsibility to provide transportation in order for a child to exercise his right to accommodation. Section 166 of the Act states that a board *may* provide transportation for a resident pupil or it *may* reimburse the parent or guardian of the child if, as a result of the distance from school, it is necessary for the parent or guardian to incur expenses with respect to the child's board, lodging or transportation. Section 149, which sets out the mandatory duties of a school board does not include that of transportation. As a complementary provision, s. 20(2)(c) excuses a child from compulsory attendance if transportation is not provided by the board and there are no schools that the child has a right to attend within certain specified distances.

The permissive nature of these sections is difficult to rationalize with the obligation of a board to provide adequate accommodation for children whose right to attend bears no transportation qualifier. The courts have recognized the importance that transportation plays in exercising the right to attend by giving strict interpretation to any non-permissive transportation-related sections such as s. 40(1), where the child has a right to attend a "more accessible" school[22] or to the method of implementing permissive provisions such as s. 166, where the board does choose to provide some transportation. With respect to the latter, it has been held that where a board has provided *any* arrangements for the transportation of children to school, it is bound to ensure that *all* children under its jurisdiction are entitled to the same benefit. An application for *mandamus* against a board was granted where the trustees had made arrangements for most of the children to be conveyed to a neighbouring school with the one exception of a family whose home was relatively isolated. The board was accordingly held

---

[20]*Re Robertson and Niagara South Board of Education* (1973), 41 D.L.R. (3d) 57 (Div. Ct.).

[21]*MacDonald et al. v. Lambton County Board of Education* (1982), 37 O.R. (2d) 221 (H.C.). And see *Alexander et al. v. Etobicoke Board of Education* (1981), 34 O.R. (2d) 76 (H.C.); *Re Arts et al. and London and Middlesex County R.C. Separate School Board* (1979), 27 O.R. (2d) 468 (H.C.); *Hatch et al. v. Board of Education for City of London* (1979), 25 O.R. (2d) 481, 104 D.L.R. (3d) 153 (H.C.); *MacDonald v. Municipal School Board of Municipality of County of Halifax* (1979), 30 N.S.R. (2d) 443 (S.C.); *Corpn. of the Town of Rayside-Balfour v. Sudbury Board of Education* (1983), 2 Admin. L.R. 280 (Ont. C.A.).

[22]See *Re Bareham and Board of Education for City of London* (1984), 46 O.R. (2d) 705 (C.A.) in which the court refused to permit a board to base its transportation decision for a student on "extraneous" policy considerations including declining enrollment, maintaining that it must be based only on the dictionary meaning of the statutory phrase "more accessible" which came down to comparative road distances and mode of transport.

liable for the cost of conveying to school the children for whom it had made no arrangements.[23]

Minority
Language
Instruction

Section 23 of the *Charter* extends the duty to accommodate by requiring French or English minority language instruction or educational facilities "where numbers warrant." Ironically, while it is unclear whether there is any constitutional guarantee that every child receive an education, where a child is entitled under statute to attend school, minority language rights, like denominational rights, now have constitutional force within the education system. Moreover, French and English minority language education rights possess reinforced constitutional strength because they are included among the rights which cannot be overridden under s. 33 of the *Charter* by an Act of Parliament or a Legislature.

Based on the wording of the section, the right belongs to the parents and is based on whether or not they are French or English-speaking, as opposed to their children. For a child to recieve instruction or be accommodated in facilities of a minority language, the parent of the child must come within one of three categories:

1) Canadian citizens whose first language learned and still understood is that of the English or French linguistic minority of the province in which they reside: s. 23(1)(a);

2) Canadian citizens whose primary school instruction in Canada was in the French or English minority language of the province in which they now reside: s. 23(1)(b);

3) Canadian citizens who are having or have had any of their children educated in French or English in Canada, have the right to have all of their children so educated: s. 23(2). Note that this particular category has no qualifying residence provision.

Where the parent qualifies under s. 23(1) or (2), the extent of the right is qualified under s. 23(3) as follows:

Language of Instruction

1) The right "applies wherever in the province the number of children of [parents who so qualify] is sufficient to warrant the provision to them out of public funds of minority language instruction".

Educational Facilities

2) The right "includes, where the number of those children so warrants, the right to have them receive that instruction in minority language educational facilities provided out of public funds."

---

[23]*Ridings v. Elmhurst School District Trustees (No. 2)*, [1927] 2 W.W.R. 159, revg [1926] 3 W.W.R. 729 (Sask. C.A.). And see *Perreault v. Board of Kinistino School* (1956), 8 D.L.R. (2d) 491 (Sask. C.A.); *Tyler v. Ardath School Trustees*, [1935] 2 D.L.R. 814 (Sask. Q.B.).

Prior to the passing of the *Charter*, a Legislature or its delegate school board had full power to establish the language of educational instruction. Even an attempt via the courts to link the protection of minority languages with religious denominational guarantees under s. 93(1) of the *B.N.A. Act* failed. The court construed the meaning of "denomination" as it was understood at the time of Confederation, concluding that it referred to a class of persons determined according to religious belief and not according to language.[24] Once the Charter passed, its first test under s. 23 was the challenge of Quebec's *Charter of the French Language*[25] which required that parents who had been educated in English in a province other than Quebec send their children to French schools. The challenge was successful as the statute was found to negate the rights under s. 23 and, as such, was of no force and effect. By total negation of the right, the s. 1 "reasonable limits" test in the *Charter* was held not to be applicable since total denial of rights cannot be a mere limitation. The court continued that if it were applicable, it could not be demonstrably established that the limitation was a reasonable one.

Applicants have tried, as well, to use s. 23 to oppose or obtain certain educational services. In one case,[26] the New Brunswick Queen's Bench held that this provision does not guarantee the right of the linguistic minority to an education in the language of the majority nor does it create a duty on the minority to exercise its rights thereunder. The Société des Acadiens failed in its attempt to restrain a school board from offering French emersion classes to Francophones in English schools and offering instruction in English to persons whose mother tongue was French. In an Ontario High Court case,[27] the applicant failed to obtain services, in this case the construction of shop facilities at a minority language instruction school so that the students would not have to travel to an English school for that particular class.

One recent major Ontario case[28] will potentially result in not only more minority language services being available but also in the control and direction of such services being more firmly in the hands of the French community. By Order-in-Council, the Attorney-General referred Ontario's laws, policies and future intentions regarding the provision of French language instruction and educational facilities to the Court of Appeal to determine whether or not they were inconsistent with the provisions of the *Charter*. The present *Education Act* in Ontario provides that a board may establish elementary and secondary schools or classes "for the purpose of providing for the use of the French language in

[24]*Mackell v. Ottawa R.C. Separate School Trustees* (1917), 32 D.L.R. 1 (S.C.) affg 24 D.L.R. 475 (P.C.).

[25]*Quebec Association of Protestant School Boards et al. v. A.-G. of Quebec et al. (No. 2)* (1982), 140 D.L.R. (3d) 33 (Que. Sup. Ct.); affd 1 D.L.R. (4th) 573 (Que. C.A.); affd [1984] 2 S.C.R. 66, 10 D.L.R. (4th) 321.

[26]*Société des Acadiens Nouveau-Brunswick Inc. et al. v. Minority Language School Board No. 50* (1983), 48 N.B.R. (2d) 361, 126 A.P.R. 361 (Q.B.).

[27]*Marchand v. Simcoe County Board of Education et al.*, summarized in (1984), 24 A.C.W.S. (2d) 196 (Ont. H.C.).

[28]*Reference Re Education Act and Minority Language Educational Rights* (1984), 47 O.R. (2d) 1, 10 D.L.R. (4th) 491 (C.A.).

instruction of French-speaking pupils'': ss. 258(1) (elementary) and 261(1) (secondary). Each section then outlines a two-level duty on the part of the board: one with respect to the provision of French language instruction which is mandatory in certain circumstances and one with respect to the provision of French language schools which is discretionary on the part of the board. In the former, written evidence must be presented to the board that ''a number of'' French speaking resident pupils have elected to be taught in the French language. Upon receipt thereof, the board must ''determine whether French-speaking pupils can be assembled for this purpose in one or more . . . groups of 25 [20 for the secondary level] or more'' in which case the board *shall* provide for the use of French-language instruction by these groups: ss. 258(2) and (3) and 261(2) and (3). With respect to the second level of duty, the board which must provide French language instruction as outlined above shall provide a French language school if, *in the board's opinion*, ''the number of [French speaking] pupils who elect to be taught in the French language so warrants'': ss. 258(4) and 261(4). There is nothing in the Act or Regulations which provide minimum criteria upon which this discretion is to be exercised. Secondary school boards alone have yet another option short of establishing a French-language school. Where, in the board's opinion, the number falls short of warranting a French-language school, the board is to consider the possibility of entering into an agreement with another board to provide for the admission of its resident French-speaking secondary school pupils to the second board's French classes or schools: s. 261(1) and (5). (Note that notwithstanding all of the foregoing, the Legislature wished to ensure the teaching of the language of the majority by providing that English *shall* be a subject of instruction from grades 5 to 12: ss. 258(5) and 271.)

The Ontario Court of Appeal was asked to consider ss. 258 and 261 as well as a government White Paper[29] proposing amendments to the minority language provisions of the Act in light of the *Charter*. Extensive materials were submitted including many comprehensive federal, provincial and private reports as well as detailed statistics on the existence and distribution of Ontario's French speaking population. The resulting decision which dealt with the government's four specific questions was equally comprehensive and was presented on the basis that s. 23 should be given a liberal interpretation in light of the fact that it created a new code of minority language education rights.

Question 1: Are Sections 258 and 261 inconsistent with the *Charter*?

The court held in the affirmative on four grounds:

Beneficiaries of the Right

    1) The rights under s. 23 are couched in terms of whether or not the *parents* are French-speaking whereas the rights under the *Education Act* are limited to *students* who are French-speaking.

---

[29]Now Bill 119 ''An Act to Amend the *Education Act, 1984*''; received second reading Oct. 23, 1984.

Exercise of Discretion

> 2) The rights under s. 23(3)(b) to French language facilities where numbers warrant cannot be left to the unfettered discretion of the local board but must be subject to legislation which provides for an "objective" assessment of same.

"Minimum Numbers" Limitations

> 3) Rights under s. 23(3) of the *Charter* are not qualified by the boundaries of each school district; the wording simply states that "wherever in the province the number . . . is sufficient to warrant." The provision under the *Education Act* for minimum numbers of 25 and 20 French-speaking students within a board's jurisdiction is therefore inconsistent since it is necessary to apply the numbers test on a local basis without any arbitrary province-wide limitation.

Regional Limitations

> 4) The geographic jurisdiction of each board imposes geographic limitations on its duty to provide French language instruction so that French-speaking parents who live relatively close to one another but who may be in different board jurisdictions do not constitute an entire group for either board to consider. Accordingly, the approach is inconsistent with the *Charter* which "transcends geographic boundaries" in providing the right "wherever in the province . . . numbers warrant."

Question 2: Is the *Education Act* inconsistent with the *Charter* in light of the fact that the French-speaking community does not possess the right to manage and control the French language instruction?

The court again held in the affirmative having regard to:

1) the ordinary meaning of the words used in s. 23;
2) s. 23 interpreted in light of the other provision of the *Charter*;
3) the mischief that s. 23 was intended to remedy; and
4) the category of person who would participate in the management and control of minority language educational facilities:

> The rights conferred by [s. 23] . . . impose a duty on the Legislature to provide for educational facilities which, viewed objectively, can be said to be of or appertain to the linguistic minority in that they can be regarded as part and parcel of the minority's social and cultural fabric. The quality of education to be provided to the minority is to be on a basis of equality with the majority.[30]

---

[30]*Reference Re Education Act and Minority Language Educational Rights, supra,* note 28, at p 43.

The decision went on to confirm the recommendations of the government's White Paper regarding

1) guaranteed representation of minority language persons on boards which administer minority language instruction, and
2) that those representatives have *exclusive* authority to make decisions regarding the provision of minority language instruction including the preparation of financial estimates.

Specifically, a board would be required to establish a "minority language section" when it has 500 or more minority language pupils or such pupils make up 10 per cent or more of the total enrollment. The number of minority language trustees would be proportionate to existing trustees but would not be less than four or more than eight.

Questions 3 and 4: Do the rights determined under Questions 1 and 2 apply equally to denominational school boards?

The court again held in the affirmative finding that s. 23 draws no distinction and that, rather than s. 23 of the *Charter* and s. 93(1) of the *B.N.A. Act* being in conflict, the former constitutes an addition to the rights under the latter. This latter conclusion was necessary in the face of s. 29 of the *Charter* which provides that nothing therein is to "abrogate or derogate" from any of the rights guaranteed to denominational schools under the *B.N.A. Act*.

Denominational Schools

Although the *B.N.A. Act* expressly provides that laws with respect to education are a provincial matter, s. 93(1) nevertheless goes on to safeguard the rights enjoyed by "any class of persons" with respect to denominational schools "at the Union" by forbidding provincial legislation to "prejudicially affect" such rights.[31] Section 29 of the *Charter* reinforces this provision by stating that nothing in the *Charter*

. . .abrogates or derogates from any rights or privileges guaranteed by or under the Constitution of Canada in respect of denominational, separate or dissentient schools.

Case law has developed an interpretation of s. 93(1) over the years which must be considered, both with respect to a citizen's denominational educational rights in general and with respect to any new educational rights which may be claimed via the *Charter* (and which may not infringe upon these existing rights), under, for example, s. 2 (freedom of religion), s. 15 (equality rights on the basis of

---

[31]See s. 93(1) of the *Constitution Act, 1867* (entrenched in the *Charter of Rights*, s. 29):

s. 93(1) In and for each Province the Legislature may exclusively make Laws in relation to Education, subject to and according to the following Provisions.

(1) Nothing in any such Law shall prejudicially affect any Right or Privilege with respect to Demoninational Schools which any Class of Persons have by law in a Province at the Union.

And see as well Bargen, P.F., *The Legal Status of the Canadian Public School Pupil* (Toronto: McMillan and Company, 1961), at pp. 14-36.

religion), s. 23 (language rights on education) and s. 27 (preservation and enhancement of multi-cultural heritage).

A Quebec Superior Court judgment[32] undertook a comprehensive review of the wording of s. 93(1) in the context of the rest of the *B.N.A. Act*, of the history behind the wording and of the case law on this section in Canada up to 1976. Irwin Coulter, in his article "Freedom of Assembly, Association, Conscience and Religion"[33], sets out a convenient summary of the principles gleened from that case law, some of the highlights are as follows:

1) The rights conferred under s. 93(1) are of a denominational, not educational character so that the right alleged to be "prejudicially affected" must be found in itself to be of a denominational character and not just possessed by one who is part of a separate school system.

2) The rights must have existed at the time of Confederation. They must also have been enforceable under the law of that time (which varied from province to province) and not simply in existence by sufferance or tradition. Accordingly, in Ontario, the Legislature and the courts have interpreted s. 93(1) to freeze only Catholic and Protestant rights[34] and those only to grade 10, to the extent of creating a publicly-funded separate school system. Regardless of the legal position, the Premier of Ontario recently announced the govenrment's intention to provide public funds to extend publicly-funded separate school education to grade 13.

3) "Any class of persons" under s. 93(1) to whom rights are reserved refers to "a class of persons determined according to religious belief and not according to race or language".[35]

4) With respect to individual provinces at the time of Confederation — Ontario, New Brunswick — Protestant (as majority) and Catholic (as minority) rights existed: s. 93(1) applies; Quebec — Catholic (as majority) and Protestant (as minority) rights existed with a possibility of enforceable Jewish rights existing: s. 93(1) applies; Nova Scotia, British Columbia and P.E.I. — no laws in existence to enforce any denominational rights: s. 93(1) does not apply; Manitoba, Alberta and Saskatchewan — a modified form of s. 93(1) applies. As well, Mr. Coulter notes that Manitoba abolished the denominational school system in 1890 and that the issue is ripe for challenge today; Newfoundland — a modified version of s. 93(1) applies; rights were recognized for Roman Catholics, Church of England, United Church of Canada, Salvation Army, Presbyterian, Congregational, Seventh Day Adventists and Pentacostal Assemblies.

---

[32]*Bureau Métropolitain des Ecoles Protestantes de Montréal v. Le Ministre de L'éducation du Québec*, [1976] C.S. 430.

[33]Irwin Colter, "Freedom of Assembly, Association, Conscience and Religion" in *Canadian Charter of Rights and Freedoms: Commentary*, eds. W.S. Tarnopolsky and G.A. Beaudoin (Carswell: Toronto, 1982), at pp. 188–190.

[34]See *Re North York Board of Education and Ministry of Education* (1978), 19 O.R. (2d) 547 (Ont. H.C.).

[35]*Ottawa R.C. Separate School Trustees v. MacKell, supra*, note 24.

(For discussion of religious freedoms generally within the education system, see below under "Religious Freedoms".)

Equality Rights Fallout

The *Charter* introduces a new set of entrenched rights and freedoms which may be used not only as a shield but also as a sword with respect to the implementation of the specific linguistic and denominational educational rights, given their selective nature (linguistic rights limited to French and English and denominational rights limited to Catholic and Protestant for the most part) and given the inevitable fact that resources will be limited to implement the rights even between the selected minorities. Provisions such as s. 2 (freedom of religion), s. 15 (equality under the law and equal benefit of the law) and s. 27 (preservation and enhancement of multi-cultural heritage) are the basis of potential challenges both as to the method of implementation of the linguistic and educational rights and as to the selective nature of these rights.

With the entrenchment of both minority linguistic and denominational educational rights, Canada may find itself in a conundrum regarding the desirability of a "separate but equal" structure of education. In practical terms, the obligation that flows from minority language protection without any right of accommodation at a particular school introduces the spectre of "busing." Tax-paying parents of the minority or majority language will now face an extension of educational segration based not only on religion but language. In both Manitoba and Ontario, the courts have upheld decisions of school boards to designate an entire school for the purpose of conducting a French emersion program where its effect was to displace children who formerly attended the school located in their neighbourhood. In so doing, the court concluded that the students who formerly attended the school had no vested right to attend that school and that the school trustees had the right to move them to another school within the board's jurisdiction.[36]

To date, the clash of group rights vs. individual rights in Ontario with respect to denominational education has largely been avoided because a Catholic parent may opt for either a separate or public school, giving them a compromise. As noted above under "Right to Attend Qualification", there is also some opportunity for non-Catholic parents to send their children to Catholic schools although this may or may not involve a fee. The opportunity of election has not been available in other provinces, giving rise to some friction. For example, a girl in Saskatchewan, refused access to the public school system because her parents were Catholic, relied on the Saskatchewan *Bill of Rights* to obtain access. The court over-ruled her application based on its interpretation of s. 93(1) of the *B.N.A. Act*.[37] On the other hand, it is arguable that nothing in s. 93 requires obligatory attendance at a separate school by reason of the religion of the parents. In an analogous issue based on the implication of linguistic educational rights, the court so held.[38]

---

[36]*Damus et al. v. Board of Trustees of St. Boniface School Division No. 4 and Minister of Education of Manitoba*, [1980] 3 W.W.R. 197 (Man. Q.B.); *Crawford v. Ottawa Board of Education, supra,* note 18; *Lapointe v. Board of School Trustees, School District No. 3, supra,* note 18.

[37]*Bintner v. Regina Public School Board*, (1965), 55 D.L.R. (2d) 646 (Sask. C.A.).

[38]*Société des Acadiens du Nouveau-Brunswick Inc. et al. v. Minority Language School Board No. 50, supra,* note 26.

The intention under s. 15 to ensure that every individual is equal before and under the law with the right to equal protection and equal benefit of the law without discrimination, coupled with s. 27, the "multi-cultural heritage" provision, suggests that a minority Portuguese, Italian or Chinese-speaking parent should be entitled to the same segregated educational rights as those afforded the minority French-speaking or English-speaking parent. The same is true for the Jewish, Greek Orthodox or Moslem parent with respect to Catholic and Protestant educational rights in Canada. The question is, will the argument that French/English/Protestant/Catholic have superior status due to their being part of the 1867 Contract of Union keep the finger in the dyke? American jurisprudence in this area will be of little assistance as the U.S. Constitution does not include the concept of segregated rights based on religion or language and indeed, with respect to the former, specifically forbids an overlap of church and state.

The Ontario *Education Act* presently provides only a passive response to the problem of multi-culturalism and equality rights by ensuring under s. 50 that a pupil is allowed to receive such religious instruction as the parent or guardian desires (which does not, in itself, create a duty on the board to so provide) and that no pupil in a public school shall be required "to read or study in or from a religious book, or to join in an exercise of devotion or religion objected to by his parent or guardian." The provisions ensure a secular education for any child such that a separate school board, for example, may not impose religious instructions as a condition to continued accommodation where the only publicly-funded facility in the municipality was a separate school.[39] However, the provisions obviously do not satisfy those ethnic, racial or religious groups who want the same status as the French/English/Protestant/Catholic groups. Not only do they not have the same rights and privileges but, with respect to denominational schooling, it is prohibited to use public funds for other than Catholic/Protestant schooling. For example, it was held to be *ultra vires* for a school board to incorporate Jewish schools into the public school system by requiring students at one or more of the schools to attend Hebraic studies and to re-assign students whose parents objected thereto to other schools in the same district.[40] The decision was based on the conclusion that the intention of the Legislature is frustrated by such action and it thereby contravenes the Legislation. The board's argument that a child who does not wish to participate in parochial Jewish education can attend another school in the board's jurisdiction and thereby retain his right to accommodation was not tenable and in so doing it contravened s. 50 of the *Education Act* which preserves the right of any pupil to claim exemption from any religious instruction provided at any school within the board's jurisdiction.

Private School   Nothing precludes a parent who can afford the fee from opting out of publicly-funded education and enrolling the child in a private school facility. Needless to say, private school attendance is not a publicly-funded right. Section 15 of the *Education Act* permits the operation of a "private school" which is

---

[39]See *Chabot v. Les Commissaires d'Ecoles dè LaMorandière*, [1957] Que. Q.B. 707 (C.A.).
[40]*Re North York Board of Education and Ministry of Education, supra*, note 34.

defined as an institution at which instruction in any of the public school subjects is provided at any time between 9 a.m. and 4 p.m. on any school day for five or more school age pupils: s. 1(1), para. 40. The Ministry regards the last qualification in the definition to mean five or more unrelated persons, presumably to distinguish a private school from home instruction which, although allowable, is not subject to the requirements of s. 15. In order for a private school to operate it must notify the Ministry of its existence, and upon request, supply the Ministry with prescribed information regarding enrollment, staff and courses of study. In the "Notice of Intention to Operate a Private School", the applicant must indicate whether the Ontario curriculum is to be followed and if courses at the honour graduation level (grade 13) are to be offered.[41]

The "compulsory attendance" section of the Act exempts a child of school age if he or she is "receiving satisfactory instruction at home or elsewhere." (For discussion of this exemption generally, see below under "Duty to Attend: Statutory Exemptions".) The simple listing of a private school with the Ministry via the prescribed notice does not in itself qualify the school as one which provides "satisfactory instruction."[42] In addition, the child can obtain a secondary school diploma only by complying with Ministry policies. Private school students may be granted credits leading to a diploma only if:

1) the teachers of the courses concerned hold appropriate qualifications;
2) the courses followed are from Ministry of Education guidelines or have been approved by the Ministry;
3) the school is inspected by a Ministry official who finds that the work of the students, the teaching, the time allotted to each of the subjects, the assessment of achievement, the organization, the accommodation and the equipment are satisfactory.

The report permitting or denying the granting of credits is issued subsequent to an inspection. In some cases, the Ministry may permit the granting of credits or diplomas by the principal of the private school; in others, the signature of the Ministry supervisory officer may be required after recommendation by the principal.[43]

Duty to Attend

The right to accommodation is complemented not only by the duty of a board to provide facilities and instruction, but also by the duty of the school age child to attend school and the duty of his parents to cause the attendance. Such a blatant and unabashed infringement on the child's and parents' absolute freedom has been justified not only on an individual "best interests" level but also on the macro-level of society's interest in producing a "responsible citizenry".[44]

---

[41]The *Education Act*, s. 15(3) and prescribed form "Notice of Intention to Operate a Private School, School year 1983–84."

[42]From "Information Regarding the Establishment of a New Private School" provided by Ministry of Education for Ontario as of February 1, 1984.

[43]From "Information Regarding the Establishment of a New Private School", from the Ministry of Education for Ontario as of March, 1984.

[44]*Ottawa Roman Catholic Separate School Trustees v. Ottawa* (1915), 24 D.L.R. 497 (S.C.); affd 30 D.L.R. 770 (S.Q.); revd [1917] A.C. 76, 32 D.L.R. 10 (P.C.).

The duty of the child to attend is found under s. 20(1)(a) which states that every child who becomes six years old on or before the 1st day of school in September in any year "shall attend an elementary or secondary school on every school day from the first school day in September in that year until he attains the age of 16 years." (Section 20(1)(b) deals with children who become six years old after the first school day in September.) The Act then sets out eight exemptions to this duty which will be discussed below.

The duty on the parent is found under s. 20(5) which directs that the parent or guardian "shall cause the [school age] child to attend school." For the sole purpose of the compulsory attendance provisions, the definition of "guardian" is expanded from that of a person who has lawful custody of a child (s. 1(1) para. 22 of the Act) to include "any person who has received into his home another person's child who is of compulsory school age and is resident with him or in his care": s. 17. Accordingly, this liability would apply to a foster parent or a group home supervisor or a Children's Aid Society. Indeed, s. 45 of the *Child Welfare Act* (and s. 57(3) of the proposed *Child and Family Services Act*) provides that a Society shall ensure that a child placed in their care as a ward receives an education while s. 40 of the *CWA* provides that a Society has and shall assume all the rights and responsibilities of a legal guardian of every child who is committed as a ward into their care.

Statutory Exemptions

Section 20(2) of the Act lists all of the possible circumstances in which a child may be exempted from compulsory attendance. The discussion under "Enforcement", below, outlines the adjudication procedures in which these exemptions are utilized as a "defence" to a charge of unlawful absence.

Section 20(2)(a) provides that a child is excused from attendance at school if "he is receiving satisfactory instruction at home or elsewhere." This kind of exemption has formed the basis of many court challenges in Canada stemming from a parent's desire to retain more control over the way his child is educated. It has led to parents either keeping their children at home to educate them or placing them in small private schools, usually of a religious nature, which had not been given prior certification by the provincial Ministry of Education. A British Columbia Court of Appeal decision (both pre-*Charter* and pre-*Bill of Rights*) held that *bona fide* education laws that infringe indirectly on religious freedom do not give the individual parent the right to remove his child from public schooling.[45] On the other hand, a 1978 decision of an Alberta Provincial Court relied upon the Alberta *Bill of Rights* to conclude that "where it can be shown in a particular case that religious beliefs are irrefutably and irrevocably linked to education, a foundation has been laid for the application of the Bill of Rights or freedom to educate children in conformity with those beliefs is infringed upon."[46] The defendant's objection in the Alberta case was based on the public school's use of radio programming and the child's exposure to vulgar language and sex discussions in the classroom, all of which were presumably absent in the

---

[45]*Perepolkin v. Supt. of Child Welfare (No. 2)* (1957), 120 C.C.C. 67 (B.C.C.A.). And see *R. v. Hildebrand; R. v. Doerksen* (1919), 31 C.C.C. 419 (Man. C.A.); *Brooks v. Ulmer* (1923), 1 W.W.R. 1 (Alta. C.A.).

[46]*R. v. Wiebe*, [1978] 3 W.W.R. 36 (Alta. Prov. Ct.).

proposed Mennonite School. In another recent Alberta Provincial Court case,[47] parents were acquitted under the compulsory education law of that province based on the s. 7 "due process" protection of the *Charter of Rights*. A pastor was charged with three counts of truancy for refusing to send his children to public school, while educating them and 20 other children in a program he created called "Western Baptist Academy" without seeking certification. The judge found that the process of obtaining an alternate schooling exemption from compulsory attendance was unfair in that the only evidence to be offered was submitted by "persons associated with the prosecutor of the unlawful attendance section." The court found this to be the equivalent of saying that the defence — "not guilty by reason of insanity" — could only be established by the evidence of a Crown psychiatrist. It held that the section should be interpreted to allow any evidence relevant to the issue of efficient instruction in order to permit the accused to make a full answer in defence. An Ontario Provincial Court has interpreted the legislative intention to be that the alternative program must be of a quality comparable to that of a public school system and that in the absence of such an assessment from a Ministry official, it was within the court's jurisdiction to decide the issue. The court concluded that as a quasi-criminal proceeding, there is a criminal burden of proof upon the state and while the onus may be upon the parent or guardian to establish the adequacy of the alternative education, the onus does not arise until the state proves beyond a reasonable doubt that a parent has not provided an adequate educational alternative.[48] On the other hand, another Ontario Provincial Court has decided that the onus is initially upon the defendant to satisfy the court that the child is receiving satisfactory instruction at home or elsewhere.[49]

Compulsory school attendance laws may potentially spawn more challenges under the *Charter of Rights*. For example, in the United States, the rights of Amish parents to keep children out of the public school system has been upheld by the Supreme Court based on the joinder of parental constitutional rights to freedom of religion and privacy of the family.[50] In Canada, if a limitation of a fundamental freedom such as religion can be proved under the *Charter*, it could be fortified by combining the s. 2 infringement with a s. 15 infringement (discussed above) wherein certain religions or cultures are guaranteed separate schooling. A further basis for constitutional challenge rests on the s. 1 requirement that the limitation of the fundamental freedom be "prescribed by law" which has been interpreted to mean that the limitation cannot be "vague,

---

[47]*R. v. Jones* (1983), 29 Alta. L.R. (2d) 349 (Prov. Ct.). The case was reversed on appeal, but solely on the ground that Mr. Jones could not challenge the validity of the section without first having applied for a certificate and having been turned down: 33 Alta. L.R. (2d) 281 (C.A.).

[48]*The Lambton County Board of Education v. Beauchamp* (1979), 10 R.F.L. (2d) 354 (Ont. Prov. Ct.).

[49]*R. v. P.F. McM.*, unreported, May 13, 1983 (Ont. Prov. Ct. Fam. Div.), *per* Glowacki J.; *R. v. Vucovic*, unreported, January 5, 1981 (Ont. Prov. Ct.).

[50]*Wisconsin v. Yonder* (1972), 406 U.S. 205 (U.S.S.C.).

[51]*Re Ont. Film and Video Appreciation Society and Ontario Board of Censors* (1983), 41 O.R. (3d) 583, at 592, 147 D.L.R. (3d) 58 (Div. Ct.); affd (1984), 45 O.R. (2d) 80, 5 D.L.R. (4th) 766 (C.A.). Leave to appeal to S.C.C. granted (Apr. 4/84), 55 N.R. 318*n*.

undefined and totally discretionary . . . and cannot be left to the whim of an official''[51] such as a school attendance counsellor. It is suggested that under the present system the courts do not have the necessary information or process to make a fair determination as to whether Montessori, Western Baptist, Church of Scientology, Chassidic or parental home instruction constitutes alternative satisfactory instruction thereby leaving the school board's agent as the real decision-maker.

The above-noted cases also give rise to the question of whether the courts can assume an identity between the constitutional rights of the parents and those of the child. In the above-noted U.S. Supreme Court case, the argument was made that the exercise of the parents' freedom of religion as it affected the child should not violate the child's constitutional rights to his own freedom of religion and to an education. (Note that some U.S. courts have read a right to education into "liberty" rights.) In his dissenting opinion, the late Mr. Justice Douglas stated:

> If the parents in this case are allowed a religious exemption, the inevitable effect is to impose the parents' notion of religious duty upon their children. Where the child is mature enough to express potentially conflicting desires, it would be an invasion of the child's rights to permit such an imposition without canvassing his views (p. 242). While the parents, absent dissent, normally speak for the entire family, the education of a child is a matter on which the child will often have a decided view. It is the future of the student, not the future of the parents, that is imperiled by today's decision. (pp. 244–5)[52]

The dissenting argument calls not for an Official Guardian-type of representative to offer an opinion as to the best interests of the child regarding his education, but simply that the child be heard if he is mature enough. Based on this argument, ensuring that the child is a party to any proceeding that decides his educational future would satisfy the concern.

The danger in relying simply on the s. 1 "reasonable limits" test when a parent wants to educate his child in an unorthodox manner is that the issues may be limited to the parents' religious freedoms or right to direct their child's education and the state's belief that the mainstream education that it offers serves the child's best interests, without every considering the child's rights and wishes.

Section 20(2)(b) provides that a child is exempted from compulsory attendance if he is unable to attend school by reason of sickness or other unavoidable cause. (Where a child is absent from school for a lengthy period, the child may apply to the school for home instruction: s. 34, O. Reg. 262/80.) What constitutes "unavoidable cause" is not defined other than under the directions in s. 20(3) stating that a child who is blind, deaf or mentally handicapped is not, *per se*, excused from attendance if he is eligible for admission to the Ontario School for the Blind, School for the Deaf or a school or class for trainable retarded children. The meaning of "other unavoidable cause" is unclear unless by reason of statutory interpretation it is read *eusdem generus* with the condition of

---

[52]*Wisconsin v. Yonder, supra,* note 50.

sickness. Alternatively, the phrase might refer to any necessary condition that requires the child to be at home. For example, some provincial legislation allows the child to remain out if his employment is necessary to maintain himself or someone who is dependent on him, or if the parent needs the child for urgent household duties or necessary employment.[53]

Section 20(2)(c) exempts a child from attendances if transportation is not provided by a board and there is no school that he has a right to attend within specified distances. In one Manitoba decision, it was held that a board's duty to provide transportation does not mean "door-to-door" bus service even though the applicable statutory provision said "to and from" school. The court observed that a duty of transportation must be interpreted reasonably and that the school's duty was not to encourage "laziness".[54] (For further discussion on transportation as a right, see above under "Right to Attend: Transportation".)

Section 20(2)(d) exempts a child if he has obtained a secondary school graduation diploma or has completed a course that gives him an equivalent standing. The secondary school graduation diploma is received upon completion of grade 12 requirements set by the Ministry. An "equivalent standing" claim must be assessed by a person authorized by the Ministry of Education.

Section 20(2)(e) exempts a child if he is absent from school for the purpose of receiving instruction in music and the period of absence does not exceed one-half day in any week. Note that there is no Ministerial discretion in this regard so that as long as the absence can be related to some kind of musical instruction for the period so stipulated, the child will be excused.

Section 20(2)(f) exempts a child if he is suspended, expelled or excluded from attendance under the Act. Without this exemption, the board would have a blanket obligation to provide accommodation to every child in Ontario regardless of the school's inability to control the child's behaviour or to provide appropriate instruction to a child who suffers from a severe disability. (For further discussion, see below under "Exclusion".)

Section 20(2)(g) exempts a child if he is absent on a day regarded as a holy day by the church or religious denomination to which he belongs. Again, the Minister has no discretion as to what constitutes a "holy day." Note that this provision presumably allows for absence on a particular day, to be distinguished from the cases discussed above concerning the complete removal of a child from school due to the religious convictions of a parent.

Finally, s. 20(2)(h) exempts a child if he is absent as authorized under the Act and Regulations. This section must refer, *inter alia*, to s. 10(7) of the Act which provides for the legal absence of children from compulsory education through Ontario's "Early School Leaving" Regulation, discussed below.

Enforcement   Enforcement of compulsory attendance, like the duty, has two streams: against the parent and against the child. Ontario still utilizes a punitive or quasi-criminal process to enforce the obligation upon a child, whereas some other provinces have limited the use of quasi-criminal sanctions to the parent,

---

[53]See Appendix, *Provincial Education Acts,* at the end of the chapter.
[54]*Kowalski v. Oak Bluff School District,* [1937] 3 D.L.R. 500 (Man. K.B.).

leaving the issue of a child's responsibility to attend school as a matter of civil child welfare law.[55]

The sanctions against the parent under s. 29(1) and (2) are as follows:

s. 29(1) A parent or guardian of a child of compulsory school age who neglects or refuses to cause the child to attend school is, unless the child is legally excused from attendance, guilty of an offence and on conviction is liable to a fine of not more than $100.

(2) The court may, in addition to or instead of imposing a fine, require a person convicted of an offence under subsection (1) to submit to the Treasurer of Ontario a personal bond in the sum of $200 . . . [which would be conditional on] the person [causing] the child to attend school . . . [U]pon breach of the condition[s] the bond is forfeit to the Crown. [As a provincial offence, the *Provincial Offences Act* applies such that the onus is upon the accused parents to prove an exemption from the obligation set out in the Act, an exemption which would be based on the legal excuses listed under s. 20(2).]

The liability of the child is set out as an offence under s. 29(5):

A child who is required by law to attend school and who refuses to attend or who is habitually absent from school is guilty of an offence and on conviction is liable to the penalties provided for children adjudged to be juvenile delinquents under the *Juvenile Delinquents Act* (Canada), and the child and his parent or guardian may be summoned to appear before the Provincial Court (Family Division), and the court has the same powers to deal with such child and his parent or guardian, including the imposition and payment of fines, as it has with respect to a juvenile delinquent and his parent or guardian under the *Juvenile Delinquents Act* (Canada), and subsection *237(2)* applies in any proceeding under this section.

As a result of the proclamation of the *Young Offenders Act* (hereinafter known as the *YOA*) and with it, the repeal of the *Juvenile Delinquents Act* (hereinafter known as the *JDA*), the validity of dispositions under s. 29(5) has been called into question. The new legislation clearly states that young offenders, as was always true of adult offenders, may no longer be subject to criminal sanction by reason of "quasi-criminal" municipal or provincial offences. Section 79(1) of the *YOA* specifically stipulates that no proceeding may be commenced under the *JDA* in respect of a delinquency as defined in that Act which has included a violation of a provincial statute such as the *Education Act*. The *Education Act* does not require a finding of delinquency nor did it require such a finding when proceedings were commenced under the *JDA*. In fact, as noted by one Ontario Provincial Court, s. 29(5) permits a school board simply to charge a child as an offender against a provincial statute which has become accepted procedure in a few Provincial Courts for many years, although in many other jurisdictions the child has been charged under the *JDA*.[56] The same court determined that a

---

[55]See *The Public Schools Act* of British Columbia and see Appendix, *infra* for a comparison of the different provincial approaches.

[56]*Re L.K.*, summarized in (1984), 7 F.L.R.R. 18 (Ont. Prov. Ct.).

violation of Ontario's *Education Act* still rendered the child liable to the penalities provided under the *JDA*, albeit the original Act that created those powers no longer existed. The court came to this conclusion after having been satisfied that the *Education Act* still contains reference to valid dispositional powers and relied upon a rule of statutory construction stipulating that where the provisions of one statute are incorporated into another by reference and the earlier statute is afterwards repealed, the provisions so incorporated continue in force so far as they form part of the second enactment. Yet another Provincial Court came to the opposite conclusion and held that the *JDA* provisions no longer apply.[57] It is suggested that the liability, in terms of sentencing, for a child under the repealed *JDA* has been substantially varied with the enactment of the *YOA*, reflecting the clear and expressed intention that children should not be subjected to criminal sanction when in violation of a provincial offence but simply to the lesser punishment provided under the *Provincial Offences Act*.

Before court proceedings are ever contemplated, the Act sets out administrative procedures to deal with inquiries into the legitimacy of non-attendance as well as enforcement matters through the authority of the Provincial School Attendance Counsellor, appointed by the Lieutenant Governor in Council: s. 23(1). As well, every board appoints one or more local school attendance counsellors: s. 24. Section 25(1) of the Act gives the school attendance counsellor the authority to act if he:

1) has reasonable and probable grounds for believing that a child is illegally absent from school and
2) has the written request of the parent or guardian or of the principal.

The counsellor may then take the child to his parent or guardian or to the school from which he is absent, provided that if exception is taken to his entry into a dwelling place he cannot enter without a warrant. Section 25(4) requires the counsellor to inquire into every case of failure to attend school within his knowledge or when requested to do so "by the appropriate supervisory officer or the principal of a school or a ratepayer." Note that a "ratepayer" is anyone paying school taxes (which includes both property owners and tenants: s. 125) presumably even outside of the school section in which the student lives. Note further that the school attendance counsellor has no discretion once having received a request under s. 25(4).

Having so investigated and presumably having satisfied himself that the child is unlawfully absent from school, the counsellor must, under s. 25(4):

1) give written warning of the legal consequences of the child's failure to attend to the parent or guardian;
2) give written notice to the parent or guardian to cause the child to attend school "forthwith";
3) advise the parent or guardian in writing of s. 23(2) which provides for an administrative inquiry in the event a parent or guardian believes their child to be legally excused from compulsory attendance.

---

[57]*Shalla L.*, summarized in (1984), 7 F.L.R.R. 18 (Ont. Prov. Ct.).

Section 23(2) of the Act provides as follows:

> s. 23(2) Where the parent or guardian of a child considers that the child is excused from attendance at school under subsection 20(2) [statutory exemptions outlined above], and the appropriate school attendance counsellor or the Provincial School Attendance Counsellor is of the opinion that the child should not be excused from attendance, the Provincial School Attendance Counsellor shall direct that an inquiry be made as to the validity of the reason or excuse for non-attendance and the other relevant circumstances, and for such purpose shall appoint one or more persons who are not employees of the board that operates the school that the child has the right to attend to conduct a hearing and to report to him the result of the inquiry and may, by order in writing signed by him, direct that the child,
>
> (a) be excused from attendance at school; or
>
> (b) attend school,
>
> and a copy of the order shall be delivered to the board and to the parent or guardian of the child.

Both sections 25(4) and 23(2) are concerned with the notification of legal consequences and the receipt of a reply from only the parent, ignoring the consequences to or explanation from the student. Presumably, only the parent then can precipitate a s. 23(2) inquiry, a parent who may or may not be *ad idem* with his child.

The school attendance counsellor may pass over the inquiry stage and simply institute a charge by way of laying an information against the child and/or the parent for unlawful absence from school under ss. 29(1) and (5). Nevertheless, s. 29(7) allows the court to refer the matter back to the Provincial School Attendance Counsellor to conduct a s. 23(2) inquiry before proceeding if it appears to the judge that the child may have a legal excuse under s. 20(2). The counsellor is then to report back to the judge rather than make an order. It is suggested that if a parent is charged with causing his child to be absent from school unlawfully and he does not receive warning or notice as to the provision of s. 23(2), an essential prerequisite of the offence is lacking and the charge should be dismissed.

Section 29(7) may also give some redress in the case of the student seeking an inquiry without the support of his parent although it is not clear whether the child, who is clearly a party to the charge of unlawful absence before the court, will retain that party status for the purpose of the court-directed administrative inquiry. The section does allow that a s. 23(2) inquiry be held "with necessary modifications" which may allow a judge to direct that the student be a party or at least have the equivalent rights of the parent. It is submitted that without such a direction, the inquiry will be of little use to the courts if the parents will either not be participating or will be echoing the position of the attendance counsellor.

While the report of the counsellor is not binding, it will certainly carry great weight insofar as it may be seen by the court as the "expert" ministerial opinion as to whether, for example, the alternate education is adequate. Given the reluctance of the courts to make decisions that are "educational" in nature, a judge will likely tend to rely heavily upon the report of the counsellor in deciding whether a legal exemption exists under s. 20(2). Further, given the importance and potential conclusiveness of the report, the validity of the administrative proceeding is certainly open to challenge based on the principles of procedural fairness, especially since a student may not be a party or since the prosecutor, the school attendance counsellor, is the same person who is appointing member(s) to the tribunal, or since the court may be delegating its duty to make a decision to the attendance counsellor.[58] Indeed, for these reasons it may be more beneficial for the student's counsel to block a s. 23(2) inquiry altogether, opting for courtroom accountability instead.

As a final evidentiary note, the legislation provides that in prosecutions under s. 29, the certificate as to attendance or non-attendance signed by the principal of the school "is *prima facie* evidence of the facts stated therein without any proof of the signature or appointment of the principal": s. 30(2). Unless the contrary is proved, the child is deemed to be of compulsory school age if he appears so to the court (s. 30(3)) and any finding of the s. 23(2) tribunal is admissible in evidence in a prosecution for unlawful absence "only where the prosecution is in respect of a school year for which the order was made": s. 30(4).

Exclusion

A student may be excluded from attending school via "suspension" or "expulsion", thereby denying him his right to attend, for various reasons and on a temporary or permanent basis. Section 20(2)(f) is the matching statutory exemption from compulsory attendance which relieves the board from having to house a student once it has suspended or expelled him.

Suspension

Section 22 of the Act provides the principal with the authority to suspend a pupil for a period not in excess of that established by the board on the following grounds:

1) persistent truancy;
2) persistent opposition to authority;
3) habitual neglect of duty;
4) the wilful destruction of school property;
5) the use of profane or improper language;
6) conduct injurious to the moral tone of the school or to the physical or mental wellbeing of others in the school.

When a pupil has been suspended, the principal must immediately notify the pupil, teachers, the parent or guardian, the school board, the School Attendance Counsellor and the supervisory officer of the suspension and provide all of them with the reasons therefor and notice of the right of appeal of the parent or guardian or adult pupil (18 years of age). The parent, guardian or adult pupil may, within seven days of commencement of suspension, appeal to the board against the suspension and the board "after hearing the appeal or where no appeal is made", may remove, confirm or modify the suspension as well as exercising a discretion to direct the record of the suspension to be expunged from the pupil's record: s. 22(2). Accordingly, the board may review the suspension

---

[58] See *R. v. Jones*, *supra*, note 47. (On appeal) where the judge held that this conflict of interests violated the principles of natural justice.

and give directions regarding same on its own initiative, even if no appeal is launched. The parties to the hearing by way of appeal from the principal's decision of suspension are the parent or guardian, the pupil but only if he is an adult, and the principal of the school: s. 22(4).

Some past cases in upholding suspensions on judicial review have confirmed the following. A pupil who stays away from school because he finds his school work uninteresting, or because he does not like the manner of teaching, may be guilty of "persistent opposition to authority" and liable to be suspended.[59] A student's hairstyle or manner of dress can be subject to board policy or provincial legislation and the flaunting of any such policy or regulation can be grounds for suspension as "persistent opposition to authority" or "conduct injurious to the moral tone of the school."[60] Even non-participation in daily patriotic exercise can form a basis for justifiable suspension.[61]

The Ontario government has imposed requirements of behaviour on students through the Regulations (s. 24, O. Reg. 262/80) in addition to those which an individual board or principal may impose. Their violation may presumably also form the basis for suspension.

s. 24(1) A pupil shall,

(a) attend classes punctually and regularly;

(b) exercise self-discipline;

(c) accept such discipline as would be exercised by a kind, firm and judicious parent;

(d) be clean in his person and habits, diligent in his studies, courteous to his fellow pupils and obedient and courteous to teachers; and

(e) take such tests and examinations as are required by or under the Act.

(2) When a pupil returns to school after an absence, his parent, or where the pupil is an adult, the pupil, shall, orally, or in writing as the principal requires, give the reason for the absence.

(3) A pupil may be temporarily absent from school at any time at the oral or written request of his parent or, where the pupil is an adult, at the request of the pupil, and in either case with consent of the principal.

(4) Where the principal believes that an unjustifiable use is being made of the privilege referred to in subsection (3), he shall promptly notify the board and inform the parent or, where the pupil is an adult, inform the pupil of such notification.

(5) Every pupil is responsible to the principal of the school he attends for his conduct,

(a) on the school premises;

(b) on out-of-school activities that are part of the school program; and

(c) while travelling on a school bus that is owned by, or on a school bus or bus that is under contract to a board.

Expulsion

Expulsion is a more severe disciplinary power than suspension which can be

[59]*Finlayson v. Powell*, [1926] 1 W.W.R. 939 (Alta. C.A.).
[60]*Ward v. Blaine Lake School Board*, [1971] 4 W.W.R. 161 (Sask. Q.B.).

exercised only by board decision, to be distinguished from that of the principal, and which may result in an indefinite absence from all schools under the board's jurisdiction. Note, however, that the same board has the discretion to re-admit the student after an expulsion: s. 22(5). Under s. 22(3), authority to expel can be exercised if the conduct of the pupil "is so refractory that his presence is injurious to other pupils" and:

1) the principal and the appropriate supervisory officer recommend the pupil's expulsion;

2) the pupil and his parent or guardian have been notified in writing of the recommendation of the principal and the supervisory officer, and of the right of the pupil, if he is an adult, and otherwise the right of his parent or guardian to make the representations at a hearing to be conducted by the board;

3) the teacher or teachers of the pupil have been notified of the intended expulsion; and

4) the expulsion hearing has been conducted.

The parties to an expulsion hearing are increased from those at a suspension proceeding to include not only the parent, guardian or the adult pupil and the principal, but also the appropriate supervisory officer: s. 24(4).

Examples of judicial review cases on expulsion which have upheld the board's decision to expel a student include cases in which (i) a principal believed the student to be trafficking in drugs at school, even though the student had not been convicted of trafficking,[62] and (ii) a mentally retarded pupil, "whether his conduct is deliberate or involuntary", was expelled "in justice to the other pupils in his class and to their distraught teacher."[63]

Judicial Review   The courts have generally been reluctant to interfere with the principal's or board's discretion in deciding to suspend or expel. For example, in response to an application for a *mandamus* to have re-admitted two mentally retarded children who had been expelled, the court explained:

In conformity to general rules already stated, *mandamus* will lie to compel the performance of the ministerial duty of admitting to school duly qualified pupils unlawfully excluded, or of reinstating them in case of illegal expulsion; but the writ will not lie where expulsion or refusal of admission was made in exercise of discretionary powers vested in school authorities and not arbitrarily. Even when the writ might otherwise issue, it will be denied where the right to admission is not clearly established, where the probable result of the reinstatement of the pupil would be to break down the authority of the teacher, where the facts do not show expulsion, or where performance of the act commanded by the writ would be impossible.

Whether or not a child possesses the qualifications entitling him to admission to school is a matter within the discretion of the proper authorities

---

[61]*Ruman v. Lethbridge School Board of Trustees*, [1943] 3 W.W.R. 340 (Alta. S.C.). But see *Donald v. Hamilton Board of Education*, [1945] O.R. 518, [1945] 3 D.L.R. 425 (C.A.).

[62]*Wilkes v. Halifax School Board* (1978), 26 N.S.R. (2d) 628 (T.D.).

[63]*Bouchard v. Commissaires d'Ecoles de St. Mathiew de-Dixville*, [1949] Que. K.B. 30; affd [1950] S.C.R. 479.

and *mandamus* does not lie to review their discretion in the absence of any showing that it was abused.[64] [Translation]

On the other hand, decisions of a school board or its agents, as one Ontario Supreme Court has already noted, are not unassailable where there is an issue of elementary procedural fairness.[65] It is hard to conceive of a more elementary deficiency in fairness than the lack of party status for the subject whose rights are most affected. The principle of procedural fairness as articulated by the Supreme Court of Canada[66] arguably applies where an attempt to achieve party status and full legal participation in an educational proceeding has been denied. There also exists the structural ''bias'' inherent in a tribunal constituted of employees of the board where the prosecuting parties include two board employees: the principal and a supervisory officer.

The substantive reasons underlying the tribunal's decisions are obviously much more invulnerable to a court's review than are procedural deficiencies but it seems inconceivable that such an important and cherished statutory right as the right to attend school can be summarily withdrawn, based on any board policy as to student action including, for example, suspension of a student because his hair was too long.[67] Indeed, if the basis for the school administration's authority by common law is derived from a delegated *in loco parentis* status, then the court should be all the more willing to intervene when the welfare of children is at issue, exercising its inherent jurisdiction to supervise all guardians or custodial agents of children, especially when the legislation does not give adequate procedural protections.[68] It would seem encumbent upon the court at least to attempt to reconcile the concept of education as a right that belongs to the child and not simply the parent[69] with its willingness to support the arbitrary nature of the discretion that is given school authorities regarding the infringement of that right.

The apparently unlimited powers of the state with respect to suspension and expulsion suggests the possibility of challenges under the *Charter*, both with respect to process as well as substantive underlying reasons for the decision, the latter arguably being limited by constitutional guarantees of fundamental freedoms under s. 2.[70] (See below for discussion of specific rights and

---

[64]*Ibid.*, [1949] Que. K.B. 30 at 40, citing with approval *Corpus Juris* (1925), t. 38, Vo. *Mandamus*, n.339, p. 734; and see as well *Re McCallum and Brant Board of Public School Trustees* (1889), 17 O.R. 451 (Q.B. Div.); *Re Minister of Education; McIntyre v. Blanchard Public School Trustees* (1886), 11 O.R. 439, at 441 (C.A.).

[65]*MacDonald et al. v. Lambton County Board of Education* (1982), 37 O.R. (2d) 221 (H.C.).

[66]*Nicholson v. Regional Municipality of Haldimand*, [1979] 1 S.C.R. 311, 88 D.L.R. (3d) 671, 23 N.R. 410.

[67]*Ward v. Blaine Lake School Board, supra,* note 60.

[68]*Re Squire* (1974), 16 R.F.L. 266 (B.C.S.C.).

[69]See *Wilkinson v. Thomas,* [1928] 2 W.W.R. 700 (Sask. K.G.); *Campbell and Cosans v. United Kingdom* (1982), 4 E.H.R.R. 293.

[70]See, *e.g.,* the landmark American case of *Tinker v. Des Moines Independent Community School District* (1969), 393 U.S. 503 (U.S.S.C.), in which it was held that a school board could not prohibit students from wearing black arm bands to protest the Vietnam war because it infringed their freedom of speech. The court further held that limitations on such fundamental freedoms could only be justified when the actions interfere substantially with school discipline.

freedoms.) If one can succeed in the argument, as posited above under "Right to Attend: Nature of the Right", that the right to education is inherent in the s. 7 right to "life, liberty and security of the person", then the way is also clear to a challenge of the process under the *Charter*. The U.S. Supreme Court considered the matter in a case in which high school students had been suspended from school for misconduct for up to 10 days without a hearing.[71] The students brought a class action against the school officials, seeking a declaration that the statute permitting such suspensions was unconstitutional and an order enjoining the officials to remove the references to the suspensions from the students' records. In this decision, the court concluded:

> 1) That students facing temporary suspension from a public school have property and liberty interests that qualify for protection under the due process clause of the Fourteenth Amendment, and that therefore the students' legitimate entitlement to a public education could not be deprived without there first occurring fair procedures to determine whether misconduct had, in fact, occurred.
> 2) Since suspension results in a notation in the student's records, there is also the question of the student's reputation which might well interfere with his later educational and employment opportunities, and therefore the state cannot claim the right to determine the issue of misconduct both unilaterally and without due process.
> 3) A 10-day suspension from school is not *de minimis* and may not be imposed in disregard of the requirement of due process. Due process requires, in connection with the suspension of 10 days or less, that the student be given oral or written notice of the charges against him and, if he denies them, an explanation of the evidence the authorities have and an opportunity to present his version. Generally, notice and hearing should precede the student's removal from school since the hearing may also immediately follow the misconduct, but if prior notice and hearing are not feasible, as where the student's presence endangers persons or property or threatens disruption of the academic process, thus justifying immediate removal from school, then the necessary notice and hearing should follow as soon as is practicable.

Discipline and Corporal Punishment

Although the school's authority to discipline is found in the *Education Act*, the underlying common law principle is the delegation to the teacher of the parents' right to discipline (and the child's duty to submit) by the act of sending the child to school. Moreover, because the teacher's power is seen as necessary not simply for meting out parental punishment but for maintaining order in the classroom, the teacher can exercise the "necessary" discipline even over the objections of a parent.[72] Such disciplinary powers entrusted to the teacher have been held to extend outside of the school "if the effects of the act . . . reach within the school room during school hours [and] are detrimental to good order in

---

[71]*Goss v. Lopez* (1975), 419 U.S. 565 (U.S.S.C.).
[72]*Murdoch v. Richards*, [1954] 1 D.L.R. 766 at 769 (N.S.). *R. v. Newport (Salop)* Justices; *Ex parte Wright*, [1929] 2 K.B. 416 at 428; *R. v. Metcalfe* (1927), 49 C.C.C. 260 (Sask. Dist. Ct.). But see

the best interests of pupils''.[73] Nevertheless, the punishment resulting from the misconduct of the child outside of school must be related to the teacher-pupil relationship. A teacher, for example, cannot rely on his status to justify the use of force against the child during a semi-professional baseball game in which both are players.[74] Generally, the teacher enjoys a wide scope of discretion including immunity from what otherwise would be criminal conduct, that is, assault. One magistrate has written ''he was beaten at school, the implication, of course, being that the beating made him the fine fellow he is.''[75]

The authority for parent and teacher alike to employ corporal punishment is codified by s. 43 of the *Criminal Code*:

> Every schoolteacher, parent or person standing in the place of a parent is justified in using force by way of correction toward a pupil or child, as the case may be, who was under his care, if the force does not exceed what is reasonable under the circumstances.

Given the common law delegation of power from parent to teacher, this section thus provides the teacher with a clear right to inflict corporal punishment, for that punishment to cause bodily harm[76] and for the teacher's corporal punishment to be considered justifiable even if the pupil had, in fact, not misbehaved but the court had found that there were reasonable and probable grounds for the teacher to believe that he had misbehaved.[77]

Assuming as a point of law that a teacher-pupil relationship exists, any attempt to redress the student's rights to security of the person will usually be based in an action of assault against the teacher. The student will allege that the teacher's disciplinary conduct was excessive and that therefore, the teacher cannot rely on the defence available under s. 43 of the *Code*. The question of excessive or unreasonable punishment is one of fact and depends upon the circumstances of the particular case. P.F. Bargen, in his book *The Legal Status of the Canadian Public School Pupil* [78] outlines guidelines based on Canadian

---

Campbell and Cosans v. United Kingdom (1982), 4 E.H.R.R. 293 (European Ct. of Human Rights) (cited by MacKay, *Education Law in Canada* (Toronto: Edmond-Montgomery Publications Ltd., 1984), at p. 84 in which the court ruled that British parents had the right to prevent school authorities from administering corporal punishment to their children. It further concluded that the mere threat of punishment hanging over the heads of school children was a breach of Article 2 of Protocol No. 1 under the European Convention on Human Rights:

> In the exercise of any functions which it assumes in relation to education and to teaching, the state shall respect the right of parents to ensure such education and teaching in conformity with their own religious and philosophical views.

[73]*Burdick v. Babcock* (1871), 31 Iowa 562, at 575 (Iowa); and see *Cleary v. Booth,* [1893] 1 Q.B. 465.

[74]See Sumption, M.R.: ''The Control of Public Conduct by the School'' in 20 *Law and Contemporary Social Problems* (1955) (No. 1), 80 at 89.

[75](June 27, 1933), 75 *Solicitors' Journal.*

[76]*Campeau v. R.* (1951), 103 C.C.C. 355 (Que. C.A.).

[77]*R. v. Dimmel* (1980), 55 C.C.C. (2d) 239 (Ont. Dist. Ct.).

[78]Bargen, P.F., *The Legal Status of the Canadian Public School Pupil* (Toronto: McMillan and Company, 1961).

case law to determine what is "excessive" or "unreasonable" punishment, some of which include the following:

1) Punishment is not unreasonable simply because a parent is unaware of school regulations, the breach of which may call for punishment.[79]

2) Unless the punishment results in permanent injury or was inflicted *mala fides*, corporal punishment *per se* is not necessarily unreasonable.[80]

3) Punishment has been considered reasonable where:

    (a) temporary marks on the skin or discolouration lasting for a few days resulted;[81]

    (b) a teacher pulling a resisting child out from his desk, shoving him along the aisle, the pupil falling and hitting his head on the floor; or a teacher tripping a pupil, sitting on him, and with a ruler, hitting him on the shoulder and backs of the hands, causing bruises and welts.[82]

        Note that in both cases under (a) and (b), the court assessed the teacher's actions in light of the child's resistance or intimidating appearance.[83]

    (c) as recently as September, 1980, it was considered not unreasonable for a teacher to shake a pupil after the latter refused to fill out a school form properly, resulting in the trading of punches.[84]

4) Punishment is considered unreasonable:

    (a) if the place on the body receiving the blows is inappropriate. As a result of strapping in one case, the child received a severe blow on her breasts leaving her with a chronic condition of mastitis. The punishment was unreasonably excessive because, if reasonable care had been exercised such as taking hold of the child's wrists, the blows of the strap could have been confined to the palms of her hands as they should be.[85]

    (b) if there clearly is a risk of permanent injury (which can be related to the place on the body on which the blows were inflicted). The court in one case noted:

---

[79]*Mansell v. Griffin*, [1908] 1 K.B. 160.

[80]*R. v. Metcalfe*, [1927] 3 W.W.R. 194, 49 C.C.C. 260 (Sask. Dist. Ct.). And see *State v. Pendergrass*, 2 Dev. and B. 365 (N. Car.), 31 Am. Dec. 416, as cited in *R. v. Metcalfe, ibid.* (W.W.R. at 198).

[81]*R. v. Metcalfe, ibid.; R. v. Robinson* (1889), 7 C.C.C. 52 (N.S. Co. Ct.); *R. v. Corkum* (1937), 67 C.C.C. 114 (N.S. Co. Ct.); *R. v. Gaul* (1904), 8 C.C.C. 178 (N.S.C.A.).

[82]*Murdoch v. Richards, supra,* note 72; *R. v. Zinck* (1910), 18 C.C.C. 456 (N.S. Co. Ct.).

[83]But see MacKay, *supra,* note 72, at pp. 85 and 103*n*, discussing the case cited in *The Times,* February 27, 1982 in which significant damages were awarded to a 14-year-old girl who had been caned by her headmistress as a result of a complaint made under the European Convention on Human Rights. The girl received £1,200 as a settlement, since the beating had been extreme, producing weals on the buttocks and hands. MacKay notes that although there was an apparent infringement of Article 3 of the European Convention on Human Rights concerning inhuman and degrading treatment, the issue was not conclusively decided because there was a "friendly settlement" between the parties.

[84]*R. v. Dimmel, supra,* note 77.

[85]*Andrews v. Hopkins*, [1932] 3 D.L.R. 459 (N.S.C.A.).

There will be no disagreement that if a teacher strikes a pupil on the head by way of discipline his act is completely unjustified; the reason, of course being that there is danger of doing permanent harm by striking a delicate part of the body such as the head. For the same reason to hit a child on the spine with a hard object such as a ruler, would in my opinion be unjustified no matter what his offence. Also though to a lesser degree, to discipline a 9-year old child and one of 6 years by banging their knuckles on the corner of a desk is dangerous and may be unjustified. The covering over the bones on the back of the hands is very thin and the risk of permanent injury is correspondingly great.[86]

In addition to criminal charges against the teacher, it has been held that, in view of the master-servant relationship between a board and teacher, a board may be held civilly liable as well.[87] In this respect, note s. 150(1), para. 17(ii)

s. 150(1) A board may,

. . .

17. pay the costs, or any part thereof, incurred by any member of the board or by any teacher, officer or other employee of the board in successfully defending any legal proceeding brought against him,

. . .

ii. for assault in respect of disciplinary action taken in the course of duty.

Moreover, the s. 235(1) of the Act and s. 24(1)(c) of the Regulations set out the disciplinary duties of the teacher and child respectively:

s. 235(1) It is the duty of a teacher,

. . .

(e) to maintain, under the direction of the principal, proper order and discipline in his classroom and while on duty in the school and on the school ground.

. . .

O. Reg. 262/80,

s. 24(1)(c) A pupil shall,

(c) accept such discipline as would be exercised by a kind, firm and judicious parent;

Present attitudes towards the use of corporal punishment range from outright banishment by some boards as serving no pedagogical purpose, to restricted use only for student control, and to the 1911 Court of Appeal position that it allows "for education in its truest and widest sense. Such education induces the inculcation of habits of order and obedience and courtesy, habits which are

---

[86]*Campeau v. R., supra,* note 76, at p. 360–61. And see *R. v. Bick* (1979), 3 W.C.B. 287 (Ont. Co. Ct.) where a vice principal's conduct was not excused under s. 43 after he struck a 12-year-old child four times on the head, although the first three times did not make contact. The vice-principal was found guilty because of the possible danger of permanent harm from striking a child on the head.

[87]*Murdoch v. Richards, supra,* note 72; and *Duchesne v. Montreal Catholic School Commissioners* (1923), 61 Que. L.R. 442.

taught by giving orders."[88] The implementation of the *Charter* with its s. 7 protection of "liberty and security of the person", s. 12 protection from cruel and unusual punishment or treatment and s. 15 assurance of equal protection before and under the law, may serve as an appropriate forum to test the reasonableness and usefulness of the practice. The present common law protection, on the other hand, seems to be limited to the one vague criterion: namely, whether the physical correction applied did or did not exceed what is reasonable under the circumstances. It does not guarantee accountability for the method of execution, the quality of the punishment or the conditions of its application.[89] For example, some would argue that the common law test used in a recent Ontario District Court decision in which it was held acceptable for a teacher to repeatedly shake a student because he was not filling out a form properly[90] was applied without regard to contemporary and perhaps more relevant pedagogical conclusions concerning the effectiveness of physical correction for the purpose of discipline in the education of young people. The Toronto Board of Education forbids all forms of corporal punishment, while the North York Board of Education limits the means of corporal punishment to that of strapping. In terms of consistency with other areas of law, can one reconcile the legalized practice of assault with child welfare law which imposes very strict limitations on the use of any direct physical force for the purpose of correction.[91] The contradiction becomes readily apparent when one considers that a parent using a strap would very likely be subject to an investigation for child abuse.[92] Indeed, the criminal law defence conveys a message to the abusing parent that strapping and other forms of physical assault on children are permissible in our society.

A United States Supreme Court decision illustrates an unsuccessful constitutional attack on a school board Regulation that contains specific directions and limitations authorizing punishment to a student's buttocks with a wooden paddle. The pupils in a junior high school filed an action for damages and injunctive and declaratory relief against the respondent school officials alleging that the pupils had been subjected to disciplinary corporal punishment in violation of their constitutional rights and in particular, the cruel and unusual punishment clause of the Eighth Amendment and the due process clause of the Fourteenth Amendment. Reading from the syllabus of the reported decision, the majority of the court concluded with respect to the due process clause:

---

[88]*Smith v. Martin and Kingston-upon-Hull Corp.*, [1911] 2 K.B. 775, at 784 (C.A.).

[89]For the applicability of these guidelines see with respect to "cruel and unusual treatment or punishment" A. Morel, "Certain Guarantees of Criminal Procedure", in *The Canadian Charter of Rights and Freedoms: Commentary,* eds. W.S. Tarnopolsky and G.A. Beaudoin (Carswell: Toronto, 1982) at pp. 389–94.

[90]*R. v. Dimmel, supra,* note 77.

[91]As discussed in Chapter 2, "Child Protection and Adoption", provisions of the *Child Welfare Act* not only prohibit any form of abuse which includes infliction of "physical harm" but directs that every person who has information as to the infliction of abuse upon a child shall report it to a Children's Aid Society: ss. 47 and 49 (now s. 75 of the proposed *Child and Family Services Act*).

[92]See *F.W. (No. 2)* and *R. v. Baptiste,* both summarized in (1980), 2 F.L.R.R. 104 for a comparison of the civil and criminal tests for child abuse.

Although liberty within the meaning of the Fourteenth Amendment is implicated where public school authorities acting under colour of state law, deliberately punish a child for his conduct by restraint and infliction of appreciable physical pain and although freedom from bodily restraint is within the liberty interest and personal security that has historically been protected from state deprivation without due process of law, the Fourteenth Amendment does not require notice and a hearing prior to the imposition of corporal punishment as that practice is authorized and limited by the common law and the judicial common law remedies are fully adequate to afford due process. Imposing additional administrative safeguards as a constitutional requirement would significantly intrude into the area of educational responsibility that lies primarily with the public school authorities. Prior procedural safeguards require diversion of education resources and school authorities may abandon corporal punishment as a disciplinary measure rather than incur the burden of complying with procedural requirements. The incremental benefit of invoking the Constitution to impose prior notice and a hearing cannot justify the costs.[93]

In the Canadian context, the courts, once finding an infringement of the s. 7 right to "liberty and security of the person", will not only consider the due process implications but must also consider the s. 1 "reasonableness" of the infringement in the first place, especially in light of the s. 15 "equal protection under the law." The likelihood is great that many judges would find no difficulty, with little or no evidence before them, in finding the practice with its common law restrictions to fall within the terms of s. 1. Nevertheless, the potential of the forum is there for an objective assessment of the usefulness and fairness of the practice in light of present day pedagogical knowledge.

The American decision also considered the argument that corporal punishment constituted cruel and unusual punishment:

The history of the Eighth Amendment and the decisions of the Supreme Court make it clear that the prohibition against cruel and unusual punishment was designed to protect those convicted of crime. There is no need to wrench the Eighth Amendment from its historical context and extend it to public school disciplinary practices. The openness of the public school and its supervision by the community affords significant safeguards against the kinds of abuses from which that amendment protects convicted criminals. These safeguards are reinforced by the legal constraints of the common law, whereby any punishment going beyond that which is reasonably necessary for the proper education and discipline of the child may result in both civil and criminal liability.[94]

Query whether in the Canadian context, the omission of any reference to "excessive bail" and "excessive fines" as included in the American provision, and the inclusion of the word "treatment" connected by the disjunctive "or" to "punishment", might widen the traditional criminal law application.

---

[93]*Ingraham et al. v. Wright et al.* (1977), 430 U.S. 651 (U.S.S.C.).
[94]*Ibid.*

Censorship   In addition to the state's authority under the *Criminal Code* to censor that which "tends to corrupt morals", the school board/principal and the Ministry possess their own authority within the school world to censor what the student may read or learn about, who the student may listen to and how the student may express himself. The board's and principal's authority to make policies as to student activities and deportment on the basis of maintaining order under ss. 149, para. 10 and 150(1), para. 34 (board) and 236(a) (principal) has already been discussed above under "Exclusion: Suspension". Recent decisions by local boards to remove certain books from their school libraries focuses on the more classic form of censorship.[95] In this connection, under s. 236(h), the principal of a school must ensure that all textbooks used by pupils are those which have been approved by the board, and in the case of subject areas for which the Minister approves textbooks, those which have been approved by the Minister. Section 8(1)(b), (d), (e) and (f) give the Minister the power to prescribe the courses of study, to establish procedures by which and the conditions under which books and other learning materials are selected and approved by the Minister, to purchase and distribute textbooks and other learning materials for use in schools and to select and approve for the use in the schools textbooks, library books, reference books and other learning materials. Finally, s. 26 of O. Reg. 262/80 prohibits any advertisement or announcement from being placed on school property or distributed or announced to pupils on school property without the consent of the board, except announcements of school activities. The power of the board under this regulation is presumably derived from s. 149, para. 10 which obligates the board to ensure that its schools are conducted in accordance with the Act and the Regulations. Furthermore, the principal is under a legal duty pursuant to s. 236(m) to refuse to admit any person to the school or classroom whose presence in the school would, in his judgment, be detrimental to the physical or mental well-being of the pupils, this decision being subject to an appeal to the board.

There is little Canadian case law in this area, although the advent of the *Charter* may engender some challenges. One case contained the issues but was dealt with on the basis of trespass. Some university students returned to their old high school to inform the present students about the inadequacies of the education system and in so doing, distributed literature and talked to the students in the halls. The case was decided against the the students based on the law of trespass and therefore the right of the administration to ban the distribution of literature did not arise.[96] In terms of censorship and freedom of expression, a recent Alberta case is worth noting. A child was suspended for wearing bluejeans and a T-shirt. The court dismissed the application, showing its deference to the school authorities when stating: "It would be just as senseless to create a school system without the power of disciplining the students as it would be to build a school house without doors through which to enter it."[97]

---

[95] See MacKay, A.E., "School Censorship and Free Expression: Old Issues in a New Context" (1983), 2 *Can. School Exec.* (No. 7).

[96] *R. v. Burko* (1968), 3 D.L.R. (3d) 330 (Ont. M.C.).

[97] *Choukalos v. Board of Trustees of St. Albert Protestant School,* unreported decision cited in (1981), 1 *Can. School Exec.* (No. 2), at p. 10 as discussed in MacKay, *supra*, note 72, at p. 302).

The blanket delegation of power to the school authorities bears up none too well under the scrutiny of various social commentators as well as of the United States Supreme Court, the latter noting that ''The nation's future depends upon leaders trained through wide exposure to that robust exchange of ideas which discovers 'truth out of a multitude of tongues' than through any kind of authoritative selection.''[98] MacKay summarizes the principles gleaned from United States decisions on student publications as follows:

> The U.S. response to free-speech issues involving student publications has been mixed.[99] While judges in the United States have been reluctant to uphold general bans on publication, restrictions on time, place and manner of publication have been accepted.[100] There must be clear and objective rules by which material can be judged; broad and excessively vague rules have been invalidated in the U.S.[101] Once again, the burden is on school officials to show likely disruption. The fact that materials relate to sensitive topics, such as sex, is not enough.[102] There is a general presumption against prior restraint except in extreme cases.[103]

With respect to book banning specifically, American courts have dealt with the issue and MacKay summarizes the effect by noting that the court will be more likely to uphold censorship of reading material if there is a clear and reliable due process for their removal. In one case,[104] the U.S. Supreme Court considered a board's decision to remove books which the board described as ''anti-American, anti-Christian, anti-Semitic, and just plain filthy''. The court decided that the removal of the books violated the students' First Amendment rights finding that it is not sufficient for a local school board to remove books ''simply because they dislike the ideas contained in those books and seek by their removal to prescribe what shall be orthodox in politics, nationalism, religion or other matters of opinion.''[105] In deciding the case, the court also concluded that the right to receive ideas is a ''necessary predicate to the recipient's meaningful exercise of his own rights of speech, press and political freedom,'' a principle that could have profound implications with respect to the issue of censorship in schools. Our own courts have also held that freedom of expression extends to the recipients as well as to the originators of the communication.[106]

---

[98]*Keyishian v. Board of Regents* (1967), 385 U.S. 589, at 603, quoting *United States v. Associated Press* (1943), 52 F. Supp. 362, at 372 (S.D.N.Y.).

[99]J.L. Huffman and D.M. Trough, ''High School Students' Publication Rights and Prior Restraint'' (1981), 10 *J. of Law and Education* (No. 4) 485, as cited by MacKay, *supra*, note 72, at p. 315*n*.

[100]*Riseman v. School Community* (1971), 439 F. 2d 148 (1st Cir.), as cited by MacKay, *ibid.*

[101]*Nitzberg v. Parks* (1975), 525 F. 2d 378 (4th Cir.). A more precise rule about disruption was upheld in *Eisner v. Stanford Board of Education* (1971), 440 F. 2d 803 (2nd Cir.), as noted by MacKay, *ibid.*

[102]*Bayer v. Kimzler* (1974), 343 F. Supp. 1164 (E.D.N.Y.) and *Gambino v. Fairfax School Board* (1977), 564 F. 2d 147 (4th Cir.), as cited by MacKay, *ibid.*

[103]MacKay, *Education Law in Canada* (Toronto: Edmond-Montgomery Publications Ltd., 1984), at p. 304.

[104]*The Board of Education, Island Trees, etc. v. Pico* (1982), 102 S.C. 2799, at 2808.

[105]*Ibid.*, at 2810.

[106]*Re Ontario Film and Video Appreciation Society and Ontario Board of Censors* (1984), 45 O.R. (2d) 80, 5 D.L.R. (4th) 766 affg. (1984), 41 O.R. (2d) 583, 147 D.L.R. (3d) 58 (C.A.).

Finally, with respect to student expression, the U.S. Supreme Court held in the case of *Tinker v. Des Moines Independent Community School District*[107] that a school board could not prohibit students from wearing black arm bands to protest the Vietnam war since it interfered with their freedom of speech. Note that one Alberta Queen's Bench *Charter* case[108] defined "freedom of expression" as "the right to express orally, in writing or in whatever manner. . . thoughts, beliefs and opinions" a definition which could easily include a manner of dressing to protest a war. In the *Tinker* case, the equivalent "reasonable limit" test was whether the restriction was implemented to prevent the activity from interfering with school discipline.

Privacy

Lockers

The issue of privacy for a pupil usually arises with respect to his locker which, in fact, belongs to the school board while the pupil, in effect, has a licence to use it. In terms of authority over its use, see s. 12(2)(g) of O. Reg. 262/80 which directs the principal to instruct the pupils in the care of school premises and s. 236(j) of the Act which requires that the principal give "assiduous attention" to the care and to the condition and appearance of the school buildings. These sections, read in conjunction with s. 236(a) of the Act which obligates the principal to maintain proper order and discipline in the school, would appear to give the principal some degree of discretion in deciding to search a student's locker, particularly in an emergency situation, or alternatively to request that a student open his locker in order that it may be checked. A school official or principal is not a police officer and therefore presumably may not exercise the right to search a pupil's person or property on the grounds of reasonable criminal suspicion as may the police officer under such Acts as s. 10 of the *Narcotics Control Act*, and s. 37 of the *Food and Drug Administration Act*. On the other hand, MacKay notes a series of American decisions which affirm the right of a principal or school official to search lockers if the search is reasonable.[109]

If the student refuses to allow his locker to be searched, he might be found to be showing "persistent opposition to authority" and be subject to suspension proceedings. At best, a pupil who is concerned about the privacy of his personal property within the school locker should check with the board in advance of leaving it there. Some boards have policies which prevent a principal from opening a student's locker unless there is an emergency or unless he has the consent of the pupil or his parents. Some boards will require the school principal to ensure that the pupil has the opportunity to nominate a teacher as a witness if a locker is to be opened on a day when it is known that the pupil will be absent. It remains to be seen whether and/or how s. 8 of the *Charter* (protection against unreasonable search and seizure) will apply to these circumstances. The first question to decide would be whether the principal's action constitutes a "state action" caught by the *Charter* and only then can one determine whether it is

---

[107]*Tinker v. Des Moines Independent Community School District* (1969), 393 U.S. 503 (U.S.S.C.).

[108]*Re Edmonton Journal and A.-G. for Alberta et al.* (1983), 42 A.R. 383, 4 C.C.C. (3d) 59 (Q.B.).

[109]MacKay, *supra,* note 103, at 221 and 234*n*, citing *State v. Stein* (1969), 456 P. 2d 1 (Kan. S.C.); *People v. Overton* (1969), 283 N.Y.S. 2d (C.A.) and E.J. Younger, *Law in the School* (Montclair, N.J.: Patterson-Smith Publishing Company, 1973), at p. 47.

reasonable. One commentator suggests[110] that it extends to security checks on airlines and customs inspections, the former being done presumably by airport personnel. Accordingly, an employee of a public body such as a school board which obtains its authority and funding from the government is also arguably caught by the section.

Records

A "pupil record" means a record concerning a pupil that is established and maintained by a principal of a school in accordance with the Regulations: O. Reg. 271/80, s. 1(1)(d). Such a record is to consist of a record folder, achievement forms on the pupil, documents, photographs and information in writing inserted in the record folder with the approval of the principal, an index card and, if the pupil is enrolled in a program of instruction in French as a second language, a record of French instruction completed in accordance with the Regulation: s. 2, O. Reg. 271/80.

Other sections of the Regulation and prescribed forms thereunder dictate in detail when and what kind of information is to be included in the record. For example, information regarding special health problems of the pupil that in the opinion of the principal are likely to interfere with the pupil's achievement are to be included in Part E of the record folder and the parents (as well as the adult student) are to be consulted before the inclusion of such information: s. 14, O. Reg. 271/80. Part H of the folder may be used to record among other things the referrals of the pupil to any services or agencies, any talent or special ability of the pupil or any other information which, in the opinion of the principal, would be beneficial to teachers in the instruction of the pupil: s. 17, O. Reg. 271/80. Part K may include information as to the destination of the pupil, either in employment or further education upon his "retiring" from school: s. 20, O. Reg. 271/80. The record folder is kept by the school or by the board for 70 years after the student "retires" from the school: s. 34(1), O. Reg. 271/80. The information and materials stored in the record folder are to be destroyed after 90 days of the student "retiring" from school, if not requested by the pupil or his parent: s. 32, O. Reg. 271/80.

Under s. 24 of the Regulation the achievement form, a copy of which is sent to the parents, will include among other items,

> s. 24(a) . . .a concise statement of the program of study undertaken by the pupil sufficient to enable a teacher to understand the objectives, content and degree of difficulty of the courses included in the program of study; and
>
> (b) . . .a detailed statement provided by an anecdotal description of each program of study undertaken by the pupil, a percentage mark, a letter grade or any other means that indicates the level of achievement of the pupil in such program of study: s. 24, O. Reg. 271/80.

The achievement form is retained for three years after the pupil "retires" from school: s. 33, O. Reg. 271/80.

The index card contains extensive information on the child's vital statistics, including evidence of any adoption or marriage as proof that a child may have

---

[110]Francois Chevrette, "Protection Upon Arrest or Detention Against Retroactive Penal Law", in *Canadian Charter of Rights and Freedoms: Commentary, supra,* note 89, at p. 294.

had his name changed: s. 8(3), O. Reg. 271/80. The index card will remain stored at the school from which the pupil transfers or retires or at a central records office established by the board for a period of 70 years from the date upon which the pupil transfers to another school or to a private school or retires, as the case may be: s. 6(3), O. Reg. 271/80.

Finally, s. 30 of O. Reg. 271/80 permits the principal to delete information from the record if it "is not conducive to the improvement of instruction of the pupil" and either give it to the pupil or parent or destroy it. In addition, this section outlines a certain class of information which the principal may delete on the same basis and may go so far as to destroy the record and then re-create it without the offending information so no indication will be left that the information ever existed: s. 30(1). This class of information is as follows:

1) a pupil has been admitted to or committed to an institution for treatment of alcoholism, drug addiction or a mental disorder;

2) a pupil has been sent to a training school or sentenced to a penal or correctional institution; or

3) a pupil has been convicted of a provincial or *Criminal Code* offence or an offence under any other jurisdiction.

When a pupil transfers to another school, the record is usually automatically transferred unless the receiving school is a private school, in which case the latter must provide written assurance that it will maintain, transfer and dispose of the pupil record according to the Act and the Regulation: s. 29(3), O. Reg. 271/80. If the private school is unauthorized, the principal can only send the pupil's record when he has the consent of the parent or adult pupil: s. 29(4), O. Reg. 271/80. If the receiving school is out of province and the record is needed for enrollment, a copy and not the original of the record will either be sent to the school with parental or adult pupil approval or will be given to the parent or adult pupil: s. 29(5), O. Reg. 271/80.

When the pupil "retires" from school, the adult pupil or otherwise the parent is entitled to request a true copy of the record folder (exclusive of the achievement forms) as well as the information and material stored therein. (A pupil "retires" from school when he withdraws from a school other than for a temporary period with the consent of the principal or transfers to another school: s. 1(2), O. Reg. 271/80.) At any other time, the parent or adult pupil has the right to examine the entire record although some schools require that a school official must sit with the parent or adult pupil while doing so: s. 237(3) of the Act. Otherwise, the record is to remain privileged for the use of supervisory officers, the principal and teachers of the school (not restricted to the student's own teachers) "for the improvement of instruction of the pupil": s. 237(2). In addition, the information is not admissible in any trial or administrative proceeding or generally available for inspection without the parents or adult pupil's permission: s. 237(2).[111] Provision is made for the parent or adult pupil to

---

[111]See *Re C.A.S. of Belleville and M.* (1980), 28 O.R. (2d) 795 (Prov. Ct.) wherein the court held that the CAS having temporary custody of children was the "guardian" under the *Education Act* for the purpose of consenting to release of school records.

dispute the accuracy of information on the record or whether its inclusion is "conducive to the improvement of instruction of the pupil" with the principal and, if not satisfied, to appeal to a supervisory officer and then to a tribunal with a mandatory hearing: s. 237(4), (5). Note also the following sub-sections:

s. 237(7) Nothing in this section prevents the compilation and delivery of such information as may be required by the Minister or by the board.

(8) No action shall be brought against any person in respect of the content of a record.

(9) Except where the record has been introduced in evidence as provided in this section, no person shall be required in any trial or other proceeding to give evidence in respect of the content of a record.

(10) Except as permitted under this section, every person shall preserve secrecy in respect of the content of a record that comes to his knowledge in the course of his duties or employment, and no such person shall communicate any such knowledge to any other person except,

(a) as may be required in the performance of his duty; or

(b) with the written consent of the parent or guardian of the pupil where the pupil is a minor; or

(c) with the written consent of the pupil where the pupil is an adult.

. . .

(13) Nothing in this section prevents the use of a record in respect of a pupil by the principal of the school attended by the pupil or the board that operates the school for the purposes of a disciplinary proceeding instituted by the principal in respect of conduct for which the pupil is responsible to the principal.

The extent to which these records are truly privileged has been the subject of a few court cases.[112] Student records have been found to be relevant and admissible under the *Canada Evidence Act* in juvenile delinquency proceedings and the federal criminal legislation was held to prevail over the provincial education statute.[113] There have been cases in the United States where damages have been assessed against school officials for divulging confidential information[114] although as noted by Professor MacKay, while the constitutional right of privacy has been found to apply to records by the United States courts, "educational institutions [in the United States] have escaped its reach".[115] If privacy rights are found to extend to students' records in Canada, Ontario's provisions may fair well as to the due process involved in keeping the records except for the fact that the student himself has no right to see or challenge the record if under 18.

Psychological Testing

Related to the question of privacy of school records is the increasing controversy about psychological or other professional testing of students, especially as it relates to classification and streaming. Section 12(2)(s) of O.

[112]For a review of Canadian law, see Edward H. Humphreys *Privacy in Jeopardy: Student Records in Canada* (Toronto: O.I.S.E. Press, 1980), as cited in MacKay, *supra*, note 103 at p. 316n.

[113]*R. v. B.* (1979), 2 Fam. L.R. 213 (Ont. Prov. Ct.).

[114]*Blair v. Union Free School* (1971), 324 N.Y.S. 2d 222 (Dist. Ct.).

[115]MacKay, *supra*, note 1 at 308, citing B. McLaughlin, "Educational Records and the Right to Privacy" (1981), 15 *U.B.C. L. Rev.* 175, at 176.

Reg. 262/80 stipulates that a principal must obtain written permission from the parent or the adult pupil before any psychological examination or test is administered to the pupil. Registered professional psychologists are bound by their own code of ethics including a confidentiality requirement between a client and the psychologist as well as the practice of not releasing the testing results directly to the client.[116] The problem then arises as to who the client is: the school board who employs the psychologist or the pupil and his parents? Can one assume that the pre-requisite parental consent also applies to the release of test results to anyone other than the parent, or does the school ensure that that aspect was included in the original consent to avoid any future problems? The difficulties may be compounded by the number of parties involved — the student, the school, the parents and the professional — and the conflict of interests which can arise between or among any of them. At best, the parent should be aware that psychological testing is not objective but requires subjective interpretation by the psychologist and, in fact, much of the purported standardized or objective testing has been found to be biased in favour of the average, middle class, white student.[117] If psychological testing becomes necessary for the student's educational advancement, it is suggested that the parent and school board agree on the selection of a psychologist and the psychologist not be associated with nor employed by the board.

Board Meetings

A final privacy issue, albeit from a reversed perspective, is the parents' and students' access to board meetings and their records. Section 183(1) of the *Education Act* directs that any meeting of a board or committee of the board must be open to the public unless the board decides that it shall not be. If it is open, no person is to be excluded from the meeting with the exception of those exhibiting improper conduct. As well, s. 183(3) provides that any person (which presumably includes the student) may at all reasonable hours inspect and obtain copies of the board's Minute Book, its audited annual financial report and the current accounts of a board. A 1964 Ontario Court of Appeal decision dealt with the nature of the "privacy" of the board meetings.[118] A radio reporter was excluded from the meeting when he attended to tape-record its proceedings. The radio station was unsuccessful in its legal challenge, the court deciding that the board had an inherent power to control its own proceedings and that power enabled the board to determine that a tape recorder would undermine the protocol of the meeting. The decision appeared once more to reflect the court's traditional

---

[116]See *e.g.* Standards of the ruling body of the Ontario Psychological Association, the Ontario Board of Examiners in Psychology, which do not absolutely prohibit release of information to the client but which require a psychologist to ensure proper use and interpretation of their findings and, in exercising their professional judgment, a psychologist may decide that releasing data to a client is not in the client's best interests.

[117]See *e.g. Hobson v. Hansen* (1967), 269 F. Supp. 401. See also David Kirp, "Student Classification, Public Policy and the Courts", *The Rights of Children* (Cambridge: Harvard Educational Review, Reprint Series No. 9, 1974), at pp. 279–327; Merle McClung, "School Classification: Some Legal Approaches to Labels" in (1973), 14 *Inequality in Education.*

[118]*Radio Chum 1050 Ltd. v. Toronto Board of Education*, [1964] 2 O.R. 207, 44 D.L.R. (2d) 671 (Ont. C.A.).

Religious Freedoms

reluctancy to interfere with educational authorities in their seemingly separate and unique world.

This subject area has been touched upon earlier in discussing the denominational separate schooling system. This section will deal with religious freedoms within a particular school. Each school day in a public school is to be opened or closed with religious exercises consisting of the reading of Scriptures "or other suitable readings" and the repeating of the Lord's prayer "or other suitable prayers", the selection of which shall be by the school board or, in its absence, the principal: s. 28 O. Reg. 262/80. In addition to this, s. 28(6) of the Regulation stipulates that religious instruction is to be given by the teacher and issues of a "controversial or sectarian nature be avoided". Note however that s. 28(15) of the Regulation allows a board to apply to the Minister for its school to be exempted from giving religious instruction. A board does have the option to designate clergy of any denomination or more than one denomination or a lay person selected by the clergy to give religious instruction instead of a teacher: s. 28(7) and (8), O. Reg. 262/80. Note also that no religious emblem of a denominational nature may be exhibited in a secondary school during school hours except during the time alloted by the principal to religious instruction: s. 29(11), O. Reg. 262/80. On the other hand, every teacher is under a duty "to inculcate by precept and example respect for religion and the principles of Judaeo-Christian morality": s. 235(1)(c) of the Act.

The exempting provision is s. 28(10) of O. Reg. 262/80 which provides that no pupil in a public school is "required to take part in any religious exercise or be subject to any instruction in religious education" if his parent or he, as an adult pupil, applies for exemption. The pupil, through the direction of his parent, may choose to leave or stay in the classroom during the religious instruction or exercise: s. 28(11), (12), and (13), O. Reg. 262/80. Finally, s. 50 of the Act provides that subject to these regulations, a pupil shall be allowed to receive such religious instruction as his parent or as he, as an adult pupil desires, and no pupil in a public school shall be required to read or study a religious book or to join in an exercise of devotion or religion objected to by his parent or by him as an adult pupil. Note, however, that a Quebec Court of Appeal allowed exemption from religious instruction even in a Catholic separate school, prohibiting the board from making a child's attendance conditional on participation in religious exercises, where no alternative schooling was available.[119] The court confirmed the authority of the parent, in this case a Jehovah's Witness, to guide and govern the education of his child, his "natural" right to freedom of religion prevailing over provincial education legislation.

Unlike religious instruction, there is no provision for a pupil's exemption from traditional patriotic exercises, such as the daily singing of the national anthem in some schools. In fact, s. 235(1)(c) of the Act states that it is the duty of every teacher to "inculcate by precept and example. . . the highest regard for truth, justice, loyalty, *love of country*, humanity, benevolence, sobriety, industry, frugality, purity, temperance and all other virtues" [emphasis added]. In a 1945 Ontario case, the court held that "patriotic exercises" may have a

---

[119]*Chabot v. Les Commissaires d'Ecoles de LaMorandière*, [1957] Que. Q B 707.

religious significance and consequently fall within the provisions for religious instruction exemption.[120]

With the advent of the *Charter*, the fundamental freedom of conscience and religion has taken on the same entrenched status as that of s. 91(3) of the *B.N.A. Act* (preservation of certain denominational education rights). In the United States, on the other hand, the entrenched concept also includes a separation of church and state so that the U.S. Supreme Court has prohibited any religious activity at all in the schools, including the reading of Bible scripture and the recital of voluntary and non-denominational prayers in the classroom.[121] In a pre-*Charter* Canadian case, a Catholic parent in Alberta who wished to send his child to a public school rather than a separate Catholic school was asked to pay a special levy to the public board of education or sign a document indicating that he did not practice Catholicism. His action against the school board based on religious discrimination succeeded at trial but was reversed by the Appellate Court which found that any claim for discrimination had to be construed within the context of the Constitution which implicitly provided for a discriminatory denominational school structure.[122] Query whether s. 2 of the *Charter* coupled with s. 15 (equal benefit under the law) would combine to change the results of this decision or whether s. 29 of the *Charter* (preserving the rights under the B.N.A. *Act*) would elicit the same decision today.

Another issue is the potential conflicting religious freedom rights of the student versus the parent. Under present legislation and common law[123] it is the parent who has the right to decide whether or not the student under 18 receives religious instruction. In a major U.S. Supreme Court case, Mennonite parents wished to withdraw their children from the secondary school system on religious grounds. While the majority affirmed the parents' right to do so, the late Mr. Justice Douglas registered a dissent based on the interests and wishes of the child. He stated that when a child is mature enough to express what may be a conflicting desire, the court should not act without first being apprised of the child's views.[124]

---

[120]*Donald v. Hamilton Board of Education*, [1945] O.R. 518, [1945] 3 D.L.R. 425 (C.A.). And see *West Virginia Board of Education v. Barnette* (1943), 319 U.S. 624; *New York v. Sandstrom* (1939), 279 N.Y. 523.

[121]*Engle v. Vitale* (1962), 370 U.S. 420.

[122]*Schmidt v. Calgary Board of Education*, [1975] 6 W.W.R. 279 (Alta. S.C.); revd [1976] 6 W.W.R. 717 (Alta. C.A.) without comment as to whether human rights legislation applies to schools as facilities customarily available to the public.

[123]See *Chabot v. Les Commissaires d'Ecoles de LaMorandière, supra,* note 118 and *Re Maestrello* (1975), 20 R.F.L. 285 (Ont. S.C.).

[124]*Wisconsin v. Yonder* (1972), 406 U.S. 205 (U.S.S.C.), at p. 241 where Douglas J. observes:

> The court's analysis assumes that the only interest at stake in the case are those of the Amish parents on the one hand and those of the state on the other. The difficulty with this approach is that, despite the court's claim, the parents are seeking to vindicate not only their free exercise claims, but also those of their high school children. . . .
>
> Religion is an individual experience. It is not necessary, nor even appropriate, for every Amish child to express his views on the subject in the prosecution of a single adult. Crucial, however, are the views of the child whose parent is the subject of the suit. . . .
>
> On this important and vital matter of education, I think the children should be entitled to be heard. While the parents, absent dissent, normally speak for the entire family, the education of the child

Peaceful Assembly and Association

Section 2 of the *Charter* guarantees the freedom of peaceful assembly and association. As noted above under "Censorship", the courts have held that a board and/or principal is entitled to decide who may enter upon school premises for what purposes without examining in any way the elementary issue of whether the learning process at the school would be disruptive. In the above-noted case, former students had returned in an attempt to inform present students of some of the failings of the education system. The pre-*Charter* court dismissed the former student reliance on the right to freedom of assembly, concluding that the dissemination of information or ideas without the permission of the proper authorities might be contrary to the public good, particularly if those ideas are not in accordance with the curriculum established by the state.[125] Professor MacKay advises of a 1971 memorandum in a similar vein from the New Brunswick Minister of Education to school boards and principals in the province, written apparently with legal advice from the Federal Minister of Justice, stating that any board could ban political clubs in the schools even if they were meeting outside regular classroom hours. Professor MacKay goes on to note that no court challenge to this memorandum was made at the time but that the enactment of the *Charter* would certainly make such action more likely.[126] A useful basis for construing the s. 1 "reasonable limits" test might be the American approach based on a "substantial disruption" test, considering the facts of each case.[127]

Equality Rights

Section 15 of the *Charter of Rights* may prove to be the most important vehicle for pursuing the educational rights of the child in Canada. (For a discussion of children's rights generally, see Chapter 1 "Introduction: Children's Rights".):

> s. 15(1) Every individual is equal before and under the law and has the right to the equal protection and equal benefit of the law without discrimination and, in particular, without discrimination based on race, national or ethnic origin, colour, religion, sex, age or mental or physical disability.

This part of the chapter will deal specifically with three of the categories of discrimination as they affect education: age, sex and mental or physical disability.

Age Discrimination

The age at which a child has a right, without payment of fee, to attend school raises several important issues which includes the rights and interests of children as well as their parents. It has become trite to say that the earlier the child begins to learn, or more precisely, to have his curiosity stimulated and satisfied, the better developed he will become both mentally and emotionally. Entire libraries of educational, psychological and sociological research developed over the past decades will provide the necessary objective data to lend

---

is a matter on which the child will often have decided views. He may want to be a pianist, or an astronaut or an oceanographer. To do so, he will have to break from the Amish tradition.

[125]See *R. v. Burko* (1968), 3 D.L.R. (3d) 330 (Ont. H.C.).

[126]MacKay, *supra*, note 103, at p. 306.

[127]See *Goldberg v. University of California* (1967), 248 Cal. App. 2d 867 (Dist. C.A.); *Gay Liberation v. University of Missouri* (1977), 558 F. 2d 848 (8th Cir.); *Healy v. James* (1971), 408 U.S. 169.

credence to the truism. Further, medical professionals, both practitioners and researchers, will readily attest to the benefits if not the necessity of detecting childhood maladies early from the simple physical problems of poor sight or hearing to more complex emotional and learning problems. Finally, the massive political issue of day care rights of parents overlaps with that of age-based school attendance rights.

In Ontario, the right to be accommodated at school without payment of fee exists for any person until the last school day in the year in which that person attains the age of 21 years, and from September 1st of the year in which the child attains:

1) six years; or
2) five years if the child resides in a board's jurisdiction which operates a kindergarten; or
3) four years if the same board operates a junior kindergarten; or
4) if the board also provides "beginner's classes", those children who turned five or six between January 1 and July 1 in anticipation of the following kindergarten or grade one year respectively: ss. 32 and 33.

Note that any attendance rights under six years are dependent on the board's totally discretionary decision making as to whether to allocate resources for kindergarten, junior kindergarten or beginner's classes.

Pursuant to s. 32(3) of the Act, the parent or guardian must "submit evidence that the child has a right to attend an elementary school, including proof of age." As will be discussed below under the discriminatory category of "mental or physical disability", it is possible for a child to be excluded prior to admission on the basis of a conclusion, based on pre-school diagnostic assessments, that the child will be "unable to profit by instruction".[128] This exclusion can be made in spite of the wording of s. 32(3) that suggests that no evidence other than age is required. A more equitable interpretation would have been that a child could only be excluded under s. 34 of the Act ("inability to profit from instruction") once admitted so that he could avail himself of all the appellate and resource rights of a pupil who, by definition, must be enrolled.

Provincial human rights legislation frequently includes age as a prohibited class but its applicability to education rights is weak. In the first place, provinces such as Ontario or Alberta define the age category to apply only with respect to the other end of the spectrum, that is, our senior citizens rather than our junior citizens. Secondly, for those provinces (and Parliament) who do not so define the age category, the question then becomes one of whether the protection applies to school boards. In a pre-*Charter* decision, a Manitoba court held that schools were not a "facility customarily available to the public" under Manitoba human rights legislation and therefore were not covered by the age-discrimination provisions of the legislation.[129] The *Charter*, on the other hand, applies to "all matters within the authority of the legislature" of each province which includes school boards and their policies: s. 32(1)(b), *Charter of Rights*.

---

[128] See *Maw et al. v. Scarborough Board of Education et al.* (1983), 43 O.R. (2d) 694 (Div. Ct.). But see Bette Stevenson's quote at p. 453.

[129] *Winnipeg School Division (No. 1) v. McArthur*, [1982] 3 W.W.R. 342 (Man. Q.B.).

Under s. 15 of the *Charter*, one might argue that the child and/or parent is being deprived of equal educational benefits of the law based on the age of the child and that the limitation is unreasonable under s. 1 both because six years is too late a starting date based on the educational objectives of publicly-funded legislation in light of all the recent research *and* that the limits are applied inconsistently and are not "prescribed by law."[130] While the former argument is unlikely to succeed given the obvious political/financial nature of the decision, the latter arguments may have more force in light of the unfettered discretion of a local board in deciding whether to provide classes earlier than age six, thereby triggering a right to accommodation for the child. Probably the most important criterion which goes into the decision is the availability of resources to that particular board which in turn will essentially depend on the wealth of the area. The difference in the quality of educational facilities between those of Northwestern Ontario and those of central Toronto is stark evidence of this factor.[131]

In a U.S. Supreme Court case,[132] this method of financing which led to inconsistent quality of education was challenged under the equal protection clause of the Fourteenth Amendment on the basis of economic discrimination. Although this particular court found that education was "not among the rights afforded explicit protection under the Federal Constitution"[133] it also found no economic discrimination in the context of a minimal scrutiny approach accorded the classifications based on income in the United States, thereby holding that the financing scheme need only "bear some rational relationship to legitimate state purpose". Although age discrimination is a specifically protected classification under our Canadian "equal protection" clause subject to the specifically defined scrutiny of s. 1 of the *Charter*, it remains to be seen how our courts will deal with income as an unenumerated classification.

Sex Discrimination

Discrimination on the basis of sex within the school system may arise from limiting specific courses to either girls or boys, such as shop and home economics, or to segregating or financing extra-curricular activities, especially sports. Again, the school board may be a facility which is outside the jurisdiction of human rights legislation while subject to the *Charter's* jurisdiction, as discussed above under age discrimination. Section 15 of the *Charter* not only distinguishes sex as a specific category but is fortified by the esoteric s. 28, if only by preventing any province from opting out of sexual equality rights under s. 33. Note however, that sex-based discrimination may not only be saved by a successful "reasonable limits" argument under s. 1, but also by an "affirmative

---

[130]See *Re Ontario Film and Video Appreciation Society and Ontario Board of Censors, supra,* note 106, which is cited for the proposition that "a limit that is prescribed by law" contemplates limitations prescribed by statute, regulation or the common law and must have legal force. A limitation simply left to administrative discretion cannot therefore be considered to be one prescribed by law.

[131]See *Annual Report 1983* of Ontario's Provincial auditor (Queen's Printer: Toronto) in which the disparity of resource distribution in Ontario evidences a disparity in availability and quality of educational resources for children across the province.

[132]*San Antonio Independent School District v. Rodriguez* (1973), 93 S. Ct. 1278 (U.S.S.C.).

[133]*Ibid.,* at p. 1297.

action'' argument under s. 15(2) in which the s. 15(1) prohibition against discrimination ''does not preclude any. . . program or activity that has as its object the amelioration of conditions of disadvantaged individuals or groups.'' ''Protectionism'' as an apologia is a complex issue known only too well to both natives and women in their equality struggles in Canada.

In an American case, a Minnesota school, like many Ontario schools, segregated boys from girls in their athletic teams and programs and prohibited any interchange. Two girls wanted to get involved in two activities, notably the non-contact sports of tennis and cross-country skiing, which were only offered to boys. The application to court succeeded, the court concluding that the denial of these activities to girls was discriminatory:

> Discrimination on the basis of sex can no longer be justified by reliance on out-dated images of women as particularly delicate and impressionable creatures in need of protection from the rough and tumble of unvarnished humanity.[134]

Mental or Physical Disability

Until the recent introduction of special education amendments to Ontario's *Education Act*, the rights which a child possessed to appropriate instruction to suit that particular child's needs and capabilities were very clearly limited. Generally every qualified pupil has the right to be enrolled in an elementary school, proceed through the school's primary and junior divisions, and then be eligible for admission into a secondary school where he will advance to the intermediate and senior divisions. If he is not promoted from elementary school, he may still be admitted into a secondary school if the principal of the secondary school is satisfied that the applicant is competent to undertake the school work: s. 1(1), paras. 38, 26, 24, 58. An appeal may be taken to the appropriate board from a principal's negative decision: s. 42(3). Furthermore, upon a child's admission into a secondary school, the principal has the power to prevent the pupil from undertaking a certain course of studies if he concludes that the pupil is not competent to do so. In this case, the pupil may take a prerequisite course presumably to gain the required competency, or he may select, with the approval of the principal, an appropriate alternative course: s. 42(4). Note that there is no appeal from this competency decision, a decision which may effectively determine the child's stream of studies and future employment possibilities.[135]

It is clear from this description that there is no obligation in these general provisions to ensure that the instruction is appropriate for the child and that the child does indeed learn and develop. It is as if the schools are grocery stores and if one has sufficient funds (read ''average'' capabilities), one can proceed along the aisles, picking up the goods and graduate through the check-out counter. What was clearly lacking from this ''average'' model was provisions for those children who do not reflect the average, especially those with mental or physical handicaps or who are extremely bright.

In recent years, there has developed a great deal of research evidence

---

[134]*Brenden v. Independent School District* (1973), 477 F. 2d 1202 (U.S.C.A. 8th Cir.), as discussed in MacKay.
[135]See *supra*, note 117.

illustrating the fact that a large percentage of children who were thought to be irretrievably "slow" or mildly retarded or possessing emotional problems were actually suffering from treatable "learning disabilities." These children might actually have an I.Q. equal to if not greater than the "average" or "typical" child, but because of a disability in one area of learning such as the inability to reduce thought processes into written form, they had been categorized as slow or retarded or possessing emotional or family difficulties. In fact, much of the behaviour problems, the withdrawal or the acting out, actually stemmed from not being able to learn and keep up with their peers.[136] It became clear that the public school system was ill-equipped both to identify the learning problems and to provide appropriate educational resources to remedy the problems.

Ontario's answer to "problem children" was to establish accommodation rights at segregated public schools for the blind and the deaf and segregated schools or classes for the "trainable retarded child": ss. 12 and 72. "Trainable retarded child" is defined under the Act as "an exceptional pupil whose intellectual functioning is below the level at which he could profit from a special education program for educable retarded pupils": s. 1(1), para. 68. Under s. 1(1), para. 21 an "exceptional pupil"

> means a pupil whose behavioural, communicational, intellectual, physical or multiple exceptionalities are such that he is considered to need placement in a special education program by a committee, established under subparagraph iii of paragraph 5 of subsection 10(1). . .

There is no definition for "educable retarded pupils" although in a September, 1981 Secondary School Report the Ontario Ministry of Education gives a detailed definition of the distinction between "educable" and "trainable":

> *Educable:* includes pupils who because of slow mental development are unable to profit from the demands of a regular class without considerable program change and supportive services, but who are considered to have potentialities for development at minimum levels at academic learning, for independent social adjustment, and for economic self support.

> *Trainable:* includes a person 21 years of age or under whose intellectual functioning is below the level at which he could profit from a special education program for educable retarded children.

Psychologists employed by the school board use I.Q. testing to winnow out the trainable retarded from the educable retarded and the retarded from the "average" child but it is only the "trainable retarded" who have special accommodation rights in a segregated stream.

Segregated schooling does not address the special education needs of all the children who do not fall within the strict definition of blind, deaf or "trainable retarded" but who are also not of "average" capabilities. They may possibly have received some remedial training or extra attention in some urban schools but

---

[136]See M. Kinsbourne, P. Caplan, *Children's Learning and Attention Problems* (Boston: Little, Brown & Co., 1979).

they have no rights in this respect and the funding for the appropriate special education resources simply has not been there. Unfortunately, many of the child's learning problems are classified by school authorities as stemming from emotional, behavioural, family, medical or psychiatric problems from which there is no solution within the school system. The child and his family is then referred out to child welfare or mental health authorities.

In addition, because these segregated schools and classes are earmarked for "problem" children and because they are out of the mainstream, many children, especially those whose learning difficulties disturb the educational process for others in regular classes, find their way into and languish in trainable retarded programs which are totally unsuited to their needs.

In addition to segregated schooling or hit and miss remedial help in the mainstream, the Legislature also provided school authorities with a "last resort" solution to the "problem children" and that was excluding the child from the system altogether with no accompanying duty to finance private educational resources. This could be accomplished through the expulsion provision, s. 22(3), for those students whose "conduct is so refractory that his presence is injurious to other pupils" since the frustration of being unable to learn and keep up with peers very often leads to "acting out" behaviour on the part of the student.[137] This exclusion provision is complemented by s. 20(2)(f) which relieves the board of the duty to compel the expelled student to attend. A more subtle form of exclusion comes in the form of the "Early School Leaving" provision under O. Reg. 261/80 pursuant to s. 10(7) of the Act. It allows a student who is 14 years or older to be excused from compulsory attendance if he conforms to a program, which is approved by a board committee, "directed towards the child's needs and interests" and which may simply amount to taking any job in the work force. There is no prerequisite "inability to profit from instruction" or "refractory conduct" to trigger the use of this section. Although it is couched in parental rights terms such that it is the parent who applies for the exemption and can reject the committee's program in favour of continued school attendance, it is another form of "last resort" for frustrated parents and teachers let alone the student himself. Finally, as mentioned earlier, young children who have been tested before entering school and found "unable to profit by instruction" have been excluded from enrollment in the first place.[138]

The parents of some of these children did manage to secure public funds for special education schooling and private schools by the "back door route" under vocational rehabilitation legislation. This was based on a judicial interpretation of "pre-vocational training" to include special education to raise a child's learning faculties, thereby making such education eligible for Ministry of

---

[137]See, *e.g. Bouchard v. Commissaires d'Ecoles de St. Mathiew de-Dixville,* [1949] Que. K.B. 30; affd [1950] S.C.R. 479 where the Supreme Court of Canada upheld the decision to expel a mentally retarded pupil whether or not his conduct was deliberate or involuntary since his disruptive presence was an "injustice to the other pupils in his class and to their distraught teacher."

[138]See *Maw et al. v. Scarborough Board of Education et al., supra,* note 128.

Community and Social Services funding.[139] The parents who pursued this route had steadfastly refused to accept the school board's categorization of trainable or educable retarded for which Ministry of Education resources were available and had also rejected non-education-focused diagnoses of family, psychiatric or emotional difficulties. The "back door" route diffused some of the dissatisfaction and frustration felt by a great many parents who knew their children needed the kind of education which the present system was not providing.

In December, 1980, the Ontario government proclaimed amendments to its *Education Act* which appeared, at first glance to be the most progressive and all-encompassing special education legislation in Canada. While retaining segregated streams for blind, deaf and "trainable retarded" students, the Minister of Education advised that the amendments were intended to ensure rights of appropriate education for every student in Ontario:

> This Bill does two things: First, the basis for universal access contained within this Bill guarantees the right of all children, condition notwithstanding, to be enrolled in the school. No longer will retarded children be enrolled after an assessment procedure established in law which has in fact denied universality of access. All children will now have a basic right to be enrolled. Second, school boards must assume responsibility for providing suitable programming for all children. This will include the provision of special education programs and special education services for its exceptional pupils in the language of instruction of such pupils.[140]

A starting point of the amendments is s. 8(2) of the Act:

> s. 8(2) The Minister shall ensure that all exceptional children in Ontario have available to them, in accordance with this Act and the Regulations, appropriate special education programs and special education services without payment of fees by parents or guardians resident in Ontario, and shall provide for the parents or guardians to appeal the appropriateness of the special education placement, and for these purposes the Minister shall,
>
> (a) require school boards to implement procedures for early and ongoing identification of the learning abilities and needs of pupils, and shall prescribe standards in accordance with which such procedures be implemented; and
>
> (b) in respect of special education programs and services, define exceptionalities of pupils, and prescribe classes, groups or categories of exceptional pupils, and require boards to employ such

---

[139]*Re Anderson and Director of Vocational Rehabilitation Services Branch* (1977), 15 O.R. (2d) 207 concerning the *Vocational Rehabilitation Services Act,* then R.S.O. 1970, c. 484 (now R.S.O. 1980, c. 525).

[140]Statement by the Honourable Bette Stephenson, M.D., Minister of Education, Minister of Colleges and Universities on the introduction of a Bill regarding the provision of special education: Hansard, May 23, 1980.

definitions or use such prescriptions as established under this clause.[141]

There are then four operative definitions:

1) s. 1(1), para. 21: "Exceptional pupil" means a pupil whose behavioural, communicational, intellectual, physical or multiple exceptionalities are such that he is considered to need placement in a special education program by a committee, established under s. 10(1), para. 5(iii) of the board,

(i)   of which he is a resident pupil,

(ii) that admits or enrolls the pupil other than pursuant to an agreement with another board for the provision of education, or

(iii) to which the cost of education in respect of the pupil is payable by the Minister.

2) Para 63: "special education program" means, in respect of an exceptional pupil, an educational program that is based on and modified by the results of continuous assessment and evaluation and that includes a plan containing specific objectives and an outline of educational services that meets the needs of the exceptional pupil;

3) Para 64: "Special education services" means facilities and resources, including support and personnel and equipment, necessary for developing and implementing a special education program;

4) s. 34(1)(b): "Hard to serve pupil" means a pupil who, under this section, is determined to be unable to profit by instruction offered by a board due to a mental handicap or a mental and one or more additional handicaps;

From these definitions it becomes apparent that the amendments have created two categories of "problem children": the "exceptional pupil" who is to receive special education services within the school system and under the board's authority, and the "hard to serve pupil" for whom the board cannot offer suitable special education services and who will be placed outside the school system at provincial expense. Given the spectre of high costs associated with the latter category, it is obvious that the Ministry will provide that the board make every effort to retain the child within the public system.

---

[141]Note that school boards do not have to comply with duties imposed by s. 8(2) of the Act until September 1, 1985. Section 149 of the Act reads as follows:

s. 149, para. 7 Every board shall, before the first day of September, 1985, provide or enter into an agreement with another board to provide in accordance with the regulations special education programs and special education services for its exceptional pupils in the English language or, where the pupil is enrolled in a school or class established under Part XI, the French language, as the case may be;

Prior to the September, 1985 deadline, each board must prepare a plan for their special education program. O. Reg. 274/80 states:

s. 3(1) Each board shall prepare and approve a plan in accordance with a planning guide provided by the Minister that will disclose the methods by which and the times within which the board shall comply with [s. 149] of the Act in relation to exceptional pupils of the board who are not trainable retarded pupils.

(2) A plan referred to in sub-section (1) shall be submitted to the Minister not later than the 1st day of May, 1982 for review by the Minister.

"Exceptional Pupil"

In order for any child to receive special education, he must first be referred to a "Special Education Identification Placement Review Committee" (hereinafter known as the "IPRC") established pursuant to O. Reg. 554/81 under the *Education Act* by the principal of the school which the child attends or is to attend. The IPRC is to consist of not fewer than three persons, all of whom are on the list of approved persons compiled by the school board and one of whom must be a supervisory officer or principal employed by the board: s. 3, O. Reg. 554/81. A member or trustee of the school board is not eligible to be appointed as a member of the IPRC. The IPRC has the mandate of identifying the nature of the child's learning problems and then designating the appropriate program offered by the board. If the parent disagrees either with the identification of the pupil as exceptional or the lack of identification of same, or with the designated placement of the pupil, he may appeal the IPRC's decision but upon launching an appeal, the parent is deemed to withhold his consent to the committee's placement, and accordingly, the board will not place the child in the program which it was prepared to make available: s. 6, O. Reg. 554/81. In other words, if the board and parent agree that a child is exceptional but disagree on the intensity of the program needed (for example, the board recommends five half days per week whereas the parent wants a full-time program), the child receives neither as long as the parents proceed with their appeal.

The appeal is heard by a new committee known as the Special Education Appeal Board which consists of three persons, none of whom may be a member, trustee, employee or former employee of the school board: s. 7(3), O. Reg. 554/81. One member must hold qualifications as a supervisory officer while another is appointed by the school board and the third member may be appointed by the parent of the pupil as long as he belongs to a "local association" defined as "an association or organization of parents that operates locally within the area. . . that is affiliated with an association or organization that is not an association or organization of professional educators but that is incorporated and operates throughout Ontario to further the interests and well-being of one or more groups of exceptional children or adults": s. 181(1)(c), *Education Act*. If there is no "local association", then a member of the local community can be nominated by the parent of the pupil. The regulation gives the parent no clear right to be represented by counsel but provides only that "any person who, in the opinion of the Appeal Board, may be able to contribute information with respect to the matters before the Appeal Board shall be invited to attend the discussion which shall be conducted in an informal manner": s. 7(8), O. Reg. 554/81. In fact, the Minister of Education has stated that "It wasn't the intention of the Act that it become a vehicle for a field day for lawyers. The Act is not designed to develop an adversary situation, which I don't believe will help the kids."[142]

The decision of the Special Education Appeal Board is not binding but simply takes the form of a report to the Board of Education who must either

---

[142]Dr. Bette Stephenson, Minister of Education as reported in the *Toronto Globe and Mail*, August 10th, 1981.

accept or reject it within 30 days: s. 7(10) and (11), O. Reg. 554/81. As a result, the *Statutory Powers Procedure Act* will not apply since the Appeal Board does not make the decision. If the board rejects the conclusions of the report, it must advise the parent of their right under s. 36(1) of the Act to apply to the secretary of a Special Education Tribunal — to be distinguished from the Special Education Appeal Board established under the Regulations — for a hearing for leave to appeal to a regional tribunal established by the Minister with respect to the issues of either identification or placement. If leave is granted, a "regional tribunal" is established by the Minister to hear the appeal: s. 36(2). On the other hand, if the parties agree, the Special Education Tribunal may hear and dispose of the appeal in lieu of granting leave to proceed to a regional tribunal: s. 36(3). The decision of the Special Educational Tribunal or regional tribunal is final and binding upon the parties (s. 36(5)) although this section does not preclude a Superior Court from reviewing the process for any unfair procedure or practice.[143] The regional or Special Education Tribunal may either dismiss or grant the appeal and make such order as it considers necessary with respect to the identification or placement of the pupil: s. 36(6).

Initially, there were some conflicting decisions as to whether the Special Education Tribunal has the power in deciding the issue of placement to determine the teaching strategies, methodology, teacher qualifications, program of studies or the philosophy of education of the program which the board is or will be offering. Ontario's Divisional Court[144] has apparently resolved the conflict, at least with respect to the phase-in period between 1980 and 1985, by ruling that they would not go behind the Minister's approval of the board's plans and programs. It also noted that the "notion of the 'appropriate' placement . . . found in s. 8(2) of the Act" is essentially watered down by s. 2 of O. Reg. 554/81 which does not use the word "appropriate." The wording also separates the functions of identifying the needs of the pupil and recommending a placement. The decision was specific in confirming that the latter function was to be based not only on the needs of the pupil but also on the availability of programs and services. Although it was also specific in noting that the decision would be *obiter* for placements after Sept. 1/85, which is the deadline for the boards to have all of their programs in place, it is probable that the courts will maintain the position that decisions about educational services requiring the expenditure of taxpayers' dollars is best left to the Ministry and boards. It remains to be seen whether the implementation of the *Charter* and especially s. 15 will affect this position in any way (see below for further discussion about constitutional rights and special educational needs).

---

[143]For discussion of effect of privative clause, see J.M. Evans, H.N. Janisch, D.J. Mullan, R.C.B. Risk, *Administrative Law* (Toronto: Edmond-Montgomery, 1980), at pp. 337–38.

[144]*Re Dolmage et al. and Muskoka Board of Education et al.* (1985), 49 O.R. (2d) 546 (Div. Ct.). This decision effectively overturns the position taken by a Central Ontario Special Education Tribunal in *Re Barger and the Board of Education for the City of North York,* unreported, June 27, 1984 (Ont. Div. Ct.) as well as disagreeing with an American court's approach in *Howard et al. v. Friendsward Independent School District* (1978), 454 Fed. Supp. 1142 (Dist. Ct., Texas).

''Hard to Serve Pupil''

Rather than utilizing special programming within the board's jurisdiction, a principal or parent may initiate a process under s. 34 of the Act to determine whether or not the child can come within the category of ''hard to serve'' and thereby be placed outside the public system at government expense: s. 34(17). To be categorized as ''hard to serve'', the student must be found to be ''unable to profit from instruction offered by a board due to a mental handicap or a mental and one or more additional handicaps.'' Upon notice to the board, it must appoint a committee consisting of three persons including a supervisory officer, a principal and a ''legally qualified medical practitioner who has expertise in respect of the mental or other handicap of the pupil'' to hold a hearing. Although the governing section does not direct that the committee hold a hearing *per se*, the committee must nonetheless inquire into (1) the alleged inability of the pupil to profit by instruction offered by the board and (2) the handicap(s) of the pupil, to arrive at a determination of whether or not the pupil is ''hard to serve'': s. 34(3). In so doing, the committee is obligated to study all existing reports in respect of the pupil, hear the teachers, the parent or guardian of the pupil, where reasonably possible the pupil, and any other person who may be able to contribute information bearing upon the matter and may, with the consent of the parent or guardian or adult pupil, obtain an assessment to be conducted by a person ''considered by the committee [not the parent] to be competent for the purpose.'' If the ''hard to serve'' committee decides that the pupil is indeed ''hard to serve'', the decision takes the form of a report to the board and the board may adopt or reject the conclusion: s. 34(7). If the committee decides that the child can profit from the board's instruction and determines that he only needs special education programming, the board *shall* refer the matter to an IPRC assessment, discussed above under ''Exceptional Pupil'': s. 34(8).

If the committee finds the pupil to be ''hard to serve'' and the board and parent agrees, the board is to assist the parent in locating a placement suited to the needs of the pupil and reimburse the parent for any expenses incurred in locating such placement: s. 34(9). The province must then pay the cost, if any, of the placement: s. 37(17). If the parent disagrees with the ''hard to serve'' finding of both committee and board, or with the proposed placement, within 15 days of notification from the school board or any time prior to placement, he may appeal through the principal to a Special Educational Tribunal: s. 34(10). That Tribunal must conduct a hearing under s. 34(12) reviewing the committee's report and all the documentation, and make one of the following findings:

1) the pupil is hard to serve;
2) the pupil needs special education within the board's system; or
3) the proposed placement for the ''hard to serve'' pupil is or is not suited to the pupil's needs.

If the finding falls under (2), there is no wording that specifically gives the Tribunal the authority to specify particulars of the special education program, nor do the provisions obligate the board, upon receiving the decision, to do anything more specific than ''provide a special education program/services'' for the pupil, although it must subsequently inform the Minister of the services that have been provided: s. 34(13).

If the Tribunal's findings fall under (1) or (3), the board must assist the parent to find a placement or new placement, as the case may be, "suited to the needs of the pupil": s. 34(14). Again, neither the wording of the section giving authority to the Tribunal nor the wording of the section determining the duty of the board on receipt of the Tribunal's finding allows for any particulars to be dictated by the Tribunal to the board.

If the finding of the Tribunal is set aside by a judicial review, the court may make no substantive decision, but simply direct that the board's original decision based on the "hard to serve" committee's report be appealed to yet another Special Educational Tribunal: s. 34(15).

Note that by the definition of "exceptional pupil" and "pupil", the child must be actually enrolled and attending a school within the board's jurisdiction in order to be entitled to the remedies with respect to exceptional pupils and "hard to serve" pupils.[145]

As a result of the introduction of these amendments to the *Education Act,* funding relief for private placements that was previously available under the *Vocational Rehabilitation Services Act* through the Ministry of Community and Social Services[146] will be eliminated as of September 1st, 1985 (with some possibility of a brief extension) to correspond with the date upon which the board (as opposed to the Minister) must assume all special education responsibilities as described under the *Education Act:* s. 149, para. 7. Until that time, funding is available only if a school board clearly indicates, in writing, that it does not have an appropriate program for the child, a letter which has seldom been forthcoming since the new provisions were enacted. The effect is an almost complete elimination of funding for children who previously received benefits under the vocational rehabilitation legislation as a result of learning disabilities that were not categorized as trainable retarded, blind or deaf. On the other hand, the practical effect of the amendments for the parent of a child with learning disabilities may arguably be regressive. The parent discovers that in order for his child to qualify for publicly-funded special education either inside or outside the board's system, the child must be attending the board's school even though the parent may have removed the child from that school because of the very fact that the board's conclusions about the child's needs were not, in the parents' opinion, helping the child. Once enrolling the child and participating in an IPRC review, if the parent disagrees with the assessment and/or appeals the assessment, then the child receives neither the proposed special education as offered by the school board nor the special education the child was receiving under vocational rehabilitation legislation before the enactment of the amendments. The child remains in a non-special education classroom until all of the appeal rights are exhausted which, to date, has a punitive effect due to the number of months which must elapse. If the parent, watching his child deteriorate daily, removes the child from the school in the course of the rather convoluted, complicated proceedings or at any time believing the child to be "hard to serve" then, as

---

[145]*Maw et al. v. Scarborough Board of Education, supra,* note 128.

noted above, the child will not be entitled to any of the appeal rights under the Act. The Kafkaesque effect on the parents and child of all the hearings, time limitations, notice requirements and non-binding, non-detailed appellate tribunal decisions have created extreme frustration and anxiety for those who have attempted to play the game. In addition to the procedural problems, a further and perhaps more significant failing is that of the lack of independence of decision makers and professionals who give evidence throughout the various processes. The decision makers are appointed by the school boards for the most part and those giving evidence as to the child's needs and capabilities and the appropriateness of special education programs are often the teachers and school psychologists employed by the board with no provision for the costs of an independent assessor on whom both the board and the parents agree and rely.

Given the tendency of courts to decline to go behind the decision making of educational authorities as illustrated throughout this chapter, it is not surprising that seeking judicial review of the special education processes is not very fruitful. There is also the civil liability route which has not been tested in Canada in which parents or groups of parents sue the school boards for negligence in classification resulting in the child losing out on an education. The essential issue would presumably be the extent of the duty of the professional and the school boards. In the United States at trial level, a mother was awarded $500,000 in damages because of an error in classification. On appeal, the award was rescinded and the board was found to be not liable. The court took the position that it would only intervene in education issues in extreme cases, asserting that the courtroom was not the appropriate forum to determine the appropriateness or adequacy of student placements.[147]

The *Charter*, on the other hand, may offer some concrete possibilities of seeking more accountability and fairness of process. (Its applicability to school boards is dealt with under "Equality rights: Age discrimination".) Section 15 ensures "equal benefit of the law without discrimination and, in particular, without discrimination based on . . . mental or physical disability." The operative hurdle is to convince a court to adopt the U.S. District Court's approach, that is, that the benefit intended by the *Education Act* is the opportunity to be educated rather than simply be accommodated. The statements to the press and the Legislature by the Minister of Education of the high flown intentions of the amendments may be of some use. Another fortification for this position is the statutory intention of s. 8(2) of the Act which requires that the Minister ensure that all exceptional children in Ontario have available to them appropriate special education programs and services without payment of fee albeit "in accordance with the Act and Regulations". Generally, there can be no justification for the state to require someone to attend an institution full-time for 10 years, backed up by employment legislation effectively preventing the person from working as an alternative, without some accountability from the state regarding the quality and appropriateness of that education for that particular

[146]See O. Reg. 943/81 pursuant to the *Vocational Rehabilitation Services Act.*
[147]*Hoffman v. Board of Education of New York* (1978), 410 N.Y.S. 2d 99 (App. Div.); revd (1979), 424 N.Y.S. 2d 376 (App. Div.).

person. There is no justification for a democratic state to force a person to sit at a desk and stare at a blackboard for 10 years, other than for the opportunity to learn, and learning is a function of individual needs. By the same token, if discrimination is established, the "reasonable limits" test under s. 1 of the *Charter* should not be interpreted so as to justify the state being exempted from providing this opportunity to learn because certain children, because of "mental or physical disability", learn through teaching techniques that are different from those required by the "average" child. "Equal benefit of the law" must mean more than "equality is equity"; the equality must be in the opportunity to learn and not in the method of teaching.

In the United States, the parents chose a constitutional rights route beginning with the landmark Supreme Court case of *Brown v. The Board of Education*[148] which was based on a challenge of racial discrimination within the education system. The court held that separate educational facilities for white and black children violated their constitutional guarantee of equal educational opportunity under the Fourteenth Amendment. The court was willing to go behind the discretion of the institutional decision maker and behind the defence of equal accommodation to the quality and purpose of education as it related to the special needs of one particular group.[149] A concept of equal educational opportunity in the United States was then extended to include discrimination on the basis of mental or physical handicap in *Mills v. Board of Education for the District of Columbia.*[150] In this case, a group of parents brought a class action seeking a declaration of their rights, an order enjoining the school board from excluding certain children and an order compelling the defendant board to provide all children with immediate and adequate education and educational facilities in the public schools or an alternative placement at public expense. The United States District Court for the District of Columbia held, both under legislation and the Constitution, that the failure of the Board of Education to provide publicly supported, specialized education for "exceptional" children could not be excused by the board's claim that there were insufficient funds. Although the court did not specifically direct that more funds be made available for special education, it did state that available funds "must be expended equitably in such a manner that no child is entirely excluded from a publicly supported education consistent with his needs and ability to benefit therefrom." This was based on the position that shortages of funds or "administrative inefficiencies" could not be a defence for a school system wherein the special needs child effectively has less opportunity to learn than the other children. The decision concluded with copious directions to the education authorities, some of which are as follows:

> 1. That no child eligible for a publicly supported education in the District of Columbia public schools shall be excluded from a regular public school assignment by a Rule, policy, or practice of the Board of Education of the District of Columbia or its agents unless such child is provided (a) adequate

---

[148]*Brown v. Board of Education* (1954), 347 U.S. 483 (U.S.S.C.).
[149]*Ibid.*, at pp. 493-94.

alternative educational services suited to the child's needs, which may include special education or tuition grants, and (b) a constitutionally adequate prior hearing and periodic review of the child's status, progress, and the adequacy of any educational alternative.

. . .

3. The District of Columbia shall provide to each child of school age a free and suitable publicly-supported education regardless of the degree of the child's mental, physical or emotional disability or impairment. Furthermore, defendants shall not exclude any child resident in the District of Columbia from such publicly-supported education on the basis of a claim of insufficient resources.

. . .

13. Hearing Procedures:

(a) Each member of the plaintiff class is to be provided with a publicly-supported educational program suited to his needs, within the context of a presumption that among the alternative programs of education, placement in a regular public school class with appropriate ancillary services is preferable to placement in a special school class.

(b) Before placing a member of the class in such a program, defendants shall notify his parent or guardian of the proposed educational placement, the reasons therefor, and the right to a hearing before a Hearing Officer if there is an objection to the placement proposed. Any such hearing shall be held in accordance with the provisions of Paragraph 13.c., below.[151]

The court also delineated extremely detailed procedural requirements for implementation including free independent diagnostic services for the parent, as well as various constitutional hearing procedures including full rights to cross-examine public school officials. The burden of proof of ''appropriateness'' was to be borne by the school board and, most importantly, the Tribunal was to consist of an independent hearing officer ''who shall be an employee of the District of Columbia, but shall not be an officer, employee or agent of the public school system''. In other words, the United States District Court recognized not only the inherent right of equal educational opportunity based on individual needs, but also recognized that the local board was an interested party and should therefore have an arms length relationship with the tribunal, as well as with the professional witness who presents the crucial evidence based on their assessments.

---

[150]*Peter Mills et al. v. Board of Education for the District of Columbia et al.* (1972), 348 F. Supp. 866 (U.S. D.C.).

[151]*Ibid.*, at pp. 878, 880.

Appendix: Provincial Education Acts

PROVINCE	COMPULSORY ATTENDANCE	REMEDIES	LEGAL EXCLUSION WHICH COULD POSSIBLY BE USED FOR WORK
Alberta	*The School Act*, R.S.A. 1980, c. S-3, s. 142(1): all children 6-15 years shall attend.	*Child* s. 157: apprehension: institute legal proceedings against pupil. ss. 171, 172: general penalty provision: fine $500; in default, imprisonment 90 days. *Parent/Third Party* s. 157(c): institute legal proceedings against anyone assisting pupil. ss. 171, 172, 181: fine/imprisonment as above; alternative $1,000 Bond. s. 180: strict liability fines on parent: $100/first offence, $250/second; $500/third; in default of payment imprisonment 60 days.	s. 143(1)(d): non-special exclusionary clause with board/principal agreement in consultation with parents. s. 143(1)(f): no suitable program offered for 15 year old. s. 170: work experience program.
British Columbia	*The School Act*, R.S.B.C. 1979, c. 375, s. 113(1): over 7 years and under 15 years.	*Child* s. 116: The board shall enforce compulsory attendance provisions. *Parent* s. 113: Parent who fails or neglects to cause child to attend commits an offence with $10 fine per offence.	s. 113(2)(d): no school available to go further in education constitutes a defence to compulsory attendance.
Manitoba	*The Public Schools Act* S.M. 1980, c. 33, s. 258(1)(b): over 7 years and under 15 years.	*Child* s. 267: apprehension. s. 271: all prosecutions may be brought before provincial judge *Parent/Third party* ss. 260, 268: strict liability on parents; subject to summary	s. 78(4): mention of work education program off school premises.

PROVINCE	COMPULSORY ATTENDANCE	REMEDIES	LEGAL EXCLUSION WHICH COULD POSSIBLY BE USED FOR WORK
		conviction, fine $500 ''or such other penalty court deems proper s. 262: employer subject to summary conviction, fine $500.	
New Brunswick	*The School Act*, R.S.N.B. 1973, c. S-5, s. 59: from 7 to 15 years of age inclusive	*Child* s. 62: apprehension s. 66: can be charged with violation of the Act or placed with child welfare agency. *Parent/Third Party* s. 59(7): Parents who do not cause their child to attend, liable to conviction, fine $20 (first offence); $40 (second and subsequent); default of payment imprisonment or fine and imprisonment. s. 60: employer subject to conviction, fine $20; in default, imprisonment.	s. 59(3): non-specific exemption under Minister's certificate. s. 61: non-specific parental request with Ministerial compliance gives up to 6 weeks.
Newfoundland	*The School Attendance Act*, S.Nfld. 1970, c. 78, s. 3: 6 years and under 15 years	*Child* *Parents/Third Party* ss. 4, 5, 6: Duty on parent re enrollment and attendance; s. 13: Parent subject to summary conviction and daily fine of $25;	

PROVINCE	COMPULSORY ATTENDANCE	REMEDIES	LEGAL EXCLUSION WHICH COULD POSSIBLY BE USED FOR WORK
		s. 15: Anyone who by threat or otherwise prevents and interferes with the child's attendance is subject to summary conviction and liable to fine of $200 or imprisonment 30 days.	
Nova Scotia	*The Education Act* R.S.N.S. 1967, c. 81, s. 79, Regs. 91: 6 to 16 years	*Child* s. 99 of the *Act*: conviction and committal to reformatory. *Parent/Third Party* ss. 79, 80 of the *Act*: duty on parents s. 96 of the *Act*: failure to cause child's attendance, liability to offence and fine ($10/first; $20/second; $30/third+); imprisonment 30 days in default of payment; *not* liable if unable to induce child. s. 98 of the *Act*: employer liable to $20 fine; imprisonment 30 days in default of payment.	s. 94 of the **Regulation**: 12 years old and required temporarily by parents for necessary employment. s. 95 of the **Regulation**: 13 years old and if school Board satisfied that it is necessary for child's maintenance.
Ontario	*The Education Act* R.S.O. 1980, c. 129, s. 20: 6 to 16 years	*Child* s. 25: apprehension. s. 29(5): guilty of an offence and liable to penalties under *JDA* (see Chapter 7 herein); s. 30(1)	s. 10(7): early school leaving program for 14 years — 16 years.

PROVINCE	COMPULSORY ATTENDANCE	REMEDIES	LEGAL EXCLUSION WHICH COULD POSSIBLY BE USED FOR WORK
		Parent/Third Party s. 29: parent who neglects or refuses to cause child's attendance guilty of offence, fine $100 or bond of $200; s. 29(3)(4): employer guilty of an offence; fine $100.	
Prince Edward Island	*The School Act*, R.S.P.E.I. 1974, c. S-2, ss. 1(b) and 49; 8 to 15 years	*Child* ss. 34, 35: board ensures enforcement; may expel/suspend for cause. *Parent* s. 49(4)(5): parent shall cause child to attend; neglect or refusal to do so makes him guilty of an offence.	s. 49(3)(e): non-specific power to Minister to certify non-attendance.
Quebec	*The Education Act*, R.S.Q. 1977, c. I-14, s. 256: 6-15 years	*Child, Parent/Third Party* ss. 454, 458: general penalty for non-compliance; fine $5-$10 for each offence. *Parent/Third Party* s. 261: Parent shall see that child complies. s. 274, 5: after being notified and parent does not see that child attends, liable on summary proceeding to fine: $20 each offence or bond of $100. s. 260: employer liable to fine $20.	s. 258(3): remoteness from school s. 259: release by Board up to 6 weeks when required by parents for farm work, or urgent/necessary work at home or for maintenance of child.

PROVINCE	COMPULSORY ATTENDANCE	REMEDIES	LEGAL EXCLUSION WHICH COULD POSSIBLY BE USED FOR WORK
Saskatchewan	*The Education Act, 1978* (Supp.) c. E-01, ss. 2(g), 149(a), 2(ee); 7-15 years	*Child* ss. 153, 154, 157(2), 158: suspension/expulsion s. 161: apprehension s. 365, 6: general penalty for not performing, guilty of offence with fine $50; for contravening, fine $100. *Parent/Third Party* s. 155: Parent shall take all steps that are necessary to ensure attendance. s. 163(2): Anyone who prevents or interferes with attendance: guilty of offence, fine $100. s. 148: Employer guilty of offence; summary conviction, fine $100.	s. 156(f): Director/Superintendent decides that continued attendance not productive or detrimental to pupil or school. s. 156(g): engaged in work experience program.
Yukon	*School Ordinance* R.S.Y.T. 1974 (2d) c. 14, s. 29(1): 6 years, 8 months to 16 years.	*Child* s. 29(6): child habitually absent commits an offence. s. 39(1): Suspension for persistent truancy. *Parent* s. 29(3): parent who neglects or refuses to cause attendance, guilty of offence, summary conviction, fine $25 or bond; failure to comply with bond, summary conviction: fine $250 or imprisonment 30 days or both with each day's continuance as separate offence.	s. 29(2)(a): by reason of illness or other unavoidable cause. s. 29(e): authorized by Regulations. s. 29(h): reasonable parental request: temporary absence. s. 17(1)(d): Superintendent may, on parental application, allow 14-16 year olds to cease attendance where (i) no further progress, or (ii) best interests of child.

PROVINCE	COMPULSORY ATTENDANCE	REMEDIES	LEGAL EXCLUSION WHICH COULD POSSIBLY BE USED FOR WORK
Indian Act	*The Indian Act*, R.S.C. 1970, c. I-6; ss. 116 and 123: 7 to 15 years (Minister may require 6 year olds to attend). s. 116(2)(c) Minister may require attendance until student becomes 18 years.	*Child* s. 119(2)(6): apprehension. s. 120: expelled/suspended. *Parent* s. 119(3): if child does not attend 3 days after parents receive notice, parents guilty of an offence, fine $5 or imprisonment 10 days, or both.	s. 117(b): up to 6 weeks to assist in husbandry or urgent and necessary household duties. s. 117(d): insufficient accommodation.

NOTES:

1. The ages in the "Compulsory Attendance" column are inclusive.
2. All fines, bonds and periods of imprisonment are usually stated in the Statute as "no more than" or "not exceeding".
3. "Parent" in the "Remedies" column usually includes anyone having care and control of the child.
4. All references to Acts include its amendments up to present time.
5. Many of the Sections in the "Legal Exclusion" column are governed by detailed regulations.
6. "Apprehension" usually includes the right to enter anywhere (a warrant being needed only if it is a private dwelling house and he is refused entry), plus the right to take the child home or to school.

Chapter 8: Readings

Abramson, P. and Chaiton, H., "A Defence Lawyer's Guide to Truancy Prosecutions" (1978), 1 *Fam. L. Rev.* 258.

"Analysis of the Rowley Decision (equal educational opportunity for deaf children): *Hendrick Hudson Central School District Board of Education v. Rowley*" (October, 1982), 16 *Clearinghouse Rev.* 422.

Ashline, N.F., Pezzullo, T.R. and Norris, C.I. (eds.), *Education, Inequality and National Policy* (Lexington, Mass., 1976).

Balderson, J. and Kolmes, J., *Legal Issues in Canadian Education: Proceedings of the 1982 Canadian School Executive Conference* (Edmonton: Canadian School Executive, 1983).

Bargen, P.F., *The Legal Status of the Canadian Public School Pupil* (Toronto: MacMillan of Canada, 1961).

Berkeley, H., Gaffield, C. and West, W.G. (eds.), *Children's Rights: Legal and Educational Issues* (Toronto: Ontario Institute for Studies in Education, Symposium Series #9, 1978).

Brent, A.S., "The Right to Religious Education and the Constitutional Status of Denominational Schools" (1976), 40 *Sask. L. Rev.* 239.

Brooks, I.R., "Native Education in Canada and the U.S.: A Bibliography" (Calgary: Indian Students University Program, Office of Educational Development, University of Calgary, 1976).

Center for Law and Education, Inc., *Special Education: Guidelines for Advocates* (Cambridge: Center for Law and Education).

Colby, K.W., "When the Family Does not Pray Together: Religious Rights Within the Family" (Summer, 1982), 5 *Harv J.L. and Pub. Pol* 37.

Coleman, J.S. et al., *Equality of Educational Opportunity* (U.S. Dept. of Health, Education and Welfare, Washington, D.C., 1966).

Commission on Emotional and Learning Disorders in Children, *One Million Children: A National Study of Canadian Children with Emotional and Learning Disorders* (Toronto: CELDIC, 1969–70).

"Constitution Law-School Board Removal of Books" (Fall, 1981), 30 *Kan L. Rev.* 146; see also (1982), 61 *Neb L. Rev.* 98; (Summer, 1981), 4 *West New Engl. L. Rev.* 1.

"Creating an Implied Educational Malpractice Action for the Handicapped in N.Y." (Winter, 1982), 46 *Albany L. Rev.* 520.

Gilbert, U.K., Martin, R.A., Sheehan, A.T. and Stewart, B.C., *A Hard Act to Follow: Notes on Ontario School Law* (Revised Edition) (Toronto: University of Toronto Faculty of Education, 1984).

Gleidman, J. and Roth, W., *The Unexpected Minority: Handicapped Children in America* (N.Y.: Carnegie Council on Children, 1980).

Holt, J., *Escape from Childhood* (New York: Ballantine, 1974).

Hudon, E.G., "Church, State and Education in Canada and the U.S.: A Study in Comparative Constitutional Law" (1980), 21 *C. de D.* 461.

Huffman, Trauth, "High School Students' Publication Right and Prior Restraint", (Oct/81) 10 *J.L. and Educ.* 485.

Humphreys, E.H., *Privacy in Jeopardy: Student Records in Canada* (Toronto: OISE Press, 1981).

Hunter, W.R., "Reviewability of Enforcement of School Board Regulations Relating to Dress and Grooming", (1971–72), 36 *Sask. L. Rev.* 479.

Illich, I., *Deschooling Society* (1971).

International Year of the Child Working Group on Education, "The Rights of the Child to Education" (1979), 19 *Education Canada* (No. 4) 14.

Janisch, H., "Educational Malpractice: Legal Liability for Failure to Educate" (1980), 38 *The Advocate* 491.

Jenks, C. et al., *Inequality: A Reassessment of the Effect of Family and Schooling in America* (N.Y.: Basic Books, 1972).

Kingsbourne, M. and Caplan, P., *Children's Learning and Attention Problems* (Boston: Little, Brown & Co., 1979).

Kirp, D., *Doing Good by Doing Little: Race and Schooling in Britain* (Berkeley: University of California Press, 1979).

_____, *Just Schools: The Idea of Racial Equality in American Education* (Berkeley: University of California Press, 1982).

_____, "Proceduralism and Bureaucracy: Due Process in the School Setting" (1976), 28 *Stanford L. Rev.* 841.

_____, "Schools as Sorters: The Constitutional and Policy Implications of Student Classification" (April, 1973), 121 *U. of Penn. L.R.* 705 (longer and more amply footnoted version of "Students classification, Public Policy and the Courts").

Kirp, D., Yudof, L. and Mark, G., *Educational Policy and the Law: Cases and Materials* (Berkeley: McCutchan Publishing Corp, 1974).

MacKay, A. Wayne, *Education Law in Canada* (Toronto: Emond-Montgomery Publications Ltd., 1984).

_____, "Protecting Ethnic Rights under the Canadian Charter of Rights and Freedoms" (1983), 6 *Multiculturalism* (No. 4) 23.

_____, "Public Education in Nova Scotia: Legal Rights, Fleeting Privileges or Political Rhetoric" (1984), 8 *Dal. L.J.* 137.

Magnet, J.E., "Minority Language Educational Rights" (1982), 4 *S. Ct. L. Rev.* 195.

Manley-Casimir, M. (ed.), *Charter of Rights and Freedoms: Catalyst for Educational Reform* (Toronto: OISE Press, forthcoming).

Manley-Casimir, M.E., "A Case Study Approach to Discretion in School Discipline", *Interchange on Children's Rights* (Toronto: OISE Press, 1978).

McLaughlin, B.M., "Educational Records and the Right to Privacy" (1981), 15 *U.B.C. L. Rev.* 175.

Mosteller, F. and Moynihan, D. (eds.), *On Equality of Educational Opportunity* (N.Y.: Random House, 1972).

National Women's Law Center, *Sex Discrimination in Education: Legal Training Materials* (Washington: National Women's Law Center, 1983).

Neill, A.S., *Summerhill* (N.Y.: Hart Publishing Co., 1960).

Organization for Economic Cooperation and Development, *External Examiner's*

Report on Educational Policy in Canada (Toronto: Canadian Association for Adult Education, University of Toronto, 1976).

Pogany, ''Education: The Rights of Children and Parents Under the European Convention on Human Rights'', (April, 1982), 132 *New L.J.* 344.

Polk, K. and Schafer (eds.), *Schools and Delinquency* (N.Y.: Prentice-Hall, 1972).

Rebell, ''Implementation of Court Mandates Concerning Special Education: The Problems and the Potential'', (July, 1981), 10 *J.L. and Educ.* 335.

Reutter, E.E., *The Supreme Court's Impact on Public Education* (Bloomington: Phi Delta Kappa, 1983).

Rhode, D.L., ''Class Conflicts in Class Actions'' (education), (1981/82), 34 *Stanf. L.R.* 1183.

Rogow, S., ''The Right to an Equal Education: Is it Happening for Blind Children in Canada?'' (1976), 16 *Education Canada* (No. 2).

''Selected Survey of Educational Policy Literature'', (Ap/82) 11 *J.L. and Educ.* 275.

''Student Displacement/Exclusion: Violations of Civil and Human Rights'' (11th National Education Assoc. Conference) (Washington, D.C.: NEA, 1973).

''Supreme Court Interprets Free, Appropriate Education under P.L. 94–142'', (July/August, 1982), 6 *Mental Disab. L. Rep.* 235.

''Title VI, Bilingual Education, Remedial Language Instruction and Proof of Discriminatory Purpose: A Suggested Approach'' (1981), 17 *Colo. J. of Law and Social Problems* 99.

Tye, ''School Closures'' (April, 1982), 15 *Clearinghouse Rev.* 1010.

U.S. Commission on Civil Rights, *More Hurdles to Clear: Women and Girls in Competitive Athletics* (Washington, D.C.: Clearinghouse Publication No. 63, 1980).

White, Burton et al., *The Origins of Human Competence: The Final Report of the Harvard Preschool Project* (Lexington, Mass: Lexington Books, 1979).

Yohalem, D. and Dinsmore, J., *Special Education: A Guide for Parents and Advocates* (Washington, D.C.: Children's Defence Fund, 1979).

Zeitlin, J. and Campbell, N., ''Availability of Child Care for Low-Income Families'', (1982) 16 *Clearinghouse Rev.* 285.

Chapter 9

The Child as Immigrant

One of the governing objectives of the *Immigration Act, 1976* is to facilitate the reunification in Canada of the close family members of a Canadian citizen or permanent resident (*i.e.* someone who is lawfully living and working in Canada, but who is not a Canadian citizen): s. 3(c), *Immigration Act* (hereinafter referred to as the *Act*). On the other hand, it also has as one of its objectives the promotion of a strong and viable Canadian economy (s. 3(h), *Act*), which necessitates the authorities allowing into Canada only those who are able and/or willing to support themselves or who will be supported by someone other than Canada's social services network: s. 19(1)(a), (b), *Act*; ss. 8–11, C.R.C. 1978, vol. IX, c. 940 (hereinafter referred to as Regs.). Therefore, the minor immigrant will only succeed in obtaining "landing" (lawful permission to come into Canada to establish permanent residence) as a family member rather than as an independent individual. The Act pointedly omits "age" when stating that admission standards do not discriminate on the basis of "race, national or ethnic origin, colour, religion or sex": s. 3(f), *Act*.

Gaining Permanent Residence in Canada

As a family member, the minor may be granted landing (1) by accompanying an adult spouse or a parent who has been granted a visa for landing in Canada; (2) by being sponsored by a Canadian citizen or permanent resident who is a spouse or parent; or (3) by convincing an immigration or visa officer that there are sufficient humanitarian and compassionate reasons to warrant landing.

Accompanying Adult Immigrant

An adult immigrant, if accepted for landing in Canada, can obtain a visa for himself as well as his accompanying "dependants" (s. 9(1), Regs.) who include his spouse and any unmarried child of his or his spouse who is under 21: s. 2(1), Regs. If he or any of his dependants is not granted landing, all accompanying dependants will also not be granted landing: s. 19(2)(c), *Act*. Note that the Regulations direct that the child of the adult immigrant must either have been legitimate, if the father had been domiciled in Canada at the time of birth, or be the biological child of an accompanying immigrant mother (definition of "daughter", "son" and "dependant": s. 2(1) Regs. The child may also be adopted if this is done before the age of 13 years.) In other words, the definition discriminates against unmarried biological fathers. (The definitions of "nephew" and "niece" are also subject to differential treatment under s. 2 of the Regs.) However, the Immigration Commission has effectively overruled this discriminatory approach by issuing policy directives to accept and process sponsorship applications from biological fathers for their children born out of wedlock who are unmarried and under 21 years and presumably the Regulations will change accordingly.

These definitions as they stand are inconsistent with the Federal Court of Appeal's interpretation of "father" as defined in the Regulations.[1] In that case, it was held that "father" includes both biological and "legitimate" father. The definitions of "son" and "daughter" were challenged under s. 1(b) of the Canadian *Bill of Rights,* as denying equality before the law, in relation to the sponsorship sections of the Act (see below), but the Federal Court held that the section was not discriminatory.[2] The Federal Court cited *Re A.-G. of Canada and Bliss*[3] in stating that the sponsorship section conferred a privilege on the parent and as such

> . . .if the difference of treatment is based on a relevant distinction or even a distinction that could be conceived as possibly relevant, the right to equality before the law is not offended.[4]

The "relevancy" in this case would be the assertion that it is more difficult to prove paternity than maternity. It seems unlikely that the same conclusion would be reached in an action under s. 15 of the *Charter* which prohibits discrimination on the basis of sex subject to a s. 1 "reasonable limits" test which has been held to require more than a "relevant distinction".[5]

Section 19 of the *Immigration Act* lists the "inadmissible classes" and those who fall within them would normally be denied entry. If the immigrant child himself happens to belong to any of these classes, then the authorities have the discretion to refuse landing to that child, to the immigrant adult parent as well as the parents' other dependants, even if the inadmissible child remained in the home country. (This is presumably on the likelihood that the parent would at some future time attempt to sponsor the child into the country): s. 9(1)(a) and 9(2), Regs. Section 9(2) of the Regulations, however, exempts a separated

---

[1]*Re Gill and Minister of Employment and Immigration,* [1979] 2 F.C. 782, 102 D.L.R. (3d) 341, 30 N.R. 596 (C.A.).

[2]*Re Germain and Malouin,* [1978] 2 F.C. 14, 80 D.L.R. (3d) 659; affd, [1979] 2 F.C. 784, 101 D.L.R. (3d) 384 (C.A.).

[3]*Re A.-G. of Canada and Bliss* (1977), 77 D.L.R. (3d) 609, 16 N.R. 254 (S.C.C.).

[4]*Ibid.*

[5]See *e.g. Public Service Alliance of Canada v. R. in Right of Canada* (1984), 11 D.L.R. (4th) 387 (Fed. C.A.), affg (1984), 11 D.L.R. (4th) 337 (Fed. Ct. T.D.). Leave to appeal to S.C.C. granted (1984), 57 N.R. 161*n.* (s. 1 test more than reasonable rationale and more than showing that in Legislature's judgment, the limitation was justified which only goes to "prescribed by law".)

spouse or a child living with that spouse from being included in such an assessment.

Inadmissible classes include:

1) persons suffering from any disease, disorder, disability or other health impairment by which they may endanger public health or safety or make excessive demands on health or social services: s. 19(1)(a), *Act*;

2) persons who will be unwilling or unable to support themselves or their dependants: s. 19(1)(b), *Act*; (Note that anyone under 18 years is deemed dependent and therefore is not subject to this provision.)

3) persons who have been convicted of two or more offences which are the equivalent of summary offences: s. 19(2)(b), *Act*. Offences under the *Juvenile Delinquents Act* and the new *Young Offenders Act* are considered to be summary offences.

Sponsorship by Canadian Citizen or Permanent Resident

In compliance with the "family reunification" objectives of the Act, the Regulations permit any Canadian citizen or permanent resident who is residing in Canada and who is 18 years or older to "sponsor" (financially support or assist in becoming successfully established: s. 6(1)(b), Regs.; "undertaking" definition: s. 2(1), Regs.) a member of his or her "family class" (defined in s. 4, Regs.) or to assist in the application of an "assisted relative" (defined in s. 2(1), Regs.). The "family class" category of immigrants enjoy first priority status in processing (along with "Convention refugees") ahead of all other classes of immigrants: s. 3, Regs. "Assisted relatives", on the other hand, have no special priority. In addition, "family class" members are exempted from having to score points under the Commission's employability assessment schedule before being granted landing: s. 8, Regs., Schel. 1. "Assisted relatives" must enter the scoring race like any other independent immigrant although they do not have to score as high or be judged in as many categories as the non-sponsored independent immigrant: ss. 8(1)(d), 10, Regs.

It is obviously highly desirable for any immigrant to be sponsored as a member of a family class and accordingly, the rules and Regulations covering the process detail not only anyone who qualifies as a family class member but they additionally impose a concrete, long-term responsibility on the sponsor which may amount to total financial support for 10 years (and longer under provincial support laws) if the immigrant is a minor. In addition, unless the immigrant is the sponsor's spouse or child, unmarried and under 21 with no issue, the immigration officer must assess the sponsor's circumstances, especially financial, to determine whether the sponsor will be able to fulfill his undertaking: ss. 6(1)(b)(iii), 6(2), 6(3), Regs. Note that if he sponsors *both* spouse and child, he will also be subject to this financial assessment, an assessment which uses Statistics Canada's "Low Income Cut-Off Guidelines". Finally, the sponsor, if he is a permanent resident, may suffer deportation himself if he fails to support those relatives whom he sponsors and/or who are financially dependent on him (s. 27(1)(f), *Act*, s. 2(3), Regs.) although in practice, this section is rarely used.

''Family Class''

Members of a family class are defined under s. 4(1) of the Regulations as the sponsor's

1) spouse,

2) unmarried son or daughter under 21 at the time of visa application, and under 23 at the time of visa issuance,

3) father, mother, grandfather or grandmother 60 years of age or over,

4) father, mother, grandfather or grandmother under 60 if they or their spouses are incapable of gainful employment or if they are widowed,

5) brother, sister, nephew, niece, grandson or granddaughter who is an orphan, under 18 years of age and unmarried,

6) fiancée,

7) child under 13 years of age whom the sponsor intends to adopt and who is
   (a) an orphan,
   (b) an abandoned child whose parents cannot be identified,
   (c) a child born outside of marriage who has been placed with a child welfare authority for adoption, or
   (d) a child whose parents are separated, and who has been placed with a child welfare authority for adoption;

8) if the sponsor has no one from (1) to (7) to sponsor, he can sponsor one relative, regardless of age or relationship to him.

A recent case[6] confirmed that, when a wife and children were being sponsored, the question of the children's admissibility was separate and apart from that of their mother's. The mother was refused admission but the children's refusal was set aside. Note that this would be inapplicable if the children were determined to be dependent on the mother and not the sponsor who was living in Canada.

As in the case of children accompanying adult immigrants, the Commission's policy directives allow the sponsorship by biological fathers of their children born out of wedlock even though the definitions in the Regulations state otherwise. All that is needed is sufficient evidence of paternity. Presumably the Regulations will be amended accordingly.

Some sponsors have turned to adoption as a method of overcoming hurdles to the infant relative becoming a member of a family class, especially if he is a brother or sister who is not an orphan. The Regulations before April, 1978 permitted sponsorship of any adopted son or daughter of the sponsor who was adopted under the age of 18 years and who was under 21 years of age and unmarried. ''Adopted'' is now defined as

. . .adopted in accordance with the laws of any Province of Canada or of any country other than Canada or any political subdivision thereof where the adoption created a relationship of parent and child: s. 2(1), Regs.

Note that the present Regulations require that the child be adopted under *13*

---

[6]*Re Toor and Minister of Employment and Immigration* (1983), 144 D.L.R. (3d) 554 (Fed. C.A.).

years of age in order to be sponsored as a "son" or "daughter" and thus the adoption must occur outside of Canada. If attempted inside Canada, the courts may not approve such an adoption if it is done only to circumvent the Act, especially if the Commission does not give approval in principle (see case law discussed below).

Under s. 4(g) of the Regulations, the following classes of children may be sponsored before the adoption actually takes place as long as an intention to adopt is shown:

(i) an orphan,

(ii) an abandoned child whose parents cannot be identified,

(iii) a child born outside of marriage who has been placed with a child welfare authority for adoption, or

(iv) a child whose parents are separated and who has been placed with a child welfare authority for adoption.

Note that these classes of children must be under 13 years of age when the sponsorship application is made but the adoption may occur after the 13th birthday. Further, note that no immigrant visa may be issued to such children unless the provincial child welfare authorities have done a home study and state that it finds no objection to the proposed adoption: s. 6(1)(c), Regs. In fact, this statement is also a prerequisite to someone sponsoring a sibling who is an orphan as a family class member under s. 4(e) of the Regulations: s. 6(1)(c), Regs.

The courts will not grant adoption orders if, in all the circumstances of the particular case, the process is a "sham" or an "accommodation adoption" to circumvent the Act since there is no intent by the sponsor to develop a parent-child relationship with the immigrant child. On the other hand, if such an intent is found, the fact that the sponsor is circumventing the Act will not be held against him. Factors such as age proximity, history of support relationship, length of time in Canada with the sponsor, and type of relative (e.g. a sibling versus an aunt or grandparent) will all bear on the judge's conclusion.[7] In other words, the classic test of "best interests of the child" in tandem with the prerequisite of "parent-child" relationship is to guide the judge in whether or not to grant the order, using immigration status only as a factor in such decision.[8]

The particular case of a biological father applying to adopt his child born out of wedlock in order to bring the child within the Act's "family class" has been litigated and although such adoptions are no longer necessary under present Ministry policy directives (see above), the decisions may be useful for other immigration-related adoptions. It has been held[9] that the fact that the father was circumventing the Immigration Act did not diminish the advantages to the child of formalizing her relationship with her father, a parent-child relationship which

---

[7]Age proximity and sibling relationship: Re Khan (1978), 21 O.R. (2d) 748, 92 D.L.R. (3d) 287 (sub nom. Re K.), 8 R.F.L. (2d) 97 (C.A.); history of support, length of time in Canada: Re S.M.S. (1983), 40 O.R. (2d) 257 (Co. Ct.), revg (1982), 35 O.R. (2d) 385, [1982] C.C.L. 5727 (Prov. Ct.).

[8]See s. 76(b) of the C.W.A./s. 140(1) of the C.F.S.A.; Re S.M.S., ibid.; Re Rai (1980), 27 O.R. (2d) 425 (C.A.); Re K.M.K., unreported, May 31, 1984 (Ont. Prov. Ct.).

[9]Re S.M.S., supra, note 7.

was found to be *bona fide* and in the child's best interests, especially since the mother had given her consent. The further issue of whether a biological parent can adopt his or her own child was considered in light of the silence of the province's *Child Welfare Act* (which will be the proposed *Child and Family Services Act*, see Table of Concordance in Chapter 3) on the subject. The judge followed a liberal construction of the intent of the Act, finding that such an adoption was acceptable since it was not specifically barred by the Act. Finally, the judge dealt with the following section in the *Child Welfare Act:*

> s. 74(1) The court shall not make an adoption order,
>
> . . .
>
> > (b) where the applicant is unmarried, a widow, a widower, a divorced person or living apart from his or her spouse. . .
>
> unless the court is satisfied that there are special circumstances that justify the making of the order.

It was held simply that "those special circumstances clearly are to be found here"[10], presumably referring to the benefits gained by the child in moving to Canada from Jamaica and developing a relationship with her father despite her having to give up her on-going relationship with her mother.[11]

In another case,[12] the Provincial Court judge refused the adoption application of the biological father for his three children despite the mother's consent, finding that the "more pleasant" circumstances of Canada versus Jamaica did not constitute enough reason to award an adoption order since this was the plight of every immigrant. Nevertheless, this decision apparently can be distinguished from the above decision in that the judge found that the net effect of an adoption order on the parent-child relationship would be to "lose a mother and add nothing in her stead . . . best interests must be in the context of adoption rather than immigration although the latter is a factor." Presumably, if the family relationship which the father had to offer had been more advantageous and suitable for the children, the judge would have followed the above-noted decision.

The *Child Welfare Act* imposes a residency requirement as a prerequisite to an adoption order: s. 72, *CWA*. Although some earlier Ontario County Court decisions[13] held that residency could not be claimed by an immigrant child under a visitor's visa, the more recent Ontario Court of Appeal case of *Re Rai*[14] has clearly held that immigration status is only one factor in determining whether the child is resident:

> But, apart from exceptional cases, the purpose of the statutory requirement of residence will have been met if there is a reasonable connection between the child and Ontario, and if the child has lived here for sufficient time to enable an effective investigation to be made into the suitability of the

---

[10]*Ibid.,* at p. 263.
[11]See also *Re K.M.K., supra,* note 8.
[12]*Re Stephenson,* unreported, May 15, 1980 (Ont. Prov. Ct.).
[13]*Re Khan, supra,* note 7.
[14]*Re Rai, supra,* note 8.

adopting parents and whether the proposed adoption order would be in the best interests of the child.[15]

Assisted Relatives

The Act provides a route whereby "assisted relatives" can be sponsored. "Assisted relative" is defined under s. 2(1) of the Regulations to be a relative of the sponsor, other than a member of the family class, who is:

(a) a brother or sister, a grandfather or grandmother, a father or mother, a son or daughter, or an unmarried niece or nephew less than twenty-one years of age, or

(b) an aunt or uncle, a grandson or granddaughter, a married niece or nephew or a niece or nephew twenty-one or more years of age.

Some infant family members who do not fall into the "family class" definition may be covered by the "assisted relative" definition (*e.g.* married or separated sibling under 18 years of age). However, such a minor would not be able to qualify because this classification of persons must also have pre-arranged employment in Canada, that is, a job which has been approved by a Canada Employment Counsellor (s. 11, Regs.), in order to gain sufficient points to qualify for landing. The Regulations also permit persons who have occupations for which there is a demand in Canada to qualify but in mid-1982, this provision was effectively cancelled and has not been reinstated. Section 11(3) of the Regulations does permit a visa officer to obtain approval for landing a person if the assessment points are inadequate but it is rarely used and is even less likely to be applicable in the case of a minor, especially if he is applying independent of his adult family members.

Finally, it may be useful to remember that s. 4(1)(h) and s. 5(2) of the Regulations allow a sponsor who does not have anyone who would qualify as a member of his family class to sponsor one relative "regardless of his age or relationship to him".

Humanitarian and Compassionate Grounds

There exists a provision for discretionary admission to a person otherwise inadmissible. A Minister's Permit (s. 37, *Immigration Act*) may be issued to allow admission and it is valid for one year. It may be extended or cancelled at the Minister's discretion although there is a duty to act fairly towards the permit holder prior to cancellation or refusal to extend. The Act and Regulations give no criteria for the exercise of this discretion although the Commission has issued public guidelines which outline various situations in which a permit could be granted. Permits may be granted for example to allow a mentally retarded child to accompany his parents to Canada or to allow a child who is admissable but cannot be processed in time to travel with his parents. Normally a child admitted on a permit is landed after a period of time by an Order-in-Council under s. 115(2) of the Act. This section permits the Governor in Council to exempt the person from the requirements of the Regulations or otherwise facilitate the person's admission on humanitarian and compassionate grounds. As well, any

---

[15]*Ibid.*, at p. 430.

person who remains in Canada for more than five years on a Minister's Permit may request landing under s. 38 of the Act, even though the person may still not qualify for landing because of some disability which would make him inadmissable under the Act for landing.

Loss of Permanent Residence

Once the minor has been granted landing and is living in Canada, he is still in jeopardy of being removed in his own right as an individual or as a dependant of a permanent resident in the event of this person's removal from the country. A Deportation Order or a Departure Notice (having less severe future consequences but still requiring the person's removal), when made against a member of a family on whom other members are dependent, can also include the said dependants unless they are Canadian citizens or over 18 years of age: s. 33(1), *Act*. "Family" in this subsection includes any relative who is dependent for support on the member of the family against whom the Deportation Order or Departure Notice is made: s. 2(4), Regs. Further, all consequences arising from the order against a person equally apply to those family members included in the order, including all appeal rights[16] with the exemption that such dependent family members are not required to obtain the consent of the Minister before returning to Canada: s. 33(3), *Act*. Conversely, when a Deportation Order against a mother was quashed, the Deportation Order against the included minor should also be quashed.[17]

Removal Proceedings

Section 27(1) of the *Immigration Act* directs an immigration officer, in effect, to commence the removal hearing process (s. 32(2), *Act*) if the permanent resident falls into any of six categories which include the commission of crimes (s. 27(1)(d), *Act*), misrepresentation to the immigration authorities (s. 27(1)(e), *Act*), or breaching terms and conditions of his immigration visa (s. 27(1)(b), *Act*). Of more specific concern to the minor is s. 27(1)(f) which focuses on the permanent resident who "wilfully fails to support himself or any dependent member of his family in Canada". For the purpose of this subsection, "family" includes those persons who were granted admission as members of the family class or assisted relatives of that person: s. 2(3), Regs. However, this section is rarely used by the Commission which regards intra-familial support issues as relevant only to domestic family law objectives. The same is likely true if a child of the permanent resident is apprehended under child protection legislation. In this context, note also that while a person may be denied admission if suffering from a disorder or disease that would cause excessive demands on health or social services, there is no such reason under s. 27 of the Act for removing the person once he has been granted landing.

Whether a family member is dependent upon another member is a question of fact and not automatically assumed due to a familial relationship.[18] In addition, there may be some potential in resorting to s. 52(1) of the Act if there is an outstanding custody order in favour of the person being removed with specified terms of access to a person who is remaining in Canada. Section 52(1) prohibits the execution of any removal order (which includes a Deportation

---

[16]*Ali* (1977), 11 I.A.C. 284 (Imm. App. Bd.).
[17]*Allen v. Minister of Immigration (No. 2)* (1978), 22 N.R. 537 (Fed. C.A.).
[18]*Morataya v. Minister of Manpower and Immigration*, [1977] 1 F.C. 571 (Fed. C.A.).

Order) which would directly result in a violation of any other order made by any judicial body or officer in Canada. Most cases under this section have arisen due to probation or bail orders. It seems unlikely that a custody/access order which is by nature variable based on change in circumstances would succeed in blocking a deportation order. For those situations in which the child remains and the parent who is being removed has been granted access or has support liability, the Commission has taken the position that removal does not prevent the parent from returning to visit or from sending money from abroad.

In one case,[19] a dependent child who was a Canadian citizen unsuccessfully argued that to deport her mother would violate the child's rights under the *Canadian Bill of Rights* since it would oblige the mother to take the child also, thus exiling her contrary to s. 2 of the *Bill of Rights*. In dismissing her appeal, the court held that her leaving the country would not be a direct and unavoidable result of the application of the law of Canada, but simply of the mother's decision to take the child with her. Query whether this would be the court's answer to s. 4(2) of the *Immigration Act* which guarantees a Canadian citizen's right to remain in Canada, or s. 6 of the *Charter of Rights* which guarantees that every citizen of Canada has the right to remain in Canada. Given the family orientation of Canada's laws when dealing with children, it is probable that this limitation on the child's rights would be justified under s. 1 of the *Charter*, especially since the departure from Canada would not in any way affect the child's Canadian citizenship at a future date when he or she may wish to return.

Final consideration under this part should be given to the possibilities of deportation based on the activities of the child himself, in particular, criminal or quasi-criminal activities. As a permanent resident, independent of his family, it would seem that unless a child is engaged in activities that fall under s. 19(1)(e), (f) or (g) of the Regs. ("acts of espionage or subversion" or "acts of violence") a finding of guilt *per se* will not render the child subject to special enquiry proceedings. Those sections which establish a liability to deportation as a consequence of a conviction for a criminal offence do not include convictions under the *Juvenile Delinquents Act* (now the *Young Offenders Act*) since under that Act a person cannot be subject to imprisonment and the offence is deemed a summary conviction, both results of which are not sufficient for criminal status as defined in the *Immigration Act*. The situation is, of course, different if the child is proceeded against in adult court. (See Chapter 7, "Crime and the Child".) As a final note, it has been held that failure of a child to adhere to the *Immigration Act* or to its Regulations does not constitute an offence of delinquency.[20]

If an immigration officer forwards to the Deputy Minister information which might lead to a person's removal under s. 27(1) of the Regulations, an inquiry must be held if the Deputy Minister wishes to proceed with removal: ss. 27(3), 32(2), *Act*. Since any dependent family member (with the exception of a Canadian citizen or permanent resident over 18 years) may be included in a Deportation Order or Departure Notice (s. 33(1), *Act*), they also have the right to

---

[19]*Denis v. R.*, [1976] 1 F.C. 499 (C.A.).
[20]*Mari* (1970), 5 I.A.C. 408 (Imm. App. Bd.).

be heard at the inquiry (s. 33(2), *Act*) and the adjudicator of the hearing must satisfy himself that each such family member is aware (s. 27(1), Regs.):

(a) of the time and place of the inquiry;

(b) that he may obtain counsel at his own expense to represent him at the inquiry; and

(c) that he may participate at the inquiry by examining evidence, cross-examining witnesses and presenting evidence.

Particularly relevant to minors is the following section:

s. 29(4) Where an inquiry is held with respect to persons under the age of eighteen years or any person who, in the opinion of the adjudicator, is not able to appreciate the nature of the proceedings, such person may, subject to sub-section (5), be represented by a parent or guardian.

(5) Where at an inquiry a person described in subsection (4) is not represented by a parent or guardian or where, in the opinion of the adjudicator presiding at the inquiry, the person is not properly represented by a parent or guardian, the inquiry shall be adjourned and the adjudicator shall designate some other person to represent that person at the expense of the Minister.

In one case,[21] the child was represented by a non-lawyer who was a second cousin with whom the child was living. The Appellate Court set aside the original Deportation Order, determining that the sections of the Act were not complied with. The court went to great pains to define "guardian" in its narrow sense as being one who *legally* has the care and management of the person or estate of the child, not simply on a *de facto* basis. In another Federal Court of Appeal case,[22] it was held that these representation sections give minors the right to be represented by a parent or guardian in addition to the right to be represented by counsel and are not merely directory. As such, a Deportation Order against the minor was set aside because he was not represented by a guardian. Interestingly, the child was represented by a lawyer. This presents a problem in principle in that a parent or guardian is considered sufficient representation for a child in extremely important legal proceedings whereas a lawyer alone is considered insufficient. Presumably, the optimum situation is to have parent or guardian retain a lawyer for the child, but this is not a prerequisite. Not only do the sections leave the child's destiny in the hands of lay persons in these legal proceedings, but also they apparently direct that it cannot be in the hands of a professional lawyer unless via a parent or guardian. Query whether the principle of these two cases would remain the same if the resulting orders sought to be set aside were favourable to the child?

In practice, if no guardian comes forward for the child, the Commission

---

[21]*Azdo v. Minister of Employment and Immigration*, [1980] 2 F.C. 645, 36 N.R. 361 (C.A.).

[22]*Kissoon v. Minister of Employment and Immigration*, [1979] 1 F.C. 301 (*sub nom. Re Kisson and Minister of Employment and Immigration*) 90 D.L.R. (3d) (*sub nom. Kissoon v. Minister of Immigration*), 23 N.R. 82 (Fed. C.A.).

Abandonment of
Canada

appoints a lawyer from a roster of lawyers to act as guardian. If a parent or other guardian is available, the Commission expects him to retain his own lawyer.

A person can lose his status of ''permanent resident'', other than through deportation, if he ''leaves or remains outside Canada with the intention of abandoning Canada as his place of permanent residence.'' It has been held that someone under 18 years is incapable of forming an independent intent to voluntarily reside outside of Canada and thereby lose Canadian domicile.[23] On the other hand, it has also been held that, for the purposes of immigration law, a child at the age of 14 years *is* capable of forming an intention such as to establish independently a domicile of his own.[24] This issue becomes important in situations in which parents send their permanent resident children out of the country and the children, in attempting to return, argue that they had not wished to leave in the first place. Those children who are capable of registering objections *before* being sent out of the country can usually seek assistance under child protection legislation as a child ''in need of protection'' or under domestic custody legislation if there is another adult in Canada willing to take over legal custody.

Note that these decisions use the concepts of ''domicile'' in relation to infant permanent residence. Such a concept is defined under the *Immigration Act* but it has been held that the domicile of a legitimate child is, during the lifetime of the father, the same as and changes with the domicile of the father, absent evidence that guardianship has been transferred.[25] To the extent that a court or tribunal may find useful provincial legislation relating to non-immigration situations, Ontario's *Family Law Reform Act* outlines a definition of ''domicile'' which attempts to minimize the arguable discriminatory aspect of the Immigration Appeal Board's approach:

s. 68(1) Subject to subsection (2), a child who is a minor,
    (a) takes the domicile of his or her parents, where both parents have a common domicile;
    (b) takes the domicile of the parent with whom the child habitually resides, where the child resides with one parent only;
    (c) takes the domicile of the father, where the domicile of the child cannot be determined under clause (a) or (b); or
    (d) takes the domicile of the mother, where the domicile of the child cannot be determined in clause (*c*).

(2) The domicile of a minor who is or has been a spouse shall be determined in the same manner as if the minor were of full age.

Students and
Visitors

Many persons under 18 years enter Canada under a student or visitor's visa: s. 9, 10, *Act*. As a student, he must be intending to

---

[23]*Wittkamper* (1969), 6 I.A.C. 369 (Imm. App. Bd.).
[24]*Wynia v. Minister of Manpower and Immigration*, unreported, August 11, 1970 (I.A.B.); see also *Fryer (Eric Amfrid) v. Minister of Manpower and Immigration* (1972), 5 I.A.C. 159, 164 cited in *Whelan* (1973), 7 I.A.C. 113.
[25]*Dutheil* (1971), 2 I.A.C. 223 (Imm. App. Bd.).

1) attend any university or college authorized by statute or charter to confer degrees, or

2) take any academic professional or vocational training course at any university, college or other institution not described in (1).

If he is a visitor and the immigration officer is satisfied that his entry would not be contrary to the Act or Regulations, the officer *may* grant entry and may "impose terms and conditions of a prescribed nature": s. 14(3), *Act*. A visitor's permit usually is for a maximum of 3 months (s. 26(2), *Act*) although he may apply for an extension: s. 16(1)(b), *Act*.

A common occurrence related to these types of status is that the student or visitor or his parents may wish him to stay on as a permanent resident and commence an application for same. If the parent does so and then abandons the application, the student or visitor who may no longer be qualified as such, may be removed either by the parent sending him home or by the Immigration Department intervening due to a violation of the Act. In these circumstances, the student or visitor could apply to remain on humanitarian grounds which may be successful if there are other relatives in Canada who offer to be responsible.

Finally, note that students and visitors are subject to removal if they stray outside the original conditions on which they entered in the first place (s. 26, *Act*) or for other specified reasons: s. 27(2), *Act*.

Citizenship

With reference to the *Citizenship Act* (hereinafter referred to as *CA*), note the following:

1) A person born in Canada after February 15th, 1977 will be a Canadian citizen: s. 3(1)(a), *CA*.

2) A person will be a Canadian citizen if, after February 15, 1955, he was born outside of Canada, and one of his parents other than a parent who adopted the child, was a Canadian citizen at the time of the child's birth: s. 3(1)(b), *CA*.

3) A child who has been lawfully admitted to Canada and has within the last four years immediately preceding the date of his application for citizenship, accumulated at least three years of residence in Canada according to the rules of s. 5 of the *Citizenship Act* and further conditions therein, may be granted citizenship upon the age of 18 years. The Minister may waive the requirement concerning the age of 18 years or length of residence for persons under a disability if there are humanitarian and compassionate grounds to do so: s. 5(3)(b), *CA*.

4) If a child before apparently attaining the age of seven years is first found in Canada as a deserted child, the child shall be deemed to be Canadian born for the purposes of s. 3(1)(a), (citizenship by Canadian birth) unless the contrary is proven within 7 years from the date he was first found: s. 4(1), *CA*.

5) If a child is born after the death of one of his parents, the child is deemed to have been born before the death of that parent for the purpose of s. 3(1)(b) (citizenship by citizenship of parent): s. 4(2), *CA*.

6) A person born after December 31, 1946 will be a Canadian if he was born in Canada, or on a Canadian ship, or if he was born outside of Canada elsewhere than on a Canadian ship and:
   i) his father, or in the case of a child born out of wedlock, his mother, at the time of the birth was a Canadian citizen, and
   ii) the fact of the birth is registered within two years after its occurrence or such extended period as the Minister may authorize pursuant to s. 4 of the *Citizenship Act*: s. 3(1)(e), *CA*.

7) If a child is born outside Canada after February 15th, 1955 and is a citizen because of s. 3(1)(b) or s. 3(1)(e) (paragraphs 2 and 6 above, respectively), he will lose his Canadian citizenship if, before 28 years of age, he does not make application to retain his citizenship and registers as a citizen and either resides in Canada for a period of at least one year preceding the date of his application or establishes a substantial connection with the country: s. 7, *CA*.

Chapter 9: Readings

Clark, G.B. ''Undocumented Aliens-Equal Protection and the Right to a Free Public Education'' (1981), 33 *Ala. L. Rev.* 181.

Kohn, A., ''Rights Upheld for Children Born in U.S. of Illegal Aliens: Day Care Benefits Ordered by Federal Judge'' (Nov. 4, 1982), 188 *N.Y.L.J.* p. 1, Col. 2.

Index